The INTERNATIONAL LIBRARY of MUSIC

for HOME AND STUDIO

WAGNER

THE INTERNATIONAL LIBRARY OF MUSIC

FOR HOME AND STUDIO

MUSIC LITERATURE

VOLUME IV

THE OPERA

History and Guide

The Origin and Development of Opera—Stories of the
Operas—Biographies of Opera Composers and
Singers—Woman in Music

Containing Chapters by

MORITZ MOSZKOWSKI   CECILE CHAMINADE   VICTOR MAUREL
RUGGIERO LEONCAVALLO   CHARLES GOUNOD   JULES MASSENET

and others

THE UNIVERSITY SOCIETY
NEW YORK

CONTENTS

THE OPERA—HISTORY AND GUIDE

STORIES OF THE OPERA

CONTENTS

CONTENTS

CONTENTS

CONTENTS

CONTENTS

THE OPERA—HISTORY AND GUIDE

THE ORIGIN AND DEVELOPMENT OF OPERA

THE term "opera," derived, or rather abbreviated, from the words *opera in musica* (works in music —i.e., a musical work), is only a convenient title that has found favor by its brevity and through lack of a better. Translate it and read "works," and we see that it is a meaningless term in all else than that it is something created.

And what is this "something" that has been created, that is in people's mouths so often, and that we designate by the word opera? The least cultured will be able to answer that it is a work for the stage, in which music plays a prominent part; that it is this, and something more, must be shown as we study its rise and development.

Since ordinary feelings or emotions are by no means naturally expressed by musical sounds, opera must be admitted to be a thing of artificiality. Some will ask: Since the introduction of music into a dramatic work admits an unreal element into that which might otherwise receive a natural interpretation, how can its existence be justified? The answer is: Whatever may be the feelings or actions to be expressed by the stage characters, proper and suitable music will express them with far greater intensity and far greater power than will spoken words or mere gesture. Such are the emotional qualities of the art of music that a phrase of quite ordinary significance in words may become, if wedded to expressive music, a thing of beauty and life; an emotional feeling may be roused in the auditor that the mere spoken word could never have touched. In the case of words that may themselves contain beautiful ideas, their loveliness can be greatly enhanced by the addition of music, their meaning intensified, their impressiveness doubled.

Artificial, then, as opera is, and must be, it can justify its artificiality. A drama is put upon the stage, and in order that its situations, its sentiments, and its meaning may be more fully expounded, music is called in to elucidate, to express, and to beautify. Admitting the possibility of this—which no one who has the least feeling for music, or who is at all moved emotionally by the art of sweet sounds, can deny—we find that opera justifies its existence, despite its unreality and its unlikeness to life.

But not all opera is sung throughout. There are many musical works under this name having spoken dialogue. Justification for these is more difficult, for it may be readily understood that one form of expression should be used throughout, and that this modified form of opera (known as singspiel), being neither one thing nor the other, is a hybrid form, which really has no right of admission to the title of opera at all. The fact that it is often effective and highly popular hardly excuses its violation of art-form. So many plays of this kind with musical numbers were written at a certain period of the history of the art, and classed as operas, that their claims cannot be overlooked; but modern taste in opera demands that one medium of expression be made use of throughout, and thus a return has been made to the early and more artistic form of *opera in musica*—the true form, of which the singspiel is only an offshoot.

An opera, then, is a play designed for the stage, with scenery, costumes, and action used as accessories as in all stage plays, but with the additional use of music to intensify the meanings of the lines uttered by the characters, to heighten the effect produced by the other combined arts, and to add an emotional element that might otherwise be lacking.

It is a curious and interesting fact that the birth of opera should be due more or less to accident, and should owe its origin to a group of amateurs; but so it is, and to the blind gropings in the dark after a something (they knew not what) of a small circle of polished scholars we owe the form of opera as we have it to-day.

It is impossible to trace back to the earliest times the addition of music to a stage play; but from the constant references to the use of the art made by the Greek poets, we know that it was a handmaid to the drama from very early days. In the Middle Ages, as there is plenty of evidence to show, at certain stated intervals in the course of the drama music was introduced; but such music as this was always written in the Church style of the period, and had no significance of its own.

It was the annoying and incongruous presentation of polyphonic music (written in strict contrapuntal style, and in the Church manner) with the performance of dramas, in which such music was utterly out of place, that led the group of amateurs to search for a more suitable means of clothing the dramatic ideas and stage situations.

This band of dilettanti is generally known by the name of the "Palazzo Bardi" coterie, from the fact that their chief representative was a certain Count Bardi, and that their meetings were usually held at his palace in Florence. This city, at the period of which we write (the last part of the sixteenth century), was highly interested in the masterpieces of literary antiquity, more especially in the magnificent dramas of the older Greek poets. Although the Florentines knew that these tragedies had some form of musical accompaniment, they were quite in the dark as to what that music was. They felt, however, that the one prevalent kind of music of their day—sacred music —was by no means adequate for the expression of the ideas to be represented. The Bardi amateurs therefore turned the steps of their native musicians toward other paths, and induced them to write music of a kind which they believed to be dramatically fit and suitable. That this music was a failure does not matter in the least, for although it was unable to give any genuine idea of what these enthusiasts sought—a reproduction of Greek tragedy consistent with its original form—it invented a new medium and method of expression, of which composers soon availed themselves in setting to music the dramatic productions of the day.

The first of these early composers to achieve success in this field was Peri, who produced in 1594 (or 1597) "Dafne," and a few years later (1600) "Euridice." "Dafne" was semiprivately performed, but "Euridice" was put before the world, and achieved such success that its method and style of composition were soon taken as models for stage music. Hence the date 1600 is assigned as that of the birth of real opera. The same year saw the production of the first real oratorio, as we now understand the term.

Peri led the way; others followed. Within a decade Northern Italy produced a whole school of writers who had grafted their ideas on those of the composer of "Euridice," chief among them being Caccini, who won great fame in the new style. But the chief merit must be accorded to Peri, for it is to him that we owe the invention of the dramatic recitative; that is to say, instead of coupling the dialogue to music that might have been designed for the Church, as his predecessors had been content to do, he endeavored in his operas to allow the singing voice to depict the ideas expressed by inflections such as would be made by the speaking voice under similar circumstances.

Thus was opera, in our modern meaning of the term, begun, and this, too, on a proper, logical, esthetic basis. It was in 1600 a new form, an untried and questionable innovation; but it contained the elements of strength and endurance, and by rapid steps grew and developed, until within a few years all other methods of accompanying stage plays by music were obsolete, and the new monodic style held unquestioned sway.

Opera in Italy, after its initial stages, as represented by the works of Peri and Caccini, fell under the commanding sway of Monteverde, of whom we shall further speak.

Monteverde was followed by his pupil Cavalli, who worked in Venice, and who improved the recitative; in his operas, male sopranos (castrati) were first employed on the stage—a practice in vogue for many years subsequently. Cavalli also foreshadowed the aria, or set melody, soon to become so prominent a feature of Italian opera. Among other prominent composers of this period are Cesti and Legrenzi, Caldara and Vivaldi.

These men, however, stand completely overshadowed by that colossus of early opera, Alessandro Scarlatti. Naples was the scene of his activity, and here he wrote, among countless other compositions, over one hundred operas, most of which made their mark. In Scarlatti we have the turning-point between antiquity and modernity in stage music. His great genius for melody caused him to modify very considerably the stiff, though dramatically correct, recitative of earlier composers, and to substitute beautiful, if sometimes inappropriate, airs in its place.

In this dangerous method of exalting the music at the expense of the other arts employed in music-drama he was followed by almost all composers for many years—until, in fact, the recognition by Gluck of the falseness of the situation. Opera writers there were by the hundred, the names of most of whom are now forgotten. Rossi, Caldara, Lotti, Bononcini, all had their successes, and contributed in various degrees to the development of early Italian opera.

But before this, opera had found its way to France; the world-renowned "Euridice" had been performed in Paris as early as 1647, and its influence was quickly felt. Robert Cambert was the first French writer to produce opera. He was ousted from his deservedly high position as the founder of French opera by the unscrupulous and brilliant Lulli.

Coming from Florence to Paris at an early age, Lulli quickly saw his way to improving on the popular operas of Cambert, and his inventive and fertile talent soon put the older writer into the background. Lulli's great gift lay less in aptitude for the conception of melody, less even in his skill with the orchestra, than in the powers he possessed of writing truly dramatic and suitably expressive recitative. Moreover, he employed his chorus as an integral factor in the situation, not as a mere collection of puppets encumbering the stage; he is credited, too, with the invention of the "French" overture, a form in which an introductory slow movement is followed by another in quick fugal style, with a third short dance movement to conclude. His mark upon French opera exists till this day.

Germany at the same period can boast of no name of like importance, but operatic development was also taking place in that country. The chief agent in its progress was Keiser, who produced a great number of operas in Hamburg. Although not the first to write such works in Germany, he is important as being an early factor in the popularization of opera during the forty years in which he labored in this direction. He had also many followers, among whom must be named Handel, who wrote a few operas for Hamburg at an early period of his career. German opera at this time, however, gave but little promise of the grand future before it: the operas of Keiser and Hasse contain but few indications of the glories of a school of composers that includes Mozart, Beethoven, and Weber.

In England Henry Purcell was in part occupied by

the composition of operas. Many of these are operas by courtesy only, for in only one of them, "Dido and Æneas," is the music continuous throughout. This, however, may claim for itself the title of the first English opera. The wholly sound and esthetically true national influence of Purcell would undoubtedly have been large, and it is not too much to say that an early school of genuine English opera might have flourished, had it not been that Handel, within a few years of Purcell's death, was turning his attention to the production of opera in London. For although Handel produced operas in Germany and Italy as well as in England, it was in London that the great majority of his pieces first saw the light, and that he achieved the greatest success. Between the date of the first performance of "Rinaldo" at the Haymarket in 1711 and that of his last opera, "Deidamia," in 1741, Handel composed no less than forty-two grand operas. With indomitable energy, and in face of very frequent misfortune, he poured forth these works, many of which contain powerful music. Few now, however, would care to sit through a performance of any of Handel's operas, or indeed of those by any of the composers above mentioned.

The changes that have taken place in opera during the three hundred years which constitute the life of modern music are far more prominent and important than those that have been undergone by the ordinary dramatic work. The arts of elocution, gesture, and stage action are very old, and have seen little radical change for many centuries. Great progress has been made through the use of modern mechanical devices and inventions in the mounting of stage pieces—in the scenery employed, the lighting, and stage effects generally. These all appeal to the eye; but the appeal to the ear is not, in an ordinary dramatic work, more powerfully made than it was in the days of the Greek dramatist. But when music is added, then appeal to the ear of a most powerful kind takes place, and during its whole life improvements and growth in musical technique and expression have been grafted upon opera with continuously progressive power and effect. As musical skill and knowledge grew, as additional instruments were added to the orchestra, as knowledge of forms developed, all these improvements found their way into operatic music, with the result that the difference between, say, a seventeenth and an eighteenth century opera is very wide, while a vaster difference still may be seen between one of the eighteenth and one of the twentieth century.

This difference is mainly due to men who were not content to leave opera where they found it. They set themselves to the construction of new works as examples of what could and should be done. First of these reformers came Monteverde. So many innovations are connected with his name that he would appear to have been a reformer of music in general. Certainly opera before his time was a very different thing from opera subsequent to that period. He applied the same daring innovations to his operatic music which he had employed in his compositions for the Church. These consisted mainly in an utter disregard for the principles of strict counterpoint, and a free use of unprepared discords.

So great was Monteverde's success, so dramatic and expressive his music, that all composers since his day have followed in his footsteps, and have composed operas on the model of free and unfettered writing originated by him. A century and more later we find a new reformer in Gluck. What had happened in the meantime? Opera had fallen under the great and commanding influence of Alessandro Scarlatti, whose methods, if not amounting to reform, had certainly led to change, in some respects to abuse. Scarlatti invented beautiful melodies and cast them into a regular mold, so that an audience knew that it only had to wait while a second part was gone through to hear again a first part that had perhaps given much pleasure. This was his famous use of the da-capo aria. It was a kind of encore, granted without trouble or uncertainty. We can imagine the melody-loving Italians of the day welcoming this beautiful and artistic innovation. But the beauty and charm of the idea compassed its own ruin; for, being but a formal procedure, it did not equally suit every situation; indeed, it may readily be understood that there must have been many occasions when it was little short of absurd, for stage purposes, to go twice through the same emotional aspects and crises. Apart from its dramatic unfitness, the real mischief of the da-capo aria lay in the fact that it attracted too much attention from the plot. The real origin of opera was lost sight of, dramatic considerations were practically ignored, and the performance became of a lyrical, rather than of a dramatic, nature.

Gluck had written many operas on this plan before it occurred to him to try to reform it, but his artistic nature at last revolted against the absurdities of works of this type. He set himself the task of remodeling the music, in a manner which can best be explained by quoting his own words, written in the famous preface to the score of "Alceste":

"When I undertook to set the opera of 'Alceste' to music, I resolved to avoid all those abuses which had crept into Italian opera through the mistaken vanity of singers and the unwise compliance of composers, and which had rendered it wearisome and ridiculous, instead of being, as it once was, the grandest and most imposing stage of modern times. I endeavored to reduce music to its proper function, that of seconding poetry, by enforcing the expression of the sentiment, and the interest of the situations, without interrupting the action, or weakening it by superfluous ornament."

Gluck had many battles to fight before he gained public opinion to his side; but eventually he brought the artistic world round to his point of view, with the result that a complete change of method was again adopted by composers.

Years passed away, and operas both good and bad were written. Mozart, with his beautiful and delicate pen; Beethoven, with his imperishable picture of the faithful wife; Weber, the composer *par excellence* of Romantic opera; Spohr, and others all left their influences—in the main thoroughly artistic and beautiful—upon music-drama. But to this chain of great classics succeeded a group of lesser luminaries whose tendencies were less truthfully artistic, whose leanings were popular rather than esthetic, and whose influence was to a great extent mischievous. Opera was again straying from the right lines; again the singers, with their executive abilities, were distracting attention from the equally important dramatic meaning of the works performed. Again the aria and duet were usurping the place of music that should have been defining the stage situation, and conveying to the ear of the auditor a tone-picture to match the scenic representation and help to carry on the action of the piece.

It needed a strong hand to stem the tide on this occasion, and a strong hand was available in the person of Richard Wagner, whose efforts have revolutionized opera to so great an extent that it is unlikely that any great work for the stage will ever be conceived in the future which will not show traces of his influence. For he took no half-measures, but went to the root of the matter, and that in so thorough a way that he really invented an utterly new phase of expression.

Wagner, whose great idea it was that in the rendering of opera the arts of music, action, poetry, and scenery should stand on an equal footing, was unable to allow attention to be devoted to the music in the very special way in which it was drawn when set forms of song or air were admitted. He gradually worked his way to the construction of what was, until his time, an absolutely unknown form of dramatic accompaniment. The great and original innovation of Wagner was his use of melody (a feature non-existent in the works of the monodic writers); not melody of the stereotyped nature which we designate as tune, nor even the rhythmic, square-cut, and often beautifully appropriate melody of a Mozart or a Beethoven. Wagner's melodies were so constructed that they had, generally speaking, definite signification. Every subject (or *Leitmotiv*, as it was called) was intended to suggest to the mind of the hearer some definite idea connected with something occurring upon or suggested by the stage. Since the stage action or words would very often describe or suggest many ideas at the same time, these themes would be often superimposed; with the result that the music of Wagner's operas—at any rate the later ones—is not so much a stream of melody as a flow of many combined melodies, working together in contrapuntal richness and fertility into a harmonious whole, which can be listened to either casually (in which case it may or may not please the auditor) or after considerable study, when it will undoubtedly awake interest and admiration.

The lazy, pleasure-loving portion of mankind was immediately up in arms against such startling methods as these, and even to-day, although the Wagner cult is a very considerable one, it is to be doubted whether the real tastes of the majority of operatic listeners are not rather for something demanding less careful and close attention. Whether this be so or not, the point remains that Wagner's innovations, when once understood and grasped, were seen to be so dramatically true and fitting that all composers of operas, since his works became widely known, have come under his influence, and have in large measure framed their dramatic music on the lines laid down by him.

Here, then, was another revolution, and an important one. Formal melody still exists on the stage, but the continuous interconnecting links of melos are derived from Wagner, while the wondrous harmonies and chord combinations which he was the first to introduce into the realm of opera have been so many additions to the material which the modern composer has for manipulation.

PHASES OF OPERATIC HISTORY, AND MISCELLANY

I. ENGLISH OPERA FROM THE EIGHTEENTH TO THE PRESENT CENTURY

"The Beggar's Opera" — Arne — Bishop — Balfe — Wallace—
Thomas—Sullivan—Living Composers.

THERE is not much to boast of, so far as English operatic music is concerned, from the death of Purcell to about the middle of the nineteenth century. Purcell's work, in its limited field, was excellent, but Handel's powerful personality attracted so much attention to the Italian methods of composition that no other style found real favor for many years.

Opera, of course, existed in England, but it was of the Italian order: indeed, there was so much said against the unfortunate English language as a medium of vocal expression that native talent had little or no chance of distinguishing itself. The only work that stands out during this period as being essentially English was a curious medley of songs and airs called "The Beggar's Opera" produced in 1728, but even this was arranged by Pepusch, a German. The old genuine English tunes were, however, used in this, and its one or two successors, but the music is not of a serious type. The airs are simple and simply harmonized, and make no comparison with the Handel or Bononcini operas.

One of the first Englishmen to write opera on the prevalent Italian model was Thomas Arne, whose chief work was "Artaxerxes." He also wrote many masques or plays with incidental music. To-day he is best known as the reputed author of "Rule Britannia," and of the popular and tuneful setting of Shakespeare's words "Where the Bee sucks."

The English style of composition of this period, which is in the main vigorous, manly, and bold, was not at all suited to the taste of the fashionable public, who were led to believe that the florid and effeminate Italian airs were the only true method of operatic composition; consequently we are not surprised that native talent was overlooked and ignored, and that England has nothing to show that will compare with what was going on in Italy, Germany, and France at a corresponding period.

Arne's name is still remembered and his tunes sung, but the same can hardly be said of his followers and successors, Shield, Storace, Kelly, and others. Although these men attempted dramatic composition in the style of Arne, they had no very definite model upon which to work, and they were more successful in the glee and madrigal than in stage work. Some of their songs are heard now and then, but their influence on national opera was very slight.

The eighteenth century is indeed a period of blank in English operatic history, and in spite of the work of Henry Bishop, who wrote effective concerted numbers, the earlier part of the nineteenth century had but little more to show. Bishop was content to leave the English "ballad opera" where he found it, although he had the ability to found a national school of opera had he possessed the requisite energy and initiative.

The first English composer after Arne to produce anything attaining to real popularity, and really deserving the name of opera, was Balfe, who, following an example set by John Barnett in his opera "The Mountain Sylph," produced in 1835 "The Siege of Rochelle," and eight years later the well-known "Bohemian Girl." That these operas are not of a particularly exalted type must be admitted; the airs are tuneful and mostly commonplace. There can be no comparison, for example, between "The Bohemian Girl" and "Faust"; for although both make a ready and immediate appeal, the artistic standard is much lower in the English than in the French work. But still the work of Balfe was an immense advance on the poorly constructed ballad opera that had hitherto found acceptance, and it helped to pave the way to higher ideals and better methods.

On about the same plane is Wallace, whose most popular work is "Maritana"—even more trying to listen to (for the cultured hearer) than "The Bohemian Girl." These works, although poor and of no interest to the musician, yet play a part in the education of the people. Those quite unenlightened in the forms of opera can make a good start by at first listening to works of this type; and as their experience grows, so their taste will undoubtedly improve, and ripen to an appreciation of better things. The admiration of the crowd for such works as these, although now less than formerly, is not to be altogether condemned, seeing that it may in some cases be the means of raising the masses to an appreciation of something better and more musically satisfactory.

As musical education in England gradually improved, so we find the composers more artistic in their outlook and more solid in their work. The operas of Benedict (1804-85) and Macfarren (1813-87), although seldom performed now, are the output of talented and cultured musicians, who possessed, moreover, gifts of melody and dramatic characterization which must not be overlooked. Benedict's best opera was "The Lily of Killarney," produced in 1862.

Greater heights still were reached by Arthur Goring Thomas (1850-92), who wrote "Esmeralda" and "Nadeshda," both works of merit, and from which excerpts are frequently given in concert-rooms.

Last of deceased English opera-composers we name Sir Arthur Seymour Sullivan (1842-1900), who wrote one serious opera, "Ivanhoe" (1891), and a host of delightful works of slighter scope to which it is hard to give a class-name. They are not quite of the opera comique type, nor do they partake of the farcical nature of opera bouffe. Perhaps a nondescript term such as "light opera" answers as well as any other to the charming, harmonious, graceful class of "Singspiel" which found such favor not only in England and America, but in the case of some works (such as "The Mikado"), also on the European continent. Their popularity, immense some twenty years ago, lately appears to be somewhat on the wane; but they are still models of refinement and of good sound musicianship.

More serious attention has been paid to opera in English by composers still living (1910) than by any yet named here. With the exception of Sir C. Hubert H. Parry, all the chief living composers of English nationality have made a bid for fame in grand opera, though with only partial success. Those whose efforts appear to have led to the best results are Stanford and Mackenzie. In England there is less opportunity for operatic composers than in almost any other country: works when written have little chance of being publicly staged. Occasionally the management of the Grand Opera invites a work from an English musician, but even then it is sometimes coupled with the condition that it be performed in a foreign language. Opera is not the delight of the man in the street, as it is in many European countries, and the works that find favor at Covent Garden seem to be chosen according to the wishes of the boxholders and members of the syndicate.

Besides Stanford and Mackenzie, among the composers making brave endeavors in face of such adverse conditions are Bunning, Corder, Cowen, De Lara, MacCunn, and others. But, notwithstanding what these have accomplished or attempted, it is acknowledged by native critics that, while English opera suffers much from lack of opportunity, it suffers more from want of individuality. Were English composers able to graft on to their style some trace of natural characteristics, as we find the Russians and Bohemians of to-day have done, there is little doubt but that their productions would command a greater interest and a more enduring success.

II. SLAVONIC OPERA

Early Russian Composers—Glinka—Dargomijsky—Borodin—César Cui—Rimski-Korsakov—Tchaikovsky—Polish Opera—Bohemian Opera—Smetana—Dvořák—Other European Countries.

THE operas of the Russians, Poles, and Bohemians, in so far as they possess points of individual interest, do so by virtue of their natural characteristics. It is unnecessary, therefore, to trace back the history of opera in these countries to its foundation, as we should find that, in the main, it was a borrowed and foreign art, employing only methods that had derived their origin elsewhere, generally in Italy.

Although, therefore, we find that opera in Russia was produced as early as 1737 on the Italian model, and even in the vernacular with some attempt at national style in 1756, these early attempts soon gave way before the popular style of light Italian pieces, and the work of such composers as Volkov, Titov, and Cavos may be passed over as unimportant in the history of opera. Even the music of that much greater musician, Anton Rubinstein, so far as his dramatic work goes, is a negligible quantity, in so far as it is Teuton in style and without distinction or national signification.

The acknowledged pioneer in this school was Glinka (1804-57), who wrote but one work of lasting worth, "A Life for the Czar." This opera, however, laid such hold upon the Russian peoples as to have become the most popular opera in their repertoire, and we are told that it is played invariably for the opening night of the season both at Moscow and at St. Petersburg. It is intensely national in subject, and although the music shows many traces of Italian influence, which is not surprising considering its date of production (1836), there is still much that has its origin in national song and folk theme. Glinka afterward wrote and produced a still more national but less successful work entitled "Russlan and Ludmilla."

Glinka's one popular opera is not only important in itself; it is still more worthy of notice as the stimulating motive which enabled a large number of younger Russians to write works of a similar nature. It must be conceded that here the names of these men are hardly anything but names; yet in their own country they mean much to the people. The extremely intimate nature of the music of the operas written by such men as Dargomijsky, Serov, César Cui, Rimsky-Korsakov, Borodin, Tchaikovsky, and Arensky, while making for popularity in the country of their production, is a factor against their performance in countries where the folk songs and themes introduced would be unknown and unappreciated.

Dargomijsky (1813-69), who has been claimed as the founder of modern Russian opera, wrote two fairly well-known works, "The Water-Sprite" and "The Stone Guest," the story of the latter being closely allied to that of Mozart's "Don Giovanni." In his operas Dargomijsky seems to have been more or less unconsciously working on the lines of Wagner in the construction of his intermediary recitative sections, and his whole method is one of greater advancement than that of Glinka. His chief follower was Mussorgsky (1839-81), a composer much influenced also by Wagner. He was also an able literary critic. His most famous work was entitled "Judith."

Borodin (1834-87), a capable chemist as well as a skilled musician, has a name for the composition of clever examples of chamber music. To the operatic repertoire he contributed "Prince Igor," a work following Italian methods to some extent, but still possessing much that stamps its Russian origin. It is one of the few members of its class that are bright and cheerful in tone, with an absence of that pessimism which is the prevalent feature of so much Russian music.

César Cui (born 1835) has composed "Ratcliff," "Angelo," "Le Flibustier," and other works, the last mentioned having been produced in Paris. Cui is well known for his able literary articles and contributions to the Russian journals and magazines. Rimsky-Korsakov (1844-1908) wrote several works, among them "Pskovitjanka" and "A May Night."

The name of Tchaikovsky (1840-93) is well enough known in the concert-rooms of the world. Of all Russian composers his is the name to conjure with, and although one cannot pass unrestrictedly favorable criticism upon all that he composed, we undoubtedly owe to him a very great deal that is surpassingly rich, beautiful, and likely to endure. His genius, however, did not shine at its brightest in the theater, and although, like the Bohemian Dvořák, he was attracted again and again to the stage, his work for it has not met with such universal success as that done in other spheres.

Besides his "Eugen Onegin," which we give, several more fine works proceeded from his fertile pen, some of them still very popular in their own country. The chief are "The Oprichnik," "Joan of Arc," "Mazeppa," and "The Enchantress." Tchaikovsky attempted many styles, but his individuality was always apparent, sometimes with good results and sometimes not. When the subject of the opera was in accordance with the general trend of his thought, the result was felicitous, but he holds a lower place as a writer of opera than as a creator of symphony, song, and tone-poem.

The sister country of Poland has at present made little claim to achievement in the opera house: the national dances, the polonaise, valse, mazurka, etc., have been utilized by Glinka very effectively, but the only record of Polish opera to hand is the work of the great pianist Paderewski, whose "Manru" is included in our selection. Its music is described as German rather than Polish, and it is not likely to found a new school of composition.

Of more interest is the national opera of Bohemia, with its headquarters at Prague. Among its composers we find the names of Tomaschek (1774-1850), Napravnik (born 1839), and Fibich (1850-1900). More important than these is Smetana (1824-84), who settled in Prague in 1866, at a time when national freedom of thought and language was gaining position in Bohemia. Smetana took advantage of the enthusiasm with which everything national was greeted, and by his incorporation of the folk-songs of the people into his operas, introduced to his country a new form of opera which at once took root and flourished there. The melodies he chose were dear to the hearts of the people; moreover, they were simply and yet effectively treated, with due knowledge of and consideration for stage effect; consequently Smetana's operas are in Bohemia looked upon as the realization of a national ideal.

His pupil and follower, Dvořák (1841-1904), whose name as a composer of symphonies and chamber music is an exalted one, also wrote much for the stage; indeed, just before his death a new opera by him, "Armida," was produced in Prague. But his success, although so great and well deserved in other fields, is not comparable with that of Smetana, nor has he ever in the same way touched the hearts of the people. Other works by him are "King and Collier," "Wanda," "Der Bauer ein Schelm," "Demetrius," and "Rusalka." There is a promising young group of composers working at Prague, of whose doings we may some day hear more than at present.

Here we may glance at the conditions that govern opera in some of the other European countries, which give evidence of a certain amount of activity; this has, in the main, confined itself up to the present within its own borders. The Scandinavian composers, such as Gade, Grieg, Sinding, etc., whose names are world-known in other fields, have nothing to show us in respect of opera. The opera houses of Christiania and Copenhagen are active and busy, but they produce little indigenous opera, nor does the fame of that little travel very far. The Spaniards and Portuguese also have no claim to distinction as composers of opera, the name of Arrieta, we take it, being little known, although he is the most famous of Spanish musicians so far as dramatic writing is concerned. Interest in the opera of these countries is the work of the specialist, rather than of the general writer.

III. OPERA TO-DAY IN ITALY, GERMANY, AND FRANCE

Boito—His Interesting Personality—Mascagni—Leoncavallo—
Puccini—Cilea—German Composers—Goldmark and Hum-
perdinck—Richard Strauss—The French School—Saint-
Saëns—Massenet—Bruneau—Debussy.

TO-DAY the art of operatic composition appears to
be returning for its best results to its much-loved
home, Italy; the young Italian composers, among all
its devotees of all nationalities, appear to be putting
forth the strongest work. Contemporary English,
French, and German operas, with a few notable exceptions, are rarely heard beyond the borders of the land
which gives them birth, but the works of Mascagni,
Puccini, and Leoncavallo find a home in every opera
house.

At the outset of our review of living Italian opera
composers we meet the strange figure of Arrigo Boito
(born 1842), more famous for one opera than are
many composers who have endowed the world with
dozens of such works. The charm of his personality
has aided its success, while the ill fortune which
dogged its birth and its intimate relationship to a great
home have also contributed to its world-wide fame.

Not that Boito's "Mefistofele" is a work in the repertoire of every opera house; rather, its performances
seem to be limited in number, and yet all the world
knows of its composer as the capable litterateur and
musician who, amidst intense excitement, brought his
"Mefistofele" before the Milanese public at La Scala
in 1868, and by the novelty of its form and musical
treatment so displeased a very large number of his
would-be admirers that he fell from the height of
popularity to which expectation had elevated him almost to the depth of extinction so far as his musical
efforts were concerned. "Mefistofele" has been re-
written; it was a work in advance of its time, and
honor must be given to Boito for the artistic beauty
of his conceptions, and for his courage and skill in the
wielding of them to the ultimate conviction of an unwilling public. This fascinating but tantalizing composer still stimulates interest by the fact that he keeps
two other and newer operas, "Nerone" and "Oresti-
ade," in his desk, and refuses, at any rate for the present, to bring them to the light.

We now come to a composer whose music, or part of
it, at any rate, must have been heard by everybody—
Pietro Mascagni (born 1863), whose most famous
opera, "Cavalleria Rusticana," is one of the most popular modern works in the operatic repertoire. It was
produced in 1890, and soon attained to fame; this was
due, to some extent, to the introduction of a new device—namely, the performance of an orchestral intermezzo dividing the work into two parts, the curtain remaining up and disclosing an empty stage (a street
scene). Possibly the original intention in leaving the
curtain up was to prevent the buzz of conversation
which always accompanies its fall, and precludes the
possibility of careful attention to the music; but in
this instance the music is so melodious, tuneful, and
cleverly scored that it assured the success of the opera.
Succeeding works from the same pen—"L'Amico
Fritz," "I Rantzau," "Guglielmo Ratcliff," "Iris," and
others—have not yet found equal success.

Very frequently coupled upon the same playbill with
Mascagni's "Cavalleria" is the short modern Italian
opera "I Pagliacci" (The Strolling Players), the work
of Leoncavallo (born 1858), and written upon much
the same general lines as its forerunner. Its prologue,
for a solo barytone, is popular in concert-halls. In the
opera it occurs as part of the overture, the singer pushing his way through the curtain, and retiring again
after his performance, before the stage scene is actually
disclosed. Leoncavallo has written many other works,
but his chief distinction of later date has been that upon
him fell the choice of the German Emperor to write a
typically German opera on the subject of "Roland of
Berlin." The work was produced in Berlin in 1905,
but without giving full satisfaction, the general opinion
being that a German composer should have been
chosen to clothe so essentially national a subject with
music, and that Leoncavallo's attempt was uninspired,
grandiose, and lacking in the elements of beauty.

Other followers of Mascagni are Giordano (born
1867), composer of "Andrea Chenier"; Spinelli
(born 1865), chiefly known by "A Basso Porto";
and Franchetti (born 1850). More famous than
these is Francesco Cilea, a young composer of
promise, whose "Adriana Lecouvreur" contains
music of great beauty and charm. The method of
Mascagni is closely followed, even to the introduction
of a tuneful and charmingly scored intermezzo, but
there is independence of melodic phrase and real grip
in the music. "Adriana" was originally produced at
Milan in 1902, and was staged at Covent Garden,
London, during the autumn visit of the San Carlo
company, two years later.

Undoubtedly the greatest of the modern Italian
composers is Giacomo Puccini (born 1858), who has
made himself famous not merely by one opera but
by several. His earlier works, "Manon Lescaut," etc.,
hardly represent him at his best, although they contain much fine music; but in "La Bohème," in "La
Tosca," and most of all in "Madame Butterfly," this
clever musician has found himself and has risen to
great heights. He is most happy in the way in

which his music paints the situation to be depicted, and he has a most wonderfully ready power of melody. The continuous use of distinctive and rhythmic melody and the absence of any definite characterization by means of the *Leitmotiv* differentiates his work very largely from that of the Wagner school—it is altogether on a lighter basis, but the melody has an irresistible attractiveness, which accounts largely for the favor which his operas are finding at the present day.

Puccini's latest work, "The Girl of the Golden West," deals with an American subject. It was produced at the Metropolitan Opera House, New York, during the season of 1910-11.

Germany to-day can hardly be held to have produced such an array of familiar names, but that of Humperdinck (born 1854) has become famous through his setting of the delightful fairy tale "Hänsel und Gretel." There is, however, still living a senior to Humperdinck in the person of Goldmark (born 1830), whose "Cricket on the Hearth" is well known. Goldmark became famous by his opera "The Queen of Sheba," produced in Vienna in 1875. He has penned much music, and other operas, but the two above named are his best-known contributions to operatic literature.

More interesting, because his fairy opera has been seen by almost every one, is Humperdinck, who has skillfully applied Wagnerian methods to opera on a comparatively light subject. The story of "Hänsel und Gretel," from Hans Andersen, is worked up into a charming plot, and if some of the incidents seem, upon the modern stage, somewhat trivial and childish, the music is so perfect in form and matter that the ear is delighted throughout. The use of folk-songs and simple melodies which appeal to all is supplemented by a wonderfully capable and polyphonic use of the orchestra, which shows the master hand in every bar of the score.

"Hänsel und Gretel" can be appreciated alike by the smallest child and by the skilled musician, and therein lies its great charm, for much study must usually precede appreciation of work so elaborate and complex. Humperdinck's succeeding works, several in number, have not risen to the same level, either of beauty or of popularity. His "Die Heirat wider Willen" was produced with a fair measure of success under Strauss at Berlin in April, 1905.

Richard Strauss, the well-known composer of orchestral tone-poems, has made several bids for fame in opera: his early works, such as "Guntram" and "Feuersnot," have not attracted so much attention as have "Salome," produced at Dresden in 1906, and the "Elektra" staged in 1909. Strauss, the most conspicuous of recent musical innovators, writes very boldly, often with a startling lack of blend between orchestra and voice.

Other living composers of German opera are Max Schillings (born 1868); Weingartner (born 1863), the great orchestral conductor; Siegfried Wagner (born 1869), son of the great master; Nessler (born 1841), composer of "Der Trompeter von Säkkingen" (a wonderfully popular work, which, however, is not of the first rank); and many others whose fame may or may not be enduring. Modern German opera

since Wagner has hardly, with the exception of "Hänsel und Gretel," the distinction, power, and originality which we find in the followers of the young Italian school.

More famous are the men of the French school, the natural followers of Gounod, Ambroise Thomas, and their fellows. Progress is noticeable from the type of music which prevails in "Faust," in the works of such composers as Saint-Saëns, Massenet, and Bruneau, and the influence of Wagner is quite apparent. But in French opera the traditions which belonged to the Académie of old, and which have descended to the more modern grand opera, combine with a certain Gallic grace and charm to preserve individuality to this school.

Foremost among French composers in every branch is that versatile and gifted man Saint-Saëns (born 1835). Like Boito, he possesses an interesting personality, prominent among his characteristics being a habit of suddenly disappearing for months together from the eyes of a world of which he has grown temporarily weary. He will then come back from some half-civilized or totally barbarous district of Africa or elsewhere, bearing with him piles of manuscript, which soon finds a ready publisher. The music so composed often bears some impress of the surroundings amid which it has been penned, which adds in no small degree to its acceptance by the public. Saint-Saëns has written many operas both for the grand and the comique stage without any very marked success. The work best known here is "Samson et Dalila," a dramatized version of the Bible story. His "Henry VIII" is perhaps the best known of his other works, which include "Proserpine," "Ascanio," "Phryne," "Les Barbares," and "L'Ancêtre."

Jules Massenet (born 1842) is the author of many operas, of which mention may be made of "Don César de Bazan," "Le roi de Lahore," "Hérodiade," "Manon," "Le Cid," "Esclarmonde," "Werther," "Thaïs," "La Navarraise," and "Le Jongleur de Notre-Dame." "Hérodiade" is really a dramatic version of the Bible story of St. John and Salome. It is perhaps the best of the Massenet operas, "Manon" and "La Navarraise" approaching it nearest in popular esteem. Massenet has had much success with "Le Jongleur de Notre-Dame," produced at Monte Carlo in 1902.

A most earnest and serious-minded composer, who more closely follows Gluck and Wagner in his desire for operatic truth, is Alfred Bruneau (born 1857), one of the finest of French musicians. From the first his style has been revolutionary, and owing to crudities somewhat hard to accept; but while sometimes musically deficient, his dramatic grip and sincerity of purpose are so strong that there is doubtless a future before his operas. "Le rêve," "L'attaque du moulin," "Messidor," and "L'Ouragan" are the titles of his chief works, the third named of these being perhaps the best. Bruneau was fortunate in securing the services of Zola as his librettist, several prose-poems by the great novelist having been intrusted to his care.

André Messager (born 1853) has chiefly distinguished himself by a charming light work, "La

Basoche," which has had much attention at English hands. Dubois, Paladihle, and others are still at work in the field of French opera, but perhaps its most prominent modern representative is Gustave Charpentier (born 1860), whose opera "Louise" has made a great hit, and shows possession of great gifts from which much more may be expected. Vincent d'Indy (born 1851), another of the younger school,

is the composer of a fairly successful work, "Fervaal."

Claude Debussy (born 1862), a composer who has written an amount of successful music of a unique kind, in that it employs mostly a scale of whole tones, rather than one of tones and semitones, produced in 1902 "Pelléas et Mélisande," based on Maeterlinck's drama of the same name. This original and distinctive work has become widely popular.

IV. THE CHIEF OPERA HOUSES OF THE WORLD

Covent Garden—La Scala—San Carlo—Venice—Rome—Paris and the Grand Opéra—Vienna—Budapest—Prague—Berlin—Dresden—Munich—Bayreuth—Russia — Other European Countries—Egypt—America.

ARCHITECTURALLY speaking, Covent Garden Theater, the leading English opera house, is not one of the sights of London. Hidden away somewhat ignominiously in a side street, it has little appearance, in spite of its size, and by no means forms so conspicuous a feature in the way of public building as do the majority of the houses in European capitals.

Covent Garden Theater is situated on Bow Street, where the first building was opened in 1732. Several structures on the site were destroyed by fire. The present building was opened in 1858. Many musical productions, including operas, had been given earlier at Covent Garden, but it was not till 1846 that the theater was converted specially into an opera house. Here Mario, Grisi, Alboni, Tamburini, and many other renowned artists have sung. At Covent Garden Adelina Patti made her first appearance before a European audience. English as well as foreign opera has at times flourished at this famous house. Under the management of the Royal Opera Syndicate it still maintains its rank as one of the world's great musical houses—this in spite of the fact that it is "nothing but an ordinary theater," and is not, like the opera houses of the Continent, practically sacred to the performance of opera. At Covent Garden, besides opera are given musical festivals, promenade concerts, fancy dress balls, etc. Only at certain seasons of the year is the theater exclusively devoted to opera. The Royal Opera Syndicate runs a season of grand opera from the end of April to the end of July, performances being given nightly.

Turning to the opera houses of the European continent, we at once think of the famous La Scala theater at Milan. This house has a seating capacity

for 3600 persons. Apart from its size, there is the musical and artistic interest which this house derives from the production of many works here for the first time. Since its opening date, August 3, 1778, hundreds of operas have been staged, and the triumphs of Rossini, Meyerbeer, Bellini, Donizetti, and Verdi have been witnessed. It is enough to state that such works as Rossini's "La Gazza ladra," Bellini's "Norma," Donizetti's "Lucrezia Borgia," Verdi's "I Lombardi," Boito's "Mefistofele," and Ponchielli's "La Gioconda" first saw the light of day in La Scala to establish for it a claim to notice on the part of operagoers. Some time ago the municipal grant toward the expenses of the establishment was close upon $50,000, but since 1902 the annual subsidy has been reduced.

Even older than La Scala, as it dates originally from 1737, is its Neapolitan rival San Carlo. The new house, built after a fire in 1816, is of great size, and at one time vied with La Scala in the importance of new works produced; but less financial support has been forthcoming from Naples than is the case at Milan, and although an annual grant of some $16,000 is given by the municipality, the San Carlo productions, while of very high rank, are perhaps hardly on a level with those at La Scala. But San Carlo has had its triumphs, and has seen the first production of Rossini's "Mosè in Egitto," "Zelmira," and other works, and of Donizetti's "Lucia di Lammermoor," besides numbers of other operas of less fame.

Although Venice looms large in the history of music, and its doings in opera have been very considerable, there appears to be no theater solely devoted to this class of work, nor is there any regular grant. The Fenice Theater has figured largely in Venetian operatic history. It is interesting to remember that Rossini's "Semiramide" and "Tancredi" were both first performed at that house.

Rome in older days nad pride of place among opera houses, and Hadow speaks of it as being at one time the highest school in which a musician could graduate. Here was produced Rossini's "Il Barbiere" and many another famous work. To-day opera at Rome, if indeed it is on an equal level, hardly seems to be of higher importance than that in other Italian cities. It has no subsidy at the present time, and has to depend on its own resources for its maintenance.

The French opera house is one of the most imposing sights of Paris; well situated and finely conceived, it is a worthy home for that art product for which it is intended. The history of French opera from the earliest recorded performances of the sixteenth century is, of course, very extensive. As long ago as 1672 the name of Lulli made Parisian opera famous, and although for a time its home was transferred to the Palais Royal, the site has borne testimony to many a fine building, the present one, inscribed Académie Nationale de Musique, dating from 1874 (commenced in 1861). Although its seating capacity of 2156 is much less than that of La Scala, it is the largest house in the world, and covers almost three acres of ground.

Besides Lulli, the names of Rameau, Gluck, Cherubini, Spontini, Hérold, Auber, Meyerbeer, and Berlioz are all indissolubly connected with the opera of Paris. There is no house in all musical history that can claim so great a measure of variety and incident, nor make such interesting reading, as that of the Académie de Musique. Its fortunes have fluctuated, but it has done wonderful work, and a mere recapitulation of names of fine operas which had their original production here would be far too long for quotation. The glory of Parisian grand opera has always held a spell over the nations, and has been a thing apart from all else in music. We know something of the hold of the Académie upon Wagner, and if there is to-day somewhat less of a glamour cast by it than in the days when Lulli held despotic sway, or Spontini or Meyerbeer dominated all, there is still a charm and delight to be found within its walls, which are difficult to equal in houses where the traditional uses are less sacredly adhered to.

The French are very jealous of its traditions, and although modern times have not allowed the directors to fall behind in their efforts to keep pace with the strides operatic music has made under Wagner's influence, it is only quite recently that the works of the composer have been welcomed in Paris. Popular feeling, partly on patriotic grounds, for long kept his operas in the background. Parisians would have none of them. The result has been, perhaps, even more rigidly to preserve those customs of grand opera, such as the inclusion of a ballet, which are among its most distinctive features.

Touching upon the question of finance, we find that the French Government allows the very large subsidy of $160,000 per annum toward the expenses of grand opera; in return, however, opera is supposed to be staged three or four times during the week. The prices of admission are not high, ranging from 17 francs to 2 francs. France loves its opera, and does not hesitate to lay out good round sums for its support; nor are its people behindhand in their attendance; a crowded house is the rule rather than the exception, appreciation, while critical, being still keen.

Comparing not unfavorably in dignity of conception and splendor of adornment with the French house is the Imperial Opera of Vienna, an ornament in that encircling ring of fine buildings which is so distinctive a feature of the Austrian capital. Vienna has been the home of so many of the giants of music that it is not surprising that it should have witnessed the first production of many a work now world-famous: Gluck's "Orfeo," Mozart's "Figaro," "Cosi fan tutte," and "Zauberflöte," Beethoven's "Fidelio." These alone would suffice to cause Vienna to stand high in musical fame. Not that the present opera house witnessed their production, for the building which to-day stands as an abode of opera dates from a more recent time; the cost of its erection was more than $2,500,000. Belonging to the state, its affairs are administered by the Lord Chamberlain's department, any deficit being made good from the Emperor's civil list.

The Royal Opera House at Budapest, Hungary, receives from the state a large subsidy, a specific sum for salaries, and a liberal grant from the Emperor.

Reference must also be made to Prague, famous for the production of Mozart's "Don Giovanni" in 1787. More recently Prague has been the home of works of the Bohemian school, as exemplified by Smetana, Dvořák, Fibich, and others. Smetana's "Bartered Bride" was staged at Prague in 1866, and from that date to the time of the appearance of Dvořák's "Armida," in 1904, the National Theater has witnessed a constant succession of works of a characteristically national tone which make an unfailing appeal to the Czechs. The Czech theater has a state grant.

The Berlin Opera House also has claims to notice, for was not Weber's "Der Freischütz" mounted here for the first time? Moreover, Berlin being the capital of Germany, the house is the scene of many fine state performances much patronized by royalty. The building itself, although standing well in the fine "Linden" promenade, will not compare with Paris or Vienna from an architectural point of view. The Opera House and Playhouse of Berlin together receive annually $270,000 toward their working expenses.

Leipzig and Dresden have fine theaters. The Dresden Court Theater, used as an opera house, is specially famous for its associations with Weber and Wagner. It is a fine building, magnificently situated in an imposing position, and having considerable architectural pretensions. The King of Saxony pays about $155,000 for the opera, theater, and orchestra, and also makes good any deficit that arises. At this theater Richard Strauss has produced his "Salome" and "Elektra."

Munich has of late come to the front in operatic matters; the Court Theater, administered from the civil list, has long devoted much attention to opera, but interest is now centered somewhat on the new Prince Regent Theater, where an attempt is being made to outvie Bayreuth itself in the Wagner productions. Nor have the performances been confined to Wagner, for Mozart's operas have been interspersed with his. It is as yet too early to say what influence, if any, the new Munich house will have on the fortunes of Bayreuth, but it seems probable that a theater even better fitted up than Bayreuth itself for Wagnerian performances, and in a locality so much more central and easily reached, may in the near future materially affect the fortunes of the older house.

Almost every German town of any size has its opera house, and detailed description of all is manifestly impossible, notwithstanding that much interest attaches to some of them. We must therefore conclude our account of the German theaters with a short description of that built by Wagner at Bayreuth according to his own ideas of what such a house should be.

There is little doubt that at the present time the Bayreuth Opera House is the most famous in the world. Worship of Wagner is still widespread, the halo surrounding his name and his home casts a glow upon the little town which he selected as the scene of his final labors, and from all parts of the world, when the Bayreuth theater opens its doors, pilgrimages are made and devotees flock with an intense enthusiasm which has no parallel. To the true Wagnerian, Bayreuth is a sacred spot inspiring a reverence quite distinct from that felt for any other.

It was in May, 1872, that the foundation-stone was laid, and the completion of the building, delayed by lack of funds, took place in 1876, when "The Ring" was performed. Since then performances have taken place on a grand scale at intervals of a year or two years in the summer. A feature in the construction was that an equally good view should be obtained from every point of view. This was done by raising every seat a little above the one immediately in front of it, and by putting each spectator where he could see between the heads of the two persons before him. Another feature was the submerged orchestra—i.e., below the level of the floor of the house. Even the conductor, although he has the stage in view, cannot be seen by the audience, and part of the orchestra (the brass) is actually under the stage—an experiment which seemed doubtful at first, but which has on the whole proved successful. The machinery and scenery were as good as could possibly be obtained, and the management still keeps up to date in this

respect. Although open to competition both from New York and from Munich, Bayreuth seems likely to hold its own for some years to come, whenever it may choose to open its doors.

In Russia, and more especially at St. Petersburg and Moscow, theatrical attendance is looked upon as an educational matter, and therefore it is possible to see opera for a very small sum. Of course this means large imperial help. The two cities have fine houses, with interest for us in that they have witnessed the production of most of the operas of the young Russian school. The ballet is much beloved in Russia, and forms one of the regular objects of representation.

Space forbids us to go into detail as to the opera houses of Sweden (Royal Theater of Stockholm), Norway (National Theater, Christiania), Spain, Holland, Belgium (Brussels, Théâtre de la Monnaie), Denmark (Copenhagen, Royal Theater), or Portugal. San Carlos, at Lisbon, is, however, of special interest in being one of the oldest houses of its kind, having been erected in 1793.

Egypt has opera houses at Cairo and Alexandria. That at Cairo saw the production of Verdi's "Aïda" in 1871.

In New York, the Metropolitan Opera House witnesses magnificent performances, and commands the best and most expensive talent in the world. It was opened October 22, 1883. Its stage is one of the largest in the country and the house has a seating capacity of 3700. That of the Manhattan, now given up to lighter productions, is 3000. (For many particulars relating to the opera houses in New York and other cities of the United States the reader is referred to the section on "Music in America," Chapter II.)

A few words should be added here concerning the Boston Opera House, in some respects the finest in America. It was inaugurated under the brightest auspices for art in the musical city which it adorns. It was brilliantly opened on November 8, 1909, with a performance of Ponchielli's "La Gioconda." The house has a seating capacity of 2750, and all its appointments are admirably suited to their purposes. The stage has been said by experts to have no equal in this country. It is 90 feet high, 70 feet deep, and 150 feet wide. It is divided into numerous platforms which can be raised or lowered by ingenious machinery to suit the requirements of any performance.

V. OFFSHOOTS AND CURIOSITIES OF OPERA

Operetta—Musical Comedy—Ballad Opera—Masque—Ballet—
Objections Thereto—Curiosities of Construction—Pasticcio—Mixed Language—Stereotyped Casts—Curiosities of
Stage Requirements—Wagner's Supernatural Requirements—Curiosities of the Music—Vocal Cadenzas.

THE chief offshoot of opera proper is opéra comique, or Singspiel—opera interspersed with
spoken dialogue, not necessarily of a humorous
nature. The mere fact, however, of the introduction
of such dialogue confers on the work the title of opéra
comique in France and that of Singspiel in Germany.
When one remembers that such works as Beethoven's
"Fidelio" and Weber's "Der Freischütz" belong to
this type, it is evidently of great importance, and
a very large number of operas by a variety of composers come under this heading.

Next, perhaps, in interest is the operetta, or short
opera, originally a one-act light opera frequently
employing spoken dialogue; the general style, moreover, is lighter and of less imposing proportions than
serious opera. In later days, operettas are often
prolonged into two or more acts and have been made
very familiar by the long series of works by Gilbert
and Sullivan, which, properly speaking, belong to
this category.

Of a somewhat lower grade is musical comedy, a
popular type of stage piece making considerable use
of music, but of only the less exalted forms of the
art. No serious pretensions to artistic beauty are
claimed by these works, the taste for which seems to
be, at the present time, somewhat on the wane.

A form of opera for which the English have always
had an affection is the ballad opera, really a string of
airs, often by different composers, thrown more or
less promiscuously into a story, with which they often
appear to have no very close connection. There is
practically no concerted music, and the whole bears
some resemblance to a ballad concert. The renowned
"Beggar's Opera," which for years was a model for
English entrepreneurs, belonged to this category, and
set an example for hosts of imitators to follow.
Indeed, England is only now beginning to shake herself free from the trammels of this class of work, to
which such operas as "The Bohemian Girl" and
"Maritana" tend to approximate. The ballad opera
also took root in America, where hundreds of such
works flourished for a time, and it is not unknown in
Germany, where it is called Liederspiel.

Of more artistic merit and interest is the masque,
which really preceded opera. Originally developing
in carnival processions through the streets of Italian
towns, it was adopted in England during the reigns
of Henry VIII and some succeeding monarchs. The

plan of such works was the presentation of some
allegorical idea upon a stage, with descriptive music,
both vocal and instrumental, and a large proportion
of dancing. Campion, Lock, Coperario, and many
others took part in the composition of these divertissements, which were in great demand for such functions
as royal weddings. They were staged in the most
sumptuous manner, great attention being paid to
stage machinery, costume, etc. Much of the music
has been lost, but what remains shows it to have been
excellent of its class, and it is effective even in performance to-day.

In early days of operatic history there was no
radical difference between the masque and the ballet.
An entertainment of vocal and instrumental music
in celebration of the marriage of the Duke of Joyeuse
in 1581 (costing three and a half million francs to
produce) was termed "Ballet comique de la Royne."
As an illustration of the dance alone, which is its
present signification, the ballet appears to date from
the foundation of the opera in France, with which
it has had a very close and lasting connection.

Indeed, until recently grand opera without a ballet
was unknown. Beginning with Lulli, and continuing
even up to the present day, the ballet has maintained
a position of great importance; and although it has
never appealed to other peoples to the same extent
as it appears to have done to Continental nations, it
has been transported with the works in which it was
introduced and has become a familiar feature to
operagoers everywhere.

The great disadvantage of the ballet is that it breaks
up the continuity of the story; the development of the
interest of the opera is arrested, and so far as the
music is concerned a complete difference in style is
often necessary, the result being that the old train
of thought and idea is often only to be resumed with
difficulty. Hence it happens that, with a growing
appreciation for artistic truth in opera, the ballet has
fallen into the background, and most operas seen to-
day do not include any performance of what is,
at best, a somewhat irrelevant interlude. A few
attempts, such as that by Wagner in "Tannhäuser,"
to introduce a ballet as an integral factor in the
dénouement, have not been specially successful, nor
have they been widely imitated. As a separate form
of entertainment, apart from opera, the ballet has
had excellent music written for it by Adam, Sullivan,
Tchaikovsky, and others (in Russia it is a very
popular amusement); but in England its appearances
are now mainly confined to the music hall, where it
is wedded to music of a light and charming character.
In our own country the ballet, at its best, is generally

enjoyed along with other features of the opera in which it occurs.

A few words as to curiosities of opera. These may be grouped somewhat as follows: (1) Curiosities of construction and design; (2) curiosities of stage requirements; (3) curiosities of the music.

The old manner of collecting a mass of heterogeneous materials in the way of airs and songs, and of turning them into a kind of opera, is certainly curious. The name pasticcio, or pie, is very applicable to this hybrid growth, which, however, has at times attained to great popularity. One of the most famous instances of its kind is "Muzio Scevola," produced in 1771. This work was in three acts: the first composed by Ariosti, the second by Bononcini, and the third by Handel. The last-named great composer, with an easy manner of doing things which would certainly not pass muster at the present day, also brought out in 1738 an opera almost entirely made up of favorite airs from his other works; an example which Gluck followed a few years later. The day for this kind of thing is fortunately past, and no composer of serious operatic work would revert to a procedure which is more suggestive of the construction of a pantomime.

The singing by different performers in different languages at the same time is another defunct custom. So little regard was paid to the importance of the libretto that it used to be quite a common occurrence for each person on the stage to sing in whatever language came easiest. On the Continent the airs would perhaps be sung in Italian and the recitatives in German, with an inconsistency that is almost incredible. When, however, agility in vocalization was the chief attraction in operatic representation, it is to be presumed that intelligibility of utterance was not an important consideration.

To the same cause must be attributed the extraordinary fact that the dramatis personæ were the same for nearly all operas during a certain period. Whatever the story or plot to be unfolded, it was essential that there should be six principal characters —a high soprano, a mezzo, and a contralto, a male soprano, a tenor, and a bass. Of course slight modifications in the character of the voices was occasionally allowed, but the main lines followed were as above. And whether it suited the story or not, each singer expected to have an important air to sing in each act, and woe betide the unhappy composer who wrote a more attractive piece for one of them than was supplied to a rival singer! From this stereotyped form of bondage, with all its artificiality, opera is now free; and it is due to the observance of these conventions that works of Handel and other composers, who wrote really good music, are absolutely dead.

Apart from the construction in the form of the opera, there have been from time to time interesting experiments made with regard to the housing of that integral portion of it—the orchestra. Wagner's innovation, the placing of the band out of sight and below the stage, although it necessitated the increase of the string sections, has proved on the whole good. Other designs have been the entire covering in of the orchestra with a thin transparent substance, which has had the effect of subduing the sound, but which

has also proved disastrously hot for the poor players. One idea emanated from the New York Metropolitan, when Conried suggested the placing of the brass players upon a movable platform, which could move up or down at will; if it is desired that their instruments shall sound prominently they will be raised into the air; if, on the other hand, a subdued effect is required, they will be lowered a few feet; a long crescendo will, presumably, be effected by a gradual elevation of this movable floor! One has yet to wait to see this invention adopted.

In days when enormous groups of performers were considered indispensable for grand effects in opera, one reads of many extravagances in the way of display. In modern scenic dramatic works, in the ballet, and in pantomime, these effects are no doubt legitimate enough; but inasmuch as the cumbering of the stage with voiceless supers hardly helps on the cause of opera, it is a matter for congratulation that these exceptional stage demands are no longer made to any great extent.

Here, for instance, is the modest list of performers that took part in Freschi's "Berenice" in 1680:

  100 Virgins.
  100 Soldiers.
  100 Horsemen in iron armor.
   40 Cornets on horseback.
    6 Mounted trumpeters.
    6 Drummers.
    6 Ensigns.
    6 Sackbuts.
    6 Flutes.
   12 Minstrels playing on Turkish instruments, etc.
    6 Pages.
    3 Sergeants.
    6 Cymballers.
   12 Huntsmen.
   12 Grooms.
   12 Charioteers.
    2 Lions led by 2 Turks.
    2 Elephants.
    4 Horses with Berenice's triumphal car.
   12 Horses drawing 6 cars.
    6 Chariots.
  A stable with 100 living horses.
  A forest filled with wild boar, deer, and bears.

However magnificent and imposing in effect such a spectacle may be, its proper sphere is not opera. With Meyerbeer, Spontini, and other composers of grand opera these ideas have found favor; but they are a bar to the production of their works to-day, not only on the score of very considerable expense, but also because the artistic sense that delights in beautiful music wedded to appropriate drama will hardly find pleasure in such merely sensuous effects of the eye.

The difficulties of modern stage management occur chiefly in the presentation of the supernatural. Huge crowds are easy enough to put upon the stage, but to make a bird fly across naturally is a more involved matter. In many of the Wagner operas these supernatural features are essential elements of the situation; the Rhine maidens *must* appear to be swimming in real water, the bird *must* fly ahead of Siegfried to show him the rock on which Brünnhilde sleeps, and round that rock living flames of fire *must* dart and play. It is such points as these which are difficult to stage convincingly. Has any one ever felt much frightened at the dragon Fafner? The fire has a way of coming out of his mouth at the wrong time, his head and his tail seem to have little connection with one another, and the impressive effect of his deeply sonorous utterances is often marred by the very visible megaphone through which they are uttered. In these strange beasts, for which machinery is ineffective, there is still scope for improvement in modern stage management.

Curiosities in the music occur now and then: such, for instance, is the weird portion in the middle of Weber's "Euryanthe" overture, where the curtain rises momentarily to display a gruesome tomb: such is the thrusting aside of the stage curtain in the midst of Leoncavallo's "Pagliacci" prelude for one of the characters to sing a song; such is the curious vocal scherzo upon one reiterated note, for the chorus of seraphim in Boito's "Mefistofele."

On a bigger scale is the curious experiment made by Michael in the opera "Utal," in writing his work without any violins in the orchestra. Of more frequent occurrence than the omission of instruments is the inclusion of various unusual effects, such as the introduction of a mandolin for the serenade in Mozart's "Don Giovanni," of the Glockenspiel for Papageno in "The Magic Flute," of peal of bells in many works, and so forth, whereas Handel sighed for a cannon, and Tchaikovsky actually used one in his "1812" overture. The maximum of stage noise

in this way was probably reached by Spontini, who in his opera "Alcidor" had a number of anvils upon the stage tuned to certain notes! An anvil accompaniment, not ineffectively used, may be heard in Gounod's "Philémon et Baucis."

Among curiosities of the music must be mentioned the vocal cadenzas, etc., written for exceptional singers; and in the days when these singers used to include male sopranos and contraltos (termed castrati) the majority of singers appear to have been exceptional. For a man to develop a high soprano voice seems not only unnatural but inartistic; and these singers, some of them most famous, belong to an order of things that obtains no longer, being contrary both to modern ethics and to good taste. What the male soprano could do can usually be done equally well by a good woman singer, and of these there is usually a sufficient supply.

For women singers with voices of exceptional compass special music has often been written, as witness the part of "Queen of the Night" in Mozart's "Zauberflöte," much of which lies abnormally high. Even where not written, singers of Italian opera have often introduced elaborate and wonderful cadenzas for the purposes of display, and these, although not tolerated in opera of the most exalted kind, may still be frequently heard.

Nowadays little of this kind of music is written for the voice, so far as opera is concerned. The work required of the modern operatic singer is more dramatic by nature, and makes demands upon technique of a different order.

VI. POTPOURRI

NOW and again it happens that opera rubs shoulders with politics, and acquires some importance in the affairs of nations. Lulli's power at court in the days of Louis XIV was notorious, and none too generously exercised so far as his fellow-musicians were concerned. But influence with monarchs, such as that which he acquired, is rarer now, and less powerful than in those earlier days. Lulli profited by the royal favor bestowed on him, but some great composers have been less fortunate.

Cherubini, for instance, was detested by the great

Napoleon, who lost no opportunity of inflicting slights upon him. Cherubini's sympathies were clearly manifested in his "Water Carrier" opera, as on the side of revolution, but distinctly contrary to the excesses to which it often led. So enraged were some ruffians with him that he was in 1794 dragged out of his house, marched through Paris, and finally compelled to provide music for the pleasure of his captors. Napoleon frequently called him into his presence in order to praise other composers, suggesting that he compared unfavorably with them. When Cherubini replied with some little spirit, he was promptly punished by being compelled to conduct various concerts and state performances with no reward whatever.

Napoleon was sometimes given to indulging his

sardonic humor at the expense of those who waited on his favors. It is related by one who knew him well that once at a social function he indulged his whim by pretending to humiliate the composer Grétry. Coming face to face with him several times, Napoleon repeatedly asked the musician, "And who are you?" At last, tired of identifying himself, he replied, "Sire, I am still Grétry."

Napoleon, for a time, could not do enough for Spontini. He commanded the production of "La Vestale," and rewarded him with a present of 10,000 francs, loading him, moreover, with praises and honors. This did not, however, last for very long, for the downfall of the great conqueror was at hand, and anxieties and cares claimed his attention.

Political feeling has probably never run so high over operatic matters as it did in Paris after the Franco-German war. For years no German work was tolerated, at any rate so far as new matter was concerned, and the determination of the management to produce Wagner's "Lohengrin" in 1891 was the signal for a riotous uproar. Public feeling ran high; some of the leading singers, considering discretion the better part of valor, caused frequent postponements of the performance by means of convenient indispositions, and when the work actually came to presentation cordons of police were called out to guard the opera house, both inside and out. M. Lamoureux, who conducted, did so with a pistol in his pocket. Opposition inside the theater made itself felt by an objectionable device of setting floating in the auditorium little balloons of foul gas; while opposition in the street was met by cavalry charges and frequent arrests. The whole occasion was made one of political import, but fortunately common sense prevailed, and no serious issues resulted. Happily for opera, such scenes as these are infrequent and unusual.

Opera is not a fortune-making business for the majority of those who embark on such enterprises. So far as the composition of opera is concerned, financial result is usually very small. Nowadays an opera cannot be lightly tossed off in a few days. It is true that Handel composed "Rinaldo" in fourteen days, Rossini "Il Barbiere" in thirteen (a wonderful performance), and Pacini his "Saffo" in four weeks; but these are very exceptional instances, and may fitly be contrasted with the labor of Wagner, who had his "Meistersinger" and "The Ring" on hand for something like twenty years. Modern opera, with its polyphonic orchestral background and amorphous movements, demands years of work, and for the majority of those who give so much of their lives to it there is little to show in return from a pecuniary point of view.

Operatic management, too, is very speculative; Handel lost his whole fortune and became bankrupt through his operatic ventures, and yet his works had enormous success in their day. The example set by him has been followed by many a subsequent manager, and is perhaps yet in store for many another.

The chief item in expenditure is, of course, the enormous amount swallowed up in the fees paid to the singers. Handel paid Senesino 1400 guineas for the season in 1731, and even allowing for the greater value of money in those days, that is a comparatively small amount. Here, for example, is the contract made by Jenny Lind with Lumley, the London manager, in 1846 (far less liberal, by the way, than such a singer would receive to-day):

"1. An honorarium of 120,000 francs (£4800) for the season (April 14th-August 20th, 1847).

"2. A furnished house, carriage, and pair of horses.

"3. A sum of £300 should she desire to have a preliminary holiday in Italy.

"4. Liberty to cancel the engagement should she feel dissatisfied after her first appearance.

"5. An agreement not to sing elsewhere for her own emolument."

(See Jenny Lind's vastly more remunerative dealings with P. T. Barnum, as related in the section on "Vocal Music and Musicians," Chapter X.)

It generally happens that a singer commands higher fees for private than for public singing, the advantage of the latter being as a rule a guaranteed number of appearances. Farinelli, for example, the chief singer engaged by the noble faction that set up in opposition to Handel in 1734, received only £1500 per annum, but his private engagements made up his income to £5000 a year—a large one at that date. This singer afterward visited the court of Philip V of Spain; that monarch was suffering from mental depression, from which nothing aroused him until the advent of Farinelli. The Queen was so delighted to see her royal spouse once more interested in anything that she engaged Farinelli at a salary of 50,000 francs to remain in Madrid. This he did, singing the same four songs to the King every night for ten years! Eventually Philip V succumbed, but he must have been a patient monarch.

It does not always happen that singers of equal merit receive the same payments, some being more fortunate than others. Catalani, for example, in 1807 received in London £5000 for the season, and with her concerts and provincial tours netted a profit for the year of £16,700. A more famous singer, Lablache, in 1828 could only command £1600 for four months; while Malibran in 1835 received £2755 for twenty-four appearances in London, and 45,000 francs for one hundred and eighty-five performances a few years later at La Scala.

But these fees are as nothing compared with those commanded by the leading singers of to-day, more especially in America, where money is "poured out like water," and where artists are sometimes retained at high fees by one opera house, even if they do not sing a single note during the whole season, so that a rival house shall not secure their services. It is not very unusual for a singer to receive $5000 per performance in the twentieth century. Madame Patti has stated that she received $6000 per night for two seasons of sixty nights each. Caruso has been paid $100,000 for eighty performances, and about $40,000 per annum for singing into gramophones; his contract for four years at $200,000 per annum with the New York Metropolitan is probably a record in this direction.

Of course the amounts received by those who compose the music never approximate to such figures as these. For "Don Giovanni" Mozart received only 500 thalers, and for "Figaro" 100 ducats. Weber's payment for "Der Freischütz" was 80 Friedrich d'ors, out of which he had to pay the librettist; after the treasury had netted 30,000 thalers from this work Weber was presented with 100! There are, however, a few examples of fair bargains made by musicians. Spontini, in 1814, was offered a salary, then liberal, equal to $3750 per annum for two operas each year in Berlin; in 1819 he accepted a ten years' engagement at the court of Frederick William III, Berlin, at a salary of 4000 thalers, a benefit of 1050 thalers, a free concert, and a pension. He was well treated, but did not himself behave very well, allowing his servant to sell free admissions to the theater, and grumbling because his first-night presentations did not bring in as much as he wished. He finally ended by a demand for compensation for 46,850 thalers, and that in face of the fact that he was convicted of lese-majesty and sentenced to nine months' imprisonment—an indignity from which his new monarch graciously released him.

Sometimes an agreement is made with the composer by which he receives a royalty or lump sum for each performance of his work. To the composer of an opera that takes the public fancy this spells fortune, and vast sums have now and again been made in this way. Isouard, for example, received for the performances of his "Cendrillon" in Paris alone over 100,000 francs in 1810, while Rossini and others have by similar strokes of luck easily acquired wealth. So small, however, is the proportion of new works to-day which become popular that the chances of such good fortune are very small; a "Cavalleria Rusticana" only makes its appearance now and then, nor is the composer of such a work often able to repeat his success.

Although rarely recognized, the work of the author of the libretto is of vast importance. In the days when the story meant little or nothing, provided so many pegs were provided on which to hang the arias, the share of the librettist was a less conspicuous one; to-day no inconsiderable part of the failure of an opera is due to a poor libretto. It therefore frequently happens that composers, finding it impossible to obtain a poem to please them, write their own libretti, the chief example of this dual work being Wagner, whose dramas are often very fine considered from a literary point of view alone.

Most famous of the librettists of early operas is Metastasio (1698-1782), some of whose poems were set by thirty and forty different composers: he wrote dramas used by such composers as Handel, Hasse, Jomelli, Porpora, Graun, Gluck, Meyerbeer, Caldara, Haydn, Cimarosa, and Mozart. In later days mention may be made of the dramatist Scribe (1791-1861), a French poet who provided a vast number of works for various composers, including Auber, Adam, Boieldieu, Donizetti, Hérold, Halévy, Meyerbeer, and Verdi. Quite one hundred of his operas were staged and performed, to say nothing of light dramatic and other pieces.

Scattered here and there in literature that deals with opera may be found endless stories of singers, composers, and art-patrons. Most fruitful in providing amusing tales are the prime donne, whose jealousies and bickerings, although unpleasant enough for those who have to contend against them, make sufficiently good reading. The prima donna generally knows her power, and is autocratic. There is not found every day a Handel to take such a one forcibly by the scruff of her neck and hang her suspended from a window in mid-air until his will is obeyed. When such a fractious lady has a husband in the same cast consequences may be very bad indeed. The tenor Arsani, for example, the teacher of the Garcias, had a wife who was a prima donna; but instead of acting together, so jealous were they of each other, that when one was receiving the plaudits of the audience the other would go round into the auditorium and hiss!

Rivalry is not always, however, so apparent, and when fine singers are willing to coöperate, very great results are sometimes obtained. The most notable ensemble in this respect was probably that of the four great singers Grisi, Rubini, Tamburini, and Lablache, a combination of talent very seldom equaled, which delighted auditors of the early Victorian era.

Nowadays, although a person of power, the great singer has not the field so entirely to himself as to be able to dictate regarding what he will or will not do. A certain tenor, for example, at Marseilles early in 1905 withdrew his promise to sing at a certain concert for the reason that a rival tenor had been engaged. Great was his amazement to find that this refusal by no means jeopardized the concert, as he had hoped, but rather became an additional source of amusement; for the management, having advertised him, determined that he should be seen upon the stage; so a ridiculous effigy of him was brought forward, and a trio from "Faust" was sung by other singers grouped round it. This may not have been very dignified, or even witty, but a few drastic measures of this kind might induce singers to be a little more reasonable in their treatment of the public.

Strange measures are sometimes taken to prevent the success of an opera. A hired body of fellows to hiss in opposition to the organized claque is by no means a rare sight in a French house; but sometimes more militant measures are taken. Rousseau's "Le devin du village," for example, received its *coup de grâce* in 1828 from the fact that some person (supposed to have been Berlioz) threw a huge powdered wig on to the stage in the midst of the performance. So threatening was the opposition to Jomelli's "Armida," produced in 1750, that its composer fled the house for his life by a back door. The opposition to "Lohengrin" in Paris has already been commented upon, but that to "Tannhäuser," organized by the Jockey Club in 1866, was even stronger. Noise and disorder filled the theater; people in the pit played flageolets, while the gallery sang riotous songs. So prejudiced was public opinion that a fair hearing was not accorded to the work. Under these conditions it is not altogether incredible that Mérimée should have exclaimed that he could write similar music after hearing his cat walk up and down the pianoforte!

Of composers, there are perhaps more amusing stories of Spontini than of any other single opera writer. This very opinionated and high-handed Italian thought much of himself, and little of all else, with the result that his life is very amusing reading.

He *would* have what he wanted. If his cellos could not play loud enough, they were made to sing their parts as well; if, after six hours' rehearsal, his prima donna fainted, he suggested that some one with more physique should be engaged. He did not, however, always have his own way. When "La petite maison" was produced in 1804, the audience dashed on the stage and smashed everything, while "La Vestale" was greeted with laughing, snoring, and the putting on of nightcaps. His orchestra, although moderate in volume in comparison with what often obtains to-day, was considered very noisy, so much so that it is said that a certain doctor who had a very deaf patient thought he might be made to hear by attending a performance of "La Vestale." After a specially noisy passage the deaf man with delight turned to his doctor: "I can hear," said he. His remark met with no response, for the reason that the doctor himself had been deafened by the noise.

Spontini felt such opposition very keenly; others are less affected by hostility. When Rossini's "Il Barbiere" was produced at Rome in 1816, it was hooted and hissed, much to the chagrin of several of the composer's friends. Thinking to commiserate with him on the failure of his work, they called at his house, expecting to find him in the depths of despair. Instead of that, the maestro was safely tucked up in bed and fast asleep!

Stories of singer and composer might fill many chapters of such a work as this, but there are books such as Sutherland Edwards's "History of the Opera" and Ella's "Musical Reminiscences" to which those interested may readily turn and find them; therefore such anecdotes need not be multiplied here.

A wealth of amusement may be derived from the daily papers, and in our time impresarios, in one country or another, often seem to be the most persecuted persons in the world. Opera has its worries and troubles, but to those who love it it is a constant source of refreshment and of artistic joy.

VII. THE TASK OF THE PRIMA DONNA

By Lillian Nordica

Marring the Performance—Success and Failure—Stern Necessities—Self-denials—A Day's Work—Stage and Dressing-room—The Prima Donna's Offering to Art.

A BROKEN note! It cannot be sung over again. The orchestra goes on. Another singer takes up the cue. The performance continues. You take up your rôle again at the proper moment. It is all so relentless!

The broken note does not fall into a net like the acrobat who has missed his footing and has another trial. You cannot stop the performance and sing the unfortunate phrase over again. No—to that extent you have marred the performance, and however well you may sing through the rest of the opera, that broken note will break again in every newspaper the next morning.

Fortunately there are singers to whom this never has happened and never will happen so long as they conscientiously consider themselves able to fulfill their missions as artists. It is not only because they have voice and method, but because they also possess the will-power to impose upon themselves the rigid régime which should govern the life of a singer

There are hundreds of beautiful voices. But why does one see almost always the same names leading the list of prima donnas at the great opera houses? It is not a fad. It is a necessity, because those singers —that handful—are the only ones who can stand the strain of a grand opera season in a house of large dimensions and give satisfaction to the public.

Where are all the other lovely voices that promised so much? They have failed. Why? Because their owners were unwilling to adapt themselves to the stern necessities that govern the life of a prima donna. It is a grand triumph to feel a great audience "rising" at you; but it is a triumph gained at the sacrifice of almost all the pleasures of life. I have questioned many of my distinguished colleagues. Always it is the same story—a story of continual sacrifice, not from the moment of the first success, nor even from the first step upon the stage, but from further back, from girlhood, from the period when the work of preparation began. The sacrifice of everything that interferes with her art and her career is what makes a "great" prima donna of the woman with the requisite voice and method. Even the athlete can learn a lesson in training from the prima donna, with this difference: the athlete can "break training," but the prima donna never can.

I am naturally active. Yet in a season of fifteen weeks I have set foot upon the street for a short walk just once. The chief part of the time it was driving from my residence to the opera house for rehearsal or performance and back again to my residence for study or rest.

Society? How fond I should be of it if I could enjoy its entertainments with a free mind! But the functions I feel I can attend during a season without fear that my so doing will interfere with my obligations as an artist, you can count on fewer fingers than those of one hand. I had an opera box at my disposal. I doubt if I occupied it more than three or four times in fifteen weeks. If I had sung Tuesday night in Philadelphia and was obliged to sing Kundry on Thursday, do you think, much as I longed to see a performance, that I would jeopardize my task and run the risk of not doing my full duty toward my public by attending the opera on Wednesday? No, I would rest from the strain of Tuesday the better to be ready to bear the strain of Thursday. It is one thing to be one of a great public, another to sing for that great public. Once I went to an afternoon concert just to treat myself to some singing that I wasn't doing myself. As I was leaving with the rest of the audience, a woman, a total stranger, came up to me.

"Please go right home and go to bed," she said. "'Götterdämmerung' to-morrow!"

And she was right. I felt she was. So I went home—and went to bed.

Take a day when rehearsal has been called for half-past ten in the morning. I am up at eight. By nine o'clock my accompanist is at the piano and I go over some of the uncertain passages. An opera, and especially a Wagner music-drama, is such a big affair that even if you have sung it many times it still is necessary to "get up" on it every time you sing it and to rehearse it, no matter how long it has been in the repertoire. At half-past ten I am at the opera house and, if it is a music-drama that is in rehearsal, I am not likely to get away till half-past four or five in the afternoon. I have been standing and acting and singing most of the time, and usually without stopping for anything to eat, for it is not well to sing until some time after a meal. Yet when I get home, hot and tired, the first thing is the bath, and even then only something light to eat, for the system is too exhausted from the strain to assimilate the dinner that an ordinary person would eat after such an arduous day and so long a fast.

But even then work is not over. Supposing that you have been rehearsing "Tristan" that day, and the following night you are to appear in "Gioconda." These are works of totally different schools, and to be "up" on them practically at the same time is a great test of vocal method. I have to turn at once from "Tristan" to the Italian work so as to become permeated with it before I go on the stage the next night. But I am too tired to stand at the piano and sing. So I rest on the sofa and listen to my accompanist while he plays over the music of my rôle.

After that I take the score to bed with me—literally—so that if, during a wakeful hour in the night or in the early morning, I should think of some point (and one often does at such times), I am able to turn to the music and work it out. Thus practically the whole time a singer's mind is on her task.

Some people think a prima donna has a chance to rest in her dressing-room between the acts. Let me dispel that illusion. When I sing Valentine in "Les Huguenots," I do not appear until the second act, but in order to have time to dress and to "warm up" my voice, I am at the opera house at seven o'clock. As for rest between the acts—the Valentine costumes are elaborate, and all my time, when not on the stage, is occupied in dressing. For Donna Anna in "Don Giovanni," I get to the opera house by half past six, for I am obliged to be on the stage soon after the raising of the curtain. As soon as my first scene is over I hasten to my dressing-room and hurry into the black costume which I wear later in the same act. Even after that I have no leisure, for I am obliged to change to another black costume.

After the first act of "Tristan und Isolde," the Isolde is happy if she still is alive, for the act is very long and Isolde is constantly on the stage, and almost constantly active. Yet she has no time to rest. She knows that no matter how much she hurries, the stage will be ready before she can change her costume, and she fairly races so as not to keep the stage waiting any longer than necessary.

You might think that during the long, long wait between the second act and Isolde's cue late in the third act (for she does not go on until nearly the end of the third act) the prima donna would have an agreeable relaxation from the great scenes of the first and second acts. Yet that hour and twenty minutes in the dressing-room is the severest strain of all. Do I rest during this long interval? Oh, no. I keep walking about my dressing-room and singing. Otherwise the vocal organs would sink into a state of lethargy and I should not be able to key them up for Isolde's tremendous scene, the "Love Death," over Tristan's prostrate form.

When I sing Selica in "L'Africaine," I begin dressing at half-past five, for I have to "make up dark" for the rôle—stain my face and arms. There are hurried changes of costume in this opera too. One night, between the acts of "L'Africaine," one of the directors of the opera house brought Lord Charles Beresford and Sir Cavendish-Bentinck to call on me behind the scenes. I was obliged to remain standing during their call while various barbaric ornaments were being fastened to my costume.

One Saturday afternoon, after the second act of "Tristan," my little niece, thinking I would have a long time for rest and relaxation, came back to pay me a visit. After watching me a while from the lounge, she exclaimed:

"Why, Aunt Lillian! If I'd known you carried on so, I wouldn't have come in. I thought this was your time for rest."

Rest? The prima donna never rests. Every girl who really is going to be a prima donna is at it when she is young and keeps at it till she retires—that is, if she has the inborn love of it. Often I hear young women who are starting out to become singers say: "I will do anything, I will make every sacrifice for my art!" But they won't.

The real prima donna says nothing. She makes the sacrifices, and when she stands before the public and finds herself in good voice and sees her audience hanging on every note and thrilled by every sound that issues from between her lips, she feels that all her sacrifices have not been sacrifices at all, but a joyous offering to her art.

VIII. WAGNER'S PERSONALITY

By Gustav Kobbé

Home Life—Wagner at a Banquet—Personal Appearance—After-dinner Speech—Love of Animals—Affection and Generosity — Activity and Determination — Wagner's Humor—His Sincerity.

IN the fierce contest which for nearly fifty years waged around Wagner his personality was not spared. His enemies, not content with pouring vituperation upon his music, assailed his private life and character. Yet his widow and son worship his memory; and the only one of his intimate friends whose reminiscences of him have been published—Ferdinand Präger—has much to say of his personal worth, and draws a charming picture of the composer's home life with his second wife, Cosima Liszt.

In spite of all his enemies may have said, or indeed still say, the mutual devotion of Wagner and Cosima and his love for his son Siegfried have become almost historical. The visitor to Wahnfried, Wagner's house at Bayreuth, may see, inscribed over the entrance, the following lines:

Hier, Wo Mein Wähnen Frieden Fand,
"Wahnfried," Sei Dieses Haus Von Mir Genannt.

Wähnen means longing, or rather the strenuous striving, amounting almost to madness, of an artist for the fulfillment of his aspirations and the triumph of his art. "Wahnfried" means rest from longing, and the lines over the entrance to Wagner's house signify that there at last he found the repose of soul and the respite from the world for which he had yearned. Fate, relenting toward the genius who had been fighting his way for half a century, had sent him the complement to his nature—a wife who loved him for himself and at the same time was in full sympathy with his aspirations. Cosima comprehended the man and the artist.

Präger speaks of the high spirits with which at times Wagner seemed fairly to bubble over. During a sojourn in Bayreuth in 1882, when "Parsifal" was produced, I myself had the opportunity to observe this exuberance; for I often saw and heard Wagner. One does not forget the first sight of a great man, and the occasion on which I first saw Wagner is indelibly impressed on my memory. He gave a banquet to his artists, the evening after the final dress rehearsal of "Parsifal," at a restaurant high up on the hill and near the Wagner Theater. At one end of the large dining-hall the floor was slightly sunk below the level of the rest. The long table for Wagner and his guests was set on this lower portion. The public was admitted to dinner in the other and larger part of the hall, so that whoever cared to pay the comparatively small price of the dinner was privileged to watch the proceedings below. This part of the hall was simply crowded; not a seat at any of the tables was unoccupied, and long after the tables were full many other people vainly sought admission.

The artists had arrived and had been waiting for some time when the door swung open and Wagner entered rapidly. On his arm was Cosima; and following them were his father-in-law, Franz Liszt, and young Siegfried Wagner, who looked like a miniature presentment of his father. Hardly had Wagner entered when he dropped Cosima's arm, and with short, quick steps hurried toward his artists; giving each in turn, from the highest to the lowest, a warm handshake, and smiling and laughing as he passed from one to the other. The wait for him had been tedious, but the moment he entered every one's spirits went up. His own exuberance was contagious.

After he had greeted his artists he looked up to where we were sitting, straining our necks to see all that was going on. Exclaiming "Da ist ja auch das Publicum!" (Hello, there is the public!) in a half amused, half contemptuous tone of voice, he dashed up the short flight of steps which led to where we were, and in a moment was hurrying in and out among us, stopping to shake hands here and there with a friend. He was closely pursued by Judith Gautier, a daughter of Théophile Gautier, who seemed to want to obtain some favor from him which he did not wish to grant, but which he was too good-natured to deny outright. Occasionally he would half turn around and laughingly say something to her, and then keep on his way while she persistently followed. He finally reached the steps, dashed down them, and was again in the holy of holies among his artists, whither she did not dare follow him.

At last Wagner seated himself, and the banquet began. On either side of him were Cosima and his father-in-law, Liszt. Seeing them in such close proximity it was easy to note the remarkable resemblance between Liszt and his daughter. They had the same strongly marked aquiline features. At the same table was a protégé of Liszt, the pianist D'Albert, then a very youthful celebrity, but since become a famous pianist.

But, of course, I was most interested in looking at Wagner himself. I frankly confess that when he first entered and came forward with quick, short, almost mincing steps, I was greatly disappointed in his personal appearance. He was diminutive in stature, and his attire was spick and span—something which in a genius seems to me unpardonable. Every genius should be at least a little disheveled in order to come up to the public's idea of what. he ought to be. If I remember rightly Wagner had on a black cutaway, light gray trousers, and immaculate lavender kid gloves. Over one arm was flung a light overcoat, and in his hand he carried a brown derby. He certainly did not at that moment realize the portrait that I had formed of him in my mind's eye.

But when he was seated and I had an opportunity to examine his features more closely, I could not help being impressed with the marvelous brow, which seemed fairly to protrude with intellect and the power of applied energy. Then, as he talked, now with his wife, now with Liszt, occasionally flinging remarks across the table to Materna, Winckelmann, Gudehus, Scaria, or some of the other artists, his eyes sparkled with good humor, and his features were wonderfully mobile. At times, as if too full of vitality to remain long quiet, he would jump up from his chair and make the round of the table, with some pleasant verbal quip for each of his friends.

I had always supposed that after-dinner speaking was a horror confined to the United States. But after the cigars had been lighted one of the local dignitaries of Bayreuth arose and began a long and uninteresting speech full of lavish laudation of Wagner. Another followed, and administered one of the most effective sleeping-potions which it has ever been my fate to partake of—more effective even than that which Sieglinde administers to Hunding. But of a sudden every one was wide awake. Wagner was on his feet and speaking. Then it was I mentally conceded that, after all, after-dinner speaking was not such a bad habit.

Wagner's speech was as brief as the others had been long. He patted papa-in-law Liszt on the shoulder and spoke feelingly of him as one of the

first who had befriended him, and as the man who had given to him his precious wife. I shall always remember the flood of emotion that he poured into the words "die teuere Gattin." He concluded with an eloquent tribute to his singers. After thanking those who had contributed to the fund for the "Parsifal" productions, he concluded: "But after all I am more indebted to my devoted, self-sacrificing artists; for art is not created by money, but is made possible only by artists." The singers who were gathered at Bayreuth in 1882 were a noble band, and passionately devoted to the great composer.

Indeed, Wagner's master mind seemed to control everything and everybody at Bayreuth. I once wrote that near the Wagner Theater was an insane asylum with cells and strait-jackets for any anti-Wagnerites who were apprehended in Bayreuth, and a penitentiary with a special lockup for small boys who were caught whistling anything but leading motives. But this really conveys an idea of how completely everything at Bayreuth was Wagnerized and how thoroughly it was dominated by Wagner's genius. During one of the "Parsifal" performances I chanced to see Wagner's head protrude from behind a bit of scenery. He was not trying to observe how closely the audience was following his work, but had his eyes on the stage. After the performance Materna explained to me that at rehearsals Wagner had not only indicated the positions on the stage which he wished the various characters to take, but had actually made little chalk marks in order to be sure that his directions were followed. He was so anxious that they should be properly observed that at the moment I saw him he had incautiously thrust his head too far forward from the wings.

Combined with his restless energy Wagner had many lovable traits, not the least of which was his affection for animals. When he was a boy he witnessed the killing of an ox by a butcher. He grew so excited that he would have rushed upon the man had not his companions forcibly led him from the scene. For a long time afterward he was unable to touch meat. To dogs he was devotedly attached. Whoever visited Wahnfried in 1882 rarely failed to notice the stately St. Bernard, Wotan, between whom and its master such mutual affection existed that, when in the following February Wagner's remains were laid at rest in Bayreuth, the dog refused to be comforted and could not be led away from the tomb, it becoming necessary to even feed it there.

Wagner and the various dogs he owned were almost inseparable companions. He delighted to engage in long conversations with them, himself supplying their answers, "infusing into these much of that caustic wit which philosophers of all ages and countries have so often and powerfully put into the mouth of animals." Wagner was fond of quoting Weber's remark to a disobedient dog: "If you go on like that you will at last become as silly and as bad as a human being." In Boulogne, where he arrived in the late thirties, after a visit to London, a huge Newfoundland dog appeared with him so constantly in the streets that he became known as "le petit homme avec le grand chien."

When the composition of "Tannhäuser" was nearing its completion, while the ill success of his works outside of Dresden had made him morbid and despondent, the love of a few friends and that of his dog was almost his only solace. He often remarked that his dog had helped him compose "Tannhäuser." When he was seated at the piano singing boisterously while composing, the dog would leap from its place at its master's feet on to the table, peer into his face, and begin to howl. Then Wagner would shake the animal's paw, exclaim, "What, it does not suit you?" and add, quoting from Shakespeare, "Well, I will do thy bidding gently."

While an exile in Zurich he would take his dog Peps with him on his long walks. Sometimes he would declaim violently against his persecutors. Then Peps, the "human Peps," as Wagner called him, would bark and snap as if aiding his master; returning after each sally to be praised and petted. "Peps," he once remarked, "has more sense than all your wooden contrapuntists."

In 1855, when Wagner was conductor of the London Philharmonic, he found that a large Norwegian dog belonging to Präger was kept in a small back yard. He expostulated against what he called the cruelty of such close confinement, and made it a point when he went out on his daily constitutional to take the dog with him. This duty he continued to perform during his stay in London, notwithstanding the fact that he was often tugged hither and thither by the spirited animal, which rejoiced at its semi-freedom. Every day while in London Wagner bought a supply of French rolls, and went to the small bridge over the ornamental water in Regent's Park, to feed the ducks as well as a regal swan, of which he used to say that it was fit to draw the chariot of Lohengrin. "The childlike happiness, full to overflowing, with which this innocent occupation filled Wagner, was an impressive sight, never to be forgotten. It was Wagner you saw before you, the natural man, affectionate, gentle and mirthful."

In one of his first letters to Präger, when he had returned to Zurich after this season in London, he asked if Präger's cat still had its bad cold. Shortly afterward his dear Peps died in its master's arms, "passing away without a sound quietly and peacefully. I cried incessantly, and since then have felt bitter pain and sorrow for the dear friend of the past thirteen years, who ever worked and walked with me."

Präger relates that Wagner almost came to blows in the London streets with a grocer who had cruelly beaten his horse; and one of the latest literary efforts of his life was an essay against vivisection. Certainly a man who throughout his life showed in so many ways his love for dumb animals must have been innately affectionate and tender; and if he ever showed himself otherwise, it was because of the irritability created by the fierce attacks of which he was constantly a victim.

Though naturally affected with the colossal egotism which seems to be part of the make-up of every intense creative genius, he was not lacking in gratitude. His letters to Liszt teem with expressions of the most affectionate recognition of all that composer had done for him; and I have already quoted his grateful reference to Liszt at the Bayreuth banquet. He fairly worshiped the memory of his stepfather Geyer; and when late in Wagner's life one of Geyer's long-forgotten little comedies was played for him at a private performance, as a birthday surprise, his delight was almost childish. His mother, "lieb' Mütterchen," as he always called her, he adored; and he poured his love for her into the exquisite music of "Siegfried" whenever the young hero of that music-drama alludes to his mother. All Wagner's references to his mother were, according to Präger, "of affection, amounting almost to idolatry."

Nor did Wagner's egotism warp his judgment of the composers of the past. When he was a conductor at the Royal Opera in Dresden, he successfully revived interest in Gluck's and Mozart's operas. The ultimate appreciation of Beethoven's Ninth symphony was largely due to performances of that work under Wagner's baton, and to the analysis of the symphony which he wrote. When he proposed to give it in Dresden opposition was raised on account of the expense. Accordingly he went to all the trouble of borrowing the orchestral parts from Leipzig, learning the symphony by heart to avoid the outlay for an orchestral score, and inducing choir-boys from neighboring churches to assist in the performance.

Nor are there lacking instances of warm-hearted sympathy on Wagner's part toward those who were unfriendly to him. The attitude of Berlioz toward Wagner was decidedly frigid. Yet when Wagner was invited in London to meet a French musical amateur in the confidence of the Emperor—the idea being that something might thus be accomplished toward awakening the latter's interest in Wagner's music—what did Wagner do? He implored the Frenchman to persuade the Emperor to espouse Berlioz's cause.

Wagner was a man of great physical as well as mental activity. I have spoken of the quick manner in which he moved about among the guests at the Bayreuth banquet. It was characteristic of the man. When he was a schoolboy he threw a schoolmate's cap high upon a steep roof. The lad began to cry. This was more than Wagner could stand. At great risk to his life he climbed the roof, threw down the cap to the boy, and then, letting himself down through the manhole into the garret, hid there to escape the reprimands of his teachers, who appeared incensed at his recklessness, though, probably, they secretly admired it.

Präger, who went to visit him in Tribschen in the summer of 1871, tells a capital anecdote of the composer's buoyant, active temperament, which years had not lessened. They were sitting on an ottoman in the drawing-room, when the composer of "The Ring of the Nibelung," "Tristan," and the "Meistersinger" suddenly rose and stood on his head upon the ottoman. Just then the door opened and Madame Wagner entered. Seeing her husband in this curious position, she hastened forward exclaiming, "Aber! lieber Richard! lieber Richard!" Quickly resuming his natural position Wagner explained to her that he was not insane, but was merely proving to his friend Ferdinand that he could stand on his head at sixty.

Coupled with this activity was great determination. When he was in London his crossing of crowded thoroughfares was so intrepid as to border upon the reckless. He would go straight across; leaving it to the drivers of the various vehicles which were bearing down upon him to take care that they did not run over him. This recklessness is interesting as a physical manifestation of his mental attitude toward his art. No man ever dared more in art than Wagner. The energy with which he went to work to produce the Ninth symphony in Dresden as already related, was characteristic. He did everything thoroughly and with the full conviction that he was bound to succeed.

Ill success only seemed to inspire him to greater energy. The return of his scores of "Rienzi," "The Flying Dutchman," and "Tannhäuser," unopened by managers, resulted in his working with redoubled zeal upon "Lohengrin." When he saw no immediate prospect of securing the production of that opera, he began the composition of an art-work even more advanced—"The Ring of the Nibelung." It is a matter of history that nearly a quarter of a century went by before that cycle saw the light of a theater. Meanwhile he composed "Tristan" and "The Meistersinger." There is no greater example of energy in the history of art than Wagner. If some one could be induced to count all the musical notes and words that Wagner wrote during his life, the figures would be found to be simply appalling.

Even when his cause had been espoused by the King of Bavaria the spirit of independence, fostered by his immense creative force, did not forsake him. Once after an interview with the King in which they disagreed, he remarked to a friend, who cautioned him to be more diplomatic, "I have lived before without the King, and I can do so again." He was thoroughly absorbed in his art. Everything seemed to him to center around it. When preparations were under way for the production of his "Ring of the Nibelung" at Bayreuth, he wrote to Präger: "It appears to me that the whole German Empire is created only to aid me in attaining my object."

In view of the length of most of his works, it is interesting to note that even as a boy he planned things on a large scale. While at school his passion for Shakespeare led him to write a drama which, he himself says, was a jumble of "Lear" and "Hamlet," and was so long that, all the characters having died, he was obliged, in the last act, to bring their ghosts on the stage in order to keep the play going. Wagner's unbounded admiration for Shakespeare continued throughout his life. When he first entered Westminster Abbey he immediately sought out the Shakespeare monument; and the first Christmas present he made to Cosima, after she became his wife, was a costly edition of Shakespeare's works, which he imported from London.

When his energy was not expended in his art work, it found vent in many humorous sallies. I have already related how he stood on his head for Präger. That was physical humor. But he was also fond of joking. He once quoted his teacher's remark that he would never learn to play the piano. "But," he added, "I play a great deal better than Berlioz." The waggishness of this remark lies in the fact that Berlioz could not play at all. During a rehearsal of the "Rienzi" overture in Dresden the trombones were too loud. Instead of rebuking them angrily, he said, with a laugh: "Gentlemen, we are in Dresden, not marching around the walls of Jericho." After "Tannhäuser" was brought out a German composer of little note, named Chellard, said that the "Song to the Evening Star" was wrongly harmonized, and suggested certain harmonies which should be substituted for those employed by Wagner. When Wagner was among friends it was one of his favorite diversions to seat himself at the piano and sing the "Song to the Evening Star" à la Chellard.

Just as this buoyancy and fondness for amusement were the result of his wonderful activity of mind, so also this fundamental trait of his character made him an enemy to all sham. The Duke of Coburg had composed an opera which he asked Wagner to score for him: offering him a sum equivalent to a thousand dollars, besides two months' residence in his palace. The offer came to Wagner when he was in comparatively needy circumstances, but he promptly declined it. He did not care to clothe another's work in his orchestral garb. To a tailor who expressed surprise that he wanted silk for the back of his waistcoat, because it was not seen, Wagner exclaimed: "Not seen! Sham, sham in everything, is the tendency of the age. Whatever is not seen may be shabby, provided the exterior be richly gilded."

It is pleasant to know that, through many years of strife, Wagner had his indomitable will-power, his love for his friends, and his spirit of humor to fall back upon. It is even more pleasant to reflect that he lived to see the art work of his life triumphant, and to know of a happy home. During those latter years of his life a wonderful sense of peace seems to have pervaded his being. "God make every one happy. Amen!" is a sentence in one of his last letters to Präger. What more fitting answer to the detractors of his personal character?

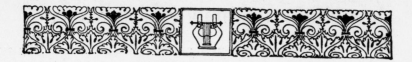

IX. THE BUSINESS SIDE OF GRAND OPERA

By Gustav Kobbé

Duties of a Manager—Work and Diplomacy—Earnings and Expenditures—A Manager's Trials—Dealings with Singers—Expenses at the Metropolitan—Performances There—The Box Office—Rules for Ticket-sellers—Lost Articles.

BROADLY speaking, the duties of an opera manager are to keep an eye on everybody and everything connected with his company, from the principal prima donna, who receives $1700 a performance, to the "practical" property monkey which opens its jaws and shows its gums in one of the scenes in "The Magic Flute." This statement will perhaps convey some idea of the variety which enters into the life of a manager of grand opera.

The most important representative of this active species in this country is the "managing director" of the company which sings at the Metropolitan Opera House, New York.

While the leading members of this company appear in perhaps six or eight performances a month, the director may be said to give a continuous performance all the year round. For when the singers are not in a scene before the audience, they are apt to be making a scene in the impresario's office. The plot and situations of these private representations are generally based on the numerous intricacies always to be found in opera singers' contracts.

To an ordinary mortal, a contract of this kind appears like a labyrinth, without a kindly Ariadne to furnish the thread enabling him to find his way out of the maze of conditions. Considering that a grand opera impresario has not one such contract, but a whole stack of them, it is wonderful how he can remember just what he can call upon each of his singers to do. Some idea of the work and diplomacy required to "sign" the leading members of an opera company like that at the Metropolitan may be gathered from a clause in the contract which the director had with the subcompany by which he was employed before the owners of the opera house themselves financed the enterprise and placed the director on a salary. It provided that should he be disabled or die at any time after he had engaged his artists for the ensuing season—even before the season began, and in fact before the artists engaged abroad sailed for this country—his heirs should nevertheless be entitled to draw out his share of the profits during the entire season. In other words, he was considered to have earned his money before the curtain rose on the first performance—in fact, even before the company assembled in this country. Not only had he to exercise the shrewdness necessary to meet the whims and demands of the singers whom he wished to engage, but a large amount of money passed through his hands while he was still closing the contracts. For it is a peculiarity of operatic contracts that they call for advance payments, and an opera director, while engaging his company during the summer, is obliged to pay out about $100,000 in advances.

The public is apt to hear of large earnings on the tours, and of enormous advance sales in New York, but knows little about the expenses of an opera company and the worries of its manager. It sounds very grandiose to say that, including the money taken in on tour and the advance sales in New York, the curtain at a first performance at the Metropolitan Opera House last season rose on over a million dollars. But when it is stated that one season one tenor, Jean de Reszke, was paid in round figures $100,000, that during another season one prima donna, Mme. Calvé, would have earned even more, had it not been for her illness during the tour, and that she was only one of a large number of high-priced artists in the company, it will be seen that the salary list of an impresario, quite aside from the rest of his expense account, is enormous.

Melba received $3000 a performance and Caruso the same amount. These are the highest honoraria paid on the stage. But in addition Caruso had a guarantee of eighty performances a year, so that his three years' contract brought him in the sum of $720,000. This contract was made by Heinrich Conried, Maurice Grau's successor, and on Conried's death was taken over by the opera house itself.

Doubtless, however, the impresario would consider the drawing of checks to meet such expenses a comparatively agreeable occupation, especially in the case of a drawing card like Caruso, if it would insure him against the personal trials which are the bane of his life. The late Maurice Grau at one time issued a prospectus of each season. He ceased doing so. The artists nearly worried the life out of him because this one wanted to be first in the list of prima donnas, tenors, barytones, or bassos; this one last with the magic word "and" before his name. That "and" was a great invention. It made the first and last on the list about coequal and enabled the manager to satisfy at least two singers in each branch of his company. But the relief was only temporary. There soon were as many candidates for the "and" as there had been for the head of the list. So Grau got out of the difficulty by abandoning the prospectus altogether. He did, indeed, issue a prospectus for the tour, in which he diplomatically, as he thought, printed the names in their alphabetical order. But this raised a hubbub, compared with which the storm in "Die Walküre" and the crash in the finale of "Götterdämmerung" were as the whispering of spring breezes.

By abandoning the prospectus, a director of opera

rids himself of one worry. But there are others which probably will never cease until opera singers' natures undergo a complete change. To look upon the splendid physical proportions of some of the principal singers you would hardly suppose they were such delicate creatures as they sometimes appear to be. But whether it is "indisposition" or a mere whim prompted, perhaps, by jealousy, there is no going behind a physician's certificate, even if it is not sent to the opera house earlier than an hour or two prior to the performance in which the singer was to have taken the leading rôle. Then perhaps the impresario recalls the scene in his office a day or two before, when the singer, suddenly "indisposed," wanted to know why he let another prima donna sing Aïda when it was her rôle; or why he should have cast Mme. A. for Elisabeth in the first performance of "Tannhäuser" when it had always been her—Mme. B.'s—privilege to sing that rôle in the first representation of the opera. Nor does it add a touch of pleasure to his reflections as he contemplates the physician's certificate, to recall the fact that it was he who made that prima donna's fortune.

To revert again to Grau, who was our most famous opera director, he conducted several tours for Sarah Bernhardt. She appeared about 1500 times under his direction. During that entire period there were only five performances in which she disappointed her audiences. In physique she was almost a shadow compared with some opera singers who disappointed him as often as five times a month. Naturally, he concluded that there is some constitutional difference between actors and singers. One could hardly apply the old quip, "An empty cab drove up and out stepped Sarah Bernhardt," to a Brünnhilde. Yet it has happened that some Brünnhildes are more apt to vanish into thin air on the eve of a performance than the great French actress, whose slender physique furnished so much amusement to the paragraphers.

An opera director not infrequently works the greater part of two days and far into the nights arranging a week's repertoire. For the repertoire must be made up with a view to many conditions. It must be sufficiently varied, so that Mrs. C., who has a certain box on "even nights and odd matinées," is not required to listen too often to the same opera; while similar consideration must be paid to Mrs. D., who has the same box for "odd nights and even matinées."

But this is a trifling matter compared with the guarantees of the singers which the impresario must observe in making out the repertoire. A prima donna will have, for instance, a guarantee that he will give her forty performances in four months, or ten performances a month, at a thousand dollars a performance. This means that he must arrange for her to appear exactly ten times during each month. He cannot crowd twelve or fifteen performances into one month for her, and then let her sing a correspondingly fewer number of times during the remaining months. For every performance above the guaranteed ten which she gives during a month she receives an extra thousand dollars, with the privilege of appearing the regular ten times during the next month. If, however, the impresario should fail to

arrange for her to sing more than eight times during a month, he would nevertheless still be obliged to pay her for ten performances. For this reason, unless her guarantees are carefully observed by the manager when he is making out the repertoire, every mistake he makes with regard to this particular prima donna costs him a thousand dollars. There are singers at the Metropolitan Opera House a mistake with whom would cost the impresario from $1000 to $3000. It is no wonder, therefore, that the director makes out a week's repertoire with a sort of checker-board before him divided into squares for each performance in and out of town, and with slips of paper containing the names of the singers for pawns, while before him, for the rules of the game, he has an abstract of his various contracts showing what each singer has been guaranteed as regards rôles and number of performances.

Even after all this work has been gone through with, there is still the question "Will this repertoire stand?" The director has such a dread of physicians' certificates coming in at the last moment, that he does not feel safe until, from his seat in the parquet, he sees the curtain rise. It is bad enough to have to change prima donnas at the last moment, although that is a matter that can generally be arranged over the telephone. But when several principal singers in a cast have become indisposed, and it is found necessary to change the opera, quick work is required. Half a dozen messengers are sent scurrying in all directions. The manager may have thought of putting on "Lohengrin." He must be sure of an Elsa. Therefore, a messenger is sent to each of the prima donnas who have this rôle in their repertoire. Neither of them may be able to sing, and so, although the hour is late, another opera may have to be substituted for "Lohengrin." As many as four changes in the opera for the night may have been made in an afternoon, and at times it has been only by a hair's breadth that the house has not remained dark.

One season, in order to save a performance of "Rheingold," the famous Lilli Lehmann, who had never sung the rôle of Fricka, was obliged to learn it in an afternoon. Fortunately, she was familiar with the music from often having heard the opera. Her sister, Marie Lehmann, who was with her, had sung the rôle many times, but could not step into the breach because, being a pensionaire of the Vienna Opera House, she would forfeit her pension if she sang on any other stage. She was, however, able to assist Mme. Lehmann materially in "swallowing" the rôle, and prompted and coached her from the wings.

Grau had a very large company, and was sometimes considered an extravagant manager because he had so many prima donnas and so many tenors on his list. He was greatly amused at this point of view, for there were many occasions when he found that instead of having too many singers he had too few.

The expenses of an opera company like that at the Metropolitan average from $40,000 to $45,000 a week, or about $1,000,000 a season. How greatly the principal singers figure in the expense list may be judged from the statement that their guarantees amount to about one-half, or $500,000. If all of Caruso's eighty guaranteed appearances occurred here the figures would be much larger. Quoting the exact figures from a season's balance-sheet, it is found that the prima donnas received $216,800, and the principal men singers $316,000, a total of $532,800. Is it policy to pay such high salaries? The question is answered by the statement that the performances which cost most pay best. The public knows when it is getting a great cast, and is willing to put out money to hear it. It may have cost over $10,000 to raise the curtain on the "seven dollar" performance of "Les Huguenots" with Melba, Nordica, "Jean," "Edouard," Lasalle and Maurel. But the public paid nearly $14,000 to hear it. The record production is "Parsifal." Costing in round figures $100,000 to produce, its ten performances during its first season at the Metropolitan brought in $160,000.

Speaking of the boxes, it is an interesting fact that ownership of a box at the Metropolitan Opera House has proved itself a profitable investment. The parterre boxes which are held by the stockholders represent $35,000 in stock. One of the boxes belonging to an estate could recently have been sold for $75,000; but the estate preferred to keep it. There have been instances of the letting of stockholder boxes for $6000 for the season. This is certainly paying high for the privilege of sitting within the charmed circle of the "glittering horseshoe."

I have referred to the half a million dollars paid during a season to the principal singers. The next largest item is $90,000 for the orchestra, and next to that comes $25,000 for transportation. In speaking of expensive performances, I have mentioned that of "Les Huguenots" when it cost over $10,000 to raise the curtain. At that performance, however, scenery, costumes, and properties were not new. When an opera is produced for the first time the cost of these must be added to the salaries for the night.

To see that the production of the new work is properly prepared for is one of the chief duties of a grand opera manager. Besides "Parsifal," one of the most elaborately mounted series of performances at the Metropolitan was the revival of Mozart's "Magic Flute." With what care it was planned, and with how much expense it was carried out, may be gathered from the fact that the director traveled to Munich and took several of the heads of his departments with him to witness the revival of the work there. It was calculated that the production of the work here cost about $35,000, exclusive of the running expenses of the evening. Various improvements on the Munich production were planned and the manager had to study and approve of these, as well as keep control of the general scheme of production. In the scenic department alone fifteen new scenes and a double panorama over three hundred feet long from "gridiron" to cellar, and representing the passage of the hero and heroine through earth, fire, and water, had to be provided. Here was one instance in which the German production was greatly improved upon. In Germany the panorama moved across the stage; here it worked downward, so that the hero and heroine seemed to ascend. Here, moreover, the panorama was double, the characters standing behind a moving front gauze, adding greatly to the effectiveness of the scene. Another improvement was introduced almost at the outset of the performance, with the quick change of scene at the entrance of the Queen of the Night. Here she descended seated on a moon over a dome of stars. The dome effect was admirably reproduced, and the back drop was studded with no less than a thousand stars, all electrically lighted. While such details are studied out by the scene-painter and the electrician of the opera house, they are submitted to the director and have to be carefully considered by him before receiving his final approval.

The same thing applies to the properties. For "The Magic Flute" a complete menagerie was required. In the property room upstairs, behind the scenes, this operatic zoo was produced. It consisted of five snakes, four lions, one giraffe, one tiger, one elephant, one camel, two alligators, four monkeys, and about one hundred birds. The director found himself, besides a grand opera manager, a Barnum on a small scale, but fortunately the animals in his menagerie did not require to be fed. Speaking of the camel reminds me of a contretemps at the opera house some years ago, which shows how thoroughly a manager has to keep his eyes open while a production is in preparation. An opera was given which had a procession with several camels in it. Each camel was worked by two men concealed in the body and representing the front and hind legs. Through an oversight, the men in these camels kept step like soldiers on parade as they came on the stage, and the result was absolutely ridiculous. The opera was withdrawn after a few performances, but the "pacing camels," as they were called, were long a source of amusement. The stage manager was responsible for the mistake, but the final consequence had to be borne by the director.

Fortunately there is another side to the story of operatic management besides worry and expense. The window of the box office is a wee orifice compared with the size of the house, but through it flows the elixir of life—the money of the public. The receipts of a New York season amount to more than $1,200,000.

If the public could get more than just a peep at the box office, it would learn a number of interesting things. For each performance 3425 tickets are required, and it takes the box-office staff two days to separate the single sale from the subscription tickets for each week, so that the latter shall not be sold in duplicate. All the tickets must be "racked" by Wednesday night, because the sale for the next week begins on Thursday. As a rule, a performance is not sold out until the night itself. But the treasurer, who presides over the box office at the Metropolitan Opera House, remembers a Patti performance when the box office opened at nine o'clock in the morning and the house was sold out by one o'clock in the afternoon. The box-office window at the Metropolitan Opera House drops with the curtain at night. There are two sellers on duty during the week, and three on Sunday night, because a Sunday night concert audience is what is known as a "late audience." It puts off buying tickets until the last moment.

A former treasurer of the Metropolitan has considerable reputation among the theater treasurers of the country as the author of a set of rules for the guidance of ticket-sellers, some of which are as follows:

"You must be a mind-reader."

"Never assert your rights."

"When a lady stands an hour or two, selecting a seat, don't suggest to her to bring her sewing and spend the afternoon, as she might be offended."

"When a man comes up to the window smoking a bad cigar and blows the smoke in your face, smile as if you like it, and ask him where you can buy the same brand."

"When a person leaves a quarter, be sure to call him back, for he will come back later and declare he left a dollar."

Articles lost at the opera house are turned in at the box office, where they are tagged and kept, ready to be delivered to the one who can prove ownership. They form a most heterogeneous collection. One season, over one thousand keys were found, and in a closet in the box office there is a stack of umbrellas on one side and a heap of rubbers on the other. A few seasons ago a bracelet of diamonds and emeralds, certainly of over $10,000 in value, was found in one of the boxes. The next morning it was sent up to the house of the boxholder and promptly recognized. The most curious part of the incident was that the bracelet had not been missed by the lady who had worn it. The first she knew of its loss was its return. Among the most remarkable finds have been a set of false teeth, a morphine fiend's outfit, and two silk hats. How two men could have deliberately walked out of the opera house of a winter's night without realizing that they were minus their hats is a mystery. Possibly the charms of music had turned their heads.

Notwithstanding much able assistance, the director himself is the final and responsible head of the opera enterprise. Were it a failure, it would be he who would have to drain the bitter cup to the dregs. He is the nerve-center of the opera season, whether it is regarded from the artistic or the business standpoint. The Metropolitan has been so liberal with the public, and established such a high standard for opera in this country, that it is pleasant to reflect that while an opera company is an enormous hole into which to shovel money, some of it is occasionally found at the end of the season to have stuck to the shovel.

* * * *

The conditions described as referring to the Metropolitan opera also apply in many respects to the other permanent American opera company established in Chicago. Both of these organizations have had a marked influence in the development of opera support in the United States although the local results have been the more important. It is true the opportunity benefits chiefly those who live in these cities; but, in addition, there are the considerable number who come to New York and Chicago during the opera season to enjoy what can be heard there.

These visitors represent, in a measure, one of the factors working against the establishment of permanent opera in other cities. Philadelphia and Boston in the East have made efforts to supply opera to their citizens but without continued success. When one recalls that every important city in Europe, outside the British Isles, has its own opera establishment, it is reasonable to inquire why American cities outside of New York and Chicago are without their own opera organizations.

While it is true that the conditions are dissimilar, it is not true that the American cities are not wealthy enough to support local opera. In European countries the state and municipal governments contribute to the expenses of musical establishments. The same orchestra gives concerts as well as plays for the opera company. The community enjoys the advantage of an establishment such as the city can afford. That means that competent singers are employed but no great stars. The public goes to hear an opera adequately presented but not to worship at the shrine of a famous prima donna.

The American public differs. It has been accustomed to the "star" system and is unwilling to support anything but the best. The music lovers who have sufficient means make a few visits to New York or Chicago to hear grand opera. They have proven that they will not support a company such as their communities could afford. They will not approve of anything not up to the standards of New York and Chicago, a standard impossible to duplicate in the other cities. In the European cities wealth and social influence are wielded by persons who have been brought up on the standard operas, presented in their own languages. The general public also has this tradition. Not so in an American city. Money is controlled largely by persons without any such background. In some cases they will attend performances to please their socially ambitious wives, but they have little disposition to pay out large sums to support a regular establishment presenting a form of entertainment which has little interest for them. Grand opera is not an attraction to the average American. Were it not for the social prestige connected with the opera in New York and Chicago the permanent companies would not continue. There is no such social influence in other cities; at least, not to the same extent.

In other words, permanent opera in many American cities is not practicable, because performances of a high standard would require a financial outlay beyond that which would be furnished by the general public, and there is not a social body large enough, wealthy enough, and liberal enough, to make up the inevitable deficit. If a community were willing to accept performances of a lower standard, yet equal to that of the average European city of the same population and wealth, it might be a possibility—even a probability.

Were it not for the visits of the traveling opera company the American public would have but little opportunity to hear musico-dramatic works of this sort. Perhaps the handling of the situation has not been such as would develop a taste for this sort of "amusement." Instead of "one-night stands" a good company, of the standard now sent out from New York, might, in a two weeks' season, build up profitable houses. The probabilities, however, are that the motion picture establishments and other purveyors of amusement are shrewder judges of the public taste, and recognize that it is not art but something more in the nature of sensation that is wanted. This the public gets in the "movie" at a moderate price. Opera, even at prices from $2.00 to $5.00 per seat, can hardly be made to pay.

In the final analysis the business side of opera organization has much to do with the fact that New York and Chicago are the only cities with high-grade opera establishments.   Lacking governmental and municipal subvention a condition which has not yet been approved by the American people, artistic performances of grand opera are possible only through the liberal support of men of wealth; yet under our democratic governmental system all efforts to secure this support, other than through social prestige, have failed.

STORIES OF THE OPERA

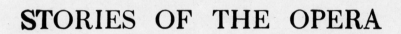

LIST OF OPERAS PRODUCED AT THE METROPOLITAN OPERA HOUSE, NEW YORK, DURING TEN SEASONS; ALSO INDEX TO PAGES CONTAINING THE STORIES OF THE OPERAS

Title	Composer	Performances	Page
Aïda	VERDI	72	350
Amore dei tre rè	MONTEMEZZI	15	416
Amore Medico	WOLF-FERRARI	4	
André Chenier	GIORDANO		431
Ariane et Barbe-Bleue	DUKAS	7	417
Armide	GLUCK	7	351
Ballo in Maschera	VERDI	10	351
Barbiere di Siviglia	ROSSINI	19	354
Bohème	PUCCINI	64	355
Boris Godounov	MOUSSORGSKY	32	418
Canterbury Pilgrims	DE KOVEN	6	
Carmen	BIZET	35	356
Cavalleria Rusticana	MASCAGNI	51	357
Contes d'Hoffmann	OFFENBACH	9	358
Coq d'Or	RIMSKY-KORSAKOV	6	418
Cyrano de Bergerac	DAMROSCH	5	
Dance in Place Congo (ballet)	GILBERT	4	
Don Pasquale	DONIZETTI	7	362
Donne Curiose	WOLF-FERRARI	8	419
Elisir d'amore	DONIZETTI	14	
Euryanthe	WEBER	5	
Falstaff	VERDI	5	367
Fanciulla del West	PUCCINI	22	420
Faust	GOUNOD	31	367
Fidelio	BEETHOVEN	9	368
Figlia del Reggimento	DONIZETTI	5	369
Fra Diavolo	AUBER	3	371
Francesca da Rimini	ZANDONAI	9	421
Freischütz	WEBER	1	372
Germania	FRANCHETTI	7	
Gioconda	PONCHIELLI	30	
Götterdämmerung	WAGNER	24	374
Goyescas	GRANADOS	5	
Haensel und Gretel	HUMPERDINCK	36	376
Huguenots	MEYERBEER	8	377
Iphigenia auf Tauris	GLUCK	5	379
Iris	MASCAGNI	4	
Jenufa	JANACEK		433
Julien	CHARPENTIER	5	
Königskinder	HUMPERDINCK	30	422
Lakmé	DELIBES	3	
Lobetanz	THUILLE	5	
Lodoletta	MASCAGNI	5	
Lohengrin	WAGNER	42	381
Lucia di Lammermoor	DONIZETTI	12	383
Madama Butterfly	PUCCINI	68	385
Madame Sans-Gêne	GIORDANI	14	
Madeleine	HERBERT	4	
Manon	MASSENET	26	387
Manon Lescaut	PUCCINI	23	
Marouf	RABAUD	6	433
Marta	FLOTOW	12	388
Meistersinger	WAGNER	37	390
Mona	PARKER	4	423
Nozze di Figaro	MOZART	11	392
Oracolo	LEONI	14	426
Orfeo	GLUCK	20	394
Otello	VERDI	18	394
Pagliacci	LEONCAVALLO	67	395
Parsifal	WAGNER	31	396
Pêcheurs de Perles	BIZET	3	
Pipe of Desire	CONVERSE	2	398
Pique Dame	TSCHAIKOWSKY	4	
Prince Igor	BORODIN	9	427
Prophète	MEYERBEER	5	400
Puritani	BELLINI	4	401
Rheingold	WAGNER	13	401
Rigoletto	VERDI	31	402
Romeo et Juliette	GOUNOD	3	404
Rosenkavalier	STRAUSS	22	427
Samson et Dalila	SAINT-SAENS	14	404
Segreto di Susanna	WOLF-FERRARI	7	
Shanewis	CADMAN	5	429
Siegfried	WAGNER	27	405
Sonnambula	BELLINI	3	406
St. Elizabeth	LISZT	5	
Stradella	FLOTOW	3	
Tannhäuser	WAGNER	35	406
Thaïs	MASSENET	11	407
Tiefland	d'ALBERT	4	408
Tosca	PUCCINI	55	408
Tote Stadt	KORNGOLD		429
Traviata	VERDI	33	410
Tristan und Isolde	WAGNER	42	410
Trovatore	VERDI	43	411
Verkaufte Braut	SMETANA	13	412
Versiegelt	BLECH	4	
Villi	PUCCINI	5	
Walküre	WAGNER	48	413
Wally	CATALANI	5	
Werther	MASSENET	2	413
Widerspenstigen Zähmung	GOETZ	2	
Zauberflöte	MOZART	28	415

1,531

STORIES OF THE OPERAS

NOTE—These stories are arranged alphabetically according to titles. For operas not found in this series see "Stories of Modern Operas," beginning on page 418.

L'AFRICAINE

Opera in five acts by Giacomo Meyerbeer.
Text by Scribe.

THE first act is laid in Lisbon. Donna Ines, Admiral Diego's daughter, is to give her hand to Don Pedro, a counselor of the King of Portugal. But she has pledged her faith to Vasco da Gama, who has been sent with Dias, the navigator, to double the Cape, in order to seek for a new land, containing treasures similar to those discovered by Columbus. Reports have reached Lisbon that the whole fleet has been destroyed, when suddenly Vasco da Gama appears before the assembled council of state.

He eloquently describes the dangers of the unknown seas near the Cape and gives an account of the shipwreck, from which he alone has escaped. He then places his maps before the council, endeavoring to prove that beyond Africa there is another country, yet to be explored and conquered.

Vasco has on his way home picked up a man and a woman of an unknown race. Those slaves, however, stubbornly refuse to betray the name of their country, and a lively debate ensues between the Grand Inquisitor and the younger, more enlightened members of the council, as to the course which should be adopted with Vasco. At last, owing to the irritation caused by his violent reproaches, fanaticism is victorious, and instead of being furnished with a ship to explore those unknown lands, he is thrown into prison, on the plea of his being a heretic, for having mantained the existence of countries which were not mentioned in the Holy Scriptures.

The second act takes place in a cell of the Inquisition, in which Vasco has been languishing for a month past, in the company of the strange slaves Nelusco and Selica. The latter has lost her heart to the proud Portuguese, who saved her and her companion from a slave-ship. But Vasco is only thinking of Ines, and Nelusco, who honors in Selica not only his Queen, but the woman of his love, tries to stab Vasco—the Christian, whom he hates with a deadly hatred. Selica hinders him and rouses the sleeping Vasco, who has been dreaming of and planning his voyage to the unknown country.

Selica now shows him on the map the way to her native isle, and he vows her eternal gratitude. His liberty is indeed near at hand, for hardly has he given his vow than Ines steps in to announce that Vasco is free. She has paid dearly for her lover's deliverance, however, for she has given her hand to Vasco's rival Don Pedro, who, having got all Vasco's plans and maps, is commissioned by government to set out on the voyage of discovery.

Ines has been told that Vasco has forgotten her for Selica the slave. In order to prove his fidelity, our ungrateful hero immediately presents her with the two slaves, and Don Pedro resolves to make use of them for his exploration.

In the third act we are on board of Don Pedro's ship in the Indian seas. Donna Ines is with her husband and Nelusco has been appointed pilot. Don Alvar, a member of the council and Don Pedro's friend, warns the latter that Nelusco is meditating treason, for they have already lost two ships; but Pedro disregards the warning. A typhoon arises, and Nelusco turns the ship again northward. But Vasco has found means to follow them on a small sailing vessel; he overtakes them and, knowing the spot well where Dias was shipwrecked, he entreats them to change their course, his only thought being Donna Ines's safety. But Pedro, delighted to have his rival in his power, orders him to be bound and shot. Ines, hearing his voice, invokes her husband's mercy. Just then the tempest breaks out, the vessel strikes upon a rock and the cannibals inhabiting the neighboring country leap on board to liberate their Queen Selica and to massacre the whole crew, in the fulfillment of which intention they are, however, arrested by Selica.

In the following acts Selica resides as Queen on the Isle of Madagascar. The people render her homage, but her priests demand the strangers' lives as a sacrifice to their gods, while the women are condemned to inhale the poisoned perfume of the Manzanillo-tree. In order to save Vasco, Selica proclaims him her husband and takes Nelusco as witness, swearing to him that if Vasco is sacrificed she will die with him. Nelusco, whose love for his Queen is greater even than his hatred for Vasco, vouches for their being man and wife, and the people now proceed to celebrate the solemn rites of marriage.

Vasco, at last recognizing Selica's great love, and believing Ines dead, once more vows eternal fidelity to her, but alas! hearing the voice of Ines, who is about to be led to death, he turns pale and Selica but too truly divines the reason.

In the fifth act Selica is resolved to put her rival to death. She sends for her, but perceiving Ines's love, her wrath vanishes, her magnanimity soars above her hatred of the Christians, and she orders Nelusco to bring Ines and Vasco on board of a ship about to sail for Portugal.

Selica herself, unable to endure life without her beloved one, proceeds to the Cape, where the Manzanillo-tree spreads his poisonous shade. Her eyes fastened on the vast ocean and on the white sail of the retiring vessel, she inhales the sweet but deadly perfume of the blossoms, and the returning Nelusco finds her dying, while an unseen chorus consoles her with the thought that in Love's eternal domain all are equal.

AÏDA

Grand Romantic Opera in four acts by Giuseppe Verdi.
Text by Ghislanzoni.

THE scene of action is alternately Memphis and Thebes, and the story belongs to the period when the Pharaohs sat on the throne.

In the first act we see the King's palace at Memphis. Ramphis, the high priest of Pharaoh, announces to the Egyptian general Radamès that the Ethiopians are in revolt and that the goddess Isis has decided who shall be leader of the army sent out against them. Radamès secretly hopes to be the elected, in order to win the Ethiopian slave Aïda, whom he loves, not knowing that she is a king's daughter.

Enter Amneris, daughter of Pharaoh. She loves Radamès without his knowledge and so does Aïda. Amneris, suspecting this, swears to avenge herself, should her suspicion prove correct.

The King's messenger announces that Amonasro, the Ethiopian king (Aïda's father), is marching to the capital, and that Radamès is chosen to conquer the foe. Radamès goes to the temple to invoke the benediction of the goddess and to receive the sacred arms.

In the second act Amneris, in order to test Aïda's feelings, tells her that Radamès fell in battle, and finds her doubts confirmed by Aïda's terror. Amneris openly threatens her rival, and both hasten to receive the soldiers, who return victorious. In Radamès's suite walks King Amonasro, who has been taken prisoner, disguised as a simple officer. Aïda recognizes her father, and Amonasro, telling his conqueror that the Ethiopian king has fallen, implores his clemency. Radamès, seeing Aïda in tears, adds his entreaties to those of the Ethiopian; and Pharaoh decides to set the prisoners free, with the exception of Aïda's father, who is to stay with his daughter. Pharaoh then gives Amneris to Radamès as a recompence for his services.

In the third act Amonasro has discovered the mutual love of his daughter and Radamès and resolves to make use of it. While Amneris prays in the temple that her bridegroom may give his whole heart to her, Amonasro bids his daughter discover the secret of the Egyptian war-plans from her lover. Amonasro hides himself, and Aïda has an interview with Radamès, in which he reveals all to her. She persuades him to fly with her, when Amonasro shows himself, telling him that he has heard all and confessing that he is the Ethiopian king. While they are speaking, Amneris overtakes and denounces them. Amonasro escapes with his daughter, Radamès remains in the hands of Ramphis, the high priest.

In the fourth act Radamès is visited in his cell by Amneris, who promises to save him from the awful death of being buried alive, if he renounces Aïda. But Radamès refuses, though she tells him that Aïda has fled into her country, her father being slain on their flight.

Amneris at length regrets her jealousy and repents, but too late! Nothing can save Radamès, and she is obliged to see him led into his living tomb. Amneris curses the priests, who close the subterranean vaults with a rock. Radamès, preparing himself for death, discovers Aïda by his side. She has found means to penetrate into his tomb, resolved to die with her lover. While she sinks into his arms, Amneris prays outside for Radamès's peace and eternal happiness.

ALCESTE

Opera in three acts by Christoph Willibald Gluck.
Text by Calzabigi.

ADMETOS, King of Pheræ, who is lying dangerously ill, causes an inquiry to be made of the oracle of Apollo as to the issue of his illness, and is told in reply that he will die unless some one can be found who would willingly lay down his life for him. Although the whole country bewails the threatened fate of its sovereign no one comes forward to save him at this terrible price. At length Alceste, the devoted wife of the unhappy King, nobly offers to sacrifice herself for his sake. Admetos in consequence is restored to health, but Alceste, on the evening of the same day, is ordered by the high priest to descend into the underworld. In vain the King implores his beloved wife to give up her resolve. As all his remonstrances prove fruitless, he determines to die with her. The spirits of the underworld have already got possession of their victim and are carrying her off. Admetos strives to gain admittance, but the entrance is barred against him.

At this moment his friend Heracles appears, who is justly celebrated far and near for his prodigious strength, a proof of which he will now give, having heard what has happened. He consoles the despairing King and rushes after the vanishing Alceste. A hot contest ensues, but finally Heracles seizes the god of death in his strong arms and restores the wife to her husband. Apollo, appearing in a cloud, praises the courageous friend and the faithful pair, promising them everlasting honor.

L'AMICO FRITZ

Lyric Comedy in three acts by Pietro Mascagni.
Text after Erckmann-Chatrian's novel.

FRITZ KOBUS, a well-to-do landowner, receives the felicitations of his friends on his fortieth birthday. At the same time his old friend Rabbi David, as consummate a match-maker as Fritz is an inveterate bachelor, receives from the latter a loan of 1200 francs, which is to enable a poor girl to marry her lover. Friend Fritz gives it very graciously, congratulating himself that he is free from marriage bonds.

He treats his friends to a hearty dinner, in which Susel, his tenant's daughter, who comes to present her landlord with a nosegay of violets, joins. Fritz makes her sit beside him, and for the first time remarks the growing loveliness of the young maiden. While they are feasting, a gypsy, Seppel, plays a serenade in honor of the birthday, which makes a deep impression on fair Susel. When the latter has departed, the joviality of the company increases. Hanczo and Friedrich, two friends, laughingly prophesy to the indignant Fritz that he will soon be married, and David even makes a bet which, should he prove right, will make him owner of one of his friend's vineyards. At the end of the first act a procession of orphans hail the landlord as their benefactor.

In the second act we find Friend Fritz as guest in the house of his tenant. Susel is sedulously engaged in selecting flowers and cherries for her landlord, who, coming down into the garden, is presented by her with flowers. Soon she mounts a ladder, and plucking cherries, throws them to Fritz, who is uncertain which are the sweeter, the maiden's red lips or the ripe cherries which she offers him. In the midst of their enjoyment the sound of bells and cracking of whips is heard. Fritz's friends enter. He soon takes them off for a walk; only old David stays behind with Susel, pleading fatigue. Taking occasion of her presenting him with a drink of fresh water, he makes her tell him the old story of Isaac and Rebecca and is quite satisfied to guess at the state of her feelings by the manner in which she relates the simple story. On Fritz's return he archly communicates to him that he has found a suitable husband for Susel, and that he has her father's consent. The disgust and fright which Fritz experiences at this news reveal to him something of his own feelings for the charming maiden. He decides to return home at once, and does not even take farewell of Susel, who weeps in bitter disappointment.

In the third act Fritz, at home again, can find no peace anywhere. When David tells him that Susel's marriage is a decided fact he breaks out, and in his passion forbids the marriage. At this moment Susel appears, bringing her landlord a basket of fruit. She looks pale and sad, and when Fritz sarcastically asks her whether she comes to invite him to her wedding, she bursts into tears. Then the real state of her heart is revealed to him, and with passionate avowal of his own love, Fritz takes her to his heart. So David wins his wager, which he settles on Susel as a dowry, promising at the same time to procure wives before long for the two friends standing by.

ARMIDE

Grand Heroic Opera in five acts by Christoph Willibald Gluck.
Text by Quinault.

THE libretto is founded on an episode of Tasso's "Jerusalem Delivered." The scene is laid in Damascus, where during the crusade of the year 1099, the crusaders have arrived at the palace and gardens of Armide, the Queen and enchantress. Rinaldo, the greatest hero in Godfrey of Bouillon's army, is the only one who not only does not stoop to adore the beautiful Armide, but on the contrary pursues and hates her. He has been banished from Bouillon's presence, charged with the rash deed of another knight, who has not dared to confess his guilt, and he now wanders lonely in the forest.

Warned by a fellow-warrior, Artemidor, to avoid Armide's enchanting presence, he scorns the warning, saying that love for a woman is to him a thing unknown. In reality, however, Armide is already ensnaring him with her sorcery. He presently hears exquisitely sweet and dreamy melodies, and, finding himself in a soft, green valley, he lies down and falls asleep.

Armide's opportunity has come and she means to stab him, but love conquers hatred and the dagger sinks from her hand. She vainly invokes the furies of hate; none can change her passion for the hero, and at last, ceasing to strive against her tender feelings, she surrenders herself entirely to him, and even succeeds by her charms and her devotion in enthralling him. Meanwhile Bouillon has sent two of his knights, Ubalt and a Danish warrior, to recall Rinaldo to his duty. They are detained by Armide's witchery; the Danish knight meets a demon, who has taken his bride's face and tenderly calls him to her, but Ubalt destroys the charm and both succeed in approaching Rinaldo, who, his love-dream dissipated by the call of honor, resolves to return to the army with his companions. In vain Armide tries to change his resolution. In despair she curses him and her love, but being unable to kill the man she loves, she suffers him to go away and turns her beautiful palace and gardens into a desert.

UN BALLO IN MASCHERA

Lyric Drama in five acts by Giuseppe Verdi.
Text by Piave.

THE libretto is almost identical with Auber's "Ballo in Maschera," which follows.

Count Richard, governor of Boston, is adored by the people but hated by the noblemen, who resolve upon his death. He loves Amelia, the wife of his secretary and best friend René, who in vain tries to warn him of the plots of his enemies, but who faithfully watches over his safety.

An old sorceress of negro blood, Ulrica, is to be banished by the decree of the high judge, but Richard's page Oscar speaks in her favor, and the Count decides to see her himself and test her tricks. He invites his lords to accompany him to the sibyl's dwelling, and orders Oscar to bring him a fisherman's disguise. His enemies, Samuel and Tom, follow him.

The second act shows Ulrica in her cottage seated at a table, conjuring Satan. A crowd of people are around her, among them Richard in disguise. A sailor, Sylvan, advances first to hear his fate, and while Ulrica is prophesying that better days await him, Richard slips a roll of gold with a scroll into Sylvan's pocket and so makes the witch's words true. Sylvan, searching in his pockets, finds the gold and reads the inscription on the scroll: "Richard to his dear officer Sylvan," and all break out into loud praises of the clever sibyl.

A short while after a servant announces Amelia, and the sorceress, driving the crowd away, ushers her in, while Richard conceals himself. He listens with delight to the confession of her sinful love for himself, against which she asks for a draught, which might enable her to banish it from her heart. Ulrica advises her to pluck a magic herb at midnight, which grows in the fields where the criminals are executed. Amelia shudders but promises to do as she is bidden, while Richard secretly vows to follow and protect her.

Amelia departs and the people flock in again. Richard is the first to ask what is his fate. The sibyl reluctantly tells him that his life is to be destroyed by the first person who shall touch his hand on this very day. Richard vainly offers his hand to the bystanders, they all recoil from him, when suddenly his friend René comes in, and heartily shakes Richard's outstretched hand. This seems to break the spell, for everybody knows René to be the Count's dearest friend, and now believes the oracle to be false. Nevertheless Ulrica, who only now recognizes the Count, warns him once more against his enemies, but he laughs at her, and shows the sorceress the verdict of her banishment, which, however, he has canceled. Full of gratitude Ulrica joins in the universal song of praise, sung by the people to their faithful leader.

The third act opens on the ghostly field where Amelia is to look for the magic herb. She is frozen with horror, believing that she sees a ghost rise before her. Richard now turns up, and breaks out into passionate words, entreating her to acknowledge her love for him. She does so, but implores him at the same time not to approach her, and to remain true to his friend. While they speak René surprises them. He has followed Richard to save him from his enemies, who are waiting to kill him. Richard wraps himself in his friend's cloak, after having taken René's promise to lead the veiled lady to the gates of the town without trying to look at her. René swears, but fate wills it otherwise, for hardly has Richard departed, when the conspirators throng in, and enraged at finding only the friend, try to tear the veil off the lady's face. René guards her with his sword, but Amelia springing between the assailants lets fall her veil, and reveals her face to her husband and to the astonished men, thereby bringing shame and bitter mockery on them both. René, believing himself betrayed by wife and friend, asks the conspirators to meet him in his own house on the following morning, and swears to avenge the supposed treachery.

In the fourth act in his own house René bids his wife prepare herself for death. He disbelieves in her protest of innocence, but at length, touched by her misery, he allows her to take a last farewell of her son. When she is gone, he resolves rather to kill the seducer than his poor weak wife. When the conspirators enter he astonishes them by his knowledge of their dark designs, but they wonder still more when he offers to join them in their evil purpose. As they do not agree who it shall be that is to kill Richard, René makes his wife draw the lot from a vase on the table. The chosen one is her own husband. At this moment Oscar enters with an invitation to a masked ball from the court. René accepts, and the conspirators decide to seize the opportunity to put their foe to death. They are to wear blue dominos with red ribbons. Their password is "death."

The next scene shows a richly decorated ballroom. René vainly tries to find out the Count's disguise, until it is betrayed to him by the page, who believes that René wants to have some fun with his master. Amelia, waylaying Richard, implores him to fly, and when he disbelieves her warnings, shows him her face. When he recognizes her, he tenderly takes her hand, and tells her that he too has resolved to conquer his passion,

and that he is sending her away to England with her husband. They are taking a last farewell, but alas! fate overtakes Richard in the shape of René, who runs his dagger through him. The crowd tries to arrest the murderer, but the dying Count waves them back, and with his last breath tells his unhappy friend that his wife is innocent. Drawing forth a document and handing it to René, the unfortunate man reads the Count's order to send them to their native land. Richard pardons his misguided friend and dies with a blessing on his beloved country.

BALLO IN MASCHERA, or GUSTAVUS THE THIRD

Grand Historic Opera in five acts by Daniel F. E. Auber.
Text by Scribe.

THIS opera has had a curious fate, its historical background having excited resistance and given rise to scruples. The murder of a king was not thought a fit subject for an opera, and so the libretto was altered and spoiled.

The Italians simply changed the names and the scene of action; Verdi composed a new opera from the same matter and succeeded admirably; nevertheless Auber's composition is preferred in Germany, Scribe's libretto being by far the better, while the music is original and vivacious, as well as full of pleasant harmony and fine instrumentation.

The scene is laid in Stockholm in the year 1792. Gustavus III, King of Sweden, loves the wife of his friend and counselor Ankarström, and is loved in return, both struggling vainly against this sinful passion. Ankarström has detected a plot against the King's life, and warning him, asks that the traitor be punished, but Gustavus refuses to listen, trusting in his people and in his friend's fidelity. His minister Kaulbart desires him to condemn a sorceress named Arvedson, who is said to be able at will by means of certain herbs and potions to cause persons to love or hate each other. The King refuses to banish the woman unheard and decides to visit her. Ankarström tries to dissuade, but the King insists, and accordingly goes to Arvedson in disguise. During the witch's conjuration Malwina, his lady-love, appears, who seeks help from the sorceress against her forbidden passion. The concealed King hears Arvedson tell her to go at midnight and gather a herb, which grows on the graves of criminals, and triumphant in his knowledge of Malwina's confessed love, Gustavus decides to follow her there.

When she has gone, he mockingly orders the witch to tell him his fortune, and hears from her that he shall be killed by the man who first tenders him his hand. Just then Ankarström, who comes to protect the King against his enemy, enters and they shake hands.

In the third act Malwina meets the King on the dismal spot to which she had been directed; but Ankarström, whose watchful fidelity never suffers him to be far from the King, and who is utterly ignorant of the deception being practised upon him, saves the lovers from further guilt. After a severe conflict with himself, Gustavus consents to fly in his friend's cloak, Ankarström having pledged his honor not to ask the veiled lady's secret, and to conduct her safely back to the city. This plan is frustrated by the conspirators, who rush in and are about to attack the King. Malwina throws herself between him and the combatants, and the husband then recognizes in the King's companion his own wife. Full of indignation he turns from her and joins the conspirators, promising to be one of them. He swears to kill his unhappy wife, but not until another has first fallen.

In the fourth act the conspirators have a meeting in Ankarström's house, where they decide to murder the King. The lots being cast, the duty to strike the death-blow falls on Ankarström, and Malwina herself draws the fatal paper. At this moment an invitation to a masked ball is brought by the King's page Oscar, and the conspirators resolve to take advantage of this opportunity for the execution of their design.

In the last act the King, happy to know Malwina safe from discovery, resolves to sacrifice his love to honor and friendship. He is about to give Ankarström the proof of his friendship, by naming him governor of Finland, and the minister is to depart with his wife on the morning after the ball. Meanwhile the King is warned by a missive from an unknown hand not to appear at the ball, but he disregards it. He meets Malwina at the ball. His page, thinking to do the King a service, has betrayed his mask to Ankarström. Malwina warns the prince, but in vain, for while he presents her with the paper which is to send her and her husband to their own beloved country, Ankarström shoots him through the heart. Gustavus dies, pardoning his murderer.

DER BARBIER VON BAGDAD
(The Barber of Bagdad)

Comic Opera in two acts by Peter Cornelius.

THE scene takes place in Bagdad, in the house of a wealthy young Mussulman called Nureddin. He is lying on a couch, surrounded by his servants, who think him dying. But it is only the flame of love which devours his strength and deprives him of all energy. As soon as Bostana, an old relative and companion of his lady-love, appears, in order to tell him that Margiana, his adored, is willing to receive him, Nureddin forgets his illness and only longs for the promised interview. The ensuing duet between him and Bostana, wherein she gives instruction about time and hour of the rendezvous, is delightfully fresh and piquant.

As Nureddin has neglected his personal appearance during his malady, his first wish is for a barber, who is speedily sent to him by Bostana. This old worthy, Abul Hassan Ali Ebe Bekar, the barber, makes him desperate by his vain prattle. Having solemnly saluted to Nureddin, he warns him not to leave the house, as his horoscope tells that his life is in danger. The young man not heeding him, Abul Hassan begins to enumerate all his talents as astrologer, philosopher, etc. When Nureddin orders him to begin his shaving he relates the fate of his six brothers, who all died before him and always of love. At last Nureddin's patience giving away, he calls his servants in to throw the old dotard out of doors, but Abul drives them all back. Nureddin tries to pacify him with flattery and finally succeeds.

Now Abul is curious, as all barbers are, and having heard Nureddin's sighs, he determines to find out all about the young man's love. This scene is most ludicrous, when Abul sings his air "Margiana," which name he has heard from Nureddin's lips, and the latter is in despair at being left with only one side of his head shaved. This great work done at last, Abul wants to accompany the young lover to the house of the cadi Baba Mustapha, Margiana's father. Nureddin again summons his servants, who begin to surround Abul, pretending to doctor him. Nureddin escapes, but Abul, after having shaken off the servants, runs after him.

The second act takes place in the cadi's house. Margiana is full of sweet anticipation, while her father, who has already chosen a husband for his daughter in the person of an old friend of his youth, shows her a large trunk full of gifts from the old bridegroom. Margiana admires them obediently. A musical scene of surpassing beauty follows, where we hear the call of the muezzin summoning the faithful to prayer. It is also the sign for Nureddin to appear. The cadi hurries to the mosque and Bostana introduces the lover. Here ensues a charming love-duet, accompanied, originally enough, by a song from the old barber, who watches before the house. Suddenly they are interrupted by cries of alarm, and with dismay they learn from Bostana that the cadi has returned to punish a slave, who has broken a precious vase.

Nureddin, unable to escape unobserved, is hidden in the big trunk. Meanwhile Abul, having heard the slave's cries and mistaking them for Nureddin's, summons the latter's servants and breaks into the cadi's house to avenge his young friend, whom he believes to be murdered. Bostana angrily bids him carry away the trunk, signifying to him whom she has hidden in it, but the cadi intervenes, believing the servants to be thieves who want to rob his daughter's treasure. The rumor of the murder gradually penetrates the whole town; its inhabitants gather before the house, and the appointed wailing-women mingle their doleful lamentations with the general uproar. At last the Calif himself appears in order to settle the quarrel.

The cadi accuses the barber of theft, while Abul calls the cadi a murderer. To throw light upon the matter, the Calif orders the trunk to be opened, which is done with great hesitation by Margiana. When the lid gives way Nureddin is lying in it in a deep swoon. All are terrified, believing him to be murdered; but Abul, caressing him, declares that his heart still throbs. The Calif bids the barber show his art, and Abul wakens Nureddin by the love-song to Margiana. The young man revives and the truth dawns upon the deceived father's mind. The Calif, a very humane and clement prince, feels great sympathy with the beautiful young couple, and advises the cadi to let his daughter have her treasure, for he had told them himself that it was Margiana's treasure that was kept hidden in the trunk.

The cadi consents, while the Calif bids the funny barber come to his palace to entertain him with stories, and invites all present to the wedding of the betrothed pair, to the great satisfaction of the people. The brilliant finale is full of energy, and is especially noteworthy on account of its melody.

IL BARBIERE DI SEVIGLIA

Comic Opera in two acts by Gioachino Antonio Rossini. Text by Sterbini.

COUNT ALMAVIVA is enamored of Rosina, the ward of Doctor Bartolo. She is most jealously guarded by the old man, who wishes to make her his own wife. In vain the Count serenades her; she does not appear, and he must needs invent some other means of obtaining his object. Making the acquaintance of the light-hearted and cunning barber Figaro, the latter advises him to get entrance into Bartolo's house in the guise of a soldier possessing a billet of quartering for his lodging. Rosina herself has not failed to hear the sweet love-songs of the Count, known to her only under the simple name of Lindoro; and with southern passion, and the light-heartedness which characterizes all the persons who figure in this opera, but which is not to be mistaken for frivolity, Rosina loves her nice lover and is willing to be his own. Figaro has told her of Almaviva's love and in return she gives him a note, which she has written in secret. But the old Doctor is a sly fox, he has seen the inky little finger, and determines to keep his eyes open.

When the Count appears in the guise of a half-drunken dragoon, the Doctor sends Rosina away, and tries to put the soldier out of the house, pretending to have a license against all billets. The Count resists, and while Bartolo seeks for his license, makes love to Rosina, but after the Doctor's return there arises such an uproar that all the neighbors and finally the guards appear, who counsel the Count to retire for once.

In the second act the Count gains entrance to Bartolo's house as a singing-master, who is deputed to give a lesson instead of the fever-stricken Basilio. Of course the music-lesson is turned into a love-lesson.

When all seems to be going well, the real maestro, Basilio, enters and all but frustrates their plans. With gold and promises Figaro bribes him to retreat, and the lovers agree to flee on the coming night.

Almost at the last moment the cunning of Bartolo hinders the projected elopement. He shows a letter, which Rosina has written, and makes Rosina believe that her lover, whom she only knows as Lindoro, in concert with Figaro is betraying her to the Count. Great is her joy when she detects that Lindoro and Count Almaviva are one and the same person, and that he loves her as truly as ever. They bribe the old notary, who has been sent for by Bartolo to arrange his own (Bartolo's) wedding with Rosina. Bartolo signs the contract of marriage, with Figaro as witness, and detects too late that he has been duped, and that he has himself united the lovers. At last he submits with pretty good grace to the inevitable, and contents himself with Rosina's dowry, which the Count generously transfers to him.

DIE BEIDEN SCHÜTZEN
(The Two Guardsmen)

Comic Opera in three acts by Gustav Albert Lortzing. Text adapted from the French.

THE scene is in a little country town, where we find Busch, a wealthy innkeeper, making preparations for the arrival of his only son. The young man had entered a grenadier regiment at the age of sixteen, ten years before, so the joyful event of his home-coming is looked forward to with pleasure by his father and sister Süschen, but with anxiety by a friend of hers, Caroline, to whom young Busch had been affianced before joining his regiment.

Enter two young grenadiers from the regiment on leave, the younger of whom falls in love with Süschen at first sight. However, as the elder grenadier, Schwarzbart, dolefully remarks, they are both almost penniless, and he reflects how he can possibly help them in their need. His meditations are interrupted by the arrival of the landlord, who, seeing the two knapsacks and recognizing one of them as that of his son, naturally supposes the owner to be his offspring, in which belief he is confirmed by Schwarzbart, who is induced to practise this deceit, partly by the desire of getting a good dinner and the means of quenching his insatiable thirst, partly by the hope of something turning up in favor of his companion in arms, Wilhelm. As a matter of fact the knapsack does not belong to Wilhelm at all. On leaving the inn at which the banquet following the wedding of one of their comrades had been held, the knapsacks had inadvertently been exchanged much to Wilhelm's dismay, his own containing a lottery ticket which, as he has just learned, had won a great prize. The supposed son is of course received with every demonstration of affection by his fond parent; but, though submitting with a very good grace to the endearments of his supposed sister—the maiden with whom he has fallen in love so suddenly—he resolutely declines being hugged and made much of by the old landlord, this double part being entirely distasteful to his straightforward nature. Nor does his affianced bride, the daughter of the bailiff, fare any better, his affections being placed elsewhere, and their bewilderment is only somewhat appeased by Schwarzbart's explanation that his comrade suffers occasionally from weakness of the brain.

In the next act Peter, a youth of marvelous stupidity, a cousin of the bailiff, presents himself in a woeful plight, to which he has been reduced by some soldiers at the same wedding festivities, and shortly after Gustav, the real son, appears on the scene. He is a manly fellow, full of tender thoughts for his home. Great is his surprise at finding himself repulsed by his own father, who, not recognizing him, believes him to be an impostor. All the young man's protestations are of no avail, for in his knapsack are found the papers of a certain Wilhelm Stark for whom he is now mistaken. When silly Peter perceives him he believes him to be the grenadier who had so ill-treated him at the wedding, though in reality it was Schwarzbart. Gustav is shut up in a large garden-house of his father's; the small town lacking a prison.

In the third act the magistrate has found out that Wilhelm's papers prove him to be the bailiff's son, being the offspring of his first love. He had been with a clergyman, and after the death of the bailiff's wife was vainly sought for by his father. Of course this changes everything for the prisoner, who is suddenly accosted graciously by his gruff guardian Barsch, and does not know what to make of his mysterious hints.

Meanwhile Caroline's heart has spoken for the stranger who had addressed her so courteously and chivalrously; she feels that, far from being an impostor, he is a loyal and true-hearted young fellow and therefore decides to liberate him. At the same time enters Wilhelm with Schwarzbart, seeking Süschen; Peter slips in for the same reason, seeking her, for Süschen is to be his bride. Gustav (the prisoner), hearing footsteps, blows out the candle in order to save Caroline from being recognized, and so they all run about in the dark, playing hide-and-seek in an infinitely droll manner. At last the bailiff, having heard that his son has been found, comes up with the innkeeper. The whole mystery is cleared up, and both sons embrace their respective fathers and their brides.

LA BOHÈME

Opera in four acts by Giacomo Puccini.
Text by Giacosa and Illica.

THE first act opens in a garret in Paris, in about 1830, and shows us Marcel the painter and Rudolph the poet, from whose Bohemian mode of life the opera derives its name, at work. Alas! there is no fire in the grate, and the cold is so intense that Marcel is about to break up a chair for firewood.

Rudolph prevents him and kindles a fire with his manuscript instead, crying: "My drama shall warm us." The second act of the manuscript follows the first one, by the blaze of which the artists joyfully warm their half-frozen hands. The paper is quickly burned to ashes, but before they have time to lament this fact the door is opened by two boys bringing food, fuel, wine, and even money. Schaunard, a musician, brings up the rear, to whom neither Marcel nor Rudolph pays the least attention.

It seems that an Englishman engaged Schaunard to sing to his parrot till it dies, but after three days Schaunard becomes so heartily sick of his task that he poisons the bird and runs away.

He suggests that they all go out for supper, it being Christmas eve. They decide to drink some of the wine first, but they are interrupted by the landlord, who demands his quarter's rent. He soon imbibes so much of the wine that he becomes intoxicated and correspondingly jovial. After being joked about his love adventures he finds himself standing outside the door in pitch darkness. The others meanwhile prepare to go out to supper, with the exception of Rudolph, who remains behind to finish a manuscript article.

A pretty young girl soon knocks, carrying a candle and a key. He begs her to come in and be seated, and she swoons while refusing. He revives her with some wine, and she goes off with her relighted candlestick, but forgets her key, which she has dropped in her swoon, and for which she at once comes back. A draft blows out the candle and Rudolph keeps the key, while pretending to look for it. Suddenly he clasps the girl's hand and he and she exchange confidences, while confessing their love for each other.

When Rudolph's friends call him he invites Mimi, who is a flower-girl, to accompany him.

The second act takes place before the well-known Café Momus in the Quartier Latin, where Rudolph and Mimi join Schaunard and Marcel.

Rudolph has bought her a pink bonnet and introduces her to his friends, the fourth of whom is Colline the philosopher.

The party eat and drink amid the noise and bustle of the fair, when Marcel suddenly sees his old love Musette, gorgeously arrayed and leaning upon the arm of an old man. Marcel turns pale, while his friends make fun of the fantastic couple, much to Musette's anger. She at once begins to make overtures to Marcel, who feigns utter indifference. Musette's old admirer orders supper, in the hope of pacifying her, while she addresses Marcel in fond whispers. The others watch the scene with amusement, but Rudolph devotes all his attentions to Mimi. Musette suddenly complains that her shoes hurt her and sends her aged lover off for another pair. Then she proceeds to make friends with Marcel. When the waiter brings the bill, Musette tells him that the old gentleman will settle for everything after his return.

The party profit by the approach of the patrol, who causes a turmoil, in the midst of which they all escape. Alcindor, the old admirer, finds only two bills awaiting him when he returns with the new shoes. Musette has been carried away shoeless by her old friend.

The third act takes place on the outskirts of Paris called "Barrière de l'Enfer" (The Tollgate of Hell). To the left there is a tavern, over which hangs Marcel's picture "The Crossing of the Red Sea," as a signboard. The day is breaking, the customhouse officials are still sleeping around the fire, but the scavengers coming from Chantilly soon awake them.

The gate is opened to admit milk-women, carters, peasants with baskets, and finally Mimi.

She looks wretched and is at once seized with a terrible fit of coughing. As soon as she can speak, she asks the name of the tavern, where she knows Marcel is working. When he emerges from the inn she implores his help, saying Rudolph is killing her by his insane jealousy. Marcel promises to intervene, and when Rudolph comes out of the tavern Mimi hides behind the trees.

She hears Rudolph say she is doomed to die, and coughs and sobs so violently that her presence is revealed.

Rudolph remorsefully takes the poor weak creature in his arms, and they decide to make it up.

Their reconciliation is interrupted by Marcel, who is upbraiding Musette. This flighty damsel has one lover after another, although she really loves Marcel alone.

The fourth and last act takes us back to the garret, where Marcel and Rudolph are alone, Musette and Mimi having left them. They each kiss mementos of their lady-loves, when Schaunard appears with bread and herring. Gaiety is soon restored and a regular frolic takes place. Musette enters in a state of great agitation, to say that Mimi, who is in the last stage of consumption, is there and wants to see Rudolph once more. The latter carries her on the little bed. As there is nothing in the house with which to revive her, Musette decides to sell her earrings in order to procure medicines, a doctor, and a muff, for which Mimi longs.

Schaunard also goes out, so that the lovers are left alone. A touching scene follows, when Rudolph shows Mimi the pink bonnet he has cherished all the time. Musette and Marcel soon return with medicines and a muff, upon which Mimi sinks into the sleep that knows no awakening, with a contented smile.

THE BOHEMIAN GIRL

Opera in three acts by Michael William Balfe.
Text by Bunn.

THE opera opens with a scene on Count Arnheim's grounds near Presburg. Count Arnheim's retainers are waiting to accompany him to the hunt. He appears with his foppish nephew Florestein, who is afraid of a gun. He bids farewell to his little daughter Arline, and she goes up a mountain path with Buda, her nurse, and Florestein. Thaddeus, a Polish exile, enters exhausted from pursuit. Gypsies appear, headed by Devilshoof. They attempt to rob Thaddeus, but after some parley he decides to join their band. Devilshoof takes everything he has except his commission, but gives him a ragged gypsy dress in return. He mingles with the gypsies just as a troop of soldiers come to apprehend him. Huntsmen return in excitement; Florestein appears, terrified. Arline has been attacked by a wild animal. Thaddeus rescues her, and the Count in gratitude invites him to a feast, during which he refuses to drink to the Emperor. He is repudiated by all, but Devilshoof comes to his aid. As a reward for the rescue of Arline the Count offers the exile a purse, which he proudly refuses. Thaddeus and Devilshoof are imprisoned, but the latter escapes and carries off Arline. He is seen by the Count and his guests crossing a frail bridge between two rocks with the child in his arms. He breaks down the bridge and disappears.

The second act reveals a street in Presburg twelve years later. We see the tent of the gypsy Queen. Arline sleeps while Thaddeus keeps watch. Devilshoof and others enter with a new project to rob Florestein, who is flushed with wine. They secure his valuables, but the Queen makes them return everything. Florestein is solicitous about a medallion which has disappeared and which is an heirloom of great value. Devilshoof has secreted it. Arline awakens and tells Thaddeus her dream in the aria "I dreamt I dwelt in marble halls." Thaddeus and Arline declare their love. The Queen, through jealousy, is angry, but, ridiculed by Devilshoof, joins their hands according to the gypsy rite.

The scene shifts to another street where a fair is being held. Count Arnheim and Florestein appear. Florestein compliments Arline, which amuses her, until he tries to kiss her, when she slaps him vigorously. The Queen, recognizing him, gives Arline the stolen medallion, so that she will be accused of robbing him. This plan succeeds, but Thaddeus and the gypsies protect Arline. Nevertheless, she and Thaddeus are imprisoned.

The final scene of the act shows Count Arnheim's apartments with a portrait of Arline in her childhood. The Count enters sadly, and gazes at the portrait. He sings "The heart bowed down." The captain of the guard reports Arline's capture. She is brought in and pleads her innocence, but in her humiliation is about to stab herself. The Count, while stopping her, observes a scar by which he recognizes her as his daughter, and Thaddeus, who enters at that moment, as her preserver.

The last act takes place in the Count's castle. Ar-line, in rich attire, is sad and lonely. She looks with longing at her gypsy dress. Devilshoof boldly enters the room and begs her to rejoin the tribe. Thaddeus appears at the window. He sings "Then you'll remember me." The two men hide themselves as the guests enter. The Queen of the gypsies suddenly appears and tells the Count that Thaddeus is concealed in his daughter's room. The Count denounces his daughter. Thaddeus comes from his hiding-place, and declares Arline innocent. He proclaims his identity as a Polish noble. The Count is reassured, but the Queen tries to kill Thaddeus, and Devilshoof, while attempting to snatch the rifle from her hands, accidentally shoots her. The joy of the lovers is too great to be marred, and all ends happily.

CARMEN

Opera in four acts by Georges Bizet.
Text by Meilhac and Halévy, founded on the story of Prosper Mérimée.

CARMEN, the heroine, is a Spanish gypsy, fickle and wayward, endowed with all the wild graces of her nation. She is adored by her people, and so it is not to be wondered at that she has many of the stronger sex at her feet. She tries to charm Don José, a brigadier of the Spanish army; of course he is one out of many; she soon grows tired of him, and awakens his jealousy by a thousand caprices and cruelties.

Don José is betrothed to the sweet and lovely Micaëla, waiting for him at home, but she is forgotten as soon as he sees the proud gypsy.

Micaëla seeks him out, bringing to him the portrait and the benediction of his mother, aye, even her kiss, which she gives him with blushes. His tenderness is gone, however, so far as Micaëla is concerned, as soon as he casts one look into the lustrous eyes of Carmen. This passionate creature has involved herself in a quarrel and wounded one of her companions, a laborer in a cigarette manufactory. She is to be taken to prison, but Don José lets her off, promising to meet her in the evening at an inn kept by a man named Lillas Pastia, where they are to dance the seguedilla.

In the second act we find them there together, with the whole band of gypsies. Don José, more and more infatuated by Carmen's charms, is willing to join the vagabonds, who are at the same time smugglers. He accompanies them in a dangerous enterprise of this kind, but no sooner has he submitted to sacrifice love and honor for the gypsy than she begins to tire of his attentions. José has pangs of conscience, he belongs to another sphere of society and his feelings are of a softer kind than those of nature's unruly child. She transfers her affections to a bullfighter named Escamillo, another of her suitors, who returns her love more passionately. A quarrel ensues between the two rivals. Escamillo's knife breaks and he is about to be killed by Don José, when Carmen intervenes, holding back his arm. Don José, seeing that she has duped him, now becomes her deadly foe, filled with sudden hatred and longing for revenge.

Micaëla, the tender-hearted maiden, who follows him everywhere like a guardian angel, reminds him of his lonely mother, everybody advises him to let the fickle Carmen alone—Carmen who never loved the same man for more than six weeks. But in vain, till Micaëla tells him of the dying mother asking incessantly for her son; then at last he consents to go with her, but not without wild imprecations on his rival and his faithless love.

In the fourth act we find ourselves in Madrid. There is to be a bullfight; Escamillo, its hero, has invited the whole company to be present in the circus.

Don José appears there too, trying for the last time to regain his bride. Carmen, though warned by a fellow-gypsy, Frasquita, knows no fear. She meets her old lover outside the arena, where he tries hard to touch her heart. He kneels at her feet, vowing never to forsake her and to be one of her own people, but Carmen, though wayward, is neither a coward nor a liar, and boldly declares that her affections are given to the bullfighter, whose triumphs are borne to their ears on the shouts of the multitude. Almost beside himself with love and rage, José seizes her hand and attempts to drag her away, but she escapes from him, and throwing the ring, José's gift, at his feet, rushes to the door of the arena. He overtakes her, however, and just as the trumpets announce Escamillo's victory, in a perfect fury of despair he stabs her through the heart, and the victorious bullfighter finds his beautiful bride a corpse.

CAVALLERIA RUSTICANA
(Rustic Chivalry)

Opera in one act by Pietro Mascagni.
Text by Targioni-Tozzetti and Menasci, after Verga's drama.

THE following are the very simple facts of the story, which takes place in a Sicilian village.

Turridu, a young peasant, has loved and wooed Lola before entering military service. At his return he finds the flighty damsel married to the wealthy carrier Alfio, who glories in his pretty wife and treats her very well. Turridu tries to console himself with another young peasant girl, Santuzza, who loves him ardently, and to whom he has promised marriage.

The opera only begins at this point.

Lola, the coquette, cannot bear to know that her former sweetheart should love another woman. She flirts with him, and before the curtain has been raised after the overture Turridu's love-song is heard for Lola, who grants him a rendezvous in her own house.

This excites Santuzza's wildest jealousy. She complains to Turridu's mother, who vainly tries to soothe her. Then she has a last interview with Turridu, who is just entering the church. She reproaches him first with his treachery, then implores him not to forsake her and leave her dishonored.

But Turridu remains deaf to all entreaty, and flings her from him. At last, half mad through her lover's stubbornness, Santuzza betrays him and Lola to Alfio, warning the latter that his wife has proved false. After church Alfio and Turridu meet in mother Lucia's tavern. Alfio refusing to drink of Turridu's wine, the latter divines that the husband knows all. The men and women leave while the two adversaries after Sicilian custom embrace each other, Alfio biting Turridu in the ear, which indicates mortal challenge. Turridu, deeply repenting his folly, as well as his falsehood

toward poor Santuzza, recommends her to his mother. He hurries into the garden, where Alfio expects him. A few minutes later his death is announced by the peasants, and Santuzza falls back in a dead swoon; with which the curtain closes over the tragedy.

LE CID

Lyric Drama in three acts by Peter Cornelius.

THE scene is laid in Burgos in Castile in the year 1064. The first act opens with a large concourse of people, assembled to celebrate the victory of Ruy Diaz over the Moors.

In the midst of their rejoicings a funeral march announces Chimene, Countess of Lozan, whose father has been slain by Diaz. While she wildly invokes the King's help against the hero the latter enters, enthusiastically greeted by the people, who adore in him their deliverer from the sword of the infidels.

He justifies himself before King Fernando, relating with quiet dignity how he killed Count Lozan in open duel to avenge his old father, whose honor the Count had grossly attacked. Nevertheless he is ready to defend himself against anybody who is willing to fight for Donna Chimene, and for this purpose he throws down his glove, which is taken up by Alvar Farnez, his friend and companion in arms, who is madly in love with Chimene. While they are preparing for the duel the Bishop Luyn Calvo, an uncle of Diaz, intervenes, entreating his nephew to desist from further bloodshed and to surrender his sword Tizona into the mediator's hands. After a hard struggle with himself the hero, who secretly loves Chimene, yields, and hands his sword to Calvo, who at once offers it to Chimene, thereby giving the defenseless hero into her hands.

Exultingly she swears to take vengeance on Diaz, who stands motionless, looking down with mournful dignity on the woman whom he loves and who seems to hate him so bitterly.

In the midst of this scene the war-cry is heard. The enemy has again broken into the country and has already taken and burned the fortress of Belforad. All crowd around Diaz, beseeching him to save them. While he stands mute and deprived of his invincible sword, Chimene, mastering her own grief at the sight of her country's distress, lays down Tizona at Fernando's feet. Ruy Diaz now receives his sword back from the hands of the King, and brandishing it high above his head he leads the warriors forth to freedom or death.

The second act takes place in Chimene's castle. Her women try to beguile their mistress's sorrow by songs, and when they see her soothed to quiet they retire noiselessly. But hardly does she find herself alone than pain and grief overcome her again. She longs to avenge her father's death on Diaz, and yet deep in her heart there is a feeling of great admiration for him. In vain she wrestles with her feelings, invoking the Almighty's help to do what is right. In this mood Alvar finds her. He once more assures her of his devotion and repeats that he will fight with Diaz as soon as the country is freed from the enemy. He leaves her, and night comes on. In the darkness Diaz steals in, for he cannot resist his heart's desire to see

Chimene once more before the battle. In the uncertain rays of the moonlight she at first mistakes him for her father's ghost, but when he pronounces her name she recognizes him, and violently motions him away, but he falls on his knee and pours out his hopeless love. At last his passion overcomes all obstacles; she forgives him, and at his entreaty she calls him by his name, saying: "Ruy Diaz, be victorious!" Full of joy he blesses her and goes to join his men, who are heard in the distance calling him to lead them to battle.

The third act is played once more in Burgos.

Diaz has been victorious. The whole army of captives defiles before the throne, and a rejoicing assemblage of nobles and people does homage to the King. Even the Moorish kings bend the knee voluntarily; they have been unfortunate, but they have been conquered by the greatest hero of the world; they are conquered by "the Cid"! When the King asks them what the name means, they tell him that its signification is "Master"; full of enthusiasm, all around adopt this name for their hero. The Cid will be his title henceforth, immortal as his glorious star!

The people loudly call for Diaz to appear, but are told that immediately after the battle Alvar had sent the hero a challenge. At the same time Alvar enters unhurt, and Chimene, who stands near the King with her women ready to greet the victor, grows white and faint, believing that Diaz has been killed by Alvar. She impetuously interrupts the latter, who begins to relate the events, and unable to control her feelings any longer she pours out her long pent-up love for Diaz, at the same time bewailing the slain hero and swearing faithfulness to his memory unto death. "He lives," cries Alvar, and at this moment the Cid, as we must now call him, appears, stormily hailed by great and small.

Deeply moved he lays down his victorious sword at the feet of his King, who embraces him, pronouncing him Sire of Saldaja, Cardenja, and Belforad. Then he leads him to his lady, who sinks into his arms supremely happy. The Bishop blesses the noble pair, and all join in his prayer that love may guide them through life and death.

LES CONTES D'HOFFMANN
(Hoffmann's Tales)

Fantastic Opera in three acts by Jacques Offenbach. Text by Barbier.

THE first scene, a prologue, is laid in Luther's famous wine-cellar in Nuremberg.

The hero of the opera, Hoffmann himself, is there, drinking with a number of gay young students, his friends. He is in a despondent mood, and when urged by his companions to tell them the reason of his depression he declares himself ready to relate the story of his three love adventures, while his friends sit round a bowl of flaming strong punch.

Now the scene changes and the curtain rises on the first act. We find Hoffmann in Spalanzani's house. This man is a famous physiologist, and Hoffmann has entered his house as his pupil in order to make the acquaintance of the professor's beautiful daughter Olympia, whom he has seen at a distance.

This daughter is nothing more than an automaton that has been manufactured by Spalanzani and his friend, the wizard Coppelius. This doll can sing, dance, and speak like a human being. Spalanzani hopes to become rich by means of this clever work of art. As half of Olympia (this is the doll's name) belongs to Coppelius, Spalanzani buys her from him, paying him by a draft on the Jew Elias, though he knows him to be bankrupt. Hoffmann has been persuaded by Coppelius to purchase a pair of spectacles, through which he looks at Olympia, and taking her for a lovely, living maiden, falls violently in love with her.

Spalanzani now gives a grand entertainment at which he presents his daughter Olympia (the automaton), who surprises everybody by her loveliness and fine singing. Hoffmann is completely bewitched, and as soon as he finds himself alone with her he makes her an ardent declaration of love and is not at all discouraged by her sitting stock-still and only answering from time to time a dry little "ja ja." At last he tries to embrace her, but as soon as he touches her she rises and trips away.

Hoffmann's friend Niklas finds him in the seventh heaven of rapture and vainly endeavors to enlighten him as to the reason of the beauty's stiffness and heartlessness.

When the dancing begins Hoffmann engages Olympia, and they dance on, always faster and faster, until Hoffmann sinks down in a swoon, his spectacles being broken by the fall. Olympia spins on alone as fast as ever and presently dances out of the room, Cochenille vainly trying to stop her. Coppelius now enters in a fury, having found out that Spalanzani's draft on Elias is worthless. He rushes to the room into which Olympia has vanished, and when Hoffmann revives he hears a frightful sound of breaking and smashing, and Spalanzani bursts in with the news that Coppelius has broken his valuable automaton. Thus Hoffmann learns that he has been in love with a senseless doll. The guests, who now enter, shout with laughter at his confusion, while Spalanzani and Coppelius load each other with abuse.

The second act takes place in Giulietta's palace in Venice. Everything breathes joy and love. Both Niklas and Hoffmann are courting the beautiful lady. Niklas warns his friend against her, but Hoffmann only laughs at the idea that he is likely to love a courtezan. The latter is entirely in the hand of the wizard Dapertutto, who acts toward Hoffmann as an evil spirit under three different names in each of his three love affairs. Giulietta has already stolen for him the shadow of her former lover Schlemihl; now Dapertutto wounds her vanity by telling her that Hoffmann has spoken disdainfully of her, and makes her promise to win the young man's love and by that means to make him give her his reflection from a looking-glass.

She succeeds easily, and there ensues a charming love-duet during which they are surprised by the jealous Schlemihl. Giulietta tells Hoffmann that her former lover has the key of her apartments in his pocket, she then departs leaving the two lovers and Dapertutto alone. When Hoffmann peremptorily demands the key from Schlemihl the latter refuses to give it up. The result is a duel, for which Dapertutto offers Hoffmann his sword.

After a few passes Schlemihl is killed and Dapertutto disappears. A few moments afterward Giulietta's gondola passes before the balcony and Hoffmann sees her leaning on Dapertutto's arm singing a mocking farewell to the poor deserted lover.

The third act takes place in Rath Krespel's house. His daughter Antonia has inherited her mother's gift of a beautiful voice, but also her tendency to consumption. The greatest joy of her life is singing, which, however, her father has forbidden, knowing this exertion to be fatal to his darling.

She is engaged to be married to Hoffmann, but Krespel is averse to the marriage, seeing in it another danger for his daughter's health, as Hoffmann is musical and encourages Antonia to sing. Krespel has forbidden his servant Franz to let anybody see Antonia while he goes out of the house, but Franz, who is very deaf, misunderstands his master's orders and joyously welcomes his mistress's suitor. A delicate love-scene follows, during which Antonia shows her lover that her voice is as fine as ever. When they hear Krespel returning, Antonia retires to her own room, but Hoffmann hides himself in an alcove, determined to learn why Antonia is so closely hidden from the world.

Immediately after the father's return Doctor Mirakel enters. Krespel is mortally afraid of this mysterious man, as he believes him to have killed his wife with drugs, and that now he aims at his daughter's life.

This Mirakel is a demon who acts as in the two former instances as Hoffmann's evil genius. From the conversation of the two men Hoffmann learns the secret of his bride's dangerous inheritance, and when Mirakel has at last been driven out of the room and Krespel has left it too, the lovers both come back again. Hoffmann by earnest entreaty succeeds in gaining Antonia's promise never to sing any more. But when he has left, Mirakel returns and by invoking the spirit of her mother he goads her on to break her promise. She begins to sing and he urges her on, until she sinks back exhausted. It is thus that her father and her lover find her, and after a few sweet words of farewell she dies in their arms.

The epilogue takes us back to Luther's cellar, where Hoffmann's companions are still sitting over their punch, the steam of which forms clouds over their heads, while they thank their poor, heart-broken friend for his three stories with ringing cheers.

COSI FAN TUTTE

Comic Opera in two acts by Wolfgang Amadeus Mozart. Text by Da Ponte, newly arranged by Schneider and Devrient.

DON FERNANDO and Don Alvar are betrothed to two Andalusian ladies, Rosaura and Isabella.

They loudly praise their ladies' fidelity, when an old bachelor, named Onofrio, pretends that their sweethearts are not better than other women and accessible to temptation. The lovers agree to make the trial and promise to do everything which Onofrio dictates. Thereupon they announce to the ladies that they are ordered to Havana with their regiment, and after a tender leave-taking, they depart to appear again in another guise, as officers of a strange regiment. Onofrio has won the ladies' maid, Dolores, to aid in the furtherance of his schemes, and the officers enter, beginning at once to make love to Isabella and Rosaura, but each, as was before agreed, to the other's affianced.

Of course the ladies reject them, and the lovers begin to triumph, when Onofrio prompts them to try another temptation. The strangers, mad with love, pretend to drink poison in the young ladies' presence. Of course these tender-hearted maidens are much aggrieved; they call Dolores, who bids her mistresses hold the patients in their arms; then coming disguised as a physician, she gives them an antidote. By this clumsy subterfuge they excite the ladies' pity and are nearly successful in their foolish endeavors, when Dolores, pitying the cruelly tested women, reveals the whole plot to them.

Isabella and Rosaura now resolve to enter into the play. They accept the disguised suitors, and even consent to a marriage. Dolores appears in the shape of a notary, without being recognized by the men. The marriage contract is signed, and the lovers disappear to return in their true characters, full of righteous contempt. Isabella and Rosaura make believe to be conscience-stricken, and for a long while torment and deceive their angry bridegrooms. But at last they grow tired of teasing, present the disguised Dolores, and put their lovers to shame by showing that all was a farce. Of course the gentlemen humbly ask their pardon, and old Onofrio is obliged to own himself beaten.

CZAR UND ZIMMERMANN
(Czar and Carpenter)

Comic Opera in three acts by Gustav Albert Lortzing.

PETER THE GREAT of Russia has taken service on the wharfs of Saardam as simple ship-carpenter under the assumed name of Peter Michaelov. Among his companions is another Peter, named Ivanov, a Russian renegade, who has fallen in love with Marie, the niece of the burgomaster Van Bett.

The two Peters being countrymen and fearing discovery, have become friendly, but Ivanov, instinctively feeling his friend's superiority, is jealous of him, and Marie, a little coquette, nourishes his passion.

Meanwhile the ambassadors of France and England, each of whom wishes for a special connection with the Czar of Russia, have discovered where he must be, and both bribe the conceited simpleton Van Bett, who tries to find out the real Peter.

He assembles the people, but there are many Peters among them, though only two strangers. He asks them whence they come, then takes aside Peter Ivanov, cross-questioning him in vain as to what he wishes to know.

At last, being aware of Peter's love for Marie, he gives him some hope of gaining her hand, and obtains in exchange a promise from the young man to confess his secret in presence of the foreign nobleman. The cunning French ambassador, the Marquis de Châteauneuf, has easily found out the Czar and gained his purpose, while the phlegmatic English lord, falsely directed by the burgomaster, is still in transaction with Ivanov. All this takes place during a rural festivity, where the Marquis, notwithstanding the claims upon his attention, finds time to court pretty Marie, exciting Ivanov's hate and jealousy.

Ivanov with difficulty plays the rôle of Czar, which personage he is supposed to be both by Lord Syndham and Van Bett. He well knows that he deserves punishment if he is found out on either side. The burgomaster, getting more and more confused, and fearing himself surrounded by spies and cheats, examines one of the strangers after the other, and is of course confounded to hear their highflown names; at last he seizes the two Peters, but is deterred from his purpose by the two ambassadors. They are now joined by a third, the Russian General Lefort, who comes to call back his sovereign to his own country. In the third act Van Bett has prepared a solemn demonstration of fealty for the supposed Czar whom he still mistakes for the real one, while the real Czar has found means to go on board of his ship with the Marquis and Lefort.

Before taking farewell Czar Peter promises a passport to Ivanov, who is very dubious as to what will become of him. Meanwhile Van Bett approaches the Czar with his procession to do homage, but during his long and confused speech cannon-shots are heard and an usher announces that Peter Michaelov is about to sail away with a large crew. The background opens and shows the port with the Czar's ship. Everybody shouts "Long live the Czar!" and Ivanov, opening the paper which his high-born friend left to him, reads that the Czar grants him pardon for his desertion and bestows upon him a considerable sum of money.

LA DAME BLANCHE

Comic Opera in three acts by François Adrien Boieldieu.
Text by Scribe.

THE scene is laid in Scotland, the plot being taken from two of Sir Walter Scott's novels, "The Monastery" and "Guy Mannering."

George Brown, the hero of the opera, a young lieutenant in the English service, visits Scotland. He is hospitably received by a tenant of the late Count Avenel, who has been dead for some years. When he arrives the baptism of the tenant's youngest child is just being celebrated, and seeing that they lack a godfather, he good-naturedly consents to take the vacant place.

Seeing the old castle of the Avenels, he asks for its history, and the young wife Jenny tells him that according to the traditions of the place it is haunted by a ghost, as is the case in almost every old castle. This apparition is called the White Lady, but unlike other ghosts she is good, protecting her sex against fickle men. All the people around believe firmly in her and pretend to have seen her themselves. In the castle is a statue which bears the name of this benevolent genius, and in it the old lord has hidden treasures. His steward Gaveston, a rogue, who has taken away the only son of the Count in the child's earliest days, brings the castle with all its acres to public sale, hoping to gain it for himself.

He has a charming ward, named Anna. It is she who sometimes plays the part of the White Lady. She has summoned the young tenant Dickson, who is sincerely devoted to her, into the castle, and the young man, though full of fear, yet dares not disobey the ghostly commands.

George Brown, thirsting for a good adventure, and disbelieving in the ghost story, declares that he will go in Dickson's place.

In the second act George, who has found entrance into the castle, calls for the White Lady, who appears in the shape of Anna. She believes that Dickson is before her and she reveals her secret to him, imploring his help against her false guardian Gaveston, who means to rob the true and only heir of his property. She knows that the missing son of the Avenels is living, and she has given a promise to the dying Countess to defend his rights against the rapacious Gaveston. George gives his hand to the pretended ghost in token of fidelity, and the warm and soft hand which clasps his awakes tender feelings in him. On the following morning Dickson and his wife, Jenny, are full of curiosity about George's visit, but he does not breathe a word of his secret.

The sale of the castle, as previously announced, is to begin, and Dickson has been empowered beforehand by all the neighboring farmers to bid the highest price, in order not to let it fall into the hands of the hateful Gaveston. They bid higher and higher, but at length Dickson stops, unable to go further. Gaveston feels assured of his triumph, when George Brown, recalling his vow to the White Lady, advances boldly, bidding one thousand pounds more. Anna is beside him, in the shape of the specter, and George obediently bids on, till the castle is his for the price of £300,000. Gaveston, in a perfect fury, swears to avenge himself on the adventurer, who is to pay the sum in the afternoon. Should he prove unable to do so, he shall be put into prison. George, who firmly believes in the help of his genius, is quietly confident, and meanwhile makes an inspection of the castle. Wandering through the vast rooms, dim recollections arise in him, and hearing the minstrel's song of the Avenels, he all at once remembers and finishes the romance which he heard in his childhood.

The afternoon comes and with it MacIrton, the justice of peace. He wants the money, and George begs to await the White Lady, who promised her help. Anna appears, bringing the treasure of the Avenels hidden in the statue, and with it some documents which prove the just claims of Edwin, Count Avenel. This long-lost Count she recognizes in George Brown, whose identity with the playmate of her youth she had found out the night before. Gaveston approaches full of wrath to tear aside the ghost's white veil, and see his own ward, Anna.

The happy owner of castle and country holds firm to the promise which he gave the White Lady, and offers hand and heart to the faithful Anna, who has loved him from her childhood.

LA DAMNATION DE FAUST
(The Damnation of Faust)

Opera in four parts by Hector Berlioz.

IN the first part Faust, the learned philosopher, wanders in the fields, near a German village, at sunrise, meditating upon nature. He observes a crowd of peasants who dance and sing, jesting rudely. The Hungarian troops approach to martial music. Great excitement prevails among the peasants. Faust alone remains cold and unmoved.

The second part opens with Faust in his study, deploring his unhappy lot. Neither in nature, nor in books, nor in old memories has he found solace. He decides to take poison; but as he raises the cup to drink, the strains of an Easter hymn turn his thoughts toward good. Even then the fiend Mephisto is at his elbow, tempting him with promises of earthly joys. He succumbs and goes forth with the fiend in search of pleasure. They enter a wine-cellar in which a number of boon companions are carousing. Mephisto joins them, but Faust is disgusted by their uproarious ribaldry. Led by Mephisto to a garden on the banks of the Elbe, he falls asleep amid the music of a chorus of sylphs, and dreams of Marguerite, a fair unknown peasant girl. As the sylphs dance about him he awakens, still thinking of Marguerite and desiring to find her. A troop of soldiers march by, returning from war and eager for pleasure. They are joined by a band of students, who proclaim in song the joys of wine and love.

Part third begins with distant drums and trumpets sounding the retreat. Faust impatiently awaits Marguerite in her dwelling. Mephisto warns him of her coming, and he conceals himself in her room. Marguerite enters, musing upon a strange dream of an unknown lover. She braids her hair, singing dreamily of the faithful King of Thule. Mephisto invokes the powers of evil and begins a mocking serenade, while in the garden without the will-o'-the-wisps dance. Faust appears before Marguerite, who is startled, but in an ardent love-scene they declare their mutual passion, and Marguerite at last is persuaded to give herself to her lover. The entrance of Mephisto, to tell them that the villagers are coming to warn Marguerite's mother of her danger, terrifies the bewildered girl. She and Faust part reluctantly, while Mephisto exults over the enslavement of his victim. The villagers approach muttering threats, as Mephisto forces Faust to depart.

In part fourth Marguerite, heavy-hearted, sits alone, thinking of her lover, who comes not. Soldiers march by singing of the glories of war. Faust, alone in his study, has found solace in nature, but Mephisto disturbs him with the news that Marguerite is in prison, condemned to death for the murder of her mother, Marthe, to whom the fiend had given too powerful a sleeping potion. Faust signs a paper which he believes will free Marguerite, but which really gives over his own soul to perdition. Faust and the fiend then set forth on a wild ride through the darkness. As they gallop along they hear women and children praying. Strange shapes close around them presaging death. The horses tremble and snort with fear. Faust imagines that it rains blood. Everywhere he sees horrible visions, and at last he is hurled into the abyss to which the fiend has craftily led him, and is forever lost. The Prince of Darkness appears attended by infernal spirits, who exult over his downfall.

With a change of scene a celestial chorus is heard, and the spirit of Marguerite, saved by faith and repentance, is received into heaven. With her apotheosis the drama ends. This opera is noteworthy as being among those in which Berlioz introduced some of his most astonishing technical effects.

DINORAH

Comic Opera in three acts by Giacomo Meyerbeer.
Text by Barbier and Carré.

DINORAH, the heroine, is a poor peasant girl and the betrothed of a goatherd named Hoël. They are about to be married in the church at Auray, when a terrible thunderstorm suddenly interrupts the ceremony.

The cottage of Dinorah's father is destroyed, and Hoël gives up all his property to enable him to rebuild his house. Hoël is told by a sorcerer that he could gain great wealth if he would only consent to hide himself for a year in the forest. He follows this advice, and Dinorah, who thinks she is forsaken by her lover, loses her reason. After the year has expired, Hoël is informed that a vast treasure is buried in a certain spot. His joy at this news turns into dismay when he hears that the first person who moves the stone placed over the treasure will die within a year. He therefore induces Corentin, an avaricious fellow, to do this in his stead by promising him a share of the booty. When Corentin is on the point of removing the stone, a voice is heard, which reveals to him the legend of the treasure, and the fatal conditions imposed upon the finder.

Corentin, though enraged at the cunning trick Hoël has played on him, still cannot forego all hope of gaining the treasure. He discovers that the singer whose voice had warned him is no other than the mad girl Dinorah, and he resolves to make use of her, as formerly Hoël had made use of him, by persuading her to move the fatal stone. This she is about to do when the bell on her favorite goat diverts her attention, and causes her to fly this accursed place. In her flight, she is in danger of being carried away by an inundation, but is saved from drowning by Hoël. The sound of his beloved voice acts like a talisman, she recovers her reason, and there is now no drawback to their marriage. The union of the lovers closes the opera.

LE DOMINO NOIR
(The Black Domino)

Comic Opera in three acts by Daniel F. E. Auber.
Text by Scribe.

THE scene is laid in Madrid in the last century. The Queen of Spain gives a masked ball, at which our heroine, Angela, is present, accompanied by her companion, Brigitta. There she is seen by Horatio di Massarena, a young nobleman, who met her a year before at one of these balls and fell in love with her, without knowing her.

This time he detains her, but is again unable to discover her real name, and confessing his love for her he receives the answer that she can be no more than a friend to him. Massarena detains her so long that the clock strikes the midnight hour as Angela prepares to seek her companion. Massarena confesses to having removed Brigitta under some pretext, and Angela in despair cries out that she is lost. She is in reality a member of a convent, and destined to be lady abbess, though she has not yet taken the vows. She is very highly connected, and has secretly helped Massarena to advance in his career as a diplomatist. Great is her anxiety to return to her convent after midnight, but she declines all escort, and walking alone through the streets, she comes by chance into the house of Count Juliano, a gentleman of somewhat uncertain character, and Massarena's friend. Juliano is just giving a supper to his gay friends, and Angela bribes his housekeeper, Claudia, to keep her for the night. She appears before the guests disguised as an Aragonese waiting-maid, and charms them all, and particularly Massarena, with her grace and coquetry. But as the young gentlemen begin to be insolent, she disappears, feeling herself in danger of being recognized. Massarena, discovering in her the charming black domino, is very unhappy to see her in such company. Meanwhile Angela succeeds in getting the keys of the convent from Gil Perez, the porter, who had also left his post, seduced by his love of gormandizing, and had come to pay court to Claudia. Angela troubles his conscience, frightens him with her black mask, and flees. When she has gone the housekeeper confesses that her pretended Aragonese was a stranger, by all appearance a noble lady, who sought refuge in Juliano's house.

In the third act Angela reaches the convent, but not without more adventures. Thanks to Brigitta's cleverness, her absence has not been discovered. At length the day has come when she is to be made lady abbess, and she is arrayed in the attire suited to her future high office, when Massarena is announced to her. He comes to ask to be relieved from a marriage with Ursula, Lord Elfort's daughter, who is destined for him, and who is also an inmate of the convent, but whom he cannot love. Notwithstanding her disguise he recognizes his beloved domino, who, happily for both, is released by the Queen from her high mission and permitted to choose a husband. Of course it is no other than the happy Massarena; while Ursula is consoled by being made lady abbess, a position which well suits her ambitious temper.

DON GIOVANNI

Opera in two acts by Wolfgang Amadeus Mozart.
Text by Da Ponte.

THE hero, spoiled by fortune, and blasé, is ever growing more reckless. He even dares to attack the virtue of Donna Anna, one of the first ladies of a city in Spain, of which her father, an old Spanish grandee, as noble and as strict in virtue as Don Giovanni is satiated and frivolous, is governor. The old father, coming forward to help his beloved daughter, with drawn dagger attacks Don Giovanni, who, compelled to defend himself, has the misfortune to stab his assailant.

Donna Anna, a lady not only noble and virtuous, but proud and high-spirited, vows to avenge her father's death. Though betrothed to a nobleman named Octavio, she will never know any peace until her father, of whose death she feels herself the innocent cause, is avenged. Her only hope is death, and in that she offers the liveliest contrast to her betrothed, who shows himself a gentleman of good temper and qualities, but of a mind too weak for his lady's high-flown

courage and truly tragic character. Though Octavio wants to avenge Donna Anna's father, he would do it only to please her. His one aim is marriage with her. Her passionate feelings he does not understand.

Don Giovanni, pursued not only by Donna Anna, but also by his own neglected bride, Donna Elvira, tries to forget himself in debauches and extravagances. His servant Leporello, in every manner the real counterpart of his master, is his aider and abettor. A more witty, a more amusing figure does not exist. His fine sarcasm brings Don Giovanni's character into bold relief; they complement and explain each other.

But Don Giovanni, passing from one extravagance to another, sinks deeper; everything he tries begins to fail him, and his doom approaches. He begins to amuse himself with Zerlina, the young bride of a peasant named Masetto, but each time, when he seems all but successful with the little coquette, his enemies, who have united against him, interfere and present a new foe in the person of the bridegroom, the plump and rustic Masetto. At last Don Giovanni is obliged to take refuge from the hatred of his pursuers. His flight brings him to the grave of the dead governor, in whose memory a life-size statue has been erected in his own park. Excited to the highest pitch and almost beside himself, Don Giovanni even mocks the dead; he invites him to a supper. The statue moves its head in acceptance of the dreadful invitation of the murderer.

Toward evening Donna Elvira comes to see him, willing to pardon everything if only her lover will repent. She fears for him and for his fate. She does not ask for his love, only for the repentance of his follies; but all is in vain. The half-drunken Don Giovanni laughs at her, and so she leaves him alone. Then the ghostly guest, the statue of the governor, enters. He too tries to move his host's conscience. He fain would save him in the last hour. Don Giovanni remains deaf to those warnings of a better self, and so he incurs his doom. The statue vanishes, the earth opens, and the demons of hell devour Don Giovanni and his splendid palace.

DON PASQUALE

Comic Opera in three acts by Gaetano Donizetti.
Text after "Ser Marcantonio" by Cammerano.

THE wealthy old bachelor Don Pasquale desires to marry his only nephew to a rich and noble lady; but finding a hindrance in Ernesto's love for another, he decides to punish his headstrong nephew by entering himself into marriage and thus disinheriting Ernesto.

His physician Malatesta, Ernesto's friend, pretends to have discovered a suitable partner for him in the person of his (Malatesta's) sister, an "ingénue," educated in a convent and utterly ignorant of the ways of the world.

Don Pasquale maliciously communicates his intentions to the young widow Norina, telling her to distrust Malatesta. The latter, however, has been beforehand with him, and easily persuades Norina to play the part of his (Malatesta's) sister, and to endeavor, by the beauty of her person and the modesty of her demeanor, to gain the old man's affections. Should she succeed in doing so, Don Pasquale and Norina are to go through a mock form of marriage—a notary, in the person of a cousin, named Carlo, has already been gained for the purpose—after which Norina, by her obstinacy, extravagance, capriciousness, and coquetry, is to make the old man repent of his infatuation and ready to comply with their wishes.

Urged on by her love for Ernesto, Norina consents to play the part assigned to her, and the charming simplicity of her manners, her modesty and loveliness so captivate the old man that he falls into the trap and makes her an offer of his hand. The marriage takes place, and one witness failing to appear, Ernesto, who happens to be near, and who is aware of the plot, is requested to take his place. Besides appointing Norina heiress of half his wealth, Don Pasquale at once makes her absolute mistress of his fortune. Having succeeded in attaining her aim, Norina throws aside her mask, and by her self-will, prodigality, and waywardness drives her would-be husband to despair. She squanders his money, visits the theater on the very day of their marriage, ignoring the presence of her husband in such a manner that he wishes himself in his grave, or rid of the termagant, who has destroyed the peace of his life. The climax is reached on his discovery among the accounts, all giving proof of his wife's reckless extravagance, a billet-doux pleading for a clandestine meeting in his own garden. Malatesta is summoned and cannot help feeling remorse on beholding the wan and haggard appearance of his friend. He recommends prudence, advises Don Pasquale to assist, himself unseen, at the proposed interview, and then to drive the guilty wife from the house. The jealous husband, though frankly confessing the folly he had committed in taking so young a wife, at first refuses to listen to Malatesta's counsel, and determines to surprise the lovers and have them brought before the judge. Finally, however, he suffers himself to be dissuaded and leaves the matter in Malatesta's hands.

In the last scene the lovers meet, but Ernesto escapes on his uncle's approach, who is sorely disappointed at having to listen to the bitter reproaches of his supposed wife, instead of being able to turn her out of doors.

Meanwhile Malatesta arrives, summons Ernesto, and in his uncle's name gives his (Don Pasquale's) consent to Ernesto's marriage with Norina, promising her a splendid dowry.

Don Pasquale's wife, true to the part she has undertaken to play, of course opposes this arrangement; and Don Pasquale, too happy to be able to thwart his wife, hastens to give his consent, telling Ernesto to bring his bride. His dismay on discovering that his own wife, whom he has only known under the name of Sophronia, and his nephew's bride are one and the same person, may be easily imagined. His rage and disappointment are, however, somewhat diminished by the reflection that he will no longer have to suffer from the whims of the young wife who had inveigled him into the ill-assorted marriage, and he at length consents, giving the happy couple his blessing.

Considered as representative of the modern Italian opera, this work, one of Donizetti's latest compositions, properly takes a high rank among those of its class. It affords excellent opportunities for vocal artists, and its bright music and witty text render it particularly enjoyable when well performed.

LES DRAGONS DE VILLARS
(The Hermit's Bell)

Comic Opera in three acts by Louis Aimé Maillart.
Text after the French by Ernst.

THE scene is laid in a French mountain village near the frontier of Savoy toward the close of the war in the Cévennes in 1704.

In the first act peasant women in the service of Thibaut, a rich country squire, are collecting fruit. Georgette, Thibaut's young wife, controls their work. In compliance with a general request she treats them to a favorite provençal song, in which a young girl, forgetting her first vows, made to a young soldier, gives her hand to another suitor. She is interrupted by the sound of trumpets. Thibaut, hurrying up in great distress, asks the women to hide themselves at once, because soldiers are marching into the village. He conceals his own wife in the pigeon-house. A detachment of dragoons arrive, and Belamy, their corporal, asks for food and wine at Thibaut's house. He learns that there is nothing to be had and in particular that all the women have fled, fearing the unprincipled soldiers of King Louis XIV, sent to persecute the poor Huguenots or Camisards, who are hiding in the mountains—further that the "Dragons de Villars" are said to be an especially wild and dissolute set.

Belamy is greatly disgusted, and after having had his dinner and a sleep in Thibaut's own bed, decides to march on. The squire gladly offers to accompany the soldiers to St. Gratien's grotto near the hermitage, where they have orders to search for the Huguenot refugees.

While Belamy is sleeping, Thibaut calls his servant Silvain and scolds him because, though best of servants, he has now repeatedly been absent overlong on his errands; finally he orders him to saddle the mules.

Stammering, Silvain owns that they have gone astray in the mountains, but that he is sure of their being found in due time. While Thibaut expresses his fear that they may be stolen by the fugitives, Rose Friquet, an orphan girl, brings the mules, riding on the back of one of them. Thibaut loads her with reproaches, but Silvain thanks her warmly, and though she mockingly repudiates his thanks, he discovers that she has taken the mules in order not to let the provost into Silvain's secret. The fact is that Silvain carries food every day to the refugees, and Rose Friquet, the poor goatkeeper, who is despised and supposed to be wicked and malicious, protects him in her poor way, because he once intercepted a stone which was meant for her head.

While the soldiers are dining, Belamy, who has found Georgette's bonnet, demands an explanation.

Thibaut, confused, finds a pretext for going out, but Rose betrays to Belamy first the wine-cellar and then Georgette's hiding-place. The young wife cries for help and Rose runs in to bring Thibaut. Belamy is delighted with the pretty Georgette, but she tells him rather anxiously that all the wives of the village must needs remain entirely true to their husbands, for the hermit of St. Gratien, though dead for two hundred years, is keeping rigid watch, and betrays every case of infidelity by ringing a little bell, which is heard far and wide.

Belamy is somewhat desirous to try the experiment with Georgette, and asks her to accompany him to the hermitage instead of her husband.

After having found the other women in the village, the soldiers, to Thibaut's great vexation, decide to stay and amuse themselves. Silvain rejoices, and after a secret sign from Rose resolves to warn the refugees in the evening.

In the second act Rose and Silvain meet near St. Gratien. Rose, after telling him that all the paths are occupied by sentries, promises to show him a way for the refugees which she and her goat alone know. Silvain, thanking her warmly, endeavors to induce her to care more for her outward appearance, praising her pretty features. Rose is delighted to hear for the first time that she is pretty, and the duet ensuing is one of the most charming things in the opera. Silvain promises to be her friend henceforth, and then leaves in order to seek the Camisards. After this Thibaut appears seeking his wife, whom he has seen going away with Belamy. Finding Rose he imagines he has mistaken her for his wife, but she laughingly corrects him, and he proceeds to search for Georgette. Belamy now comes and courts Thibaut's wife. But Rose, seeing them, resolves to free the path for the others. No sooner has Belamy tried to snatch a kiss from his companion than Rose draws the rope of the hermit's bell, and she repeats the proceeding until Georgette takes flight, while Thibaut rushes up at the sound of the bell. Belamy reassures him, intimating that the bell may have rung for Rose (though it never rings for girls), and accompanies him to the village. But he soon returns to look for the supposed hermit who has played him this trick and finds Rose instead, who does not perceive him. To his great surprise, Silvain comes up with the whole troop of refugees, leading the aged clergyman, who had been a father to him in his childhood. Silvain presents Rose to them as their deliverer and vows to make her his wife. Rose leads them to the secret path, while Silvain returns to the village, leaving Belamy triumphant at his discovery.

In the third act we find the people on the following morning speaking of nothing but Silvain's wedding with Rose and of the hermit's bell. Nobody knows who has been the culprit, but Thibaut slyly calculates that the hermit has rung beforehand when Rose the bride kissed the dragoon. Having learned that the soldiers had been commanded to saddle their horses in the midst of the dancing the night before, and that Belamy, sure of his prey, has come back, he believes that Rose has betrayed the poor Camisards in order to win the price set on their heads, and this opinion he now communicates to Silvain.

To keep Belamy away from Georgette, the sly squire has conducted him to the wine-cellar, and the officer, now half-drunk, admits having had a rendezvous with Rose. When Thibaut has retired, Belamy again kisses Georgette, and lo, the bell does not ring this time!

Meanwhile Rose comes down the hill, neatly clad and glowing with joy and pride, and Georgette, disregarding Thibaut's reproofs, offers her the wedding garland. The whole village is assembled to see the wedding, but Silvain appears with dark brow, and when Rose radiantly greets him he pushes her back fiercely, believing that she betrayed the refugees, who are, as he has heard, caught. Rose is too proud to defend herself, but when Georgette tries to console her she silently draws from her bosom a paper containing the information that the refugees have safely crossed the frontier. Great is Silvain's shame and heartfelt his repentance. Suddenly Belamy enters, beside himself with rage, for his prey has escaped and he has lost his patent as lieutenant, together with the remuneration of two hundred pistoles, and he at once orders Silvain to be shot. But Rose bravely defends her lover, threatening to reveal the dragoon's neglect of duty. When, therefore, Belamy's superior appears to hear the important news of which the messenger told him, his corporal is only able to stammer out that nothing in particular has happened; and so, after all, Georgette is saved from discovery and Rose becomes Silvain's happy bride.

ELEKTRA

Opera in one act by Richard Strauss.
Text by Hofmannsthal.

LIKE nearly all the works of this composer in larger form, "Elektra" gave rise to a merry war among the critics. It was roundly abused and ardently praised, but both friendly and adverse reviews have merely served to extend its fame, and although the first performance only took place in the Royal Dresden Opera House on January 25, 1909, it was billed for production within a year in both Americas, as well as in the principal music centers of Europe.

Æschylus, Sophocles, and Euripides all based tragedies on the story of Elektra, but it may be conceded that while the characters in the old Greek plays are merely puppets in the hands of the Olympian gods, Hofmannsthal preferred to base his book on the primitive passions of humanity.

Klytemnestra, with the aid of her lover Ægisthus, murders her royal husband, Agamemnon. Then, believing that if allowed to grow to manhood, Orestes will in turn slay her to avenge his father's death, she plans the destruction of her own son. A pilgrim steals him away from the palace, however, and removes him to a place of safety. Elektra, one of the daughters of Agamemnon and Klytemnestra, cherishes hope that this brother may survive as an instrument of destruction, but failing this, determines to be the avenger herself. Chrysosthemis, her sister, accepts conditions as they are, and becomes the favorite in the wretched household, where Elektra is the drudge. Tortured by an evil dream, Klytemnestra asks Elektra to interpret it for her. She replies that "the dreams will only cease when the blood of a certain person has been shed," meaning her mother.

Wishing to know Elektra's precise feelings toward her, Klytemnestra causes the girl to be informed that Orestes is dead—killed by a fall from his horse.

Klytemnestra and Ægisthus are convinced from Elektra's attitude under this great grief that she too is dangerous, but before they can destroy her, their plot is revealed by Chrysosthemis. Thus Elektra, already bent on murder, must either slay or be slain.

Orestes, now grown into manhood, returns to carry out the vengeance which has been the one object of his life. Elektra does not know him, but when he has convinced her, by means of a ring, that he is indeed her brother, she is overjoyed. She digs up the hatchet with which their father was slain, gives it to Orestes, and almost forces him into the castle where the guilty mother and her paramour are asleep. The death of Klytemnestra is announced a moment later by a frightful shriek. Then Ægisthus runs forth, closely followed by Orestes, who strikes him down. Elektra, drunk with blood, dances in mad exultation until she falls dead.

DIE ENTFÜHRUNG AUS DEM SERAIL
(The Abduction from the Seraglio)

Opera in three acts by Wolfgang Amadeus Mozart.
Text after Bretzner by Stephanie.

CONSTANZE, the betrothed bride of Belmonte, with her maid Blondchen and Pedrillo, Belmonte's servant, is captured by pirates. All three are sold as slaves to Selim Pasha, who keeps the ladies in his harem, taking Constanze for himself, and giving Blondchen to his overseer Osmin. Pedrillo has found means to inform his master of their misfortune, and Belmonte comes seeking entrance to the Pasha's villa, in the guise of an artist. Osmin, who is much in love with Blondchen, though she treats him haughtily, distrusts the artist and tries to interfere. But Pedrillo, who is gardener in the Pasha's service, frustrates Osmin's purpose and Belmonte is engaged. The worthy Pasha is quite infatuated with Constanze and tries hard to gain her affections. But Constanze has sworn to be faithful till death to Belmonte, and great is her rapture when Blondchen brings the news that her lover is near.

With the help of Pedrillo, who manages to intoxicate Osmin, they try to escape, but Osmin overtakes them and brings them back to the Pasha, who at once orders that they be brought before him. Constanze advancing with noble courage, explains that the pretended artist is her lover, and that she will rather die with him than leave him. Selim Pasha, overwhelmed by this discovery, retires to think about what he shall do, and his prisoners prepare for death, Belmonte and Constanze with renewed tender protestations of love, Pedrillo and Blondchen without either fear or trembling.

Great is their happiness and Osmin's wrath when the noble Pasha, touched by their constancy, sets them free, and asks for their friendship, bidding them remember him kindly after their return into their own country.

ERNANI

Opera in four acts by Giuseppe Verdi.
Text adapted from Victor Hugo's "Hernani" by Piave.

ERNANI, an Italian rebel of obscure parentage, is the accepted lover of Donna Elvira, the high-born niece of Don Ruy Gomez de Silva, grandee of Spain.

Donna Elvira is also coveted by Don Carlos, King of Spain, and by her old uncle Silva, who is about to wed her, much against her will.

Ernani comes to Silva's castle in the garb of a pilgrim and finds the King in Donna Elvira's room trying to lure her away. Here they are surprised by Silva, who, failing to recognize his sovereign, challenges both men to mortal combat. When he recognizes the King in one of his foes he is in despair and humbly craves his pardon, which is granted to him. At the same time Don Carlos sends Ernani away on a distant errand, hoping to rid himself of him once for all; but Donna Elvira vows to kill herself rather than belong either to the King or to her uncle, and promises unwavering constancy to her lover Ernani.

Nevertheless, the second act shows Elvira on the eve of her wedding with her uncle Silva.

Ernani, once more proclaimed an outlaw, seeks refuge in Silva's castle, again disguised as a pilgrim. But when Ernani hears of Donna Elvira's approaching marriage with Silva, he reveals his identity and offers his head to the old man, telling him that his life is forfeited and that a reward is offered for his capture. Silva is too generous to betray his rival; he orders the gates of the castle to be barred at once. While this is being done Ernani violently reproaches Elvira for having played him false. She answers that she has been led to believe him dead. Dissolved in tears, they embrace tenderly. Thus they are surprised by Silva, who, though for the time being bound by the laws of hospitality, swears to destroy Ernani wherever he may find him.

For the moment, however, he conceals his foe so well that Don Carlos's followers cannot find him. Though the King threatens to take the old man's life, the nobleman remains true to his word, and even makes the greatest sacrifice by delivering Elvira as a hostage into the King's hands.

Left alone, he opens Ernani's hiding-place and challenges him to fight, but when the latter proves to him that Don Carlos is his rival and wants to seduce Elvira, Silva's wrath turns against the King.

He accepts Ernani's offer to help him in frustrating the King's designs, but at the same time he reminds him that his life is forfeited. Ernani declares himself satisfied and gives Silva a bugle, the sound of which is to proclaim that the hour of reckoning between the two foes has come.

The third act takes place at Aix-la-Chapelle.

The King has heard of the conspiracy against his life. While the conspirators assemble in the imperial vaults he is concealed behind the monument of Charlemagne, and frustrates their designs by advancing from his hiding-place and proclaiming himself emperor.

At the same moment the people rush in and do homage to Charles V. Ernani surrenders to his foes, but Elvira implores the Emperor's pardon, which is granted; and Charles crowns his gracious act by uniting the lovers and creating Ernani Duke of Segorbia.

Both Elvira and Ernani go to Seville to celebrate their nuptials. But in the midst of their bliss Ernani hears the sound of his bugle, and Silva appears and claims his rival's life. In vain the lovers implore his mercy; Silva is inexorable, and relentlessly gives Ernani the choice between a poisoned draught and a dagger. Seizing the latter, Ernani stabs himself, while Donna Elvira sinks senseless beside his corpse, leaving the aged Silva to enjoy his revenge alone. So ends this very dramatic work of Verdi's, which has been more appreciated lately than when first produced.

ESMERALDA

Opera in four acts by Arthur Goring Thomas.

THE first act takes place in the Court of Miracles in Paris, where the beggars are assembled and discuss the edict condemning the poet Gringoire to death unless some girl will accept him as her husband. Only Esmeralda, a gypsy, is willing to rescue Gringoire at such a sacrifice. When she has saved the poet, however, guards seize her, at the instigation of Archdeacon Frollo, who is madly in love with her. Esmeralda escapes.

The second act takes place in the home of Fleur de Lys, a room opening into a garden. Seeing a girl dancing in the court, the ladies demand that she be brought before them, and when she enters they are astonished at her beauty. Fleur de Lys recognizes in Esmeralda the dancing girl who has presumed to become her rival in the affections of Captain Phœbus, and finds her in possession of a scarf which she had herself embroidered and presented to the gallant captain. She then denounces Phœbus for his infidelity, and threatens Esmeralda, who throws herself on the protection of Phœbus and compels the acknowledgment of their love.

In the third act Esmeralda's garret is shown. Gringoire finds that though Esmeralda has saved his life, she intends to be his wife in name only, so he philosophically goes to bed, leaving her *tête-à-tête* with Captain Phœbus. While the lovers are thus occupied, Frollo and Quasimodo enter through a window. Frollo pledges himself not to injure the girl, and thereupon Quasimodo retires, as Frollo hides behind a curtain. Phœbus and Esmeralda sing an impassioned duet, which is abruptly ended by Frollo. The unfortunate priest is overcome by insane jealousy, and stabs Phœbus, then escapes through the window. The guards arrive, and Esmeralda is arrested for attempting the murder of Phœbus.

In the fourth act Esmeralda, who has been condemned to death, is visited by Frollo. He assures her of his great love, and promises to save her life if she will return his affection. At this juncture Gringoire arrives, followed by Captain Phœbus. Enraged at the sight of Phœbus, Frollo again tries to kill him, but Quasimodo throws himself between them, and receives the fatal blow intended for the captain. Frollo is imprisoned as a murderer, and Phœbus and Esmeralda are united.

EUGEN ONEGIN

Opera in three acts by Peter Ilyitch Tchaikovsky.
Text adapted from Pushkin's tale.

THE first act shows a garden, in which Frau Larina, owner of a country estate, is preserving fruit and listening to the song of her daughters. It has been familiar to her since youth, when she loved a careless officer, but was compelled to marry an unloved husband. She has gradually accustomed herself to her fate, however, and has found happiness in the love of a good man. The peasants bring in the harvest wreath. Larina's daughter Tatjana grows pensive with the music, while her lively sister, Olga, prefers to dance. All are astonished at the pallor of Tatjana, and believe she is affected by the contents of a book she is reading. Lenski arrives in a wagon, accompanied by his neighbor Onegin. It soon appears that Tatjana loves Onegin, while Lenski is attracted to Olga. The latter soon comes to an agreement, while Onegin remains stiffly polite to Tatjana.

The scene changes to Tatjana's room. She is about to retire, and begs the nurse Filipjewna to tell her stories. While listening she tries to conceal her emotion. At last she confesses to the old nurse that she is in love, and sends her away. Instead of sleeping, she writes letters, but tears them up when written. At last she finishes one and seals it. She remains at the window the rest of the night, and when Filipjewna arrives in the morning, she sends the latter secretly to Onegin.

Again we are taken to the garden. A number of maids gather berries and sing. Tatjana arrives, running in excitement, and throws herself on the sward, followed by Onegin, who has received her letter. He explains to her coldly that he honors the candor of her confession, but cannot fulfill her hopes, as he is a profligate and not suited to the marriage state. A maiden's love is only fantasy, and she must overcome it. Deeply hurt, Tatjana departs.

The second act begins in a room in Larina's house, filled with a merry crowd. Lenski dances with Olga, Onegin with Tatjana. They are compelled to endure the tattling of the older dames. Notwithstanding the protest of Lenski, Onegin asks Olga to dance. Lenski is angry with Olga because she is flirting with Onegin, and becomes so jealous that the girl, to punish him, says that she will dance the quadrille with Onegin. Before it begins, the Frenchman Triquet sings a song of doubtful character to the praise of Tatjana, which is received with applause. Onegin dances with Olga, a captain with Tatjana, and Lenski stands moodily apart. When Onegin asks him what is wrong, he answers angrily; a quarrel ensues, and the dance is interrupted. Amid general consternation Lenski asks his friend to fight a duel.

Now follows a change of scene to a mill. It is early in the morning. Lenski and his second, Saretzki, are impatiently awaiting their opponents. At last Onegin arrives, accompanied only by his servant, who is to act as second. While he arranges with Saretzki, the erstwhile friends regret that they are now enemies. Lenski falls dead, struck by the bullet of Onegin, and Onegin, overwhelmed with grief, falls upon the body of his friend.

The third act, six years later, discloses a hall in the palace of Prince Gremin, where company is gathered. The hostess is Princess Gremina (Tatjana). Onegin is among her guests. He has found no peace, and is constantly troubled with pangs of conscience. He learns that the Princess is Tatjana, and she is profoundly agitated when she meets him. The Prince tells Onegin that he loves his wife passionately, and introduces him to her. She addresses a few indifferent words to him, and is led away by her husband. Onegin gazes after her. He feels that he loves her, laments his former conduct, and resolves to gain her affection.

The closing scene takes place in the reception-room

in the palace of the Prince. Tatjana has received a message from Onegin that he will visit her. She still loves him, but she wishes to retain her peace of mind, and when he appears she reminds him with deep emotion of the conversation in the garden. She has pardoned him and acknowledges that he had acted rightly, but declares it to be his duty to leave and never return. Notwithstanding his outbreak of passion, she remains firm and leaves him. Completely cast down, he stands silent, and then rushes away in despair.

FALSTAFF

Lyric Comedy in three acts by Giuseppe Verdi.
Text by Boito.

THE first scene is laid in the Garter Inn at Windsor, England. After a quarrel with the French physician Dr. Caius, who has been robbed while drunk by Falstaff's servants Bardolph and Pistol, the servants are ordered off by Falstaff with two love-letters for Mrs. Ford and Mrs. Page. The knaves refusing indignantly to take the parts of go-betweens, Falstaff sends them to the devil and gives the letters to his page Robin.

In the second act the two ladies having shown each other the love-letters, decide to avenge themselves on the old fat fool. Meanwhile Falstaff's servants betray their master's intentions toward Mrs. Ford to her husband, who swears to guard his wife, and to keep a sharp eye on Sir John. Then ensues a love-scene between Fenton and Mrs. Ford's daughter Anne, who is destined by her father to marry the rich Dr. Caius, but who by far prefers her poor suitor Fenton.

After a while the Merry Wives assemble again, in order to entice Falstaff into a trap. Mrs. Quickly brings him an invitation to Mrs. Ford's house in the absence of the lady's husband, which Sir John accepts triumphantly.

Sir John is visited by Ford, who assumes the name of Brook, and Falstaff is nothing loath to drink the old Cyprus wine which the other has brought with him. Brook also produces a purse filled with sovereigns, and entreats Falstaff to use it in order to get admittance to a certain Mrs. Ford, whose favor Brook vainly sought. Falstaff gleefully reveals the rendezvous which he is to have with the lady, and thereby leaves poor disguised Ford a prey to violent jealousy.

The next scene contains Falstaff's interview with mischievous Alice Ford, which is interrupted by Mrs. Page's announcement of the husband.

Falstaff is packed into a clothes-basket, while husband and neighbors search for him in vain. This scene, in which Falstaff, half suffocated, alternately sighs and begs to be let out, while the women tranquilly sit on the basket and enjoy their trick, is extremely comic. The basket, with Falstaff, soiled clothes and all, is turned over into a canal, while the fat knight hears the women's laughter.

In the third act Mrs. Quickly succeeds once more in enticing the old fool. She orders him to another rendezvous in the park at midnight, and advises him to come in the disguise of Herne the Black Huntsman. The others hear of the joke, and all decide to punish him thoroughly for his fatuity. Ford, who has promised Dr. Caius to unite Anne to him that very night,

tells him to wear a monk's garb, and also reveals to him that Anne is to wear a white dress with roses. But his wife, overhearing this, frustrates his designs. She gives a black monk's garb to Fenton, while Anne chooses the costume of a fairy queen. When Falstaff appears in his disguise he is attacked on all sides by fairies, wasps, flies, and mosquitos, and they torment him until he cries for mercy. Meanwhile Caius, in a gray monk's garb, looks for his bride everywhere until a tall veiled female in flowing white robes (Bardolph) falls into his arms; on the other side Anne appears with Fenton. Both couples are wedded, and only when they unveil is the mistake discovered. With bitter shame the men see how they have all been duped by merry and clever women, but they have to make the best of a bad case, and so Ford grants his benediction to the happy lovers, and embraces his wife, only too glad to find her true and faithful.

FAUST

Opera in five acts by Charles François Gounod.
Text by Barbier and Carré, founded on Goethe's drama.

FAUST, a celebrated old doctor, is consumed by an insatiable thirst for knowledge; but having already lived through a long life devoted to the acquirement of learning and to hard work as a scholar, without having his soul-hunger appreciably relieved, he is dissatisfied, and in his disappointment wishes to be released from this life, which has grown to be a burden to him. At this moment Mephisto, the fiend, appears and persuades him to try life in a new shape. The old and learned doctor has only known it in theory, Mephisto will now show it to him in practice and in all the splendor of youth and freshness. Faust agrees and Mephisto endows him with youth and beauty. In this guise he sees earth anew. It is Easter-time, when all is budding and aglow with freshness and young life, and on such a bright spring day he first sees Marguerite and at once offers her his arm.

But this lovely maiden, pure and innocent, and well guarded by a jealous brother named Valentin, refuses his company somewhat sharply. Nevertheless she cannot help seeing the grace and good bearing of the fine cavalier, and the simple village maiden is inwardly pleased with his flattery. A bad fate wills it that her brother Valentin, who is a soldier, has to leave on active service, and after giving many good advices and warnings for his beautiful sister's welfare, he goes, and so Mephisto is able to introduce Faust to the unprotected girl by means of a message which he is supposed to have received for Martha, an old aunt of Marguerite's. This old gossip, hearing from Mephisto that her husband has been killed in battle, lends a willing ear to the flatteries of the cunning fiend; and Marguerite is left to Faust, who wins her by his love and easy manners. She is only a simple maiden, knowing nothing of the world's ways and wiles, and she accepts her lover's precious gifts with childish delight.

By and by her brother Valentin returns victorious from the war, but too late! He challenges his sister's seducer; Mephisto, however, directs Faust's sword, and the faithful brother, much against Faust's own will, is slain, cursing his sister with his last breath.

Now Marguerite awakes to the awful reality of her situation and she shrinks from her brother's murderer. Everybody shuns her, and she finds herself alone and forsaken. In despair she seeks refuge in church, but her own conscience is not silenced; it accuses her more loudly than all the pious songs and prayers. Persecuted by evil spirits, forsaken and forlorn, Marguerite's reason gives way and she drowns her new-born child.

Meanwhile Mephisto has done everything to stifle in Faust the pangs of conscience. Faust never wills the evil, he loves Marguerite sincerely, but the bad spirit urges him onward. He shows him all the joys and splendors of earth, and antiquity in its most perfect form in the person of Helena, but in the midst of all his orgies Faust sees Marguerite. He beholds her, pale, unlike her former self, in the white dress of the condemned, with a blood-red circle round the neck. Then he knows no rest, he feels that she is in danger and he bids Mephisto save her.

Marguerite has actually been thrown into prison for her deed of madness, and now the executioner's axe awaits her. She sits on the damp straw, rocking a bundle which she takes for her baby, and across her poor, wrecked brain there flit once more pictures of all the scenes of her short-lived happiness. Then Faust enters with Mephisto and tries to persuade her to escape with them. But she instinctively shrinks from her lover, loudly imploring God's and the saints' pardon. God has mercy on her, for, just as the bells are tolling for her execution, she expires, and her soul is carried to heaven by angels, there to pray for her erring lover. Mephisto disappears into the earth.

FEUERSNOT

(The Fire Famine)

Lyric Poem in one act by Richard Strauss.
Text by Wolzogen.

IT is proof of the versatility of Richard Strauss, if proof were needed, that the man whose choice of material in "Salome" and "Elektra" in itself sufficed to provoke controversy of the most acrimonious kind, should have attained no less success in his musical setting of "Feuersnot."

Here is a folk-tale, modernized as to poetic and musical treatment, and made serve as the legends of the meistersingers of Nuremberg served Wagner, to confound the enemies and critics of the composer.

In the hero of this opera Strauss is portraying himself. Perhaps for this reason it caused less of a sensation in the world than his other works, but it continues to make its way in the permanent repertoire of the world's great opera houses, in which alone it can be rightly performed. In Germany it has always been well received since the original production in Dresden, November 21, 1901.

The action takes place in Munich in a "fabulous no-time." Children are gathering wood for the bonfires which are to make part of the celebration that night. The burgomaster has given a liberal donation, and they now clamor at the Wizard's house, disturbing the meditations of Kunrad, the student who dwells there. Once aroused, however, Kunrad gleefully joins the children in their labors, and helps them to tear off the shutters of his old house to add to their stock of fuel.

In the throng is Diemut, the burgomaster's daughter, with whom the student instantly falls in love. Kunrad takes her in his arms and kisses her passionately. Naturally the girl is mortified and indignant, and her friends are about to avenge what they can only interpret as an insult, when Diemut begs to be allowed to punish the youth in her own way. That evening, when the burgomaster invites his daughter to join him in a stroll about the town, she refuses. A moment later Diemut is seen combing her long hair in her balcony. Kunrad renews his protestations of affection, and begs the maiden to grant an interview. To this she finally consents, and Kunrad steps into a basket in which wood had been lowered to the children, Diemut promising to draw him up. Three of her girl friends, who have been watching Diemut's efforts to ensnare her too ardent lover, voice their delight in song, for when the basket is halfway between the balcony and the ground, Diemut pretends that her strength has failed, and when Kunrad tries to seize her long hair, she draws away with a little scream, leaving Kunrad hanging in mid-air.

The townspeople gather about to deride Kunrad, and congratulate Diemut on the success of her plan, but their triumph is brief. Invoking the aid of the Wizard, who is at once his friend and master, Kunrad plunges the entire city into darkness. The women and children are weeping with fright, and the burghers are threatening vengeance, when the moon shines forth clear and full, and Kunrad, now standing on the balcony, addresses the people. First he upbraids them for having driven from his home the great master, Richard Wagner. Then he adds that, as Wagner's successor, he is determined to carry on his chosen work, despite all opposition. Even Diemut, whom he has chosen as his helpmate, has failed to understand, and so he has put out their lights and fires to show them how cold and dark the world can be without love.

Diemut now opens her door, admitting Kunrad. The citizens have been convinced by his eloquence, and sound his praises. And Diemut too has been convinced, for again the windows glow with lights, the bonfires give forth a cheerful glare—sure token of the happiness of the lovers within.

FIDELIO

Opera in two acts by Ludwig van Beethoven.
Text from the French of Bouilly by Sonnleithner.

FLORESTAN, a Spanish nobleman, has dared to blame Don Pizarro, the governor of the state prison, a man as cruel as he is powerful. Pizarro, thus become Florestan's deadly foe, has seized him secretly and thrown him into a dungeon, reporting his death to the minister, Don Fernando.

But this poor prisoner has a wife, Leonore, who is as courageous as she is faithful. She never believes in the false reports, but disguising herself in male attire, resolves not to rest until she has found her husband.

In this disguise, calling herself Fidelio, she has contrived to get entrance into the fortress where she supposes her husband imprisoned, and by her gentle and courteous behavior and readiness for service of all kinds has won not only the heart of Rocco, the jailer, but that of his daughter Marcelline, who falls in love with the gentle youth and neglects her former lover Jaquino. Fidelio persuades Rocco to let her help him in his office with the prisoners. Quivering with mingled hope and fear, she opens the prison gates to let the state prisoners out into the court, where they may for once have air and sunshine.

But seek as she may she cannot find her husband, and in silent despair she deems herself baffled.

Meanwhile Pizarro has received a letter from Sevilla announcing the minister's forthcoming visit to the fortress. Pizarro, frightened at the consequences of such a call, resolves to silence Florestan forever. He orders the jailer to kill him, but the old man will not burden his soul with a murder, and refuses firmly. Then Pizarro himself determines to kill Florestan, and summons Rocco to dig a grave in the dungeon in order to hide all traces of the crime.

Rocco, already looking upon the gentle and diligent Fidelio as his future son-in-law, confides to him his dreadful secret, and with fearful forebodings she entreats him to accept her help in the heavy work. Pizarro gives his permission, Rocco being too old and feeble to do the work quickly enough if alone. Pizarro has been rendered furious by the indulgence granted to the prisoners at Fidelio's entreaty, but a feeling of triumph overcomes every other when he sees Rocco depart for the dungeon with his assistant.

Here we find poor Florestan chained to a stone. He is wasted to a skeleton, as his food has been reduced in quantity week by week by the cruel orders of his tormentor. He is gradually losing his reason; he has visions and in each one beholds his beloved wife.

When Leonore recognizes him she well-nigh faints, but with a superhuman effort she rallies and begins her work. She has a piece of bread with her which she gives to the prisoner, and with it the remainder of Rocco's wine. Rocco, mild at heart, pities his victim sincerely, but he dares not act against the orders of his superior, fearing to lose his position, or even his life.

While Leonore refreshes the sick man, Rocco gives a sign to Pizarro that the work is done, and bids Fidelio leave: but she only hides herself behind a stone pillar, waiting with deadly fear for the coming event, and decides to save her husband or to die with him.

Pizarro enters, secretly resolved to kill not only his foe but also both witnesses of his crime. He will not kill Florestan, however, without letting him know who his assailant is. So he loudly shouts his own much-feared name; but while he raises his dagger Leonore throws herself between him and Florestan, shielding the latter with her breast. Pizarro, stupefied like Florestan, loses his presence of mind. Leonore profits by it and presents a pistol at him, with which she threatens his life should he attempt another attack. At this critical moment the trumpets sound, announcing the arrival of the minister, and Pizarro, in impotent wrath, is compelled to retreat. They are all summoned before the minister, who is shocked at seeing his old friend Florestan in this sad state, but not the less delighted with the noble courage of Leonore.

Pizarro is conducted away in chains; and the faithful wife with her own hands removes the fetters which still bind the husband for whom she has just won freedom and happiness.

Marcelline, feeling inclined to be ashamed of her mistake, returns to her faithful lover Jaquino.

LA FIGLIA DEL REGGIMENTO

(The Daughter of the Regiment)

Comic Opera in two acts by Gaetano Donizetti. Text by St. George and Bayard.

THE scene in the first act is laid near Bologna in the year 1815; the second act in the castle of the Marchesa di Maggiorivoglio.

Mary, a vivandière, has been found and educated by a French sergeant, named Sulpice, and therefore belongs in a sense to his regiment, which is on a campaign in Italy. She is called the "daughter" of the regiment, which has adopted her, and she has grown up a bright and merry girl, full of pluck and spirit, the pet and delight of the whole regiment.

Tonio, a young Swiss, who has fallen in love with Mary, is believed by the grenadiers to be a spy, and is about to be hanged. But Mary, knowing that he has only come to see her, tells them that he lately saved her life when she was in danger of falling over a precipice.

This changes everything, and on his expressing a desire to become one of them the grenadiers suffer the Swiss to enlist into their company. After the soldiers' departure he confesses his love to Mary, who returns it heartily. The soldiers agree to give their consent, when the Marchesa di Maggiorivoglio appears, and by a letter once affixed to the foundling Mary, addressed to a marchesa of the same name and carefully kept by Sulpice, it is proved that Mary is the Marchesa's niece. Of course this noble lady refuses her consent to a marriage with the low-born Swiss and claims Mary from her guardian. With tears and laments Mary takes leave of her regiment and her lover, who at once decides to follow her. But he has enlisted as a soldier and is forbidden to leave the ranks. Sulpice and his whole regiment curse the Marchesa, who thus carries away their joy.

In the second act Mary is in her aunt's castle. She has masters of every kind for her education, in order that she may become an accomplished lady; but she cannot forget her freedom and her dear soldiers, and instead of singing solfeggios and cavatinas, she is caught warbling her "rataplan," to the Marchesa's grief and sorrow. Nor can she cease to think of Tonio, and only after a great struggle has she been induced to promise her hand to a nobleman, when she suddenly hears the well-beloved sound of drums and trumpets. It is her own regiment, with Tonio as their leader, for he has been made an officer on account of his brave behavior. Hoping that his altered position may turn the Marchesa's heart in his favor, he again asks for Mary, but his suit is once more rejected. Then he proposes flight, but the Marchesa, detecting his plan, reveals to Mary that she is not her niece, but her own daughter, born in early wedlock with an officer far beneath her in rank, who soon after died in battle. This fact she has concealed from her family, but as it is now evident that she has closer ties with Mary, the poor girl dares not disobey her, and, though broken-hearted, consents to renounce Tonio.

The Marchesa invites a large company of guests to celebrate her daughter's betrothal to the son of a neighboring duchess. But Mary's faithful grenadiers suddenly appear to rescue her from those hateful ties, and astonish the whole company by their recital of Mary's early history. The obedient maiden, however, submissive to her fate, is about to sign the marriage contract, when at last the Marchesa, touched by her obedience and her sufferings, conquers her own pride and consents to the union of her daughter with Tonio. Sulpice and his soldiers burst out into loud shouts of approbation, and the high-born guests retire silently and in disgust.

DIE FLEDERMAUS
(The Bat)

Comic Operetta in three acts by Johann Strauss.
Text by Haffner and Genée.

A SERENADE, which is listened to by Adèle, Rosalind Eisenstein's maid, but is intended for her mistress, begins the first act. Adèle has just received an invitation from her sister Ida to a grand entertainment to be given by a Russian prince, Orlovsky by name. She is longing to accept it, and attempts to get leave of absence for the evening from her mistress, when the latter enters, by telling her that an aunt of hers is ill, and wishes to see her. Rosalind, however, refuses to let Adèle go out, and the maid disappears, pouting. While Rosalind is alone, her former singing-master and admirer Alfred suddenly turns up. He it was who had been serenading her, and Rosalind, succumbing to her old weakness for tenors, promises to let Alfred return later, when her husband is not at home. Herr Eisenstein, a banker, has just been sentenced to five days' imprisonment, a misfortune which his hot temper has brought upon him. The sentence has been prolonged to eight days through the stupidity of his lawyer, Dr. Blind, who follows Eisenstein on to the stage. The banker finally turns Dr. Blind out of the house, after upbraiding him violently. Rosalind tries to console Eisenstein, and finally decides to see what a good supper will do toward soothing his ruffled spirits. While she is thus occupied Eisenstein's friend Dr. Falck appears, bringing his unlucky friend an invitation to an elegant soirée which Prince Orlovsky is about to give. Eisenstein is quite ready to enjoy himself before going to prison, and when Rosalind reënters she finds her husband in excellent spirits. He does not, however, partake of the delicious supper she sets before him with any great zest. But he takes a tender, although almost joyful, leave of his wife, after donning his best dress-suit. Rosalind then gives Adèle leave to go out, much to the maid's surprise. After Adèle has gone, Alfred again puts in an appearance. Rosalind only wishes to hear him sing again, and is both shocked and frightened when Alfred goes into Herr Eisenstein's dressing-room, and returns clad in the banker's dressing-gown and cap. The tenor then proceeds to partake of what is left of the supper, and makes himself altogether at home. But a sudden ring at the door announces the arrival of Franck, the governor of the prison, who has come with a cab to fetch Eisenstein. Rosalind is so terrified at being found tête-à-tête with Alfred that she introduces him as her husband. After a tender farewell Alfred good-naturedly follows the governor to prison.

The second act opens in the garden of a café, where the guests of Prince Orlovsky are assembled. Adèle enters, dressed in her mistress's best gown and looking very smart. Eisenstein, who is also present, at once recognizes her, as well as his wife's finery. But Adèle and the whole party pretend to be very indignant at his mistaking a fine lady for a maid. Prince Orlovsky proceeds to make Eisenstein most uncomfortable, by telling him that Dr. Falck has promised to afford him great amusement, by playing some practical joke at Eisenstein's expense. The last guest who enters is Rosalind, whom nobody recognizes, because she is masked. Dr. Falck introduces her as a Hungarian countess, who has consented to be present at the soirée only on condition that her incognito be respected. She catches just a glimpse of Eisenstein, who is flirting violently with Adèle instead of being in prison, and determines to punish him. Noticing the magnificent attire and fine form of the supposed countess, Eisenstein at once devotes himself to the newcomer. He even counts her heart-beats with the aid of a watch which he keeps for that purpose, without, however, giving it away as he always promises to do. But Rosalind suddenly takes possession of the watch, and slips away with it. The whole party finally assembles at supper, where Eisenstein becomes very jovial, and tells how he once attended a masquerade ball with his friend Falck, who was disguised as a bat. Eisenstein, it appears, induced his friend to drink so heavily that he fell asleep in the street, where Eisenstein left him. Falck did not wake up till morning, when he had to go home amid the jeers of a street crowd, by whom he was nicknamed "Dr. Fledermaus." Eisenstein's story creates much amusement, but Dr. Falck only smiles, saying that he who laughs last, laughs best.

After a champagne supper and some dancing, Eisenstein remembers, when the clock strikes six, that he ought to be in prison. Both he and Dr. Falck take a merry leave of the boisterous party.

The third act begins with Franck's return to his own room, where he is received by the jailer. Frosch has taken advantage of his master's absence to get drunk, while Franck himself has likewise become somewhat intoxicated. He grows drowsy while recalling the incidents of Prince Orlovsky's fête, and finally falls fast asleep.

Adèle and her sister Ida interrupt his slumbers, in order to ask the supposed marquis to use his influence in the former's behalf. Adèle confesses that she is in reality a lady's maid, but tries to convince Franck, the supposed marquis, and her sister (who is a ballet dancer), of her talents by showing them what she can do in that line. A loud ring soon puts an end to the performance. While the jailer conducts Adèle and Ida to No. 13, Eisenstein arrives and gives himself up. Franck and he are much surprised to find themselves face to face with each other in prison, after each had been led to suppose the other a marquis, at the fête.

They are naturally much amused to learn each other's identity. Meanwhile Dr. Blind enters, to undertake the defense of the impostor Eisenstein. He proves to be the genuine Eisenstein, who again turns Blind out of doors, and possesses himself of his cap and gown and of his spectacles, in which he interviews his double. Alfred has been brought in from his cell, when Rosalind also enters, carrying her husband's watch, and prepared for revenge. Both Alfred and she alternately state their grievances to the supposed lawyer, who quite loses his temper when he learns of Alfred's tête-à-tête with his wife, and how completely she has fooled him. Throwing off his disguise, he reveals his identity, only to be reviled by his wife for his treachery. He in turn vows to revenge himself on Rosalind and on her admirer, but the entrance of Dr. Falck, followed by all the guests who were at Prince Orlovsky's fête, clears up matters for all concerned. While making fun of the discomfited Eisenstein, he explains that the whole thing is a huge practical joke of his invention which he has played on Eisenstein in return for the trick Eisenstein played on him years ago, which he related at the fête. All the guests had been bidden to the fête by Dr. Falck with the consent of the prince in order to deceive Eisenstein. The latter, when convinced of his wife's innocence, embraces her. All toast one another in champagne, which they declare to be the king of wines.

DER FLIEGENDE HOLLÁNDER
(The Flying Dutchman)

Romantic Opera in three acts by Richard Wagner.

THE Flying Dutchman is a sort of Wandering Jew, condemned to sail forever on the seas until he has found a woman whose love to him is faithful unto death.

In the first act we find ourselves by the high seas. Daland, a Norwegian skipper, has met with several misfortunes on his way home, and is compelled to anchor on a deserted shore. There he finds the Flying Dutchman, who vainly roves from sea to sea to find death and with it peace. His only hope is doomsday. He has never found a maiden faithful to him, and he knows not how often and how long he has vainly tried to be released from his doom. Once in every seven years he is allowed to go on shore and seek a wife. This time has now come again, and hearing from Daland that he has a daughter, sweet and pure, he begins to hope once more, and offers all his wealth to the father for a shelter under the Norwegian's roof and for the hand of his daughter Senta. Daland is only too glad to accept for his child what to him seems an immense fortune, and so they sail home together.

In the second act we find Senta in the spinning-room. The servants of the house are together spinning and singing. Senta is among them, but her wheel does not turn; she is dreamily regarding an old picture. It is that of the Flying Dutchman, whose legend so deeply touches her that she has grown to love its hero without having in reality seen him.

Senta has a wooer already in the person of Erik the hunter, but she does not care much for him. With deep feeling she sings to the spinning maidens the ballad of the doomed man as she has heard it from Mary, her nurse:

An old captain wanted to sail round the Cape of Good Hope, and as the wind was against him, he swore a terrible oath that he never would leave off trying. The devil heard him and doomed him to sail on to eternity, but God's angel had pity on him, and showed him how he could find deliverance through a wife faithful unto the grave.

All the maidens pray to God to let the maiden be found at last, when Senta ecstatically exclaims, "I will be his wife!" At this moment her father's ship is announced. Senta is about to run away to welcome him, but is detained by Erik, who tries to win her for himself. She answers evasively; then Daland enters and with him a dark and gloomy stranger. Senta stands spellbound: she recognizes the hero of her picture. The Dutchman is not less impressed, seeing in her the angel of his dreams and as it were his deliverer; and so, meeting by the guidance of a superior power, they seem created for each other, and Senta, accepting the offer of his hand, swears to him eternal fidelity.

In the third act we see the Flying Dutchman's ship; everybody recognizes it by its black mast and its blood-red sail. The Norwegian sailors call loudly to the mariners of the strange ship, but nothing stirs, everything seems dead and haunted. At last the unearthly inhabitants of the Dutch ship awake; they are old and gray and wrinkled, all doomed to the fate of their captain. They begin a wild and gloomy song, which sends a chill into the hearts of the stout Norwegians.

Meanwhile Erik, beholding in Senta the betrothed of the Dutchman, is in despair. Imploring her to turn back, he calls up old memories and at last charges her with infidelity to him.

As soon as the Dutchman hears this accusation he turns from Senta, feeling that he is again lost. But Senta will not break her faith. Seeing the Dutchman fly from her, ready to sail away, she swiftly runs after him and throws herself from the cliff into the waves.

By this sacrifice the spell is broken, the ghostly ship sinks forever into the ocean, and an angel bears the poor wanderer to eternal rest, where he is reunited to the bride who has proved faithful unto death.

FRA DIAVOLO
(Brother Devil)

Comic Opera in three acts by Daniel F. E. Auber.
Text by Scribe.

THE scene is laid at Terracina in Italy. Fra Diavolo is a celebrated and much-feared chief of brigands. The Roman court of justice has set a price of 10,000 piasters on his head. In the first act we meet with the Roman soldiers, who undertake to win the money. Their captain Lorenzo has a double aim in trying to catch the brigand. He is Zerline's lover, but having no money, Zerline's father Matteo, the owner of a hotel, threatens to give her to a rich farmer's son. Meanwhile Fra Diavolo has forced his society on a rich English lord, Cockburn by name, who is on his wedding tour with his fair young wife Pamela. Lord Cockburn looks jealously at Fra Diavolo, though he does not recognize in him a brigand. The English are robbed by Diavolo's band. Disgusted with the insecurity of "la bella Italia," they reach the inn at Terracina, where the dragoons, hearing the account of this new robbery, believe that it was Fra Diavolo with his band, and at once decide to pursue him.

Shortly afterward Fra Diavolo arrives at the inn disguised as the Marquis of San Marco, under which name the English lord has already made his acquaintance. He is not enchanted by the arrival of this marquis; he fears a new flirtation with his own fair wife. Pamela wears most valuable diamonds, and these strike the eye of Fra Diavolo.

He sees that the English have been clever enough to conceal the greater part of their wealth and resolves to put himself speedily into possession of it.

He is flirting desperately with Pamela, and looking tenderly at the pretty Zerline, when the soldiers return, having captured twenty of the brigands and retaken the greater part of Lord Cockburn's money and jewels. Lorenzo, the captain of the dragoons, is rewarded by the magnanimous lord with 10,000 lire, and may now hope to win Zerline's hand. But Fra Diavolo vows to avenge the death of his comrades on Lorenzo.

In the second act he conceals himself behind the curtains in Zerline's sleeping-room, and during the night he admits his two companions Beppo and Giacomo. Zerline enters and is about to retire to rest after praying to the Holy Virgin for protection. During her sleep Giacomo is to stab her, while the two others are to rob the English lord.

But Zerline's prayer and her innocence touch even the robbers. The deed is delayed, and this delay brings Lorenzo upon them. Fra Diavolo's two companions hide themselves, and the false marquis alone is found in Zerline's room. He assures Lorenzo that he had a rendezvous with his bride, and at the same time whispers into the lord's ear that he came by appointment with his lady, showing her portrait, of which he had robbed her the day before, as proof. The consequence of these lies is a challenge from Lorenzo, and a meeting with Diavolo is fixed. The latter is full of triumphant glee; he has arranged a deep-laid plan with the surviving members of his band and hopes to ensnare not only Lorenzo but his whole company. Ordinarily Diavolo is a noble brigand; he never troubles women, and he loads poor people with gifts, taking the gold out of rich men's purses only; but now he is full of ire and his one thought is of vengeance.

Finally he is betrayed by the carelessness of his own helpmates. Beppo and Giacomo, seeing Zerline, recognize in her their fair prey of the evening before and betray themselves by repeating some of the words which she had given utterance to. Zerline, hearing them, is now able to comprehend the wicked plot which was woven to destroy her happiness. The two banditti are captured and compelled to lure their captain into a trap. Diavolo appears, not in his disguise as a marquis, but in his own well-known dress with the red plume waving from his bonnet, and being assured by Beppo that all is secure, is easily captured. Now all the false imputations are cleared up. Milord is reconciled to his wife and Lorenzo obtains the hand of the lovely Zerline.

Scribe's text, which is full of life and witty passages, largely shares in the qualities that make this opera the most popular of Auber's works.

DER FREISCHÜTZ
(The Free Shot)

Romantic Opera in three acts by Karl M. von Weber
Text by Kind.

A YOUNG huntsman, Max, is in love with Agathe, daughter of Kuno, the chief ranger of Prince Ottokar of Bohemia. Max woos her; but their union depends on a master-shot which he is to deliver on the following morning.

During the village festival he has all day been unlucky in shooting, and we see him, full of anger and sorrow, being mocked at by peasants more lucky than he.

His comrade, Caspar, one of the ranger's older huntsmen, is his evil genius. He has sold himself to the devil, is a gloomy, mysterious fellow, and hopes to save his soul by delivering some other victim to the demon. He wants to tempt Max to try enchanted bullets, to be obtained at the cross-roads during the midnight hour by drawing a magic circle with a bloody sword and invoking the name of the mysterious huntsman. Father Kuno, hearing him, drives him away, begging Max to think of his bride and to pray to God for success.

But Max cannot forget the railleries of the peasants; he broods over his misfortunes, and when he is wellnigh despairing, Caspar, who meanwhile calls Samiel (the devil in person) to help, encourages him to take refuge in stimulants. He tries to intoxicate the unhappy lover by pouring drops from a vial into his wine. When Max has grown more and more excited, Caspar begins to tell him of nature's secret powers, which might help him. Max first struggles against the evil influence, but when Caspar, handing him his gun, lets him shoot an eagle soaring high in the air, his huntsman's heart is elated and he wishes to become possessed of such a bullet. Caspar tells him that they are enchanted and persuades him to a meeting in the Wolf's Glen at midnight, where the bullets may be molded.

In the second act Agathe is with her cousin Aennchen. Agathe is the true German maiden, serious and thoughtful almost to melancholy. She presents a marked contrast to her light-hearted cousin, who tries to brighten Agathe with fun and frolic. They adorn themselves with roses which Agathe received from a holy hermit, who blessed her but warned her of impending evil. So Agathe is full of dread forebodings, and after Aennchen's departure she fervently prays to Heaven for her beloved. When she sees him come to her through the forest with flowers on his hat, her fears vanish and she greets him joyously. But Max only answers hurriedly that, having killed a stag in the Wolf's Glen, he is obliged to return there. Agathe, filled with terror at the mention of this ill-famed name, wants to keep him back, but ere she can detain him he has fled. With hurried steps Max approaches the Wolf's Glen, where Caspar is already occupied in forming circles of black stones, in the midst of which he places a skull, an eagle's wing, a crucible, and a bullet-mold. Caspar then calls on Samiel, invoking him to allow him a few more years on earth. To-morrow is the day appointed for Satan to take his soul, but Caspar promises to surrender Max in exchange. Samiel, who appears through the cleft of a rock, agrees to let him have six of the fatal balls, reserving only the seventh for himself.

Caspar then proceeds to make the bullets, Max only looking on, stunned and remorseful at what he sees. His mother's spirit appears to him, but he is already under the influence of the charm; he cannot move. The proceeding goes forward amid hellish noise. A hurricane arises, flames and devilish forms flicker about, wild and horrible creatures rush by and others follow in hot pursuit. The noise grows worse, the earth seems to quake, until at length, after Caspar's reiterated invocations, Samiel shows himself at the word "seven." Max and Caspar both make the sign of the cross, and fall on their knees more dead than alive.

In the third act we find Agathe waiting for her bridesmaids. She is perturbed and sad, having had frightful dreams and not knowing what has become of Max. Aennchen consoles her, diverting her with a merry song, until the bridesmaids enter, bringing flowers and gifts. They prepare to crown her with the bridal wreath, when, instead of the myrtle there lies in the box a wreath of white roses, the ornament of the dead.

Meanwhile everybody is assembled on the lawn near Prince Ottokar's tent to be present at the firing of the master-shot. The Prince points out to Max a white dove as an object at which to aim. At this critical moment Agathe appears, crying out: "Don't shoot, Max, I am the white dove!" But it was too late; Max has fired, and Agathe sinks down at the same time as Caspar, who has been waiting behind a tree and who now falls heavily to the ground, while the dove flies away unhurt. Everybody believes that Max has shot his bride, but she is only in a swoon; the bullet has really killed the villain Caspar. It was the seventh, the direction of which Samiel reserved for himself, and Satan, having no power over the pious maiden, directed it on Caspar, already forfeited to him. Max confesses his sin with deep remorse. The Prince scornfully bids him leave his dominions forever. But Agathe prays for him, and at last the Prince follows the hermit's advice, giving the unhappy youth a year of probation, during which to prove his repentance and grow worthy of his virtuous bride.

GENOVEVA

Opera in four acts by Robert Schumann.
Text after Hebbel and Tieck.

SIEGFRIED, Count of the Palatinate, is ordered by Charles Martel to join him in the war with the infidels, who broke out of Spain under Abdurrahman. The noble Count recommends his wife Genoveva and all he possesses to the protection of his friend Golo, who is, however, secretly in love with his master's wife. After Siegfried has said farewell she falls into a swoon, which Golo takes advantage of to kiss her, thereby still further exciting his flaming passion. Genoveva finally awakes and goes away to mourn in silence for her husband.

Golo being alone, an old hag, Margarethe, whom he takes for his nurse, comes to console him. She is in reality his mother and has great schemes for her son's future happiness. She insinuates to him that Genoveva, being alone, needs consolation and will easily be led on to accept more tender attentions, and she promises him her assistance. The second act shows Genoveva's room. She longs sadly for her husband and sees with pain and disgust the insolent behavior of the servants, whose wild songs penetrate into her silent chamber.

Golo enters to bring her the news of a great victory over Abdurrahman, which fills her heart with joy. She bids Golo sing, and sweetly accompanies his song, which so fires his passion that he falls upon his knees and frightens her by glowing words. Vainly she bids him leave her; he only grows more excited, till she repulses him with the word "bastard." Now his love turns into hatred, and when Drago, the faithful steward, comes to announce that the servants begin to be more and more insolent, daring even to insult the good name of the Countess, Golo asserts that they speak the truth about her. He persuades the incredulous Drago to hide himself in Genoveva's room, the latter having retired for the night's rest.

Margarethe, listening at the door, hears everything. She tells Golo that Count Siegfried lies wounded at Strasburg; she has intercepted his letter to the Countess and prepares to leave for that town, in order to nurse the Count and kill him slowly by some deadly poison. Then Golo calls quickly for the servants, who all assemble to penetrate into their mistress's room. Full of wounded pride, she repulses them, but at last she yields, and herself taking the candle to light the room, proceeds to search, when Drago is found behind the curtains and at once silenced by Golo, who runs his dagger through his heart. Genoveva is led into the prison of the castle.

The third act takes place at Strasburg, where Siegfried is being nursed by Margarethe. His strength defies her perfidy, and he is full of impatience to return to his loving wife, when Golo enters bringing him the news of her faithlessness.

Siegfried, in despair, bids Golo kill her with his own sword. He decides to fly into the wilderness, but before fulfilling his design, he goes once more to Margarethe, who has promised to show him all that passed at home during his absence. He sees Genoveva in a magic looking-glass, exchanging kindly words with Drago, but there is no appearance of guilt in their intercourse. The third image shows Genoveva sleeping on her couch, and Drago approaching her. With an imprecation Siegfried starts up, bidding Golo avenge him, but at the same instant the glass flies in pieces with a terrible crash, and Drago's ghost stands before Margarethe, commanding her to tell Siegfried the truth.

In the fourth act Genoveva is being led into the wilderness by two ruffians, who have orders to murder her. Before this is done, Golo approaches her once more, showing her Siegfried's ring and sword, with which he has been told to kill her. He tries hard to win her, but she turns from him with scorn and loathing, preferring death to dishonor. At length, relinquishing his attempts, he beckons to the murderers to do their work and hands them Count Siegfried's weapon. Genoveva in her extreme need seizes the cross of the Saviour, praying fervently, and detains the ruffians till, at the last moment, Siegfried appears, led by the repentant Margarethe. There ensues a touching scene of forgiveness, while Golo rushes away to meet his fate by falling over a precipice.

GOTTERDÄMMERUNG
(Twilight of the Gods)

Third Day of the Nibelungen Ring by Richard Wagner.

THE third day in Wagner's great tetralogy opens with a prelude showing the three Norns weaving the world's fate. When the cord breaks, they fly; the dawn of another world is upon them.

In the first act Siegfried bids Brünnhilde farewell. His active soul thirsts for deeds, and Brünnhilde, having taught him all she knows, does not detain him. He gives her the fatal ring in token of remembrance, confiding her to the care of Loge. Then we are transported to the Gibichungs' hall on the Rhine. Gunther and his sister Gutrune sit there together with their gloomy half-brother Hagen. The latter advises his brother to marry, telling him of the beautiful woman guarded by the flames. When he has sufficiently excited Gunther's longing, he suggests that, as Siegfried is the only one able to gain Brünnhilde, Gunther should attach him to his person by giving him Gutrune as wife. This is to be achieved by a draught which has the power of causing oblivion. Whoever drinks it forgets that ever a woman has existed besides the one who has tendered the potion. Hagen well knows of Siegfried's union with Brünnhilde, but Gunther and Gutrune are both ignorant of it.

Siegfried arrives and is heartily welcomed. All turns out as Hagen has foretold. By the fatal potion Siegfried falls passionately in love with Gutrune so that he completely forgets Brünnhilde. He swears blood-brothership to Gunther, and promises to win Brünnhilde for him. Then the two depart on their errand.

Meanwhile the Valkyr Waltraute comes to Brünnhilde and beseeches her to render Siegfried's ring to the Rhine-daughters in order to save the gods from destruction. Brünnhilde refuses to part with the token of her husband's love; and hardly has Waltraute departed than fate overtakes her in the person of Siegfried, who ventures through the flames in Gunther's shape. She vainly struggles against him, he snatches the ring from her, and so she is conquered. Siegfried holds vigil through the night, his sword separating him and the woman he wooed; and in the early dawn he leads her away to her bridegroom, who takes Siegfried's place unawares.

In the second act Alberich appears to Hagen. He tells his son of the story of the ring and bids him kill Siegfried and recover the stolen treasure for its owner. Siegfried appears announcing Gunther's and Brünnhilde's arrival. The bridal pair are received by all their men, but the joy is soon damped by Brünnhilde recognizing in the bridegroom of Gutrune her own husband. Siegfried does not know her, but she discovers her ring on his hand, and as she asserts that Gunther won it from her, this hero is obliged to acknowledge the shameful rôle he played. Though Siegfried swears that his sword Nothung guarded him from any contact with Gunther's bride, Brünnhilde responds in a most startling manner, and both swear on Hagen's spear that it may pierce them should their words prove false. All this makes a dreadful impression on the weak mind of Gunther.

When Siegfried has withdrawn in high spirits with his bride Gutrune, Hagen, hoping to gain the ring, offers to avenge Brünnhilde on the faithless Siegfried. Brünnhilde, in her deadly wrath, betrays to him the only vulnerable spot beneath Siegfried's shoulder. Gunther consents reluctantly to their schemes.

The third act opens with a scene on the Rhine. The Rhine-daughters try to persuade Siegfried to render them the ring. He is about to throw it into the water when they warn him of the evil which will befall him should he refuse their request. This awakens his pride. Laughing, he turns from them, he, the fearless hero. His fellow-hunters overtake him, and while he relates to them the story of his life Hagen mixes an herb with his wine, which enables him to remember all he has forgotten. Hagen then treacherously drives his spear into Siegfried's back, killing him. He dies with Brünnhilde's praise on his lips. The funeral march, which here follows, is one of the most beautiful ever written. When the dead hero is brought to the Gibichungs' hall, Gutrune bewails him loudly. A dispute arises between Hagen and Gunther about the ring, which ends by Hagen slaying Gunther. But when Hagen tries to strip the ring off the dead hand the fingers close themselves and the hand raises itself, bearing testimony against the murderer. Brünnhilde appears to mourn for the dead; she drives away Gutrune, who sees too late that under the influence of the fatal draught Siegfried forgot his lawful wife, whom she now recognizes in Brünnhilde. The latter, taking a long farewell of her dead husband, orders a funeral pile to be erected. As soon as Siegfried's body is placed on it, she lights it with a firebrand, and when it is in full blaze she mounts her faithful steed, leaping with it into the flames.

When the fire sinks the Rhine-daughters are seen to snatch the ring, which is now purified from its curse by Brünnhilde's death.

Hagen, trying to wrench it from them, is drawn into the waves and so dies.

A dusky light, like that of a new dawn, spreads over heaven, and through a mist Valhalla, with all the gods passing away, may be perceived, in flames.

GUILLAUME TELL

Grand Opera in three acts by Gioachino Antonio Rossini. Text by Bis and Jouoy.

THE text is founded on the well-known story of William Tell, who, according to tradition, delivered his fatherland from one of its most cruel despots, the Austrian governor Gessler.

The first act opens with a charming introductory chorus by peasants, who are celebrating a nuptial fête. Tell joins in their pleasures, though he cannot help giving utterance to the pain which the Austrian tyranny causes him. Arnold von Melchthal, son of an old Swiss, has conceived an unhappy passion for Mathilda,

Princess of Hapsburg, whose life he once saved; but he is Swiss and resolves to be true to his country. He promises Tell to join in his efforts to liberate it. Meanwhile, Leuthold, a Swiss peasant, comes up. He is a fugitive, having killed an Austrian soldier to revenge an intended abduction of his daughter. His only safety lies in crossing the lake, but no fisherman dares to row out in the face of the coming storm. Tell steps forth, and seizing the oars brings Leuthold safely to the opposite shore. When Rudolf von Harras appears with his soldiers, his prey has escaped, and nobody being willing to betray the deliverer, old father Melchthal is imprisoned.

In the second act we find the Princess Mathilda returning from a hunt. She meets Arnold and they betray their mutual passion. Arnold does not yet know his father's fate, but presently Tell enters with Walther Fürst, who informs Arnold that his father has fallen a victim to the Austrian tyranny. Arnold, cruelly roused from his love-dream, awakes to duty, and the three men vow bloody vengeance. This is the famous oath taken on the Rütli. The deputies of the three cantons arrive, one after the other, and Tell makes them swear solemnly to establish Switzerland's independence. Excited by Arnold's dreadful account of his father's murder, they all unite in the fierce cry "To arms!" which is to be their signal of combat.

In the third act Gessler arrives at the market-place of Altdorf, where he has placed his hat on a pole to be greeted instead of himself by the Swiss who pass by.

They grumble at this new proof of arrogance, but dare not disobey the order, till Tell, passing by with his son, disregards it. Refusing to salute the hat, he is instantly taken and commanded by Gessler to shoot an apple off his little boy's head. After a dreadful inward struggle, Tell submits. Fervently praying to God and embracing his fearless son, he shoots with steady hand, hitting the apple right in the center. But Gessler has seen a second arrow, which Tell has hidden in his breast, and he asks its purpose. Tell freely confesses that he would have shot the tyrant had he missed his aim. Tell is fettered, Mathilda vainly appealing for mercy. But Gessler's time has come. The Swiss begin to revolt. Mathilda herself begs to be admitted into their alliance of free citizens, and offers her hand to Arnold. The fortresses of the oppressors fall; Tell enters free and victorious, having himself killed Gessler; and in a chorus at once majestic and grand the Swiss celebrate the day of their liberation.

HANS HEILING

Romantic Opera in three acts, with a prelude, by Heinrich Marschner. Text by Devrient.

HANS HEILING, King of the gnomes, has fallen in love with a daughter of the earth, the charming Anna. This maiden, a poor country girl in the first freshness of youth, has been induced by her mother to consent to a betrothal with the rich stranger, whom Anna esteems, but nothing more, her heart not yet having been touched by love.

In the prelude we are introduced into the depths of earth, where the gnomes work and toil incessantly carrying glittering stones, gold and silver, and accumulating all the treasures on which men's hearts are set.

Their King announces to them that he will no longer be one of theirs; he loves, and therefore he resigns his crown. All the passionate entreatings of his mother and of the gnomes are of no avail. At the Queen's bidding he takes with him a magic book, without which he would lose his power over the gnomes. After giving him a set of luminous diamonds, the mother parts with her son—Heiling rejoicing in his heart, the Queen in tears and sorrow.

In the first act Heiling arises from the earth, forever closing the entrance to the gnomes. Anna greets him joyously and Gertrud, her mother, heartily seconds the welcome. Heiling gives his bride a golden chain, and Anna, adorning herself, thinks with pleasure how much she will be looked at and envied by her companions. She fain would show herself at once, and begs Heiling to visit a public festival with her. But Heiling, by nature serious and almost taciturn, refuses her request. Anna pouts, but she forgets her grief when she sees the curious signs of erudition in her lover's room. As she looks over the magic book, the leaves turn by themselves, quicker and quicker; the strange signs seem to grow, to threaten her, until, stricken with horrible fear, she cries out, and Heiling, turning to her, sees too late what she has done. Angry at her curiosity, he pushes her away, but she clings to him with fervent entreaties to destroy the dreadful book. His love conquers his reason, and he throws the last link which connects him with his past into the fire. A deep thunder-peal is heard. Anna thanks him heartily, but from this hour the seed of fear and distrust grows in her heart.

Heiling, seeing her still uneasy, agrees to visit the festival with her upon condition that she refrains from dancing. She gladly promises, but as soon as they come to the festival Anna is surrounded by the village lads, who entreat her to dance. They dislike the stranger, who has won the fairest maiden of the village, and Conrad the hunter, who has long loved Anna, is particularly hard on his rival. He mocks him, feeling that Heiling is not what he seems, and tries to lure Anna away from his side. At last Heiling grows angry, forbidding Anna once more to dance. She is wounded by his words and, telling him abruptly that she is not married yet, and that she never will be his slave, she leaves him. In despair Heiling sees her go away with Conrad, dancing and frolicking.

In the second act we find Anna in the forest. She is in a deep reverie; her heart has spoken, but alas! not for her bridegroom, whom she now fears; it beats only for Conrad, who has owned his love to her. Darkness comes on, and the gnomes appear with their Queen, who reveals to the frightened girl the origin of her bridegroom and entreats her to give back the son to his poor bereft mother. When the gnomes have disappeared, Conrad overtakes Anna, and she tells him all, asking his help against her mysterious bridegroom. Conrad, seeing that she returns his love, is happy. He has just obtained a good situation and will now be able to wed her.

He accompanies her home, where Gertrud welcomes them joyously, having feared that Anna had met with an accident in the forest.

While the lovers are together, Heiling enters, bringing the bridal jewels. Mother Gertrud is dazzled, but Anna shrinks from her bridegroom. When he asks for an explanation, she tells him that she knows of his origin. Then all his hopes die within him; but, determined that his rival shall not be happy at his cost, he hurls his dagger at Conrad and takes flight.

In the last act Heiling is alone in a ravine in the mountains. He has sacrificed everything and gained nothing. Sadly he decides to return to the gnomes. They appear at his bidding, but they make him feel that he no longer has any power over them, and by way of adding still further to his sorrows they tell him that his rival lives and is about to wed Anna. Then indeed all seems lost to the poor dethroned King. In despair and repentance he casts himself to the earth. But the gnomes, seeing that he really has abandoned all earthly hopes, swear fealty to him once more and return with him to their Queen, by whom he is received with open arms.

Meanwhile Conrad, who only received a slight wound from Heiling's dagger and has speedily recovered, has fixed his wedding day and we see Anna, the happy bride, in the midst of her companions, prepared to go to church with her lover. But when she looks about her, Heiling is at her side, come to take revenge. Conrad would fain aid her, but his sword breaks before it touches Heiling, who invokes the help of his gnomes. They appear, but at the same moment the Queen is seen, exhorting her son to pardon and to forget. He willingly follows her away into his kingdom of night and darkness, never to see earth's surface again. The anxious peasants once more breathe freely and join in common thanks to God.

HÄNSEL UND GRETEL

Fairy Opera in three acts by Engelbert Humperdinck. Text by Wette.

THE first act represents the miserable little hut of a broom-maker. Hänsel is occupied in binding brooms, Gretel is knitting and singing old nursery-songs, such as "Susy, dear Susy, what rattles in the straw?" Both children are very hungry, and wait impatiently for the arrival of their parents. Hänsel is particularly bad-tempered, but the merry and practical Gretel, finding some milk in a pot, soon soothes his ruffled feelings by the promise of a nice rice-pap in the evening. Forgetting work and hunger, they begin to dance and frolic until they roll on the ground together. At this moment their mother enters, and seeing the children idle, her wrath is kindled and she rushes at them with the intention of giving them a sound whipping. Alas! instead of Hänsel, she strikes the pot and upsets the milk. The mother's vexation cools and only sorrow remains, but she quickly puts a little basket into Gretel's hands and drives the children away, bidding them look for strawberries in the woods. Then, sinking on a chair utterly exhausted, she falls asleep.

She is awakened by her husband, who comes in singing and very gay. She sees that he has had a drop too much, and is about to reproach him, but the words die on her lips when she sees him unfold his treasure, consisting of eggs, sausages, coffee, etc. He tells her that he has been very fortunate at the church-ale (kermess), and bids her prepare supper at once. Alas! the pot is broken, and the mother relates that, finding the children idle, anger got the better of her and the pot was smashed to pieces. He good-naturedly laughs at her discomfiture, but his merriment is changed to grief when he hears that their children are still in the forest, perhaps even near the Ilsenstein, where the wicked fairy lives who entices children in order to bake and devour them. This thought so alarms the parents that they rush off to seek the children in the forest.

The second act is laid near the ill-famed Ilsenstein. Hänsel has filled his basket with strawberries and Gretel is winding a garland of red hips, with which Hänsel crowns her. He presents her also with a bunch of wild flowers and playfully does homage to this queen of the woods. Gretel, enjoying the play, pops one berry after another into her brother's mouth; then they both eat while listening to the cuckoo. Before they are aware of it they have eaten the whole contents of the basket and observe with terror that it has grown too dark either to look for a fresh supply or to find their way home. Gretel begins to weep and to call for her parents, but Hänsel, rallying his courage, takes her in his arms and soothes her until they both grow sleepy. The sandman comes, throwing his sand into their eyes, but before their lids close they say their evening prayer; then they fall asleep and the fourteen guardian angels, whose protection they invoked, are seen stepping down the heavenly ladder to guard their slumber.

In the third act the morning dawns. Crystal drops are showered on the children by the angel of the dew; Gretel opens her eyes first and wakes her brother with a song. They are still entranced by the beautiful angel-dream they have had, when suddenly their attention is aroused by the sight of a little house made entirely of cake and sugar. Approaching it on tiptoe they begin to break off little bits, but a voice within calls out, "Tip, tap, tip, tap, who raps at my house?" "The wind, the wind, the heavenly child," they answer, continuing to eat and to laugh, nothing daunted. But the door opens softly and out glides the witch, who quickly throws a rope around Hänsel's throat. Urging the children to enter her house she tells her name, Rosina Sweet-tooth. The frightened children try to escape, but the fairy raises her staff and by a magic charm keeps them spellbound. She imprisons Hänsel in a small stable with a lattice door and gives him almonds and currants to eat, then turning to Gretel, who has stood rooted to the spot, she breaks the charm with a juniper-bough and compels her to enter the house and make herself useful.

Believing Hänsel to be asleep, she turns to the oven and kindles the fire; then, breaking into wild glee, she seizes a broom and rides on it round the house singing, Gretel all the while observing her keenly. Tired with her exertions the witch awakes Hänsel and bids him show his finger, at which command Hänsel stretches out a small piece of wood. Seeing him so thin, the witch calls for more food, and while she turns her back Gretel quickly takes up the juniper-bough and, speaking the formula, disenchants her brother. Meanwhile the witch, turning to the oven, tells Gretel to creep into it in order to see if the honey-cakes are ready, but the little girl, affecting stupidity, begs her to show how she is to get in. The witch impatiently bends forward, and at the same moment Gretel, assisted by Hänsel, who has escaped from his prison, pushes her into the hot oven and slams the iron door. The wicked witch burns to ashes, while the oven cracks and roars and finally falls to pieces. With astonishment the brother and sister see a long row of children, from whom the honey-crust has fallen off, standing stiff and stark. Gretel tenderly caresses one of them, who opens his eyes and smiles. She now touches them all, and Hänsel, seizing the juniper-bough, works the charm and recalls them to new life. The cake-children thank them warmly, and they all proceed to inspect the treasures of the house, when Hänsel hears their parents calling them. Great is the joy of father and mother at finding their beloved ones safe and in the possession of a sweet little house. The old sorceress is drawn out of the ruins of the oven in the form of an immense honey-cake, whereupon they all thank Heaven for having so visibly helped and protected them.

DAS HEIMCHEN AM HERD
(The Cricket on the Hearth)

Opera in three acts by Karl Goldmark.
Text after Dickens's tale by Willner.

THE scene is laid in an English village. The cricket, a little fairy, lives with a postilion, John, and his wife Dot. They are a happy couple, the only thing wanting to their complete happiness being children, and even this ardent wish Dot knows will be fulfilled before long.

A young doll-maker, May, visits Dot to unburden her heavy heart. The young girl is to marry her old and rich employer Tackleton, in order to save her foster-father from want, but she cannot forget her old sweetheart, a sailor named Edward, who left her years ago, never to come back. Dot tries to console her, and gives her food for her old father. When May has taken leave, Dot's husband John enters, bringing a strange guest with him.

It is Edward, who has, however, so disguised himself that nobody recognizes him. Dot receives him hospitably, and while he follows her in another room, a very lively scene ensues, all the village people flocking in to receive their letters and parcels at John's hands.

In the second act John rests from his labor in his garden, while Dot, who finds her husband, who is considerably older than herself, somewhat too self-confident and phlegmatic, tries to make him appreciate her more by arousing his jealousy. While they thus talk and jest May enters, followed by her old suitor, who has already chosen the wedding ring for her. Edward listens to his wooing with ill-concealed anxiety, and Tackleton, not pleased to find a stranger in his friend's house, gruffly asks his name. The strange sailor tells him that he left his father and his sweetheart to seek his fortune elsewhere, and that he has come back rich and independent, only to find his father dead and his sweetheart lost to him. His voice moves May strangely, but Tackleton wants to see his riches. Edward shows them some fine jewels, which so delight Dot that she begins to adorn herself with them and to dance about the room. Edward presents her with a beautiful cross, and seizes the opportunity to reveal to her his identity, entreating her not to betray him. Then he turns to May, begging her to choose one of the trinkets, but Tackleton interferes, saying that his promised bride does not need any jewels from strange people. Dot is greatly embarrassed, and Tackleton, mistaking her agitation, believes that she has fallen in love with the sailor, and insinuates as much to her husband, whom he invites to have a glass of beer with him.

This unusual generosity on the part of the avaricious old man excites the clever little wife's suspicion. May having withdrawn, she greets the friend of her youth with great ostentation (knowing herself secretly watched by John and Tackleton), and promises to help him to regain his sweetheart. John and his friend, who suddenly return, see them together, and poor old John gets wildly jealous. But when he is alone, he falls asleep and the faithful cricket prophetically shows him his wife fast asleep in a dream, while a little boy in miniature postilion's dress plays merrily in the background.

In the third act Dot adorns May with the bridal wreath, but the girl is in a very sad mood. All at once she hears the sailor sing. Dot steals away, and May, vividly reminded of her old love by the song, decides to refuse old Tackleton at the last moment, and to remain true to Edward till the end of her life. The sailor, hearing her resolve, rushes in tearing off his false gray beard, and catches May, who at last recognizes him, in his arms. Meanwhile Tackleton arrives gorgeously attired. He brings a necklace of false pearls and invites May to drive with him to the wedding ceremony in the church at once. A whole chorus of people interrupt this scene; they greet him, saying they are his wedding guests, exciting the miser's wrath. At last May, who had retired to put on her bridal attire, reappears, but instead of taking Tackleton's arm she walks up to Edward, who courteously thanks the old lover for the carriage standing at the door, and suddenly disappears with May. The chorus detains the furious old Tackleton until the lovers are well out of the way.

Meanwhile Dot has explained her behavior to John, and whispering her sweet secret into his ear, makes him the happiest man on earth. The cricket, the good fairy of the house, chirps sweetly, and the last scene shows once more a picture of faithfulness and love.

LES HUGUENOTS

Opera in five acts by Giacomo Meyerbeer.
Text by Scribe.

THE scene is laid in France at the time of the bloody persecutions of the Protestants or Huguenots by the Catholics. The Duke of Guise has apparently made peace with Admiral Coligny, the greatest and most famous of the Huguenots, and we are introduced into the castle of Count Nevers, where the Catholic noblemen receive Raoul de Nangis, a Protestant, who has lately been promoted to the rank of captain. During their meal they speak of love and its pleasures and everybody is called on to give the name of his sweetheart. Raoul begins by telling them that once when taking a walk he surprised a band of students molesting a lady in a litter. He rescued her, and as she graciously thanked him for his gallant service he thought her more beautiful than any maiden he had ever before seen. His heart burned with love for her, though he did not know her name. While Raoul drinks with the noblemen, Marcel, his old servant, warns him of the danger of doing so.

Marcel, who is a strict old Protestant, sings a ballad of the Huguenots to the young people, a song wild and fanatic. They laugh at his impotent wrath, when a lady is announced to Count Nevers. In her Raoul recognizes the lady of his dreams.

Of course he believes her false and bad, while as a matter of fact she only comes to beseech Nevers, her destined bridegroom, to set her free. Nevers does so, though not without pain. When he returns to his companions he conceals the result of the interview and presently Urbain, a page, enters with a little note for Raoul de Nangis in which he is ordered to attend a lady, unknown to him. The others recognize the seal of Queen Marguerite of Valois, and finding him so worthy at once seek to gain his friendship.

In the second act we find Raoul with the beautiful Queen, who is trying to reconcile the Catholics with the Protestants. To this end the Queen has resolved to unite Raoul with Valentine, her lady of honor and daughter of the Count of St. Bris, a staunch Catholic. Valentine tells her heart's secret to her mistress, for to her it was that Raoul brought assistance, and she loves him. The noble Raoul, seeing Marguerite's beauty and kindness, vows himself her knight, when suddenly the whole court enters to render her homage. Recognizing her at last to be the Queen, Raoul is all the more willing to fulfill her wishes and offers his hand in reconciliation to the proud St. Bris, promising to wed his daughter. But when he perceives in her the unknown lady whom he believes to be so unworthy he takes back his word. All are surprised, and the offended father vows bloody vengeance.

In the third act Marcel brings a challenge to St. Bris, which the latter accepts, but Maurevert, a fanatical Catholic nobleman, tells him of other ways in which to annihilate his foe. Valentine, though deadly offended with her lover, resolves to save him. Seeing Marcel, she bids him tell his master not to meet his enemy alone. Meanwhile Raoul is already on the spot, and so is St. Bris with four witnesses. While they fight, a quarrel arises between the Catholic and the Protestant citizens, which is stopped by Queen Marguerite. The enemies accuse each other, and when the Queen is in doubt as to whom she shall believe, Valentine appears to bear witness. Then Raoul hears that her interview with Nevers had been but a farewell, sought for but to loosen forever the ties which her father had formed for her against her will; but the knowledge of his error comes too late, for St. Bris has once more promised his daughter to Nevers, who at this moment arrives with many guests, invited for the wedding. The presence of the Queen preserves peace between the different parties, but Raoul leaves the spot with death in his heart.

In the fourth act the dreadful night of St. Bartholomew is already beginning.

We find Valentine in her room despairing. Raoul comes to take a last farewell, but almost immediately St. Bris enters with a party of Catholics and Raoul is obliged to hide in the adjoining room. There he hears the whole conspiracy for the destruction of the Protestants, beginning with their leader, Admiral Coligny. The Catholics all assent to this diabolical plot; Nevers alone refuses to soil his honor and swears only to fight in open battle. The others, fearing treason, decide to bind him and keep him prisoner until the next morning. Raoul prepares to save his brethren or die with them. Vain are Valentine's entreaties; though she confesses to her love for him, he yet leaves her, though with a great effort, to follow the path of duty.

In the last act Raoul rushes pale and bloody into the hall where Queen Marguerite sits with her husband Henry, surrounded by the court.

He tells them of the terrific events which are going on outside and beseeches their help. It is too late, however; Coligny has already fallen and with him most of the Huguenots.

Raoul meets Valentine once more; she promises to save him if he will go over to her faith. But Marcel reminds him of his oath, and Valentine, seeing that nothing can move her lover's fortitude and firmness, decides to remain with him. She accepts his creed and so they meet death together, Valentine falling by the side of her deadly wounded lover, both praising God with their last breath.

IPHIGÉNIE EN AULIDE
(Iphigenia in Aulis)

Grand Opera in three acts by Christoph Willibald Gluck. Text of the original rearranged by Wagner.

THIS opera may be called the first part of the tragedy, and "Iphigénie en Tauride" very beautifully completes it. The music is sure to be highly relished by a cultivated hearer, characterized as it is by a simplicity which often rises into grandeur and nobility of utterance.

The first scene represents Agamemnon rent by a conflict between his duty and his fatherly love; the former of which demands the sacrifice of his daughter, for only then will a favorable wind conduct the Greeks safely to Ilion. Kalchas, the high priest of Artemis, appears to announce her dreadful sentence. Alone with the King, Kalchas vainly tries to induce the unhappy father to consent to the sacrifice.

Meanwhile Iphigenia, who has not received Agamemnon's message which ought to have prevented her undertaking the fatal journey, arrives with her mother Klytemnestra. They are received with joy by the people. Agamemnon secretly informs his spouse that Achilles, Iphigenia's betrothed, has proved unworthy of her and that she is to return to Argos at once. Iphigenia gives way to her feelings. Achilles appears, the lovers are soon reconciled and prepare to celebrate their nuptials.

In the second act Iphigenia is adorned for her wedding and Achilles comes to lead her to the altar, when Arkas, Agamemnon's messenger, informs them that death awaits Iphigenia.

Klytemnestra in despair appeals to Achilles and the bridegroom swears to protect Iphigenia. She alone is resigned in the belief that it is her father's will that she should face this dreadful duty. Achilles reproaches Agamemnon wildly and leaves the unhappy father a prey to mental torture. At last he decides to send Arkas at once to Mykene with mother and daughter and to hide them there until the wrath of the goddess be appeased. But it is too late.

In the third act the people assemble before the royal tent and with much shouting and noise demand the sacrifice. Achilles in vain implores Iphigenia to follow him. She is ready to be sacrificed, while he determines to kill any one who dares touch his bride. Klytemnestra then tries everything in her power to save her. She offers herself in her daughter's stead, and finding it of no avail, at last sinks down in a swoon. The daughter, having bade her an eternal farewell, with quiet dignity allows herself to be led to the altar. When her mother awakes she rages in impotent fury; then she hears the people's hymn to the goddess, and rushes out to die with her child. The scene changes. The high priest at the altar of Artemis is ready to pierce the innocent victim. A great tumult arises. Achilles, with his native Thessalians, makes his way through the crowd in order to save Iphigenia, who loudly invokes the help of the goddess. But at this moment a loud thunder peal arrests the contending parties, and when the mist, which has blinded all, has passed, Artemis herself is seen in a cloud with Iphigenia kneeling before her.

The goddess announces that it is Iphigenia's high mind which she demands and not her blood; she wishes to take her into a foreign land, where she may be her priestess and atone for the sins of the blood of Atreus.

A wind favorable to the fleet has risen, and the people, filled with gratitude and admiration, behold the vanishing cloud and praise the goddess.

IPHIGÈNIE EN TAURIDE
(Iphigenia in Tauris)

Opera in four acts by Christoph Willibald Gluck.
Text by Guillard.

THE libretto follows pretty exactly the Greek original. Iphigenia, King Agamemnon's daughter, who has been saved by the goddess Diana (or Artemis) from death at the altar of Aulis, has been carried in a cloud to Tauris, where she is compelled to be high priestess in the temple of the barbarous Scythians. There we find her after having performed her cruel service for fifteen years. Human sacrifices are required, but more than once she has saved a poor stranger from this awful lot.

Iphigenia is much troubled by a dream, in which she saw her father deadly wounded by her mother, and herself about to kill her brother Orestes. She bewails her fate in having at the behest of Thoas, King of the Scythians, to sacrifice two strangers who have been thrown on his shores. Orestes and his friend Pylades,

for these are the strangers, are led to death loaded with chains.

Iphigenia, hearing that they are her countrymen, resolves to save at least one of them in order to send him home to her sister Elektra. She does not know her brother Orestes, who, having slain his mother, has fled, pursued by the Furies, but an inner voice makes her choose him as a messenger to Greece. A lively dispute arises between the two friends; at last Orestes prevails upon Iphigenia to spare his friend by threatening to destroy himself with his own hands, his life being a burden to him. Iphigenia reluctantly complies with his request, giving the message for her sister to Pylades.

In the third act Iphigenia vainly tries to steel her heart against her victim. At last she seizes the knife, but Orestes cries, "So you also were pierced by the sacrificial steel, O my sister Iphigenia!" and the knife falls from her hands. A touching scene of recognition ensues.

Meanwhile Thoas, who has heard that one of the strangers was about to depart, enters the temple with his bodyguard, and, though Iphigenia tells him that Orestes is her brother and entreats him to spare Agamemnon's son, Thoas determines to sacrifice him and his sister Iphigenia as well. But his evil designs are frustrated by Pylades, who, returning with several of his countrymen, stabs the King of Tauris. The goddess Diana herself appears and, helping the Greeks in their fight, gains for them the victory. Diana declares herself appeased by the repentance of Orestes and allows him to return to his country with his sister, his friend, and all his followers.

LE JONGLEUR DE NOTRE-DAME
(The Juggler of Notre-Dame)

Opera in three acts by Jules Massenet.
Text by Léna.

IN Cluny, on a market-day (the first of May), the juggler Jean wanders hungry and miserable through the countryside, but rejoices in his freedom. It does not satisfy his wants, however, and he is unsuccessful in gaining the attention of the people, who deride his performance. They care nothing for his globes, his hoops, his old songs and dances. They do applaud a ribald song, "Alleluia to wine," and although in his heart Jean is a good Christian, his stomach remains egotistical, and he sings a parody on the mass. The prior appears, and the crowd disperses, leaving Jean to his fate. The juggler is about to be excommunicated for his blasphemy, when he confesses his guilt, and is received among the monks. Hunger overcomes him, and he relinquishes his freedom, sorely tempted by the rich food of the abbey.

In the second act, in the study at the abbey, musicians, poets, painters, and sculptors labor for the feast of the Holy Mother, but Jean takes no part—he knows no Latin. Brother Boniface, the cook, consoles him, and Jean resolves to serve the Holy Mother in his own way.

The last act takes place in the chapel of the abbey, in which stands the image of the Blessed Virgin. Jean slowly approaches. He puts off his monastic garb, and appears in his juggler's dress. He offers to Mary the only gift he possesses, his songs and dances. In his ecstasy, he fails to notice the entrance of the monks, and dances on unheeding. The prior in horror is about to throw himself upon Jean, when the Holy Mother interferes; a miracle takes place, for the image raises its hands, and places them in benediction upon the head of the juggler. The monks now acclaim him a saint, and as they sing, led by Boniface, "Sancta Maria, ora pro nobis," Jean declares in softly childish tones, "Oh, dear, I understand Latin now!" Overcome with joy at the favor of the Holy Mother, the juggler sinks to the ground and dies.

JOSEPH

Opera in three acts by Etienne Nicolas Méhul.
Text after Duval.

JOSEPH, the son of Jacob, who was sold by his brothers, has by his wisdom saved Egypt from threatening famine; he resides as governor in Memphis under the name of Cleophas. But though much honored by the King and all the people, he never ceases to long for his old father, whose favorite child he was.

Driven from Palestine by famine, Jacob's sons are sent to Egypt to ask for food and hospitality. They are tormented by pangs of conscience, which Simeon is hardly able to conceal, when they are received by the governor, who at once recognizes them. Seeing their sorrow and repentance, he pities them, and promises to treat them with all hospitality. He does not reveal himself, but goes to meet his youngest brother, Benjamin, and his blind father, whose mourning for his lost son has not been diminished by the long years. Joseph induces his father and brother to partake of the honors which the people render to him. The whole family is received in the governor's palace, where Simeon, consumed by grief and conscience-stricken, at last confesses to his father the selling of Joseph. Full of horror, Jacob curses and disowns his ten sons. But Joseph intervenes. Making himself known, he grants full pardon and entreats his father to do the same. The old man yields, and together they praise God's providence and omnipotence.

LA JUIVE

(The Jewess)

Opera in five acts by Jacques Halévy.
Text by Scribe.

THE scene of action is laid in Constance, in the year 1414, during the Council.

In the first act the opening of the Council is celebrated with great pomp. The Catholics, having gained a victory over the Hussites, Huss is to be burned, and the Jews, equally disliked, are oppressed and put down still more than before. All the shops are closed, only Eleazar, a rich Jewish jeweler, has kept his open and is, therefore, about to be imprisoned and put to death when Cardinal de Brogni intervenes and saves the Jew and his daughter Recha from the people's fury. The Cardinal has a secret liking for Eleazar, though he once banished him from Rome. He hopes to gain news from him of his daughter, who was lost in early childhood. But Eleazar hates the Cardinal bitterly. When the mob is dispersed Prince Leopold, the imperial commander-in-chief, approaches Recha. Under the assumed name of Samuel he has gained her affections, and she begs him to be present at a religious feast which is to take place that evening at her father's house. The act closes with a splendid procession of the Emperor and all his dignitaries. Ruggiero, the chief judge in Constance, seeing the hated Jew and his daughter among the spectators, is about to seize them once more, when Prince Leopold steps between and delivers them, to Recha's great astonishment.

In the second act we are introduced to a great assembly of Jews, men and women, assisting at a religious ceremony. Samuel is there with them. The holy act is, however, interrupted by the Emperor's niece Princess Eudora, who comes to purchase a golden chain which once belonged to the Emperor Constantine, which she destines for her bridegroom Prince Leopold. Eleazar is to bring it himself on the following day. Samuel, overhearing this, is full of trouble. When the assembly is broken up and all have gone he returns once more to Recha and, finding her alone, confesses that he is a Christian. Love prevails over Recha's filial devotion and she consents to fly with her lover, but they are surprised by Eleazar. Hearing of Samuel's falseness, be first swears vengeance, but, mollified by his daughter's entreaties, he only bids him marry Recha. Samuel refuses and has to leave, the father cursing him, Recha bewailing her lover's falseness.

In the third act we assist at the imperial banquet. Eleazar brings the chain and is accompanied by Recha, who at once recognizes in Eudora's bridegroom her lover Samuel. She denounces the traitor, accusing him of living in unlawful wedlock with a Jewess, a crime punishable by death.

Leopold (alias Samuel) is outlawed, the Cardinal pronounces the anathema upon all three, and they are put in prison.

In the fourth act Eudora visits Recha in prison and by her prayers not only overcomes Recha's hate but persuades her to save Leopold by declaring him innocent. Recha, in her noble-mindedness, pardons Leopold and Eudora and resolves to die alone.

Meanwhile the Cardinal has an interview with Eleazar, who tells him that he knows the Jew who once saved the Cardinal's little daughter from the flames. Brogni vainly entreats him to reveal the name. He promises to save Recha should Eleazar be willing to abjure his faith, but the latter remains firm, fully prepared to die.

In the fifth act we hear the clamors of the people, who furiously demand the Jew's death.

Ruggiero announces to father and daughter the verdict of death by fire. Leopold is set free through Recha's testimony. When in view of the funeral pile Eleazar asks Recha if she would prefer to live in joy and splendor and to accept the Christian faith, but she firmly answers in the negative. Then she is led on to death, and she is just plunged into the glowing furnace when Eleazar, pointing to her, informs the Cardinal that the poor victim is his long-lost daughter; then Eleazar follows Recha into the flames, while Brogni falls back senseless.

DIE KÖNIGIN VON SABA
(The Queen of Sheba)

Grand Opera in four acts by Karl Goldmark.
Text by Mosenthal.

A MAGNIFICENT wedding is to be celebrated in King Solomon's palace at Jerusalem. The high priest's daughter, Sulamith, is to marry Assad, King Solomon's favorite. But the lover, who in a foreign country has seen a most beautiful and haughty woman bathing in a forest pool, is now in love with the stranger and has forgotten his destined bride.

Returning home, Assad confesses his error to the wise King, and Solomon bids him wed Sulamith and forget the heathen. Assad gives his promise, praying to God to restore peace to his breast.

Then enters the Queen of Sheba in all her glory, followed by a procession of slaves and suitors. Next to her litter walks her principal slave, Astaroth.

The Queen comes to offer her homage to the great Solomon with all the gifts of her rich kingdom. She is veiled, and nobody has seen her yet, as only before the King will she unveil herself.

When she draws back the veil, shining in all her perfect beauty, Assad starts forward; he recognizes her; she is his nymph of the forest. But the proud Queen seems to know him not, she ignores him altogether. Solomon and Sulamith try to reassure themselves, to console Assad, and the Queen hears Solomon's words: "To-morrow shall find you united to your bride!" She starts and casts a passionate look on the unfortunate Assad.

The Queen is full of raging jealousy of the young bride. But though she claims Assad's love for herself, she is yet too proud to resign her crown, and so, hesitating between love and pride, she swears vengeance on her rival. Under the shade of night Astaroth allures Assad to the fountain, where he finds the Queen, who employs all her arts again to captivate him, succeeding only too well.

Morning dawns, and with it the day of Assad's marriage with Sulamith. Solomon and the high priest conduct the youth to the altar, but just as he is taking the ring, offered to him by the bride's father, the Queen of Sheba appears, bringing as wedding gift a golden cup filled with pearls.

Assad, again overcome by the Queen's dazzling beauty, throws the ring away and precipitates himself at her feet. The Levites detain him, but Solomon, guessing at the truth, implores the Queen to speak. Assad invokes all the sweet memories of their past, the Queen hesitates, but her pride conquers. For the second time she disowns him. Now everybody believes Assad possessed by an evil spirit, and the priests at once begin to exorcise it; it is all but done, when one word of the Queen's, who sweetly calls him "Assad," spoils everything. He is in her bands: falling on his knees before her he prays to her as to his goddess. Wrathful at this blasphemy in the temple, the priests demand his death.

Assad asks no better, Sulamith despairs, and the Queen repents having gone so far. In the great tumult Solomon alone is unmoved. He detains the priests with dignity, for he alone will judge Assad.

Now follows a charming ballet, given in honor of the Queen of Sheba. At the end of the meal the Queen demands Assad's pardon from Solomon. He refuses her request. She now tries to ensnare the King with her charms as she did Assad, but in vain. Solomon sees her in her true light and treats her with cold politeness. Almost beside herself with rage, the Queen threatens to take vengeance on the King and to free Assad at any risk.

Solomon, well understanding the vile tricks of the Queen, has changed the verdict of death into that of exile. Sulamith, faithful and gentle, entreats for her lover, and has only one wish: to sweeten life to her Assad, or to die with him.

We find Assad in the desert. He is broken down and deeply repents his folly, when the Queen appears once more, hoping to lure him with soft words and tears. But this time her beauty is lost upon him: he has at last recognized her false soul; with noble pride he scorns her, preferring to expiate his follies by dying in the desert. He curses her, praying to God to save him from the temptress. Henceforth he thinks only of Sulamith and invokes Heaven's benediction on her. He is dying in the dreadful heat of the desert, when Sulamith appears, the faithful one who without resting has sought her bridegroom till now. But in vain she kneels beside him couching his head on her bosom; his life is fast ebbing away. Heaven has granted his last wish; he sees Sulamith before his death, and with the sigh, "Liberation!" he sinks back and expires.

LOHENGRIN

Romantic Opera in three acts by Richard Wagner.

THE scene is laid near Antwerp where "Heinrich der Vogler," King of Germany, is just levying troops among his vassals of Brabant to repulse the Hungarian invaders. The King finds the people in a state of great commotion, for Count Frederick Telramund accuses Elsa of Brabant of having killed her young brother Godfrey, heir to the Duke of Brabant, who died a short time before, leaving his children to the care of Telramund. Elsa was to be Telramund's wife, but he wedded Ortrud of Friesland and now claims the deserted duchy of Brabant.

As Elsa declares her innocence, not knowing what has become of her brother, who was taken from her during her sleep, the King resolves to decide by a tourney in which the whole matter shall be left to the judgment of God. Telramund, sure of his rights, is willing to fight with any champion who may defend Elsa. All the noblemen of Brabant refuse to do so and even the King, though struck by Elsa's innocent appearance, does not want to oppose his valiant and trustworthy warrior.

Elsa alone is calm; she trusts in the help of the heavenly knight who has appeared to her in a dream, and publicly declares her intention of offering to her defender the crown and her hand. While she prays a knight arrives in silver armor; a swan draws his boat. He lands, Elsa recognizes the knight of her dream, and he at once offers to fight for the accused maiden on two conditions: first, that she shall become his wife; and second, that she never will ask for his name and his descent.

Elsa solemnly promises and the combat begins. The strange knight is victorious, and Telramund, whose life the stranger spares, is with his wife Ortrud outlawed.

The latter is a sorceress; she has deceived her husband, who really believes in the murder of Godfrey, while as a matter of fact she has abducted the child. In the second act we see her at the door of the ducal palace, where preparations for the wedding are already being made. She plans vengeance. Her husband, full of remorse and feeling that his wife has led him on to a shameful deed, curses her as the cause of his dishonor. She derides him and rouses his pride by calling him a coward. Then she pacifies him with the assurance that she will induce Elsa to break her promise and ask for the name of her husband, being sure that then all the power of this mysterious champion will vanish.

When Elsa steps on the balcony to confide her happiness to the stars, she hears her name spoken in accents so sad that her tender heart is moved. Ortrud bewails her lot, invoking Elsa's pity. The Princess opens her door, urging the false woman to share her palace and her fortune. Ortrud at once tries to sow distrust in Elsa's innocent heart.

As the morning dawns a rich procession of men and women throng to the church where Elsa is to be united to her protector. Telramund tries vainly to accuse the stranger; he is pushed back and silenced. As Elsa is about to enter the church Ortrud steps forward claiming the right of precedence. Elsa, frightened, repents too late having protected her. Ortrud upbraids her with not even having asked her husband's name and descent. All are taken aback, but Elsa defends her husband, winning everybody by her quiet dignity.

She turns to Lohengrin for protection, but the venom rankles in her heart.

When they again turn to enter the church Telramund once more steps forth, accusing Lohengrin and demanding from the King to know the stranger's name. Lohengrin declares that his name may not be told unless his wife asks it. Elsa is in great trouble, but once more her love conquers and she does not put the fatal question.

But in the third act, when the two lovers are alone, she knows no rest. Although her husband asks her to trust him, she fears that he may leave her as mysteriously as he came, and at last she cannot refrain from asking the luckless question. From this moment all happiness is lost to her. Telramund enters to slay his enemy, but Lohengrin, taking his sword, kills him with one stroke. Then he leads Elsa before the King and loudly announces his secret. He tells the astounded hearers that he is the keeper of the Holy Grail. Sacred and invulnerable to the villain, a defender of right and virtue, he may stay with mankind as long as his name is unknown. But now he is obliged to reveal it. He is Lohengrin, son of Parsifal, King of the Grail, and is now compelled to leave his wife and return to his home. The swan appears, from whose neck Lohengrin takes a golden ring, giving it to Elsa, together with his sword and golden horn.

Just as Lohengrin is about to depart Ortrud appears triumphantly declaring that it was she who changed young Godfrey into a swan and that Lohengrin would have freed him too had Elsa not mistrusted her husband. Lohengrin, hearing this, sends a fervent prayer to Heaven, and loosens the swan's golden chain. The animal dips under water and in his stead rises Godfrey, the lawful heir of Brabant. A white dove descends to draw the boat in which Lohengrin glides away, and Elsa falls senseless in her brother's arms.

LOUISE

Opera in four acts by Gustave Charpentier.

CHARPENTIER has taken for his subject the romance of the everyday working-girl, just such a tale as one may find in the popular story-papers, or in the so-called melodrama of the cheaper theaters. But to this commonplace text he has wedded a truly Wagnerian musical setting, elaborate in orchestration, full of the "recitative which is aria, and the aria which is recitative," and with an ever-recurring *Leitmotiv* typical of the joy of Paris. First performed February 2, 1900, at the Opéra Comique in Paris, "Louise" rapidly passed into the repertoire of the world's principal lyric theaters.

The first act opens in a working-man's home in Paris. The attic is scantily furnished, but clean, and Louise, at the open window, is listening to the ardent pleadings of Julien, her lover. The girl's mother enters in time to hear Julien tell Louise that, since her parents will not permit them to wed, they must elope. The mother pulls her daughter from the window, dismisses the lover, then lectures the girl on the bad character of her suitor. The father enters, and greets his family affectionately. He has received a letter from Julien, who begs to be accepted as a son-in-law. But while the father is rather favorably impressed by the young man's letter, his wife is not, and with the antipathy of her class for artists, she repeats all the gossip she has heard to Julien's discredit. The father then exacts a promise from Louise that she will see Julien no more.

An allegory portraying Paris introduces the second act. A night-walker, a ragpicker, and the rabble of a great city in the early dawn are shown. Julien enters with a party of friends, to whom he describes his plans for the abduction of Louise. He hides as the working-girls come by on their way to the shops. Louise enters with her mother, and the moment they part, Julien approaches the girl, and again begs her to elope with him. She refuses and he turns sadly away. The scene now shifts to the interior of a dressmaking shop, where Louise is at work with her companions. The girls chatter as they work, and the noises of the street are heard through open windows in the back. Presently Julien is heard singing to the accompaniment of his guitar. The girls flock to the windows. Julien, not seeing Louise, sings in sadder vein, and the girls lose interest —all but Louise. Unable longer to resist her lover's pleadings, she pretends to be ill, and dons her coat and hat as though going home. A moment later the girls at the window cry out in excitement. Louise has gone off with the singer.

The third act takes place in the garden of a house on Montmartre overlooking Paris. Louise tells Julien that she regrets nothing, that she is happy. Julien speaks of her parents as Mother Routine and Father Prejudice, and tells her that the selfishness of her parents must be met with selfishness. The city lights up, and the lovers sing the praise of Paris, of life, of love. When night has fallen, a crowd of Julien's Bohemian associates come to celebrate the happy union. They crown Louise "Queen of Montmartre," but the festivities are interrupted by the arrival of Louise's mother. The father has fallen ill, and she begs Louise to go home with her. Julien consents, on the promise of Louise that she will return.

In the last act we return to the humble home in Paris, where the father, broken in health, is declaiming against the ingratitude of children. Louise makes no reply, but looks longingly out into the night. Called to help her mother in the kitchen, Louise is treated to another tirade against her lover. The girl recalls the promise that she should be free. The mother refuses to let her go. The father draws her to his knee, and sings her a lullaby, promising that the child shall have whatever she wants if she will be good. Louise answers that she can be happy only by returning to her lover. Then the songs in the streets excite her to the verge of hysteria. Finally, in a fit of rage, the father drives her from home. He immediately repents and calls her back, but it is too late. She has gone to rejoin Julien. "Oh, Paris!" cries the father, shaking his fist in impotent anger at the city.

LUCIA DI LAMMERMOOR
(The Bride of Lammermoor)

Tragic Opera in three acts by Gaetano Donizetti.
Text from Scott's romance by Cammerano.

HENRY ASHTON, lord of Lammermoor, has discovered that his sister Lucia loves his mortal enemy Sir Edgar of Ravenswood. He confides to Lucia's tutor Raymond that he is lost if Lucia does not marry another suitor of his (her brother's) choice.

Lucia and Edgar meet in the park. Edgar tells her that he is about to leave Scotland for France in the service of his country. He wishes to be reconciled to his enemy Lord Ashton, for, though the latter has done him all kinds of evil, though he has slain his father and burned his castle, Edgar is willing to sacrifice his oath of vengeance to his love for Lucia. But the lady, full of evil forebodings, entreats him to wait and swears eternal fidelity to him. After having bound himself by a solemn oath, he leaves her half-distracted with grief.

In the second act Lord Ashton shows a forged letter to his sister, which goes to prove that her lover is false. Her brother now presses her more and more to wed his friend Arthur, Lord Bucklaw, declaring that he and his party are lost and that Arthur alone can save him from the executioner's axe. At last, when even her tutor Raymond beseeches her to forget Edgar, and, like the others, believes him to be faithless, Lucia consents to the sacrifice. The wedding takes place in great haste, but just as Lucia has finished signing the marriage contract, Edgar enters to claim her as his own.

With grief and unbounded passion he now sees in his bride a traitress, and tearing his ring of betrothal from her finger, he throws it at her feet.

Henry, Arthur, and Raymond order the raving lover to leave the castle, and the act closes in the midst of confusion and despair.

The third act opens with Raymond's announcement that Lucia has lost her reason and has killed her husband in the bridal room. Lucia herself enters to confirm his awful news; she is still in bridal attire, and in her demented condition believes that Arthur will presently appear for the nuptial ceremony. Everybody is full of pity for her, and her brother repents his harshness too late—Lucia is fast dying, and Eliza leads her away amid the lamentations of all present.

Edgar, hearing of these things while wandering amid the tombs of his ancestors, resolves to see Lucia once more. When dying she asks for him, but he comes too late. The funeral bells toll, and he stabs himself, praying to be united to his bride in heaven.

LUCREZIA BORGIA

Tragic Opera in three acts by Gaetano Donizetti.
Text by Romani after Victor Hugo's drama.

THE heroine, whose part is by far the best and most interesting, is the celebrated poisoner and murderess, Lucrezia Borgia. At the same time she gives evidence, in her dealings with her son Gennaro, of possessing a very tender and motherly heart, and the songs in which she pours out her love for him are really fine as well as touching.

Lucrezia, wife of Don Alfonso, Duke of Ferrara, goes to Venice in disguise to see the son of her first marriage, Gennaro. In his earliest youth he was given to a fisherman, who brought him up as his own son. Gennaro feels himself attracted toward the strange and beautiful woman who visits him, but hearing from his companions, who recognize her and charge her with all sorts of crimes, that she is Lucrezia Borgia, he abhors her. Don Alfonso, not knowing the existence of this son of an early marriage, is jealous, and when Gennaro comes to Ferrara and in order to prove his hatred of the Borgias tears off Lucrezia's name and scutcheon from the palace-gates, Rustighello, the Duke's confidant, is ordered to imprison him. Lucrezia, hearing from her servant Gubella of the outrage to her name and honor, complains to the Duke, who promises immediate punishment of the malefactor.

Gennaro enters, and Lucrezia, terror-stricken, recognizes her son. Vainly does she implore the Duke to spare the youth. With exquisite cruelty he forces her to hand the poisoned golden cup to the culprit herself, and, departing, bids her accompany her prisoner to the door. This order gives her an opportunity to administer an antidote by which she saves Gennaro's life, and she implores him to fly. But Gennaro does not immediately follow her advice, being induced by his friend Orsini to assist at a grand festival at Prince Negroni's.

Unhappily all those young men who formerly reproached and offended Lucrezia so mortally in presence of her son are assembled there by Lucrezia's orders. She has mixed their wine with poison, and herself appears to announce their death. Horror-stricken, she sees Gennaro, who was not invited, among them. He has partaken of the wine like the others, but on her offering him an antidote he refuses to take it; its quantity is insufficient for his friends, and he threatens to kill the murderess. Then she reveals the secret of his birth to him, but he only turns from this mother, for whom he had vainly longed his whole life, and dies. The Duke, coming up to witness his wife's horrible victory, finds all either dead or dying, and Lucrezia herself expires, stricken down by deadly remorse and pain.

DIE LUSTIGEN WEIBER VON WINDSOR
(The Merry Wives of Windsor)

Comic Opera in three acts by Otto Nicolai.
Text by Mosenthal.

THIS admirable opera is, it need hardly be said, taken from Shakespeare's famous comedy. Falstaff has written love-letters to the wives of two citizens of Windsor, Mrs. Fluth and Mrs. Reich. They discover his duplicity and decide to punish the infatuated old fool.

Meanwhile Mr. Fenton, a nice but poor young man, asks for the hand of Anna Reich. But her father has already chosen a richer suitor for his daughter in the person of the silly young squire Spärlich.

In the following scene Sir John Falstaff is amiably received by Mrs. Fluth, when suddenly Mrs. Reich arrives, telling them that Mr. Fluth will be with them at once, having received notice of his wife's doings. Falstaff is packed into a clothes-basket and carried away from under Mr. Fluth's nose by two men, who are bidden to put the contents in a canal near the Thames, and the jealous husband, finding nobody, receives sundry lectures from his offended wife.

In the second act Mr. Fluth, mistrusting his wife, makes Falstaff's acquaintance, under the assumed name of Bach, and is obliged to hear an account of the worthy fat knight's gallant adventure with his wife and its disagreeable issue. Fluth persuades Falstaff to give him a rendezvous, swearing inwardly to punish the old coxcomb for his impudence.

In the evening Anna meets her lover Fenton in the garden, and ridiculing her two suitors, Spärlich and Dr. Caius, a Frenchman, she promises to remain faithful to her love. The two others, who are hidden behind trees, must perforce listen to their own dispraise.

When the time has come for Falstaff's next visit to Mrs. Fluth, who of course knows of her husband's renewed suspicion, Mr. Fluth surprises his wife and reproaches her violently with her conduct. During this controversy Falstaff is disguised as an old woman, and when the neighbors come to help the husband in his search, they find only an old deaf cousin of Mrs. Fluth's who has come from the country to visit her. Nevertheless the hag gets a good thrashing from the duped and angry husband.

In the last act everybody is in the forest, preparing for the festival of Herne the hunter. All are masked, and Sir John Falstaff, being led on by the two merry wives, is surprised by Herne (Fluth), who sends the whole chorus of wasps, flies, and mosquitos on to his broad back. They torment and punish him, till he loudly cries for mercy. Fenton, in the mask of Oberon, has found his Anna in Queen Titania, while Dr. Caius and Spärlich, mistaking their masks for Anna's, sink into each other's arms, much to their mutual discomfiture.

Mr. Fluth and Mr. Reich, seeing that their wives are innocent and that they only made fun of Falstaff, are quite happy, and the whole scene ends with a general pardon.

THE MACCABEES

Opera in three acts by Anton Rubinstein.
Text by Mosenthal, taken from Otto Ludwig's drama.

THE hero is the famous warrior of the Old Testament. The scene takes place one hundred and sixty years before Christ, partly at Modin, a city in the mountains of Judah, and partly in Jerusalem and its environs.

The first act shows Leah with three of her sons, Eleazar, Joarim, and Benjamin. Eleazar is envious of Judah, the eldest son, whose courage and strength are on everybody's lips, but his mother consoles him by a prophecy that Eleazar shall one day be high priest and king of the Jews.

The fête of the sheep-shearing is being celebrated, and Noëmi, Judah's wife, approaches Leah with garlands of flowers asking for her benediction. But she is repulsed by her mother-in-law, who is too proud to recognize the low-born maid as her equal and slights her son Judah for his love. She tries to incite him into rebellion against the Syrians, when Jojakim, a priest, appears. He announces the death of Osias, high priest of Zion, and calls one of Leah's sons to the important office. As Judah feels no vocation for such a burden, Eleazar, his mother's favorite, is chosen, and so Leah sees her dream already fulfilled. They are about to depart when the approaching army of the Syrians is announced. Terror seizes the people as Gorgias, the leader of the enemy, marches up with his soldiers and loudly proclaims that the Jews are to erect an altar to Pallas Athene, to whom they must pray henceforth. Leah seeks to inflame Eleazar's spirit, but his courage fails him. The altar is soon erected, and as Gorgias sternly orders that sacrifices are to be offered to the goddess, Boas, Noëmi's father, is found willing to bow to the enemy's commands. But the measure is full, Judah steps forth, and striking Boas, the traitor to their faith, dead, loudly praises Jehovah. He calls his people to arms and repulses the Syrians, and Leah, recognizing her son's greatness, gives him her benediction.

The second act represents a deep ravine near Emmaus; the enemy is beaten and Judah is resolved to drive him from Zion's walls, but Jojakim warns him not to profane the coming Sabbath.

Judah tries to overrule the priests and to excite the people, but he is not heard and the enemy is able to kill the psalm-singing soldiers like lambs.

The next scene shows us Eleazar with Cleopatra, daughter of King Antiochus of Syria.

They love each other, and Eleazar consents to forsake his religion for her, while she promises to make him king of Jerusalem.

In the next scene Leah in the city of Modin is

greeted with acclamations of joy, when Simei, a relative of the slain Boas, appears to bewail Judah's defeat. Other fugitives coming up confirm his narrative of the massacre. Leah hears that Judah fled and that Antiochus approaches conducted by her son Eleazar. She curses the apostate. She has still two younger sons, but the Israelites take them from her to give as hostages to King Antiochus. Leah is bound to a cypress-tree by her own people, who attribute her misfortunes to her and to her sons. Only Noëmi, the despised daughter-in-law, remains to liberate the miserable mother, and together they resolve to ask the tyrant's pardon for the sons.

In the third act we find Judah, alone and unrecognized, in the deserted streets of Jerusalem. Hearing the prayers of the people that Judah may be sent to them, he steps forth and tells them who he is, and all sink at his feet swearing to fight with him to the death. While Judah prays to God for a sign of grace, Noëmi comes with the dreadful news of the events at Modin, which still further rouses the anger and courage of the Israelites. Meanwhile Leah has succeeded in penetrating into Antiochus's presence to beg the lives of her children from him. Eleazar, Gorgias, and Cleopatra join their prayers to those of the poor mother, and at last Antiochus consents, and the two boys are led into the room.

But the King only grants their liberty on condition that they renounce their faith. They are to be burned alive should they abide by their heresy. The mother's heart is full of agony, but the children's noble courage prevails. They are prepared to die for their God, but the unhappy mother is not even allowed to share their death. When Eleazar sees his brothers' firmness his conscience awakens, and notwithstanding Cleopatra's entreaties he joins them on their way to death. The hymns of the youthful martyrs are heard, but with the sound of their voices suddenly mingles that of a growing tumult. Antiochus falls, shot through the heart, and the Israelites rush in, headed by Judah, putting the Syrians to flight. Leah sees her people's victory, but the trial has been too great; she sinks back lifeless. Judah is proclaimed King of Zion, but he humbly bends his head, giving all glory to the Almighty God.

MADAME BUTTERFLY

Japanese Lyric Tragedy in three acts by Giacomo Puccini. Founded on the book of John Luther Long and the drama by David Belasco. Text by Illica and Giacosa.

THE scene is laid in Nagasaki in our own time. The first act takes place on a hill, from which there is a grand view of the ocean and of the town below.

Goro, a marriage broker, shows his new Japanese house to an American naval lieutenant, Pinkerton, who has purchased it in Japanese fashion for 999 years, with the right of giving monthly notice. He is waiting for his bride Cho-Cho-San, called Butterfly, whom he is about to wed under the same queer conditions for one hundred yens (a yen about one dollar).

Butterfly's maid Suzuki and his two servants are presented to him, but he is impatient to embrace his sweetheart, with whom he is very much in love.

Sharpless, the United States consul, who tells him much good of the little bride, warns him not to bruise the wings of the delicate butterfly, but Pinkerton only laughs at his remonstrances.

At last Butterfly appears with her companions. At her bidding, they all shut their umbrellas and kneel to their friend's future husband, of whom the girl is very proud. Questioned by the consul about her family, she tells him that they are of good origin, but that, her father having died, as a geisha (dancing-girl) she has to support herself and her mother. She is but fifteen and very sweet and tender-hearted.

When in procession her relations come up, they all do obeisance to Pinkerton. They are all jealous of Butterfly's good luck and prophesy an evil end, but the girl perfectly trusts and believes in her lover and even confides to him that she has left her own gods, to pray henceforth to the God of her husband.

When Pinkerton begins to show her their house, she produces from her sleeve her few precious belongings. These are some silken scarfs, a little brooch, a looking-glass, and a fan; also a long knife, which she at once hides in a corner of the house. Goro tells Pinkerton that it is the weapon with which her father performed hara-kiri (killed himself). The last things she shows her lover are some little figures representing the souls of her ancestors.

When the whole assembly is ready, they are married by the commissary. Pinkerton treats his relations to champagne, but soon the festival is interrupted by the dismal howls of Butterfly's uncle, the bonze (Buddhist monk), who climbs the hill and tells the relations that the wretched bride has denied her faith, and has been to the mission-house, to adopt her husband's religion. All turn from her with horror and curse her. But Pinkerton consoles his weeping wife, and the act closes with a charming love-duet.

The second act shows Butterfly alone. Pinkerton has left her, and she sits dreamily with her faithful maid Suzuki, who vainly implores her gods to bring back the faithless husband. The young wife, who has been waiting three long years for his return, still firmly believes his promise to come back when the robin should build its nest. She refuses a proposal of marriage from Prince Yamadori, who has loved her for years, and now tries again to win the forsaken wife. She answers him with quiet dignity, that, though by Japanese law a wife is considered free as soon as her husband has left her, she considers herself bound by the laws of her husband's country, and Yamadori leaves her.

Sharpless now enters with a letter he has received from Pinkerton. Not daring to let her know its contents at once, he warns her that her husband will never return, and advises her to accept Prince Yamadori's offer. Butterfly is at first startled and alarmed, but soon she recovers herself, and beckoning to Suzuki, she shows Sharpless her little fair-haired, blue-eyed boy, begging the consul to write and tell her husband that his child is awaiting him.

Sharpless, deeply touched, takes leave of her, without having shown the letter, when Suzuki enters screaming and accusing Goro, who has goaded her to fury, by spreading a report in the town that the child's father is not known.

"You lie, you coward!" cries Butterfly, seizing a knife to kill the wretch. But suppressing her wrath she throws away the weapon and kicks him from her in disgust. Suddenly a cannon-shot is heard. Running on to the terrace, Butterfly perceives a war-ship in the harbor, bearing the name "Abraham Lincoln." It is Pinkerton's ship.

All her troubles are forgotten; she bids her maid gather all the flowers in the garden; these she scatters around in profusion. Then she brings her boy, and bids Suzuki comb her hair, while she herself rouges her pale cheeks and those of her child. Then they sit down behind a partition, in which they have made holes, through which they may watch the ship and await Pinkerton's arrival.

The third act finds them in the same position. Suzuki and the child have fallen asleep, while Butterfly, sleepless, watches for Pinkerton. Suzuki waking sees that it is morning and begs her mistress to take some rest. Butterfly, taking her child in her arms, retires into the inner room.

A loud knock is heard, and Suzuki finds herself in the presence of Sharpless and Pinkerton. The latter signs to her not to waken Butterfly. Suzuki is showing him the room adorned with flowers for his arrival, when she suddenly perceives a lady walking in the garden and hears that she is Pinkerton's lawful American wife.

Sharpless, taking the maid aside, begs her to prepare her mistress for the coming blow and tells her that the foreign lady desires to adopt her husband's little boy. Pinkerton himself is deeply touched by the signs of Butterfly's undying love. Full of remorse, he entreats Sharpless to comfort her as best he can, and weeping, leaves the scene of his first love-dream.

His wife Kate returning to the foot of the terrace, sweetly repeats her wish to adopt the little boy, when Butterfly, emerging from the inner room, comes to look for her long-lost husband, whose presence she feels with the divination of love. Seeing Sharpless standing by a foreign lady, and Suzuki in tears, the truth suddenly bursts upon her. "Is he alive?" she asks, and when Suzuki answers "yes," she knows that he has forsaken her.

Turned to stone, she listens to Kate's humble apologies and to her offer to take the child. By a supreme effort she controls herself. "I will give up my child to him only; let him come and take him; I shall be ready in half an hour," she answers brokenly.

When Sharpless and Kate have left her, Butterfly sends Suzuki into another room with the child. Then, seizing her father's long knife, she takes her white veil, throwing it over the folding screen. Kissing the blade, she reads its inscription, "Honorably he dies who no longer lives in honor," and raises it to her throat. At this moment the door opens, and her child runs up to his mother with outstretched arms. Snatching him to her bosom, she devours him with kisses, then sends him into the garden. Seizing the knife once more, Butterfly disappears behind the screen, and shortly afterward the knife is heard to fall.

When Pinkerton's call, "Butterfly," is heard, she emerges once more from the background and drags herself to the door; but there her strength fails her and she sinks dead to the ground.

MANON

Opera in four acts by Jules Massenet. Text by Meilhac and Gille.

THE subject of this opera is based on Prévost's famous novel "Manon Lescaut." The scene is laid in France in 1721.

The first act takes place in the courtyard of a large inn at Amiens. Several young cavaliers are amusing themselves by paying attentions to three pretty ladies. They impatiently call upon their host to bring dinner, and at last it is brought to them in great state.

While they are dining in the large saloon above, the stage-coach arrives with a large number of travelers; among them is young Manon, a country girl of sixteen; this is her first journey, and is to end in a convent, an arrangement made by her parents, who think her taste for worldly pleasures is greater than it should be. She is expected by her cousin Lescaut, of the Royal Guard, and while he is looking for her luggage, the young beauty is accosted by Guillot Marfontaine, an old roué and rich farmer, who annoys her with his equivocal speeches and offers her a seat in his carriage. He is quickly driven away by Lescaut on his return; the young man is, however, enticed away by his comrades to play a game of cards, for which purpose he leaves his cousin a second time. Before long another cavalier approaches Manon; this time it is the Chevalier des Grieux, a young nobleman, whose good looks and charming manners please the young girl much better. They quickly fall in love with each other, and when Des Grieux offers to take her to Paris, Manon gladly consents, thankful to escape the convent. Remembering Guillot's offer, she proposes to make use of the farmer's carriage, and they drive gaily off just before Lescaut returns to look for his cousin. When this worthy soldier hears that the fugitives have gone off in Guillot's carriage, he abuses the farmer with great fury and swears that he will not rest until he shall have found his little cousin.

The second act takes place in a poorly-furnished apartment in Paris. Des Grieux is about to write to his father, whom he hopes to reconcile to his purpose of marrying Manon by telling him of the girl's beauty, of her youth and innocence. They are interrupted by the entrance of Lescaut, who, accompanied by De Brétigny, another victim of Manon's charms, comes to avenge the honor of the family. While Des Grieux takes Lescaut aside and pacifies him by showing him the letter he has just written, De Brétigny tells Manon that her lover will be kidnapped this very evening by his father's orders. Manon protests warmly against this act of tyranny, but De Brétigny warns her that her interference would only bring greater harm to both of them, while riches, honors, and liberty will be hers if she lets things take their course.

Manon, who on the one hand sincerely loves Des Grieux, while on the other hand she has a longing for all the good things of this world, is very unhappy, but allows herself to be tempted. When Des Grieux leaves her to post his letter she takes a most tender farewell of the little table at which they have so often sat, of the one glass from which they both drank, and of all the objects around. Des Grieux, finding her in tears, tries to console her by picturing the future of his dreams, a little cottage in the wood where they are to live forever happy and contented. A loud knock interrupts them; Manon, knowing what will happen, tries to detain him, but he tears himself from her and, opening the door, is at once seized and carried off.

The third act opens on the promenade Cour-la-Reine in Paris, a scene of merry-making where all the buying, selling, and amusements of a great fair are going on. The pretty ladies of the first act, Yavotte, Poussette, and Rosette, are being entertained by new lovers, while rich old Guillot looks in vain for a sweetheart.

Manon, who appears on De Brétigny's arm, is the queen of the festival. She has stifled the pangs of conscience which had troubled her when she left Des Grieux, and her passion for jewels and riches is as insatiable as ever. Guillot, who hears that De Brétigny has refused to comply with her last wish, which is to order the ballet of the grand opera to dance in the open market-place for her own amusement, rushes off to pay for this whim himself, hoping thereby to gain the young lady's favor.

Manon slowly wanders about in search of new and pretty things to buy, while De Brétigny suddenly finds himself face to face with the old Count des Grieux. When he asks for news of his son the Count tells him that the young man has renounced the world and become an abbé and is a famous preacher at St.-Sulpice. He cuts De Brétigny's expressions of astonishment short by telling him that this turn of things is due to De Brétigny's own conduct, meaning that the latter had done a bad turn to his friend by crossing his path in relation to a certain pretty young lady. De Brétigny, indicating his lady-love by a gesture, says, "That is Manon," and the Count, perceiving her beauty, quite understands his son's infatuation.

But Manon's quick ears have also caught bits of the conversation, and beckoning to her lover she sends him away to buy a golden bracelet for her. She then approaches the Count and asks if his son has quite overcome his passion for the lady who, she says, was a friend of hers. The old man acknowledges that his son had had a hard struggle with his love and grief, but adds, "One must try and forget," and Manon repeats the words and falls into a fit of sad musing.

Meanwhile Guillot has succeeded in bringing the ballet-dancers, who perform a beautiful gavotte and other dances. When these are ended he turns to Manon in hope of a word of praise, but the willful beauty only turns from him to order her carriage, which is to take her to St.-Sulpice, saying lightly to Guillot that she has not cared to look at the ballet after all.

The next scene takes place in the parlor of the seminary in St.-Sulpice. A crowd of ladies has assembled to praise the new abbé's fine preaching. They at last disperse when the young abbé enters with downcast eyes. He is warmly greeted by his father, who has followed him. The father at first tries to persuade him to give up his newly chosen vocation before he finally takes the vows, but, seeing him determined, the Count hands him over his mother's inheritance of 30,000 livres and then bids him good-by. The young man retires to find strength and forgetfulness in prayer.

When he returns to the parlor he finds Manon. She has also prayed fervently that God would pardon her and help her to win back her lover's heart. A passionate scene ensues in which Manon implores his forgiveness and is at last successful. Des Grieux opens his arms to her and abandons his vocation.

The fourth act opens in the luxurious drawing-rooms of a great Paris hotel. Games of hazard and lively conversation are going on everywhere. Manon, arriving with Des Grieux, is joyously greeted by her old friends. She coaxes her lover to try his luck at play and is seconded by her cousin Lescaut, himself an inveterate gambler, who intimates that fortune always favors a beginner. Guillot offers to play with Des Grieux, and truly fortune favors him. After a few turns, in which Guillot loses heavily, the latter rises, accusing his partner of false play.

The Chevalier, full of wrath, is about to strike him, but the others hold him back and Guillot escapes, vowing vengeance. He soon returns with the police headed by the old Count des Grieux, to whom he denounces young Des Grieux as a gambler and a cheat and points out Manon as his accomplice. Old Count des Grieux allows his son to be arrested, telling him he will soon be released. Poor Manon is seized by the guards, though all the spectators, touched by her youth and beauty, beg for her release. The old Count says she only gets her deserts.

The last scene takes place on the high road leading to Havre. Cousin Lescaut meets Des Grieux, whom he promised that he would try to save Manon from penal servitude by effecting her escape. Unfortunately the soldiers he employed had meanly deserted him, on hearing which Des Grieux violently upbraids him. Lescaut pacifies the desperate nobleman by saying that he has thought of other means of rescuing Manon. Soon the wagons conveying the convicts to their destination are heard approaching. One of these wagons stops. Lescaut, accosting one of the soldiers in charge, hears that Manon is inside, dying. He begs that he may be allowed to take a last farewell of his little cousin, and bribing the man with money, he succeeds in getting Manon out of the wagon, promising to bring her to the nearest village in due time.

Manon, sadly changed, totters forward and finds herself clasped in her lover's arms. For a little while the two forget all their woes in the joy of being together; Manon deeply repents of her sins and follies and humbly craves his pardon, while he covers her wan face with kisses. Then he tries to raise her, imploring her to fly with him, but alas! release has come too late; she sinks back and expires in her lover's embrace.

MANRU

Opera in three acts by Ignace Jan Paderewski.
Text by Nossig.

THE scene is laid in the Hungarian Tatra mountain district.

Manru, a wandering gypsy, has fallen in love with a peasant girl, Ulana, and has married her against her mother's wishes.

In the first act mother Hedwig laments her daughter's loss. While the village lasses are dancing and frolicking, Ulana returns to her mother to ask her forgiveness; she is encouraged by a hunchback, Urok, who is devoted to her, and who persuades the mother to forgive her child, on condition that she shall leave her husband. As Ulana refuses, though she is in dire need of bread, Hedwig sternly shuts her door upon her daughter. Ulana turns to Urok, who does his best to persuade her to leave her husband.

Urok is a philosopher; he warns the poor woman that gypsy blood is never faithful, and that the time will come when Manru will leave wife and child. Ulana is frightened. Finally she obtains from Urok a love-potion, by which she hopes to secure her husband's constancy.

When she tries to turn back into the mountains, she is surrounded by the returning villagers, who tease and torment her and the hunchback until Manru comes to their rescue. But his arrival only awakes the villagers' wrath. They fall upon him, and are about to kill him, when mother Hedwig comes out and warns them not to touch the outlaws on whom her curse has fallen.

The second act takes place in Manru's hiding-place in the mountains. The gypsy is tired of the idyl. He longs for freedom, and quarrels with his wife, whose sweetness bores him. She patiently rocks her child's cradle and sings him to rest. Suddenly Manru hears the tones of a gypsy fiddle in the distance. He follows the sound, and soon returns with an old gypsy, who does his best to lure him back to his tribe. But once more love and duty prevail; and when Ulana sweetly presents him the love-potion he drains it at one draught. Immediately feeling the fire of the potent drug, he becomes cheerful, and receives his wife, who has adorned herself with a wreath of flowers, with open arms.

In the third act Manru rushes out of the small close hut. His intoxication is gone; he gasps for air and freedom. Wearily he stretches himself on the ground and falls asleep. The full moon shines on him and throws him into a trance, during which he rises to follow the gypsy tribe, whose songs he hears. In this state he is found by Asa, the gypsy Queen, who loves him and at once claims him as her own.

But the tribe refuse to receive the apostate, and Oros, their chief, pronounces a terrible anathema against him. However, Asa prevails with her tribe to pardon Manru. Oros in anger flings down his staff of office and departs, and Manru is elected chief in his place. Once more he hesitates, but Asa's beauty triumphs; he follows her and his own people.

At this moment Ulana appears. Seeing that her husband has forsaken her, she implores Urok, who has been present during the whole scene, to bring Manru back to her. Alas! it is in vain. When Ulana sees Manru climbing the mountain path arm in arm with Asa, she drowns herself in the lake.

But Manru does not enjoy his treachery. Oros, hidden behind the rocks, is on the watch for him, and tearing Asa from him, he precipitates his rival from the rocks into the lake.

In this opera Paderewski has shown great skill in his treatment of the story, which conveys the spirit of his people as expressed in their songs and dances, and reveals the weird nature of the wandering tribes whose music he likewise adapts with telling effect. In his choice of the subject, no less than in the handling of it, he displays a true talent for dramatic work.

MARTHA

Comic Opera in four acts by Friedrich von Flotow. Text by St. George and Friedrich.

LADY HARRIET DURHAM, tired of the pleasures and splendors of court, determines to seek elsewhere for pastime, and hoping to find it in a sphere different from her own, disguises herself and her confidante Nancy as peasant girls, in which garb they visit the fair at Richmond, accompanied by Lord Tristan, who is hopelessly enamored of Lady Harriet and unwillingly complies with her wish to escort them to the adventure in the attire of a peasant. They join the servant girls who are there to seek employment and are hired by a tenant, Plunkett, and his foster-brother Lionel, a youth of somewhat extraordinary behavior, his air being noble and melancholy and much too refined for a country squire, while the other, though somewhat rough, is frank and jolly in his manner.

The disguised ladies take the handsel from them without knowing that they are bound by it, until the sheriff arrives to confirm the bargain. Now the joke becomes reality and they hear that they are actually hired as servants for a whole year.

Notwithstanding Lord Tristan's protestations, the ladies are carried off by their masters, who know them under the names of Martha and Julia.

In the second act we find the ladies in the company of the tenants, who set them instantly to work. Of course they are totally ignorant of household work, and as their wheels will not go round, Plunkett shows them how to spin. In his rough but kind way he always commands and turns to Nancy, with whom he falls in love, but Lionel only asks softly when he wishes anything done. He has lost his heart to Lady Harriet and declares his love to her. Though she is pleased by his gentle behavior, she is by no means willing to accept a country squire and wounds him by mockery. Meanwhile Plunkett has sought Nancy for the same purpose, but she hides herself, and at last the girls are sent to bed very anxious and perplexed at the turn their adventure has taken. But Lord Tristan comes to their rescue in a coach and they take flight, vainly pursued by the tenants. Plunkett swears to catch and punish them, but Lionel sinks into deep melancholy from which nothing can arouse him.

In the third act we meet them at a court hunt, where they recognize their hired servants in two of the lady hunters. They assert their right, but the ladies disown them haughtily, and when Lionel, whose reason almost gives way under the burden of grief and shame which overwhelms him at thinking himself deceived by Martha, tells the whole story to the astonished court, the ladies pronounce him insane and Lord Tristan sends him to prison for his insolence, notwithstanding Lady Harriet and Nancy's prayer for his pardon.

Lionel gives a ring to Plunkett, asking him to show it to the Queen, his dying father having told him that it would protect him from every danger.

In the fourth act Lady Harriet feels remorse for the sad consequences of her haughtiness. She visits the prisoner to crave his pardon. She tells him that she has herself carried his ring to the Queen and that he has been recognized by it as Lord Derby's son, once banished from court, but whose innocence is now proved.

Then the proud lady offers hand and heart to Lionel, but he rejects her, believing himself duped. Lady Harriet, however, who loves Lionel, resolves to win him against his will. She disappears, and dressing herself and Nancy in the former peasant's attire she goes once more to the fair at Richmond, where Lionel is also brought by his friend Plunkett. He sees his beloved Martha advance toward him, promising to renounce all splendors and live only for him; then his melancholy vanishes, and he weds her, his name and possessions being restored to him, while Plunkett obtains the hand of pretty Nancy, alias Julia.

MASANIELLO, or LA MUETTE DE PORTICI
(The Dumb Girl of Portici)

Opera in five acts by Daniel F. E. Auber.
Text by Scribe.

IN the first act we witness the wedding of Alfonso, son of the viceroy of Naples, with the Spanish princess Elvira. Alfonso, who has wronged Fenella, the Neapolitan Masaniello's dumb sister, and abandoned her, is tormented by doubts and remorse, fearing that she has committed suicide. During the festival Fenella rushes in to seek protection from the viceroy, who has kept her a prisoner for the past month. She has escaped from her prison and narrates the story of her undoing by gestures, showing a scarf which her lover gave her. Elvira promises to protect her and proceeds to the altar, Fenella vainly trying to follow. In the chapel Fenella recognizes her betrayer in the bridegroom of Elvira. When the newly married couple come out of the church, Elvira presents Fenella to her husband and discovers from the dumb girl's gestures that he was her faithless lover. Fenella flees, leaving Alfonso and Elvira in sorrow and despair.

In the second act the fishermen, who have been brooding in silence over the tyranny of their foes, begin to assemble. Pietro, Masaniello's friend, has sought for Fenella in vain, but at length she appears of her own accord and confesses her wrongs. Masaniello is infuriated and swears to have revenge, but Fenella, who still loves Alfonso, does not mention his name. Then Masaniello calls the fishermen to arms and they swear perdition to the enemy of their country.

In the third act we find ourselves in the market-place in Naples where the people go to and fro, selling and buying, all the while concealing their purpose under a show of merriment and carelessness. Selva, the officer of the viceroy's bodyguard, from whom Fenella has escaped, discovers her, and the attempt to rearrest her is the sign for a general revolt, in which the people are victorious.

In the fourth act Fenella comes to her brother's dwelling and describes the horrors which are taking place in the town. The relation fills his noble soul with sorrow and disgust. When Fenella has retired to rest, Pietro enters with comrades and tries to excite Masaniello to further deeds, but he only wants liberty and shrinks from murder and cruelties.

They tell him that Alfonso has escaped and that they are resolved to overtake and kill him. Fenella, who hears all, decides to save her lover. At this moment Alfonso begs at her door for a hiding-place. He enters with Elvira, and Fenella, though at first disposed to avenge herself on her rival, pardons her for Alfonso's sake. Masaniello, reëntering, assures the strangers of his protection, and even when Pietro denounces Alfonso as the viceroy's son he holds his promise sacred. Pietro, with his fellow-conspirators, leaves him full of rage and hatred. Meanwhile the magistrate of the city presents Masaniello with the royal crown and he is proclaimed King of Naples.

In the fifth act we find Pietro with the other fishermen before the viceroy's palace. He confides to Moreno that he has administered poison to Masaniello in order to punish him for his treason and that the King of one day will soon die. While he speaks Borella rushes in to tell of a fresh troop of soldiers marching against the people with Alfonso at their head. Knowing that Masaniello alone can save them, the fishermen entreat him to take the command of them once more, and Masaniello, though deadly ill and half bereft of his reason, complies with their request. The combat takes place while an eruption of Vesuvius is going on. Masaniello falls in the act of saving Elvira's life. On hearing these terrible tidings Fenella rushes to the terrace, from which she leaps into the abyss beneath, while the fugitive noblemen again take possession of the city.

MEFISTOFELE

Opera in four acts, with prologue and epilogue, by Arrigo Boito.

IN the prologue Mefistofele is commanded to visit the earth, where he is to tempt the doctor and philosopher Faust, who is self-satisfied in his own wisdom. The cherubim prostrate themselves before the Most High, and the voices of repentant sinners are heard in prayer. Angelic voices swell the chorus, which is full of beauty and strength.

The first act takes us to Frankfort on a festival day. Bells are ringing in merry chorus. Soldiers, students, and peasants mingle in the crowd, cheering as the elector appears. The peasants take partners for the dance, and Faust enters with Wagner, a student. In the crowd they observe a friar, clad in a gray robe, and strangely sinister in appearance. Wherever they go they find him at Faust's elbow. Finally Faust declares that it must be the devil. To escape the man, Faust returns to his study, but Mefistofele—for the friar is none other—stands in a dark corner awaiting him. Faust apostrophizes Nature, and, soothed by pastoral musings, opens his Bible. The fiend, with a loud scream, shows himself, but recovering, answers Faust's questions as to his identity and his business there, by proclaiming himself as the Evil One. His gray robe falls from him, and he appears richly dressed. He is ready to do Faust's bidding in exchange for his soul. On his magic cloak he carries the philosopher away.

In the second act we see Faust and Marguerite walking arm in arm in a garden, while Mefistofele makes violent love to Martha, Marguerite's mother, who is greatly flattered. The lovers wander off under the trees, and forget time and space, until Mefistofele reminds Faust that they must leave. The scene changes to the Brocken. It is the Witches' Sabbath. The witches dance and sing in weird revelry; they make incantations, bringing before Faust a realistic picture of Marguerite's sorrowful fate. Mefistofele receives from them a crystal ball, which he balances on his hand, saying, "Behold the earth." To the sound of diabolic music the witches disappear.

Act third shows Marguerite in prison. She has been convicted of killing her child, and is about to be executed. She becomes insane, calling upon God for pardon. Faust appears to take her away, but she scarcely understands his words. The day breaks, and Mefistofele summons Faust to depart, just as Marguerite falls back dead. Angelic voices chant of pardon and peace.

In the fourth act we are taken to the banks of a river in Greece. Here Faust and Mefistofele meet Pantalis and Helen of Troy, to whom Faust makes ardent love. Helen dramatically describes the fall of Troy, and the tragic events to which it gave rise. A change of scene introduces the epilogue. Faust is in his study considering his past life, which he regrets bitterly. Mefistofele, appearing once more, offers to transport him on his cloak anywhere he desires to go. Faust refuses to accompany him, and angel voices are heard as in the prologue and in the third act. Baffled, the fiend surrounds Faust with voluptuous women, who tempt him with every art in their power. Once more the philosopher opens his Bible, and therein reads that the vilest sinner if repentant can be saved. He prays fervently for protection from evil, and dies. Roses cover his body in token of Heaven's forgiveness. Mefistofele vanishes, utterly discomfited. In a magnificent finale angelic voices proclaim that the powers of evil are vanquished, and Faust receives his pardon.

DIE MEISTERSINGER VON NURNBERG
(The Mastersingers of Nuremberg)

Opera in three acts by Richard Wagner.

IN the first act we see St. Catherine's Church in Nuremberg, where divine service is being celebrated in preparation for St. John's day. Eva, the lovely daughter of Master Pogner the jeweler, sees the young knight Walther von Stolzing, who has fallen in love with Eva and who has sold his castle in Franconia to become a citizen of Nuremberg. She tells him that her hand is promised to the winner of the prize in the mastersingers' contest, to be held on the following morning.

We are now called to witness one of those ancient customs still sometimes practised in old German towns. The mastersingers appear and the apprentices prepare everything needful for them. Walther asks one of them, called David, an apprentice of Hans Sachs, what he will have to do in order to compete for the prize. He has not learned poetry as a profession like those worthy workmen, and David vainly tries to initiate him into their old-fashioned rhyming. Walther leaves him, determined to win the prize after his own fashion.

Pogner appears with Beckmesser the clerk, who has the wish to be his son-in-law. Beckmesser is so infatuated that he does not doubt of his success. Meanwhile Walther comes up to them, entreating them to admit him into their corporation as a mastersinger.

Pogner consents, but Beckmesser grumbles, not at all liking to have a nobleman among them. When all are assembled, Pogner declares his intention of giving his daughter to the winner of the contest on the day of St. John's festival, and all applaud his resolution. Eva herself may refuse him, but never is she to wed another than a crowned mastersinger. Sachs, who loves Eva as his own child, seeks to change her father's resolution, at the same time proposing to let the people choose in the matter of the prize, but he is silenced by his colleagues. They now want to know where Walther has learned the art of poetry and song, and as he designates the book of Walther von der Vogelweide, they shrug their shoulders.

He begins at once to give a proof of his art, praising Spring in a song thrilling with melody. Beckmesser interrupts him; he has marked the rhymes on the black tablet, but they are new and unintelligible to this dry verse-maker, and he will not let them pass. The others share his opinion; only Sachs differs with them, remarking that Walther's song, though not after the old rules of Nuremberg, is justified all the same, and so Walther is allowed to finish it, which he does with a bold mockery of the vain poets, comparing them to crows oversounding a singing-bird. Sachs alone feels that Walther is a true poet.

In the second act David the apprentice tells Magdalene, Eva's nurse, that the new singer did not succeed, at which she is honestly grieved, preferring the gallant younker for her mistress to the old and ridiculous clerk. The old maid loves David; she provides him with food and sweets, and many are the railleries which he has to suffer from his companions in consequence.

Evening coming on, we see Sachs in his open workshop; Eva, his darling, is in confidential talk with him. She is anxious about to-morrow, and rather than wed Beckmesser she would marry Sachs, whom she loves and honors as a father. Sachs is a widower, but he rightly sees through her schemes and resolves to help the lovers.

It has now grown quite dark and Walther comes to see Eva, but they have not sat long together when the sounds of a lute are heard.

It is Beckmesser trying to serenade Eva, but Sachs interrupts him by singing himself, and thus excites Beckmesser's wrath and despair. At last a window opens and Beckmesser, taking Magdalene for Eva, addresses her in louder and louder tones, Sachs all the time beating the measure on a shoe. The neighboring windows open, there is a general alarm, and David, seeing Magdalene at the window apparently listening to Beckmesser, steals behind this unfortunate minstrel, and begins to slap him. In the uproar which now follows, Walther vainly tries to escape from his refuge under the lime-tree, but Sachs comes to his rescue and takes him into his own workshop, while he pushes Eva unseen into her father's house, the door of which has just been opened by Pogner.

In the third act we find Sachs in his room. Walther enters, thanking him heartily for the night's shelter. Sachs kindly shows him the rules of poetry, encouraging him to try his luck once more. Walther begins and quite charms Sachs with his love-song. After they have left the room, Beckmesser enters and, reading the poetry which Sachs wrote down, violently charges the shoemaker with wooing Eva himself. Sachs denies it and allows Beckmesser to keep the paper. The latter, who has vainly ransacked his brains for a new song, is full of joy, hoping to win the prize with it.

When he is gone Eva slips in to get her shoes, and she sees Walther stepping out of his dormitory in brilliant array. He has found a third stanza to his song, which he at once produces. They all proceed to the place where the festival is to be held, and Beckmesser is the first to try his fortunes, which he does by singing the stolen song. He sadly muddles both melody and words, and being laughed at, he charges Sachs with treachery, but Sachs quietly denies the authorship, pushing forward Walther, who now sings his stanzas inspired by love and poetry. It is needless to say that he wins the hearers' hearts as he has won those of Eva and Sachs, and that Pogner does not deny him his beloved daughter's hand.

MIGNON

Opera in three acts by Ambroise Thomas.
Text by Barbier and Carré, based on Goethe's "Wilhelm Meister."

THE first two acts take place in Germany. Lothario, a half-demented old man, poorly clad as a wandering minstrel, seeks his lost daughter Sperata. Mignon comes with a band of gypsies, who abuse her because she refuses to dance. Lothario advances to protect her, but Jarno, the chief of the troop, only scorns him, until a student, Wilhelm Meister, steps forth and rescues her, a young actress named Philine compensating the gypsy for his loss by giving him all her loose cash. Mignon, grateful for the rescue, falls in love with Wilhelm and wants to follow and serve him, but the young man, though delighted with her loveliness and humility, is not aware of her love. Nevertheless he takes her with him. He is of good family, but by a whim just now stays with a troop of comedians, to whom he takes his protégée.

The coquette Philine loves Wilhelm and has completely enthralled him by her arts and graces. She awakes bitter jealousy in Mignon, who tries to drown herself but is hindered by the sweet strains of Lothario's harp, which appeal to the noble feelings of her nature. The latter always keeps near her, watching over the lovely child. He instinctively feels himself attracted toward her; she recalls his lost daughter to him and he sees her as abandoned and lonely as himself. Mignon, hearing how celebrated Philine is, wishes that the palace, within which Philine plays, might be struck by lightning, and Lothario at once sets the house on fire.

While the guests rush into the garden, Philine orders Mignon to bring her nosegay, the same flowers which the thoughtless youth offered to his mistress Philine. Mignon, reproaching herself for her sinful wish, at once flies into the burning house, and only afterward does her friend Laertes perceive that the theater has caught fire too. Everybody thinks Mignon lost, but Wilhelm, rushing into the flames, is happy enough to rescue her.

The third act carries us to Italy, where the sick Mignon has been brought. Wilhelm, having discovered her love, which she reveals in her delirium, vows to live only for her. Lothario, no longer a minstrel, receives them as the owner of the palace, from which he had been absent since the loss of his daughter. While he shows Mignon the relics of the past, a scarf and a bracelet of corals are suddenly recognized by her. She begins to remember her infantine prayers, she recognizes the hall with the marble statues and her mother's picture on the wall. With rapture Lothario embraces his long-lost Sperata. But Mignon's jealous love has found out that Philine followed her, and she knows no peace until Wilhelm has proved to her satisfaction that he loves her best.

At last Philine graciously renounces Wilhelm and turns to Friedrich, one of her many adorers, whom to his own great surprise she designates as her future husband. Mignon at last openly avows her passion for Wilhelm. The people, hearing of the arrival of their master, the Marquis of Cipriani, alias Lothario, come to greet him with loud acclamations of joy, which grow still louder when he presents to them his daughter Sperata and Wilhelm, her chosen husband.

NORMA

Tragic Opera in two acts by Vincenzo Bellini.
Text by Romani.

NORMA, daughter of Orovist, chief of the druids and high priestess herself, has broken her vows and secretly married Pollio, the Roman proconsul. They have two children. But Pollio's love has vanished. In the first act he confides to his companion Flavius that he is enamored of Adalgisa, a young priestess in the temple of Irminsul, the druids' god.

Norma, whose secret nobody knows but her friend Clotilde, is worshiped by the people, being the only one able to interpret the oracles of their god. She prophesies Rome's fall, which she declares will be brought about not by the prowess of Gallic warriors but by its own weakness. She sends away the people to invoke alone the benediction of the god. When she also is gone, Adalgisa appears, and is persuaded by Pollio to flee with him to Rome. But remorse and fear induce her to confess her sinful love to Norma, whom she, like the others, adores. Norma, however, seeing the resemblance to her own fate, promises to release her from her vows and give her back to the world and to happiness, but hearing from Adalgisa the name of her lover, who just then approaches, she of course reviles the traitor, telling the poor young maiden that Pollio is her own spouse. The latter defies her, but she bids him leave. Though as he goes he begs Adalgisa to follow him, the young priestess turns from the faithless lover and craves Norma's pardon for the offense she has unwittingly been guilty of.

In the second act Norma, full of despair at Pollio's treason, resolves to kill her sleeping boys. But they awake and the mother's heart shudders as she thinks of her purpose; then she calls for Clotilde and bids her bring Adalgisa.

When she appears Norma entreats her to be a mother to her children and to take them to their father Pollio, because she has determined to free herself from shame and sorrow by a voluntary death. But the noble-hearted Adalgisa will not hear of this sacrifice. She promises to bring Pollio back to his first love. After a touching duet, in which they swear eternal friendship to each other, Norma takes courage again. Her hopes are vain, however, for Clotilde enters to tell her that Adalgisa's prayers were of no avail. Norma, distrusting her rival, calls her people to arms against the Romans and gives orders to prepare the funeral pile for the sacrifice. The victim is to be Pollio, who was captured in the act of carrying Adalgisa off by force. Norma orders her father and the Gauls away that she may speak alone with Pollio, to whom she promises safety if he will renounce Adalgisa and return to her and to her children. But Pollio, whose only thought is of Adalgisa, pleads for her and for his own death. Norma, denying it to him, calls the priests of the temple to denounce as victim a priestess, who, forgetting her sacred vows, has entertained a sinful passion in her bosom and betrayed the gods. Then she firmly tells them that she herself is this faithless creature, but to her father alone does she reveal the existence of her children.

Pollio, recognizing the greatness of her character, which impels her to sacrifice her own life in order to save him and her rival, feels his love for Norma revive, and stepping forth from the crowd of spectators, he takes his place beside her on the funeral pile. Both commend their children to Norma's father Orovist, who finally pardons the poor victims.

LE NOZZE DI FIGARO
(The Marriage of Figaro)

Comic Opera in four acts by Wolfgang Amadeus Mozart. Text by Da Ponte.

COUNT ALMAVIVA, though married to Rosina and loving her ardently, cannot bring himself to cease playing the rôle of a gallant cavalier; he likes pretty women wherever he finds them, and notwithstanding his high moral principles, is carrying on a flirtation with Rosina's maid, the charming Susanna. This does not hinder him from being jealous of his wife, who is here represented as a character both sweet and passive. He suspects her of being overfond of her page, Cherubino. From the bystanders, Doctor Bartolo and Marcellina, we hear that their old hearts have not yet ceased to glow at the touch of youth and love; Bartolo would fain give his affections to Susanna, while Marcellina pretends to have claims on Figaro. These are the materials which are so dexterously woven into the complicated plot and furnish so many funny passages.

In the second act we find Cherubino in the rooms of the Countess, who, innocent and pure herself, sees in him only a child; but this youth has a passionate heart and he loves his mistress ardently. Mistress and maid have amused themselves with Cherubino, putting him into women's dresses. The Count, rendered suspicious by a letter, given to him by Basilio, bids his wife open her door. The women, afraid of his jealousy, detain him a while, and only open the door when Cherubino has got safely through the window and away over the flower-beds. The Count, entering full of wrath, finds only Susanna with his wife. Ashamed of his suspicions, he asks her pardon and swears never to be jealous again. All blame in the matter of the letter is put on Figaro's shoulders, but this cunning fellow lies boldly, and the Count cannot get the clue to the mystery. Figaro and Susanna, profiting by the occasion, entreat the Count at last to consent to their wedding, which he has always put off. At this moment the gardener Antonio enters, complaining of the spoiled flower-beds. Figaro, taking all upon himself, owns that he sprang out of the window, having had an interview with Susanna and fearing the Count's anger. All deem themselves saved, when Antonio presents a document which the fugitive has lost. The Count, not quite convinced, asks Figaro to tell him the contents; but the latter, never at a loss, and discovering that it is the page's patent, says that the document was given to him by the page, the seal having been forgotten. The Count is about to let him off, when Bartolo appears with Marcellina, who claims a matrimonial engagement with Figaro. Her claim is favored by the Count, who wishes to see Susanna unmarried. Out of this strait, however, they are delivered by finding that Figaro is the son of the old couple, the child of their early love; and all again promises well. But the Countess and Susanna have prepared a little punishment for the jealous husband as well as for the flighty lover.

They have both written letters in which they ask the men to an interview in the garden. Susanna's letter goes to the Count, Rosina's to Figaro. Under cover of night each of the two women meets her own lover, but Susanna wears the Countess's dress, while Rosina has arrayed herself in Susanna's clothes.

The Countess, not usually given to such tricks, is very anxious. While she awaits her husband, Cherubino approaches, and taking her for Susanna he, like a little Don Juan as he is, makes love to her. Hearing the Count's steps, he disappears. Almaviva caresses the seeming Susanna, telling her nice things and giving her a ring, which she accepts. They are observed by the other couple, and the sly Figaro, who has recognized Susanna notwithstanding her disguise, denounces the Count to her, vows eternal love, and generally makes his bride burn with wrath. In her anger she boxes his ears, upon which he confesses to having known her from the first, and at once restores her good humor.

Seeing the Count approach, they continue to play their former rôles, and the false Countess makes love to Figaro, till the Count accosts her as "traitress." For a while she lets him suffer all the tortures of jealousy, then the lights appear and the Count stands ashamed before his lovely wife, recognizing his mistake. The gentle Countess forgives him, and the repenting husband swears eternal fidelity. He speedily unites the lovers Figaro and Susanna, and forgives even the little page Cherubino.

DIE NÜRNBERGER PUPPE
(The Nuremberg Doll)

Comic Opera in one act by Adolphe Charles Adam. Text by Leuven and Beauplan.

THE scene takes place in a toy-shop at Nuremberg. Cornelius, the owner, has an only son, Benjamin, whom he dearly loves notwithstanding his stupidity; while he is most unjust to his orphan nephew, Heinrich, whom he keeps like a servant after having mis-appropriated the latter's inheritance.

The old miser wants to procure a wife for his dar-ling, a wife endowed with beauty and every virtue; and as he is persuaded that such a paragon does not exist in life, he has constructed a splendid doll which he hopes to endow with life by the help of Doctor Faust's magic-book.

He only awaits a stormy night for executing his de-sign. Meanwhile he enjoys life, and when presented to us is just going with Benjamin to a masked ball, after sending at the same time his nephew supperless to bed. When they have left, Heinrich reappears in the garb of Mephistopheles. He claps his hands and his fiancée Bertha, a poor seamstress, soon enters.

Sadly she tells her lover that she is unable to go to the ball, having given all her money, which she had meant to spend on a dress, to a poor starving beggar-woman in the street.

Heinrich, touched by his love's tender heart, good-humoredly determines to lay aside his mask, in order to stay at home with Bertha, when suddenly a bright idea strikes him. Remembering the doll, which his uncle hides so carefully in his closet, which has, how-ever, long been spied out by Heinrich, he shows it to Bertha, who delightedly slips into the doll's beautiful clothes, which fit her admirably.

Unfortunately Cornelius and his son are heard re-turning while Bertha is still absent dressing. The night has grown stormy, and the old man deems it favorable for his design; so he at once proceeds to open Faust's book and to begin the charm.

Heinrich, who has hardly had time to hide himself in the chimney, is driven out by his cousin's attempts to light a fire. He leaps down into the room and the terrified couple take him for no other than the devil in person, Heinrich wearing his mask and being besides blackened by soot from the chimney. Perceiving his uncle's terror, he profits by it, and at once beginning a conjuration he summons the doll, that is to say, Bertha in the doll's dress. Father and son are delighted by her performances, but when she opens her mouth and reveals a very willful and wayward character, Corne-lius is less charmed. The doll peremptorily asks for food, and Mephistopheles indicates that it is to be found in the kitchen. While the worthy pair go to bring it, Mephistopheles, hastily exchanging words with his lady-love, vanishes into his sleeping-room.

The doll now begins to lead a dance which makes the toymaker's hair stand on end. She first throws the whole supper out of the window, following it with plate, crockery, toys, etc. Then, taking a drum, she begins to drill them, slapping their ears, mouths, and cheeks as soon as they try to approach her.

At last, when they are quite worn out, she flies into the closet. But now the father's spirit is roused, he resolves to destroy his and the devil's work; however, he is hindered by Heinrich, who now makes his ap-pearance and seems greatly astonished at the uproar and disorder he finds in the middle of the night. He only wants to gain time for Bertha to undress and then escape.

Resolutely the old man walks into the closet to slay the doll. But he returns pale and trembling, having destroyed her while asleep and believing to have seen her spirit escape through the window with fiendish laughter. Yet, awed by his deed, he sees Heinrich re-turning, who confesses to his uncle that he has found out his secret about the doll, and that, having acciden-tally broken it, he has substituted a young girl. Cor-nelius, half dead with fright, sees himself already ac-cused of murder; his only salvation seems to lie in his nephew's silence and instant flight. Heinrich is will-ing to leave the country provided his uncle give him back his heritage, which consists of 10,000 thalers. After some vain remonstrances the old man gives him the gold. Heinrich, having gained his ends, now intro-duces Bertha, and the wicked old fool and his son see too late that they have been the dupes of the clever nephew.

OBERON

Romantic Opera in three acts by Karl Maria von Weber.
English text by Planché.

IN the first act we find Oberon, the elf-king, in deep melancholy, which no gaiety of his subjects, however charming, avails to remove. He has quarreled with his wife Titania, and both have vowed never to be reconciled until they find a pair of lovers faithful to each other in all kinds of adversity. Both long for the reunion, but the constant lovers are not to be found.

Oberon's most devoted servant is little Puck, who has vainly roved over the world to find what his master needs. He has, however, heard of a valiant knight in Burgundy, Huon, who has killed Carloman, the son of Charlemagne, in a duel, having been insulted by him. Charlemagne, not willing to take his life for a deed of defense, orders him to go to Bagdad, to slay the favor-ite, sitting to the left of the Calif, and to wed the Calif's daughter Rezia. Puck resolves to make this pair suit his ends. He tells Oberon the above-men-tioned story, and by means of his lily-scepter shows Huon and Rezia to him. At the same time these two behold each other in a vision, so that when they awake both are deeply in love.

Oberon wakes Huon and his faithful shield-bearer Scherasmin, and promises his help in every time of need. He presents Huon with a magic horn, which will summon him at any time; Scherasmin receives a cup, which fills with wine of itself. Then he immediately transports them to Bagdad.

There we find Rezia with her Arabian maid Fatima. The Calif's daughter is to wed Babekan, a Persian prince, but she has hated him ever since she saw Huon in her vision. Fatima has discovered the arrival of Huon. It is high time, for in the beginning of the second act we see the Calif with Babekan, who wants to celebrate the nuptials at once. Rezia enters, but at the same time Huon advances, recognizing in Rezia the fair one of his dream. He fights and stabs Babekan. The Turks attack him, but Scherasmin blows his magic horn and compels them to dance and laugh, until the fugitives have escaped.

In the forest they are overtaken, but Huon and Scherasmin, who has come after his master with Fati-ma, put the pursuers to flight.

Oberon now appears to the lovers, and makes them promise upon oath that they will remain faithful to each other under every temptation. He immediately after transports them to the port of Ascalon, from which they are to sail homeward. Oberon now puts their constancy to the proof. Puck conjures up the nymphs and the spirits of the air, who raise an awful tempest. Huon's ship sinks; the lovers are shipwrecked. While Huon seeks for help, Rezia is captured by the pirates, and Huon, returning to save her, is wounded and left senseless on the beach. Oberon now causes him to fall into a magic sleep, which is to last seven days.

In the third act we find Scherasmin and his bride, Fatima, in Tunis dressed as poor gardeners. A corsair has saved the shipwrecked and sold them as slaves to the Emir of Tunis. Though poor and in captivity, they do not lose courage and are happy that they are permitted to bear their hard lot together.

Meanwhile the seven days of Huon's sleep have passed. Awaking, he finds himself, to his astonishment, in Tunis, in the Emir's garden, with his servant beside him, who is not less astonished at finding his master.

Fatima, coming back, relates that she has discovered Rezia in the Emir's harem. Huon, who finds a nosegay with a message which bids him come to the myrtle-bower during the night, believes that it comes from Rezia and is full of joy at the idea of meeting his bride. Great is his terror when the lady puts aside her veil and he sees Roschana, the Emir's wife. She has fallen in love with the noble knight, whom she saw in the garden, but all her desires are in vain; he loathes her and is about to escape, when Emir enters, captures him, and sentences him to be consumed by fire. Roschana is to be drowned. Rezia, hearing of her lover's fate, implores the Emir to pardon him. But she has already offended him by her unwillingness to listen to his protestations of love, and when he hears that Huon is her husband, he condemns them to be burned together. Their trials, however, are nearing their end. Scherasmin has regained his long-lost horn, by means of which he casts a spell on everybody, until, blowing it with all his might, he calls Oberon to their aid. The elf-king appears accompanied by Queen Titania, who is now happily reconciled to him, and thanking the lovers for their constancy, he brings them safely back to Paris, where Charlemagne holds his court. The Emperor's wrath is now gone and he warmly welcomes Sir Huon with his lovely bride, promising them honor and glory for their future days.

ORFEO ED EURIDICE

Opera in three acts by Christoph Willibald Gluck.
Text by Calzabigi.

ORFEO (Orpheus), the Greek legendary musician and singer, has lost his wife Euridice. His mournful songs fill the groves where he laments, and with them he touches the hearts not only of his friends but of the gods. On his wife's grave Amor appears to him and bids him descend into Hades, where he is to move the Furies and the Elysian shadows with his sweet melodies, and win back from them his lost wife.

He is to recover her on a condition, which is, that he never casts a look on her on their return to earth; for if he fails in this, Euridice will be forever lost to him.

Taking his lyre and casque Orfeo promises obedience, and with new hope sallies forth on his mission. The second act represents the gates of Erebus, from which flames arise. Orfeo is surrounded by furies and demons, who try to frighten him; but he, nothing daunted, mollifies them by his sweet strains and they set free the passage to Elysium, where Orfeo has to win the happy shadows. He beholds Euridice among them, veiled; the happy shadows readily surrender her to him, escorting the pair to the gates of their happy vale.

The third act beholds the spouses on their way back to earth. Orfeo holds Euridice by the hand, drawing the reluctant wife on, but without raising his eyes to her face; on and on through the winding and obscure paths which lead out of the infernal regions. Notwithstanding his protestations of love and his urgent demands to her to follow him, Euridice never ceases to implore him to cast a single look on her, threatening him with her death should he not fulfill her wish. Orfeo, forbidden to tell her the reason of his strange behavior, long remains deaf to her cruel complaints, but at last he yields and looks back, only to see her expire under his gaze. Overwhelmed by grief and despair Orfeo draws his sword to destroy himself, when Amor appears and stays the fatal stroke.

In pity for Orfeo's love and constancy he reanimates Euridice (contrary, however, to the letter of the Greek tragedy), and the act closes with a beautiful chorus sung in Amor's praise.

OTELLO

Opera in four acts by Giuseppe Verdi.
Text by Boito.

THE first scene represents the people following excitedly the course of the ship that bears Otello (Othello), which battles with the waves. After he has landed and informed the assembly of his victory over the Turks, shouts of joy and exultation rend the air.

Then follows a convivial chat between Cassio, Rodrigo, and Iago, in the course of which the latter makes Cassio drunk. Iago's demoniacal nature is masterfully depicted here, where he soon succeeds in ruining Cassio, who loses his rank as captain.

In the third scene we see Desdemona with her husband, both rejoicing in the felicity of their mutual love.

In the second act Iago proceeds to carry out his evil intents, by sending Cassio to Desdemona, who is to intercede for him with Otello. Iago then calls Otello's attention to the retiring Cassio, and by making vile insinuations inflames his deadly jealousy. Desdemona appears, surrounded by women and children, who offer her flowers and presents. She comes forward to plead for Cassio, and Otello suspiciously refuses. She takes out her handkerchief to cool her husband's aching forehead with it, but he throws it down and Emilia, Iago's wife, picks it up. Iago wrenches it from her and hides it.

In the next scene Iago's villainous insinuations work upon Otello, who becomes wildly suspicious. Iago relates a dream of Cassio's, in which he reveals his love for Desdemona, then he hints that he has seen Otello's first love-token, her lace handkerchief, in Cassio's hands, and both swear to avenge Desdemona's infidelity.

In the third act Otello, pretending to have a headache, asks for Desdemona's lace handkerchief. She has lost it, she tells him, but he is incredulous and charges her with infidelity. All her protests are useless, and at length he forces her to retire. Meanwhile Iago has brought Cassio and urges Otello to hide himself. Cassio has a lady-love named Bianca, and of her they speak, but Iago dexterously turns the dialogue so as to make Otello believe that they are speaking of his wife. His jealousy reaches its climax when Cassio draws forth Desdemona's handkerchief, which Iago has deposited in Cassio's house. All his doubts now seem to be confirmed. A cannon-shot announcing the arrival of a galley interrupts the conversation and Cassio quickly leaves.

In the following scene Iago advises Otello to strangle his wife. Otello consents, and gives Iago a captaincy.

Lodovico, an ambassador of Venice, arrives, with other nobles, to greet their liberator Otello. Desdemona once more asks pardon for Cassio, but is roughly rebuked by her husband. Otello reads the order which has been brought to him, and tells Cassio that he is to be general in his stead by will of the Doge of Venice; but while Cassio is confounded by this sudden change of fortune, Iago secretly vows his death, instigating his rival Rodrigo to kill him. At last Otello faints, overcome by conflicting emotions.

In the fourth act Desdemona, filled with sad forebodings, takes a touching farewell of Emilia. When she has ended her fervent prayer (one of the most beautiful things in the opera), she falls into a peaceful slumber. Otello wakes her with a kiss, and tells her immediately thereafter that she must die. She protests her innocence, but in vain, for Otello, telling her that Cassio can speak no more, smothers her. Hardly has he completed his ghastly work than Emilia comes up, announcing that Rodrigo has been killed by Cassio. Desdemona with her dying breath once more asserts her innocence, while Emilia loudly screams for help. When the others appear, Emilia discovers her husband's villainy. Iago flees, and Otello stabs himself at the feet of his innocent spouse.

PAGLIACCI
(The Players)

Musical Drama in two acts, with a prologue, by Ruggiero Leoncavallo.

IN the prologue, a wonderful piece of music, Tonio, the clown, announces to the public the deep tragic sense which often is hidden behind a farce, and prepares them for the sad end of the lovers in this comedy.

The introduction, with its wonderful largo, is like a mournful lamentation; then the curtain opens, showing the entry of a troop of wandering actors, so common in Southern Italy. They are received with high glee by the peasants, and Canio, the owner of the troop, invites them all to the evening's play. Canio looks somewhat gloomy, and he very much resents the taunts of the peasants, who court his beautiful wife Nedda and make remarks about the clown's attentions to her. Nevertheless Canio gives way to his friends' invitation for a glass of wine, and he takes leave of his wife with a kiss, which, however, does not quite restore her peace of mind, Nedda's conscience being somewhat disturbed. But soon she casts aside all evil forebodings and vies with the birds in warbling pretty songs, which, though reminding the hearer of Wagner's Siegfried, are of surpassing harmony and sweetness. Tonio spying the moment to find Nedda alone, approaches her with a declaration of love, but she haughtily turns from him, and as he only grows more obtrusive and even tries to embrace her, she seizes a whip and slaps him in the face. Provoked to fury, he swears to avenge himself. Hardly has he turned away when the peasant Silvio appears on the wall. He is Nedda's lover, and, having seen Canio sitting in the tavern, he entreats Nedda to separate herself from the husband she never loved and take flight with him. Nedda hesitates between duty and passion, and at last the latter prevails and she sinks into his arms. This love-duet is wonderful in style and harmony. Tonio unfortunately has spied out the lovers and returns with Canio. But, on perceiving the latter's approach, Silvio has leaped over the wall, his sweetheart's body covering his own person so that Canio is unable to recognize his rival; he once more reminds Nedda to be ready that night, and then takes flight. With an inarticulate cry Canio rushes after him, and Nedda falls on her knees to pray for her lover's escape, while Tonio triumphs over her misery. The husband, however, returns defeated; panting, he claims the lover's name, and Nedda's lips remaining sealed he is about to stab his wife when Beppo (Harlequin) intervenes. Wrenching the dagger from his unfortunate master's hands, he intimates that it is time to prepare for the play. While Nedda retires Canio breaks out into a bitter wail over his hard lot, which compels him to take part in the farce, which for him is bitter reality. With this air the tragic height of the opera is reached.

In the second act the spectators throng before the small stage, each of them eager to get the best seat. Nedda appears dressed as Columbine, and while she is collecting the money she finds time to warn Silvio of her husband's wrath. The curtain opens and Nedda is seen alone on the stage listening to the sentimental songs of Harlequin, her lover in the play. Before she has given him the sign to enter, Tonio, in the play called Taddeo, the fool, enters, bringing the food which his mistress has ordered for herself and Harlequin. Just as it really happened in the morning, the poor fool now makes love to her in play; but when scornfully repulsed he humbly retires, swearing to the goodness and pureness of his lady-love. Harlequin entering through the window, the two begin to dine merrily, but Taddeo reënters, in mocking fright, to announce the arrival of the husband. Canio, however, is in terrible earnest, and when he hoarsely exacts the lover's name the lookers-on, who hitherto have heartily applauded every scene, begin to feel the awful tragedy hidden behind the comedy.

Nedda remains outwardly calm, and mockingly she names innocent Harlequin as the one who had dined with her. Then Canio begins by reminding her how he found her in the street a poor waif and stray, whom he nursed, petted, and loved, and Nedda remaining cold, his wrath rises to fury and he wildly curses her, shrieking, "The name, I will know his name!" But Nedda, though false, is no traitress. "Should it cost my life I will never betray him!" she cries, at the same time trying to save her life by hurrying from the stage among the spectators. Too late, alas! Canio already has reached and stabbed her, and Silvio, who rushes forward, also receives his death-stroke from the hands of the deceived husband, who has heard his name slip from the dying lips of his wife. All around stand petrified; nobody dares to touch the avenger of his honor, who stands by his wife's corpse limp and broken-hearted. "Go," says he, "go, the farce is ended."

PARSIFAL

Consecrational Stage Festival Drama by Richard Wagner.

THE last, and in the opinion of the composer and his family, the greatest of Wagner's compositions, was intended exclusively for the Festspielhaus in Bayreuth, where the stage equipment was especially designed to permit of complete fidelity to the master's directions as to its performance. For years "Parsifal" continued to draw pilgrims from every part of Europe and America to the little Bavarian town, and had the terms of Wagner's will been obeyed, it would have remained unknown, save to these pilgrims, until 1913. But American enterprise had not been reckoned with. Heinrich Conried, in 1903, found this work an excellent medium for drawing the attention of the whole musical world to the Metropolitan Opera House in New York. There followed litigation, protests from the Wagner family, and attacks from the pulpit, and when Conried had sold out his house with the stalls at $10, seats were sold at a premium as high as $85. Then Henry W. Savage gave an excellent production in English, and in two years' time America knew its "Parsifal" as well as its "Mikado."

The first scene is laid in a forest on the grounds of the keepers of the Grail near Castle Monsalvat. Old Gurnemanz awakes two young squires for their morning prayer, and bids two knights prepare a bath for the sick King Amfortas, who suffers cruelly from a wound, dealt him by the sorcerer Klingsor, the deadly foe of the Holy Grail. The Grail is a sacred cup, from which Christ drank at the last Passover, and which also received his blood. Titurel, Amfortas's father, has built the castle to shield it, and appointed holy men for its service. While Gurnemanz speaks with the knights about their poor master's sufferings, in rushes Kundry, a sorceress in Klingsor's service, condemned to laugh eternally as a punishment for having derided Christ while he was suffering on the cross. She it was who with her beauty seduced Amfortas and deprived him of his holy strength, so that Klingsor was enabled to wrest from the King his holy spear Longinus, with which he afterward wounded him. Kundry is in the garb of a servant of the Grail; she brings balm for the King, who is carried on to the stage in a litter, but it avails him not: "a guileless fool" with a child's pure heart, who will bring back the holy spear and touch him with it, can alone heal his wound.

Suddenly a dying swan sinks to the ground, and Parsifal, a young knight, appears. Gurnemanz reproaches him severely for having shot the bird, but he appears to be quite ignorant of the fact that it was wrong, and, when questioned, proves to know nothing about his own origin. He only knows his mother's name "Herzeleid" (heart-break), and Kundry, who recognizes him, relates that his father Gamuret perished in battle, and that his mother reared him, a guileless fool, in the desert. When Kundry mentions that his mother is dead and has sent her last blessing to her son, Parsifal is almost stunned by this, his first grief. Gurnemanz conducts him to the castle, where the Knights of the Grail are assembled in a lofty hall. Amfortas is laid on a raised couch, and from behind Titurel's voice is heard imploring his son to efface his guilt in godly works. Amfortas, writhing with pain, is comforted by the prophecy:

By pity lightened, the guileless fool—
Wait for him—my chosen tool.

The Grail is uncovered, the blessing given, and the repast of love begins. Amfortas's hope revives, but toward the end his wound bursts out afresh. Parsifal, on hearing Amfortas's cry of agony, clutches at his heart, without, however, understanding his own feelings.

The second act reveals Klingsor's magic castle. Kundry, not as a demon now, but as a woman of imperious beauty, is awakened by Klingsor to seduce Parsifal. She yearns for pardon, for sleep and death, but she struggles in vain against the fiendish Klingsor.

The tower gradually sinks; a beautiful garden rises, into which Parsifal gazes with rapture and astonishment. Lovely maidens rush toward him, accusing him of having destroyed their lovers. Parsifal, surprised, answers that he slew them because they checked his approach to their charms. But when their tenderness waxes hotter he gently repulses the damsels and at last tries to escape. He is detained, however, by Kundry, who tells him again of his beloved mother, and when Parsifal is sorrow-stricken at having forgotten her in his thoughtless rambles, she consoles him, pressing his lips with a fervent kiss. This rouses the dreamy youth, he awakes to his duty, he feels the King's spear-wound burning; the unconscious fool is a fool no longer, but conscious of his mission and distinguishing right from wrong. He calls to the Saviour to save him from a guilty passion, and at last he starts up, spurning Kundry. She tells him of her own crime, of Amfortas's fall, and curses all paths and ways which would lead him from her. Klingsor, appearing at her cry, flings the holy spear at Parsifal, but it remains floating over his head, and the youth, grasping it, destroys the magic by the sign of the cross.

In the third act Gurnemanz awakes Kundry from a deathlike sleep, and is astonished to find her changed. She is penitent and serves the Grail. Parsifal enters from the woods. Gurnemanz recognizes and greets him, after his wanderings in search of the Grail, which have extended over long years. Kundry washes his feet and dries them with her own hair. Parsifal, seeing her so humble, baptizes her with water from the spring, and the dreadful laugh is taken from her; then she weeps bitterly. Parsifal, conducted to the

King, touches his side with the holy spear, and the wound is closed. Old Titurel, brought on the stage in his coffin, revives once more a moment, raising his hands in benediction. The Grail is revealed, pouring a halo of glory over all. Kundry, with her eyes fixed on Parsifal, sinks dead to the ground, while Amfortas and Gurnemanz render homage to their new King.

PAUL AND VIRGINIA

Romantic Opera in three acts by Victor (Félix Marie) Massé.
Text by Barbier and Carré.

THE opera begins with a scene in the cottage of Marguerite, Paul's mother. She and Mme. de la Tour, mother of Virginia, are discussing their children, who have always been like brother and sister, but are now unconsciously drifting into a deeper feeling. Marguerite talks of sending Paul to India for a time. Domingues, a trusted slave, starts up, protesting. Laughter and shouts are heard, when a ship from France is sighted; Mme. de la Tour hurries off, thinking it may bear news of the forgiveness of a wealthy aunt. Domingues talks of Paul and Virginia, wondering what changes the money will cause, and, as a storm arises, goes to seek the young people, who presently enter, laughing, shielded from the storm by a great banana-leaf, held above their heads. Virginia seats herself; Paul throws himself on a rug at her feet. As they innocently sing of their love and innocent pleasures, Meala, another slave, enters, footsore and weary. She is wounded by the lash of a whip. Virginia gives her food. They cannot keep an escaped slave, so Virginia offers to intercede for her with her master.

The scene changes to the plantation of St. Croix. St. Croix appears, followed by two huge negroes with whips. He kicks and cuffs the slaves, and orders bloodhounds set on Meala's track. She enters with Paul and Virginia. Virginia, kneeling at his feet, sweetly asks his forgiveness for the slave. St. Croix, moved by her girlish beauty, grants what she asks, with a mental reservation. They turn to depart. St. Croix asks them to stay and rest after their long walk. The negroes sing, dance, and play for their amusement. Meala now sings alone, and in her song warns Paul that Virginia will be in danger if she stays, as St. Croix is drinking heavily. They hurry away. St. Croix, in a rage, turns on Meala and orders her to be lashed while she can stand. He drinks himself into a stupor. Meala screams wildly, and St. Croix, rousing himself, orders the slaves to sing louder to drown her voice. Then follows an *entr'acte* in the forest.

The second act brings us to the house of Mme. de la Tour. Virginia is arrayed in festival attire and decked with jewels. Domingues sits on the floor, weaving a mat. Virginia's mother hands her a mirror. Domingues, shaking his head, declares that the gold will bring sorrow. Virginia is to go to France, and she is overcome with grief because she now realizes her love for Paul. Domingues advises her in a song not to go. Paul is at the door. He enters, but does not recognize the grand young lady before him as Virginia. She remains silent as he reproaches her, then hurries away. Marguerite, calling Paul, tells him that there is a stain upon his birth. They decide to depart forever. Meala warns them of the coming of St. Croix, who now appears. Virginia, entering, buys Meala from him with some of the gold. Meala warns Paul to keep watch, or St. Croix will carry Virginia off. A change of scene shows a fountain beneath the trees; sea in the distance. Virginia enters, singing a joyous song, then falls asleep, while Meala hums a lullaby. Virginia sees in a vision the planter's house in flames. The governor brings an order from the king for Virginia's deportation. They waken her, and she is swiftly carried to the ship.

The third act opens on the seashore. Paul, now melancholy, stands looking out to sea. He is half-crazed by grief. His mother is in despair. Paul receives a letter, in which Virginia tells of her loneliness and love for him. He sees in a vision a ballroom, with Virginia dancing a minuet, amid splendid surroundings. Her harp is brought in; she sings and her voice is wafted to her lover. He sings in unison with her, begging her to sing once more. Their voices seem to mingle regardless of intervening space. St. Croix appears in the room beside her; she repulses him, and refuses his hand. Paul is entranced, and tells Domingues what he has seen. A ship is seen on the horizon approaching the island. A storm arises, causing it to be wrecked. Paul hears Virginia calling him, and at last her body is washed up on the shore at his feet.

PELLÉAS ET MÉLISANDE

Opera in five acts by Claude Debussy.
Text adapted from Maeterlinck's play.

GOLAUD, a grandson of King Arkel, meets Mélisande while wandering in the woods. A coronet she has worn has dropped into a well, but though she cries bitterly, she will not let Golaud fish it out; nor will she tell her name or country, although dressed like a princess, if somewhat in tatters. Golaud takes the maiden to the castle where he lives with Arkel, the old Queen Genevieve, and Yniold, his son by a wife some time deceased. Six months later Golaud, contrary to a family compact, makes Mélisande his wife, and takes her away, then writes to Pelléas, his half-brother, begging him to intercede with the old King, and effect a reconciliation. Genevieve reads this letter to Arkel, and they agree to welcome home the eloping lovers. Pelléas and Mélisande meet for the first time in the castle garden when the latter returns as Golaud's bride.

In the second act Pelléas and Mélisande are disclosed chatting together near a well, into which Mélisande drops her wedding ring. Instead of telling her husband the truth when he misses the ring, Mélisande tells Golaud that she has lost it in a cavern by the sea. Golaud sends her to look for the ring, with Pelléas to guard her from danger. But the moon shines brightly as they wander together on the sands, and the two are taken in a pitfall of which the trusting husband had not dreamed.

In the third act Golaud surprises Pelléas, who is passionately kissing Mélisande's hair, which is of luxuriant growth, and streams down to him from the balcony where she stands. By way of warning, he takes Pelléas through dungeons of the castle, suggestive of death and suffering, then commands him to avoid Mélisande in future.

The next scene is at night. Golaud learns from Yniold that Pelléas and Mélisande still meet. Raising the child in his arms so that he can look into Mélisande's room, Golaud ascertains that even then Pelléas and Mélisande are together.

In the fourth act Pelléas, at last realizing that he loves his brother's wife, tells Mélisande that he is going away on a long journey. Then, as Arkel is expressing his sympathy to Mélisande, and deploring the dullness of her surroundings, Golaud enters, bitterly reproaches Mélisande for her misconduct, and swings her about by her long hair. The next scene is devoted to a childish soliloquy by Yniold, but the action is soon resumed. Pelléas and Mélisande again meet, and again he avows his determination to go away. A mutual confession of love follows, and as Golaud enters they are locked in each other's arms. Drawing his sword, Golaud strikes down Pelléas, then starts in pursuit of Mélisande, who has fled.

The fifth act takes place in Mélisande's apartment in the castle. Mélisande has been lying in a stupor, following a delirium in which she has given birth to a child. Golaud knows that she is dying, and reproaches himself for his violence. When Mélisande regains consciousness, he begs her forgiveness, which she readily grants. Then he implores her to tell him if her relations with Pelléas were innocent, and if she really loved the dead man. To this she replies that she loved him, but that they were innocent. Still Golaud is tormented by doubt, which can never be resolved; for a moment later, when Mélisande's child is brought to her, she is dead.

PHILÉMON ET BAUCIS

Opera in two acts by Charles François Gounod.
Text by Barbier and Carré.

IN the first act Jupiter comes to Philémon's hut, accompanied by Vulcan, to seek refuge from a storm, which the god himself has caused. He has come to earth to verify Mercury's tale of the people's badness, and finding the news only too true, besides being uncourteously received by the people around, he is glad to meet with a kindly welcome at Philémon's door.

This worthy old man lives in poverty, but in perfect content with his wife Baucis, to whom he has been united in bonds of love for sixty years. Jupiter, seeing at once that the old couple form an exception to the evil rule, resolves to spare them, and to punish only the bad folks. The gods partake of the kind people's simple meal, and Jupiter, changing the milk into wine, is recognized by Baucis, who is much awed by the discovery. But Jupiter reassures her and promises to grant her only wish, which is, to be young again with her husband and to live the same life. The god sends them to sleep, and then begins the intermezzo.

Phrygians are seen reposing after a festival, bacchants rush in and the wild orgies begin afresh. The divine is mocked and pleasure praised as the only god. Vulcan comes, sent by Jupiter to warn them, but as they only laugh at him, mocking Olympus and the gods, Jupiter himself appears to punish the sinners.

An awful tempest arises, sending everything to wrack and ruin.

In the second act Philémon's hut is changed into a palace; he awakes to find himself and his wife young again. Jupiter, seeing Baucis's beauty, orders Vulcan to keep Philémon apart, while he courts her. Baucis, though determined to remain faithful to her Philémon, feels, nevertheless, flattered at the god's condescension, and dares not refuse him a kiss. Philémon, appearing on the threshold, sees it, and violently reproaches her and his guest, and, though Baucis suggests who the latter is, the husband does not feel in the least inclined to share his wife's love even with a god. The first quarrel takes place between the couple, and Vulcan, hearing it, consoles himself with the reflection that he is not the only one to whom a fickle wife causes sorrow. Philémon bitterly curses Jupiter's gift; he wishes his wrinkles back, and with them his peace of mind. Throwing down Jupiter's statue, he leaves his wife to the god. Baucis, replacing the image, which happily is made of bronze, sorely repents her behavior toward her beloved husband. Jupiter finds her weeping, and praying that the gods may turn their wrath upon herself alone. The god promises to pardon both if she is willing to listen to his love. She agrees to the bargain, on condition that Jupiter shall grant her a favor. He consents, and she entreats him to make her old again. Philémon, listening behind the door, rushes forward to embrace the true wife and joins his entreaties to hers. Jupiter, seeing himself caught, would fain be angry, but their love conquers his wrath. He does not recall his gift, but giving them his benediction he promises never more to cross their happiness.

THE PIPE OF DESIRE

Romantic Opera in one act by Frederick S. Converse.
Text by Barton.

THIS opera, the first work of an American composer to be accepted for performance during the regular season of the Metropolitan Opera House, was produced there in 1910. Its first actual performance, with full stage accessories, took place January 31, 1906, in Boston. The book is highly poetic, the music admirably descriptive.

In a mountain glade, closed in by forest and rocks, through which one catches a glimpse of the valley below, the elves sing a joyous hymn, for it is spring, and the flowers are budding. Iolan, a peasant much beloved by the elves, is seen approaching, and they determine that he shall witness their festivities. It is madness, the Old One, their king, tells them, but on the first day of spring their wishes are supreme.

Iolan thinks he must be dreaming as the fairy folk surround him, but he returns their expressions of good will, and shows them a purse containing the gold with which he means to buy a farm. Then he will wed Naoia, and he invites them all to the feast. The Old One alone is gloomy, and when the elves tell Iolan that this is the mightiest of them all, he cannot understand. "Ten thousand years of life my crown," says the Old One, in explanation, "the earth my purse of gold, this Pipe, which hangs about my neck, the scepter of the world."

In accordance with their annual custom, the elves demand that the Old One pipe for them, that they may dance. He protests, but is obliged to grant their request, and the elves dance merrily. But Iolan is not in the least awed by the Pipe. Any other would have served as well, he thinks, and he declares that no power on earth or in heaven can make him dance, save with his promised bride. The elves compel the Old One to play the Pipe again, and Iolan is forced to dance. The elves jeer at him for doubting the potency of the charm, but in revenge he wrests the Pipe from the Old One, and the mirth of the elves instantly changes to terror. They offer him wealth and power if he will return this sacred instrument, for, says the Old One, "it is the Pipe God gave to Lilith and she played to man in Eden, but its charm was rent by woman." Still Iolan will not heed the warning. The Old One pronounces accursed the mortal that dares to sound the Pipe, but Iolan replies by blowing a harsh note, at which the elves, screaming with fear, retire into hiding.

Again Iolan sounds the Pipe, and as he does so, sees the vision of his utmost wish—a farm lying in a peaceful valley, and wife and children waiting to welcome him. "Naoia," he cries, "leave all! leave all and come to me."

Regaining possession of the Pipe, the Old One says, "The Pipe but played the note of your desire," and disappears. Now Iolan sees his beloved arise from bed, and, obeying his command, race toward him, dashing through streams, scaling the rocks, sometimes falling, but always coming on, on, until at last she joins her lover, trembling and exhausted. The curse is soon fulfilled, for Naoia's journey has been too much for human endurance. She dies. Maddened at this great loss, Iolan scatters the gold with which he had meant to buy a home for his bride, and cries aloud, "There is no God, and I am all alone!"

"There is a God," the Old One says, "whose laws unchanging no man may hope to disobey. Upon his Pipe you blew your one desire, forced your own will upon the ordained way. Man has his will, man pays the penalty." Iolan is about to strike the Old One with his staff, but stays his arm as the Old One says, "Strike, if you think her soul demands revenge."

The elves, who have ruined the mortal they wished to befriend, are grief-stricken. The Old One, at their petition, now plays the Song of Autumn. The season changes. The leaves are falling from the trees, and Iolan breathes his last in peace beside the body of his beloved. As the curtain falls, the elves are chanting "Nothing is wasted, nothing is wasted."

POIA

Opera in three acts by Arthur Finley Nevin.
Text by Hartley.

THIS opera will go down in history as the first American work of its kind to be produced in a foreign opera house. It was given at the Royal Opera House, Berlin, in 1910. It was first performed in concert form in Pittsburg, January 16, 1907.

The book is based on legends of Indian origin, and the action takes place among the Blackfeet Indians at a time prior to the coming of the white race.

Poia, whose name means scar-face, is so called because of the birthmark which disfigures him. He loves the daughter of a chief, Natoya, but she scorns his ugliness, preferring Sumatsi, a warrior who is bold and handsome and wicked. To banish the unwelcome wooer, she tells Poia that unless he can free himself from his disfigurement she can never wed him. Nenahu, the medicine woman, tells Poia that only the Sun God can remove this blemish, and then warns Sumatsi that only evil can result from a union with Natoya. But Natoya gladly accepts the gifts of Sumatsi, and neither heeds the warning. Poia goes forth to seek the Sun God.

When the curtain rises on the second act, Poia, in the midst of a forest, prays to the Sun God, but Natosi scorns him, even as the maiden had. Just then Poia rescues the morning star, Episua, who has been attacked by eagles, and this heroic deed avails him where prayer has failed. Poia sinks into a profound sleep, and Mola, Nepu, Moku, and Stuyi, the four seasons, dance about him at the god's behest, giving him manly beauty in place of ugliness. Natosi invites the young warrior to dwell with him among the gods, but Poia thinks of Natoya, and refuses. Then is the god enraged; but again he softens when Poia has told his story, and in the end he sends Poia back to his people with a rich robe for Natoya. And Episua is his guiding star, while Wolf Trail (the Milky Way) teaches him a song which shall command the love of woman, and presents to him a magic whistle.

In the last act we return with Poia to the camp of the Blackfeet. Poia, whose scar symbolized his mystic attributes as the scapegoat of his people, finds that troubles have come upon them in his absence, and that the people blame Natoya for driving him away. The infatuation of the maiden for Sumatsi has, indeed, grown deeper in Poia's absence, but though an impassioned love-scene is revealed between the two, the moment Natoya hears Poia's magic song in the distance, she loves the singer and hates Sumatsi. The young warrior is welcomed as the savior of his tribe. Natoya alone seems cold. She fears him because of the present he had brought from the Sun God, for the robe can be worn only by a pure woman, and Natoya is no longer pure. Sumatsi, mad with jealousy, tries to kill Poia, but Natoya intervenes, and receives the fatal blow. A ray from the Sun God slays the wicked Sumatsi, then Poia, raising the dying maiden in his arms, declares that her sacrifice has made her pure. He invests her with the sacred robe, and together they are wafted to the realms of the Sun God.

THE POSTILION OF LONGJUMEAU

Comic Opera in three acts by Adolphe Charles Adam.
Text by Leuven and Brunswick.

CHAPELOU, stage-driver at Longjumeau, is about to celebrate his marriage with the young hostess of the post-house, Madeleine. The wedding has taken place and the young bride is led away by her friends, according to an old custom, while her bridegroom is held back by his comrades, who compel him to sing.

He begins the romance of a young postilion, who had the luck to be carried away by a princess, having touched her heart by his beautiful playing on the cornet. Chapelou has such a fine voice that the superintendent of the Grand Opera at Paris, the Marquis de Courcy, who hears him, is enchanted, and being in search of a good tenor, succeeds in winning over Chapelou, who consents to leave his young wife in order to follow the Marquis's call to glory and fortune. He begs his friend Bijou, a wheelwright, to console Madeleine by telling her that he will soon return to her. While Madeleine calls for him in tenderest accents, he drives away with his protectors, and Bijou delivers his message, determined to try his fortune in a similar way. The desperate Madeleine resolves to fly from the unhappy spot, where everything recalls to her her faithless husband.

In the second act we find Madeleine under the assumed name of Mme. de Latour. She has inherited a fortune from an old aunt, and makes her appearance in Paris, as a rich and noble lady, with the intention of punishing her husband, whom she, however, still loves. During these six years that have passed since their wedding day, Chapelou has won his laurels under the name of St. Phar, and is now the first tenor of the Grand Opera and everybody's spoiled favorite. Bijou is with him as leader of the chorus, and is called Alcindor. We presently witness a comical rehearsal in which the principal singers are determined to do as badly as possible. They all seem hoarse and, instead of singing, produce the most lamentable sounds. The Marquis de Courcy is desperate, having promised this representation to Mme. de Latour, at whose country-seat near Fontainebleau he is at present staying. As soon as St. Phar hears the name of this lady his hoarseness is gone and all sing their best. We gather from this scene that Mme. de Latour has succeeded in enthralling St. Phar; he has an interview with her, and won by his protestations of love, she consents to marry him.

St. Phar, not wishing to commit bigamy, begs his friend Bijou to perform the marriage ceremony in a priest's garb, but Mme. de Latour locks him in her room along with Bourdon, the second leader of the chorus, while a real priest unites the pair for the second time.

St. Phar enters the room in high spirits, when his companions, beside themselves with fear, tell him that he has committed bigamy. While they are in mortal terror of being hanged, Mme. de Latour enters in her former shape as Madeleine, blows out the candle, and torments St. Phar, assuming now the voice of Mme. de Latour, now that of Madeleine. After she has sent her fickle husband into an abyss of unhappiness and fear, the Marquis de Courcy, who had himself hoped to wed the charming widow, appears with the police to imprison the luckless St. Phar, who already considers himself as good as hanged, and in imagination sees his first wife Madeleine rejoicing over his punishment. But he has been made to suffer enough, and at the last moment Madeleine explains everything, and Chapelou obtains her pardon.

Both in text and music this opera, which is decidedly French in all respects, deserves to be ranked among the best works of its class thus far produced.

LE PROPHÈTE
(The Prophet)

Opera in five acts by Giacomo Meyerbeer.
Text by Scribe.

THE scene is laid in Holland at the time of the wars with the Anabaptists. Fides, mother of the hero, John of Leyden, keeps an inn near Dordrecht. She has just betrothed a young peasant girl to her son, but Bertha is a vassal of the Count of Oberthal and dares not marry without his permission.

As they set about getting his consent to the marriage, three Anabaptists, Jonas, Mathisen, and Zacharias, appear, exciting the people with their speeches and false promises. While they are preaching, Oberthal enters, but smitten with Bertha's charms he refuses his consent to her marriage and carries her off, with Fides as companion.

In the second act we find John waiting for his bride. As she delays, the Anabaptists try to win him for their cause, they prophesy him a crown, but as yet he is not ambitious, and life with Bertha looks sweeter to him than the greatest honors. As the night comes on, Bertha rushes in to seek refuge from her pursuer, from whom she has fled. Hardly has she hidden herself when Oberthal enters to claim her. John refuses his assistance, but when Oberthal threatens to kill his mother he gives up Bertha to the Count, while his mother, whose life he has saved at such a price, asks God's benediction on his head. Then she retires for the night, and the Anabaptists appear once more, again trying to win John over. This time they succeed. Without a farewell to his sleeping mother, John follows the Anabaptists, to be henceforth their leader, their Prophet-King.

In the third act we see the Anabaptists' camp; their soldiers have captured a party of noblemen, who are to pay ransom. They all make merry and the famous ballet on the ice forms part of the amusements. In the background we see Münster, now in the hands of Count Oberthal's father, who refuses to surrender it to the enemy. They resolve to storm it, a resolution which is heard by young Oberthal, who has come disguised to the Anabaptists' camp in order to save his father and the town.

But as a light is struck he is recognized and is about to be killed, when John hears from him that Bertha has escaped. She sprang out of the window to save her honor, and falling into the stream, was saved. When John learns this, he bids the soldiers spare Oberthal's life that he may be judged by Bertha herself.

John has already endured great pangs of conscience at seeing his party so wild and bloodthirsty. He refuses to go farther, but, hearing that an army of soldiers has broken out of Münster to destroy the Anabaptists, he rallies. Praying fervently to God for help and victory, inspiration comes over him and is communicated to all his adherents, so that they resolve to storm Münster. They succeed, and in the fourth act we are in the midst of this town, where we find Fides, who, knowing that her son has turned Anabaptist, though not aware of his being their Prophet, is receiving alms to save his soul by masses. She meets Bertha, disguised in a pilgrim's garb. Both vehemently curse the Prophet, when this latter appears to be crowned in state.

His mother recognizes him, but he disowns her, declaring her mad, and by strength of will he compels the poor mother to renounce him. Fides, in order to save his life, avows that she was mistaken and she is led to prison.

In the last act we find the three Anabaptists, Jonas, Mathisen, and Zacharias, together. The Emperor is near the gates of Münster, and they resolve to deliver their Prophet into his hands in order to save their lives.

Fides has been brought into a dungeon, where John visits her to ask her pardon and to save her. She curses him, but his repentance moves her so that she pardons him when he promises to leave his party. At this moment Bertha enters. She has sworn to kill the false Prophet, and she comes to the dungeon to set fire to the gunpowder hidden beneath it. Fides detains her, but when she recognizes that her bridegroom and the Prophet are one and the same person, she wildly denounces him for his bloody deeds and stabs herself in his presence. Then John decides to die also, and after the soldiers have led his mother away, he himself sets fire to the vault.

Then he appears at the coronation banquet, where he knows that he is to be taken prisoner. When Oberthal, the bishop, and all his treacherous friends are assembled, he bids two of his faithful soldiers close the gates and flee. This done, the castle is blown into the air with all its inhabitants. At the last moment Fides rushes in to share her son's fate, and all are thus buried under the ruins.

I PURITANI
(The Puritans)

Opera in three acts by Vincenzo Bellini.
Text by Pepoli.

THE action takes place in England during the Great Rebellion. Lord Walton, who has promised the hand of his daughter Elvira to Ricardo, is in command of Plymouth for the Puritans. But the girl loves Arturo, a young noble who has adhered to the house of Stuart. Giorgio, brother of Lord Walton, brings his niece the news that her father has agreed that she shall marry Arturo, who is now admitted to the fortress. Within the walls is Henrietta Maria, widow of Charles I, who is under sentence of death. Arturo assists the august prisoner to escape, disguised as Elvira. Believing that she has been deserted by her lover, Elvira becomes insane. Meantime Arturo, proscribed by Parliament, is in grave danger. Giorgio then appeals to the generosity of Ricardo, who agrees that he will induce the Parliamentary leaders to pardon Arturo, provided he is taken unarmed. Arturo returns to the fortress to explain his disappearance to Elvira, and is captured. The news of his pardon arrives in time, however, and the young people are restored to happiness.

The music of this opera is considered by good judges of this form of composition to belong with Bellini's best achievements. It is rich in varied melodies, and the chorus of Puritans, with which the first act concludes, is full of strength and animation.

DAS RHEINGOLD
(The Rhinegold)

First Division of the Music-Drama "Der Ring des Nibelungen" (The Ring of the Nibelungs) by Richard Wagner.

AS first conceived, Wagner's great "festival play in three days" was a trilogy based on the mythology of the Norse and German peoples. As was usual with him, Wagner took a poet's liberties with the old legends. "Das Rheingold," written as the result of an afterthought, to serve as a "fore-evening," made of the group a tetralogy—"Das Rheingold," "Die Walküre," "Siegfried," and "Götterdämmerung"—which stands as the most perfect embodiment of Wagner's art-theories, and, with the exception of "Parsifal," his last work.

The first scene is laid in the very depths of the Rhine, where we see three nymphs frolicking in the water. They are the guardians of the Rhinegold, which glimmers on a rock.

Alberich, a Nibelung, highly charmed by their grace and beauty, tries to make love to each one of them alternately. As he is an ugly dwarf, they at first allure and then deride him, gliding away as soon as he comes near, and laughing at him. Discovering their mockery at last, he swears vengeance. He sees the Rhinegold shining brightly, and asks the nymphs what it means. They tell him of its wonderful qualities, which would render the owner all-powerful if he should form it into a ring and forswear love.

Alberich, listening attentively, all at once climbs the rock, and before the frightened nymphs can cry for help, has grasped the treasure and disappeared. Darkness comes on; the scene changes into an open district on mountain heights. In the background we see a grand castle, which the rising sun illumines. Wotan, the father of the gods, and Fricka, his wife, are slumbering on the ground. Awakening, their eyes fall on the castle for the first time. It is Valhalla, the palace which the giants have built for them at Wotan's bidding. As a reward for their services they are to obtain Freya, the goddess of youth; but already Wotan repents of his promise and forms plans with his wife to save her lovely sister. The giants Fafner and Fasolt enter to claim their reward. While they negotiate, Loge, the god of fire, comes up, relates the history of Alberich's theft of the Rhinegold, and tells Wotan of the gold's power. Wotan decides to rob the dwarf, promising the treasure to the giants, who consent to accept it in Freya's stead. But they distrust the gods and take Freya with them as a pledge. As soon as she disappears the beautiful gods seem old and gray and wrinkled, for the golden apples to which Freya attends and of which the gods partake daily to be forever youthful, wither as soon as she is gone. Then Wotan, without any further delay, starts for Nibelheim with Loge, justifying his intention by saying that the gold is stolen property. They disappear in a cleft and we find ourselves in a subterranean cavern, the abode of the Nibelungs.

Alberich has forced his brother Mime to forge a Tarnhelm for him, which renders its wearer invisible. Mime vainly tries to keep it for himself; Alberich, the possessor of the all-powerful ring which he himself formed, takes it by force and making himself invisible strikes Mime with a whip until the latter is half dead. Wotan and Loge, hearing his complaints, promise to help him. Alberich, coming forth again, is greatly flattered by Wotan and dexterously led on to show his might. He first changes himself into an enormous snake and then into a toad. Wotan quickly puts his foot on it, while Loge seizes the Tarnhelm. Alberich, becoming suddenly visible in his real shape, is bound and led away captive. The gods return to the mountain heights of the second scene, where Alberich is compelled to part with all his treasures, which are brought by the dwarfs. He is even obliged to leave the ring, which Wotan intends to keep for himself. With a dreadful curse upon the possessor of the ring Alberich flees.

When the giants reappear with Freya, the treasures are heaped before her; they are to cover her entirely, so it is decided, and not before will she be free. When all the gold has been piled up, and even the Tarnhelm thrown on the hoard, Fasolt still sees Freya's eye shine through it, and at last Wotan, who is most unwilling to part with the ring, is induced to do so by Erda, goddess of the earth, who appears to him and warns him. Now the pledge is kept and Freya is released. The giants quarrel over the possession of the ring and Fafner kills Fasolt, thereby fulfilling Alberich's curse. With lightened hearts the gods cross the rainbow bridge and enter Valhalla, while the songs and wailings of the Rhine nymphs are heard, imploring the restitution of their lost treasure.

RIGOLETTO

Opera in three acts by Giuseppe Verdi.
Text by Piave from Victor Hugo's drama "Le roi s'amuse."

THE Duke of Mantua, a wild and debauched youth, covets every girl or woman he sees, and is assisted in his vile purposes by his jester, Rigoletto, an ugly, humpbacked man. We meet him first helping the Duke to seduce the wife of Count Ceprano, and afterward the wife of Count Monterone. Both husbands curse the vile Rigoletto and swear to be avenged. Monterone especially, appearing like a ghost in the midst of a festival, hurls such a fearful curse at them that Rigoletto shudders.

This bad man has one tender point, it is his blind love for his beautiful daughter Gilda, whom he brings up carefully, keeping her hidden from the world and shielding her from all wickedness. But the cunning Duke discovers her and gains her love under the assumed name of a student named Gualtier Maldé.

Gilda is finally carried off by Ceprano and two other courtiers, aided by her own father, who holds the ladder believing that Count Ceprano's wife is to be the victim. A mask blinds Rigoletto and he discovers, too late, by Gilda's cries that he has been duped. Gilda is brought to the Duke's palace. Rigoletto appears in the midst of the courtiers to claim Gilda, and then they hear that she, whom they believed to be his mistress, is his daughter, for whose honor he is willing to sacrifice everything. Gilda enters and, though she sees that she has been deceived, she implores her father to pardon the Duke, whom she still loves. But Rigoletto vows

vengeance, and engages Sparafucile to stab the Duke. Sparafucile decoys him into his inn, where his sister Maddalena awaits him. She too is enamored of the Duke, who makes love to her as to all young females, and she entreats her brother to have mercy on him. Sparafucile declares that he will wait until midnight, and will spare him if another victim should turn up before then. Meanwhile Rigoletto persuades his daughter to fly from the Duke's pursuit, but before he takes her away he wants to show her lover's fickleness in order to cure her of her love.

She comes to the inn in masculine attire, and, hearing the discourse between Sparafucile and his sister, resolves to save her lover. She enters the inn and is instantly put to death, placed in a sack, and given to Rigoletto, who proceeds to the river to dispose of the corpse. At this instant he hears the voice of the Duke, who passes by, singing a frivolous tune. Terrified, Rigoletto opens the sack and recognizes his daughter, who is yet able to tell him that she gave her life for that of her seducer, and then expires. With an awful cry the unhappy father sinks upon the corpse. Count Monterone's curse has been fulfilled.

ROBERT LE DIABLE
(Robert the Devil)

Opera in five acts by Giacomo Meyerbeer.
Text by Scribe and Delavigne.

ROBERT, Duke of Normandy, has a friend of gloomy exterior named Bertram, with whom he travels but to whose evil influence he owes much trouble and sorrow. Without knowing it himself, Robert is the son of this erring knight, who is an inhabitant of hell. During his wanderings on earth he seduced Bertha, daughter of the Duke of Normandy, whose offspring Robert is. This youth is very wild and has, therefore, been banished from his country. Arriving in Sicily, Isabella, the King's daughter, and he fall mutually in love.

In the first act we find Robert in Palermo surrounded by other knights, to whom a young countryman of his, Raimbaut, tells the story of "Robert de Diable" and his fiendish father; warning everybody against them. Robert, giving his name, is about to deliver the unhappy Raimbaut to the hangman, when the peasant is saved by his bride Alice, Robert's foster-sister. She has come to Palermo by order of Robert's deceased mother, who sends her last will to her son in case he should change his bad habits and prove himself worthy. Robert, feeling that he is not likely to do this, begs Alice to keep it for him. He confides in the innocent maiden, and she promises to reason with Isabella, whom Robert has irritated by his jealousy, and who has banished him from her presence.

As a recompense for her service Alice asks Robert's permission to marry Raimbaut. Seeing Robert's friend, Bertram, she recognizes the latter's likeness to Satan, whom she saw in a picture, and instinctively shrinks from him. When she leaves her master, Bertram induces his friend to try his fortune with the dice and he loses all.

In the second act we are introduced into the palace of Isabella, who laments Robert's inconstancy. Alice enters, bringing Robert's letter, and he instantly follows to crave his mistress's pardon. She presents him with a new suit of armor, and he consents to meet the Prince of Granada in mortal combat. But Bertram lures him away by deceiving him with a phantom. Robert vainly seeks the Prince in the forest, and the Prince of Granada is in his absence victorious in the tournament and obtains Isabella's hand.

The third act opens with a view of the rocks of St. Irene, where Alice hopes to be united with Raimbaut. The peasant expects his bride, but meets Bertram instead, who makes him forget Alice by giving him gold and dangerous advice. Raimbaut goes away to spend the money, while Bertram descends to the evil spirits in the deep. When Alice comes Raimbaut is gone, and she hears the demons calling for Bertram. Bertram extracts a promise from her not to betray the dreadful secret of the cavern. She clings to the Saviour's cross for protection, and is about to be destroyed by Bertram, when Robert approaches, to whom she decides to reveal all. But Bertram's renewed threats at last oblige her to leave them.

Bertram now profits by Robert's rage and despair at the loss of his bride, his wealth, and his honor to draw him on to entire destruction. He tells Robert that his rival used magic arts, and suggests that he should try the same expedient. Then he leads him to a ruined cloister, where he resuscitates the guilty nuns. They try to seduce Robert first by drink, then by gambling, and last of all by love. In the last Helena, the most beautiful of the nuns, succeeds and makes him remove the cypress-branch, a talisman, by which in the fourth act he enters Isabella's apartment unseen. He awakes his bride out of her magic sleep to carry her off, but overcome by her fears and her appeal to his honor, he breaks the talisman and is seized by the now awakened soldiers; but Bertram appears and takes him under his protection.

The fifth act opens with a chorus sung by monks, which is followed by a prayer for mercy. Robert, concealed in the vestibule of the cathedral, hears it full of contrition. But Bertram is with him, and, his term on earth being short, he confides to Robert the secret of his birth and appeals to him as his father.

He almost succeeds, when Alice comes up, bringing the news that the Prince of Granada renounces Isabella's hand, being unable to pass the threshold of the church. Bertram urges Robert all the more vehemently to become one with him, suggesting that Isabella is likewise lost to him, who has transgressed the laws of the Church, when in the last extremity Alice produces his mother's will, in which she warns him against Bertram, entreating him to save his soul. Then at last his good angel is victorious, his demon father vanishes into the earth, and Robert, united by prayer to the others, is restored to a life of peace and goodness.

Although in "Robert le Diable" Meyerbeer worked with a text in many ways defective, he made it serve his purpose by means of his musical effects. The music itself, though often strong and brilliant, is felt to lack depth and earnestness; but, notwithstanding this, the opera is recognized as having a distinct place in the history of musical development, where it marks a stage of progress from the bondage of conventionality.

LE ROI L'A DIT
(The King Has Said It)

Comic Opera in three acts by Clément P. L. Delibes. Text by Gondinet.

THE Marquis de Moncontour has long wished to be presented to the King Louis XIV, and as he has been fortunate enough to catch the escaped paroquet of Mme. de Maintenon, he is at last to have his wish accomplished. By way of preparation for his audience he tries to learn the latest mode of bowing, his own being somewhat antiquated, and the Marquise and her four lovely daughters and even Javotte, the nice little ladies' maid, assist him. After many failures the old gentleman succeeds in making his bow to his own satisfaction, and he is put into a litter and borne off, followed by his people's benedictions. When they are gone Benoit, a young peasant, comes to see Javotte, who is his sweetheart. He wishes to enter the Marquis's service. Javotte thinks him too awkward, but she promises to intercede in his favor with Miton, a dancing-master, who enters just as Benoit disappears. He has instructed the graceful Javotte in all the arts and graces of the noble world, and when he rehearses the steps and all the nice little tricks of his art with her, he is so delighted with his pupil that he pronounces her manners worthy of a princess; but when Javotte tells him that she loves a peasant he is filled with disgust and orders her away.

Miton's real pupils, the four lovely daughters of the Marquis, now enter, and while the lesson goes on Miton hands a billet-doux from some lover to each of them. The two elder, Agathe and Chimene, are just in the act of reading theirs when they hear a serenade outside, and shortly afterward the two lovers are standing in the room, having taken their way through the window. The Marquis Flarembel and his friend, the Marquis de la Bluette, are just making a most ardent declaration of love when Mme. la Marquise enters to present to her elder daughters the two bridegrooms she has chosen for them. The young men hide behind the ample dresses of the young ladies, and all begin to sing with great zeal, Miton beating the measure, so that some time elapses before the Marquise is able to state her errand. Of course her words excite great terror, the girls flying to the other side of the room with their lovers and receiving the two elderly suitors, Baron de Merlussac and Gautru, a rich old financier, with great coolness and a refusal of their costly gifts. When the suitors are gone the two young strangers are detected, and the angry mother decides at once to send her daughters to a convent, from which they shall only issue on their wedding day.

When they have departed in a most crestfallen condition, the old Marquis returns from his audience with the King and relates its astounding results. His Majesty had been so peremptory in his questioning about the Marquis's son and heir that the Marquis, losing his presence of mind, promised to present his son at court on the King's demand. The only question now is where to find a son to adopt, as the Marquis has only four daughters. Miton, the ever useful, at once presents Benoit to the parents, engaging himself to drill the peasant into a nice cavalier in ten lessons. Benoit takes readily to his new position; he is fitted out at once, and when the merchants come, offering their best in cloth and finery, he treats them with an insolence worthy of the proudest seigneur. He even turns from his sweetheart Javotte.

In the second act Benoit, dressed like the finest cavalier, gives a masked ball in his father's gardens. Half Versailles is invited, but he has made the mistake of inviting many people who have long been dead. Those who do appear seem to him to be very insipid, and wanting some friends with whom he can enjoy himself, the useful Miton presents the Marquises de la Bluette and de Flarembel, who are delighted to make the acquaintance of their sweethearts' brother.

Benoit hears from them that he has four charming sisters who have been sent to a convent, and he at once promises to assist his new friends. Meanwhile Javotte appears in the mask of an Oriental queen and Benoit makes love to her, but he is very much stupefied when she takes off her mask and he recognizes Javotte. She laughingly turns away from him, when the good-for-nothing youth's new parents appear to reproach him with his levity. But Benoit, nothing daunted, rushes away, telling the Marquis that he intends to visit his sisters in the convent. Miton tries in vain to recall him. Then the two old suitors of Agathe and Chimene appear to complain that their deceased wife and grandmother were invited, and while the Marquis explains his son's mistake the four daughters rush in, having been liberated by their lovers and their unknown brother, whom they greet with a fondness very shocking to the old Marchioness. The elderly suitors withdraw, swearing to take vengeance on the inopportune brother.

In the last act Benoit appears in his father's house in a somewhat dilapidated state. He has spent the night among gay companions and met Gautru and Merlussac successively, who have both fought him and believe they have killed him, Benoit having feigned to be dead.

When the old Marquis enters he is very much astonished at receiving two letters of condolence from his daughters' suitors. Miton appears in mourning, explaining that Mme. de Maintenon's visit being expected they must all wear dark colors, as she prefers these. Meanwhile Benoit has had an interview with Javotte, in which he declares his love to be undiminished, and he at once asks his father to give him Javotte as his wife, threatening to reveal the Marquis's deceit to the King if his request is not granted. In the dilemma help comes in the persons of the two young Marquises, who present their King's condolences to old Moncontour. This gentleman hears to his great relief that his son is supposed to have fallen in a duel and he is disposed of. Nobody is happier than Javotte, who now claims Benoit for her own, while the Marquis, who receives a duke's title from the King in compensation for his loss, gladly gives his two elder daughters to their young and noble lovers.

The girls, well aware that they owe their happiness to their adopted brother, are glad to provide him with ample means for his marriage with Javotte, and the affair ends to everybody's satisfaction. The opera throughout is replete with musical delights that have called forth the highest praise.

ROMÉO ET JULIETTE

Opera in five acts by Charles François Gounod.
Text by Barbier and Carré.

THE first act takes place in the palace of the Capulets, where a masked ball is being held. Roméo, a Montague, meets the daughter of his unwilling host, and they love each other at sight. Tybalt, Capulet's nephew, recognizes in Roméo the enemy of his race, and drags Juliette away, but is prevented from attacking Roméo by Capulet himself. In the second act we have the familiar garden scene, the lovers breathing their sighs in sweetest music. In the third act the lovers are united by Friar Laurent, but Roméo, involved in combat with Tybalt, kills his adversary. The fourth act reveals the parting of the lovers, for Roméo has been banished from the city. Juliette's father insists on her marriage to the Count of Paris, and the good friar contrives to aid her to escape. In the last act, seeing Juliette apparently dead, Roméo takes poison. When Juliette, whose death has only been simulated, awakes to find her beloved dying, she resolves to join him, and with her death the opera ends.

SALOME

Opera in one act by Richard Strauss.

STRAUSS'S text of this opera is adapted from the drama with the same title by Oscar Wilde. Though the principal characters are Biblical, the story is not, for Salome is represented as loving John the Baptist, and as demanding his "head on a charger" only after the prophet has scorned her wiles and seductions. Its one great spectacular feature is the "Dance of the Seven Veils," by means of which Salome obtains from Herod his promise to grant whatever request she may prefer. Following this, Salome receives the bloody head from the hands of the executioner, and rapturously kisses the dead lips. Even Herod is unable to support this spectacle, and by his orders the soldiers crush the woman to death with their shields.

"Salome" was first performed in Dresden, December 5, 1905. Two years later it was produced by Heinrich Conried for his own benefit at the Metropolitan Opera House, New York. It was gorgeously mounted, but the impression created was so unfavorable that the owners of the opera house gave orders to Conried that it should not be repeated. In 1908-09 it was presented at the Manhattan Opera House, New York. The impresario was not, however, permitted to give the work in Boston.

SAMSON ET DALILA
(Samson and Delilah)

Opera in three acts by Charles Camille Saint-Saëns.
Text by Lemaire.

THE libretto is Biblical; the scene is laid in Gaza, in Palestine, 1150 years before Christ. In the first act the Israelites, groaning under the yoke of the Philistines, pray to God for deliverance. They are derided and insulted by Abi Melech, satrap of Gaza. Samson, unable longer to endure the blasphemy hurled by the heathen against the God of Israel, rises up in mighty wrath, and so inspires his brethren that they suddenly take up arms, and precipitating themselves on their unsuspecting oppressors, first slay Abi Melech and then rout the whole army of the Philistines.

The high priest of the heathen god Dagon, finding his friend slain, vows to be avenged upon the Israelites, but he is deserted by all his companions, who flee before Samson's wrath.

In the next scene the Israelites return victorious and are greeted with triumphant songs and offerings of flowers. Even the Philistine Delilah, the rose of Sharon, receives them with her maidens, and pays homage to the hero Samson. Delilah had enthralled him once before, and again her beauty causes him very nearly to forget his people and his duty; but an aged Israelite implores him not to listen any more to the arts and wiles of the enchantress.

In the second act Delilah has an interview with the high priest, whom she promises to avenge her people by winning Samson's love once more. She proudly refuses the reward which the high priest offers her, for it is her bitter hatred against the hero, who once loved and then forsook her, which prompts her to ruin him and to force from him by every means in her power the secret of his strength.

When the high priest has left her, Samson comes down the steep mountain path, drawn to Delilah's house against his will. She receives him with the greatest tenderness, and once more her beauty and her tears assert their power over him, so that he sinks at her feet and falters out his love for her. In vain she tries to lure his secret from him. At last she leaves with words of contempt and enters the house. This proves his undoing. Goaded beyond earthly power, he rushes after her and seals his fate. After a while the Philistines surround the house and Delilah herself delivers her unfortunate lover, whom she has deprived of his strength by cutting off his locks, into the hands of his foes.

In the third act we find Samson in prison. Bereft of his eyesight, he has to turn the heavy mill. From the outside the wailings and reproaches of his Israelite brethren are heard, who have again been subjugated by their foes. Bitterly repentant, Samson implores God to take his life as the price of his people's deliverance.

In the last scene he is led away to Dagon's temple, there to be present at the festival of the Philistines, celebrated with great pomp in honor of their victory.

On the conclusion, after an exquisite ballet, Delilah presents a golden cup to the blind hero, and jeers at him for having been fool enough to believe in her love for him, the enemy of her country. Samson maintains silence, but when they order him to sacrifice at Dagon's shrine he whispers to the child who is guiding him to lead him to the pillars of the temple.

This being done, he loudly invokes the God of Israel, seizes the pillars, and tears them down with a mighty crash, burying the Philistines under the ruins of the temple.

"Samson et Dalila," in which Saint-Saëns is seen at his best, has oftener been given in concert than in opera form. It was first heard in this country in oratorio form. For many years the work was unsuccessful, but has finally taken its place among standard operas.

SIEGFRIED

Second day of the Nibelungen Ring by Richard Wagner. Musical Drama in three acts.

THE first act represents a part of the forest where Fafner guards the Rhinegold and where Sieglinde has found refuge. We find her son Siegfried—to whom, when she was dying, she gave birth—in the rocky cave of Mime the Nibelung (brother of Alberich), who has brought up the child as his own, knowing that he is destined to slay Fafner and to gain the ring, which he covets for himself. Siegfried, the brave and innocent boy, instinctively shrinks from this father, who is so ugly, so mean and vulgar, while he has a deep longing for his dead mother, whom he never knew. He gives vent to these feelings in impatient questions about her. The dwarf answers unwillingly and gives him the broken pieces of the old sword Nothung (needful), which his mother left as the only precious remembrance of Siegfried's father. Siegfried asks Mime to forge the fragments afresh, while he rushes away into the woods.

During his absence Wotan comes to Mime in the guise of a wanderer. Mime, though he knows him not, fears him and would fain drive him away. Finally he puts three questions to his guest. The first is the name of the race which lives in earth's deepest depths, the second the name of those who live on earth's back, and the third that of those who live above the clouds. Of course Wotan answers them all, redeeming his head and shelter thereby; but now it is his turn to put three questions. He first asks what race it is that Wotan loves most, though he dealt hardly with them, and Mime answers rightly that they are the Wälsungs, whose son Siegfried is; then Wotan asks after the sword which is to make Siegfried victorious. Mime joyously names "Nothung," but when Wotan asks him who is to unite the pieces he is in great embarrassment, for he remembers his task and perceives too late what question he ought to have asked. Wotan leaves him, telling him that only that man can forge it who never knew fear. Siegfried, finding the sword still in fragments when he returns, melts these in fire, and easily forges them together to Mime's great awe, for he sees now that this boy is the one whom the stranger has meant.

In the second act we see the opening of Fafner's cavern, where Alberich keeps watch for the dragon's slayer, so long predicted. Wotan, approaching, warns him that Alberich's brother Mime has brought up the boy who is to slay Fafner in the hope of gaining Alberich's ring, the wondrous qualities of which are unknown to Siegfried. Wotan awakes Fafner, the dragon, telling him that his slayer is coming.

Mime, who has led Siegfried to this part of the forest under the pretext of teaching him fear, approaches now, and Siegfried, eager for combat, kills the dreadful worm. Accidentally tasting the blood, he all at once understands the language of the birds. They tell him to seek for the Tarnhelm and for the ring, which he finds in the cavern. Meanwhile, the brothers, Alberich and Mime, quarrel over the treasure which they hope to gain. When Siegfried returns with ring and helmet, he is again warned by the voice of a woodbird not to trust in Mime. Having tasted the dragon's blood, Siegfried is enabled to probe Mime's innermost thoughts, and so he learns that Mime means to poison him in order to obtain the treasure. He then kills the traitor with a single stroke. Stretching himself under the linden-tree to repose after that day's hard work, he again hears the voice of the wood-bird, which tells him of a glorious bride sleeping on a rock surrounded by fire; and flying before him, the bird shows Siegfried the way to the spot.

In the third act we find Wotan once more awakening Erda, to seek her counsel as to how best to avert the doom which he sees coming, but she is less wise than he, and so he decides to let fate have its course. When he sees Siegfried coming he, for the last time, tries to oppose him by barring the way to Brünnhilde, but the sword Nothung splits the god's spear. Seeing that his power avails him nothing, he retires to Valhalla, there to await the "Twilight of the Gods."

Siegfried plunges through the fire, awakes the Valkyr, and after a long resistance wins the proud virgin.

LA SONNAMBULA
(The Sleep-Walker)

Opera in two acts by Vincenzo Bellini.
Text by Romani.

THE scene of action is a village in Switzerland, where the rich farmer Elvino has married a poor orphan, Amina. The ceremony has taken place at the magistrate's, and Elvino is about to obtain the sanction of the Church to his union, when the owner of the castle, Count Rodolfo, who fled from home in his boyhood, returns most unexpectedly and, at once making love to Amina, excites the bridegroom's jealousy. Lisa, the young owner of a little inn, who wants Elvino for herself and disdains the devotion of Alessio, a simple peasant, tries to avenge herself on her happy rival. Lisa is a coquette and flirts with the Count, whom the judge recognizes. While she yet prates with him, the door opens and Amina enters, walking in her sleep and calling for Elvino. Lisa conceals herself, but forgets her handkerchief. The Count, seeing Amina's condition and awed by her purity, quits the room, where Amina lies down, always in deep sleep. Just then the people, having heard of the Count's arrival, come to greet him and find Amina instead. At the same moment Elvino, summoned by Lisa, rushes in, and finding his bride in the Count's room, turns away from her in disdain, snatching his wedding ring from her finger in his wrath, and utterly disbelieving Amina's protestations of innocence and the Count's assurances. Lisa succeeds in attracting Elvino's notice and he promises to marry her.

The Count once more tries to persuade the angry bridegroom of his bride's innocence, but without result, when Teresa, Amina's foster-mother, shows Lisa's handkerchief, which was found in the Count's room. Lisa reddens, and Elvino knows not whom he shall believe, when all of a sudden Amina is seen emerging from a window of the mill, walking in a trance and calling for her bridegroom in most touching accents.

All are convinced of her innocence, when they see her in this state of somnambulism, in which she crosses a very narrow bridge without falling.

Elvino himself replaces the wedding ring on her finger, and she awakes from her trance in his arms. Everybody is happy at the turn which things have taken; Elvino asks Amina's forgiveness and leaves Lisa to her own bitter reflections.

TANNHÄUSER

Romantic Opera in three acts by Richard Wagner.

WAGNER took his subject from an old legend which tells of a minstrel called Tannhäuser (probably identical with Heinrich von Ofterdingen), who won all prizes by his beautiful songs and all hearts by his noble bearing. So the palm is allotted to him at the yearly "Tournament of Minstrels" on the Wartburg, and his reward is to be the hand of Elisabeth, niece of the Landgrave of Thuringia, whom he loves. But instead of behaving sensibly, this erring knight suddenly disappears nobody knows where, leaving his bride in sorrow and anguish. He falls into the hands of Venus, who holds court in the Hörselberg near Eisenach, and Tannhäuser, at the opening of the first scene, has already passed a whole year with her.

At length Tannhäuser has grown tired of sensual love and pleasure, and, notwithstanding Venus's allurements, he leaves her, vowing never to return to the goddess, but to expiate his sins by a holy life. He returns to the charming vale behind the Wartburg, where he hears again the singing of the birds, the shepherds playing on the flute, and the pious songs of the pilgrims on their way to Rome. Full of repentance, he kneels down and prays, when suddenly the Landgrave appears with some minstrels, among them Wolfram von Eschenbach, Tannhäuser's best friend. They greet their long-lost companion, who, however, cannot tell where he has been all the time, and as Wolfram reminds him of Elisabeth, Tannhäuser returns with the party to the Wartburg.

It is just the anniversary of the Tournament of Minstrels, and in the second act we find Elisabeth with Tannhäuser, who craves her pardon and is warmly welcomed by her. The high prize for the best song is again to be Elisabeth's hand, and Tannhäuser resolves to win her once more. The Landgrave chooses "love" as the subject whose nature is to be explained by the minstrels. Every one is called by name, and Wolfram von Eschenbach begins, praising love as a well, deep and pure, a source of the highest and most sacred feeling. Others follow: Walter von der Vogelweide praises the virtue of love, every minstrel celebrates spiritual love alone.

But Tannhäuser, who has been in Venus's fetters, sings of another love, warmer and more passionate, but sensual. And when the others remonstrate, he loudly praises Venus, the goddess of heathen love. All stand aghast; they recognize now where he has been so long; he is about to be put to death, when Elisabeth prays for him. She loves him dearly and hopes to save his soul from eternal perdition. Tannhäuser is to join a party of pilgrims on their way to Rome, there to crave for the Pope's pardon.

In the third act we see the pilgrims return from their journey. Elisabeth anxiously expects her lover, but he is not among them. Fervently she prays to the

Holy Virgin; but not that a faithful lover may be given back to her—rather that he may be pardoned and his immortal soul saved. Wolfram is beside her; he loves the maiden, but he has no thought for himself; he only feels for her whose life he sees ebbing swiftly away, and for his unhappy friend.

Presently, when Elisabeth is gone, Tannhäuser comes up in pilgrim's garb. He has passed a hard journey, full of sacrifices and castigation, and all in vain, for the Pope has rejected him. He has been told in hard words that he is forever damned and will as little get deliverance from his grievous sin as the stick in his hand will ever bear green leaves afresh.

Full of despair, Tannhäuser is returning to seek Venus, whose siren songs already fall alluringly on his ear. Wolfram entreats him to fly, and when Tannhäuser fails to listen he utters Elisabeth's name. At this moment a procession descends from the Wartburg chanting a funeral song over an open bier. Elisabeth lies on it dead, and Tannhäuser sinks on his knee beside her, crying, "Holy Elisabeth, pray for me." Then Venus disappears and all at once the withered stick begins to bud and blossom, and Tannhäuser, pardoned, expires at the side of his beloved.

"Tannhäuser" was represented at the Dresden Theater, in June, 1890, according to Wagner's changes of arrangement, done by him in Paris, 1861, for the Grand Opera, by order of Napoleon III. This arrangement the composer acknowledged as the only correct one.

These alterations were limited to the first scene in the mysterious abode of Venus, and Wagner's motives for the changes become clearly apparent when it is remembered that the simple form of "Tannhäuser" was composed in the years 1843 and 1845, in and near Dresden, at a time when there were neither means nor taste in Germany for such high-flown scenes as those which excited Wagner's brain. Afterward success rendered Wagner bolder, and he endowed the person of Venus with more dramatic power and thereby threw a vivid light on the great attraction she exercises on Tannhäuser. The decorations are by far richer, and a ballet of sirens and fauns was added, a concession which Wagner had to make to the Parisian taste. Venus's part, now sung by the first prima donnas, has considerably gained by the alterations, and the first scene is far more interesting than before, but it is to be regretted that the Tournament of Minstrels has been shortened and particularly the fine song of Walter von der Vogelweide omitted by Wagner. All else is as of old, as indeed Elisabeth's part needed nothing to add to her purity and loveliness, which stand out now in even bolder relief against the beautiful but sensual part of Venus.

THAÏS

Opera in four acts by Jules Massenet.
Text by Gallet.

PERHAPS the most popular of all Massenet's lyric dramas, certainly the best known outside of France itself, is this, which has the advantage of an excellent libretto, founded upon a novel of great appeal. The scene is laid in Egypt in the stormy period when Christianity was battling for supremacy with paganism. Athanael and other monks, presided over by Palemon, have retired to the desert for a life of meditation and prayer, and the rising curtain reveals these holy men at their evening meal—all but Athanael, who has been in Alexandria for the brethren. Palemon has seen Athanael in a vision, and as he tells the monks that their brother is returning, the weary traveler enters. After an exchange of greetings, he tells the monks that Alexandria is given over to sin, and ruled by Thaïs, an infamous priestess of Venus, whom he had known before his conversion. Palemon sagely advises the brothers to forget the world in seeking out their own salvation.

Night falls, and in a dream Athanael sees Thaïs enacting the rôle of Aphrodite in the theater at Alexandria. The mob applauds the lovely priestess, who redoubles her efforts to charm. With the coming of the dawn the vision fades and Athanael wakes. Impressed by what he has seen, he declares that he will return to Alexandria and make of Thaïs a Christian convert. Vainly do Palemon and the monks seek to dissuade him. In the next scene we find Athanael in Alexandria, a guest in the palace of his old friend Nicias, who causes him to be newly robed and perfumed, but laughs at his idea of converting Thaïs. Then comes the priestess herself, surrounded by her admirers, and when she asks who Athanael is, and learns his mission, she too is amused, and is preparing to enact for Athanael's edification the scene which he had beheld in his dreams. Filled with loathing, Athanael rushes from the palace.

In the second act Thaïs, worn with pleasure and unhappy, kneels before the shrine of Venus, beseeching the goddess to grant her eternal beauty. Athanael comes to preach the faith of the Redeemer; but though Thaïs listens with interest, and denies herself to Nicias, the latest of her lovers, she is unconvinced. Athanael tells her that he will await her coming with the rising of the sun, and retires, meaning to spend the night in prayer before her door. Then, after an interlude by the orchestra, the scene shifts, and Athanael is shown reclining on the portico of Thaïs's house. He is aroused by Thaïs herself, who tells him that she has prayed, has wept, and having seen the nothingness of pleasure, has come in obedience to his commands. Athanael takes from Thaïs a statuette of Cupid, the one memento she has brought with her, dashes it to the ground, and bids her follow him to a convent presided over by Albine, a daughter of the Cæsars, who has embraced the religious life. Before they can depart, Nicias, who has just won a fortune at the gaming-table, brings in a party of friends to celebrate the occasion, and all are incensed at the thought of losing their favorite priestess. They attack Athanael, but their attention is distracted by flames issuing from the palace of Thaïs, who had fired it before leaving, and then Nicias adds to the confusion by flinging handfuls of gold into the street. In the scramble for money which follows, Athanael and his convert escape.

In the third act we are shown an oasis in the desert, the abode of the Christian sisterhood of whom Albine is the head. Almost at her journey's end, Thaïs faints from fatigue. Athanael kisses her feet, wounded as they are, then brings her water and fruit. The nuns enter, chanting their prayers, and when they have welcomed Thaïs she bids farewell to Athanael, whom she hopes to meet again in heaven. Then the stage picture changes, again showing the monastery in the Thebaid. Athanael has touched neither food nor drink for twenty days. As Palemon expresses it, "The triumph he has won over hell has broken him, body and soul." Athanael confesses to Palemon that he is haunted perpetually by thoughts of Thaïs, to which Palemon can only reply that he had warned Athanael not to meddle with the affairs of the world.

Again the vision of Thaïs appears to Athanael, but this time she seems to be dying, surrounded by the mournful sisterhood of the oasis. Then Athanael rushes into the night, crying as he goes that a single caress from Thaïs is more than all the delights of heaven.

In the fourth act Athanael, arriving at Albine's convent, is welcomed by the nuns, who assume that he is there to give the final benediction to Thaïs, and they describe her as a saint. The former priestess of Venus in her last moments feels the beatitudes of the Christian heaven, and is oblivious to the passionate appeal of Athanael. She dies, and with a terrible outburst of grief Athanael falls to his knees beside her.

TIEFLAND

Opera in three acts, with a prologue, by Eugen d'Albert.
Text by Lothar.

UNTIL this opera was produced in New York, the composer was known in America only as a pianist. Earlier works for the stage, while not unsuccessful, had their vogue chiefly in Germany, but "Tiefland," first performed in Berlin in 1908, was immediately claimed for the world at large. The book is based on the Catalonian play by Angel Guimera known as "Terra Baixa."

In the prologue Pedro is tending his sheep in the highlands of the Pyrenees, and when Sebastiano, his master, promises him wealth and a pretty bride in the person of Marta, a damsel from the plains, he is delighted.

In the first act the scene shifts to the lowlands, where preparations have been made for the wedding. Pedro, dazed by the change in his fortunes, and deeply in love with Marta, fails to note the jeering attitude of the villagers, and not until after the ceremony has taken place does he learn the truth. Marta, who has felt for him only contempt, experiences a complete revulsion of feeling at his profound depression when she has told her story. Daughter of a strolling player, she has aroused the admiration of Sebastiano, who bought her from her father by giving him a mill which would afford an easy living. This relationship, a common scandal in the village, had continued until Sebastiano found an opportunity of marrying a wealthy heiress. Then, as a means of freeing himself, Sebastiano had determined to provide a husband for Marta, and Pedro had been the unsuspecting victim. Enraged against his wife, Pedro becomes calmer as he realizes that she too has been the victim of Sebastiano, and he determines to revenge her as well as himself.

Sebastiano, who has never meant to relinquish his claims on Marta, comes to her home as boldly as ever, and though Marta repulses him, and calls on Pedro to protect her, the peasants who have accompanied Sebastiano eject the husband from the house, then leave Marta and Sebastiano together. Marta faints away, but recovers herself a moment later as Tommaso enters to say to Sebastiano that he has already denounced him to the family of his prospective bride.

In the third act Sebastiano, again alone with Marta, continues to force his unwelcome attentions on her, when Pedro returns. "Man to man!" cries Pedro, in whose hand a knife is gleaming. "I have no weapon," shouts Sebastiano in reply, as he seeks to escape from the house. "Then I need none," is Pedro's rejoinder, and flinging away his knife, he closes in on his former master, and after a desperate struggle succeeds in strangling him.

Meantime the noise of combat has again brought the villagers about the cottage, and they are clamoring for admittance. Having satisfied himself that Sebastiano is beyond earthly help, Pedro throws open the door, boldly proclaims his deed, then clasping his wife in his arms, leads her through the group of awestruck peasants. The lowlands shall know them no more, for in the pure surroundings of their mountain home they are to begin life anew.

LA TOSCA

Opera in three acts by Giacomo Puccini.
Text by Illica and Giacosa, after Sardou's drama.

THE scene is laid in Rome. The first act takes place in the church of Sant' Andrea alla Valle. Cesare Angelotti, a state prisoner, has escaped from jail and is hiding in a private chapel, of which his sister, the Lady Attavanti, has secretly sent him the key. When he has disappeared from view the painter Mario Cavaradossi enters the church. He is engaged in painting a picture to represent Mary Magdalen. The canvas stands on a high easel, and the sacristan, who is prowling about, recognizes with scandalized amazement and indignation that the sacred picture resembles a beautiful lady who comes to pray daily in the church. The old man, after having left a basket with food for the painter, retires grumbling at this sacrilege.

When he is gone, Angelotti comes forward, and the painter, recognizing in the prisoner the consul of the late Roman Republic who is at the same time an intimate friend of his own, puts himself at his disposal; but, hearing the voice of his fiancée Tosca, who demands entrance, he begs the prisoner, a victim of the vile Scarpia, to retire into the chapel, giving him the refreshments which the sacristan has left.

At last he opens the church door, and Tosca, a famous singer, enters looking suspiciously around her, for she is of a jealous disposition. She begs her lover to wait for her at the stage door in the evening. He assents and tries to get rid of her, when her suspicions are reawakened by the sight of the picture, which she sees is a portrait of the Lady Attavanti. With difficulty he succeeds in persuading her of his undying love, and at last induces her to depart; he then enters the chapel and urges Angelotti to fly while the way is clear. The chapel opens into a deserted garden from whence a root-path leads to the painter's villa, in which there is a well now nearly dry. Into this well the painter advises Angelotti to descend if there is any danger of pursuit, as halfway down there is an opening leading to a secret cave, where his friend will be in perfect safety.

The Lady Attavanti had left a woman's clothes for her brother to wear as a disguise. He takes them up and turns to go when the report of a cannon tells him that his flight from the fortress is discovered. With sudden resolution Cavaradossi decides to accompany the fugitive to help him to escape from his terrible enemy.

In the next scene acolytes, scholars, and singers enter the church tumultuously. They have heard that Napoleon has been defeated, and all are shouting and laughing when Scarpia, the chief of the police, enters in search of the fugitive. Turning to the sacristan he demands to be shown the chapel of the Attavanti, which to the amazement of the sacristan is found open. It is empty, but Scarpia finds a fan, on which he perceives the arms of the Attavanti, then he sees the picture and hears that Tosca's lover Cavaradossi has painted it. The basket with food is also found empty. During the discussion that ensues Tosca enters, much astonished to find Scarpia here instead of her lover. The chief of the police awakens her jealousy by showing her the fan, which he pretends to have found on the scaffolding. Tosca, recognizing the arms of the Attavanti, is goaded almost to madness by the wily Scarpia. When she departs three spies are ordered to follow her.

The second act takes place in Scarpia's luxurious apartments in an upper story of the Farnese palace. Scarpia is expecting Tosca, who is to sing this evening at the Queen's festival. He has decided to take her for his mistress and to put her lover to death, as well as Angelotti, as soon as he has got hold of both. Spoletta, a police agent, informs his chief that he followed Tosca to a solitary villa, which she left again, alone, very soon after she had entered it.

Forcing his way into the villa, he had found only the painter Cavaradossi, whom he had at once arrested and brought to the palace. Cavaradossi, who is now brought in, denies resolutely any knowledge of the escaped prisoner. When Tosca enters he embraces her, whispering into her ear not to betray anything she has witnessed in his villa.

Meanwhile, Scarpia has called for Roberto, the executioner, and Mario is led into the torture-chamber that adjoins Scarpia's apartment. Scarpia vainly questions Tosca about her visit to the villa. She assures him that she found her lover alone. Then she hears her lover's groans, which are growing more fearful, the torture under Scarpia's directions being applied with more and more violence. In the intervals Mario, however, entreats Tosca to be silent, but at last she can bear no more and gasps, "In the well in the garden." Scarpia at once gives a signal to stop the torture and Mario is carried in fainting and covered with blood. When he comes to himself he hears Scarpia say to Spoletta, "In the well in the garden," and thereby finds out that Tosca has betrayed the unfortunate prisoner. While he turns from her in bitter grief and indignation, Sciarrone, a gendarme, enters and announces, in the greatest consternation, that the news of victory has proved false, Napoleon having beaten the Italian army at Marengo. Mario exults in the defeat of his enemy, but the latter turns to him with an evil smile and orders the gendarmes to take him away to his death. Tosca tries to follow him, but Scarpia detains her. Remaining alone with her she offers him all her treasures and at last kneels to him imploring him to save her lover. But the villain only shows her the scaffold which is being erected on the square below, swearing that he will save her lover only on condition that she will be his. Tosca turns shuddering from him. Spoletta now enters to announce that Angelotti, being found and taken, has killed himself, and that Mario is ready for death.

Now at last Tosca yields, Scarpia promising to liberate her lover at the price of her honor. He suggests, however, that Mario must be supposed dead, and that a farce must be acted, in which the prisoner is to pretend to fall dead while only blank cartridges will be used for firing. Tosca begs to be allowed to warn him herself, and Scarpia consents, and orders Spoletta to accompany her to the prison at four o'clock in the morning, after having given the spy private instruction to have Mario really shot after all. Spoletta retires, and Scarpia approaches Tosca to claim his reward. But she stops him, asking for a safe conduct for herself and her lover. While Scarpia is writing it Tosca seizes a knife from the table, while leaning against it, and hides the weapon behind her back. Scarpia seals the passport; then, opening his arms, he says: "Now, Tosca, mine at last." But he staggers back with an awful scream. Tosca has suddenly plunged the knife deep into his breast. Before he can call for help, death overtakes him, and Tosca, after having taken the passport from the clenched fist of the dead man, turns to fly.

The third act takes place on the platform of the castle Sant' Angelo. The jailer informs Mario Cavaradossi that he may ask for a last favor, having only one hour to live, and the captive begs to be allowed to send a last letter of farewell to his fiancée. The jailer assents, and Mario sits down to write, but soon the sweet recollections of the past overcome him. Tosca finds him in bitter tears, which soon give way to joy when she shows him her passport, granting a free pass to Tosca and to the chevalier who will accompany her.

When she tells him of the deadly deed she has done to procure it, he kisses the hands that were stained with blood for his sake. Then she informs him of the farce which is to be acted, and begs him to fall quite naturally after the first shot, and to remain motionless until she shall call him. After a while the jailer reminds them that the hour is over. The soldiers march up, and Tosca places herself to the left of the guard's room in order to face her lover. The latter refuses to have his eyes bandaged, and bravely stands erect before the soldiers. The officer lowers his sword, a report follows, and Tosca, seeing her lover fall, sends him a kiss. When one of the sergeants is about to give the *coup de grâce* to the fallen man, Spoletta prevents him, and covers Mario with a cloak. Tosca remains quiet until the last soldier has descended the steps of the staircase, then she runs to her lover, calling him to rise. As he does not move, she bends down to him and tears the cloak off, but, with a terrible cry, she staggers back. Her lover is dead! She bewails him in the wildest grief, when suddenly she hears the voice of Sciarrone, and knows that Scarpia's murder has been discovered! A crowd rushes up the stairs with Spoletta at their head. He is about to precipitate himself upon Tosca, but she runs to the parapet and throws herself into space, with the cry: "Scarpia, may God judge between us!"

LA TRAVIATA
(The Wandering One)

Opera in three acts by Giuseppe Verdi.
Text taken from the French by Piave.

THE original of the libretto is the celebrated novel "La dame aux camélias" by the younger Dumas.

The scene is laid in and near Paris. Alfred Germont is passionately in love with Violetta Valery, one of the most frivolous beauties in Paris. She is pleased with his sincere passion, anything like which she has never hitherto known, and openly telling him who she is, she warns him herself; but he loves her all the more, and as she returns his passion, she abandons her gay life and follows him into the country, where they live very happily for some months.

Annina, Violetta's maid, dropping a hint to Alfred that her mistress is about to sell her house and carriage in town in order to avoid expenses, he departs for the capital to prevent this.

During his absence Violetta receives a visit from Alfred's father, who tries to show her that she has destroyed not only his family's but his son's happiness by suffering Alfred to unite himself to one so dishonored. He succeeds in convincing her, and, broken-hearted, she determines to sacrifice herself and leave Alfred secretly. Ignoring the possible reason for this inexplicable action, Alfred is full of wrath and resolves to take vengeance. He finds Violetta in the house of a former friend, Flora Bervoix, who is in a position similar to that of Violetta. The latter, having no other resources, and feeling herself at death's door (a state of health suggested in the first act by an attack of suffocation), has returned to her former life. Alfred insults her publicly. The result is a duel between her present adorer, Baron Dauphal, and Alfred.

From this time on Violetta declines rapidly, and in the last act, which takes place in her sleeping-room, we find her dying. Hearing that Alfred has been victorious in the duel and receiving a letter from his father, who is now willing to pardon and to accept her as his daughter-in-law, she revives to some extent; and Alfred, who at last hears of her sacrifice, returns to her, but only to afford a last glimpse of happiness to the unfortunate woman, who expires, a modern Magdalen, full of repentance and striving tenderly to console her lover and his now equally desolate father.

This opera, which at first fared poorly at the hands of the public, is now classed among the works that have most contributed to Verdi's reputation. Little can be said for the text of "La Traviata," but its faults are redeemed by the work of the master, whose music abounds in the finest melody and in special features of admirable quality.

TRISTAN UND ISOLDE

Lyric Drama in three acts by Richard Wagner.

THE first act represents the deck of a ship, where we find the two principal persons, Tristan and Isolde, together. Tristan, a Cornish hero, has gone over to Ireland to woo the Princess for his old uncle, King Marke. Isolde, however, loves Tristan and has loved him from the time when he was cast sick and dying on the coast of Ireland and was rescued and nursed by her, though he was her enemy. But Tristan, having sworn faith to his uncle, never looks at her; and she, full of wrath that he should woo her for another instead of for himself, attempts to poison herself and him. But Brangäne, her faithful attendant, secretly changes the poisoned draught for a love-potion, so that they are inevitably joined in passionate love. Only when the ship gets ashore, its deck already covered with knights and sailors who come to greet their King's bride, does Brangäne confess her fraud; and Isolde, hearing that she is to live, faints in her attendant's arms.

In the second act Isolde has been wedded to Marke, but the love-potion has worked well, and she has secret interviews at night with Tristan, whose sense of honor is deadened by the fatal draught. Brangäne keeps watch for the lovers, but King Marke's jealous friend Melot betrays them, and they are found out by the good old King, who returns earlier than he had intended from a hunt.

Tristan is profoundly touched by the grief of the King, whose sadness at losing faith in his most noble warrior is greater than his wrath against the betrayer of honor. Tristan, unable to defend himself, turns to Isolde, asking her to follow him into the desert, but Melot opposes him, and they fight, Tristan falling back deadly wounded into his faithful servant Kurvenal's arms.

The third act represents Tristan's home in Brittany, whither Kurvenal has carried his wounded master in order to nurse him. Isolde, skilled in the art of healing wounds, has been sent for, but they look in vain for the ship which is to bring her.

When at last it comes in sight, Tristan, who awakes from a long swoon, sends Kurvenal away, to receive his mistress, and as they both delay their coming, his impatient longing gets the better of him. Forgetting his wound, he rises from his couch, tearing away the bandages, and so Isolde is only just in time to catch him in her arms, where he expires with her name on his lips. While she bewails her loss, another ship is announced by the shepherd's horn. King Marke arrives, prepared to pardon all and to unite the lovers. Kurvenal, seeing Melot advance, mistakes them for foes and, running his sword through Melot's breast, sinks, himself deadly wounded, at his master's feet. King Marke, to whom Brangäne has confessed her part in the whole matter, vainly laments his friend Tristan, while Isolde, waking from her swoon and seeing her lover dead, pours forth rapturous words of devotion and, broken-hearted, sinks down dead at his side.

In "Tristan und Isolde" Wagner first fully embodied his theories regarding the drama and the orchestra in their artistic relations.

IL TROVATORE
(The Troubadour)

Opera in four acts by Giuseppe **Verdi**.
Text by Cammerano.

TWO men of entirely different station and character woo Leonora, Countess of Sergaste. The one is Count Luna, the other a minstrel named Manrico, who is believed to be the son of Azucena, a gypsy.

Azucena has, in accordance with gypsy law, vowed bloody revenge on Count Luna, because his father, believing her mother to be a sorceress and to have bewitched one of his children, had the old woman burned. To punish the father for this cruelty Azucena took away his other child, which was vainly sought for. This story is told in the first scene, where we find the Count's servants waiting for him, while he stands sighing beneath his sweetheart's window. But Leonora's heart is already captivated by Manrico's sweet songs and his valor in tournament. She suddenly hears his voice, and in the darkness mistakes the Count for her lover, who, however, comes up just in time to claim her. The Count is full of rage, and there follows a duel in which Manrico is wounded, but, though it is in his power to kill his enemy, he spares his life, without, however, being able to account for the impulse.

In the second act Azucena, nursing Manrico, tells him of her mother's dreadful fate and her last cry for revenge, and confesses to having stolen the old Count's son, with the intention of burning him. But in her despair and confusion, she says, she threw her own child into the flames, and the Count's son lived. Manrico is terrified, but Azucena retracts her words and regains his confidence, so that he believes her tale to have been but an outburst of remorse and folly.

Meanwhile he hears that Leonora, to whom he was reported as dead, is about to take the veil, and he rushes away to save her. Count Luna arrives before the convent with the same purpose. But just as he seizes his prey, Manrico comes up and liberates her with the aid of his companions, while the Count curses them. Leonora becomes Manrico's wife, but her happiness is shortlived.

In the third act the Count's soldiers succeed in capturing Azucena, in whom they recognize the burned gypsy's daughter. She denies all knowledge of the Count's lost brother, and as the Count hears that his successful rival is her son, she is sentenced to be burned. Ruiz, Manrico's friend, brings the news to him. Manrico tries to rescue her, but is seized too, and condemned to die by the axe.

In the fourth act Leonora offers herself to the Count as the price of freedom for the captives, but, determined to be true to her lover, she takes poison. She hastens to him, announcing his deliverance. Too late he sees how dearly she has paid for it, when, after sweet assurance of love and fidelity, she sinks dead at his feet.

The Count, coming up and seeing himself deceived, orders Manrico to be put to death instantly. He is led away, and only after the execution does Azucena inform the Count that his murdered rival was Luna's own long-sought brother.

THE VAMPIRE

Romantic Opera in two acts by Heinrich **Marschner**.
Text by Wohlbrück.

THE subject is taken from Lord Byron's tale of the same name. The scene is laid in Scotland in the seventeenth century and illustrates the old Scottish legend of the vampire, a phantom monster which can only exist by sucking the heart-blood of sleeping mortals.

Lord Ruthven is such a vampire. He victimizes young maidens in particular. His soul is sold to Satan, but the demons have granted him a respite of a year, on condition of his bringing them three brides young and pure. His first victim is Ianthe, daughter of Sir John Berkley. She loves the monster and together they disappear into a cavern. Her father assembles followers and goes in search of her. They hear dreadful wailings, followed by mocking laughter proceeding from the ill-fated vampire, and entering they find Ianthe lifeless. The despairing father stabs Ruthven, who wounded to death knows that he cannot survive but by drawing life from the rays of the moon, which shines on the mountains. Unable to move, he is saved by Edgar Aubrey, a relative of the Laird of Davenant, who accidentally comes to the spot.

Lord Ruthven, after having received a promise of secrecy from Aubrey, tells him who he is and implores him to carry him to the hills as the last favor to a dying man.

Aubrey complies with the vampire's request and then hastily flies from the spot. Ruthven revives and follows him, in order to win the love of Malvina, daughter of the Laird of Davenant and Aubrey's betrothed.

His respite now waxing short, he tries at the same time to gain the affections of Emma, daughter of John Perth, the steward.

Malvina meanwhile greets her beloved Aubrey, who has returned after a long absence. Both are full of joy, when Malvina's father enters to announce to his daughter her future husband, whom he has chosen in the person of the Earl of Marsden. Great is Malvina's sorrow, and she now for the first time dares to tell her father that her heart has already spoken, and to present Aubrey to him. The laird's pride, however, does not allow him to retract his word, and when the Earl of Marsden arrives, he presents him to his daughter. In the supposed earl Aubrey at once recognizes Lord Ruthven, but the villain stoutly denies his identity, giving Lord Ruthven out as a brother, who has been traveling for a long time. Aubrey, however, recognizes the vampire by a scar on his hand, but he is bound to secrecy by his oath, and so Ruthven triumphs, having the Laird of Davenant's promise that he will be betrothed before midnight to Malvina, as he declares that he is bound to depart for Madrid the following morning as ambassador.

In the second act all are drinking and frolicking on the green, where the bridal is to take place.

Emma awaits her lover George Dibdin, who is in Davenant's service. While she sings the ghastly romance of the vampire, Lord Ruthven approaches, and by his sweet flattery and promise to help the lovers, he easily causes the simple maiden to grant him a kiss in token of her gratitude. In giving this kiss she is forfeited to the Evil One. George, who has seen all, is very jealous, though Emma tells him that the future son-in-law of the Laird of Davenant will make him his steward.

Meanwhile Aubrey vainly tries to make Ruthven renounce Malvina. Ruthven threatens that Aubrey himself will be condemned to be a vampire if he breaks his oath, and depicts in glowing colors the torments of a spirit so cursed. While Aubrey hesitates as to what he shall do, Ruthven once more approaches Emma and succeeds in winning her consent to follow him to his den, where he murders her.

In the last scene Malvina, unable any longer to resist her father's will, has consented to the hateful marriage. Ruthven has kept away rather long and comes very late to his wedding. Aubrey implores them to wait for the coming day, but in vain. Then he forgets his own danger and only sees that of his beloved, and when Ruthven is leading the bride to the altar, he loudly proclaims Ruthven to be a vampire. At this moment a thunder-peal is heard and a flash of lightning destroys Ruthven, whose time of respite has ended at midnight. The old laird, witnessing Heaven's punishment, repents his error and gladly gives Malvina to her lover, while all praise the Almighty, who has turned evil into good.

DIE VERKAUFTE BRAUT
(The Bartered Bride)

Comic Opera in three acts by Friedrich Smetana.
Text by Sabina.

THE scene is laid in a village in Bohemia. It is spring kirmess, and everybody is gay. Only Mary, the daughter of the rich peasant Kruschina, carries a heavy heart within her; for the day has come on which the unknown bridegroom, chosen by her parents, will claim her hand. She loves Hans, known to her as a poor servant, who has come to her village lately, and who is in reality her bridegroom's half-brother. He consoles her, beseeching her to cheer up and be faithful to him, and then tells her that he comes of wealthy people. He lost his mother early, and his father wedded a second wife, who so estranged his heart from the poor boy that he had to gain his daily bread abroad. She deeply sympathizes with him, without guessing his real name.

Meanwhile Mary's parents approach with the match-maker Kezul, a personage common in Bohemia, who has already won Kruschina's consent to his daughter's marriage with Wenzel, son of the rich farmer Micha by a second marriage. Mary's mother insisting that her child's will is to be consulted before all, the father consents to let her see the bridegroom before she decides. Kezul, though angry at this unlooked-for obstacle, excuses the bridegroom's absence volubly, and sings his praise loudly, at the same time touching upon the elder son's absence, and hinting that he may probably be dead. When Mary steps in, Kezul woos her in due form, but is at once repulsed by her. The young girl owns to having given her heart to the humble servant Hans, in whom nobody has yet recognized Micha's son. Father Kruschina angrily asserts his

promise to Kezul, cursing Wenzel's timidity, which hindered him from making his proposal in person. Kezul, however, resolves to talk Hans over to reason.

We find him, in the second act, singing and highly praising the god of love. Afterward the would-be bridegroom Wenzel finds himself face to face with Mary, whom he does not know. When he tells her of his purpose, timidly and stammeringly, she asks him if he is not ashamed to woo a girl who loves another man, and who does not love *him* in the least. She at last so frightens the lad that he promises to look out for another bride, if his mother permits it. Mary flirts with him, until he swears never to claim Kruschina's daughter.

Meanwhile Kezul does his best to convert Hans. He promises to provide for him another bride, much richer than Mary, but Hans refuses. He offers him money, first one hundred, then two hundred, then three hundred florins. Hans, looking incredulous, asks, "For whom are you wooing my bride?" "For Micha's son," the matchmaker replies. "Well," says Hans, "if you promise me that Micha's son, and no other, shall have her, I will sign the contract; and I further stipulate that Micha himself shall have no right to reclaim the money later; he is the one to bear the whole cost of the bargain." Kezul gladly consents and departs to bring the witnesses, before whom Hans once more renounces his bride in favor of Micha's son. He coolly takes the money, at which they turn from him in disgust, and signs his name Hans Ehrentraut at the foot of the document.

The third act opens with a performance by tight-rope dancers. Wenzel, who has been quite despondent about his promised bride, is enraptured by their skill. He especially admires the Spanish dancer Esmeralda, who bewitches him so entirely that he woos her. The director of the band, being in want of a dancing-bear, is not loath to take advantage of the lad's foolishness. He engages him as a dancer, and easily overcomes Wenzel's scruples by promising him Esmeralda's hand. Just when they are putting him in bear's skin his parents appear on the scene with the marriage contract. To their great dismay, he refuses to sign it, and when pressed he runs away.

Meanwhile Mary has heard of her lover's fickleness, which she would fain disbelieve; but alas! Kezul shows her the document by which Hans renounces her. Nevertheless she refuses to wed any other man than the one her heart has chosen. Wenzel, approaching again, and recognizing in Mary the bride he had renounced, is now quite sorry to give her up, and very willing to take her if she will only yield. Mary, praying to be left alone for a little while, abandons herself to her grief, and is thus found by Hans, whom she bitterly reproaches for his faithlessness. But he only smiles, and recalls the whole chorus, coolly saying that it is his wish that Mary should wed Micha's son. That is too much for poor Mary's feelings. She declares that she is ready to do as they wish; but before she signs the contract, Hans steps forth in full view of his parents, who at last recognize in him their long-lost eldest son. Though his stepmother Agnes is in a rage about his trick, he claims his rights as son and heir, and the bride of course is not loath to choose between the two brothers.

Kezul the matchmaker retires shamefaced, and when Wenzel shows himself in the last scene as a dancing-bear, and stammeringly assures the laughing public that they need not be afraid of him, as he is "not a bear but only Wenzel," the final blow is dealt whereby he loses all favor in the eyes of Kruschina, who is now quite reconciled to give his daughter to Micha's eldest son.

DIE WALKÜRE
(The Valkyrs)

First day of the Nibelungen Ring by Richard Wagner.

IN the first scene we are introduced into the dwelling of a mighty warrior, Hunding, in whose house Siegmund, a son of Wotan and of a mortal woman, has sought refuge, without knowing that it is the abode of an enemy. Sieglinde, Hunding's wife, who, standing alone and abandoned in the world, was forced into this union against her will, attracts the guest's interest and wins his love.

When Hunding comes home from the fight, he learns, to his disgust, that his guest is the same warrior who killed his kinsmen and whom they vainly pursued. The laws of hospitality forbid him to attack Siegmund under his own roof, but he warns him that he will only await the morrow to fight him.

Sieglinde, having fallen in love with her guest, mixes a powder with her husband's potion, which sends him into profound sleep. Then she returns to Siegmund, to whom she shows the hilt of the sword, thrust deep into the mighty ash-tree's stem, which fills the middle space of the hut. It has been put there by an unknown one-eyed wanderer (Wotan, who once sacrificed one of his eyes to Erda, wishing to gain more knowledge for the sake of mankind). No hero has succeeded until now in loosening the wondrous steel. Siegmund reveals to Sieglinde that he is a son of the Wälsung, and they recognize that they are twin brother and sister. Then Sieglinde knows that the sword is destined for Siegmund by his father, and Siegmund with one mighty effort draws it out of the ash-tree. He names the sword Northung (needful). Sieglinde elopes with him and the early morning finds them in a rocky pass, evading Hunding's wrath.

In the second scene we see Wotan giving directions to the Valkyr Brünnhilde, who is to shield Siegmund in his battle with Hunding. Brünnhilde is Wotan's and Erda's child and her father's favorite. But Fricka comes up, remonstrating violently against this breach of all moral and matrimonial laws; she is the protector of marriages and most jealous of her somewhat fickle husband, and she forces Wotan to withdraw his protection from Siegmund and to remove the power of Siegmund's sword.

Wotan recalls Brünnhilde, changing his orders with heavy heart and sending her forth to tell Siegmund his doom. She obeys, but Siegmund scorns all her fine promises of Valhalla. Though he is to find his father there, and everything besides that he could wish, he prefers foregoing all this happiness when he hears that Sieglinde, who has been rendered inanimate by grief and terror, cannot follow him, but must go down to Hel after her death, where the shadows lead a sad and gloomy existence. He wins Brünnhilde by his love and noble courage, and she for the first time resolves to disobey Wotan's orders, given so unwillingly, and to help Siegmund against his foe.

Now ensues the combat with Hunding, Brünnhilde standing on Siegmund's side. But Wotan interferes, breaking Siegmund's sword; he falls, and Wotan kills Hunding too by one wrathful glance.

Then he turns his anger against the Valkyr who dared to disobey his commands and Brünnhilde flies before him, taking Sieglinde on her swift horse Grane, which bears both through the clouds.

In the third scene we find the Valkyrs arriving through the clouds on horseback one after the other. Every one has a hero lying before her in the saddle. It is their office to carry these into Valhalla, while the faint-hearted, or those of mankind not happy enough to fall in battle, are doomed to go to Hel after their death.

There are eight Valkyrs without Brünnhilde, who comes last with Sieglinde in her saddle, instead of a hero. She implores her sisters to assist her and the unhappy woman. But they refuse, fearing Wotan's wrath. Then she resolves to save Sieglinde and to brave the results of her rash deed alone. She first summons back to the despairing woman courage and desire to live, by telling her that she bears the token of Siegmund's love; then sends her eastward to the great forest with Grane, where Fafner the giant, changed into a dragon, guards the Rhinegold and the ill-fated ring, a spot which Wotan avoids.

She gives to Sieglinde the broken pieces of Siegmund's sword, telling her to keep them for her son, whom she is to call Siegfried, and who will be the greatest hero in the world.

Wotan arrives in thunder and lightning. Great is his wrath, and in spite of the intercession of the other Valkyrs he deprives Brünnhilde of her immortality, changing her into a common mortal. He dooms her to a long magic sleep, out of which any man who happens to pass that way may awaken her and claim her as his property.

Brünnhilde's entreaties, her beauty and noble bearing at last prevail upon him, so that he encircles her with a fiery wall, through which none but a hero may penetrate.

After a touching farewell the god, leading her to a rocky bed, closes her eyes with a kiss, and covers her with shield, spear, and helmet. Then he calls up Loge, who at once surrounds the rock on which Brünnhilde sleeps with glowing flames.

WERTHER

Lyric Drama in three acts by Jules Massenet. Text from Goethe by Blau, Milliet, and Hartmann.

THE scene is laid in Wetzlar, Prussia, in the year 1772. The first act takes place in the house of Lotte's father, who is a bailiff in his native city. He has assembled his younger children to teach them a new Christmas song. While they are practising, two friends of the bailiff enter and invite him to sup with them at the neighboring inn. He declines, and sits down in his armchair, while the smaller children, climbing on his knees, resume their interrupted song. During this pretty scene Werther approaches. He sees Lotte coming out of the house, becomingly attired for a country ball. She is duly admired by her father and the children. Then she acquits herself most charmingly of her household duties, distributing bread to the children. Werther meanwhile is cordially welcomed by her father. Other visitors come in, and Lotte goes to attend the ball, escorted by Werther.

Sophia, the second daughter, persuades her father to join his friends at the inn and promises to look after the children. As soon as he is gone Albert, Lotte's affianced husband, who has been on a journey, returns. On hearing that Lotte is not at home, he leaves the house again. When night comes on, Lotte returns with Werther. He is deeply in love with her, and she listens to his sweet words like one in a dream, but when her father informs her that Albert has returned she comes to her senses. In answer to Werther's questions she tells him that she promised her dying mother to wed Albert—a confession that leaves Werther a prey to gloom and despair.

The second act takes place in the autumn of the same year. Lotte is married to Albert. She has conquered her sentimental fancy for Werther and is sitting quietly with her husband, enjoying a peaceful Sabbath and the celebration of the village clergyman's golden wedding. Werther is a jealous witness of her happiness; but when Albert welcomes him as a friend he cannot but accept his overtures.

Sophia enters with a large bouquet for the clergyman. She is in love with Werther, but the unhappy young man has eyes for her sister only, who receives him coldly and bids him leave the village.

On seeing Werther so cast down, Lotte repents of her harshness and invites him to celebrate Christmas with her and her husband. But Werther refuses to be consoled and hurries away, notwithstanding Sophia's entreaties, vowing never to return.

The third act takes us to Lotte's drawing-room. She is sitting alone in deep thought. Werther's frequent and passionate letters have reawakened her dormant love for him. Her sister, coming in laden with Christmas parcels, finds her in tears. Unable to console Lotte, Sophia takes her leave after inviting her to spend Christmas eve at her old home.

Hardly has she gone when Werther appears. Unable to keep away from Lotte any longer, he reminds her of her invitation for Christmas; and seeing his letters spread out on the table, he guesses that Lotte returns his love. An impassioned love-scene follows. Half unconscious, Lotte sinks into his arms, but the first kiss of her lover brings her to herself. Tearing herself from his embrace, she flees into her room and bolts the door. After vain remonstrances, Werther rushes out half-crazed.

Albert, returning home, finds no one in. He calls Lotte. She appears, pale and distressed, and her husband perceives that something is wrong. Before she can reply to his questions a servant brings in a note from Werther, asking Albert for his pistol. The husband forces his unhappy wife to hand the weapon to the servant herself. As soon as Albert has gone

Lotte seizes her hat and cloak and hastens out to prevent the impending calamity. Alas! she comes too late.

The last scene shows Werther's room, dimly lighted by the moon. The Christmas bells toll. Lotte enters, calling her lover by name. She discovers him lying on the floor mortally wounded. Now that he is lost to her forever, she pours out all her love and for a brief space calls him back to life and sweetens his last moments by a first kiss. He expires in her arms, while from the opposite house the children's voices are heard singing their Christmas song.

ZAMPA

Opera in three acts by Louis J. F. Hérold.
Text by Mellesville.

IN the first act Camilla, daughter of Count Lugano, expects her bridegroom Alfonso di Monza, a Sicilian officer, for the wedding ceremony. Dandolo, her servant, who was to bring the priest, comes back in a fright, and with him the notorious pirate captain, Zampa, who has taken her father and her bridegroom captive. He tells Camilla who he is, and forces her to renounce Alfonso and consent to a marriage with himself, threatening to kill the prisoners if she refuses compliance.

Then the pirates hold a drinking-bout in the Count's house, and Zampa goes so far in his insolence as to put his bridal ring on the finger of a marble statue standing in the room. It represents Alice, formerly Zampa's bride, whose heart was broken by her lover's faithlessness; then the fingers of the statue close over the ring, while the left hand is upraised threateningly. Nevertheless Zampa is resolved to wed Camilla, though Alice appears once more, and even Alfonso, who interferes by revealing Zampa's real name and by imploring his bride to return to him, cannot change the brigand's plans. Zampa and his comrades have received the viceroy's pardon, purposing to fight against the Turks, and so Camilla dares not provoke the pirate's wrath by retracting her promise. Vainly she implores Zampa to give her father his freedom and to let her enter a convent. Zampa, hoping that she only fears the pirate in him, tells her that he is Count of Monza, and Alfonso, who had already drawn his sword, throws it away, terrified to recognize in the dreaded pirate his own brother, who has by his extravagances once already impoverished him.

Zampa sends Alfonso to prison and orders the statue to be thrown into the sea. Camilla once more begs for mercy, but seeing that it is likely to avail her nothing, she flies to the Madonna's altar, charging Zampa loudly with Alice's death. With scorn and laughter he seizes Camilla, to tear her from the altar, but instead of the living hand of Camilla, he feels the icy hand of Alice, who draws him with her into the waves.

Camilla is saved and united to Alfonso, while her delivered father arrives in a boat, and the statue rises again from the waves, to bless the union.

"Zampa" is generally regarded as the most important work of Hérold, and while less popular than formerly, it still keeps a place of its own.

DIE ZAUBERFLÖTE
(The Magic Flute)

Opera in two acts by Wolfgang Amadeus Mozart.
Text by Schikaneder.

PRINCE TAMINO, a youth as valiant as he is noble and virtuous, is implored by the Queen of Night to save her daughter, whom the old and sage high priest Sarastro has taken from her by force. The bereaved mother pours forth her woe in heart-melting sounds and promises everything to the rescuer of her child. Tamino is filled with ardent desire to serve her. On his way he meets the gay Papageno, who at once agrees to share the Prince's adventures. Papageno is the gay element in the opera; always cheerful and in high spirits, his ever-ready tongue plays him many a funny trick. So we see him once with a lock on his mouth by way of punishment for his idle prating. As he promises never to tell a lie any more, the lock is taken away by the three ladies of the Queen of Night. They present Tamino with a golden flute, giving at the same time an instrument made with little silver bells to Papageno, both of which are to help them in times of danger. The Queen of Night even sends with them three boy angels. These are to point out to them the ways and means by which they may attain their purpose.

Now the young and beautiful Princess Pamina is pursued by declarations of love from a negro servant of Sarastro. Papageno comes to her rescue, frightening the negro Monostatos with his feathery dress. Papageno, on the other hand, fears the negro on account of his blackness, believing him to be the devil in person. Papageno escapes with Pamina, but the negro overtakes him with his servants. Then Papageno shakes his bells, and all, forgetting their wrath, forthwith begin to dance.

Meanwhile Tamino reaches Sarastro's castle and at once asks for the high priest, poor Pamina's bitter enemy. The under priests do not allow him to enter, but explain that their master Sarastro is as good as he is sage, and that he always acts for the best. They assure Tamino that the Princess lives and is in no danger. Full of thanks the Prince begins to play on his flute; and just then he hears Papageno's bells. At this juncture Sarastro appears, the wise master before whom they all bow. He punishes the wicked negro; but Tamino and his Pamina are not to be united without first having given ample proof of their love and constancy. Tamino determines to undergo whatever trials may await him, but the Queen of Night, knowing all, sends her three ladies to deter Tamino and his comrade from their purpose. But all temptation is gallantly set aside; they have given a promise to Sarastro which they will keep.

Even the Queen of Night herself is unable to weaken their strength of purpose; temptations of every kind overtake them, but Tamino remains firm. He is finally initiated into the mysteries of the goddess Isis.

In the interval Pamina deems Tamino faithless. She would fain die, but the three celestial youths console her by assuring her that Tamino's love is true and that he passes through the most severe trials solely on her behalf.

On hearing this, Pamina at once asks to share in the trials, and so they walk together through fire and water, protected by the golden flute as well as by their courage and constancy. They come out purified and happy.

Papageno, having lost his companion, has grown quite melancholy and longs for the little wife that was promised to him and shown to him only for a few moments. He resolves at last to end his life by hanging himself, when the celestial youths appear, reminding him of his bells. He begins to shake them, and Papagena appears in feathery dress, the very counterpart of himself. All might now be well were it not that the Queen of Night, a somewhat unreasonable lady, broods vengeance. She accepts the negro Monostatos as her avenger and promises to give him her daughter. But already Sarastro has done his work. Tamino is united to his Pamina, and before the sunny light of truth everything else vanishes and sinks back into night.

STORIES OF MODERN OPERAS

•L'AMORE DEI TRE RE

(The Love of the Three Kings)

Opera in three acts by Italo Montemezzi.
Text by Sem Benelli.

ONE night the blind old King Archibaldo could not sleep. Before dawn, he had one of his servants lead him to an open place on the battlements between two chambers where a torch burned through the darkness as a signal to Manfredo, who might suddenly return from the wars. As they sat and talked there, and Archibaldo told how first, as a young chieftain, he had come into Italy, he felt that on that day Manfredo would return to the castle. Restless and perturbed he sought his chamber. . . . Then, as the dawn flamed suddenly, from her chamber, which was over against his, came the young princess, Fiora, and with her the prince, Avito. In passionate embrace they had told their love; since, before the barbarians had taken Fiora, she and Avito had been betrothed. When they heard a shepherd's pipe and saw that the torch was out, Avito knew that the day had come, and went his way. But scarcely had he gone before old Archibaldo wandered again to the battlement, and though Fiora stood in silence, yet did he feel her presence. He bade her tell him what she did there when all the castle was still asleep. She evaded his questioning and lied to him unfalteringly. By intuition and by the promptings of his suspicious spirit, he knew that she did not speak the truth, and that she had had a lover with her. But for Manfredo's sake and for the pride of his line he determined to keep the secret. Then, all of a sudden, out of the distance gleamed the trailing line of Manfredo's spearmen; soon his trumpet sounded, and now he was upon the battlement in his father's embrace and telling how he had forsaken the siege in longing for Fiora, his wife. Yet when she came from her chamber to greet him she was cold and distant, albeit in a speech of great affection Manfredo told his love for her. As they went again to her chamber, the old man, bitter and troubled, suspecting and fearing, thanked God that he was blind.

The second act deals with Manfredo's stay of many days in the castle and his frantic wooing of Fiora. Then it came to pass that he must return to the wars. When he took leave of her on the great terrace in the warm light of the afternoon, he begged her that she give some sign of her affection. She relented. Then he told her that as he and his host descended from the castle and wound away into the valley they could long see that terrace. On it she, Fiora, was to stand and wave her white scarf so long as she could see Manfredo, to be a token of her affection. She said that she would do all that he had charged her. There-

upon Manfredo departed as one distraught between loving anticipation and haunting dread. Fiora waited until Manfredo went down into the valley and until her handmaid brought her the scarf. Musing sorrowfully, she stood thus upon the highest part of the terrace.

Of a sudden, at the foot of the steps behind her, called Avito, for he had not quit the castle at dawn; one of the guardsmen, in loyalty to his prince, had harbored him. Avito entreated Fiora out of his love and despair, while she, feigning cold anger, bade him go his way, and fell a-waving of her kerchief. Yet still did Avito entreat and proclaim his passion and kiss the golden fringe, the hem of her mantle; for her hand had embroidered it. Then, more and more slowly did she wave the scarf, until at last it was as lead in her hand. Then came she swiftly down from the high place and fell weeping upon Avito's breast, giving herself utterly to him. In the sunset they sat upon the great stone seat and drank their fill of love, knowing not that old Archibaldo was stealing upon them. Though he was sightless, yet did he hear and know, and a great and bitter lust of vengeance came upon him. But Avito evaded him in his blindness, and Fiora, though she flaunted her lover cruelly in the old man's face, would not tell his name. Then the old king, beside himself, seized her by her false throat and strangled her and she lay dead upon the great seat. . . . As he stood before her body to hide it, Manfredo came striding out of the gathering night. For when he had seen the kerchief drop from Fiora's hand fear had come upon him that ill had befallen her. His father told him what ill had really befallen and what he had done. Hearing this, Manfredo cried aloud that there was such love, then in the girl's heart —a love that was stronger than life—yet she would not give it to him. He would fain know to whom she had given it. Old Archibaldo knew not, and when Manfredo shrank from him, he cast Fiora's body over his shoulder and went his way.

The third act is cast in the crypt of the castle, wherein the image of the Crucified looked down upon it, stood Fiora's bier all spread with white flowers and white candles at her head and feet. Around her the women, young and old, of the castle made their moan, and the distant choir answered them, hymning God, who is Lord of Death as He is of Life. Between their chants they whispered that Fiora had been slain in vengeance. Then out of the darkness came Avito. By Fiora's bier he knelt and cried that he might die with her. But when he kissed her cold lips they were hot with a poison that the crafty old king had smeared upon them as a snare wherein to catch him whose mistress she had been. When the poison spread through Avito's veins and he was like to die, Manfredo came also to the bier. He saw Avito and knew, but he would not slay him, since he, too, had come to die by the poison of a woman's lips. Then in the darkness, old Archibaldo seized him as Fiora's lover, but when he knew that it was his son who was dead, too, he cried that all were gone where there is only darkness.

ARIANE ET BARBE-BLEUE

(Ariane and Blue Beard)

Opera in three acts by Paul Dukas.
Text by Maurice Maeterlinck.

A LARGE and splendid hall in Blue Beard's castle ushers in the first scene. Through the windows the angry voices of a crowd of peasants are heard, who have gathered to witness the return home of the infamous Blue Beard, accompanied by his sixth wife. They know the fate that has befallen the other five, and wish to save this one—the most beautiful of all—from becoming a victim like the rest. But all they can do is to shout a warning to her and to accuse the husband who is escorting her home. . . . Suddenly the windows close, shutting out the tumult of the crowd, and Ariane, accompanied by her nurse, appears in the hall. Ariane, who has heard of the five wives, does not believe that they are dead. She tells the nurse so, and adds that through her husband's love for her she will get to know his secret. Her first act must be disobedience. He has given her six silver keys, which she may use to open his bridal treasures. But the seventh key, a golden one, she is forbidden to use. This is the most important to her; so she throws the others away. The nurse picks them up, and noticing that around the hall there are six doors with silver locks, she opens each door in turn. There are indeed treasures within! The first key unlocks a vault in which amethysts are stored in vast quantities, and which now come tumbling into the room, to the astonishment of the two women. The second vault contains the most beautiful sapphires, and these, too, roll out upon the floor. The third vault is filled with rare pearls; the fourth with emeralds; the fifth with rubies, tragic in their blood-red color, and the sixth with diamonds of the purest water, whose beauty astounds Ariane. So far it was the nurse alone that had gone into raptures over the jewels, but the diamonds are too beautiful for even Ariane to resist. She bedecks herself with them. Then, looking farther within the vault, she sees an inner door whose lock is of gold. Going in, she inserts her key and opens the door. A low, muffled chant, which grows louder as it continues, greets her ear, and she is convinced it is the voices of the other wives, entombed below. She is about to descend into the vault, in spite of the protests of the nurse, when Blue Beard enters. He demands of Ariane how she dared to disobey him, but promises to pardon her if she will forego her curiosity. This she will not do—she must "know all." Blue Beard tries to drag her away, and she cries out. Her cries are heard by the peasants without, and stones are thrown through the windows. The nurse opens the door of the hall, admitting the angry crowd which gathered, hesitatingly, upon the threshold. Blue Beard draws his sword to defend himself, but Ariane, calmly approaching the peasants, gently pushes them back and closes the door. "He has done me no harm," she tells them.

In the second act the scene has changed to the underground vaults, below Blue Beard's castle. Ariane and the nurse, taking advantage of Blue Beard's absence, set off in search of the five wives, whom Ariane suspects are imprisoned here. Ariane, with the aid of the lamp she carries, penetrates the deep gloom of this subterranean prison and discovers the five wives—Melisande, Bellangére, Alladine, Ygraine and Selysette—all huddled together in a corner. They are in rags, with disheveled hair and pallid countenances that little suggest the beauty which was formerly theirs. Ariane caresses them and tries to calm their fears, assuring them that she has come to rescue them; but they cannot believe this possible, they have been so long confined in this dark, dreary prison. While they are talking, Ariane's lamp is extinguished by accident, and the group is plunged into darkness more intense than ever. Selysette, however, knows the location of her prison and directs Ariane's attention to a distant glow that dimly illumines one corner of the vault. Ariane bravely goes on till she discovers a trap-door, which she opens. Above this trap is a glass skylight which Ariane shatters, admitting the glare of daylight. Following the example of brave Ariane, they clamber up through the opening and joyously disappear into the golden sunlight.

The third act returns to the hall in Blue Beard's castle. The jewels are still flashing upon the floor and in the niches in the wall. The five rescued wives stand before mirrors arranging their hair and adjusting the beautiful gowns they have found and appropriated. Ariane, going from one to the other, advises and assists them. They have been unable to escape from the castle, as all the gates are locked, but Ariane knows that the peasants are without, hidden behind the hedges, and that they are watching over them. She expects that Blue Beard will presently return with assistance, and she wishes his five wives to appear before him as beautiful as possible. She therefore suggests to them how best to enhance their charms by a proper attention to their costumes, and by selecting the most becoming jewels from the great abundance before them. While they are thus engaged, the nurse enters, terrified, with the news that Blue Beard is returning; this she has heard from one of the guards, who, unseen by the wives, has been watching them in their master's absence. The five wives are alarmed by the news, but Ariane reassures them. They then ascend to one of the windows, whence they watch the fight between Blue Beard (first assisted by negro attendants, later by the guards) and the enraged peasants, who, being victorious, are about to throw Blue Beard into the moat, when the wives, seeing their purpose, shout to them to spare him. Blue Beard is then brought into the castle hall where the wives are waiting in terror; all save Ariane, who calmly opens the doors to admit the angry, noisy crowd. Blue Beard, bound, and helpless with his wounds, is now at the mercy of his wives, to whom the angry peasants deliver him for vengeance. Ariane dismisses the mob and after they have gone she cuts the cords that bind Blue Beard, and, assisted by the wives, attends to his wounds and revives him. Blue Beard is astonished on opening his eyes to see these beautiful women around him, and can hardly believe that they are the wives he imprisoned. His gaze travels to Ariane, however, and when she approaches to bid him goodbye he tries to keep her. But Ariane's work is done and she must leave him to the love and attention of the others. She asks them each in turn if they will come with her, but none of them will now leave Blue Beard, and thus she goes forth alone.

BORIS GODOUNOFF

Opera in four acts and prologue by Modest Moussorgsky. Text founded upon Pushkin.

THIS story is about a Tartan upstart, one Boris Godounoff, who climbed up into a high place in the councils of the Czar Ivan the Terrible, and was made regent during the minority of Ivan's son. He used his power to bring about the murder of the heir, Demetrius, and, after pretending to hesitate and be very reluctant, he ascended the throne. Once he had attained his ambition his conscience began to trouble him, and when there arose in the west a claimant for the throne, pretending to be the murdered heir Demetrius, his fears preyed upon him day and night. Boris began to pray that the false Demetrius might prove to be the true one, so that he might be free from the guilt of murder. But the officer whom he had commissioned to execute the murder assured him that the lad had been actually killed, and Boris died terror-stricken by terrible visions.

In the first scene, a street in Moscow, the people are mourning the state of Russia, whose royal line has been extinguished, and are begging Boris to ascend the throne. He appears and refuses. The second scene, taken almost in its entirety from Pushkin, shows a lonely cell in which the monk Pimen insinuates into the mind of a young monk, Gregory, that he is the true Demetrius, son of the dead Czar. In the third scene Boris accepts the crown and is joyfully acclaimed by the populace. The fourth scene is an inn on the frontier of Lithuania, where the false Demetrius, accompanied by two drunken tramps, is seen on his way to Moscow to proclaim himself the true Czar, and narrowly escapes arrest at the hands of the police. Next we see the palace of the Czar, with Boris in conversation with his young son Feodor, and later receiving reports of the uprising of Poland on behalf of the false Demetrius. Already conscience has begun its deadly work. The two scenes following are inserted for the sake of the love *motif*. There are gay doings at the home of a noble Polish lady, Marina Minishek. In the course of the scenes Marina talks with a Jesuit priest, who knows of the pretender's attention to her and hopes through her to make the Roman Catholic religion the official faith of Russia. The second scene closes with a love duet between Marina and Gregory. The next scene shows Boris, surrounded by the Boyards, discussing measures of state. An interview with Pimen dispels any possible hope that the true Demetrius may not after all have been murdered, and the Czar, after bidding farewell to his son, falls dead. The last scene shows the gath-

ering of the people to support the pretender, and the acclamation of him as he approaches with his army. The final scene is usually played before the one preceding in order that the opera may end with the death of the chief figure. But Moussorgsky's intention in placing the scenes as he did is evident. Boris, for all the interest attaching to him, is a subordinate figure. The hero of the opera is the Russian people. It is the people which dominates the last scene, as it did the first, presenting a national drama which is greater than any individual.

LE COQ D'OR

(The Golden Cock)

Opera in three acts by Rimsky-Korsakov. Text founded upon Pushkin.

AN old astrologer opens the work by declaring that, although the opera is

A fairy tale, not solid truth, It holds a moral good for youth.

The first scene is laid in a hall in the palace of King Dodon. He is tired of his royal responsibilities, and especially of the perpetual warfare with his hostile neighbors; he wants to rest. First he asks the advice of his heir, Prince Gvidon; then of his second son, then of his generalissimo, Polkan.

Very soon the whole assembly is in an uproar over the best way out of the difficulty; then the Astrologer arrives upon the scene. He offers to give King Dodon a golden cock which will always give warning in case of danger. At first the King does not believe him, but the cock is produced and at once proclaims: "Kikeriki! Kikerikou! Be on your guard; mind what you do!"

The King is delighted and feels that he can now take his ease. He offers to give the Astrologer whatever reward he asks. Dodon's bed is brought in, and the chatelaine of the palace tucks him up and keeps watch until he falls into a sound sleep. Suddenly the shrill crowing of the Golden Cock awakens the King and his attendants. The first time this happens he has to send his unwilling sons to the war; the second time he is obliged to go himself.

In the second act, Dodon and his general, Polkan, with their army, come to a narrow pass among the rocks, after the battle is over. Here Dodon comes suddenly upon the dead bodies of his two sons, who have apparently killed each other.

The wretched egotistical King is reduced to tears at the sight. His attention, however, is soon distracted, for, as the distant mist clears away, he sees under the shelter of the hillside a large tent lit up by the rays of the rising run. He thinks it is the tent of the hostile leader. But, to the great astonishment of the King and his Voyevode, a beautiful woman emerges from the tent, followed by her slaves bearing musical instruments. She sings a song of greeting to the dawn.

Dodon approaches and asks her name. She replies modestly that she is the Queen of Shemakha. Then follows a long scene, in which she casts her wiles on the old King until he is hopelessly infatuated with her beauty. Her recital of her own attractions is very complete, and soon she has completely turned old Dodon's head. She insists on his singing and mocks at his voice; she forces him to dance until he falls exhausted to the ground, and laughs at his uncouth movements.

Finally, the Queen of Shemakha consents to return to his capital and become his bride. Amid much that is genuinely comic there are touches of grim realism in this scene, in which the indolent and sensual old King is fooled to the top of his bent by the capricious and heartless Queen.

The curtain rises in the third act upon another of those scenes of bustle and vigorous movement characteristic of Russian opera. The people are awaiting the return of King Dodon. "Jump and dance, grin and bow, show your loyalty, but don't expect anything in return," says the sardonic chatelaine, Amelfa.

Then enters a wonderful procession which reminds one of an Eastern fairy tale: the advance guard of the King; the Queen of Shemakha, in a bizarre costume, followed by a grotesque cortège of giants, dwarfs and black slaves. At this juncture the Astrologer makes his appearance, and a storm, long threatening, bursts over the city. The King gives a flattering welcome to the Astrologer and expresses his readiness to reward him for the gift of the Golden Cock. The Astrologer asks nothing less than the Queen of Shemakha herself. The King refuses with indignation and in his wrath hits the Astrologer over the head with his scepter. General consternation reigns in the crowd. The Queen laughs a cold, cruel laugh, but the King is terrified, for he thinks that he has killed the Astrologer.

Suddenly the Cock gives out a shrill, threatening cry; he flies on to the King's head, and with one blow of his beak pierces his skull. The King falls dead. A loud clap of thunder is followed by darkness, during which the sarcastic laugh of the Queen is heard. When it grows light again Queen and Cock have both disappeared, and the unhappy and bewildered people sing a mournful chorus of regret for the King.

The opera concludes with a short epilogue in which the Astrologer bids the spectators dry their tears, since the whole story is nothing but fiction, and in the kingdom of Dodon there were but two real human beings, himself and the Queen.

LE DONNE CURIOSE

(The Inquisitive Women)

Musical Comedy in three acts by Ermanno Wolf-Ferrari. Text by Luigi Sugana.

A ROOM in a clubhouse, the members playing chess and chatting, opens the play. Florindo is sighing like a furnace for his sweetheart, Rosaura, the daughter of Ottavio. The members talk over the efforts of their wives and daughters to fathom the secrets of the organization, but Florindo only sings of his sweetheart. Leandro, who is a bachelor, suggests a dinner for the evening, and they all agree to allow old Pantalone, the president, to pay for it. He comes in and agrees. His servant, Arlecchino,

appears and is told to order a fine spread for that evening at ten o'clock. Pantalone insists that the club's secrets must be absolutely kept from the women.

The next scene is laid in a room in the home of Ottavio, who is late for dinner, detained, of course, at his horrid club. His wife, Beatrice, and his daughter Rosaura, are suspicious; Beatrice feels sure they gamble there, Rosaura's theory is that they meet women there. Elenora, a neighbor, drops in and she is positive that the men are merely alchemists looking for the philosopher's stone. Colombina, a maid, rushes in breathlessly and announces that she has discovered that the club is looking for buried treasure. And now Arlecchino, who is secretly courting Colombina, comes in, the women pounce upon him with their various ideas as to the object of the club, he agrees with all of them. They turn upon him in a rage, he flees, leaving the women as mystified as ever, but each still positive that her theory is the correct one. Ottavio comes home and his wife tries to wheedle out of him the secrets of the club. He goes off in a huff, she following him. Florindo appears, but Rosaura declares that she will not give him her heart until he tells her the secret of the club. He tries to avoid the question, then Colombina suggests to Rosaura that she try the effect of swooning. She pretends to faint. Florindo is frantic and Colombina tells him that the only way to restore Rosaura is to reveal to her the secrets of the club. Thus she makes him reveal the rule of the club, that no women shall be admitted; that their motto is "Friendship," and the fact that there is to be a supper at ten o'clock; every member having his own key. Colombina then gets rid of him and speedily revives Rosaura.

A room in Lelio's house introduces the next scene. His wife is going through his pockets in true wifely fashion. She finds two new keys with a letter from Pantalone saying that the locks have just been changed. Crying "Victory! Victory!" she restores the letter, but not the keys. Lelio comes in and she asks him if he is going back to the alchemist's furnace. He is furious at her nagging, and they storm out at opposite doors.

In scene two, a room in Ottavio's house, Colombina tells all that she has learned. Only one thing is lacking—the key to get in with. Beatrice manages to get her husband to change his coat so that she may search the pockets of it. Colombina brings back the things she found in the pockets, and informs Beatrice that she has substituted the cellar keys for the club keys. Beatrice seizes the keys and tells Rosaura that she is too young to go to a men's club. Rosaura, left alone, muses over Florindo, he steals back, but she refuses to relent unless he gives her the keys, so finally he yields to her.

A street in Venice before the clubhouse, with a canal behind, opens act three. Pantalone comes out looking for Arlecchino, who appears loaded with bottles, but has forgotten the candles; he goes inside to get them, and Pantalone follows him. A gondola draws up to the landing and Elenora steps from it, as Arlecchino comes from the clubhouse. Elenora in her terror drops her keys and runs. Arlecchino pockets them and goes on his way as Colombina, disguised as a man, enters with Beatrice from a side street. Beatrice hides as Pantalone comes out, and seeing Colombina give the password "Friendship." He soon finds out that Colombina is only a disguised woman, and snatches the keys from her. She runs off, leaving Pantalone wondering who the traitor is who has given the club keys into a woman's keeping. Pantalone goes back into the club. Lelio and Ottavio come up. Lelio is puzzled at not finding his keys in his pocket. Florindo appears. Ottavio twits him about his love for the capricious Rosaura. Ottavio, about to open the club door, finds that he has the cellar keys in his pocket. He turns to Florindo for his. Florindo in some confusion says that he left them at home. The three locked out members knock, and Pantalone comes to the door in a very bad temper and shows the keys that have been found. Lelio and Ottavio follow him into the club, but Florindo remains, seeing a servant with a lantern preceding a woman. He conceals himself, and Rosaura, masked, follows her servant; the servant is about to put the key in the door when Florindo snatches it from him. Rosaura drops her mask and the servant runs away. Florindo reproaches Rosaura for trying to betray him, and entering the club, slams the door behind him. Arlecchino, who has seen this quarrel, catches Rosaura as she faints. While he is wondering what to do with his burden, Beatrice and Elenora appear. Beatrice, recognizing her daughter, faints in Arlecchino's other arm. Colombina runs and prepares to faint also, but Arlecchino reminds her that he had not arms enough for three. The women recover and begin to cry. They now round upon Arlecchino. Colombina tries to bribe him with caresses; Beatrice offers him money; Rosaura offers him earrings; Colombina offers him a dinner and kisses. But he refuses them all. Then they turn upon him in a fury, and he perforce surrenders the keys. They open the club door and enter while Arlecchino, picking up the lantern, looks up and down the street, ironically calling out, "Are there any others who want to get in?"

A room in the clubhouse, with a heavy door leading to the dining-room, is scene two. The members of the club are congratulating Pantalone, who warns them not to give to a woman the keys either to a door or to their hearts. Arlecchino announces supper, and the members enter the banquet-room. When the door is closed the four women steal from their hiding-places, somewhat surprised to find that the mysterious activity of the club consists of a simple stag supper. The men hear laughter, and the women, taking turns at the keyhole, describe what is going on. They grow hungry at the sight of the banquet, and when Arlecchino comes in at a side door with a dish of tarts, they rob him of them. They struggle so frantically for the privilege of peeping through the keyhole, that they push the door open. The club members arise in amazement from the table, and Pantalone exclaims that he has heard of showers of frogs, and showers of larks, but never before of showers of women. The women apologize for their suspicions and are forgiven. One of the members begins to play the spinet and Pantalone chucks Colombina under the chin. Arlecchino protests that her hand belongs to him, and she gives it to him—over the ear. A minuet is begun,

and it gradually develops into a livelier and livelier dance, during which Pantalone gives Arlecchino a clip over the head and sends him face downward into a large dish of whipped cream. The dance breaks up with a general cry of the club's motto, "Friendship."

LA FANCIULLA DEL WEST
(The Girl of the Golden West)

Opera in three acts by Giacomo Puccini.
Text by Zangarini and Civinini.

READERS of Bret Harte will see in the drama a picture of the life of a California which has completely passed away—the California of the 1849 gold-hunting craze, where pistols took the place of courts of law, and where a rough and ready code of honor did duty for ethics. In this atmosphere the orphan Minnie, "the Girl," has lived for some years without stain or soil, besides teaching the miners their Sunday-school lessons. She is very pretty and is looked up to as a sort of goddess. The sheriff of the neighborhood, one Jack Rance, is very much in love with her, and although married to a woman back East, is anxious to marry her. In the first act we see the goings-on of the "Polka" bar-room, where the miners gather and drink after their day's work. They gamble and nearly lynch a cheater. They hear the reports of the "greaser" robber Ramerrez, and listen to their Sunday-school lesson from Minnie. The girl, on her side, listens to Rance's proposal of marriage, and rejects him because he is married; moreover, she dislikes him. Then a certain Dick Johnson enters. Minnie knew him in the old days, and promptly falls in love with him. The miners go out in search of the robber Ramerrez, and leave Johnson and Minnie to a duet which is one of the best things in the opera.

The second act deals with the same night in Minnie's cabin. Johnson comes to call on her, as prearranged, and Minnie, amid the roaring of the wind, receives her first kiss. Johnson hides as Rance enters to tell Minnie that her beau is no other than Ramerrez the robber. After Rance has gone, Johnson confesses the truth to Minnie, but says that his life changed the moment he met her, and vows to go out and meet his fate like a man. He leaves, a moment later falling back into the cabin, bleeding with pistol wounds. Minnie's love thrusts aside every consideration and she hides him in the garret. Rance enters in search of his prey. After having gone over the whole place he is convinced that no one is there, but just as he is leaving a drop of blood falls upon his hand. Searching once more, he finds Johnson in the garret and makes him come down. Minnie pleads with him, and finally arranges to play a game of cards; the bargain being that if she wins, her lover's life is to be spared; if she loses, she is to marry the sheriff. They play, while Johnson looks on. Rance has promised to be a sport, and to abide by the result of the card game, but Minnie has not the slightest intention of losing. So she commits the most heinous sin of the times, she hides a card in her stocking and cheats to win,—without being caught. Rance loses, accepts his fate and leaves.

But Johnson still has to escape the mob. In the

last act, in the forest, they are waiting for him. While trying to escape, he is captured, and is about to be hanged when Minnie appears. She pleads with the men, and wins them one by one to her side. They agree to free her and her lover, and the two depart for another and distant home, while the sunset reddens the great trees of the forest.

FRANCESCA DA RIMINI

Opera in four acts by Riccardo Zandonai.
Text by Gabriele D'Annunzio.

FRANCESCA, daughter of Guido da Polenta, for state reasons, is to be married to Giovanni, known as Gianciotti, the malformed son of Malatesta da Verrucchio. But as Francesca would certainly refuse to marry the lame and deformed Gianciotto, she is introduced in the first act, by means of a well-laid plot, to his handsome younger brother, Paolo, known as il Bello. Under the impression that Paolo is her destined bridegroom, Francesca falls deeply in love with him at first sight; he also falls passionately in love with her, although they do not exchange a single word.

The next act shows a fight in progress between the Guelfs and Ghibellines, and on the platform of a tower of the Malatesti, Francesca, now married to Gianciotto, meets Paolo and gently reproaches him for the fraud practised on her. He protests his innocence of the plot and reveals his intense passion for her. Gianciotto brings the news of Paolo's election as Captain of the People and Commune of Florence. Paolo departs for Florence.

In the third act Francesca, in her luxurious apartment, is reading the story of Lancelot and Guinevere to her women. They then dance and sing in celebration of the advent of Spring, until, on a whispered word from her slave, Francesca dismisses them. Paolo, sick with longing for her, has returned from Florence. He enters; they continue reading the story of Guinevere together, until, no longer in control of their feelings, they let their lips meet in a long kiss.

In the fourth act Malatestino, Gianciotto's youngest brother, who himself cherishes a guilty love for Francesca, has discovered her secret meetings with Paolo, and betrays them to Gianciotto, who determines to find out the truth for himself. Accordingly, he lies in wait outside Francesca's door, and surprising her and Paolo together at early dawn, he slays them both.

I GIOJELLE DELLA MADONNA

(The Jewels of the Madonna)

Opera in three acts by Ermanno Wolf-Ferrari.
Text by Golisciani.

IT is the afternoon of the festival of the Madonna, and the little square by the sea, where stand Carmela's house, Gennaro's workshop, and Biaso's hut and tavern, is crowded with merrymakers of all sorts. Thus opens the play. When the crowd is somewhat dispersed, Gennaro works at his anvil on a wrought-iron candelabrum. Totonno twits him for being so serious. When he is gone, Gennaro kneels before the anvil as at an altar and pledges the gift to the Madonna. Maliella rushes out of the house in disarray, rebuked by her foster-mother, Carmela. Gennaro, her foster-brother, protests against her reckless ways, and she accuses him of jealousy. Biaso, the scribe, gives her a paper cap and she sings the "Canzone di Cannetella," while a chorus of Camorrists come over the bay. Then Maliella dashes out, followed by a crowd of young men; and Gennaro pours out to his mother, Carmela, the story of his jealous anguish. The mother tells how, when Gennaro was a sick baby, about to die, she vowed to adopt a misbegotten infant girl if the Madonna would spare Gennaro's life. Maliella has turned out badly, but Carmela hopes that marriage with an honest man will reform her. The Camorrists chase Biaso and threaten him because he has protested against their pursuit of Maliella. Among them is Rafaele, their chief. He seizes the girl in his arms and sings of love. She tries to escape, but they surround her and sing a mock serenade. She defends herself with a sharp hatpin, and stabs Rafaele in the hand. He kisses the wound made by her "kiss of steel," and thrusts a flower on her bosom. She throws the flower away.

The crowd now appears to watch the procession of children in white, preceding the image of the Madonna. During the procession Rafaele pours out his love and asks her if she wishes to be adored kneeling, and if she wishes him to steal the Jewels of the Madonna for her. Gennaro appears and warns her against Rafaele. When Maliella defends him, Gennaro orders her into the house, and is about to attack Rafaele; but the procession reappears, and all must kneel.

Act two is laid in the garden of Carmela's house in the evening. Maliella stands near the railing looking longingly toward the sea. Carmela bids them good-night and goes in. Maliella turns on Gennaro, saying that she is sick of this gloom and is going away. She goes inside and can be seen at her window packing her things, as she sings a popular love song. She comes out with her bundle and Gennaro checks her, lovingly embraces her and pours out his devotion. She is astounded, but says she could only love a man of reckless courage like the one who had offered to steal the Jewels of the Madonna for her. Gennaro is horrified, but when she starts to go he prevents her, and she storms back to her room in a rage, leaving him alone with his lawless temptation. At last he goes to a tool chest and, taking out skeleton keys and files, steals away like a thief.

A group of serenading Camorrists, among them Rafaele, appear and call upon Maliella to open her window. Maliella appears, Rafaele makes love to her and promises to make her queen of his band. At last she embraces him through the bars of the gate just as a warning is given that Gennaro is returning. Rafaele disappears as Gennaro comes back horror-stricken at his deed. He carries a bundle, which he opens at Maliella's feet. It contains the Jewels of the Madonna. Maliella is terrified, but Gennaro, with passion declares "The Madonna knows that I am guiltless." Fascinated, Maliella takes up the necklace and notices that it smells of incense. She puts on the diadem and the bracelets, wishing that Rafaele might see her so. Gennaro embraces her with wild fervor and she, almost in a trance of horror, imagining him to be Rafaele, yields to him.

The headquarters of the Camorra are shown in act three. Among the crude ornaments is a fresco of the Madonna, and a little altar behind a curtain. The Camorrists are drinking heavily, and three women join in their revel. When Rafaele appears the girls twit him with his infatuation for Maliella, but he sings in her praise. A curtain is drawn in front of the fresco of the Madonna, and a wild orgy begins. In the midst of it Maliella pounds on the door and rushes in, appealing for help against Gennaro and his revenge. She faints in Rafaele's arms, and he orders the Camorrists to bring him Gennaro, alive or dead. He turns upon Maliella, crying, "You belong to Gennaro, go to him," and hurls her to the ground. As she falls, her shawl falls open and exposes the jewels. The other women surround Maliella in amazement. In the distance Gennaro is heard bemoaning his sin. Then the noise of the attack upon him is heard and he bursts into the room pursued by the Camorrists. He bares his breast, calling on them to kill him. Seeing Maliella, he rushes toward her with a despairing cry, but she looks upon him with loathing, tearing off the jewels and flinging them at his feet, crying that Gennaro had stolen them from the Madonna. The men recoil, and the women drop to their knees, mumbling a litany. Rafaele declares that Maliella's soul is damned, and she dashes out to drown herself. Rafaele protects Gennaro from the attacks of the Camorrists. In the distance the church bells ring the alarm, showing that the theft has been discovered. They all flee in terror, leaving Gennaro alone. He gathers up the jewels, kisses them with reverence and staggers to the altar, where he lays them before the Madonna imploring her pity. A ray of light from the rising sun shines through the window and falls upon the jewels. Gennaro takes it for a sign of forgiveness. Finding a knife on the ground, he calls aloud for his mother not to weep for him; slowly pressing the knife into his breast. As he falls, he sees Maliella's scarlet wrap on the ground. He kisses it, and pillows his dying head on it as the birds break out into song. An angry mob appears at the door, but, seeing Gennaro dead, halts on the threshold.

LA HABAÑERA

Opera in three acts by Raoul Laparra.
Text by Raoul Laparra.

A STORY of legendary character told in three acts. Two brothers, Pedro and Ramon, living in a Castilian village, love Pilar. Pedro is the successful suitor. In the first act, during a festival of the people, Ramon gets into a quarrel with his brother over the girl and kills him while the Habañera is being sung and danced in the streets outside. The dying man prophesies that if Ramon does not confess, the Habañera will return each year, lacking a day, after the murder, to haunt him. In the second act Ramon and Pilar are married and living in their cottage. It is just a year after the murder, and Ramon is apprehensive. There are knocks at the door, and three blind musicians enter, playing a ghostly tune. Ramon recognizes it as the Habañera. Then he sees behind the blind men the ghost of Pedro, who warns him that if he does not confess he will return the next night and take Pilar with him. In the third act Pilar and Ramon are in the cemetery at midnight, just a year after the murder, paying their respects to the dead Pedro over his grave. The priests in the nearby chapel sing a death hymn. Ramon is terrified to discover that this hymn is only the Habañera in a new form. He sees Pilar becoming weak and faint over the grave. He struggles to confess his crime, but the words will not come out. Pilar sinks down dead on the grave, and Ramon in agony shrieks to the heavens the confession of his sin.

KÖNIGSKINDER

(Kingly Children)

Fairy Opera in three acts by Engelbert Humperdinck.
Text by Rosmer.

IN a small sunlit glade in the Hella Mountains the first act takes place. Here stands the hut of the Witch, and all about stretch the woods. With the Witch lives the Goose-Girl, who is discovered lying beneath a linden-tree tending her flock. The Witch appears, scolds the Girl, and orders her to assist in preparing a magic pasty that will kill whoever may eat of it. The Goose-Girl rebels and asks the Witch to allow her to go down into the world below, where she might be happy. The Witch refuses, telling her that all mankind is hateful. From the hillside comes a youth clad in a shabby hunting costume; on his stick a bundle. He is, in reality, the King's Son; and in the bundle he bears a royal crown. The King's Son tells the Goose-Girl of his wanderings through the hills and that he was once in the service of a great king. When the Goose-Girl asks what a king may be, he replies by telling her that he is a ruler who guards his subjects in much the same way that she tends her geese. He describes the joys of woodland life and begs her to go a-maying with him; takes her in his arms, and kisses her. As he does so, a gust of wind blows away a wreath of wood-flowers which the Girl has been wearing. The King's Son recovers the wreath, hides it near his heart, and in exchange for it offers the Goose-Girl his crown. The two are about to flee together, when the Girl finds herself fixed to the spot by some magic spell. Thinking that she is afraid to go with him, he says she is not worthy to be his companion. Then leaves her, vowing that she never shall see him again until a star has fallen into a lily which is blooming near by. The Witch reappears, berates the Girl for having wasted her time upon a mortal man, and drives her into the house. Now enter a fiddler, a woodcutter, and a broommaker. The King has just died and they have been sent by the town of Hellabrunn to ask the Witch where the King's Son may be found. The woodcutter and the broommaker are in terror of the old hag, but the fiddler scorns her and her powers. To their queries the Witch replies that the first person who enters the town-gate at noon the following day should wear the crown. The woodcutter and the broommaker return to Hellabrunn, the town near by, but the fiddler lingers. The Goose-Girl reappears and confides her sorrows to the fiddler, who assures her that she will wed the King's Son. The Witch jeers at this and assures the fiddler that the Goose-Girl is the child of a hangman's daughter. The Goose-Girl, however, does not lose courage, for she feels that her soul is royal. As she kneels in prayer for help, a star falls from the heavens upon the lily, and the Girl, followed by her geese, rushes into the wood to join her lover.

The second act opens in front of an inn near the town-gate of Hellabrunn. The King's Son enters, clad, as before, in his worn garments. The innkeeper's daughter gives him food and drink, and is angry because he will not respond to her advances. Townspeople enter, the tables and benches are occupied, and there is music and dancing. The King's Son offers himself to the innkeeper as an apprentice, but is told that there is no work for him, unless he is willing to become a swineherd. The counselors and well-to-do burghers appear and seat themselvees in a tribunal erected for them. The senior counselor requests the woodcutter to relate his adventures in the wood. He tells of many dangers, purely imaginary, encountered by him in the journey with the broommaker, and the King's Son is amazed at his narrative. The woodcutter asserts that on the stroke of twelve the King's Son will enter the gate in glittering raiment, drawn in a car of gold. The King's Son steps into the circle and asks if the expected monarch might not come clad in rags, but is met with ridicule from the crowd. At the twelfth stroke of the clock the gate is thrown wide open, and the Goose-Girl enters attended by her flock of geese. A few steps behind her comes the fiddler. She greets the King's Son and tells him that she has come to join him on the throne; but the crowd bursts into loud laughter and at last, despite the protests of the fiddler, drives the two forth with sticks and stones. The little daughter of the broommaker is the only one who believes that they are the true king and queen.

In the third act we return to the glade in the woods. It is now winter. The Witch has been burned at the stake for her supposed betrayal of the people, to whom she had promised a new ruler. The fiddler has been maimed and imprisoned for his defence of the two outcasts, and upon his release has come to live in the Witch's hut. He is feeding doves, left behind by the Goose-Girl, when he is interrupted by the arrival of the woodcutter and the broommaker, accompanied by a band of children. They entreat him to return to Hellabrunn, but he refuses. At last, one of the children begs him to lead them in search of the lost king and queen, and he agrees to do so. The woodcutter and the broommaker enter the hut, where, in rummaging about, they discover the poisoned pasty, in a box, which the Witch had baked. The fiddler has entered the wood in the background with the children, and now his song is heard in the distance. As it dies away, the snow begins to fall heavily and it grows darker. The King's Son and the Goose-Girl reappear, hungry and worn with wandering. They pause to rest, and the King's Son knocks at the door of the hut to beg food and shelter. The woodcutter brutally refuses to give them anything. The

Goose-Girl draws the King's Son away from the hut and leads him to the hillside. To comfort him, she pretends she is none the worse for the long travels, and, throwing off her cloak, attempts to dance and sing. She soon grows faint and falls. The King's Son then returns to the hut and barters his crown for the poisoned pasty. The outcasts eat it and soon fall asleep, believing themselves in a land of roses. The fiddler reappears with his troop of children, and, too late, they discover those whom they seek. They place the two upon a bier made of pine-branches, and singing, as they move away, a lament for the Kingly Children.

MONA

Opera in three acts by Horatio W. Parker.
Text by Hooker.

MONA was unanimously declared to be the best grand opera, composed by an American to an English libretto, by the directors of the Metropolitan Opera Company, New York, who had offered a prize of $10,000 for such a combination.

The scene of the opera is laid in southwestern Britain; the time, the close of the first century, A.D.

The first act passes in the hut of Arth, a British tribesman. Burned into the lintel above the doorway is the sign of the Unspeakable Name, indicating that here dwells a druid—Gloom, Arth's son. The other members of this household are Enya, Arth's wife; Nial, a changeling, who gazes wonderingly into the eyes of life and is wise in the lore of bird and beast, and the foster-daughter, Mona, last of the blood of the Queen Boadicea. Mona is to wed Gwynn, whose true name is Quintus, his mother having been a British captive and his father being Roman governor of Britain. Gwynn dwells among his mother's people, who are unaware of his real origin. He hopes to reconcile the British and Roman rule, and has influenced the governor toward a more humane and liberal policy. But Gloom and Caradoc, a bard, have long been chief conspirators against Rome, and Mona has been chosen, because of birthright and certain signs, to lead the revolt. She, devoutly believing in her mission and eager for usefulness, dreams of great deeds. Of all this Gwynn has suspected nothing. Mona now reveals to him that she has been "sealed" for a great adventure. Arth strides in and flings at her feet an unsheathed Roman sword, taken from a soldier whom he has slain in violation of the peace. Mona recognizes the sword as one she wielded in a strange dream she had, the meaning of which none can tell her. She is inspired to a prophetic frenzy, which is increased by the arrival of Gloom and Caradoc. Caradoc, Arth, and Gloom formally declare the peace broken; and Gwynn is led to swear fellowship in their conspiracy. Mona dons druidic robes. Gwynn seeks to sway her from her purpose; but, urged by Gloom and Caradoc, she repels and dismisses him. Arth, Gloom, and Caradoc do reverence to Mona as Queen. She half turns to follow Gwynn, lets fall the sword, and stands sobbing as the curtain falls.

The second act takes place in an open-air druid temple. Nial is discovered, at evening, dancing with his shadow and talking to the birds. The governor enters with a few soldiers, whom he orders to seize and torture Nial in order to obtain information. Gwynn suddenly appears, orders Nial's release, and explains to the governor his hope that Mona and he will yet be able to check rebellion. To his plan the governor hesitatingly agrees. When, with falling dusk, the Romans have departed, Mona and Gloom enter and make tally of the British forces. Gwynn, returning, conquers her decision regarding himself; but when he would unfold his cherished designs for peace, she, at once changed and scarcely comprehending his assertion of Roman birth, cries out "Treason!" and calls in the Britons. She cannot, however, deliver him to death, so, declaring that he is a bard, orders that he be bound and led away unhurt. The Britons rally, and to the music of a war-chant rush forth against the Roman town.

The third act is enacted on a small plateau at the forest's edge, facing the Roman town, which stands upon a corresponding rise at the other side of the valley. The attack has been successfully met, and the defeated Britons straggle back to cover. Arth has fallen; Gloom, his right arm broken, stumbles in, half carrying Mona. Mona, in dull grief, bewails the outcome. Gwynn, who in the turmoil has made his escape, finds them, reveals his origin, and seeks Mona's aid. Gloom jeers at him; and Mona, believing he lies, and blaming him for the British disaster and herself for having once spared his life, now slays him with the Roman sword that she has carried. The governor arrives with legionaries and archers, discovers Gwynn's body, in a fierce outburst denounces the Britons, and thus makes known to Mona, before she is led away, how Gwynn, whom she has slain, was the Britons' best friend and the one to have averted their fall.

MONNA VANNA

Drama in four acts by Henri Février.
Text by Maurice Maeterlinck.

AFTER a long siege by the Florentines, the garrison and inhabitants of Pisa are at the last gasp; munitions of war and supplies of food exhausted; the commandant, Guido Colonna, and his officers are desperate. Guido has sent his own father, Marco Colonna, as an envoy to Prinzivalle, the commander of the besieging army; the aged envoy overstaying the expected time, the son is a prey to the gloomiest forebodings. Marco enters unannounced. In answer to persistent questioning, after the first outburst of joy over his safe return, he tells of his hospitable reception by the dreaded foe, and finally, as it can no longer be put off, tells his son that Prinzivalle has agreed to send a great store of provisions and ammunition to relieve the starving Pisans, if Guido, in return, will consent that his wife, Giovanna, familiarly known as Monna Vanna, will come to Prinzivalle's tent the next night, unattended, and clad solely in her cloak; he promising that she shall return to Pisa at the following dawn. Guido, horrified at such a vile demand, plies his father with questions until he learns that Prinzivalle loves Giovanna, although the latter declares that she has never seen

him, and further, that Marco has already informed Giovanna of the entire affair. Pressing to know whether Giovanna had said that she would consent, the question is parried by Marco with another: Would Guido consent, and if she did? To this Guido declares that in such a case he would feel that all his love had been but a dream. Giovanna enters, and is incoherently questioned by Guido, who tells her to give his father a reply befitting the baseness of the proposal. She turns to Marco simply saying, "My father, I will go this night!" and Marco, kissing her brow, responds that he knew it. Guido, at first stunned, then frenzied, repulses Giovanna's advances. At this she goes out slowly, without turning back to look at him.

The second act opens in Prinzivalle's tent, where he is busied at a table when Vedio, his lieutenant, enters and tells him that Marco has not returned to give himself up, as he would have done had Giovanna rejected Prinzivalle's proposal. Prinzivalle falls into an ecstasy which is rudely interrupted by the approach of Trivulzio, an official sent by the Florentines to spy upon Prinzivalle, and now openly taxes him with treachery. Trivulzio attempts to stab Prinzivalle, who disarms him and turns him over to the guard. This incident shows the disfavor with which Prinzivalle is regarded by his Florentine employers, grown suspicious on account of his long stay before Pisa. Now his case is desperate indeed, even his life is no longer safe. But Prinzivalle recks not of danger— he is swallowed up in love-dreams. A shot is heard; Vedio goes out to seek the cause, and returns to usher in Giovanna, who, enveloped in her great cloak, hesitates on the threshold, saying, in a choked voice: "I have come as you wished." Prinzivalle tremblingly approaches her, sees a bloodstain on her hand, and learns that the sentry had wounded her. All tender solicitude, he inquires if she suffers,—if she has decided,—if she regrets her decision,—to which she replies: "Was it required that I should come without regrets?" He replies he will let her go free, if she wishes. "You are unclothed, save for that cloak?" and as she makes as if to open it, he prevents her with a swift gesture. Again he asks whether she had seen, on her approach, the herds and the laden wagon-train waiting for the word to depart, and whether she would like to see them move on to Pisa; the signal is given, and the relief wagons start under the flaring torchlight. He now begs her to rest on his couch; then, kneeling at its foot, he seizes her hand and pours out his heart to her, calling to her recollection their meeting in a Venetian garden years ago, when she was a child of eight and he a boy of twelve; recalling each trivial incident; how, after long wanderings, he had returned to the spot to find the house vacant, and worse, that she whom his heart had cherished all those years was the bride of a Tuscan lord. In desperation he had become a mercenary in the Florentine army, until fortune had made him general-in-chief over Pisa's besiegers. The tender, impassioned recital of his faithful love awakens slumbering memories of her childhood and touches Giovanna's heart; still she remains, outwardly at least, firm in her devotion to Guido. But his own love for her is so genuine that she now understands that he means her no harm; she feels absolutely safe with him. When he asks, "Could you have loved me?" she gently responds, "If I could tell you that I could have loved you, should I not love you already, Giannello?"— Vedio, now reentering in hot haste, informs his master that he has been proclaimed a traitor by the Florentine commissioner who has just arrived in the camp with six hundred men, and that he must fly instantly. When Giovanna asks him whither he would flee, he replies that it makes little difference. But she suggests, then insists, that he, her savior from shame, shall come with her to Pisa, promising him safety and full protection as an honored guest.

The third act opens in a great hall in Guido Colonna's palace, showing Guido, Marco and officers anxiously awaiting Giovanna's return—Guido in the depths of misery, declaring that he will pardon her when "that man" is dead; he curses his aged father as the author of his wretchedness. Outside, the shouts of the citizens are heard; it is Giovanna approaching, borne in triumph by the cheering multitude, and accompanied by Prinzivalle, who shields his face from their curious gaze. As she mounts the stair, Marco embraces her. He wishes to lead her to Guido's arms; but the latter, in imperious tones, bids the crowd and his officers depart and leave them alone. He coldly repulses Giovanna; presently catching sight of Prinzivalle, who stands motionless by himself, he snatches a halberd from a soldier and would strike him, but Giovanna interposes, crying: "It was he who saved me!" "Aye," replies Guido bitterly, "when it was too late!" But as soon as Giovanna has explained that this man who saved, spared and respected her is none other than Prinzivalle himself, Guido, his brain in a whirl, bursts out in savage exultation, calling back the crowd, disregarding Giovanna's protestations, feeling only that he has his hated foe in his grasp. In his frenzy he cannot be made to understand that Prinzivalle has treated Giovanna like a beloved sister; that she, far from being untrue to him in thought or deed, loves him as a true wife should; his distorted fancy depicts her merely as having treacherously lured Prinzivalle into the city to deliver him up to punishment. When Giovanna at last makes him hear that Prinzivalle spared her honor "because he loved her," he is stupefied, and calls upon all present to say whether they believe her; Marco cries, "I believe her!" only to be taunted with being her accomplice in crime. Worn out by conflicting emotions, Guido brokenly calls on Giovanna to tell him the truth, promising that she and the man whom Guido thinks to be her paramour shall both go free if she will but confess. Giovanna restates the exact truth; Guido's mood changes to one of ferocity; he commands that Prinzivalle be cast into the deepest dungeon, telling Giovanna that she shall never see him again. And now Giovanna, outraged, scoffed at by her own husband, and filled with the tenderest pity for the man who had given her back unsullied to her rightful lord, and trusted his life to her word, throws herself between them, wildly exclaiming, despite Prinzivalle's frantic protests, that she has lied, that Prinzivalle had really taken her as he had threatened, that she hates him and only desires vengeance, that she alone will be his jailer; feigning an ecstasy of wild triumph, and

pretending to bind Prinzivalle's hands herself while fastening them in such wise that he can readily free himself; at the same time whispering to Prinzivalle that she will rescue him—that she loves him. As he is led away, Giovanna is caught half-fainting in the arms of Marco, who alone of all present comprehends the meaning of the scene. Giovanna finally exacts Guido's promise that the key of the dungeon shall be delivered into her keeping.

The fourth act discovers Prinzivalle in his prison cell, throwing off the fetters with which he was so lightly bound. Abruptly the cell-door opens, and Giovanna herself appears. Prinzivalle rushes forward, they embrace passionately. She, disengaging herself, says, in a low voice, "Silence! we have but a moment! They do not know that I have the key to the other door—come!" And throwing open the door at the back, a flood of sunshine and the fair prospect of green fields meet the astonished eyes of Prinzivalle. It is the open country outside Pisa's walls, and together they go forth to freedom.

NATOMA

Opera in three acts by Victor Herbert.
Text by Joseph Redding.

NATOMA is an Indian girl of pure blood whose name means the "girl from the mountains." The first act is laid on the island of Santa Cruz, one of the Santa Barbara Channel islands. Here live Don Francisco Guerra, a noble Spaniard of the old school, and his daughter Barbara. She is just coming of age, and to-day returns home from her convent studies on the mainland. Don Francisco is seated upon the porch of his hacienda and muses on the flight of time. Soon comes Alvarado, accompanied by his chums, Castro, Pico, and Kagama, to hunt the wild boar in the mountains of the island. Alvarado, a fiery young Spaniard, is a cousin of Barbara and a suitor for her hand. Castro is a half-breed, part Indian and part Spaniard, who hates Spaniard and American alike. The party is received with due Spanish formality and then departs for the hunt, while Don Francisco retires for his siesta. Natoma, the playmate and handmaid of Barbara, appears at the back of the stage with Lieutenant Merrill, an American naval officer, who has visited the island several times. About her neck Natoma wears a small abalone-shell, as an amulet. Merrill bids her tell him the meaning of this amulet, and she recites the legend of her people. He salutes her as queen of this fair domain, but she responds sadly that her father's people have vanished and a stranger now rules. Replying to his questions, she describes Barbara in glowing terms, and then, falling at his feet, begs to be allowed to become his slave. Barbara arrives, accompanied by Father Peralta. Castro upbraids Natoma for spending her time with the white people and bids her come with him, but she spurns him as a half-breed. The hunting party returns. Alvarado serenades Barbara and presses his suit. He taunts her with having fallen under the influence of the *Americano,* and she abruptly leaves him. Castro explains to Alvarado how upon the morrow, when on the great fiesta day the country is assembled to do honor to Barbara at her coming of age, swift horses may be ready and the girl may be spirited away to the mountains. Don Francisco and Barbara are left on the porch in the moonlight. At last the old man retires. Lieutenant Merrill returns hurriedly and declares his love. A light appears in the hacienda and Merrill leaves. Barbara disappears in the hacienda, while Natoma is seen at the window with a lighted candle in her hands. She seats herself at a table in the window and looks silently out into the moonlight as the curtain falls.

The second act takes place on the mainland in the Plaza of Santa Barbara, with the towers of the mission church in the background. It is just before dawn. Alvarado and his cronies appear and discuss their plans. In an elaborate ensemble the soldiers cheer the flag of Spain carried by the friars on the steps of the church. The plaza begins to stir with life. Don Francisco and Barbara enter on horseback, Natoma walking at Barbara's side. Having dismounted, they ascend the grandstand, where the formal ceremony takes place. Alvarado claims the honor of a dance with Barbara, and they tread the measure of a minuet. Lieutenant Merrill and other officers enter with American sailors. After formal presentations have been made, Alvarado comes forward and demands that the dance be continued. According to the preconcerted arrangement ten or twelve couples now take part. The music breaks into the *pañuelo* or the dance of the proposal, at the climax of which each gallant places his hat upon the head of his lady. Barbara tosses Alvarado's hat to one side and rejoins her father. Castro in an ugly mood breaks through the crowd and, thrusting his dagger into the ground, demands who will dare to dance with him the dagger-dance of primitive California. Natoma responds to this challenge. Castro at first refuses to dance with her, but at last yields to her insistence. As they dance, the leather thongs supporting the railing of the grandstand are quietly unfastened, and Alvarado, smothering Barbara in his *serape,* attempts to make off with her. Natoma passes Castro in the dance and plunges her dagger into Alvarado. Castro is held by the officers. Natoma stands motionless, dagger in hand, while the crowd, quickly sensing the tragedy, is like to fall upon her and tear her to pieces. Lieutenant Merrill draws his sword and, with his men, holds the mob at bay. The great doors of the church open and Father Peralta appears. The people fall upon their knees. Natoma, letting fall her weapon, staggers toward the steps of the church and sinks at the feet of the priest, who exclaims: "Vengeance is mine, saith the Lord."

At the opening of the third act, Natoma is found alone in the mission church, where she lies huddled upon the altar crooning an Indian song. She then depicts the injustice done her race by the white man and invokes the Great Spirit to destroy the strangers. Father Peralta appears and quiets her, as, in simple language, he recalls to her her childhood days with Barbara. She realizes that by accepting the protection of the Church, although her own dream of happiness is ended, she will bring happiness to her idolized mistress. The doors of the church are thrown open and Natoma stands upon the steps of the altar. Father Peralta explains from the pulpit that a crime has been committed and punishment must follow. From the convent garden the nuns enter and kneel. Slowly Natoma descends the altar-steps and walks to where Barbara and Paul are seated. Barbara and Paul come from their pews and kneel before her, while she gently places the amulet around Barbara's neck. She then passes down between the kneeling nuns and stands in the doorway. The nuns rise and disappear into the garden. Father Peralta lifts his hands in benediction, and the orchestra sounds the chords of Natoma's Indian theme of Fate as the doors close upon her.

L'ORACOLO

(The Oracle)

A Music Drama in one act by Franco Leoni. Text based upon "The Cat and the Cherub" by C. B. Fernald.

THE play opens in the Chinese quarter in San Francisco on the fifth hour of the Chinese New Year's day. With the coming of the dawn the last straggling revellers make their way home from the opium dens, the devout part of the populace going to the temple. Chim-Fen, the proprietor of an opium den, pretends to be in love with Hua-Quee, nurse to Hoo-Chee, the son of a rich merchant named Hoo-Tsin. His real purpose, however, is to get the nurse to steal a fan from the wealthy merchant's house, and to obtain access to the house to further his plans. Win-San-Luy, the son of Win-Shee, a learned doctor, is in love with Ah-Yoe, Hoo-Tsin's niece. At break of day they meet and confess the secret of their love. From the temple comes the echo of a hymn, from the streets are heard joyful songs.

Hoo-Tsin consults the learned doctor, Win-Shee, as to the future of his little son. Win-Shee reads in the book of stars that tragic events are shadowing his life. Hence the title of "The Oracle." Chim-Fen overhears the conversation, and when the street is deserted, save for the little child and his nurse, he awaits his opportunity, and, finding the nurse's back turned for a moment, steals the child and hides him in his opium den. He then goes to the child's father, Hoo-Tsin, and asks for the beautiful Ah-Yoe in marriage should he succeed in finding and restoring the child. Hoo-Tsin accepts, but San-Luy also declares that he will find the child, and asks the same reward that Chim-Fen has asked for. San-Luy suspects Chim-Fen, watches him, and after a fierce struggle succeeds in entering his opium den. He rescues the little boy, but Chim-Fen follows him, and with a hatchet kills him. He then opens a trap-door and thrusts the child into it. Ah-Yoe, at the sight of her lover's dead body, is distraught with grief. Win-Shee, the learned doctor, overpowered with sorrow at the death of his son, determines to discover his murderer.

After an interval the scene opens on the second night. Win-Shee burns the sacred papers and begs the gods to aid him. A cry of distress from the little boy, Hoo-Chee, reaches his ears. He finds him beneath the trap-door and restores him to his father. Win-Shee now waits for Chim-Fen, and the latter, who has been drinking, approaches him. Win-Shee, with tragic calm, beckons him and makes him sit beside him on a wooden bench. Being convinced of Chim-Fen's guilt, he suddenly attacks him and strangles him with his pigtail. In the distance the step of an approaching policeman is heard. Win-Shee hastily props the body upon the bench beside him, and, as the policeman passes, appears to be quietly talking to the dead man. As soon as the policeman is out of sight the dead body falls with a thud to the ground.

PRINCE IGOR

An Opera in four acts.
Words and music by A. P. Borodin.

JUST as Prince Igor, ruler of Severok, and his followers are about to start out on a campaign against the Khan of the Polovtsy, an eclipse takes place, which is interpreted as a bad omen. Igor heeds neither the warnings of his people nor his wife, and sets out. Skoula and Eroshka, two of his subjects, are bribed by Prince Galitsky, to give him their support. He wants to usurp Igor's place. Igor, unsuspecting the prince's motives, entrusts his wife to his care.

The first scene is laid in the courtyard of Galitsky's house. The people welcome him as their prince. It is a scene of general rejoicing and feasting. A group of young women come up to the prince and ask for the return of one of their number who has been carried off by the prince. He frightens the girls and they run away. Skoula and Eroshka drink and jest.

In the next scene Yaroslavna is alone, lamenting Igor's absence. The young women come in and tell her the story of their friend who was taken away by Galitsky. Just as they are relating the story he enters and the girls run away. Yaroslavna asks him for an explanation of his misdeeds, but he only laughs at her. The Boyards come in and tell the princess that Igor is wounded, and, together with his son, is a prisoner in the enemy's camp. While they are deliberating on a plan of action the tocsin rings the alarm. Flames are seen in the distance. The Boyards draw their swords in defence.

The second act opens in the Polovtsy camp. A chorus of girls sing, accompanied by Kontchakovna, the daughter of the Khan Kontchak. Russian prisoners are led in; among them Vladimir, son of Igor. Ovlour is on guard. Vladimir is in love with Kontchakovna. She promises to be his bride, but he has misgivings, as he is sure that Igor will object to their union. Kontchakovna assures him that her father will consent to the marriage. Igor appears, very much dejected. He is anxious to return and fight for Russia. Ovlour greets him and offers him a horse on which to escape. Igor refuses the offer. Kontchak approaches. He shows great friendship for Igor, treats him with great respect and offers him freedom if he promises to cease waging war on him. He also entertains him with dancing.

In the third act the great Khan Gzak is seen riding in on horseback in triumph. The people welcome him with great rejoicing; and a council of war is held. Igor learns that his city was attacked. The Polovtsky

bring in booty. There is feasting and celebrating. Ovlour again suggests flight. The men are all drunk and the opportunity is ripe. Vladimir, the son of Igor, is taking leave of Kontchakovna. Igor tries to draw him away, but she clings to her lover. Igor seizes the opportunity and escapes. The young princess gives the alarm. When her father learns of Igor's escape he is full of admiration for him, and orders his men not to pursue him but retains the young prince as hostage and gives him his daughter. The khans resolve to march upon Russia.

Yaroslavna is alone and bewailing the absence of her husband when the last act opens, and suddenly she sees two horsemen approaching. They are Ovlour and Igor. Her joy is unbounded. Igor tells of his flight upon learning that the town was raided. The prince and his wife go to the citadel. Eroshka and Skoula, both rather tipsy, catch sight of them. They are ashamed of their state and perplexed as to what to do. They hit upon the idea of ringing the town bell. This done, the people rush in and ask what has happened. They are told that the prince has returned. At first they do not believe the news but are finally convinced of the fact. They reward the two vagabond minstrels, Eroshka and Skoula. The prince comes out of the Kremlin, accompanied by Yaroslavna, and is welcomed with great rejoicing.

DER ROSENKAVALIER

(The Rose Bearer)

Opera in three acts by Richard Strauss.
Text by Hugo von Hofmannsthal.

THE spirit of eighteenth-century Vienna shows up as the play begins with a scene in a chamber of the Princess von Werdenberg. The Princess reclines on a sofa, half embraced by the ardent Octavian who professes an all-consuming love for her. In the midst of this impassioned scene the lovers are startled by sounds which they fear are the footsteps and the voice of the Prince von Werdenberg, unexpectedly returning from hunting. Octavian quickly conceals himself, gliding behind a curtain and slipping into the dress of a lady's maid; the anxiety of the Princess is changed to amusement when the noisy, boastful and debauched Baron Ochs of Lerchenau unceremoniously enters her chamber to crave her assistance in his forthcoming marriage with Sophia Faninal. The old rake no sooner sets eyes on Octavian, disguised as a maid, than he makes love to her and invites her to sup with him. Meanwhile the Princess, as was the practice of ladies of quality in those days, has her morning interview with her attorney, head cook, milliner, hairdresser, literary adviser, animal dealer, etc., including a flute player and an Italian tenor, whose business it is to help to divert her.

When Baron Lerchenau departs the Princess asks Octavian to be the bearer of the silver rose, which the bridegroom left with her to be delivered to the bride, Sophia, according to the custom of the time. The first act ends somewhat sadly, the Princess reflecting on the day, not far distant, when her charms will have faded and her power to attract her lover passed away.

In the second act Sophia in her home receives the silver rose sent to her by the Princess in behalf of Baron Lerchenau. Unfortunately for the Baron, Octavian no sooner delivers the rose, and Sophia no sooner receives it, than the two fall desperately in love with each other. In the midst of their new-found joy the Baron enters to be formally presented to his betrothed and to have the contract duly drawn and signed. His arrogant manner and coarse language disgust Sophia. Octavian picks a quarrel with him, draws his sword and wounds him. Sophia weeps and protests she will never marry the Baron. Faninal fumes and rages, declaring his daughter shall marry the Baron or take the veil, for he is socially ambitious and seeks to ally his wealth as a merchant with an aristocratic house. Octavian sets his wits to work to upset all the marriage arrangements.

Disguised as the maid of the Princess, he makes, and keeps, an appointment with the Baron at an inn. There so many tricks are played upon the Baron that he firmly believes he has lost his reason and is in a madhouse. Faces appear in unsuspected places; a widow turns up claiming him as her husband; children rush in and hail him as "papa"; the commissary of police arrests him on a charge of leading young girls astray; and in his attempt to clear himself, he makes a hopeless muddle of it all and is in a terrible fix. The merchant, Faninal, is furious to find his prospective son-in-law in such a disgraceful brawl, and Sophia publicly renounces him. The arrival of the Princess is the signal for the police to withdraw, and for Octavian to reveal himself to the Baron in his proper garments as a man.

And so the play ends, on the whole happily, although it is not all honey to the Princess when she sees her lover carried off by another. However, the love of the Princess for the boy was but a passing fancy, innocent enough, though indiscreet. So all ends happily; everybody satisfied.

SADKO

Opera in three acts by Rimsky-Korsakov.
Founded upon a Novgorod folk story.

A POOR wandering minstrel of Novgorod, one Sadko, sings for the purse-proud merchants of his city, who jeer at him. Maddened by their scorn, he offers to wager them that he will catch goldfish in Lake Ilmen. The merchants bet their goods, and the minstrel his head on the result. Sadko charms the sea-king by his playing on the *guslee,* and secures the fish. Thus becoming rich, he sets sail with a fleet of merchant vessels in search of fresh adventures. A storm comes on, and it is necessary to sacrifice someone to the sea-god. The lot falls upon Sadko, but his good luck is still with him. Again he charms the sea-god, and the only danger is that he may fall in love with one of the beautiful sea-princesses and forget his wife in Novgorod. The king is so delighted at his playing that he dances a dance which shakes the earth and can only be stopped by the destruction of the *guslee.* Finally Sadko is allowed to return to his home and his wife. This he forthwith does, amid great rejoicing.

SNEGOUROTCHKA

(The Snow Maiden)

Opera in three acts by Rimsky-Korsakov.
Founded upon Ostrovsky.

THE Snow Maiden, daughter of King Frost and the Fairy Spring, who, hearing the songs of the shepherd Lel, begs her parents to allow her to become a mortal, is the theme of this opera. The parents consenting, entrust her to the care of two peasants. Fairy Spring tells the daughter to call on her if she ever needs help. The Snow Maiden becomes a mortal, but Lel will have none of her. She is, however, beloved by the merchant Mizgyr, who on her account deserts his affianced bride, Kupava. At the magnificent court of Berendei, Kupava demands justice, but the king, seeing the Snow Maiden, decrees that she shall belong to anyone of his courtiers who can woo her and win her within twenty-four hours. In the subsequent forest scene we see the revels of the people of Berendei. The Snow Maiden, seeing the lovers Lel and Kupava, in desperation calls upon her mother to give her human love. Granted this request she at last responds to the advances of Mizgyr, but just then the summer sun begins to shine upon her, and she melts away into the rising spring waters.

SHANEWIS

Opera in two acts by Charles Wakefield Cadman.
Text by Mrs. Nellie Eberhardt.

SHANEWIS, a beautiful Indian girl of musical promise, is sent to New York by Mrs. J. Asher Everton, a wealthy widow and prominent club woman of southern California. After several years' study, Shanewis is invited by her benefactress to spend the summer in her bungalow by the sea. A few days afterward, Amy Everton arrives home, following her graduation from Vassar and, in honor of both girls, Mrs. Everton gives a dinner, dance and musicale. Shanewis makes her first appearance before Mrs. Everton's guests.

Her initial number, "The Spring Song of the Robin Woman," a Tsimshian legend, together with the thrilling quality of her voice and her undoubted histrionic ability, create a sensation even among the older, more critical guests.

Lionel Rhodes, the childhood sweetheart and acknowledged fiancé of Amy, is fascinated by the charm and novelty of Shanewis. He names her "Enchantress," "The Robin Woman" who calls spring to the heart, and he makes love to her behind a screen of palms while the guests are out on the terrace dancing. Shanewis is at first shy but, finally, not knowing of his engagement to the daughter of her benefactress, she yields to his wooing conditionally. The condition is that he is to go with her to her home on the reservation to see if her family be any bar to his love. He consents, and their interview is terminated by the sudden entrance of Amy with a young man who seeks the next dance with the Indian girl.

Surprised and annoyed by their evident confusion

at her interruption, Amy jealously protests to Lionel, and is not reassured by his half-hearted efforts to propitiate her.

At midnight the guests hasten to take their departure, congratulating Mrs. Everton and Shanewis, and teasing Amy, laughingly, about her lover's interest in the Indian girl.

The second part takes place in Oklahoma a few days later. With a plausible excuse Shanewis has left Mrs. Everton for the reservation, where Lionel has secretly followed her. They are discovered watching the closing scenes of a big summer powwow. Instead of being repelled, the gay and brilliant pageant, the mingling of traditional and modern Indian life appeals to his strong sense of the picturesque. He watches with lively interest the crowds, the gay blankets, the Indian mothers with babies in cradle-boards, the dancers in regalia, and the white visitors in holiday attire. The ceremonial songs move him strangely, so that his impulsive love for Shanewis grows stronger. Therefore, when Philip Harjo, a fanatical young Indian devoted to the old traditions, presents Shanewis with a poisoned arrow once used by a maiden of the tribe to revenge herself upon a white betrayer, he is piqued and assures Harjo that Shanewis will never have any use for such a weapon.

Lionel and Shanewis attract much attention especially among the white people. Lionel begs Shanewis to leave early, but she insists on staying to the end. When the crowd has departed, the booths are stripped, and Shanewis has accepted the poisoned arrow from Harjo, Mrs. Everton and Amy hasten up in traveling costume. They strive to check Lionel's mad infatuation for Shanewis. He refuses absolutely to return with them. But the Indian girl, learning for the first time of his engagement to Amy, rejects his love with scorn. She insists upon surrendering him to Amy, thus repaying her debt to Mrs. Everton. Passionately she denounces the white race and its dealings with her people. She declares her intention of retiring from civilization to seek refuge in the forest, near to God, to recover from her wound. Recognizing the chasm between her and that other maid who sought revenge for treachery, she throws the bow and arrow far from her.

Though all the other Indians had left at the beginning of the altercation, Philip Harjo watches the scene from behind a tree. As Shanewis repulses Lionel, Harjo rushes out, snatches up the bow and arrow and shoots the young man straight through the heart. Shanewis runs back; she and Amy kneel beside him, while Mrs. Everton frantically attempts to drag Amy from the scene. Shanewis looks upward, saying, "'Tis well. In death thou art mine!'"

DIE TOTE STADT

(The Dead City)

Opera in three acts by Erich W. Korongold.

Text by Paul Schott, founded on G. Rodenbach's Burges le Morte.

THE story is located in Bruges, a city which is dead to the present and dreams of the past. The waterways are stagnant and the canals are destitute of barges; churches and cloisters are filled with a mystic peace. In this city which has no present, only a past, lives Paul, the hero of the opera. In his house he has made an altar to the memory of his wife, Marie. His thoughts are given to her; he spends much time in a sanctuary in which he has placed relics of her and the life they had spent together.

The first act opens at Paul's house. A traveling opera company has come to the city. Among the members is a dancer, Marietta, who bears a remarkable resemblance to the dead wife of Paul, including her beautiful golden hair. Attracted by the physical resemblance Paul is ready to transfer to the living the emotion he cherishes for the dead; in his state of mind he believes that Marie has come back to renew their happiness. The dancer comes to the house and thus strengthens the impression on the mind of Paul who is filled with a vision which is represented in the second act and part of the third.

The second act shows Paul as he sees himself in the vision on a deserted wharf near the house in which Marietta is living. He is waiting for her to appear. While he is watching he is torn with doubt and jealousy because Marietta has other lovers. This feeling is intensified when his bosom friend enters and confesses that he also is in love with the dancer who has given him a key to her house. In a violent quarrel Paul takes the key and drives the friend away.

A party of dancers now comes on the scene. They take a position before Marietta's house to serenade her. She appears with one of her lovers and is greeted with enthusiasm. Several dance and sing and are rewarded with kisses by Marietta. Then she proposes to enact a scene from Robert le Diable in which a dead woman rises from the grave. The effect is so realistic that Paul rushes from his place of concealment to protest against the mockery of things that he reverences. The crowd disperses and Marietta and Paul are left alone. In his excitement he accuses her of granting her favors to others and tells her that the passion she had inspired in him was only of the senses and that in caressing her he considered her merely a substitute for the wife whom he had lost and to whom his thoughts still turned. Angered by his taunts Marietta determines to enslave him completely and make him renounce the dead for the living. She requires him to take her to his own house from which she intends to drive the presence and memory of Marie.

In the third act, located in Paul's house, Marietta stands before Marie's picture and exults in her victory. A procession of children passes on the way to the cathedral. Paul enters and finds Marietta in the dead wife's sanctuary. When she goes toward a window to look at the procession Paul protests that she is not to be seen in his house. She cajoles him to wean his thoughts from the religious procession but in vain. In his wrought-up state of mind Paul fancies that the procession has entered his house and threatens him for his conduct. To this picture of his fancy he responds completely but Marietta mocks his superstition. She calls him a spineless hypocrite who really delights in her viciousness. In the excitement of the quarrel Marietta refuses to leave the house, rushes to a casket and takes from it a braid of golden hair which had

ENGRAVED BY W. B. CLOSSON FROM A PHOTOGRAPH MADE AT CANNES, FRANCE, IN 1866.

JENNY LIND-GOLDSCHMIDT.

SHE CREATED THE PART OF ' VIELKA" IN "EIN FELDLAGER IN SCHLESIEN."

belonged to Marie, Paul's wife. This act enrages Paul whose anger mounts when Marietta winds the hair around her neck and dances wantonly before him. In the struggle to wrest the hair from Marietta Paul strangles her.

With this the vision ends and Paul awakes to find himself in his house. Marietta comes in to get roses which she had left behind in the room as shown in the first act. She is ready to stay if invited by Paul. But he remains mute, overcome by the vision which he interprets as a warning against Marietta. Cured of his infatuation Paul also recognizes that he has made a god of his grief and that he must go away from the "dead city" out into the world of the present.

ANDRE CHENIER

Opera in four acts by Umberto Giordano.

Text by Luigi Illica.

THE central figure in this opera was a historical personage and a litterateur of the period preceding the French Revolution. He was born at Constantinople in 1762. His father was the French consul-general; the mother a Greek lady of exceptional beauty and accomplishments. Chenier was educated in Paris, entered the army in 1782 but resigned after a period of service and returned to Paris to devote himself to literary work and studies. From 1787 to 1790 he was in the diplomatic service. Attracted by the principles which led to the Revolution he later opposed the excesses of the leaders and thus incurred the disfavor of Robespierre. Accused of treason he was executed July 25, 1794.

The first act of the opera opens in the ballroom of the Chateau de Coigny which the servants are preparing for a ball. One of the servants, Gerard, is secretly in love with Madeleine, daughter of the Countess. Ambitious for a career higher than that of a lackey, Gerard has taken up with the doctrines of the revolutionary party. The Countess, Madeleine, and her friend, Bersi, now appear to receive the guests who have begun to arrive. Distinguished among the latter is Andre Chenier, a poet. One of the guests, recently from Paris, tells of the excesses of the revolutionists. The Countess asks Chenier for some verses but the poet pleads backwardness of his muse. However Madeleine challenges him to a praise of love and wins. First he lauds love of country and tells how the aristocracy has alienated the people. The indignation of the guests is aroused but music for a dance averts trouble.

Before the dance is begun a group of beggars is introduced by Gerard who announces them with the formality used to present the aristocratic guests. The Countess orders the rabble to be driven out. Gerard renounces his livery and goes out with the beggars to make his way to Paris.

The second act opens in Paris in June of 1794.

Chenier is seated alone at a cafe table. Bersi, accompanied by a spy, is at another table. Having incurred the suspicions of the revolutionists, Chenier is watched by the spy, a creature of Gerard. Roucher, friend of Chenier, enters and tells the latter that he

has brought a passport to enable him to leave the country. Chenier refuses and says that he will remain to follow the destiny which guides him, Love. He tells of mysterious letters which he has received, letters of reproof, of warning, and passion. They have aroused his feelings but he cannot find the writer.

Roucher tells him that the cafe is a resort for the aristocratic ladies and that he will point out the writer of the letters. Chenier is pained that he is interested in one of the aristocracy. Roucher advises his friend to use the passport and forget the puppet of fashion who has been playing with him.

Robespierre and a party including Gerard now appear. The spy reports to Gerard that he will show to him the woman whom he had been ordered to find. Chenier now rises to leave but is detained by Roucher whom Bersi furtively has told to keep Chenier, and that she is watched. As the gay crowd enters the cafe Bersi passes Chenier with the word that in a few minutes a lady, threatened by grievous peril, will come to him. Roucher fears a trap but Chenier waits. Darkness falls. The spy lurks near by to watch Chenier. Madeleine appears, recognizes Chenier and tells him that she needs his help. He recalls her as Madeleine de Coigny. The spy hurriedly leaves to report to Gerard. Madeleine tells Chenier how she had depended on his influence with the revolutionists to save her from one who pursued her. But now that his power had been lost she had no one to save her. They declare mutual love and pledge faith. As they are about to leave they are confronted by Gerard who tries to seize Madeleine. Roucher manages to help her to elude Gerard who is compelled to cross swords with Chenier and is wounded. Believing that he is at the point of death Gerard tells Chenier that his name is on the death list and that he should save Madeleine and both of them leave the country.

The scene at the opening of the third act is the court of the revolutionary tribunal. The crowd is asked to give to the funds to prosecute the war in defense of France. There is no response. Just then Gerard enters and is asked to use his eloquence to aid the cause. The people respond enthusiastically. The spy comes in and tells Gerard that Chenier has been arrested. No trace of Madeleine has been found but the spy insists that she will dare all to see her lover. Gerard writes a letter denouncing Chenier as a traitor to France and gives the indictment to his henchman to be delivered to the authorities. Too late he realizes that he has allowed evil passions to master him until he resorts to murder to win the woman he loves.

Madeleine enters, asks for Gerard and learns that it is he who has pursued her. Gerard tells how, as a servant, he had loved her and that now she is in his power. Madeleine threatens to denounce herself to the mob, is restrained by Gerard, and finally offers herself to him if he will save Chenier.

A messenger appears with papers for Gerard. These announce that Chenier has been arrested and that his trial is to be rushed. Gerard now promises to make an effort to save the poet. The crowd assembles, the judges and jury enter and Chenier is called to the dock. The prosecutor announces that Chenier has written against the revolution and served in the army of Du-

SEVEN STARS OF MODERN OPERA

From Photographs in Character

mouriez. Chenier defends himself. Gerard takes the stand and declares that the charges he had made were false. The prosecutor, an enemy of Chenier, insists and a verdict of guilty is given. As he is led away to prison Chenier discovers Madeleine.

The scene of the fourth act is the courtyard of the prison of St. Lazare. Chenier is writing at a table with Roucher beside him. The former has written verses to the muse of Poetry and to Death. Gerard and Madeleine enter. By a bribe of gold and jewels Madeleine arranges with the keeper that she shall be substituted for a woman who is to be executed. Gerard hastily leaves to make a final appeal to Robespierre. The lovers declare their mutual affection and their happiness in passing from life together. As the curtain falls they leave for the scaffold.

JENUFA

Opera in three acts by Leos Janacek.

Text by Gabriele Preissova.

THE music of Jenufa was composed by Janacek in 1902 to a drama on country life in Moravia. It has some parallels to Cavalleria Rusticana in its picturization of rural life.

The first act opens at a lonely mill in the hills of Moravia. Jenufa is wooed by two half-brothers and has given her love to Stewa, who betrays her. Jenufa is worried by the fear that Stewa will be drafted into the army before he marries her. In her distraction Laca, half-brother to Stewa, appears and tells of his love but is repulsed. Merrymakers now appear on the scene, among them Stewa in a state of intoxication. Incensed at Stewa and his behavior Jenufa's stepmother demands that he accept a probation of a year before he shall be allowed to marry Jenufa. This delay will be fatal to Jenufa in her condition. A controversy arises between the stepmother, the two brothers and Jenufa, in the course of which Laca is infuriated by Jenufa's scorn and slashes her cheek with a knife.

The second act begins in the stepmother's house. Jenufa's illness and the birth of her child have been concealed even from the father, Stewa. He has been summoned by the stepmother. When he appears she tells of Jenufa's misfortune and demands that the marriage take place at once. Of this visit Jenufa is unaware because she has been drugged. Stewa is no longer attracted to Jenufa because of the disfiguring scar on her face and is engaged to the daughter of the village judge. In spite of entreaties and threats Stewa refuses to marry Jenufa or to see the child. After his departure Laca appears and is told about Jenufa and her trouble. When he is told that the child is dead he agrees to marry Jenufa. After he leaves, the stepmother drowns the baby in the ice-covered river. When Jenufa awakes she is told that she has lain in a fever for two days and that the child is dead. Laca now returns and wins the consent of Jenufa who is touched with his devotion.

In the third act preparations are under way for the wedding of Jenufa and Laca. Just as the stepmother is about to bestow her blessing on the couple word is brought in that the body of a baby has been found under the ice and suspicion attaches to Jenufa. Unnerved by her deed and the discovery, the stepmother confesses and establishes the innocence of Jenufa.

Won by the deep love and devotion of Laca, Jenufa promises her affection. Together they determine to leave the locality and seek happiness in new surroundings.

MAROUF, THE COBBLER OF CAIRO

Opera in five acts by Henry Rabaud.

Text by Lucien Nepoty, after "The Arabian Nights."

THE scene opens with the cobbler on his bench expressing his envy of the fortunate men who have riches and fair wives whereas he is the husband of an old pest. The wife comes in, demands a certain honey cake, and threatens him if he does not get it for her. A neighbor, a pastry cook, takes pity on the cobbler who has no money to buy the dainty and gives him one similar to that demanded by the wife but made with sugar instead of honey. In her rage the wife refuses it and strikes it from Marouf's hands, whereupon he proceeds calmly to eat it himself. This increases her rage. She rushes to the street and cries that she has been cruelly beaten. The Kadi (judge) and two policemen come on the scene. In response to the wife's complaints Marouf is severely punished by the policemen's wooden staves and left alone to finish the cake. He decides to leave the city and his wife.

Marouf has joined a ship on its way down the Nile and then to sea. The vessel is wrecked but Marouf reaches land. While he lies unconscious a merchant sees him, has him taken up by his slaves and carried to his house in a neighboring city, Khaïtan, where the incidents of the second act take place. Ali and Marouf discover that they were schoolmates and have a joyful reunion. Ali is now the richest merchant in the city and secretly plans to honor his guest. While Ali goes to his shop in the market-place Marouf is dressed in the finest garments and then escorted to Ali's shop where he is received with great courtesy and magnificence to bear out Ali's explanation that his friend is one of the richest men in the world. Marouf enters into the play but allows himself to be carried away by his fancy and boasts of the unusually large and rich caravan which was on its way to Khaïtan. In disguise the Sultan and his Vizier are in the crowd and listen with interest. When Marouf states that among the treasures of the caravan are thirty bags of precious stones for the Sultan the latter discloses his identity and invites Marouf to dine with him.

The third act opens in the palace of the Sultan who has ordered that a marriage contract be made with the rich stranger. The Vizier suggests that they wait until the caravan arrives but the covetous Sultan fears to delay. Marouf enters into the spirit of the scene and scatters gold freely until his supplies are exhausted. After the Festivities Marouf is left alone with his Princess, still veiled. Mindful of his first wife he expects that his new bride will be old and ugly. When she unveils he is overcome by her beauty and his deceit and faints away. When the women would assist the Princess she sends them away and thus hears alone his murmured confessions as he regains consciousness. The Princess falls in love with Marouf and kisses him.

In the fourth act the Sultan has become uneasy over the delay in the arrival of the expected caravan, a state of mind which is increased by the expressed doubts of the Vizier. The latter is sent to speak with the Princess. Loyal to Marouf she fools the Vizier but is troubled by her father's request that she find out from Marouf when the caravan is to arrive. In answer to her questions Marouf confesses that the caravan has no existence, that he is only a poor cobbler who has been presented as a rich merchant by Ali as a joke on his friends. Although she laughs over the affair she knows that her father will be extremely angry and dreads the consequences of his wrath. They determine to escape. The Princess disguises herself as a boy and they ride away into the desert.

The last act shows Marouf and the princess at a fellah's hut, hungry and thirsty. While the peasant goes into the hut to prepare food Marouf continues the ploughing which their arrival had interrupted. The plow catches on an obstacle which Marouf examines. To his surprise he finds it is a ring attached to a large stone. When this is raised he finds an entrance to a cavern. The Princess has joined him and notices characters on the ring. When she rubs the ring to read the characters the fellah is changed into a splendid genie, the slave of the ring, ready to obey the commands of the holder of the ring. The Princess and Marouf ask for a caravan such as had been promised to the Sultan. While they await the execution of their command, the Vizier and a troop of soldiers arrive. Marouf is bound and brought face to face with Ali, his partner in the deceit. Just as they are to be executed the caravan arrives, the Sultan releases the two captives, and all ends happily.

THE KING'S HENCHMAN
A lyric drama in three acts by Deems Taylor
Book by Edna St. Vincent Millay

THE scene is laid in England during the reign of King Eadgar, in the tenth century. The first act takes place in the banquet hall of King Eadgar, who has gathered about him at his festive board, the lords and ladies of his court. His stalwart men are disporting themselves with tales of chivalry, of the hunt, of romance and finally of Aethelwold's aversion to the charms of women. Aethewold, Earl of East Anglia, is a foster brother and henchman of the King. The King confides to all that he has been a widower too long and would have a lovely bride that he might lavish upon her the silks, gems and riches that he, in his position, could well afford. Owing to the pressure of kingly duties at Winchester, he selects Aethelwold to seek and inspect the daughter of the Thane of Devon, Aelfrida, reputed to be the fairest maiden in all of the west country. Aethelwold accepts his commission good naturedly, pledges his troth of friendship to the King and departs.

The second act discloses a dense forest in Devon, on the eve of "All Hallow Mass." A heavy mist hangs over the forest through which Aethelwold and his com-

panion, Maccus, forge wearily on, but, driven by fatigue, Aethelwold sinks to the ground bewitched with sleep. Aelfrida, moved by a restless urge has sought the forest with her maid Ase, to evoke magic spells, such that might bring her a lover; eerie and indistinct murmurings answer her and, as the mist lifts, the moonlight falls on the sleeping form of Aethelwold. Entranced at the reward of her spell, Aelfrida sees in Aethelwold the fulfillment of her ideal and gently kisses him as he sleeps. He is startled by her gesture and springs to his feet only to find himself in her embrace.

After revealing their identity, Aethelwold finds to his horror that he has unwittingly betrayed his King. He attempts flight, but Aelfrida calls him back and he knows then that he can never leave her. He tells Maccus to return and tell the King that he has found the maiden, but that her charms are far less than reputed and, that since she was possessed of certain estate, he, having nothing of his own, would marry her himself.

The scene of the third act is laid in the hall of Aelfrida's father, Ordgar Thane of Devon, where Aethelwold has taken his bride. Aelfrida has become weary of her household duties and the dreariness of the life she has known for so long, so Aethelwold, still tormented by his treachery to the King, avows that they will depart that same night to Ghent, in Flanders, where Aelfrida will be forever rid of her drudgery and live in more befitting taste and elegance, but news of the arrival of the King himself puts an end to these plans. Aethelwold is driven to confess to his wife that, but for him, she would be queen, and begs her to retire and dim her beauty so that his infidelity would never be known. As she departs the King and his retinue enter the hall to greet Aethelwold and his bride. Suddenly Aelfrida reappears, not dimmed in beauty as Aethelwold has asked her, but radiant and dazzling, showing her beauty and charm to the utmost. The stupefied King realizes to his horror the treachery of his henchman and reproaches him sorrowfully. The tormented Aethelwold takes the only course open to him as he drives his dagger into his breast and brings to a close an epoch-making tragedy in the field of American opera.

The King's Henchman is the twelfth opera to be presented by an American composer and librettist and the first opera to be written by commission. It was first produced at the Metropolitan Opera House, New York, on February 17, 1927, where it was received with great acclaim.

LA GIOCONDA
Opera in four acts by Amilcare Ponchielli
Text by Arrigo Boito

THE scene of action is laid in Venice, in the seventeenth century. The first act opens on a holiday gathering close to the courtyard of the ducal palace in honor of a regatta. La Gioconda, a light-hearted street singer, has brought with her her blind mother, La Cieca. Barnaba, chief of the police and a spy of the Inquisition, observes the young singer and makes advances to her, but she repulses him. Not satisfied, Barnaba schemes to inveigle the mother, La Cieca, into his power and thereby secure a stronger hold on her daughter. As the victor of one of the boat races is being acclaimed, he confides to Zuane, one of the less fortunate boatsmen, that his defeat was due to an evil influence cast on him by La Cieca, whom he condemns as a witch. The report spreads rapidly among the populace who rise to demand her death, but Enzo, a Genoese nobleman, whom La Gioconda loves, arrives in time to calm the infuriated mob. Alvise, an officer of the State Inquisition, then appears with his wife, Laura; the latter effects the release of La Cieca, who presents Laura with her rosary as a token of gratitude.

As the populace enters the Church, Enzo, a former lover of Laura, is left standing alone watching her, and who, despite her marriage with Alvise, still loves him. Barnaba has watched these proceedings with cunning and finally accosts Enzo and confides to him that Laura will be on board the ship Hecate that night while her husband meets with the Council of Ten. La Gioconda overhears this confidence and Enzo's protestations of love for Laura. Embittered at his faithlessness, she enters the Church with her mother. Barnaba, in the meantime, sends a warning to Alvise advising him of Laura's contemplated treachery and love for Enzo.

The second act discloses Enzo's ship later in the evening. Barnaba and a fellow-spy, Isepo, appear disguised as fishermen; they greet the sailors, then send for the police galleys. Later, Laura appears and joins Enzo on board the ship. They decide to set sail that night, as soon as the wind rises. Enzo goes below to make final preparations for the departure, leaving Laura unattended. La Gioconda steals upon Laura intending to slay her, but in her attempt Laura holds before her the crucifix of her mother's rosary, which stays her hand. Alvise then appears in great anger to denounce his wife, who in the meantime has effected an escape with the aid of La Gioconda, mindful of her gratitude to Laura for having saved her blind mother, La Cieca. Enzo returns to the deck to find La Gioconda

instead of Laura. She condemns him for his wrongful purpose and warns him that the police are about to attack him. Enzo, in fury, sets fire to the ship.

Act three finds Alvise alone and brooding over his wife's infidelity. The scene is laid in his palace, where a masked ball is in progress. Alvise decides that Laura must die for the dishonor she has brought to his name. He sends for her, denounces her and commands her, as he leaves the room, to drink a vial of poison. La Gioconda, who has been concealed in the room, substitutes a powerful opiate for the death draught and departs. When Alvise returns to the room, seeing the recumbent form of his wife, he rejoices that his purpose has been done.

The scene then changes to the ball where Alvise returns, satisfied that Laura is dead. Barnaba seeks Enzo and whispers to him that Laura has been murdered. Enzo, in a rage, tears off his mask and denounces Alvise, and in his struggle to kill him is carried off by the police. Barnaba, sensing La Gioconda's plight, demands she come to him. This she promises to do, on condition that Enzo be released. Alvise then opens the curtain revealing the seemingly dead Laura, admitting that he has killed her.

The fourth act shows a deserted palace on an island in the Adriatic where La Gioconda has taken Laura, still unconscious. Enzo, meantime, having been sent for by La Gioconda, arrives and receives her broken-hearted condemnation for his infidelity. Laura's voice is suddenly heard and the lovers reunited. La Gioconda, remembering her promise to Barnaba, prays to the Virgin for deliverance. Barnaba overhears her prayer, but, when he confronts her, she tells him that she will keep her word and begs but to be allowed to adorn herself to do him honor. As he waits, she stabs herself with a dagger, saying: "I have sworn to be thine—take me, I am thine."

La Gioconda is the adaptation of Victor Hugo's "Angelo" and was first presented at La Scala, Milan, April 8, 1876. The opera has had phenomenal success in nearly all parts of the world and enjoys to this day a reputation for its lyric and dramatic excellence.

WOTAN'S FAREWELL TO BRÜNNHILDE

("Die Walküre")

From the Painting by Konrad Dielitz

JEAN BAPTISTE LULLI

THE first French composer of a series of operas, Jean Baptiste Lulli (or Lully), the son of Lorenzo de' Lulli, a gentleman of Florence, Italy, and Catarina del Serta, was born at Florence in 1633. An old Franciscan monk gave the gifted but mischievous child some elementary instruction, and taught him the guitar and the rudiments of music. The Chevalier de Guise took him to France, and having entered the service of Mlle. de Montpensier—"La Grande Mademoiselle"—in the kitchen, Lulli employed his leisure in learning the songs of the day and playing them upon his violin.

As his talent became known he was promoted from the kitchen to the Princess's band, where he soon distanced the other violinists. Mademoiselle, having discovered that he had composed the air of a satirical song at her expense, promptly dismissed him; but his name was sufficient to procure him a place in the King's band. Here some airs of his composition so pleased Louis XIV that he established on purpose for him a new band, called "les petits violons," to distinguish it from the large band of twenty-four violins. His new post enabled him to perfect himself as a solo-player, and gave him valuable practice as a conductor and composer for the orchestra.

Baptiste, as he was then called, had common sense as well as ambition, and soon perceived that without deeper study he could not make full use of his talents. To remedy his defective education he took lessons on the harpsichord, and in composition from the organists Métru, Gigault, and Roberdel; and at the same time lost no opportunity of ingratiating himself with men of rank, a useful process for which he had a special gift. He was soon chosen to compose the music for the court ballets, in which Louis XIV himself danced, and after the success of "Alcidiane" (1658) he was commissioned to write the divertissements for "Serse," an Italian opera by Cavalli, performed at the Louvre (November 22, 1660) in honor of the King's recent marriage with Marie Thérèse of Austria (June 9 previous), and, a year and a half later, the ballets for "Ercole amante," another opera by Cavalli, performed at the opening of the magnificent "Salle de spectacles" at the Tuileries (February 7, 1662).

It was by studying the works of this Venetian composer, and observing his method, that Lulli laid the foundation of his own individual style. In composing the divertissements for "Le mariage forcé," "Pourceaugnac," and "Le bourgeois gentilhomme," he made good use of the feeling for rhythm which he had imbibed from Cavalli, and also endeavored to make his music express the life and variety of Molière's situations and characters. The exquisitely comic scene of the polygamy in "M. de Pourceaugnac" is in itself sufficient evidence of the point to which he had attained, and of the glorious future which awaited him.

From 1658 to 1671—the year in which Molière produced his tragedy-ballet "Psyché"—Lulli composed no less than thirty ballets, all unpublished. These slight compositions, in which Lulli took part with considerable success as dancer and comic actor, confirmed him in the favor of Louis XIV, who successively appointed him composer of his instrumental music, "surintendant" of his chamber music, and in 1662 "maître de musique" to the royal family. But neither these lucrative posts nor his constantly increasing reputation were sufficient to appease his insatiable ambition.

With all his genius he possessed neither honor nor morals, and would resort to any base expedient to rid himself of a troublesome rival. His envy had been roused by the privilege conceded to the Abbé Perrin (June 28, 1669) of creating an Académie de Musique, and was still further excited by the success of Cambert's operas "Pomone" and "Les peines et les plaisirs de l'amour" (1671). With the astuteness of a courtier Lulli took advantage of the squabbles of the numerous associés-directeurs of the opera, and with the aid of Mme. de Montespan procured the transference of Perrin's patent to himself (March, 1672).

Once master of a theater, the man whom honest Boileau branded with odium proved his right to a place in the first rank among artists, though as a man he could claim neither sympathy nor respect. In the poet Quinault he was fortunate enough to discover a *collaborateur* of extraordinary merit, and in conjunction with him Lulli within fourteen years composed twenty operas or divertissements. The variety of subjects in these is surprising, but Lulli was perfectly at home with all, passing easily from lively and humorous divertissements to scenes of heroism and pathos, from picturesque and dramatic music to downright comedy, and treating all styles with equal power. He revolutionized the *ballets de la cour*, replacing the slow and stately airs by lively allegros, as rapid as the pirouettes of the danseuses whom he introduced on the stage, to the great delight of the spectators. For the recitativo secco of the Italians he substituted accompanied recitative, and in this very important part of French opera scrupulously conformed to the rules of prosody, and left models of correct and striking declamation. On the other hand, he made no attempt to vary the form of his airs, but slavishly cut them all after the fashion set by Cavalli in his operas, and by Rossi and Carissimi in their cantatas.

Lulli thoroughly understood the stage—witness the skill with which he introduces his choruses; had a true sense of proportion, and a strong feeling for the picturesque. The fact that his works are not forgotten, but are still republished, in spite of the progress of the lyric drama during the last two hundred years, is sufficient proof of his genius. Not but that he has serious faults. His instrumentation, though often labored, is poor, and his harmony not always correct: a great sameness of treatment disfigures his operas, and the same rhythm and the same counterpoint serve to illustrate the rage of Roland and the rocking of Charon's boat. Such faults are obvious to us; but they were easily passed over at such a period of musical revolution. It is a good maxim that in criticising works of art of a bygone age we should put them back in their original frames; and according to this rule we have no right to demand from the composer of "Thésée," "Atys," "Isis," "Phaëton," and "Armide" outbursts of passion or agitation which would have disturbed the solemn majesty of his royal master, and have outraged both stage propriety and the strict rules of court etiquette. The chief business of the King's surintendant de la musique undoubtedly was to please his master, who detested brilliant passages and lively melodies; and making due allowance for these circumstances we affirm that Lulli's operas exhibit the grace and charm of Italian melody and a constant adherence to that good taste which is the ruling spirit of French declamation. Such qualities as these will always be appreciated by impartial critics.

Lulli was also successful in sacred music. Ballard published his motets for double choir in 1684, and a certain number of his sacred pieces, copied by Philidor, exist in the libraries of Versailles and of the Conservatoire. Mme. de Sevigné's admiration of his "Miserere" and "Libera" was strongly declared. Readers will recall the manner of Lulli's death. While conducting a Te Deum, January 8, 1687, in honor of the King's recovery from a severe illness, he accidentally struck his foot with the baton; an abscess followed; the quack in whose hands he placed himself proved incompetent, and he died in his own house in Paris on March 22.

As both surintendant de la musique and secretary to Louis XIV, Lulli was in high favor at court, and being extremely avaricious, used his opportunities to amass a large fortune. At his death he left four houses, all in the best quarters of Paris, besides securities and appointments amounting to a considerable fortune. His wife Madeleine, daughter of Lambert the singer, whom he married July 24, 1662, and by whom he had three sons and three daughters, shared his economical tastes. For once laying aside their parsimonious habits, his family erected to his memory a splendid monument surmounted by his bust, which still exists in the left-hand chapel of the church of the Petits Pères, near the Place des Victoires.

FRANÇOIS ADRIEN BOIELDIEU

THIS celebrated French composer of opéra comique was born December 16, 1775, at Rouen, where his father held the position of secretary to Archbishop Larochefoucauld. His mother kept a milliner's shop in the same city. The union does not seem to have been a happy one. We know at least that during the Revolution the elder Boieldieu availed himself of the law of divorce passed at that time to separate from his first wife and contract a second marriage.

Domestic dissensions were perhaps the reason why the composer, when his talent for music began to show itself, exchanged the house of his parents for that of his master, Broche, organist of the cathedral, who, although an excellent musician and pupil of the celebrated Padre Martini, was known as a drunkard, and occasionally treated Boieldieu with brutality. On one occasion, it is said, the boy had stained one of his master's books with ink, and in order to evade the cruel punishment in store for him escaped from Broche's house and went on foot to Paris, where he was found after much trouble by his family. Whether he returned to Broche seems uncertain. Neither are we informed of any other master to whom the composer owed the rudimentary knowledge of his art. This knowledge, however acquired, was put to the test for the first time in 1793, when an opera by Boieldieu, called "La fille coupable" (words by his father), was performed at Rouen with considerable success. It has been believed that Boieldieu left Rouen for Paris immediately or at least very soon after this first attempt. This, however, must be a mistake, unless we accept the improbable conjecture of a second temporary sojourn in the capital. Certain it is that Boieldieu was again in Rouen October 28, 1795, when another opera by him, "Rosalie et Myrza," was performed at the theater of that city. The success of this second venture does not seem to have been brilliant, to judge at least by the "Journal de Rouen," which after briefly noticing the book observes silence with regard to the music.

Many of Boieldieu's charming ballads and chansons owe their origin to this period, and added considerably to the local reputation of the young composer. Much pecuniary advantage he does not seem to have derived from them, for Cochet, the Paris publisher of these minor compositions, told Fétis that Boieldieu was glad to part with the copyright for the moderate remuneration of twelve francs apiece. Soon after the appearance of his second opera Boieldieu left Rouen for good. Ambition and the consciousness of power caused him to be dissatisfied with the narrow sphere of his native city, particularly after the plan, advocated by him in an article in the "Journal de Rouen," of starting a music school on the model of the newly founded Conservatoire had failed.

To Paris therefore Boieldieu went for a second time, with an introduction from Garat the singer to Jadin (a descendant of the well-known Belgian family of musicians), at whose house he found a hospitable reception, and became acquainted with the leading composers of the day, Cherubini among the number. Boieldieu made his début as an operatic composer in the capital with "La famille suisse," which was performed at the Théâtre Feydeau in 1797, and had a run of thirty nights alternately with Cherubini's "Médée."

Other operas followed in rapid succession, among which we mention "Zoraime et Zulnare" (written before 1796, but not performed till 1798), "La dot de Suzette" (same year), "Beniowski" (after a drama by Kotzebue; performed in 1800 at the Théâtre Favart), and "Le Calife de Bagdad" (performed in September of the same year with enormous success). To these operatic works ought to be added some pieces of chamber music. They are, according to Fétis, a concerto and six sonatas for pianoforte, a concerto for harp, a duo for harp and pianoforte, and three trios for pianoforte, harp, and violoncello. To the success of these minor compositions Boieldieu owed his appointment as professor of the pianoforte at the Conservatoire in 1800. With the same year we may close the first period of Boieldieu's artistic career. "Le Calife de Bagdad" is the last and highest effort of this period. If Boieldieu had died after finishing it he would be remembered as a charming composer of pretty tunes cleverly harmonized and tolerably instrumented—in short, as an average member of that French school of dramatic music of which he is now the acknowledged leader.

Boieldieu's first manner is chiefly characterized by an absence of style—of individual style at least. Like most men of great creative power and of self-training, like Wagner for instance, Boieldieu began by unconsciously adopting and reproducing with great vigor the peculiarities of other composers. But every new advance of technical ability implied with him a commensurate step toward original conception, and his perfect mastery of the technical resources of his art coincided with the fullest growth of his genius. During this earlier period matter and manner were as yet equally far from maturity. This want of formal certainty was felt by the composer himself, if we may believe a story told by Fétis, which, although somewhat doubtful on chronological grounds, is at any rate plausibly invented. He relates that, during the composition of "Le Calife de Bagdad," Boieldieu used to submit every new piece as he wrote it to the criticism of his pupils at the Conservatoire. When, as happened frequently, these young purists took exception at their master's harmonic peccadillos, the case was referred to Méhul, to whose decision, favorable or adverse, Boieldieu meekly submitted. Considering that at the time Boieldieu was already a successful composer of established reputation, his modesty cannot be praised too highly. But such diffidence in his own judgment is incompatible with the consciousness of perfect formal mastership.

After one of the successful performances of "Le Calife," Cherubini accosted the elated composer in the lobby of the theater with the words "Malheureux! are you not ashamed of such undeserved success?" Boieldieu's answer to this brusque admonition was a request for further musical instruction, a request immediately granted by Cherubini, and leading to a severe course of contrapuntal training under the great Italian master. The anecdote rests on good evidence, and is in perfect keeping with the characters of the two men. Fétis strongly denies the fact of Boieldieu having received any kind of instruction or even advice from Cherubini—on what grounds it is not easy to perceive. Intrinsic evidence goes far to confirm the story. For after "Le Calife de Bagdad" Boieldieu did not produce another opera for three years, and the first work brought out by him after this interval shows an enormous progress upon the compositions of his earlier period. This work, called "Ma tante Aurore," was first performed at the Théâtre Feydeau January, 1803, and met with great success.

In June of the same year the composer left France for St. Petersburg. His reasons for this somewhat sudden step have been stated in various ways. Russia at that time was an El Dorado to French artists, and several of Boieldieu's friends had already found lucrative employment in the Emperor's service. But Boieldieu left Paris without any engagement or even invitation from the Russian court, and only on his reaching the Russian frontier was he agreeably surprised by his appointment as conductor of the Imperial Opera, with a liberal salary. It is very improbable that he should have abandoned his chances of further success in France, together with his professorship at the Conservatoire, without some cause sufficient to make change at any price desirable. Domestic troubles are named by most biographers as this additional reason. Boieldieu had in 1802 contracted an ill-advised marriage with Clotilde Mafleuray, a dancer; the union proved anything but happy, and it has been asserted that Boieldieu in his despair took to sudden flight. This anecdote, however, is sufficiently disproved by the discovered fact of his impending departure being duly announced in a theatrical journal of the time. Most likely domestic misery and the hope of fame and gain conjointly drove the composer to a step which, all things considered, one cannot but deplore.

Artistically speaking, the eight years spent by Boieldieu in Russia must be called all but total eclipse. By his agreement he was bound to compose three operas a year, besides marches for military bands, the libretti for the former to be found by the Emperor. But these were not forthcoming, and Boieldieu was obliged to take recourse to books already set to music by other composers. The titles of numerous vaudevilles and operas belonging to the Russian period might be cited, such as "Rien de trop," "La jeune femme colère," "Les voitures versées," "Aline, reine de Golconde," "Télémaque"; also the choral portions of Racine's "Athalie." Only the three first-mentioned works were reproduced by Boieldieu in Paris; the others he assigned to oblivion. "Télémaque" ought to be mentioned as containing the charming air to the words "Quel plaisir d'être en voyage," afterward transferred to "Jean de Paris."

In 1811 Boieldieu returned to Paris, where great changes had taken place in the meantime. Dalayrac was dead; Méhul and Cherubini, disgusted with the fickleness of public taste, kept silence; Niccolo Isouard was the only rival to be feared. But Boieldieu had not been forgotten by his old admirers. The revival of "Ma tante Aurore" and the first performance in Paris of an improved version of "Rien de trop" were received with applause, which increased to a storm of enthusiasm when in 1812 one of the composer's most charming operas, "Jean de Paris," saw the light. This is one of the two masterpieces on which Boieldieu's claim to immortality must mainly rest. As regards refined humor and the gift of musically delineating a character in a few masterly touches, this work remains unsurpassed even by Boieldieu himself; in abundance of charming melodies it is perhaps inferior, and inferior only, to "La dame blanche." No other production of the French school can rival either of the two in the sustained development of the excellences most characteristic of that school. The Princess of Navarre, the Page, the Seneschal, are indestructible types of loveliness, grace, and humor. After the effort in "Jean de Paris" Boieldieu's genius seemed to be exhausted: nearly fourteen years elapsed before he showed in "La dame blanche" that his dormant power was capable of still higher flights.

We will not encumber the reader's memory with a list of names belonging to the intervening period, which would have to remain names only. Many of these operas were composed in collaboration with Cherubini, Catel, Isouard, and others; only "Le nouveau seigneur de village" (1813) and "Le petit chaperon rouge" (1818), both by Boieldieu alone, may be mentioned here. After the successful production of the last-named opera, Boieldieu did not bring out a new entire work for seven years. In December, 1825, the long-expected "Dame blanche" saw the light, and was received with unprecedented applause. Boieldieu modestly ascribes part of this success to the national reaction against the Rossini-worship of the preceding years. Other temporary causes have been cited, but the first verdict has been confirmed by many subsequent audiences. The melodies sound as fresh and are received with as much enthusiasm as on that eventful night of December 10, 1825, so graphically described by Boieldieu's pupil Adam. Such pieces as the cavatina "Viens gentille dame," the song "D'ici voyez ce beau domaine," or the trio at the end of the first act, will never fail of their effect as long as the feeling for true grace remains.

"La dame blanche" is the finest work of Boieldieu, and Boieldieu the greatest master of the French school of comic opera. With Auber, Boieldieu shares verve of dramatic utterance, with Adam piquancy of rhythmical structure, while he avoids almost entirely that bane of modern music, the dance rhythm, which in the two other composers marks the beginning of the decline and fall of the school. Peculiar to Boieldieu is a certain homely sweetness of melody, which proves its kinship to that source of all truly national music, the popular song. "La dame blanche" might indeed be considered as the artistic continuation of the chanson, in the same sense as Weber's "Der Freischütz" has been called a dramatized Volkslied. With regard to Boieldieu's work this remark indicates at the same time a strong development of the amalgamating force of French art and culture; for it must be borne in mind that the subject treated is Scotch. The plot is a compound of two of Scott's novels, "The Monastery" and "Guy Mannering." Julian (alias George Brown)

comes to his paternal castle unknown to himself. He hears the songs of his childhood, which awaken old memories in him; but he seems doomed to misery and disappointment, for on the day of his return his hall and his broad acres are to become the property of a villain, the unfaithful steward of his own family. Here is a situation full of gloom and sad foreboding. But Scribe and Boieldieu knew better. Their hero is a dashing cavalry officer, who makes love to every pretty woman he comes across, the "White Lady of Avenel" among the number. Yet nobody who has witnessed an adequate impersonation of George Brown can have failed to be impressed with the grace and noble gallantry of the character.

The Scotch airs also introduced by Boieldieu, although correctly transcribed, appear, in their harmonic and rhythmical treatment, thoroughly French. The tune of "Robin Adair," described as "le chant ordinaire de la tribu d'Avenel," would perhaps hardly be recognized by a genuine North Briton; but what it has lost in raciness it has gained in sweetness.

So much about the qualities which Boieldieu has in common with all the good composers of his school; in one point, however, he remains unrivaled by any of them; namely, in the masterly and thoroughly organic structure of his ensembles. Rousseau, in giving vent to his whimsical aversion to polyphony, says that it is as impossible to listen to two different tunes played at the same time as to two persons speaking simultaneously. True in a certain sense; unless these tunes represent at once unity and divergence—oneness, that is, of situation, and diversity of feelings excited by this one situation in various minds. We here touch upon one of the deepest problems of dramatic music, a problem triumphantly solved in the second act of "La dame blanche." In the finale of that act we have a large ensemble of seven solo voices and chorus. All these comment upon one and the same event with sentiments as widely different as can well be imagined. We hear the disappointed growl of baffled vice, the triumph of loyal attachment, and the subdued note of tender love—all mingling with each other and yet arranged in separate groups of graphic distinctness. This ensemble, and indeed the whole auction scene, deserve the title "classical" in the highest sense of the word.

The remainder of Boieldieu's life is sad to relate. He produced another opera, called "Les deux nuits," in 1829, but it proved a failure, owing chiefly to the dull libretto by Bouilly, which the composer had accepted from good nature. This disappointment may have fostered the pulmonary disease, the germs of which Boieldieu had brought back from Russia. In vain he sought recovery in the mild climate of Southern France. Pecuniary difficulties increased the discomforts of his failing health. The bankruptcy of the Opéra Comique and the expulsion of Charles X, from whom he had received a pension, deprived Boieldieu of his chief sources of income. At last M. Thiers, the minister of Louis Philippe, relieved the master's anxieties by a government pension of 6000 francs. Boieldieu died October 8, 1834, at Jarcy, his country house, near Paris. The troubles of his last years were shared and softened by his second wife, to whom the composer was united in 1827 after a long and tender attachment.

GAETANO DONIZETTI

AMONG famous Italian composers we must include Donizetti, who was born at Bergamo, November 25, 1797, nearly six years after the birth of Rossini; and though he began his career at a very early age, he never achieved any important success until after Rossini had ceased to compose. Having completed his studies at the Conservatorio of Naples, under Mayr, he produced at Vienna, in 1818, his first opera, "Enrico di Borgogna," which was rapidly followed by "Il Falegname di Livonia" (Mantua, 1819). His "Zoraïde di Granata," brought out immediately after "Il Falegname" at Rome, procured for the young imitator of Rossini exemption from the conscription, and the honor of being carried in triumph and crowned at the Capitol.

The first work, however, by Donizetti which crossed the mountains and the seas and gained the ear of all Europe, was "Anna Bolena," given for the first time at Milan in 1830. This opera, which was long regarded as its composer's masterpiece, was written for Pasta and Rubini. It was in "Anna Bolena," too, as the impersonator of Henry VIII, that Lablache made his first great success. The graceful and melodious "Elisir d'Amore" was composed for Milan in 1832. "Lucia di Lammermoor," perhaps the most popular of all Donizetti's works, was written for Naples in 1835, the part of Edgardo having been composed expressly for Duprez, that of Lucia for Persiani. The lively little operetta called "Il Campanello di Notte" was produced under very interesting circumstances, to save a Neapolitan manager and his company from ruin. "If you would only give us something new our fortunes would be made," said one of the singers. Donizetti declared they should have an operetta from his pen within a week. But where was he to get a libretto? He determined himself to supply that first necessity of the operatic composer; and, recollecting a vaudeville which he had seen some years before at Paris, called "La sonnette de nuit," took that for his subject, rearranged the little piece in operatic form, and forthwith set it to music. It is said that in nine days the libretto was written, the music composed, the parts learned, the opera performed and the theater saved.

Donizetti seems to have possessed considerable literary facility. He designed and wrote the last acts both of the "Lucia" and of "La Favorita"; and he himself translated into Italian the libretto of "Betly" and "La fille du régiment." Donizetti had visited Paris in 1835, when he produced, at the Théâtre des Italiens, his "Marino Faliero." Five years later another of his works was brought out at the same establishment. This was "Lucrezia Borgia" (composed for Milan in 1834); of which the run was cut short by Victor Hugo, who, as author of the tragedy on which the libretto is founded, forbade the representations. "Lucrezia Borgia" became, at the Italian Opera of Paris, "La Rinegata"—the Italians of Alexander VI's court being changed into Turks. "Lucrezia" may be

ranked with "Lucia" and "La Favorita" among the most successful of Donizetti's operas. "Lucia" contains some of the most beautiful melodies in the sentimental style that its ingenious composer produced; it contains also a concerted finale which is well designed and admirably dramatic.

The favor with which "Lucrezia Borgia" is everywhere received may be explained partly by the merit of the music—which, if not of a very high order, is always singable and tuneful—partly by the interest of the story, partly also by the manner in which the interest is divided between four principal characters, so that the cast must always include four leading singers, each of whom is well provided for by the composer. But of the great dramatic situation, in which a voluptuous drinking-song is contrasted with a funeral chant, not so much has been made as might have been expected. The musical effect, however, would naturally be more striking in the drama than in the opera; since in the former singing is heard only in this one scene, whereas in the latter it is heard throughout the opera. "Lucrezia Borgia" may be said to mark the distance halfway between the style of Rossini, imitated by Donizetti for so many years, and that of Verdi, which he in some measure anticipated: thus portions of "Maria di Rohan" (1843) might almost have been written by the composer of "Rigoletto."

In 1840 Donizetti revisited Paris, where he produced successively "I Martiri" (which as "Poliuto" had been forbidden at Naples by the censorship); "La fille du régiment," composed for the Opéra Comique, and afterward brought out in the form of an Italian opera, with added recitatives; and "La Favorita," represented at the Académie. Jenny Lind, Sontag, Patti, Albani, all appeared with great success in "La Figlia del Reggimento," but when "La fille du régiment" was first brought out, with Madame Thillon in the chief part, it produced comparatively little effect. "La Favorita," on the other hand, met from the first with the most decided success. It is based on a very dramatic subject (borrowed from a French drama, "Le Comte de Commingues"), and many of the scenes have been treated by the composer in a highly dramatic spirit. For a long time, however, it failed to please Italian audiences. The fourth and concluding act of this opera is worth all the rest, and is probably the most dramatic act Donizetti ever wrote. With the exception of the cavatina "Ange si pur," taken from an unproduced work, "Le Duc d'Albe," and the slow movement of the duet, which was added at the rehearsals, the whole of this fine act was composed in from three to four hours.

Leaving Paris, Donizetti visited Rome, Milan, and Vienna. At Vienna he brought out "Linda di Chamouni." Coming back to Paris, he wrote (1843) "Don Pasquale" for the Théâtre Italien, and "Dom Sebastien" for the Académie. "Dom Sebastien" has been described as "a funeral in five acts," and the mournful drama to which the music of this work is wedded rendered its success all but impossible. As a matter of fact it did not succeed. The brilliant gaiety, on the other hand, of "Don Pasquale" charmed all who heard it, as did also the delightful acting and singing of Grisi, Mario, Tamburini, and Lablache, for whom the four leading parts were composed. For many years after its first production "Don Pasquale" was always played as a contemporary piece, but the singers perceived at last that there was a little absurdity in prima donna, barytone, and basso wearing the dress of everyday life; and it became usual, for the sake of picturesqueness in costume, to put back the time of the incidents to the eighteenth century. "Don Pasquale" and "Maria di Rohan" (Vienna) belong to the same year; and in this last opera the composer shows much of that earnestness and vigor for which Verdi has often been praised. Donizetti's last opera,

"Catarina Cornaro," was produced at Naples in 1844, and apparently made no mark. This was his sixty-third work, without counting two operas which have never been played—the "Duc d'Albe," composed to a libretto originally meant by Scribe, its author, for Rossini, but which Rossini returned when, after "Guillaume Tell," he resolved to write no more for the operatic stage, and a piece in one act composed for the Opéra Comique.

Donizetti, during the last three years of his life, was subject to fits of melancholy and abstraction which became more and more intense, until he was attacked with paralysis at Bergamo, where he expired April 8, 1848. Buried some little distance outside the town, his remains were disinterred in 1876 and reburied within its limits.

ST. CECILIA.

Painted by Domenichino.

ORPHEUS AND EURYDICE IN THE GARDEN.

II. EURYDICE DYING OF THE BITE OF A POISONOUS SNAKE.

CHRISTOPHER WILLIBALD GLUCK

ERNEST NEWMAN

The illustrations of Burne-Jones's famous cyclus upon the myth of Orpheus and Eurydice accompanying this article afford ground for suggestive comparison between Gluck's artistic ideas in 1762, expressed in music, and those of the great Preraphaelite artist upon the same subject a century later, expressed in color. These illustrations are from photographs by Frederick Hollyer, reproduced by permission.

AN able French critic once said, in speaking of the development of opera through Gluck, Wagner, and Berlioz, that Gluck sought and found the dramatic accent, but not the dramatic form — which is a piece of perfectly just criticism as far as it goes. As a matter of fact, the true dramatic form, being a compromise between the two arts of poetry and music, must necessarily be very difficult to attain; and — to say nothing of Berlioz — it is not quite beyond dispute that even Wagner achieved it completely more than once or twice. Yet the task of Wagner and his contemporaries was not only easier in many ways than that of Gluck, but it was easier precisely because of the example Gluck had set them. Given the essentials of dramatic speech in music, the modern composer could bestow all the more attention on the pursuit of the dramatic form — more especially as the palette of the musician had been enriched by the new colors brought to it by so many of the great immortals. But Gluck had not only to work out for himself, as best he could, the broader relations of music to poetry, but he had to invent, to a large extent, his own forms of speech — had to translate the big dramatic emotions into tone with very little assistance from the vocabulary of his contemporaries. It is scarcely to be wondered at if, under these circumstances, he spent his strength for the most part in getting veracity and poignancy of ex-

III. ORPHEUS SEEKS EURYDICE AT THE GATE OF HADES.   IV. CERBERUS, CHARMED BY THE MUSIC OF ORPHEUS, ADMITS HIM.

pression from moment to moment, and failed to recast the form of opera as a whole, to remold it on more homogeneous, more vital lines.

When he commenced his great reforming works, opera was everywhere regarded in Europe as a comparatively inferior medium of musical expression. The Italians had prostituted it to the vanity of the singers and the languors of the audience; the French, all the dramatic earnestness of Rameau notwithstanding, had made it the quintessence of dullness; while in Germany the opera-houses were mostly run by Italian troupes and stocked with Italian music. Everywhere the opera was sinking under the burdens of cheap melody, inane libretti, vain and stupid singers, and pompous scenic display. The only department in which there could be said to be any real life was that of *opera buffa*, which had been vivified by the sparkling inspiration of Pergolesi, Jomelli, and others, and which escaped a lot of the absurdities that had swallowed up *opera seria*. Satirist after satirist had laughed the opera to scorn, but apparently with little or no effect. Serious students like Algarotti made elaborate analyses of what it was and what it ought to be, but had no influence upon the practice of composers. It is probable, too, that the system of patronage current in the eighteenth century had something to do with the flaccid condition of the opera of the day, for the musician must frequently have felt his imagination hampered by the necessity of pleasing not only the public but his patron.

This was the condition of things with which Gluck had to contend. On the intellectual side he was a man of enormous volition, a combatant who believed very firmly in himself. On the artistic side he was gifted with a poetical and dramatic sense in opera far beyond that of any of his contemporaries, and with a musical imagination comparatively limited in range and complexity, but capable of profoundly moving expression when it had to deal with a strong dramatic situation. At the time when, dissatisfied with his earlier works, he set himself to consider the problem of

444

V. EURYDICE ACROSS THE FLAMES.   VI. ORPHEUS ADVANCES THROUGH THE FLAMES.

the reform of the opera, he had attained complete maturity of imagination and of technic. Critically minded as he was, and alive to the main esthetic forces of his day, he brought to bear upon the problem of music and the drama, as he conceived it, the theories of poetical and musical expression that had so great a vogue in the eighteenth century. The Aristotelian theory that art imitated nature was almost everywhere predominant; the respective spheres of the arts were not clearly defined; their sensuous sides were barely glanced at in considering their scopes and possibilities, the attention of the estheticians being fixed almost solely on the ideas to be expressed. If all the arts suffered from this esthetic confusion, music stood at a greater disadvantage than any of the others; for not only did the fallacy of the imitation of nature work the deadliest havoc there, but the art itself was a comparatively undeveloped one, and so more likely to be set traveling along a wrong path. It is clear, for example, that so long as men held a theory like Baumgarten's, that the faculty concerned in apprehending beauty is just a lower phase of reason, music had not much chance of development along the more emotional lines.

It was owing to this kind of esthetic that Gluck was prompted to the writing of the famous passage in his preface to *Alceste:* "I sought to reduce music to its true function—that of supporting the poetry, in order to strengthen the expression of the sentiments and the interest of the situations, without interrupting the action or disfiguring it with superfluous ornament. I imagined that the music should be to the poetry just what the vivacity of color and the happy combination of light and shade are to a correct and well-composed design, serving to animate the figures without altering the contours." Here the function of the musician in opera is clearly made subservient to that of the poet; and the reasons for this are to be sought partly in the comparatively undeveloped state of music in that day, partly in the current esthetic theory of the

445

need for "imitating nature," and partly in the pronounced bias of Gluck's mind to that order of musical expression that takes its inspiration and its accent from words. Everywhere in the esthetic writings of the time the musician was exhorted to be faithful to the guidance of the poet, and to "imitate nature" in tone as closely and as simply as possible. Rousseau argues at great length on the assumption that the aim of the musician should be to create in sound an esthetic product intrinsically the same as that created by the poet in words, or by the painter in lines and colors; the musician, in fact, was to "paint objects" in tone. Harris, in his "Discourse on Music, Painting, and Poetry" (1744), discussed the question as to which art — poetry, painting, or music — "imitates nature most effectively." Du Bos laid it down that "music achieves its imitations by

VII, VIII, AND IX. IN THE HOUSE OF PLUTO. ORPHEUS CHARMS THE KING OF HADES, WHO PROMISES TO RESTORE EURYDICE TO HIS ARMS IF HE WILL CONDUCT HER TO EARTH AND NOT LOOK BACK UPON HER UNTIL THE GATEWAY IS PASSED.

means of melody, harmony, and rhythm, just as painting makes its imitations by means of lines, chiaroscuro, and local colors." He even went further, summing up that "the first principles of music are the same as those of poetry and painting. Music, like the other two arts, is an imitation, and it cannot be of any value unless it conforms to the general rules of these two arts as to the choice of its subjects, its probability, and other matters." The duet was condemned by Grimm and other writers because it is "not according to nature"—it being altogether against reason for two tragic persons to be talking at the same time without either paying any attention to the other. Saint-Evremond even objected to the characters singing at all; for "can any one imagine a master calling his valet and *singing* his orders to him?" Beattie, one of the sanest esthetic writers of the day, contended that music was inferior to poetry just because

X.   THEY NEAR THE GATEWAY.   XI.   ORPHEUS IS UNABLE TO RESTRAIN HIS DESIRE TO LOOK UPON EURYDICE.

it could not make its pictures so definite as the latter. "Poetry is the most immediate and most accurate interpreter of music. Without this auxiliary, a piece of the best music, heard for the first time, might be said to mean something, but we should not be able to say what. It might incline the heart to sensibility; but poetry, or language, would be necessary to improve that sensibility into a real emotion, by fixing the mind upon some definite and affecting idea." Algarotti and others even held that the dance should be an "imitation of nature."

A glance at opinions of this kind, which were freely expressed in the musical and critical circles in which Gluck moved, makes clear to us how he came to write the music he did. For the most part he would have thought it rank heresy to set up music as higher or more expressive than poetry, or even very different from poetry in its essential features. He was content to play the part of colorist to the poet's drawing, taking care not to let his musical imagination slip the fetters the poet had imposed

XII.   EURYDICE SINKS TO THE GROUND AND FADES AWAY.

XIII.   ORPHEUS DIES AND SO REGAINS HIS EURYDICE.   HE IS BURIED BY THE MUSES.

on it.   "The melody in my operas," he wrote, "is merely a substitute for declamation,"—not a self-existing shape of beauty, finding justification in the first place in the laws of *music*. "The imitation of nature," he says again, "is the end which both poet and composer should set before themselves; that is the goal after which I have striven. . . . My music tends only to greater expressiveness and to the enforcement of the declamation of the poetry." Once more: "I have tried to be painter and poet rather than musician;" and again, "in composing, I try to forget that I am a musician." This faith found complete expression when he wrote: "I might perhaps have written something more beautiful from a *musical* point of view, and varied it so as to please your ears; but in that case *I would only have been a musician*, and would have been untrue to nature, which I must never abandon."

Thus it is clear that the ideal Gluck set before himself was a form of opera in which the music should be the handmaid of the poetry from first to last. It is almost unnecessary, at this time of day, to point out that he did not achieve this ideal, and that if he *had* done so his music would not live for the modern world as it does. His best melody is very much more than intensified declamation; it addresses itself to the musical even more than to the poetical side of our intelligence. When one finds, in our own epoch, the theory that music is an intensification of speech held by such a thinker as Herbert Spencer and by such a musician as Wagner, it is hardly surprising that this erroneous view was the prevailing one in the eighteenth century, when music, as a separate art, was not so supremely developed as now. As a matter of fact, Gluck himself, in his more incandescent moments, reached out to quite another theory of opera,

448

that "the voices, the instruments, the tones, even the pauses, should strive after one end,— expression,— and the agreement between the words and the music should be such that neither the poem should seem to be made for the music nor the music for the poem." That is quite a different theory from the other, in that it restores to the musician the right to reach brain and heart in his own way, instead of being required to do unnecessary or impossible things at the behest of the poet. But Gluck could have no more than fugitive intuitions of this; the development of music along these lines, and its consequent action upon opera, was reserved for other times and other men. Circumstanced as he was, both by temperament, by training, and in his intellectual associations, his work was necessarily cast in the mold of reticent, well-ordered classicism. If the painters worshiped line,— the painters, who might have been expected to *see* that life and nature had something more than line,— it is not to be wondered at that the musician, with no external model to instruct him, should hesitate to trust himself on the unknown seas of color. The social structure and the *salon* of the eighteenth century had first to be shattered and then reconstructed before that development became possible in music.

BY PERMISSION OF HOLLYER.

ORPHEUS AND EURYDICE.

From the painting by George Frederick Watts.

GIACOMO MEYERBEER

BY

MORITZ MOSZKOWSKI

THE 2d of May, 1894, was the thirtieth anniversary of the death of Meyerbeer, and according to the provision of his will, on that day his heirs entered into possession of his musical estate. Among other conditions to inheritance, Meyerbeer stipulated that his unpublished manuscripts be given to that one of his grandsons who should have developed most musical ability. These posthumous works, however, will not be published.

In commemoration of this anniversary of Meyerbeer's death "L'Africaine" was given at the Berlin royal opera-house, several papers made cursory reference to the import of the day, and there were occasional expressions of curiosity, in musical circles, as to the nature of the master's musical legacy. It was believed that there existed a completed opera of which the young Goethe was the hero, but the facts only partly sustain that assumption, for the work proved to be simply a drama by Blaze de Bury, entitled "La Jeunesse de Goethe," in which music is accorded an important rôle.

All of these discussions and conjectures attracted little attention from the outer world, and aroused less interest among musicians of the inner circles than could have been expected, considering the honored and popular name with which they were associated. This circumstance suggests an investigation of Meyerbeer's present position in public esteem, of what it once was, and as to what rank the verdict of future generations is likely to assign his creations.

Music is an art which rapidly alters its forms. We speak of "immortal masterpieces" of music, forgetting that barely four hundred years have passed since that epoch which we of to-day look upon as the dawn of musical art. What enormous development, what unforeseen perfection, and what wide dissemination it has attained during this period! How much has been created, admired, and afterward buried! And there has been no lack of errors of diagnosis in regard to musical works. Many have been adjudged dead that contained the life-impulse, while others have been accredited with a vitality that they did not possess. Factious critics have sometimes proved too ambitious to become grave-diggers, and at other times have worshiped musical corpses, as the Portuguese court parasites did homage to the exhumed remains of Ines de Castro, which Pedro had seated upon the throne.

Among the energetic partizans of the so-called new German school, the men whom I have denominated grave-diggers were numerous, and it strikes me that the arrangements which they made for the wholesale burial not only of Meyerbeer's operas, but of all related works, were a trifle premature. It is not to be denied that they succeeded in somewhat discrediting the value of Meyerbeer's music, and after the absolute denial of merit in his works had become an article of faith for Wagnerism there was no hesitation in its acceptance by those who desired to be modern *à tout prix.*

The public at large, which has little judgment in things musical, soon became an active participant in the war for the reformation of dramatic music; for Wagner not only illustrated his art principles through his operas, but also announced them in papers on art, which most skilfully accentuated the German national element in its esthetic ambitions. He furthermore took into consideration so much that was foreign to music, attempting to establish parallels between his reformatory ideas in his own department of art and matters which concerned apparently remote domains of thought and action, that many who had originally been totally indifferent came through this indirect path of reasoning into the Wagner fold.

The anti-Semitic propaganda found a capable champion in Wagner. Had there been no other available reasons for condemning Meyerbeer's music than the Jewish origin of its author, that, with Wagner's help, would have sufficed. The interesting discovery was made that the scores of "Robert le Diable" and "Les Huguenots" were in reality nothing but Jewish brogue, though they afforded valuable documentary proof at the same time of the existence of the famous French-Jewish alliance.[1] I will not accuse Wagner of having greeted this popularized interpretation of his ideas with satisfaction, although in his warfare against Meyerbeer and his adherents he sometimes failed to confine himself to purely artistic arguments.

It should be mentioned, however, that before Wagner's appearance

[1] A supposed alliance to combat German composers.— EDITORS.

MEYERBEER'S HOME IN PARIS, 1851.

Rue de Richelieu, corner rue St. Marc. Meyerbeer's home was at No. 91, the house
on the left. Opposite, at No. 96, Berlioz lived in 1830. At No. 89, the
second door from the corner on the left, lived Ferdinand Palt, the
operatic conductor, from 1830 until his death in 1839.

upon the field the fight against Meyerbeer had been conducted with great
personal enmity. Spontini, who was at first overestimated, and later saw
his fame fade, had done all that was possible in this reprehensible style
of warfare. As soon as he became convinced that no machinations could
prevail against the success of his hated rival, he overreached himself in
the harebrained assertion that Meyerbeer did not compose his own operas,
but that they were the products of a certain Gouin, who preferred selling
his fame to endangering his position as postal clerk by the acquisition of
musical *renommée*.

In justice it must be admitted that Meyerbeer's ardent admirers carried the glorification of their master to the borders of the ridiculous.
When Dr. Schucht, for instance, in his work on Meyerbeer, says that the
"Struensée" overture "takes first rank among classical overtures," and
when he, in discussing that early work, "Gott und die Natur," claims that

452

it evinces a command of counterpoint equal to that displayed by Händel and other masters of polyphony, every honest and intelligent person who honors Meyerbeer must regard these assertions as regrettable exaggerations.

Heine wrote of Meyerbeer in veins varying from extreme rapture to bitter mockery. In those operas composed during Meyerbeer's Italian period he found "Rossiniisms intensified by means of the most delicious exaggerations, the gold gilded, and the flowers endowed with stronger perfumes." He could not reach a similar height of absurdity in regard to "Robert le Diable" and "Les Huguenots," for their qualities precluded such a result, even though most recklessly loaded with superlative praise. With the advent of "Le Prophète" a complete change manifested itself in Heine's musical taste. He had fallen out with the composer, and thereafter saw in him only a "*maître de plaisir* of the aristocracy, and a music-corrupter, who composed morbid music," etc.

I remember that, even while a child, I was aware of the contradictions contained in the various opinions that I heard expressed in regard to Meyerbeer's music. How I longed to hear a stage-performance of one of his works! When I was about ten years old my wish was fulfilled. The third theatrical performance that I was permitted to attend made me acquainted with "Les Huguenots." I had previously heard most of the opera played upon the piano, and had not been pleased with it thus presented; but through the medium of voices and orchestra it made an immense impression on me, the details of which are still clear in my memory. It was not until some years later that I heard "Robert le Diable" and "Le Prophète." It seems strange to me that my present estimate of the comparative artistic value of these three operas should so perfectly tally with my youthful impressions. "Le Prophète" seems to me to approach "Les Huguenots" in musical value, while "Robert" is far inferior; but this order of rank does not accord with the scale of public esteem. Recent years have developed a slight disposition to glorify "Le Prophète" at the expense of "Robert"; the latter work is nevertheless thought to possess greater melodic spontaneity, and the value of this quality is certainly beyond dispute.

Notwithstanding the fact that music is largely a matter of taste, it possesses elements that may be assayed. If we compare the scores of "Robert" and "Le Prophète" in all their details, taking into consideration the attributes of each as a musical dramatic work, we find in "Le Prophète," first of all, a far more characteristic formation of the concerted numbers. The sermon of the Anabaptists and the chorus of peasantry associated with it form together a masterpiece of choral development, evincing a power of climax possessed by no earlier dramatic composer. The rhythmic structure and modulations show a true art perception, just as the two principal motifs (in C minor and C major) show a

PRESENT OPERA HOUSE IN BERLIN.

Where Meyerbeer's "Ein Feldlager in Schlesien" was first given.

gift for melodic invention. I have always regarded the beginning of the latter, with its audacious upward progression to the chord of the seventh,

as one of Meyerbeer's happiest inspirations. When this melody is repeated by the whole chorus in unison, it seems like a veritable *cri du peuple*, and the accompanying sturdy tributes of the celli, contrabassi, fagotti, and tuba sound like the dull tread of the working-classes marching to revolution. The chorus "Auf! tanzet um Leichen," in the third act, is endowed with characteristic color; but Meyerbeer's sovereign command of choral and instrumental forces is most brilliantly exemplified in the great ensemble of the church scene. The movement in D major, "Seht den König, den Propheten," is Händelian in its grandeur, and affords the most effective contrast possible to the "allegretto agitato" that succeeds it. The excitement which takes possession of the deluded people, who cannot be sure who is their betrayer, after the recognition scene between *Fidès* and *John;* the ecstatic rejoicing called forth by the seeming miracle of the

Prophet; and the final blending of the "Domine, salvum fac regem nostrum" with the triumphant cries of the people—all this is handled with such mastery, and the manifold details are so ingeniously devised, that, excepting the sword consecration in "Les Huguenots," the whole mass of opera literature furnishes no counterpart to it. The entire act is, besides, very rich in harmonic and instrumental effects, showing that Meyerbeer was, even in these spheres, a successful innovator.

It is obvious that these enormous demands upon musical and dramatic resources could have left little for the fifth act. Librettist and composer were both entirely exhausted, and could hope for a satisfactory finale only at the hands of the stage-machinists, to whom they could, to be sure, cry as does *King Philip* in "Don Carlos," "Cardinal, I have done my duty; do yours." Taking it all in all, we may say that Meyerbeer reached the zenith of his technical skill in "Le Prophète," and that his creative power had at that period hardly diminished. It is not to be denied that this work exhibits numerous weak movements. The whole of the last act does not contain one important musical number; indeed, there is much in it that is repulsive. *Fidès's* grand aria (A flat major) is a model of disagreeable and misplaced vocal bravura, and the andante in E major, in the duet between *John* and his mother, direct torture. What the composer intended to express through the almost endless repetition of B in the trumpets, and later in the hautboys and violins, is to me incomprehensible. Perhaps others may see his intention more clearly.

Of the ballet music in "Le Prophète" the skating dance alone has obtained great popularity. The other numbers are entirely ineffective. Meyerbeer evidently devoted little care to their production, because they had not the slightest import in the scheme of the opera. In comparing the ballets of "Robert" and "Le Prophète," I prefer the former. As both are incidental accessories, the superiority weighs less. It is of much more moment that the last act of "Robert" so far surpasses that of "Le Prophète" in healthy and soulful melody. The final trio of *Alice, Robert*

Final trio of Alice, Bertram, and Robert.
Andante cantabile.

and *Bertram* is one of the most beautiful parts of the opera, and the pathetic melody played by the orchestra while *Robert* reads his mother's will reconciles us to the bantering of the preceding period, out of which it grows. Unfortunately, the composer's intention is never entirely realized by our opera orchestras in the performance of this melody. Meyerbeer designed that it should be played underneath the stage, and by keyed bugles. In order to avoid the considerable difficulty of securing a perfect ensemble, and the trifling extra expense thus involved, the melody is

SCENE FROM "ROBERT LE DIABLE."

From "Album de l'Opéra."

assigned to the orchestra cornets, and loses materially in poetic effect. *Alice, Robert* and *Bertram* have another fine trio in the third act, although

Trio in the third act of the same opera.

it is effective only from the standpoint of the old Italian operatic style, on which the composer of "Robert" had turned his back. Shreds of that school adhered to him, however, for a long time. When we consider that Meyerbeer had previously written seven operas purely in Rossini's vein, it ceases to seem strange that many traces of Italianism are to be found in "Robert."

If we compare "Crociato in Egitto," the last of Meyerbeer's operas in the Italian school, with "Robert," which he began five years later, we find an astounding change of style — even greater than that shown in the

456

period of Wagner's development between "Rienzi" and "The Flying Dutchman."

Musical historians with fine perceptions, in this, as in so many similar cases, have given the world the benefit of their backward-glancing prophecies. They discover the "claws of the lion in 'Crociato.'" If one has the whole lion before him, the genuineness of the claws can no longer be questioned. Had the score of "Crociato" been submitted to me as the work of a thirty-three-year-old composer, and had I been asked for an estimate of his gifts as based thereon, I should have made a fool of myself. The whole opera impresses me as a shallow imitation of Rossini's mannerisms, and the only feature of it which I find worthy of praise is the skilful treatment of the voices. Harmony, structural forms, and impersonations are unendurably commonplace: nothing forecasts greatness.

Meyerbeer's increasing musical ability, as traceable through his successive operas, "Crociato," "Robert," and "Les Huguenots," is quite analogous to the gradual development shown in Beethoven's symphonies. Berlioz says, quite properly, of the First Symphony, "This is not yet Beethoven." No one would question that the Second Symphony bears the unmistakable impress of its creator, but not until the Third Symphony does the master exhibit the full glory of his genius. The careers of Beethoven and Meyerbeer are analogous, in that each in his own province showed not only the ripest individuality but also the most perfect mastery of art forms; for just as Beethoven is the mightiest composer that has arisen in the symphonic field, so is Meyerbeer still the foremost representative of grand opera. The gap between the highest and most ideal forms of instrumental music, and grand opera, distorted here and there through concessions to stage-machinists and ballet-dancers, is too wide to push the comparison further.

Whatever one's opinion of Meyerbeer's music in general, it cannot be denied that "Les Huguenots" is a work that exhibits entirely original invention, a rare wealth of characterization, and a wonderful mastery of technical resources. Even Richard Wagner, the most spiteful of Meyerbeer's opponents, was aroused by the fourth act to the expression of the warmest praise.

Schumann alone saw retrogression from "Robert" in "Les Huguenots"; he indeed preferred "Crociato" to "Robert."[1] This assignment of rank is incontrovertible evidence of the one-sidedness and untenableness of Schumann's opinions. The individualities of the two musicians were so unlike that they necessarily repelled each other. Schumann could accord Meyerbeer justice as long as he showed noteworthy capacity on

[1] Schumann's "Music and Musicians" (Fragments from Leipzig, No. IV): "I agree perfectly with Florestan, who clenched his criticism of the opera with the words: 'In "Crociato" Meyerbeer was a musician, in "Robert" he wavers, and from "Les Huguenots" on he is distinctly a "Franconian."'" ("Franconian" refers to a character in Schumann's writings who represents the Philistine ways of thinking.)

a Monsieur Jenny Brandus
souvenir de
Meyerbeer

accepted lines; but as Meyerbeer became more and more Meyerbeer, as his artistic physiognomy became more and more marked and significant, he lost Schumann's sympathy.

Rivalry, unhappily, often enough leads to enmity; but a no less deplorable, because unjust, antagonism often arises between artists having

SPONTINI.

Lithographed in 1823, from a painting by Jean Guérin.

irreconcilable tastes. Such was the case between Meyerbeer the positivist and Schumann the symbolist. The former was a cosmopolitan, and the latter a national artist. The one was attracted by the brilliancy of the footlights; the other reveled in clair-obscure. Meyerbeer was objective, *i. e.*, worked from the outside in. Schumann was subjective, *i. e.*, worked from the inside out.

All music that does not belong to the class that might be called abstractly contrapuntal grows obsolete. This style alone is based on the everlasting laws of unassailable logic, for its structure rests upon combinations of actualities which are inspired by the spirit of mathematics. It is therefore not subject to the changing tastes of passing time. Quite other is the fate of musical works in the conception of which imagination plays the principal rôle, which arouse a thousand varying moods in their hearers, and in which the whole range of resources of musical expression is exhaustively applied; for here we have to do with an art of individual feeling and temporary taste. Such music is not deathless, but its life may be shorter or longer—a long life certainly indicating inherent strength. If this be granted, we cannot refuse "Les Huguenots" a place among the masterpieces of musical dramatic literature. What composer would not rejoice to see his creations the subject of strife for fifty-eight years? While thus calling attention to the enduring vitality of "Les Huguenots," I should go too far did I claim that this work still presents the full vigor of youth.

There are two factors either of which may induce decadence in the effectiveness of a musical work. The one is the natural dullness of sensibilities toward any pleasure or stimulus with which we are too familiar; the other is the apparent change in our tastes. There is of course a wide difference between that loss of charm in a composition occasioned by too frequent hearing, and that caused by our having revised our estimate of its value. In the case of "Les Huguenots" we shall be obliged to concede the presence of both factors, but this may also be said of all works that belong to the same genre.

Did Rossini, Halévy, and Auber, in their operas, make less damaging concessions to the public, and to the vanity of singers? Did not their works also contain examples of those forced and artificially produced effects that Wagner quite aptly called "effects without motives"? Even if we grant that Meyerbeer is the greatest representative of the French Grand Opera, that is no justification for loading all of the shortcomings of his school upon his shoulders.

The score of "Les Huguenots" is so full of veritable musical beauties, it contains such a wealth of noble melody and ingenious dramatic settings, that one can well afford to overlook the many features of it that have become obsolete, and the few that are positively disagreeable. Its instrumentation is replete with characteristic qualities. A certain virtuoso-like treatment of certain instruments, entirely different from that found in Mozart's and Weber's writings, was one of Meyerbeer's characteristics. *Raoul's* romanza in the first act suggested to the ingenious composer the employment of the long-disused viola d'amore, the ethereal tones of which blend most exquisitely with the *mezzo voce* of the tenor singer. This is the last occurrence of this instrument in all musical literature—probably because the charm of its tone-color is fully developed in but few keys, best in D major. The bass clarinet, which Meyerbeer introduced into the opera orchestra, and which he used as solo instrument in "Les Huguenots" and

"Le Prophète," has, however, been largely adopted by later composers. Altogether Meyerbeer's treatment of the wood-wind was entirely original and suitable. Every good treatise on instrumentation contains illustrative excerpts from his works, because they show such an extraordinary sense for tone-color, and such complete familiarity with the technic of each and all instruments.

Meyerbeer's inventive faculty especially distinguished itself in producing melancholy, weird, and wild combinations. This was strikingly manifested in "Robert." The famous triplet passage for the bassoons in the cemetery scene has always ranked as one of the greatest strokes of this master's genius. He understood how to draw new and characteristic effects from this instrument. "Les Huguenots" furnishes especially numerous examples in this genre. Who does not remember the awful, hollow timbre with which the piccolo, bassoon, contrabass, and grand drum endow *Marcel's* war-song, or the hissing chromatic scales in which

the flutes, hautboys, and clarinets so horribly portray the flaming bloodthirstiness of the Catholic conspirators? Meyerbeer's employment of the trumpets to depict furious fanaticism, as in the fourth and fifth acts, was

markedly successful. In other places his treatment of the trumpets is not congenial to German taste. French and Italian operatic scores have always materially differed from German in this particular. Each of these three nations has its own physiognomic character in instrumentation.

Berlioz once said of Meyerbeer that "he not only has the luck to have talent, but he has the talent to have luck." This was equally witty and true. If it was a rare good fortune for our master to have been aided in his difficult career as operatic composer by the possession of a million thalers, there was a second good fortune, not less valuable, for which he had every reason to be profoundly thankful. This second good fortune was called Scribe. The composer had in Scribe a librettist who not only possessed astonishing dramatic inventive faculty and knowledge of stage-business, but who also had the talent of adaptability. Scribe could suit his work to the peculiar and often capricious demands of his collaborators. He complained often enough because of the changes that Meyerbeer required in his texts, but he always yielded until a difference of opinion arose with regard to "L'Africaine" which no amount of discussion could adjust. Meyerbeer in consequence laid aside this score, which was already far advanced toward completion, took up the "Prophète" libretto, and after that had been finished, wrote a comic opera, "Dinorah," for which Carré and Barbier furnished the text. In my opinion Meyerbeer's reason for the acceptance of this latter unsympathetic and also technically weak book is obvious. He wished to prove by the composition of this dubious idyl that the nature of his talent did not confine him to the heroic style; and it cannot be said that he failed to accomplish his purpose. "Dinorah" is not poor in characteristic graceful and brilliant vocal and instrumental effects. Still, it shows unmistakable evidence of decadence in inventive power, apparent in debilitating repetitions, rhythms, and in melismas from his earlier works. For this reason "Dinorah" has never secured a firm foothold in German opera repertoires, although even to-day it is highly regarded in France. The festival opera, "A Camp in Silesia," composed for the dedication of the new Berlin opera-house, has had a similar experience. The French adaptation called "L'Etoile du Nord" is seldom seen in Germany, although it has obtained considerable popularity in Paris.

"Le Prophète," "L'Etoile du Nord," "Dinorah," and several compositions intended for the concert-room and dating from the same period, had long since been performed when Meyerbeer returned to the neglected "L'Africaine." Negotiations with Scribe for the alterations of the last two acts were fruitless, and the death of the librettist, in 1861, blighted the composer's hopes of ever seeing the libretto revised to accord with his desires. He was therefore obliged to finish the opera on the original lines. What displeased Meyerbeer in the text was the circumstance that, according to Scribe, the supposed African heroine turns out to be a young

East Indian queen—a somewhat violent transformation, but one that Scribe regarded as essential. He maintained that India, with her gorgeous costumes and her pompous religious ceremonials, lent herself easily to musical illustration, whereas Africa was not operatically suggestive. He was not entirely wrong, for the first performance of "L'Africaine"—after the death of both authors—developed the fact that the most effective parts of the opera were those the scenes of which were laid in India. The composer was afforded exceedingly appropriate musical colors for the pomp of the Buddhist religious service, with its exotic magnificence of processions and dances; whereas other parts of the opera are uninterestingly dry, as might be expected from the long political and geographical discussions which they contain.

During his years of exhausting labor in the operatic field, Meyerbeer found time to compose a not inconsiderable number of small choral and orchestral works,—many of them *pièces d'occasion*,—the majority of which are to-day entirely forgotten. Such of his cantatas and church music as have become known to me are hardly worthy of earnest consideration, but I must not fail to call attention to one of Meyerbeer's works which, although small in its proportions, equals the best creations of the master in artistic significance. It is his music to Michael Beer's tragedy "Struensée." The score embraces only fourteen numbers, but it belongs to the masterworks of its genre, and may be classed with Beethoven's "Egmont," Mendelssohn's "Midsummer Night's Dream," Weber's "Preciosa," Schumann's "Manfred," and Bizet's "L'Arlesienne." Meyerbeer, with the overture to "Struensée," nullified, once for all, the reproach that he could not write orchestral pieces in symphonic form.

Few, in advance, would have accredited the great master Verdi with the ability to produce such a "Requiem" as he has given to the world; and when the painter Lenbach incidentally showed that he could paint hands as well as heads, he also did so without the permission of his critics. It is doubtless vexatious that artists sometimes venture to exhibit new features of their talent, regardless of the category to which critics have consigned them; but it is certainly most disagreeable of all when any one—like Meyerbeer, for instance—persists in living in his works, although long since declared artistically dead and buried. Yes, he lives, to the satisfaction of all unprejudiced musicians, who know no one-sidedness in art, and who will not allow doctrinaire pedants and their sterile principles to embitter their love of the beautiful.

MADAME KRAUSS.
Best latter-day "Fidès."
PHOTOGRAPH BY BARY, PARIS.

MADAME VIARDOT.
Original "Fidès" in "Le Prophète."
PHOTOGRAPH BY BARY, PARIS.

MEYERBEER'S BRANDUS CORRESPONDENCE

THE following letters, which illustrate the artistic life of Meyerbeer during the years 1859–63, are given to the public with the permission of Mr. Edward Brandus, the only son of M. Gemmy Brandus of the old music-publishing house of Brandus et Cie., Paris. The house of Brandus belongs to a group of great firms to whose exertions the literature and music of Europe owe an enormous debt. In the days of its greatest activity, character and individuality entered into the transaction of business to an extent which modern commercialism is making more and more impossible. Great works which could by no possibility bring more than a modest return for the outlay were undertaken to add to the honor of the name. A closer relation existed between the great composers and their publishers than we find to-day. Thus it was quite in accord with its habits that the house of Brandus should not only publish the works of Chopin, Rossini, Meyerbeer, Auber, Adam, Flotow, Halévy, Mendelssohn, Offenbach, Lecocq, and others, but also should be the close friend of the men themselves. Meyerbeer especially found in Louis and Gemmy Brandus his intimate

confidants. He depended on them for every care that insured his personal comfort or the fulfilment of his artistic ambitions, and in his frequent separations from his family, when he was busy rehearsing his works in Paris, he went in and out of the home of M. Gemmy Brandus, in the Faubourg Montmartre, as if it were his own.

How close the intimacy was, and to what extent the continuous interest which Meyerbeer felt in the fate of his compositions was shared by his publishers, these letters show plainly. The correspondence also gives a clue to that practical side of a successful composer's life without which the works of genius hardly survive the struggle for existence,—however great their merit,—but of which the world at large seldom takes account.

The wide-awake interest which Meyerbeer felt in the world of art and letters is clear from these pages. Much has been warmly said of his disinterested kindnesses to Wagner and other musicians—and vigorously denied. The fact is that Meyerbeer was interested in all musicians, and helpfully disposed toward them; but he did not trouble himself about their possible rivalry. He did not say with

Berlioz, who remarked to M. Gemmy Brandus as they sat together at the first performance of Gounod's "Faust," "I trust that you are not going to publish cette cochonnerie là." He would not have permitted the publication because it would have interfered with "Pardon"; but he was quite ready to have Gounod's works played under his own direction. Meyerbeer's was not a mean nature.

Mr. Edward Brandus adds the following particulars regarding the personality of his father's friend:

"How well I remember our parlor in Paris, how I peeped through the door to see Meyerbeer at the piano, teaching Marie Battu who created *Inez* in 'L'Africaine' her aria 'Adieu, mon beau rivage'; or the tenor Naudin, with his frightful accent, singing 'Zè vou, Nobles Signors' instead of 'J'ai vu Nobles Seigneurs'; or Marie Sasse, who created *Sélika*. None of the divas suited Meyerbeer; he was urged to accept La Stolz, Cruvelli, Alboni, but none came up to his ideal for the rôle. Marie Sasse created the part after his death. She relates how one evening Meyerbeer was in the front orchestra row 'when I sang the "Huguenots," and after that whenever I went to Brandus, Meyerbeer would seat himself at the piano and call out to me, "Come, Marie, and listen to this," and then he would play and sing the morceau in an undertone and beg me to sing it to his accompaniment. That was his way of trying my voice. He bequeathed the rôle of *Nelusko* to Faure and that of *Sélika* to me.'

"Meyerbeer was never weary of retouching his operas. When, after his death, the task of putting 'L'Africaine' on the stage was really undertaken, it was found that he had written at least two different settings of every scene, and the selection which finally constituted the opera as it now stands left a second complete and different version of which twenty-two pieces are published. The present correspondence, too, shows how reasonable he was, and how ready to make the best of the voices of the artists that undertook his rôles. He was very set, however, when the matter involved what he regarded as a consideration of vital interest. For instance, when, in composing the 'Huguenots,' he arrived at the third act, the idea of the great duet between soprano and bass came to him,

and he applied to his librettist, Eugène Scribe, for the words of a dialogue between *Valentine* and *Marcel*. Scribe refused on the ground that no woman of such high rank as la Comtesse de Nevers would be alone with a Huguenot soldier in one of the public squares of Paris on the night of her marriage. Meyerbeer said no more, but went to the poet Emile Deschamps, and offered him one per cent of all the royalties paid on the work if he would write the words of the duet for him. It is safe to estimate that in the sixty-odd years which have elapsed since then, Deschamps and his heirs have received at least sixty thousand dollars from this source.

"The note respecting Rossini shows a very pleasing courtesy between these rival composers; but Rossini was not without bitterness toward Meyerbeer. One day Carafa, who was accustomed to borrow of Rossini, asked for a new loan. 'Look here,' said Rossini, 'I have no money in my pocket, but take this composition to Brandus and he will buy it, and you may have the money.' So saying, he took up a manuscript lying on the piano and wrote on the cover, 'Douces Réminiscences sur "L'Africaine" de Meyerbeer, par Rossini.' The man brought the music to my father, who, glancing at the cover, bought it for 1000 francs, and sent it to the engravers without opening it, secure in the sale which 'Selections from Meyerbeer's "L'Africaine," written for the piano by Rossini,' would have. But when it came back printed ready for the market, and its contents were really looked into, the trick came to light. There were no melodies by Meyerbeer — nothing but a foolish scrawl of hideous dissonances, as unworthy of Rossini as the trick it represented.

"It is said that Meyerbeer went to Italy to become Italianized. Perhaps he did, but the fact remains that when he started on that journey he brought a trunk of compositions to our house and asked permission to leave them in our keeping. While he was gone, Donizetti produced his 'Lucia di Lammermoor,' which created a great furor. When Meyerbeer came back to Paris he opened the trunk in the presence of my father, and, sitting down at the piano, began playing over some of the half-completed scores which it contained, and there, almost note for note, was the famous septuor in 'Lucia!' Thus once more deep minds ran in the same channel.

"Meyerbeer's real name was Beer. The Meyer he added in recognition of his affection for his old music-master Meyer, who bequeathed him his name. Michael Beer, his brother, the author of 'Struensée,' and his nephew Jules, alluded to in the present correspondence, retained their original patronymic.

"The composer was of medium height, with a very prominent forehead bordered with thick curls. His manner was marked by extreme courtesy and consideration for others. When rehearsing his operas, unlike most maestri, he was never known to lose his temper. 'My dear Maître,' he would say to some humble member of the orchestra, with the utmost gentleness, 'will you forgive me, but I think you were a little in error in the phrasing of the last page.' In fact, he was much too gentle to make the best conductor of his own operas, although he was never weary of rehearsing them.

"Meyerbeer died in 1864, at a hotel in the Champs-Elysées, which, after his death, took the name of Hotel Meyerbeer, which it still bears. He died at five o'clock in the morning in the arms of my uncle Louis. My father, Doctor Nelaton, and his nephew, Jules Beer, were present. The funeral cortège, passing through rue Lafayette on its way to the Gare du Nord, was escorted by the music of the Garde Impériale, which played the composer's own 'Marche aux Flambeaux' and the 'Marche du Sacre,' while military honors were rendered, he being a Commander of the Legion of Honor. My uncle, who was the executor of the will, took the body in a special funeral train to Berlin, where Meyerbeer held the position of Director-General of Music to his Majesty the King of Prussia.

"It was in virtue of this latter position that Meyerbeer came into relations with Wieprecht, mentioned in these letters. Wieprecht, by his individual exertions, had carried out the reform of Prussian military music, including the improvement of the instruments used. These great reforms, which Meyerbeer interested himself to forward, exactly as Berlioz befriended the similar career of Sax in France, led to the composition of the military music which remains an ornament to his name.

"Meyerbeer left a widow and two daughters, one of the latter being the wife of Baron von Korff, a colonel in the German army, and the other the wife of Richter, the celebrated German painter."

The earlier of the present group of letters indicates the composer's Parisian habits. He excuses himself for missing a call on the ground that the beautiful weather tempted him to walk in the Champs-Elysées. He buys two dozen "gants Jouvain," which his wife

ROGER IN "LE PROPHÈTE."

in Baden-Baden wishes to present to a friend, and forwards them to her. He applies to his friends to purchase wood and similar housekeeping necessities for his bachelor life. He invites them to dine with him at his favorite haunts (at six o'clock) at the "Café Voisin, rue Luxembourg, corner of rue St. Gouve"; or to share his box (No. 22 torcheuse de face), which he declares to be his favorite. "Perhaps M. Gemmy Brandus has recovered from his illness," he writes, "and may like to hear for himself whether the rehearsals in his home have produced satisfactory results. If I feel well enough I may come, too; if not I shall stay at home."

He is also composing and re-composing, and requests M. Brandus to obtain a reader to go over his music so that he can get the effect of his changes from practical audition. His method of securing him is characteristic. He is in the habit of taking his siesta after dinner at M. Brandus's house. He makes an appointment on this neutral ground. He is

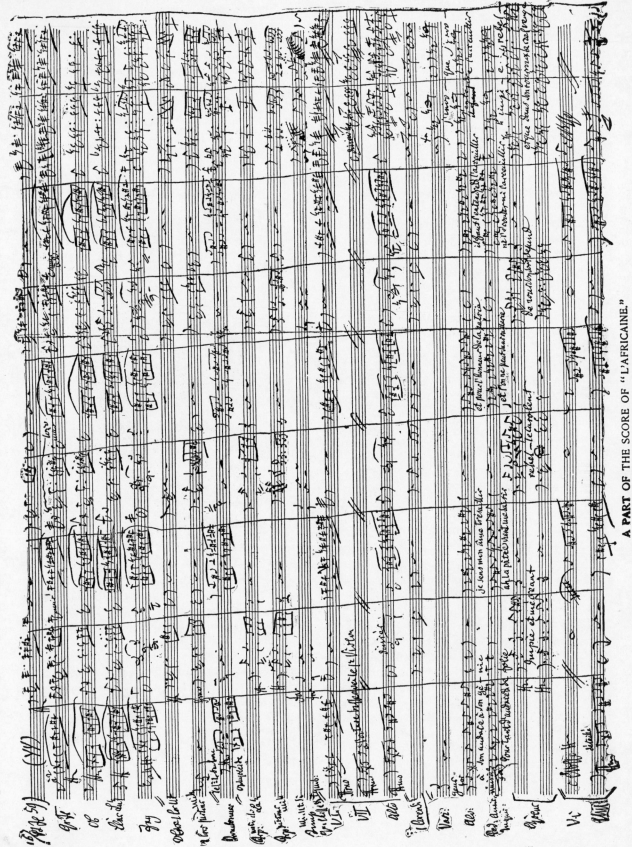

A PART OF THE SCORE OF "L'AFRICAINE."

From the collection of Edward Brandus.

467

charmed with the reader's voice, one M. Calabert, and they haggle over the terms. The price is finally made and the hour set, which the singer ignores, whereupon the injured composer speaks his mind:

"If the bass [Calabert] will bind himself to the engagement of coming to me every day at eight o'clock as he promised me yesterday (but which promise he failed to keep to-day), and if he will agree to remain until six P.M., and will discontinue the monstrous practice of losing an hour and a half over his déjeuner, I will (to avoid further complications) consider him still engaged to me for fifteen francs a day, *dear though it is.* But he must give you his word to keep the conditions faithfully. I beg you to preach him an emphatic sermon."

Meyerbeer is full of interest in everything pertaining to art. He goes to hear Ristori, and buys the words of her tragedy, "Giuditta," next day, to go over them privately. He calls on Patti, who is to sing in one of his operas, and presses forward his rehearsals and composing. All the world is at his feet, and his favorite opera, the "Pardon de Ploërmel" is to be brought out. Then the scene changes. He is away in Berlin, or at the baths, and the care of the great rôles of his operas, which is never forgotten for a moment, finds expression in letters. He has the capacity of every singer in Europe inventoried in his memory, and from behind the scenes arranges for the adequate presentation of his compositions all over the world.

"I take this opportunity of thanking you most warmly for sending me news of my dear friend Gouin's health; you would greatly oblige me by sending me word now and then how he is. I see that Herr Crosnier has given up his appointment, and that Herr Alphonse Royer has been chosen in his place; I read it in to-day's 'Revue et Gazette de Théâtres' and should like to know if it is true."

"I read in a German paper that the poet Heine's widow had given Herr Duisberg the order to correct and publish his memoirs. It would interest me greatly to know if this is really the case. I want to ask you to find it

out from him (*not in my name,* but as though *you* wanted to know).

"Is it true that the editor of the feuilletons in 'L'Assemblée Nationale,' who signs himself Ch. de Ville, is Henri Blaze?

"I am curious to see whether Herr Alphonse Royer is going to let Madame Borghi-Mamo sing again in 'Le Prophète' as he told you. I wish very much that this work could be produced again with this great artist for the chief character. If this is really the case, please let me know what impression she made upon the audience as *Fidès.*"

The three following letters show the usual order of events in Meyerbeer's diplomacy. The suggestion that Madame Lauters sing

CAROLINE DUPREZ IN "L'ÉTOILE DU NORD."

in the "Huguenots" is made to Meyerbeer through M. Brandus, and also to M. Royer through the same channel.

"Herr Formes is shortly to sing the part of the *Prophète* for the first time, which I consider is most beneficent to the opera, as until now it has always been sung by an inferior tenor. Now Herr Formes is most anxious to sing the 'Prière' in the third act, which, however, is only in the piano score and not in the grand score. It is No. 19 in the Italian piano score, and the first few words are 'Eternel Dieu Sauveur,' etc. Herr Formes heard Mario sing this prayer in London. I do not know if you have my original manuscript still in your possession. If so, please get the opera copyist Lenorne to copy it at once; if not, the copyist of the Italian Opera in Covent Garden must do it. In any case, it is most urgent and immediate. This 'Prière' is very short, only from page 217 to page 220 in the Italian piano score. If you should be obliged to have it sent from London, but only in this event, please have the coda copied too, which Costa added for Mario in the third act of the 'Couplets Bachiques.' I have not yet been able to make the corrections of the French words of the choral song 'Das Vaterland'; neither have I yet been able to correct the cavatine from the 'Crociato.' But I will do this to-morrow.

"I have quite lately composed another German chorus for men's voices, which I will send you soon, but I must first have another verse written to it, as the original has only one. I have found a third chorus among my manuscripts, so it would be best for them all to appear together, under the title of 'Drei Chorlieder für Männerstimmen ohne Begleitung.'

"Kindly send a piano score as well as the grand score of the 'Schiller Cantate' to Herr Guidi in Florence. I would also ask you to be so kind as to send one more piano score to me here in Berlin, as well as the libretto of the 'Ballo in Maschera.'

"You write that Madame Lauters is to sing the part of *Valentine* in the Grand Opera. I think it would be well if you could remind Herr Royer of the fact (he does not seem willing to pay any attention to what I say). Is it true that Madame Tedesco was nearly suffocated by opening the door of a stove too soon after it had been lighted? I should be most grateful to you if you would send me the most detailed particulars regarding the success of Auber's 'Circassienne.'

"In reply to your letter of July 21, I beg to say that you misunderstood me in thinking that I did not wish Madame Lauters to sing the part of *Valentine*; on the contrary, I most earnestly desire her to do so. I only meant that if she refused to take this part in the event of Niemann's singing the part of *Raoul* later on, in which case I should propose Sachs.

"Second, I do not wish you by any means to try and persuade Niemann to sing one of my parts; only if you should hear casually that he intends taking one, then I would ask you to advise his taking *Raoul* in the 'Huguenots.'

"Third, I will not allow my prayer from 'Le Prophète' to be orchestrated by Costa, so please don't have it copied.

"Lastly, thank you very much for your kind promise to send me full particulars of 'Tannhäuser's' third performance; it will interest me greatly to hear all about it."

In another letter he writes:

"With regard to what Herr Royer told you about Scribe's having mentioned my intention to the Minister of State, Walewsky, to produce 'L'Africaine' for a certainty next winter: please tell Herr Royer that as I have not seen Scribe for the last year or more, he cannot possibly know my intention for 'L'Africaine,' and consequently I look upon this as only the result of his fertile imagination."

"BERLIN, October 26, 1860.

"You would do me a great favor by seeing Herr Carré as soon as possible and asking him not to send me merely the second and third acts of his libretto, but to wait and send it all at the same time, when it is quite finished, as I can only judge it properly by reading the whole thing through. I am sending you by to-morrow's post the Romance of the fourth act of the 'Huguenots' for Madame Lauters. The latter writes to tell me that everybody at the Opera is talking of my bringing out 'L'Africaine' for certain next season, with Herr Niemann as the principal tenor. Now this must hurt Guymard most deeply as he has sung all my operas for so many years with such faithful love and with such great success. I do not wish to send Madame Lauters a written answer to this, but I should be exceedingly obliged if you would take her the Romance yourself, and tell her, at the same time, that I cannot possibly be responsible for all the canards which appear in the papers about me. Tell her, please, that I have as yet settled nothing with regard to the different characters, and also that I have not the faintest notion when my 'L'Africaine' is to be produced; but at any rate it will not be for a long time to come. Besides this, will you kindly tell Madame Lauters that if she finds, during the rehearsals of the 'Huguenots,' that anything seems unsuitable to her voice, I shall have great pleasure in altering whatever places she likes. Please ask her when she thinks of singing *Valentine*. Will you also tell Herr Weyll for me that I have found out the title of the book for him? It is 'The Opera of the Future,' and can be had at the Franco-German bookstore of either Avenarius or Franke. Let me have the article from the paper regarding which the inclosed notice reads:

"'The "Journal Amusant" gives Halévy as the composer of the "Huguenots." I wonder whether Meyerbeer agrees to this or not.'"

In the meantime the "Pardon de Ploërmel" was produced (1859), and, having been fairly well received, was almost immediately sought as a novelty for the United States.

The story is laid in Brittany, where pilgrimages (pardons) are still made to favorite shrines. The story is developed in a haunted valley; *Hoël*, *Dinorah*, the *Chevrière* (goatherd), and the *Faucheur* (mower) make up the principal cast.

"Spa, August 12, 1859.

"I authorize you to give the grand score of 'Pardon' to Herr Strakovitz[1] [Strakosch] as he requested for NewYork, solely on condition that he pledges to you his word to give the part of *Hoël* to the very best barytone in his company, and also promises not to give the four smaller parts to so-called stop-gap singers, but to first-class artists, as was the case in London."

"September 11, 1859.

"I should be greatly obliged if, as soon as Herr Parent has corrected the mistakes in the third act, you would send a copy to Lard with the request that it may be bound in red morocco at once, with gilt-edged leaves, and, if possible, the Würtemberg coat of arms embossed in gold on the cover. And I would be glad if he would let me know directly this score is bound.

"I am here and, unhappily, ill in bed. I do not know how long it will be necessary for me to stay here to recover. But please let me know every detail concerning the reprise

[1] The Editors have thought best to leave unaltered Meyerbeer's version of the proper names in his letters.

of 'Le Pardon de Ploërmel,' so that the game may not be played on me of performing this during my absence; for the same reason I beg you not to tell anybody of my illness, as this Roqueplan would be quite capable of performing my opera secretly, thinking that because I am away from home and ill I should not find it out.

HERMAN LÉON IN "L'ÉTOILE DU NORD."

"How does Musard play the overture to 'Pardon,' and does it seem to please the public?"

A year later the adverse criticism of Meyerbeer's enemies still vexed him.

"Berlin, March 19, 1860.

"In my previous letter I requested you to speak to Herr Le Roy. After earnest consideration I have come to the conclusion that it is better for you not to do so. By the inclosed article you will see with what malicious animosity R. is filled. One must not do him the honor of speaking to him. Unfortunately it is too late for us to withdraw the work, so we must simply leave it to its fate.

"Please be kind enough to ascertain in what month the Marchisio sisters intend making their début in the French Opera, and also if they would be willing, as I have once heard, to sing in London first in Italian."

The accompanying extract is from "Le Figaro":

LE CHÂTEAU DE CHENONCEAU.

Decoration of second act of "Les Huguenots." From "Album de l'Opéra."

" A propos de théâtre on prête un joli mot de plus à M. Nestor Roqueplan. M. Meyerbeer, dit-on, se plaignait de ce que le spirituel Directeur semblait se refroidir beaucoup à son égard. 'Le Pardon de Ploërmel' était négligé, on ne le jóuait plus assez souvent. Soyez tranquille; je la jouerai toujours, votre pièce, je la jouerai continuellement, impitoyablement jusqu'à ce qu'il n'y ait plus dans la salle qu'un unique spectateur."

The following letter, dated May 20, 1860, shows the solicitude which Meyerbeer showed for the success of all his musical offspring. One of his biographers quotes Heine as saying that he could not rest while one soul remained unconverted to his music, and the amount of importance which he attached to minutiæ usually disregarded by successful composers is unparalleled.

" As I see by the papers that the festival in the Grand Opera has been postponed for a week, I should be very grateful to you if you would kindly ask Royer *not* to put the 'Schiller Marsch' quite as near the end of the program as he has done, as by that time the audience is quite exhausted from having heard so much music. I should prefer most of all for it to come immediately after the aria 'Pietà Signor,' by Stradella, which Michant is to sing, but on no account after an important ensemble piece.

"From your brother's letter I learn that the Opéra Comique has a new Director in the person of Herr de Beaumont. I trust that he will prove more sensible than Roqueplan.

"Be kind enough to attract Herr de Beaumont's attention to the great success which Mademoiselle Boulard is having in Brussels with 'Pardon.' Please ask him to engage her for the month of June, when the Brussels theater is closed, to sing 'Pardon' at the Opéra Comique.

"You did quite right to allow Musard to play my 'Schiller Marsch,' but you certainly

471

ought to have seen that he did not put it in such a disadvantageous part of the program. He played it at each concert as the first piece on the program, when, as you know, there is never an audience. And now I find that after playing it just a few times, he has crossed it out of his repertoire altogether, thereby doing the work more harm than good. You told me that you had allowed him to compose a fantaisie from themes in 'Pardon'; then how is it that he has not once played it?

"You can understand how doubly trying this eye trouble is to me in cutting me off from all activity in music, and this happens just when I am in the midst of a new composition to which I so earnestly wished to devote my whole love and energy.

"Has nothing yet been done to engage Madame Miolan for the next season in St. Petersburg?"

"SCHWALBACH, August 25, 1860.

"Herr Wollheim writes me from Wiesbaden that Mademoiselle Panatrat has studied and intends singing the part of *Dinorah* in the Opéra Comique. And from your letter it appears that Mons. de Beaumont told Mons. Monnais that he intended taking up 'Dinorah' again. We know that Demoiselle Montrose is angry with me because I would not allow her to sing *Dinorah* at her first début. But now it would be an actual calamity for 'Dinorah' (after the long rest that this opera has had) to be revived again with an absolutely unknown singer like the Demoiselle Panatrat; indeed it would be breaking the neck of this opera forever. It would be far better for 'Dinorah' not to be given at all this season than for it to be given with Demoiselle Panatrat. So please find out immediately whether what Herr Wollheim says is really true. (Your brother who knows Victor so intimately could ascertain it better than anybody else.) And if it really is the case, you must please go to Fiorentino and beg him to help us in this matter. Tell him, I beg you, how everything stands, and get him to use every means in his power to prevent Demoiselle Panatrat from taking this part. Then beg him to get De Beaumont to give the part to Demoiselle Montrose and to persuade her to begin it immediately. Fiorentino must hear from you why Demoi-

selle Montrose is angry with me, and she must by no means be allowed to think that Herr de Beaumont feels any particular sympathy for me. The matter is by no means easy to arrange, but Fiorentino has such a mighty and influential position that when he really wants to do a thing, however difficult, he can usually carry it out. As we have to act in great haste, I think it is best that you tell him candidly that you come to him in my name with this request, and that I *beg* him to take the matter in hand and do what he can to get my wishes fulfilled. You can add, as though from yourself, that you are certain that I shall be very grateful to him for his trouble.

"I trust you will soon let me hear all about Demoiselle Duprez's début in 'Les Huguenots.'"

The plan for producing "Pardon" is more fully developed, and the next three letters relate to the filling of the other parts, all of which is managed from a distance with the aid of Meyerbeer's friends, and, as the last

BATAILLE IN "L'ÉTOILE DU NORD."

letter suggests, a slight tax on his private influence if not his purse. He finally succeeds in fitting out the following cast, but not without sleepless nights:

Hoël . . . . Mademoiselle Wertheimer.
Dinorah . . . Mademoiselle Montrose.
The Chevrière . Mademoiselle Darcier.

"September 14, 1860.

" HONORED SIR :

" I forgot to tell you in my letter yesterday that I give Charlot *carte blanche* to make any modifications he considers necessary to Mademoiselle Wertheimer's voice with regard to compass in the part of *Hoël*. The difficulties concerning Madame Ugalde in the part of the *Chevrière* might possibly be overcome in the manner suggested yesterday.

" BERLIN, September 17, 1860.

" I have just received your letter of the fourteenth, and beg you tell Herr Beaumont that of course I will gladly give up my rights of authorship for a performance connected with a charitable purpose. You know that I always do this for every charitable benefit. You might tell him at the same time that as he is taking so very much trouble with re-

AUTOGRAPH OF MEYERBEER.

Closing paragraph of a letter to Auber.

" Be kind enough to submit the idea to F.'s judgment as soon as possible. He has overcome so many great difficulties already for the Theater Directors and Composers which were caused by the vanity of the singers that perhaps he will now be able to conquer these difficulties in the way I suggested, which will be greatly to our advantage in executing this work."

It would appear from the following note that Meyerbeer did intend to compose an opera on "La Jeunesse de Goethe."

gard to choosing good singers it would be most advisable to let Varot take the part of the *Faucheur*, which he sang so admirably, again. It would be well to let him know, as if quite casually, that I am working at 'Mignon.' I am very glad indeed that Herr Beaumont has agreed to the idea of getting Madame Ugalde for the *Chevrière*. Do try and strengthen him in this idea. If the canzonetta which I wrote for Mademoiselle Nantier Didier should be either too high or too low for Madame Ugalde, she can have it transposed as she likes."

"BERLIN, September 26, 1860.

"I told you in one of my former letters that if Madame Ugalde could not sing the 'Arie des Chevrières' nobody must sing it, as the Opéra Comique would then probably give the part to some inferior singer, and thus make its success an impossibility. But now I read in the 'Entr'acte' of the 25th of this month that Demoiselle Darcier is to sing the *Chevrière*, and of course I gave my consent to it most willingly, as Demoiselle Darcier was a first-class artist whose place has not yet been filled.

"Only I cannot understand how it is that such a celebrated artist is willing to make her reappearance in such an insignificant part in the theater in which she won such a brilliant success. Or is this, perhaps, another singer with the same name? I believe that Carvalho once told me that the chansonette singer Darcier (male) had a daughter who was going on the stage; perhaps this is she. Please be kind enough to find out from Charlot (who no doubt knows it) whether she is the celebrated Darcier-Mamignard, or the daughter of the singer Darcier. And if this latter is the case, whether she has voice and talent enough to do the Arie justice, in which case she may sing it. If, however, Charlot should not consider her good enough, it would then be better to leave out the whole of the scene and (as previously) only have the scene with two peasants."

"September 29, 1860.

"I received your letter of the 25th, and beg to say in reply that if Charlot considers Demoiselle Darcier good, and that if the air, which was really written for a mezzo-soprano, suits her voice, I am willing that she should sing it. Only I make the condition that it must be carried out exactly as it was in London, viz.: Demoiselle Darcier must sing the preceding recitative, as otherwise the canzonetta would sound short and poor.

"P.S. I am very glad that Mademoiselle Wertheimer will study her part with Herr Royer; the latter is a clever, earnest, and talented musician. At the same time please advise her (though not in my name) to go through her part with Charlot also, as he, through having been present at so many re-

hearsals, knows my wishes and ideas so thoroughly."

"BERLIN, October 31, 1860.

"I hope you received my last letter, and to-day I want to ask you the following questions:

"1. In the last number of the 'Revue Musicale' I read that a certain person had paid *anonymously* to the Director of the Théâtre Lyrique 50,000 francs as security for the mise en scène of the new opera by Berlioz. Can you find out for me *who* this person is, or at least who he is supposed to be, as it is a matter of the keenest interest to me.

"2. In the last number of the 'Presse Théâtrale' I read that an article had been published in the 'Figaro' about Richard Wagner signed Guy d'Estrée, but believed to be

MOCKER IN "L'ÉTOILE DU NORD."

by Blaze de Bury. I should so much like to read this article if you would kindly send it to me.

"3. I should be very much interested to hear from you whether you think that the 'Pardon de Ploërmel' has gained or lost in musical conception since its first performance (especially on Montrose's part).

"4. I hear that the Teutonia is organizing a musical festival to honor the anniversary of Schiller's birthday. Are they going to have an orchestra, and are my 'Schiller Marsch' and 'Schiller Cantata' going to be performed? 'Dinorah' has been brought out lately in both Bremen and Linz, and (from what the papers say) has had great success.

"P. S. I see in the last number of your 'Revue Musicale' that the Editor Legouix has just published Schubert's 'Roi des Aunes' (Erlking), orchestrated by Berlioz. You would do me the greatest favor by buying this for me (but without the separate parts) and sending it to me by 'bandes croisées.'

"I saw from your letter that Faure was not engaged by Mirelli. The latter has been in Berlin since then, and, after hearing from me that I considered it advisable to engage Faure for the Italian representation of 'Dinorah' in Vienna, he consented to engage him (of course on condition that they can come to terms from a financial point of view, and also on condition that Faure can be ready to arrive in Vienna at the latest on the 18th of February, and remain until the 20th or 25th of April). Mirelli says he knows that Faure is engaged by Gay and that such engagements begin as a rule in the early part of April, but as Gay, who had also engaged Demoiselle Patti for the 1st of April, easily arranged to have her free until the 25th of April, although Patti was to have sung an important part in each performance, Mirelli hopes that Faure may also be relieved until the 25th of April. Will you have the great kindness to ask Faure from Mirelli (*but by no means in my name*) whether he would be willing to accept an engagement for the above-mentioned time, and, if so, what his conditions would be. You can tell him *this:* that Mirelli is most anxious that he should take the part of *Hoël* with Patti in Vienna. And please write your answer in a way that I can read it to Mirelli.

"Your brother wrote to me about Musard's coming to Berlin in connection with my 'London Exhibition Overture.'

"Should Faure absolutely decline coming to Vienna, I would ask you to be kind enough (through a third person—for instance through Duncan Davidson) to ask the barytone Santley in London whether he would be free, or could make himself free, from the 15th of February until the 25th of April in order to take an engagement in a large German city. He must neither guess that this question comes from me, nor that it is for Mirelli, as I do not wish to speak of it to Mirelli (who

as yet knows nothing about this idea of mine until he has Faure's answer)."

"Pardon," thanks to the anxious care of its composer and publisher, becomes a success for the public, if not for the critics. Meyerbeer is presently able to write to Louis Brandus:

"'Pardon' is being rapidly produced in all the large cities in Germany, and always with success. During the past week alone it has been given in the following towns for the first time: Darmstadt, Lubeck, Munich, Leipsic, and Breslau. Altogether it has been performed in twenty-one German theaters. I think this will interest you for the 'Revue.'"

He has no sooner settled the question of Paris and "Pardon" than he is busy with those of *Fidès* and "L'Etoile." Until the day of his death he resolutely worked up the adequate presentation of his rôles in London, Vienna, St. Petersburg, Italy, and Paris, and the success crowned his efforts that common sense and business tact command. The present correspondence has, in fact, exposed the basis of the charge of wire-pulling to which Meyerbeer's enemies loved to impute his success. It is all reduced to the reasonable activity of good business methods.

"NICE, September 11.

"Henzel has written me in Carvalho's name asking me if he had no chance of getting my new comic opera for his theater. He wished to come at once to Nice to hear my conditions. I cannot answer your brother's letter to-day, as I am busy finishing a little cantata which is to be privately performed by amateurs at the birthday celebration of a lady here. I shall probably publish it by and by."

The following group of letters gives an insight into Meyerbeer's relations toward his brother musicians. They are a sample of his habitual attitude:

"Allow me through these lines to present to you Mr. Guglielmi, who has a beautiful barytone voice. This gentleman has transposed my song 'Guide au bord ma nacelle' for barytone, and sings it with great success. If you can give him any help in his musical career in Paris I shall be grateful to you, for he is a good, amiable man, and at the same time a fellow countryman (for notwithstanding his Italian name he is a German).”

CARL FORMES.

Lithographed from a daguerreotype.

“BERLIN, September 25, 1861.

“HIGHLY HONORED SIR:

“I had hoped to hear from you yesterday whether Gounod could or could not let you have the orchestral parts of his ‘Ave Maria’ in order to perform the same in the Königsberg Court concert. We are much pressed for time in this matter, as it must all be copied and the parts well studied, and the concert is to take place on the 15th of October.

“If, on the other hand, we cannot have it,

I must begin to prepare another piece to take its place on the program.

“I am anxious to hear from you how Madame Ugalde’s voice sounded at her reappearance in ‘L’Etoile’ after her confinement, and what was your general impression of the performance.

“Receive, dear M. Brandus, the assurance of my most complete esteem.

“Your very devoted,

“MEYERBEER.”[1]

“February 2, 1861.

“Rossini has written me a kind and friendly letter about the performance in his house of

[1] This is Meyerbeer’s habitual formula.

the operetta by my nephew Julius. As I wish my answer to reach him as soon as possible, but unfortunately forget the number of his house, I am taking the liberty of sending you my letter to him, and beg you to have the great kindness to take it to him yourself brated pianist and composer Kullak (whose works you have yourself brought out). This young man is worthily treading in the footprints of his celebrated father, and is already an excellent pianist. But he wishes to perfect himself in music in all its branches, and

GRAVES OF MEYERBEER FAMILY.

In the Schönhaus Allée Cemetery, Berlin.
To the right of the spectator is the composer's grave.

the same day that you receive it. Please tell him yourself '*what intense* pleasure his letter has given me, and how *enraptured* I am with his kind attention.'

"Please, dear M. Brandus, forgive me for troubling you with this commission."

"Berlin, October 28, 1862.
"Dear Sir:
"Allow me with these lines to introduce to you Herr Franz Kullak, son of the cele-

has therefore come to Paris to study and to hear all that can be heard in the way of music. You would oblige me greatly by helping and advising him in this matter.

"I must also take advantage of your kindness and ask you to help him in regard to his new home, and also get him introduced to some German families, for he is very young, and this is the first time he has left the home of his parents."

AN EARLY PORTRAIT OF MEYERBEER.

"BERLIN, May 8, 1863.

"This letter is accompanied by the chorus from 'Struensée' for men's voices, in four parts, which vou expressed the wish to publish. I composed this chorus for the Männer-Gesangverein (men's choral club). Please put on the title-page 'Chant guerrier (de Struensée) chœur pour voix d'hommes.' Then you must have a pianoforte accompaniment written to this, which, however, must contain nothing but the exact notes of the voices, and in exactly the same position on the piano as in the vocal parts. And add that the accompaniment is solely to assist at rehearsal. Please put also on the title-page

'SCHOTT IN BRUSSELS.'

"Wieprecht told me that he was to send you in the next few days the score of 'The Torchlight Dances.' He has written the title quite wrong. Consequently I must remind you to have it printed as follows:

"'Première Marche aux Flambeaux composée pour Musique Militaire par G. Meyerbeer et arrangée pour orchestre ordinaire par W. Wieprecht.'

"Please let me know soon after the performance of the 'Vêpres Siciliennes' exactly how Villaret sang and acted, and whether he can be intrusted with a very large and important work.

"P. S. Have you heard how long Verdi is to stay in Paris, and whether he intends to go to London?"

BY PERMISSION OF BRAUN, CLEMENT & CO., NEW YORK.

G. ROSSINI

GIOACHINO ROSSINI

BY

BERNARD BOEKELMAN

ITALY has been remarkable for her success in imparting dignity, grandeur, and completeness to art forms of small dimensions. Ghiberti's gates would not be improved by raising his figures to heroic dimensions. The intaglios of Italy were large enough to portray the great myths of antiquity. In the sonnet the Italian poets could voice the noblest sentiments of the human heart; in the melody, where other nations saw but a link in a chain, Italy made of the single link a perfect and complete art form, capable of expressing sentiments exactly corresponding to those to which she had already given voice in the sonnet. In fact, an Italian melody is to music what the sonnet and its allied forms are to poetry.

It is as a writer of Italian melody that Rossini will live after the operas in which his melodies first reached the public have been dropped from the theater repertoire. "Tell," "Semiramide," "Moïse," "The Barber," are words that conjure memories of melody and, from a musical point of view, little else; but how rich, how dignified, how delicious was the feast!

In raising melody as an art form to its highest potency, Italy was pursuing the normal course of her peculiar genius. Melody is concise, simple in structure, symmetrical, and organic,—a living germ. It is capable of vigorous motion. It may be amplified and set in rich decorations, but it is complete in itself. It needs no words to express its meaning. It carries all the properties of harmony in itself. It comes into existence by a supreme act of creation. It cannot be made, and it therefore corresponds to the function of the human figure in painting and sculpture, in that it is the vehicle for the expression of life.

ST. PETRONIO AT BOLOGNA, WHERE ROSSINI SANG AS A CHILD.

Let us look for a moment at Italian architecture. It is an echo of Greece. How simple the type! how symmetrical the details! how dignified, reposeful, and delicious the colonnades and porticos! Nowhere any mystery, nowhere any aspiration. Compare it with the Gothic cathedrals of Germany, and the divergence of the initial ideal at once manifests itself. See the branching pillars, the carved grotesques, the multiplicity of ornamental detail, the aspiring towers. Everything hints at unrest, mystery, and passionate desire for expression,—a religious life reaching toward the unknown and depicting the terrors of the dim forests of the North.

Go farther, and examine the great masterpieces of Italian art. Scrutinize its Madonnas, Sebastians, Magdalens; its Adorations of Foreign Potentates; its Nativities, where maidenly mothers sit composed and cheerful in caves and stables. There is nothing mystical in the gallery of beautiful forms and faces the painter has limned. All are the presentments of his friends and neighbors, done in his best style. The composition is geometrical. Sometimes a simple pyramid suffices for the scheme of an ascending Madonna. Everything is properly and reposefully balanced. Violent pain those old painters did depict; but their aim was not to do violence to the observer's feelings. Beauty, worked out in line, perspective, modeling, grouping, and color, was the first and last aim of Italian art. The perfection of the type, and the perfection of the artistic expression of the type, were the painter's highest care. Since in due time

480

Italy gave birth to Angelo and to Raphael, it was inevitable that she should give birth to Rossini and Bellini,—that is to say, she would develop every art under the control of her peculiar temperament. The strife, the unrest, the philosophies, the desire for a speech which should utter all that language conceals, are foreign to Italian art in every phase; but they are congenial to the Gothic character. Dignity, proportion, repose, grace, sweetness, and purity would find their complete expression in every phase of Italian creativeness. Far above the turbid waves of modern emotional life towers the art of Italy, serene in its development within the laws of symmetry and proportion, cheerful, direct, and amazingly beautiful. And just as to the student of Italian painting all other art seems cold and crude, so to the ear attuned to Italian melody all other melody seems uninspired and barbarous.

This is why the name of Gioachino Rossini still awakens dread in the heart of our modern school of musical composition. An overture without a melody is a novel without a hero; but while Rossini's overtures are alive to-day because of their superb melodic contents, modern compositions are often built upon mere phrases, without exhibiting any one perfect melody. Rossini was a princely thief; but he put his mark on Italian melody, and since his day composers have never been able to find any

INTERIOR OF SANTA CROCE, FLORENCE.

This is the Florentine Pantheon, in which Rossini's body—formerly at Père Lachaise, Paris—is now interred.
His tomb is in the aisle at the left, marked by a tablet on the floor. Michelangelo and Alfieri
are buried under the same aisle, and there is a monument there to Dante.

escape from the laws of its development.   Their only resource has been
to attack melody itself as a complete entity.

Perhaps a better instance of the peculiar charm of polished Italian
melody, as it differentiates itself from mere folk-song, cannot be found
than the lovely theme from "Semiramide," which Rossini has worked over
from a melody often attributed to Mozart.   I give the two side by side
for convenience

Measures 1, 3, 5, 7, exhibit the closest similarity.   The transformation
arises principally from the substitution of *mi* for high *do* in measures 2,
6, 13, 14, and 18, by which the violent "kick" upward is avoided, and the
calmness and softness of the mediant obtained.   The chromatic interval
of E sharp in the fourth measure, utilized in the harmonization, keeps the
melodic intervals closer together, and the return to the tonic *do* adds still
more to the repose of the theme.   A modulation effected in measure 6
gives variety and affords another moment of repose on A, measure 8.   The
emotional intensity of the theme is further heightened by the introduction
of the chord of F sharp minor, measure 10, after which a return is made
to the original thesis.

By these simple touches a jerky dance tune becomes noble, refined,
and complete.   Similar differences may be traced among all varieties of
Italian melody and the corresponding forms of Gothic art.   French melody seems thin and shallow, German crude and unfinished, after studying
that of Italy.   Italian melody needs no words, no harmony,— is its own
finished and complete utterance.

There is no great modern composer who has not studied Italian melody to his profit. Berlioz, Gounod, and Bizet were each taught the charm of Italian art in Rome. How closely akin was the method of Chopin to that of Bellini comes as a revelation to the student of their creations. Even Mozart as a child studied in Italy, and his style is completely Italian.

There is no reason why Wagner, obedient to his genius, should not utter his philosophies in blank verse and prose. But the student should recognize that music, like poetry, is a congeries of many art forms, and needs them all.

Rossini will go down to posterity as the great innovator who in "Tell" gave opera the direction it has ever since been pursuing. During his career as a composer he was always in advance of his contemporaries. The school of opera which he created—the melodic school—survives in Italy. Now and then an operetta constructed on the principles in vogue when Rossini left the stage is still brought forward. The audience once more hears with delight the chaplets of melodies, each a gem complete and polished, and witnesses the natural scenes and brilliant comedy of the situations.

Every encyclopedia recites the salient facts of Rossini's career: that his best works are "The Barber of Seville," "Guillaume Tell," "Tancredi," "Otello," "Semiramide," and the "Stabat Mater"; relates that he dispensed with recitative unaccompanied (*secco*); that he increased the power of melody to a high pitch by his melodic construction, by which it gains in color and intensity; that his ornamentation is used only when it is at the same time characteristic; that his vocal parts are always natural, never trivial, and give expression to the words without lessening the melodic character.

Any enumeration of Rossini's innovations loses in picturesqueness because they were at once adopted. It is impossible, without a course of antiquarian music, to realize how music sounded before Rossini bethought him of what every one now accepts without thought. Such innovations were his introduction of concerted numbers into serious opera; his enlargements of the resources of orchestra; his unmistakable sympathy with the trend of Romantic literature; his gradual curtailments of excessive colorature; his application of crescendo and diminuendo as orchestral effects; his efforts to invest the drums and brass of his orchestra with new and special values; his final presentation, in "Tell," of an opera, logical, organic, and powerful in emotional content, which remade the operatic stage of his day as effectually as Wagner's principles of declamation and architectural construction by means of leit-motifs have since done. Rossini's work of reformation gives his figure heroic dimensions on the canvas of musical history.

Rossini still lives. Laughter and truth can never be far separated from each other. No matter how wildly mankind may wander among mysticisms and myths in the paths of tragic art, the moment the *Barber's* genial profile advances upon the operatic stage we are in the region of common sense and beauty.   For art, when it is sufficiently truthful to become immortal, is always founded on common sense; and common sense Rossini had in a remarkable degree.

TOMB OF THE ROSSINI FAMILY AT PÈRE LACHAISE, PARIS.

Here the body of Rossini was originally interred.   It was removed to the Church of Santa Croce, Florence, in 1887.

HOUSE ON AVENUE INGRES, PASSY, IN WHICH ROSSINI DIED IN 1869.

ROSSINI BETWEEN GLUCK AND WAGNER

HIS INFLUENCE ON THE MENTALITY OF THE INTERPRETER

BY

VICTOR MAUREL

IT has been averred that Monteverde, Caccini, Peri, and Strozzi sought to revive Greek tragedy in that form of art which they originated in the sixteenth century. We incline rather to the belief that the attempt was a reaction against a style of virtuoso singing that was regulated by no feeling of unity and that departed outrageously from the accent of truth. But by a strange caprice of fate the new form of art,— sustained recitative with accompaniment, — unable to stem the tide that bore Italian singers and public toward such virtuosity, became the mold into which flowed with absolute freedom the defects and mannerisms that it was intended to oppose. The outcome of fashion's passing whim seldom resists the increasing development of life, and it might be thought that the invention of this constellation of amateurs was doomed to a speedy extinction. It endured, however, through centuries, and a lucid explanation of the reason may be deduced from the critical literature of the seventeenth and eighteenth centuries.

I prefer to state the case of truth *vs.* opera as it existed in 1753 through the medium of

485

a comic writer, Dufresny, and that of Jean Jacques Rousseau. In a mocking and stinging essay on the opera the former writes:

"Here we are in the land of people that sing without knowing why; in the land of those strange beings that speak but in song, dance instead of walking, and often do both when least inclined thereto."

Rousseau in terms of moderation suggests remedies for this faulty condition of things:

"The singer requires many special qualities for success in his art besides those which he must possess in common with the dramatic actor. Thus a good speaking voice does not suffice if his singing organ be not equally good. No such connection exists between the speaking and the singing voice that the beauty of the one implies that of the other. We may forgive in the actor the absence of some quality that he flatters himself that he has acquired, but not his daring to devote himself to the stage if destitute of qualities as essential to the singer as is that of voice.

"In using the word voice, however, I mean less the force of the timbre than the compass, the trueness, and flexibility of the organ. I think that harsh and noisy voices that only dull the ear should be denied access to a stage the object of which is to move the heart by song; no matter how small the actor's voice may be, if it be true, impressive, flexible, and of sufficient compass, he has all that is required. If he know how to make himself listened to, he will always know how to make himself heard.

"Given a suitable voice, the actor needs to cultivate it by art for his own sake, even if the voice itself does not need culture, so that he can grasp and render intelligently the musical part of his rôles. Nothing is more unbearable and disgusting than to see a hero in the outbreak of his strongest passions constrained and ill at ease in his part, toiling and bending like a school-boy badly reciting his lesson, and revealing, instead of the struggles of love and virtue, those of a bad singer with time and orchestra, who shows himself more uncertain of the key he must strike into than the determination to which he must come. Without facility neither warmth nor grace can exist, and the actor will never well interpret the rôle that costs him an effort.

" It does not suffice an actor in opera that he be an excellent singer; he should be an excellent pantomimist also; for he must make one feel not only what he himself says, but also that which he permits the symphony to say. The orchestra should render no symphony which comes not from his soul; the actor's steps, his looks, his gesture, all must be in unbroken accord with the music without his appearing to think of it; even in silence he must always interest. If, while occupied with a difficult rôle, he permits his character to be forgotten in his preoccupation with the singing, he is but a musician on the boards and an actor no longer."

We see that Rousseau had an idea of the necessity of truth in the interpretation of a musical work. But let us be exact on this head. If I quote Rousseau with enthusiasm, yes, to express my deepest artistic feeling, it is because from the exclusive point of view of the interpreter of the period nothing more complete could be said. These monitions, if applied to modern interpretation, however, should be presented in a different light. These famous precepts justly present the conditions necessary for the realization of a work of pure dramatic truth; but the truth in its totality none the less eluded Jean Jacques Rousseau. When compelled to take sides in the battle of art between Gluck and Piccini, he never refrained from showing his preference for the Italian artist. If, however, the musical form of theatrical pieces then prevailing fully satisfied his conception of the musical drama, he required of the actor accuracy of expression to the fullest extent. This is what raises Rousseau above the disciples of the *arte bel canto* who merely demanded arbitrary successions of melodies in the opera. Rousseau, however, remained faithful to the frivolous tendencies of bel canto in his own works, while exacting from the lyric actor the greatest concern for expression.

The vice inherent in the genus opera consists in this precise contradiction; but in this contradiction lies the secret of the vitality of the opera. Two antagonistic elements, each responding to a different human taste, have always constituted this form of art. What pleases one hearer displeases another. Music does not hold the foremost place with Dufresny, the simple littérateur; hence, as he saw music on its artificial side only and was shocked by it, he condemned it as a whole. The case with Rousseau, musician and littérateur, is different. He demands that truth which the Gluckists were so soon to exalt, but demands it of the mimetic powers, the attitude and the stage technic of the actor only.

While we listen to these two men, the one, of positive moral character, repelled by the fictitious and unreal and denouncing both, the other hesitating as though he would effect a reconciliation between two contrary sentiments, we reach the fact accepted to-day, that the opera is a hybrid genus. History, if we note briefly its developments, will establish this fact with still greater precision, and the pungent expressions of Dufresny and Rousseau, if applied to the career of Rossini, will gain significance. How profound and felicitous might have been the influence of the latter's musical genius had he employed it when he came to France in a work of verity and life!

It was Lulli,[1] as every one knows, an Italian by birth who had received a French education in early youth, who organized the opera in accordance with French taste.

From the confused mass of heterogeneous tastes covered by the art-form which had originated with Peri's coterie, he extricated the idea of scenic music; and the element of truth markedly characteristic of the French mind — a mind clear and well balanced — seemed to him to complete the conception of opera. Rameau, who followed him, affirmed through the medium of the orchestra what Lulli only hinted; and increased the richness of harmony while making clearer than ever the demand for truth in expression. It will be remembered that the quarrel of the Buffi occurred in his lifetime, as the prelude to the more violent struggle carried on toward the end of the eighteenth century between French and Italian taste, that is to say, between purely dramatic art and that of the bel canto. The personal element in the latter case was supplied by the battle between the Gluckists and the Piccinists.

The Gluckists demanded that life should always reflect itself in the art-form, which should move freely within its boundaries. There is a spice of dogmatism in the amiability of the Italian character. To the Italian, the opera, in defiance of the situations expressed by song and giving song ground for

[1] 1633–87. Opera composer to Louis XIV.

existence, was but the characteristic method of an amusement furnished by vocalization. Faithful to their genius, they barricaded and intrenched themselves in the heart of tradition.

At an early stage of events these opposing tendencies had assumed possession of the opera, in its confused entity, and hurried it in different directions. Gluck pointed out the means of modifying these conditions. Thorough fusion would locate the heterogeneous elements — music, poetry, mimicry — in their respective and proper places; the spirit would then recognize itself as being in a harmonious ensemble such as existed in the fairest days of Greece. In the words of M. Edouard Schuré, Gluck put living men in the place of fashionable singers, and the earnestness of real tragedy in place of the futilities of the opera. He imparted meaning to the overture, dramatic character to the recitative, poignant expression to the aria, and above all he understood the necessary accord between melody and words.

French taste firmly maintained its position; the Italians represented in France could accomplish nothing against it: but amiable virtuosity continued to flourish amid the familiar landscapes. Mozart seemed inclined toward it, but Mozart — we never weary of repeating it — was the divine musician whom we are never weary of admiring, and to whom a real poet was ever wanting.

Meanwhile, France, notwithstanding her craving for verity and while holding her ground, was making no advance and was without power for self-direction. At the beginning of the nineteenth century the repertoire of the Academy of Music was very limited, while Italy at the same period was loudly proclaiming the liberation of music at the Théâtre Italien in Paris. This theatre entered upon an era of prosperity when the minister of the king's household summoned Rossini to its directorship in 1823. Rossini was then at the outset of his career, but, according to the newspapers of the period, he brought pure Italian melody with him, and his assumption of office kindled anew, though with less fury than of old, the quarrels of the previous century. Should music be subordinated to dramatic interest, or the latter to the former?

Rossini had warm and powerful partizans.

Moreover, the celebrated lyric interpreter, Adolphe Nourrit, who was suffering from the limitations of the French repertoire, greeted the young composer with enthu-

cessions to public taste were necessary to success in France. A compromise between French and Italian music was imperative; he set about effecting it, and refashioned his

ROSSINI.

From an early lithograph.

siasm. A spirit of proselytism suddenly pervaded the centers of art. Nourrit succeeded in modifying his earlier style and bending it to the exigencies of Italian work. Thanks to his popularity, he was able to guide public opinion, and to him the reformers trusted for triumph.

Rossini, on his own side, realized that con-

"Maometto Secondo," adapted it to the French stage, and had it performed August 9, 1820, under the title of "Le Siège de Corinth." Its success was great; the public thoroughly comprehended the composer's intention, and the "Moniteur" did not hesitate to say that the success of "Le Siège de Corinth" must be looked at above all as constituting a binding engagement (*un engagement d'honneur*) to the French stage.

We must have — we do not shrink from saying it — a work from him composed completely for us and which we may appropriate as we have appropriated those of the great foreign masters who have preceded him in his career and through their masterpieces have become naturalized Frenchmen.

Once launched, Rossini thought of expanding his " Mosè " and of filling it with all the melodious treasures that could enrapture his listeners. On March 26, 1827, his new work was presented at the Academy. From that day the revolution of the French lyric stage may be regarded as an accomplished fact. The most enduring prejudices yielded. The brilliant fascination of Italian music made it the mistress of the national taste.

To-day this victory can be regarded only as a deplorable recession. No artistic revolution ever sank so deep into the social strata, but never before had the people been fascinated by melodies so splendid. Rossini painted his picture solely through the medium of music; his aim was to please and charm. Perhaps the composer here obeyed a social force which made him the man of the period. After the great wars of the Empire, after the storms in which the men of his time had lived, calmness, repose, and oblivion were needed in public life. Rossini brought to his music the qualities best fitted to charm society under the Restoration, to entertain it, to lull it into pleasant dreams, and thus he made the opera strike root into contemporary manners while giving music detrimental supremacy over poetry and dancing. Has any notable change occurred in this respect? Hardly, for Gounod's " Faust " and Bizet's "Carmen," the two works that universally retain the favor of modern audiences, belong to the genus of pure opera. The facile and supple melodies best loved by the masses because they understand them demonstrate that the " théâtre chanté," drama in song, is the same form of entertainment that filled the wants of pleasure-seekers in Rossini's day.

Hence arises the present conflict between public taste in opera and the sort of music needed by the mentality of the days in which we live. The inability of the public to comprehend the new idea is due to lack of education only. Is it not easier to modify public taste by brilliant and witty productions than by offering the masses the truth in severity? If reflection casts a critical shadow on the tribute I wish to bring to the Swan of Pisaro, it is because of the thought that Rossini, who ruled the taste of the world, did not try to direct it to a more exalted conception of truth. It remained for the genius of another race to realize the reform of which the composer of " Il Barbiere di Seviglia " and " Guillaume Tell " had caught no glimpse.

A reaction has taken place ; a new era has opened to lyric art ; the work of Wagner is nearer than ever to our mentality — a work of life, a work of the present, created by a genius that lived over past epochs the better to locate them in our own time. In this Wagner differentiates himself from all preceding composers. Living art is what he sought to create, and contemplating his gigantic effort, it almost seems as if he had exhausted all the powers of art itself. But this is an illusion, for the interpretation of life can have no limits, and Wagner, as he himself said, has perhaps but pointed out the future goal. Yet so vast, so varied, so complete is Wagner's work that in it all the aspirations of this powerful artist have achieved the maximum of realization.

The musical drama is the path that lyric art must henceforth tread ; not that falsehood, the esthetic rarity, which is intelligible to the initiated only, but a drama which, by making its object the representation of life, must penetrate into the masses. What a factor of progress it may become !

How, we ask, shall the masses, subjugated by facile melody and unable to comprehend the higher art, be acted upon?

By propagating the main idea that lies at the bottom of all lyric art, by throwing aside the prejudices that raise the silliest barriers. No chasm must henceforth separate the composer from the lyric artist ; both must interpret life and coöperate in their united work ; their efforts, put forth in the same direction, must no longer be separated. For the life created by the composer is only potential. It will be realized by the new lyric artist, and by him only. Hence to yield a work perfect as a whole, and with no semblance of an arbitrary superposition of dissimilar temperament, composer and artist must live in the same atmosphere.

SIR TRISTRAM AND LA BELLE YSEULT DRINKING THE LOVE DRINK ("MORT D'ARTHUR").

From the painting by Rossetti.

What must be the future interpreter of the musical drama?

To answer this is to define the musical drama. The object of this art-form is to represent life by the aid of song, music, and gesture, so that the hearer's entire being shall be harmoniously affected. Nothing must preponderate; music, poetry, the mimic art, must be fused into one homogeneous whole. Hence the rôle of the interpreter completely changes. He is no longer the singer intended to produce upon the public one exclusive sensation; he is to represent life in its completeness. A new education, a new attitude, is therefore required.

To-day the interpreter seldom possesses any accurate notion of the function, henceforth very important, that he is to discharge in the creation of his rôles; he is still the instrument that the composer and theater manager direct at will. They do not succeed in communicating to him the sense of life. Life can be rendered truthfully by a free being only, one not subject to the will of another.

490

Let us confess that the lyric interpreter is too often powerless to follow the composer. Few singers are equipped to bring a share of real coöperation to the integral representation of the music-drama. Practical vocal teaching can nowhere offer more than empirical receipts, useless in face of the difficulties offered by the simplest rôles in modern lyric art. Yet Wagner passed this art-form from the domain of dreams into that of reality. Verdi devoted himself to it; with a power that set the world marveling, after fifty years of glory his "Falstaff" is written with a youthful vigor that no other musician, French, German, or Italian, has attained. I affirm that the great Wagnerian idea has not been apprehended in its integrity; and that the spirit that to this day informs the teaching of modern lyric art still bows to the rule of the bel canto. The musical drama is organizing. The future is within its grasp — on one condition: that an intellectual *rapprochement* be brought about between the composer and the interpreter.

WILLIAM TELL.

From "Album de l'Opéra."

A MANUSCRIPT OF BELLINI.

VINCENZO BELLINI

BY

RUGGIERO LEONCAVALLO

BELLINI! With the greatest enthusiasm, with the profoundest admiration for the artist, I agree to write about him. A new historical sketch of a life already familiar to the world is not my purpose; nor shall I investigate, with the barren pen of the critic, the great art works of this master of music. My wish is to make plain my own impressions of this great man, and to show what influence he, in my opinion, exerted over the development of modern art. I need the exquisite poetry of Messer Francesco Petrarca, or the more severe and saddening muse of Leopardi, to express the ideas and fancies that so throng my brain as completely to choke expression; my utterance will too often be inadequate to the idea; I shall not be able to repeat modestly with Massenet:

> "Ce ne sont pas des chants, ce ne sont que des larmes,
> Et je ne te dirai que ce que Dieu m'a dit."

The name of Bellini does not summon up a figure great solely from artistic merit. It is associated with a form of art new to his contemporaries. Tawdry and frivolous ornamentation had characterized the school which, starting with Cimarosa, finally reached a more exaggerated form with Pacini. Donizetti and Verdi had not been able to make the slightest concession to the taste of the time. Bellini, more courageous than either, at the outset of his career did what the great Rossini dared in his last work only, and absolutely ignored the affectations and mannerisms of a school that did not adapt itself to his genius. Writing only as he thought and felt, he really created what we call "Verismo."

Florimo, the eminent librarian (and virtual founder rather than reviver) of the library of the Conservatory of Naples, told me while I was studying there that the great Catanese frequently shut himself up to work in a certain little room which he showed me; and that he often sought inspiration in absolute seclusion. Florimo sometimes watched him through a round hole cut in the door of this room to enable the teachers to see what the pupils were doing. For an hour or two Bellini would remain absorbed in reading some classic writer, oftenest Beethoven, whom he preferred to all others. As he read his beautiful face would grow pale and tears would run down his cheeks. Then he would close his book and, going to the piano, take up a blank sheet of music-paper and write nervously in pencil.

Florimo's tale gave me the key to the secret of Bellini's power of preserving the sincerity and truth which characterize his music, while composing works of such diverse character. Listen to the first chords of the "Marcia Religiosa" in "Norma," which makes Bellini the foster-brother of that Gluck who wrote the funeral scene in "Euridice." Notice the development of the scene with the Druids from the entrance of the fierce and passionate priestess as far as "Casta diva." The inspired song "Puro astra d'argente" wells from *Norma's* own being as she gazes at the star; and such is its force that behind her, as in a vision, I see the pale face of Bellini bathed in tears, his eyes fixed upon the moon shining so clearly in the deep azure of the Sicilian sky!

Thus he wrote, and thus he could but write; for one can feel an emotion that is not sincere as little as he can experience a conviction of what he does not believe.

To this school of what I call "Verismo" I have the honor to belong. It is the same "Verismo" which you recognize in the great statues of "Laocoön" and the "Capitoline Venus," in the "Madonna of the Chair," and in the "Fates,"—"Verismo," truth without alloy or corruption.

Bellini's perception of what is true is peculiar to himself. He works according to the axiom "Simplex veri sigillum." He writes simply, and expresses what is truest and most human. This is the aim sought by the greatest, and Bellini, with inimitable confidence, writes that immortal scene in which *Norma* tries to kill her children, finds that wild note in which the chorus bursts out with the cry, "War! war!" and finally reaches the perfection of that yet more wonderful page in the history of art, the finale of "Norma." "Quale cor tradiste" sings *Norma* to *Pollione;* and from this point in the opera we know not whether we are moved more by admiration or by sympathy. Captured by an ever increasing emotion, we pass from that splendid prayer, "Deh! non volerti vittema," addressed to her father, to whom before she dies *Norma* confides her children, to that passage in the finale which will always awaken the greatest enthusiasm as long as there are men of flesh and blood to listen to it. Like the

BELLINI.

"Transfiguration" of Raphael or the "Moses" of Michelangelo, it is one of those works of art which will live through centuries, an object of veneration to all people.

In "La Sonnambula" we owe to Bellini the creation of the musical idyl, a field in which he remains not only unsurpassed, but even unequaled. Since his day another great genius has, in the opera of "Dinorah," essayed the same task. Meyerbeer has produced the musical historical drama, which was originated by Rossini in his "William Tell," in a most perfect form; but in the idyl, in spite of many beautiful passages worthy of his pen, he was manifestly unequal to the attempt. After all his exertion, not a character speaks with even rustic simplicity; and, still worse, at the

494

most dramatic moment *Hoel*, believing *Dinorah* dead, sings, "Sei vendicata assai," to music so beautiful that were Nevers resurrected from the "Huguenots" he would not be able to sing that little *morceau* without tearing his pink-and-white costume to shreds.

Contrast with this the two most dramatic movements in Bellini's works: the first (in "La Sonnambula"), where *Elvira* reproves *Amina*, saying, "Ah! perche non passo odiate?" and the second, that in which *Amina*, half unconscious, sings while looking at the withered flower, "Ah! non crediva mirarti." With how much simplicity and truth is the character of the village wanderer drawn, and with what lasting effect! And finally, as the impression of Bellini's great genius deepens while we study its last and wonderful product, "I Puritani," which of us has not wondered, in profound regret at his early death, what greater works he might have given to art, and what greater glory he might have given our Italy, if Fate had not so soon cut short the thread of his precious life?

To Bellini's glory should be credited the profound impression which his work made on the mind of Wagner, the greatest modern genius. The latter never hesitated to speak and write of the high esteem in which he held him. We can feel the weight of Bellini's influence in the construction of more than one phrase of Wagner's work. I do not refer to resemblance in the notes, but in the structure, as for instance in certain parts of "Lohengrin," such as "Ardo per to d'un puro e sancto amore!" or in "Egle e daranti me triste e dolenti!" in the "Flying Dutchman," and many another. Do not those perfect chords in E flat in which the "Marcia Religiosa," of "Lohengrin," commences seem to be own cousins to those chords which precede the "Marcia Religiosa" in "Norma"? The effect of the crescendo movement in D major after the reveille in the second act of "Lohengrin," furthermore, reminds me of that other reveille in "I Puritani," where the horns are playing alone in this same key. Finally, that splendid progression, the most marvelous of all, the death of *Isolde*, is reminiscent in notes as well as in structure of the celebrated passage in the wonderful finale of "Norma."

What do I prove by all this? my readers will ask. I prove only that Bellini was really great, and that Wagner, who was great also, knew how to value Bellini at his proper worth; and that Wagner has done well to make "blood of his blood" of those forms created by Bellini, who preceded him in the bright path of Art. And he also will do well who, having the desire to break away from the bonds of servitude and from the desire to imitate the "Wagnerian ideal," has also the genius to make "blood of his blood," as did Wagner, of whatever is new or true or sincere in the domain of Art.

For thus Art progresses, and these two great geniuses are as columns placed along her ascending course, which the critics who hissed "Norma," and who derisively call Wagner "the Master of the Future," have in vain tried to check.

GOUNOD IN ITALY AND GERMANY

REMINISCENCES OF A PENSIONNAIRE OF THE ACADEMY OF FRANCE

BY

CHARLES FRANÇOIS GOUNOD

IN 1839 I won the Grand Prix for musical composition at the Institute of France. As a consequence, it was my privilege to occupy chambers for the ensuing two years in the palace of the Villa Medici at Rome. I was at that time twenty-one years of age. Fate gave me as fellow-prizemen in other departments the painter Hébert, the architect Lefuel, the sculptor Gruyère, and the medalist engraver Vauthier. At eight o'clock in the evening of the 5th of December, Lefuel, Vauthier, and I entered the mail-coach in the court of the old Paris Hôtel-des-Postes, in the Rue Jean-Jacques Rousseau. Our first stopping-place was Lyons; thence we descended the Rhone via Avignon and Arles to Marseilles. At this point we took a vettura, which was to convey us to the end of our journey.

What memories that word "vettura" suggests to my mind! Poor old, broken-down trap, now crowded out of existence by the puffing of the steam-engine and the giddy dash of iron wheels! How it allowed you to stop, admire, and gaze at your ease on all those views through which or under which the screaming locomotive now transports you as a mere piece of luggage, projecting you through space with all the fury of a mortar-shell! The vettura bore you along tenderly, step by step, as it were, from one charming landscape to another; while this mortar-shell on rails picks you up fast asleep under the gray sky of Paris, and shoots you forth, waking, into the atmosphere of the Orient, without mental transition or change of temperature, roughly, like a bale of merchandise or an invoice of fish sent by express, with the idea only that it should get to market fresh.

If Progress, that pitiless conqueror, would at least spare the life of the vanquished! But no, the vettura is no more! I bless it for having existed, for it allowed me to enjoy in every detail that admirable Corniche Road, which prepares the traveler so thoroughly for the climate and picturesque beauties of Italy, by unfolding to his gaze a series of enchanting sights — Monaco, Mentone, Sestri, Genoa, Spezia, leading up to Pisa, Lucca, Siena, Perugia, and Florence — that progressive and ever-varying exposition of nature which explains the masters—masters who themselves in turn show you how to study nature. For nearly two months we were tasting and enjoying all this at our ease, and on the 27th of January, 1840, we made our entry into Rome, which was to become our residence, our school, and the scene of our initiation into the grand and stern beauties of nature and of art.

M. Ingres, whom my father had known when he was young, was at that time the director of the French Conservatory at Rome. On entering his salon, we found that he had been informed of our arrival, and was there to give us a cordial welcome. As soon as he saw me, he exclaimed: "You are Gounod, I am sure! How very like your father!" and he talked of my father, of his talent as a draftsman, his character, the charm of his wit and conversation, in terms that, coming from the lips of an artist of his high repute, made me proud, and furnished the most genial welcome to a new-comer. We were installed at once in our chambers, and at dinner-time were made acquainted with all our colleagues gathered at the common board in that famous hall, which was hung with portraits of all the pensionnaires who had preceded us since the foundation of the Academy.

I must confess that Rome did not at first correspond to the dreams my fancy had conceived. I was still too young in years, and especially in character, to lay hold of and to take in at first glance the deep signification of that great and austere city, which struck me as cold, dry, cheerless, and gloomy, and which speaks with a voice so low that it can be heard only by ears trained to silence and solemn contemplation. Rome is itself so many things, and those things are wrapped in such profound calm, in such quiet and serene majesty, that it is impossible at once even to suspect its marvelous whole, and the inexhaustible store of its many-sided wealth. Its past like its present, its present like its future destiny, make it the capital, not of a country, but of humanity. Any one who has lived there long knows this well; and whatever nation claims our loyalty, or whatever tongue is ours, Rome speaks a language so universal that it is impossible to turn our back upon it without feeling that we are turning away from our native land.

That first impression of austerity threw me into a profound melancholy, and a very slight occasion would have been sufficient to put me back on the road to France and to my mother's fireside. However, little by little, every day contributed its sedative effect. I set to work, and among the

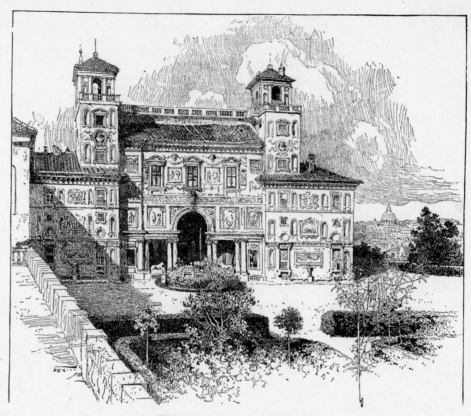

THE VILLA MEDICI AT ROME.

The home of the French students who win the *Grand Prix de Rome*.

musical ideas which marked the début of my existence as a pensionnaire I count two songs that have long remained unknown—"Le Vallon" and "Le Soir." Both of them were composed to verses by Lamartine, and the dreamy and contemplative accent of the music was in perfect accord with my feelings at the time. I wrote them a few days apart and soon after my arrival at the Villa Medici.

Some six weeks elapsed before my sadness took its flight and I grew accustomed to the town, which had impressed me like a desert. Its very silence now began to charm me, to be in itself a blessing, and I found peculiar pleasure in visiting the Forum, the ruins on the Palatine, the Colosseum, and all those other remains of greatness and power now gone, over which has been extended for ages the august and peaceful crook of the Shepherd of Nations.

My stay was begun under most favorable auspices. M. Ingres had taken a fancy to me. He was passionately fond of music, of Haydn, Mozart, and Beethoven; Gluck especially, by the nobility and the pathos of his style, seemed to him a Greek, a descendant of Æschylus, Sophocles, and Euripides. M. Ingres played on the violin. He was not a great proficient, still less a virtuoso; but he had in his youth belonged to the orchestra in the theater of Montauban, his native town, where he had taken part in the performance of Gluck's operas. I had read and studied the works of Gluck; as for Mozart's "Don Juan," I knew it by heart, and although I was not a pianist, I made a respectable enough show to be able to please M. Ingres with the remembrance of that score, which he adored. I knew likewise from memory the symphonies of Beethoven, greatly admired by him. We often spent together a portion of the night in this familiar association with the great masters, and in a short time I was wholly secure in his friendship. That was a genuine piece of good fortune for me. I owe more than I could ever express to the contact with such a solid mind, inflexible as he was in his fervent conception of the beautiful, simple and naïf as a child. He was wrongly and narrowly judged by those who did not know him well, although he was so transparent and easy to know. He was persuasive in his faith, because he allowed himself to be carried away by it even to enthusiasm and eloquence; sincerely humble and modest in the presence of masters, but dignified and proud in the presence of self-assertion and the arrogance of fools; paternal to all the pensionnaires, whom he looked on as his children, and whose rank he maintained with jealous affection in the midst of the visitors, no matter what their category who were admitted to his drawing-rooms. Such was the great and noble artist by whose precious and fruitful instruction I was to have the good fortune to profit.

One must have associated freely with men of superior genius to comprehend how their conversation influences the development of our peculiar capacities by the lessons of their experience and the light shed by their general conclusions. M. Ingres let fall in my presence words, precepts, observations, aphorisms, which have given direction to my whole life. In giving me to understand what art is, he taught me more of my own art than numberless purely technical artists ever could have done; his ideas constantly revealed in him and awoke in his hearer the perception of the conditions and laws of beauty in art. It has been said, and many have mechanically repeated it, that he was exclusive; nothing is more false. I never saw any one admire more things than he, for the very reason that he saw better than any one where and why a thing is worthy of admiration. It is true that he was discreet. He understood how far enthusiasm lures young men to infatuation for certain personal traits of this or that master, without discernment or method; that those peculiarities which are the proper and distinctive characteristic of masters, their individual physiognomy by which they are recognized as men recognize one another, are precisely the incommunicable properties of their nature; that, as a consequence, to be inclined to imitate them is but little short of plagiarism; and that, furthermore, such imitation tends to a fatal exaggeration of qualities which the imitator fashions into so many defects. That is M. Ingres's view, and the origin of the most unreasonable accusation against him on the score of exclusiveness and intolerance.

To show how sincere he was in modifying a first and superficial impression of prejudice, the following anecdote will suffice. I had just sung for him, for the first time, that admirable scene of *Charon* and the *Shades* in the "Alcestis," not by Gluck, but by Lulli. The first perform-

GOUNOD'S PARIS HOME.

No. 1 rue Montchanin.

ance had produced in him an impression of stiffness, harshness, and uncouth roughness so painful that he exclaimed: "That is frightful! That is not music; it is iron." Being but a youth, I took good care not to oppose the impetuosity of a man for whom I entertained so high a regard; I waited for the tempest to pass by. Some time after, M. Ingres recurred to the impression made on him by that piece. The impression seemed to me somewhat softened now, as he said: "Pray let us hear that scene by Lulli—*Charon* and the *Shades*. I should be glad to hear that again." I sang it anew, and this time, better acquainted, doubtless, with the primi-

GOUNOD'S SUMMER HOME AT ST. CLOUD

No. 5 rue de Gounod. Gounod died in the room just over the door.

tive and rough style of this startling picture, he was struck with the irony
and satire of *Charon's* language, and the power expressed by the lamentation of the wandering *Shades*, rejected from the Stygian bark because they
were unprovided with the passage-money. Gradually he became so attached to the character of the scene that it came to be one of his favorite
pieces, and he was constantly requesting me to repeat it. But his prevailing passion was Mozart's "Don Juan," over which we lingered occasionally till two o'clock in the morning, when Madame Ingres, tired out from
loss of sleep, would feel obliged to close the piano to separate us and pack
us off to our respective beds.

My stay at Rome, which was my permanent and regular residence, was
supplemented by authorized excursions to other parts of Italy. I shall
never forget the impression produced on me by Naples at my first visit.
The charming climate, which anticipates and suggests the sky of Greece;
that bay, blue as sapphire, set in a circle of mountains and islands, whose
slopes and peaks assume at sunset the ever-changing scale of magic hues
which would defy the richest velvet or the most brilliant gems—all this
produced the effect of a dream or a fairy-tale. The environment of this
wonderful scene—Vesuvius, Portici, Herculaneum, Pompeii, Castellam-
mare, Sorrento, the islands of Capri and Ischia, Posilipo, and, farther off,

Amalfi, Salerno, and, last of all, Pæstum, with its marvelous Doric temples bathed aforetime by the azure waves of the Mediterranean—all this seemed to me a vision indeed. It was the absolute reverse of Rome; I was at once in ecstasy. If to such seduction be added all the interest that attaches to a visit to the Museum of Naples, a unique storehouse of masterpieces of antique art, the greater part of which have been brought to light by the excavations of Pompeii and Herculaneum, the attractions that such a city must afford, and especially the pleasures that await the artist in such an environment as this, will be easily understood.

During my residence in Rome I had the good fortune to visit Naples on three distinct occasions, and among the most vivid and profound impressions which I bore away with me I give the first place to that wondrous island of Capri, all the more wild and charming by the contrast of its steep crags and its green slopes. I first visited Capri in summer; the sun shone brightly, diffusing a torrid warmth. During the day one was forced to shut himself up in a room or to plunge into the sea— an alternative which I often chose with delight. But what is difficult to portray is the glory of the nights in such a climate, and at such a season of the year. The heavens seemed literally palpitating with stars—a counterpart, as it were, of the sea, with waves of light vibrating along the infinite vault above. During the fortnight of my stay I often listened to the living silence of those phosphorescent evenings. I sat for hours on the top of some steep crag, scanning the horizon, occasionally watching large stones that I would start rolling down the almost perpendicular mountain, enjoying their crashing bounds to the sea, into which they would disappear with a cloud of spray and foam. From time to time a solitary bird passed over, uttering a plaintive note, leading my thoughts back to those fancied gulfs whose impression of terror has been so marvelously rendered by the genius of Weber in his immortal scene of "The Casting of the Bullets" in the opera of "Der Freischütz."

It was on one of those nocturnal excursions that I had the first conception of the Walpurgisnacht in Goethe's "Faust." I had read that work at the age of twenty, and it never had left my mind. I bore it with me everywhere I went, and jotted down in scattered notes the different ideas which I imagined might serve me when the time should come to try this subject as an opera—an event not realized till seventeen years later.

But at length I was obliged to return to Rome and the Academy. However delightful and seductive a residence at Naples is, I have never lived there without feeling after a certain interval the need of going back to Rome. Something like homesickness now came over me, and without sorrow I withdrew from those scenes where I confess I had spent delicious hours. The fact is that Naples, with all its brilliancy and reputation, must be set down as a loud, vulgar, bustling, high-keyed town. From morning till night crowds push, scuffle, and quarrel on its wharves, where neither rest nor silence is known. Its normal state is one of contention. You are besieged, importuned, and beset on all sides by the untiring solicitations of porters, traffickers, hackmen, and boatmen, who would take violent possession of you if they could, competing with one another in cutting down their prices and fares.

VIEW OF PARIS FROM THE TERRACE AT ST. CLOUD.
This picture is taken from the summer house built by Gounod on his favorite spot.
The view is familiar to every one who visited him.

Once more in Rome, I went to work. It was now the autumn of 1840. At this period it was customary for the musicians of the Conservatory to direct, each year by turn, the performance of a mass with orchestra specially composed for the fête of King Louis Philippe, to be celebrated on the 1st of May in the church of San Luigi de' Francesi. It fell to my lot to write the mass to be performed in May, 1841. I composed and directed personally the performance of the piece, which gained for me the title for life of Honorary Maître de Chapelle. The more I prolonged my stay in Rome the more deeply I loved its mysterious charm, its incomparable peace. After the serrated, volcanic, and swelling lines of the Neapolitan crater, the placid, solemn, noiseless lines of the Roman Campagna, encircled with the Alban hills, the mountains of Latium and the Sabine district, the majestic Mons Januarius, Soracte, the hills of Viterbo, Monte Mario and the Janiculum, all impressed me with the calm, sweet air of an open cloister. One of my favorite positions in the environs of Rome was the village of Nemi, with its lake visible to the eye at the bottom of a vast crater surrounded with woods in admirable foliage. One of the most beautiful walks imaginable is around the lake by the upper road; a beautiful day, ending with such a sunset as I have witnessed there,—with a glimpse of the sea from the heights of Genzano,—leaves an enchanting and ineffaceable remembrance. Indeed, the environs of Rome abound in wonderful spots, which furnish the traveler and the tourist with an inexhaustible variety of impressions; such as Tivoli, Subiaco, Frascati, Albano, and a thousand other places so often explored by landscape-painters, not to speak of the Tiber, whose banks exhibit such noble and majestic outlines.

Among the wonders of art found only at Rome, it would be impossible in these reminiscences of my youth to pass over that work of indescribable beauty which shares with the Sistine Chapel the interest and glory of the Vatican. I mean those immortal paintings of Raphael grouped under the common designations of the Loggie and the Stanze. Two masterpieces, among so many others, due to the pencil of that unique artist, those inimitable works the "School of Athens" and the "Dispute of the Holy Sacrament," have carried so high the note of beauty that it would seem impossible ever to surpass them. And yet, such is the irresistible privilege of genius, that the man who never had his equal, whose name the centuries have placed on the summit of glory, was disturbed at the apparition of Michelangelo! He suffered the grasp of that Titan, he bowed under the crushing weight of that Colossus, and his last works bear traces of the homage he offered to the grandiose inspiration of that powerful genius, which exceeded human proportions. Raphael is the first, Michelangelo the only. In Raphael strength dilates and expands into grace; in Michelangelo grace, on the contrary, seems to discipline and conquer strength. Raphael charms you and allures you; Michelangelo fascinates you and overwhelms you. The one is the painter of the earthly paradise, the other seems to penetrate with an eagle's eye, like the prisoner of Patmos, into the very flaming dwelling-place of the seraphim and the archangels. One would say that those two evangelists of art had been put there beside each other in the fullness of esthetic time to the end that he who had received the gift of calm and perfect beauty should be a salutary protection against the dazzling splendors revealed to the singer of the Apocalypse.

In the month of April, 1841, M. Ingres left the Academy. His term as director had expired. He was replaced by M. Schnetz, a celebrated painter, who chiefly owed his success and his popularity to qualities of sentiment and expression. Under an easy and almost rustic exterior

38

M. Schnetz veiled a refined and intelligent nature. He was very tall, of a dark, swarthy complexion, with black hair like an Italian's. His smile was very sweet, and his character had a charming gaiety. He was an excellent man. I spent my second and last year at Rome under his direction. M. Schnetz had a special fondness for Rome which was peculiarly favored by circumstances. He was for many years director of the Academy, and left there the very best impressions.

My stay was about to expire with the year 1841; but I felt unable to go away, and I continued there with the consent of the Director until my resources were exhausted and I was obliged to proceed to Germany to discharge the obligations of my third year, in order to draw the salary which I needed for my support. I shall not try to describe my sorrow when I was compelled to say farewell to the Academy, to my beloved companions, and to that Rome which had become a second home to me.

My companions bore me company as far as Ponte Molle (Pons Milvius), and after having embraced them, I got into the vettura which was to tear me away — yes, that is the word — from those dear years of the Promised Land. If I had been going direct to my poor mother and my excellent brother, the departure would have been less painful to me; but I was to live alone in a country where I knew no one, and of the language of which I was ignorant, and this prospect seemed to me cold and dark. As long as the highroad permitted, I kept my eyes fixed on the dome of St. Peter's — that "high place" of Rome, and center of the world; then the hills caught it away wholly from my sight and I surrendered myself, weeping bitterly, to my sad reflections.

ON leaving Rome to proceed to Germany my route naturally led through Florence and the north of Italy, trending to the right by Ferrara, Padua, Venice, and Trieste. Florence, as well as Rome, is inexhaustible in works of art. But there, too, in that delightful city of Florence, the scepter is in the grasp of Michelangelo, who dominates everything from the vantage-ground of that marvelous and striking Chapel of the Medici. There, as at Rome, his genius has left unique, sovereign, incomparable traces. Everybody knows this chapel by the admirable statues it contains, and which have been for years made common by copies or by photography. Wherever Michelangelo is found, he compels meditation. When he speaks, you feel that all must be silence; and that supreme authority of silence he has perhaps exercised nowhere with more power than in the terrible crypt of the Medici Chapel. What a prodigious conception is that of the "Pensiero," mute sentinel who seems to be watching over death and waiting motionless for the trumpet of Judgment! What repose and flexibility in that figure of "Night," or rather of Peace in Sleep, which forms the counterpart of that robust figure of "Day," lying there apparently chained until the dawn of the final Day of

CHURCH OF ST. EUSTACHE, PARIS.

Here the great French masses written for St. Cecilia's Day were first performed, among them Gounod's.

Days! By this profound feeling, and by the ideal, and at the same time natural, attitude, Michelangelo everywhere rises to that intensity of expression which is the peculiar mark of his powerful individuality. The amplitude of his style is as the channel wrought by the majestic river of his thought, and for this reason every imitation of his mere exterior is at once condemned as pompous and bombastic; he alone could fill and give life to the form peculiar to his own genius.

I at last reach Venice. Venice! Ah, that enchantress! She is the country of resplendent masters. Venice has thrown a sunny light over painting. She charms one's senses; and as a consequence her attraction is instantaneous. She intoxicates, but the intoxication that she excites is mingled (at least it has been so in my case) with an inexplicable melancholy, something like the sentiment of captivity. Is it the memory of those dark tragedies of which she has been the theater, and to which her very situation seems to have predestined her? It is perhaps so; although a long stay in that kind of amphibious necropolis does not seem to me possible without at last experiencing something of a smothered feeling, or falling into a state of mental depression. The sleeping waters whose gloomy silence bathes the feet of all the old palaces, that mournful shadow from the depths of which you seem to hear the groans of some illustrious victim, make Venice a kind of capital of Fear; she has preserved a sinister impression. And yet on a fair day what magic in that Grand Canal! How those lagoons flash as the waters seem transformed into life! What brilliancy in those remains of an antique splendor which seem to rival the beauty of their skies and to implore their aid against the gulf into which they are sinking farther and farther every day, to disappear at last forever! If Rome possesses the Vatican and Florence the Chapel of the Medici, Venice has also her peerless treasure in the Church of St. Mark. The magnificence of those mosaics and of that gold whose dark iridescence streams down from the height of the cupola to the base is something absolutely unique in the world. I know nothing to be compared with it in vigor of tone and power of effect.

.   .   .   .

I knew nobody at Vienna, but one of the first things I did was to attend the theater, where I heard "The Magic Flute" of Mozart. The orchestra was directed by Otto Nicolai; I got permission to be presented to him. He gave me a very cordial reception, and at once put me into relations with the artists of the theater and the orchestra. That was the first time that I had ever listened to the adorable score of "The Magic Flute." I was in raptures. The execution was superior; the part of the *Queen of Night* was admirably rendered by a cantatrice of very great talent, Mme. Hasselt-Barth; that of the High Priest, *Sarastro*, was sung by Staudigl, an artist of great reputation, with an admirable voice, which he controlled with great method and style. The other parts were all rendered with great pains, and I remember still the charming voices of the three lads who took the parts of the three genii.

Thanks to the acquaintance which I had just made with Nicolai, I felt no longer isolated at Vienna, and recovered my good spirits. Nicolai presented me to several artists of the orchestra; among others to a cornettist whose name was Lévy, the father of Richard Lévy, who was then a child of fourteen years, and who since then has held at the Vienna Opera the position of his father. Lévy made me promise to come to see him, and I received a most cordial welcome from the whole family. There were in the house three other children: the eldest, Carl Lévy, was a pianist of a good deal of talent and a distinguished composer; the second, Gustave, is to-day a publisher of music in Vienna ; and the daughter, Mélanie, a charming person, is married to the harpist Parish Alvars.

After some weeks of residence I became acquainted with Count Stockhammer, President of the Philharmonic Society of Vienna, who gave me the opportunity of bringing out in the Church of St. Charles the mass

LIBRARY OF THE PARIS OPERA-HOUSE

that I had directed at Rome the year before on the occasion of the fête of King Louis Philippe.   This execution was well received, and Count Stockhammer immediately proposed to me the composition of a requiem mass to be performed on All Souls' Day, in the same Church of St. Charles Although it was then the 14th of September, and there were only six weeks to the 2d of November, I accepted resolutely, and went to work.   I worked day and night, and was ready at the appointed moment.   A single rehearsal was sufficient—thanks to the generality of musical education which is found in Germany only, and which it is very agreeable to meet   I was especially astonished at the facility with which the boys of the schools read music at sight; they all read it as fluently as if it had been their mother tongue.   As a consequence the execution of the choruses was perfect. I had among the soloists a superb basso, Draxler by name, who was then quite young and shared with Staudigl the position of first basso at the theater. Since then Staudigl has died insane, they say; and Draxler, who replaced him, was still at the theater twenty-five years afterward, in 1868, when I returned to Vienna to bring out my opera of "Roméo et Juliette."

The success of my requiem had modified all my plans, deciding me to prolong my stay at Vienna. Count Stockhammer gave me a new order in the name of the Philharmonic Society. The proposition was to write a vocal mass, without accompaniment, designed to be performed during Lent, in the same Church of St. Charles, my patron saint. I took good care not to let slip this fresh opportunity, first of keeping myself in training, and also of hearing my own pieces rendered — a thing of such rare importance to me at the outset of my career. It was my second and final work at Vienna, whence I set out soon after for Berlin, making but a short stop in Prague and Dresden. I was, however, unwilling to leave Dresden without having visited the admirable museum.

On my arrival at Berlin, my first call was on a person I had become acquainted with in Rome. This was Mme. Hensel, sister of the illustrious composer Mendelssohn-Bartholdy, and wife of M. Hensel, at that time painter to the King of Prussia. Mme. Hensel was an extraordinary musician, a remarkable pianist, a woman of superior ability, slender in form, petite in stature, but possessed of an energy which could be seen in her penetrating glance and the flash of her eye. She was, furthermore, endowed with rare faculties as a composer, and to her are due several of the "Songs without Words" which are found published in a work for the piano under her brother's name. Mme. Hensel had resided in Rome with her husband during the winter of 1841, and often came to the soirées of the Academy, where I frequently had the opportunity and the pleasure of hearing her. She knew by heart the music of the masters, and, thanks to her prodigious memory, it was an advantage as well as a treat to listen to her interpretation of Bach, Haydn, Mozart, Beethoven, and her brother— Mendelssohn.

PATTI AS MARGUERITE.
From an early photograph.

I therefore lost no time in calling on her, as in fact she had made me promise to do; but some three weeks subsequently I fell ill, at the very moment I had written my mother that I was preparing to return home, after a separation of three years and a half. Mme. Hensel at once sent me her physician, and to him I addressed the following ultimatum:

"Sir: My mother in Paris is expecting my return, and is at this instant counting the hours. If she knows I am detained by illness, she will start for Berlin, and may go mad on the way. She is advanced in years. I must give her a reason for my delay; but it must be brief. I give you a fortnight to put me into the ground or on my feet again."

"Well," said the doctor, "if you are resolved to follow my prescriptions, you will be off in a fortnight."

And he kept his word; the fourteenth day I was *hors d'affaire*, and forty-eight hours later I found myself on the road to Leipsic, where Mendelssohn, to whom I had a letter of introduction from his sister, resided.

Mendelssohn received me admirably. I use this word purposely to characterize the condescension with which a man of his powers welcomed the child who in his eyes could be but a school-boy. During the four days I spent at Leipsic, I may indeed say that Mendelssohn gave me his whole time. He questioned me about my studies and my works with the deepest and most sincere interest. He expressed a desire to hear on the piano my latest effort, and I received from him precious words of approval and encouragement. I shall mention but one, which has made me too proud ever to forget it. I had just rendered the "Dies Iræ" of my Vienna requiem. He placed his hand on a part consisting of five solo voices, without accompani-

CLARA LOUISE KELLOGG AS MARGUERITE.

Miss Kellogg created the part of *Marguerite* in America.

ment, saying, "*Mon ami*, that might be signed Cherubini!" Such words are genuine decorations, coming from such a master, and are worn with greater pride than many a ribbon.

Mendelssohn was the director of the Gewandhaus. The orchestra did not meet at that time, the concert season having expired. He had the thoughtfulness to call it together for me, and allowed me to hear his beautiful Scotch symphony in A minor. He made me a present of the score, with a friendly word of dedication written with his own hand. Alas! the untimely death of that noble genius was soon to transform the souvenir he had left me into a precious relic. His death followed, six months later, that of the charming sister to whom I owed the honor of this acquaintance.

Mendelssohn did not limit his polite attentions to that convocation of the Gewandhaus orchestra. He was an organist of the first order, and wished to make me acquainted with several of the admirable compositions written by the great Sebastian Bach for the instrument over which he reigned supreme. To this end he had examined and put in order the old St. Thomas organ on which Bach himself had played, and for more than two hours he revealed marvels of which I had never dreamed; then, to crown all, he presented me with a collection of motets by Bach, for whom he felt a religious veneration, in whose school he had been educated from childhood, and whose grand oratorio of "The Passion according to St. Matthew" he had directed and accompanied, from memory, at the age of fourteen!

THE CONTRALTO SULZER AS SIEBEL.

In first production of "Faust" in America.

Such was the extraordinary kindness I received from this delightful man, this great artist, this astonishing musician, taken away in the flower of his life—at thirty-eight—from the center of admiration which he had won, and from the masterpieces which he would have written had his life been prolonged. But strange destiny of genius, even the most attractive,— these exquisite works, now the delight of those who attend the Conservatory, required the death of the composer to give them favor in the ears of those who once rejected them.

After my visit to Mendelssohn I had but one thought, and that was to get back to Paris as soon as possible, where a new life was about to open to me. My brother met me on the arrival of the diligence, and we both bent our footsteps at once in the direction of that dear house where I was to find again, and to which I was to bring back, so much joy.

GOUNOD IN HIS STUDY.

THE PHILOSOPHY OF GOUNOD

BY

FANNY MORRIS SMITH

THE art of Gounod is a musical exposition, delivered in the nineteenth century, of the Gospel according to St. John. For Gounod sang on but one theme,—those manifestations of benevolence, affection, and tender passion which English-speaking people recognize collectively as love. Whatever he touched was an expression of what he himself defined as " one of the three forms of that principle of separate immortality which constitutes the perpetual resurrection of hu-

512

manity at large by virtue of its three creative powers, distinct in function, though substantially identical: Love, the essence of human life; Science, the essence of truth; and Art, the essence of beauty." Gounod, like St. John, grasped the fact that love is the essence of human life, and saw truth and art through the eyes of love. In his operas he has painted the three great types of human passion, not, as we sometimes say, with a master hand, but with creative insight:

Roméo and *Juliette*, the world's personification of young affection; *Baucis* and *Philemon*, the steadfast love of old age; *Faust* and *Marguerite*, the love that burns upward through passion into immortality; and beside these he has placed a series of masses that completely express the tenderest religious sentiments of his church and century.

Gounod was intensely religious by nature and training, and he was a mystic, in just the sense that St. John was. Let us examine his philosophy in the light of a few of his sayings:

"Man, in his quality of high priest in a temple thenceforth dedicated to goodness, beauty, and truth, was destined to glorify the world by bestowing each of these."

"Man's sublime function is literally and positively that of a *new earthly* creator. His duty is to make all things what they ought to become."

"Every art demands something beyond mere technical knowledge and special handicraft, beyond the fullest, nay, the most absolutely perfect acquaintance with its various processes. These are absolutely necessary, of course, but they are only the tools with which each artist works, the outward form and development of each particular branch. But in each art there is a something, the exclusive property of none, but common to them all, higher than all, in default of which they fall to the level of mere handicrafts. This something, which, itself unseen, imbues the whole with life and soul — this constitutes the art itself."

"Art is one of the three great transformations which reality, brought into contact with the human mind and looked at in the ideal and all-powerful light of the good, the beautiful, and the true, is bound to undergo. Art is neither an utter dream, nor an exact copy. Inasmuch as it is ideal, it soars above us. Were it only real, it would be below us. Morality is the humanization, the incarnation of good; science is that of truth, and art that of beauty."

"To pass from exterior tangible realities to emotion, from emotion onward to reason, this is the progressive order of true intellectual development."

"Let us have no more flaunting of those equivocal and noisy titles, naturalism, realism,

and so forth. Art is a reparation of the failures and forgetfulness of reality."

"Have men forgotten that the artisan is but part of the artist — that is, the *man*; that it is the *man* that must be touched, enlightened, carried away, — nay, transfigured, — so that he shall be lost in passionate adoration of that immortal beauty which insures not momentary success alone, but the never ending empire of those masterpieces which have been the light and guide of human art?"

I have quoted at length from Gounod's published writings because of the extreme dignity of his position and the flood of light shed upon not his own art only, but art itself. Gounod was a poet, but when he declares that "New Jerusalem, that chosen country, is *human selection*, which lays the *new earth* regenerated, *recreated* according to the supreme formula, 'Verily, I say unto thee, except a man be born again, he can in no wise enter the Kingdom of Heaven,' at the feet of his Father and his God," he has passed beyond poetry into that form of religious clairvoyance which is the beginning of all art. As a matter of biography, he was throughout life a fervent Catholic. When young he even attended lectures at St. Sulpice in a religious dress, intending to enter the church, a resolution which resulted from the religious feeling fostered by his duties as organist.

Religious emotional life is so marked a characteristic of creative musical genius as to place the unity of art and mysticism beyond a doubt. But few, indeed, are the musical natures as well balanced and sane as Gounod's. In fact, his philosophy and his temperament were at one. His extreme personal charm was closely allied to his ideas of art. Everybody pressed forward his fortunes, and everybody was "one of his dearest friends." Berlioz gave him advice in composition and welcomed his maiden works; his first masses were written one after another on invitation of his priestly friends and admiring patrons; his first opera, "Sapho," was proposed by Madame Viardot-Garcia, who offered to sing the rôle, and who coaxed Nestor Roqueplan to stage it; and Roqueplan himself, the venomous antagonist of Meyerbeer, had faith in the tender poetry of Gounod's genius, and supported his early efforts at opera-writing to a successful issue.

Gounod was essentially a lyric poet. His melody was the melody of the French peasantry "recreated" into the highest forms of art. Not only the "King of Thule," which is deliberate reproduction both in form and tonality of the type which exists in so many tender French folk-songs, but everywhere in his music the spontaneous and natural character of his themes stamps them as the direct product of French national melody. If without education, he would have poured forth song after song, direct, simple, and tender, that would have lingered in cottage and field long after his name was forgotten. But with his fine training and culture, each poetic strophe found its place in an art work of the highest character. Gounod was an innovator of the boldest type, because what he did was done with simplicity of heart. Perfect simplicity, naturalness, and directness guided his art. His four models, on which he fed his musical life when a student, were Lulli's "Alcestis," Gluck's "Iphigenia," Mozart's "Don Giovanni," and Rossini's "William Tell." We can trace Rossini's influence in the richness and elaboration of Gounod's melodies (which, French as they are, possess Italian roundness and artistic completeness of expression), Mozart's in the purity and transparency of his harmony, Gluck and Lulli rather in his dramatic standpoint than his dramatic treatment, and all four in the romantic feeling which vivified his work.

Nevertheless, Gounod saw art through a medium altogether his own. He is one of the striking modern examples of that duality of artistic genius which was so marked a feature of the Renaissance. A man of fine education and culture, born of a father and mother both painters and draftsmen, he was so skilful an artist that Ingres, with whom he used to work when in Rome, offered to bring him back with a second *grand prix*. Gounod records that his musical education in Rome was obtained from two sources, the art-philosophy of this great artist, and the music at the Sistine Chapel. "By showing me the real nature of true art," he writes, "Monsieur Ingres taught me more about my own art than any number of merely technical masters could have done."

When Gounod went to the Sistine Chapel he listened to the music of Palestrina and looked at the frescos of Michelangelo, and "wondered whether the music and the painting were not the fruit of one and the same artistic inspiration." "Between the masterpieces of Michelangelo and Palestrina such close analogy of thought, such kinship of expression, exist, that one is almost forced to recognize the identity of the talents." he exclaims. It was, therefore, as an artist that Gounod recognized that beauty is higher than passion, at the very moment when violent expression of the passions opened the way to the fatal degradation of the music of to-day. It was not dramatic poetry, but painting that warned Gounod that "there is not the faintest analogy between the violent shock caused by some striking theatrical situation and the noble and calm delight to be derived from an exquisite and perfect work of art"; that taught him that "a whole abyss lies between the domain of mere sensation and that of intellectual feeling." One great charm of Gounod's operas consists in the pictorial quality of the scenes. What he saw as a painter but expressed as a musician, other painters have never tired of putting on canvas. Doubtless Gounod's long training as a religious composer had much to do with the elevation of his style and the dignity of his harmonies, but we know from his own lips that his standpoint in opera-writing was that of a painter. "Dramatic art is a branch of portraiture; its function is to delineate character, as that of the painter is to present feature and attitude." It was as a painter of human beings in music, as his father had painted them with pigments, that Gounod produced *Marguerite* and *Roméo*. The situation for him was but a light in which to display the individual, and each individual an idealized type of humanity. Hence the delicate charm and propriety of his art — the art of a Raphael.

Gounod has much to say in his autobiography about Michelangelo, whom he compares with Raphael. With the majestic genius of the former his own has little in common; but there are many points of sympathy between the work of Raphael and that of Gounod. Each reached the highest point of religious ecstasy. In each you find the same subtile perception of the perfection of beauty, the same sense of proportion, the same naïve truth at one moment, the same splendid mysticism at another, the same exquisite color, the same thoughtful and well-balanced composition. The delicious perfection of Gounod's loveliest passages is paralleled only by that of Raphael's types of beauty. The artist who painted the maiden mothers of Raphael's Florentine period might easily have conceived the music of "Roméo." The composer of Gounod's immortal Sanctus could have imagined the "Queen of Heaven" as the Sistine Madonna. Gounod must have drunk deep of the fountain of Raphael's art when he could know that "in art, as elsewhere, reason must counterbalance passion, and thence it follows that all artistic work of the highest class leaves an impress of calm, that sign of real power." The work of each of these men marked the opening of a new development of his art. Raphael initiated the decadence, with its Caravaggios and simpering Dolcis, its swooning Magdalens and tortured martyrs. Gounod lived to see the naturalness and feeling of his own art give place to a brutal realism which knows no reserves where *Santuzza* displaces *Marguerite* and the love of *Juliette* pales before the frenzy of the "Navarraise." Nevertheless, Raphael's painting remains for all time the unimpeachable testimony that beauty has rights of existence for beauty's sake. Gounod's influence, radical at first, has also proved wholly conservative. Thanks to *Faust* and *Roméo*, the type of an opera natural yet artistic, passionate yet chaste, has remained living upon the French stage, while too many of his successors have groveled in the lowest depths of sensational realism.

GOUNOD'S TOMB AT AUTEUIL, NEAR PARIS.

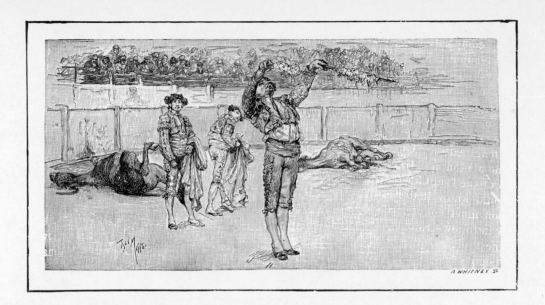

GEORGES BIZET

BY

CÉCILE CHAMINADE

SINCE the hour of triumph has come for the lamented master, snatched away in his prime,—since Bizet's work, become popular, has been acclaimed the world over, how many "prophets of the morrow" have arisen with the assurance that they first discovered the great artist! They foresaw him; they divined him! The criticisms which followed the brilliant revival of "Carmen," in 1883, afford a strangely edifying comparison with those which greeted the opera when it was first brought out The most enthusiastic admirers of the present had been the most persistent detractors in the past.

Little has been written concerning Bizet. A few brief biographies have appeared, but only one claims attention as important and abundant in good material; this was written by Mr. Charles Pigot, from the first an admirer of Bizet's, who published, in 1886, a very excellent and complete book entitled "Bizet and his Work," wherein he depicts with impassioned eloquence the noble character of the young master.

Bizet was not only a great master: he was, above all, a great artist, a great character, a large-hearted man; this is why his work bears its peculiar imprint, its so personal, so truthful aspect. In this simple sketch, for which no claim to literary excellence is advanced, I would now rehearse, through the medium of a few biographical notes drawn from most trustworthy sources, the first steps in life of this rare personality—a life simple, modest, too brief, alas! and marvelously laborious.

Bizet was born in Paris on October 25, 1838.   His father, a singing-teacher by profession, and his mother, an accomplished pianist, both wished to make their little Georges a musician.   He was sung to rest with the adagios of Mozart and Beethoven.   When but four years of age, as soon as his little fingers had sufficient strength to press down the keys of the piano, he was taught the notes simultaneously with the letters of the alphabet.   Like Mozart, like Weber and Saint-Saëns, Bizet was an infant phenomenon.   He possessed, as it were, a foreknowledge of all things; his progress was astounding.   In his ninth year he entered the Conservatoire and carried off in succession and with surprising ease all the highest prizes.   After being awarded the first prize of solfeggio,— he was then eleven,— Marmontel claimed him for his piano class, and here also, two years afterward, little Bizet bore away in sensational fashion the first prize.   The virtuoso of thirteen years already stood revealed as one of the elect.   His organ prize in the Benoist class and his prize for fugue in the Halévy class were taken with the same extraordinary facility, and, fitly to cap the climax of the series of youthful triumphs, he was given, in 1857, the "Prix de Rome" on the strength of his cantata "Clovis and Clotilde," which contains several pages of great and inspired beauty.   So passed his school-days, bathed in the sunlight of success.   He was fond of his work, which came so easy to him; his teachers worshiped him and cherished the brightest hopes of his future.   Thus, equipped with all attainable testimonials, an accomplished virtuoso, possessed of the kindest heart, of a mind of uncommon *finesse*, gifted with an overflowing imagination, Bizet's dreams must have been an enchantment, a golden vista, a maddening vision of delight.   He had just entered his twentieth year.

If an artistic career is of all careers the most attractive, the one that fascinates most powerfully all ardent imaginations aspiring to the ideal, it is also the one that has in reserve the largest measure of disappointment, bitterness, and despair.   The creative artist, even the most modest, is born ambitious, and dreams of glory.   He that feigns contentment with the sole enjoyment bestowed by the work involved in the pursuit of the Beautiful, he that parades his indifference to the approval of the public and his contempt of its applause, lacks sincerity.   One hears not seldom a young musician proclaim after a failure that he is happy and proud not to have known how to please the stupid crowd; he attempts to laugh, but his merriment has a hollow ring; his heart bleeds and is full of bitterness; the man grows bad.   If, later on, he succeeds, behold him transfigured; he exults and inclines to cry out with Guy de Maupassant: "Talent imposes itself upon the masses"; he loves the public which he once treated with such profound disdain, for now the public has restored him his confidence in himself.   How enthusiastically he once again falls to work! Yes, the artist has need of the opinion of the crowd. All sincere artists have an instinctive distrust of incense-bearers as well as of detractors; the competent critic is a *rara avis;* the kindly and impartial critic, a still more infrequent being; the public, the public at. large, is the sole authorized judge, because of its absolute independence. If it starts

MLLE. CÉCILE CHAMINADE.

From photograph by Benque.

back at the boldness of an art work, if it hesitates at sight of too abstract an achievement; if, in brief, the public does not "understand," what can be said if those whose mission it is to guide opinion, and who consequently should be qualified so to do, do not "understand" more clearly?

The premature decease of Bizet kept from him the knowledge of his glory; he foresaw it only, but, be it noted at once, he was not wholly disregarded by the Parisian public. Except in the case of "Carmen," against which the public was somewhat prejudiced, the master's works were greeted with lively interest, and fell but little short of attaining definite success. The very discordant newspaper press unfortunately brought confusion into the uncertain spirit of the public, for the public has no convictions; it feels, and feels only, and little by little the sincere but inconscient impulse of its first manifestations weakens and dies away.

While the young master is still in happy ignorance of the years of fever and strife that await him, let us follow him to Italy, through his

THE HOME OF GEORGES BIZET.
No. 22 Rue Douai.

sojourn in the Eternal City, the dream of his early youth, the supreme reward of toil and merit. Bizet did not slumber on his laurels, but fell passionately to work. His *envois* were: an Italian opera bouffe, "Don Procopio"; a symphony; an overture, "Ossian's Hunt"; and "La Guzla de l'Emir," a comic opera in one act. Little is left of these achievements of his early youth. The personality of an author seldom asserts itself in his first efforts. Bizet, a fanatic *per la musica*, steeped in the works of his favorite masters, still walked unconsciously in their shadow, and his first productions were somewhat deficient in the originality that a few years afterward became so powerful.

His correspondence from Rome is delightful. His brimming enthusiasm for the masters of all schools denotes his ardent nature and his passionate fondness for his art. He addresses to his parents letters marked by innocent and touching tenderness. He writes of his fellow-students in the Villa Medici with the greatest kindliness. Some of them have won his admiration and he delights in their success. Ernest Guiraud, his classmate, his companion in arms, is to join him, for he has just borne off the "Prix de l'Institut." Bizet rejoices at thought of meeting again the friend whose musical ethics are in such perfect accord with his own. What enthusiastic *causeries*, what projects for the future, what golden dreams were to be looked forward to, as they rambled through the lovely Roman summer land!

His first great grief was brought to him by the death of his mother. He returned to Paris in hot haste, and arrived just before she breathed her last. The blow was a terrible one for his gentle soul. For a long while he was inconsolable, seeking in work, however, the strength to overcome the sorrow that possessed him.

In 1863 Bizet wrote "Les Pêcheurs de Perles," a three-act opera, ordered of him by M. Carvalho, then manager of the Théâtre Lyrique. The book of the opera was not of a character to tempt a fiery and original composer like Bizet, but he accepted it with gratitude, without even having read it, holding himself very fortunate at being able to come at once into contact with the public, without submitting to the long and depressing period of waiting in store for almost all writers for the stage. The dullness of the subject did not discourage him, and he set about his task with a hopeful heart. "Les Pêcheurs" was represented for the first time at the Théâtre Lyrique, September 29, 1863, and met with but questionable success. Some passages of the score were enthusiastically applauded: the duet between *Nadir* and *Zurga*, the tenor air, "Je crois rêver encore," and *Leïla's* aria, "Comme autrefois dans la nuit sombre," called forth unanimous applause. These are, of course, the simplest pages of the opera, and hence those most easily understood on a single hearing. The score abounds in new and lovely thoughts; the orchestration denotes a skilful hand; the Eastern color is most felicitously evoked. Be it not forgotten that the composer was in his twenty-fifth year, and that a first step of this sort certainly deserved encouragement. Only here and there did some dull scene or some measures devoid of personality call down hostile criticism, and this was not spared the composer. Discord reigned in the newspaper press, and Bizet was taxed with following in Verdi's steps, in Félicien David's, in Grisar's! Some journalists attributed to him Wagnerian tendencies. All this seems astonishing, but so it was, and the journals of the period are still at hand to prove it. Berlioz, who foresaw what Bizet might one day become, said in the "Journal des Débats": "The score of 'Les Pêcheurs de Perles' does the greatest credit to M. Bizet, whom people will be constrained to accept as a composer, *notwithstanding* his rare talent as a pianist." Berlioz stood almost alone in doing justice to the young master. The homage paid came from so exalted a fount that it might well console the musician for many onslaughts. Bizet was not discouraged by the doubtful outcome of his first battle, and valiantly set to work without delay.

Between 1863 and 1866 he undertook several works of vastly different styles and proportions: a symphony, "Roma"; a five-act grand opera, "Ivan le Terrible"; and several instrumental pieces. During this period of his life he appears to have worked feverishly and desperately, rather than under the impulse of conviction. Perhaps he was influenced unconsciously by the contradictory comments that greeted his first effort. Had self-doubt, the sharpest pang that can afflict an artist, entered his mind? At that very moment M. Carvalho intrusted to him the book of a four-act opera, "La Jolie Fille de Perth," the score of which was to be ready in six months. Bizet accepted the task. The book pleased him, for it opened a path to his straying thoughts. Then, too, arose the hope of a complete revenge, or, better still, of a definite success. He addressed himself to the new work in the heartiest manner, setting aside for the time being all the compositions he had already commenced.

He was then a resident of Le Vésinet. The tiny house on the Route des Cultures still stands, just as it was then, isolated, hidden in foliage, a veritable hermitage. Bizet was wont to lock himself up in it for weeks; strict orders were given, and a formal authorization had to be shown to gain admission to the hermit. In a letter written to a pupil and friend, M. Edmond Galabert, he thus speaks of his country abode: "I am so thoroughly at home, safe from bores, idlers, sayers of nothing — from the world, in fine, alas!" Bizet, whose frank joyousness, wit, and humor were known to all, loved calmness, silence, and solitude. His changeful disposition was alternately fiery and meditative. He came to Paris but once a week in order to give lessons, for he was poor; his music brought him but little, and he had to live. Fancy the sufferings of an artist of genius compelled to earn his livelihood by teaching — mostly uninteresting pupils — while ten operas sing in his brain! Moreover, he gave his lessons with care, patience, and resignation that seemed incompatible with his vivacious and passionate disposition. In all he undertook, in everything he agreed to do, he threw his will, his whole heart — an honest and loyal heart in the fullest sense of the word.

During this term of excessive activity, Bizet wrote the series of charming melodies, very varied in form and color, whereof many, now celebrated, have an exquisite and penetrating flavor: "Chant d'Amour," "A une Fleur," "Pastorale," "Vieille Chanson," "Ma Vie a Son Secret," "Les

WHERE GEORGES BIZET DIED.

No. 5 Avenue de Mesmes, Bougiral (near St. Germain).

Adieux de l'Hôtesse Arabe" may be cited among the best. The latter song, especially poetic, won rare success for Mme. Carvalho, who interpreted it to perfection. He also wrote for the publishing house of Choudens numerous transcriptions for piano and some original compositions. His romances without words, entitled "Chants du Rhin" are models of form and elegance. "La Chasse Fantastique," which is very difficult in point of execution, is characterized by strange and diabolic accents suggesting ancient legends, and written with a fancy and an originality that it would seem impossible to surpass.

Bizet never consented to appear publicly as a pianist. He purposely concealed his great talent and virtuosity. Many offers had been made him, and concert tours would surely have proved less wearying and more lucrative than the work of teaching, but he invariably declined to entertain them. He no doubt dreaded the indestructible prejudice that lies in holding instrumentalists to their specialty, and denying them the gift of exalted conception. Bizet dreaded for his works, when asked to execute them, the epithet, "pianist's music," from which Liszt and Rubinstein fought themselves free with so much difficulty. Chopin, immortal

GEORGES BIZET.

PAINTED BY SCELLIER, WHO WON THE PRIX DE ROME FOR PAINTING IN THE
SAME YEAR THAT BIZET WON HIS PRIZE FOR MUSIC, AND, ACCORDING TO CUS-
TOM, PAINTED A PORTRAIT OF HIS CLASSMATE AT THE VILLA MEDICI, IN ROME.

Chopin, who made the piano the sole confidant of his dreams, his sufferings, his aspirations, found it no easy task to be taken seriously by the worthies that lay down the principle, "there is no great music written, save for the stage, or in symphonic form"—which is tantamount to proclaiming that there is no great painting found, save canvases five feet by ten. Bizet shrank from destroying his growing prestige as a dramatic musician by making himself known as a pianist, and thus it came that he kept men in ignorance of his great talent as an executant. Marmontel, in his "Symphonistes et Virtuoses," supplies a glittering description of Bizet's playing, comparing him with the greatest pianists of the period and emphasizing the personality of his style, the marvelous sensitiveness of his touch and the fullness of his tone. Liszt, who had heard him before he departed for Rome, expressed his admiration to him in strong terms, and Liszt, everybody knows, was not easily stirred to admiration.

The date was at hand when Bizet, to comply with the terms of the contract, was to complete the score of "La Jolie Fille de Perth." He worked fifteen and sixteen hours a day; a less robust nature, one less steeled, would have speedily broken down. The opera was finished in due season, but months were spent in arranging the cast, and its initial performance occurred but a year later. Too much space would be required to analyze the score—a work of real importance. I confess that I prefer "Les Pêcheurs de Perles," with its charming sincerity. "La Jolie Fille de Perth" is an achievement of broad proportions, full of life and at certain points powerfully dramatic, but it impresses me as less felicitous as to inspiration, and the very Italian *vocalizzi* that frequently appear are somewhat confusing, when the advanced ideas of the young master are kept in mind.

The opera was cordially received, but its success recalled the experience of "Les Pêcheurs de Perles": it did not endure. After twenty-five representations the work vanished from the bills, nor has it up to this writing again been performed in France. The newspaper press was again very contradictory and by no means eulogistic, with the exception of the journals represented by the great musician-critics—a slender force. These writers, although recognizing in Bizet a dangerous future rival, succeeded in silencing the utterances of instinctive jealousy, and were agreed in praising the incontestable merit of "La Jolie Fille de Perth" as they had praised "Les Pêcheurs de Perles," and in classing Bizet with the musicians of whom, henceforward, account must be taken. The numberless journalists, however, who assumed the title of "musical critics" with no other claim thereto than their own good will, formed a cabal whose operations were to begin afresh whenever a new work of the composer's appeared. The hapless artist, unnerved by excessive labor, weary of a fruitless struggle, filled with bitterness, a shining mark for envy and ill will, was all but disheartened; despite the faith he still held in his powers, he was on the eve of giving up the contest. The first symptoms of the malady that was to prove fatal a few years later were disclosed at this period.

"Djamileh," a one-act opera, followed. The music of the work is very dainty, very poetical, and intensely Oriental, but the book is scarcely interesting. The interpretation, too, was inadequate; the leading rôle, that of the slave *Djamileh*, was allotted to an admirable creature whose talent unluckily bore no proportion to her beauty, and the remaining parts were quite as poorly sustained. It may be said with justice that "Djamileh," a very delicate achievement and one not easily sung, was betrayed by its performers.

We now come to "L'Arlésienne," a masterpiece of grace, poetry, and local color, every page a lifelike, luminous picture. In this work the musician reveals himself as a colorist among painters. Without resorting to the language of the day, which endows a musician with a palette, tints, and horizons, and in compensation gives the painter a scale, tones, and harmonies, one is tempted in this instance to use the terms of the studio quite as freely as those of the music-room in dealing with this work, so wonderfully truthful for all that are familiar with Provence. Daudet could have found no co-laborer more potent to depict the scene of the evolution of his simple, lovely, and touching drama. Bizet had that rarest of gifts, the power to evoke. He had caught but a glimpse of Provence on his way to Rome a few years previous. He had been fascinated by its peculiar charm. Had he not seen it, even, he would with his marvelous intuition have divined it. This he proves in "Les Pêcheurs de Perles" and in "Djamileh," wherein he summons up the East—the East which he knows not, but into which he gives a luminous insight. Later on he will do likewise with Spain, and always with that same intensity of expression which transports one into the picture-lands.

From an esthetic standpoint, "L'Arlésienne" impresses one as Georges Bizet's most complete masterpiece. Following the beautiful symphonic prelude, the chorus, "Grand soleil de la Provence," conveys a sense of happiness and light. Then we have the "Pastorale," so graceful and fresh that it exhales a perfume of lavender and thyme; the chorus, *a bocca chiusa*, so felicitously effective; the intermezzo, in minuet form, abounding in life and sparkle; the carillon, full of picturesque harmonic "finds": the adagietto, tinged with such profound emotion that this number alone would confer immortality upon its composer; the farandole, with its satanic rhythm; and, lastly, the fine chorus, the "Marche des Rois," which is first heard at the outset of the prelude. Its motive is a Provençal song attributed by some to Lully, by others to King René. No agreement has been reached on this point, but that matters little. Bizet has treated these few measures with so admirable an art in development and scoring that he has wrought them into a symphonic page of the highest order.

Bizet, in "L'Arlésienne," is in full possession of his individuality. No trace remains of his preference for any master with whom he has been in touch in his early youth. He has reconquered his personality, and, even when he devotes himself to reproducing this or that medium, this or that atmosphere, he retains his nature, his skill, his stamp, his clear-cut, bright, and accurate style, the temperament of the Frenchmen of southern France, with its frankness, its good humor, and its sensitiveness.

The production of this admirable work was hailed with unanimous applause. This time the newspapers were eulogistic. There were heard, in truth, a few discordant notes, but they were silenced in the immense *tutti* of admirers. And yet the success was not to last. Like "Les Pêcheurs de Perles," "La Jolie Fille de Perth," and "Djamileh," "L'Arlésienne" had but a few representations. Bizet was deeply affected. In face of a spontaneous and unanimous success, he thought the game was won, and now it was to be commenced over again! To what could one attribute the general lukewarmness after the welcome of the first night? Was it that this time all the honors were borne off by the music, and that Daudet's play, touching and captivating though it was, but presented as a melodrama, a form of art-work that finds slight favor in France, failed to move the throng? Alphonse Daudet is less of a dramatic author than he is a poet, an analyst, a descriptive writer, and the public, always somewhat indolent, prefers seeing to divining.

This success without morrow would have discouraged Bizet had he not almost immediately found consolation in the transfer of his work to the popular concerts, where it was given a permanent place in the program, and where its success was definitely affirmed.

The fine overture to "Patrie" and a delicate and charming suite for orchestra were next added to the symphonic work of the young master, but the stage, whither his real vocation beckoned him, claimed him once more. "Carmen" was the song of the swan, the composer's apotheosis. The new opera was impatiently awaited, which proves that Bizet, although much discussed and contested, was nevertheless regarded as one of the most interesting personalities of the modern French school. Before the first performance occurred, footlight gossip scattered tidings that the music was "strange," the book *risqué*, the interpretation extraordinary. "Carmen" was brought out in the Salle Favart on March 3, 1875, in presence of all Paris—the world of fashion, literature, and art. The curtain rose in view of a crowded and sympathetic audience, tremulous with impatience and curiosity.

"Carmen," a work brimming with vitality and action, whose dazzling brilliancy was later on to gather and mingle in one and the same outburst of enthusiasm the public, the artists, and the critics,—"Carmen" was not understood! The listeners, astonished rather than delighted, remained cold.

How admit such an injustice, or, rather, how explain a general error bordering upon aberration? Be it added that the book of "Carmen" is itself a masterpiece, based upon Prosper Mérimée's "Carmen," an impressive, powerfully dramatic tale. The piece taken from it by MM. Meilhac and Halévy is unquestionably the most interesting, the most passion-inspiring that has ever been intrusted to a musician. Every one knows with what vigor, originality, boldness, and charm Bizet has thrown into relief the distinct characteristics of each personage. The rôle of *Micaëla* has been felicitously added for stage purposes, and is a chaste, tender, and poetic note in the somewhat too realistic strain of the drama. To this realism, though skilfully attenuated by the authors of the play, but excessive notwithstanding, must be ascribed the well-nigh hostile reception of "Carmen" on the occasion of its first performance. The public of the Salle Favart, accustomed to the gentle emotions of the ancient French opéra comique, was shocked, alarmed even, at this bold and thoroughly human work; the piece was proclaimed immoral; the word was whispered at first by a few, then repeated by all; ere long the only theme of comment was the immorality of the performance. The dainty, dazzling, but fiendish representation of Mme. Galli-Marié dismayed the family parties. The management was attacked, indignation was expressed that the Salle Favart should be given up to such spectacles, which mothers could not permit their daughters to behold. In brief, the *tolle* became general.

All this occurred twenty-four years ago; the Parisian public is no longer so prudish, if one may judge by many plays of the modern repertoire, concerning which much might be written in a far more censorious vein; moreover, the early interpreters of the opera at least had sufficient talent and tact to constrain acceptance of certain scenes which may be violent, somewhat brutal, perhaps, but are never vulgar. Among the performers may be mentioned Mme. Galli-Marié, the matchless, the inimitable *Carmen*; M. Shéry, as *Don José*, the accomplished artist, the captivating singer and comedian; Mlle. Chapuy, an angelic *Micaëla*; M. Bouhy, the superb and arrogant *Toreador;* and Mlles. Ducasse and Chevalier, delightful in the subsidiary rôles of *Frasquita* and *Mercedes.*

Yet this complete masterpiece, sustained by the artists just enumerated, failed to impress the Parisian public — a public so enlightened, so spontaneous in its demonstrations! A few days after its production it found increased favor, but the opera reached its thirty-seventh performance with difficulty. In 1883, "Carmen," acclaimed in foreign lands, laden with laurels garnered outside of France, returned, and in the same Salle Favart where the opera failed of comprehension, in presence of the same public and of the same critics, was greeted with transports of enthusiasm.

But Bizet was no longer at hand to enjoy his glory, too long awaited, so dearly bought. He died a few weeks after the first representation of "Carmen." The heart disease that had appeared some years previous had become visibly aggravated during the laborious rehearsals of his last achievement. During the long hours of study he had alternately hoped and yielded to despair; then, as the work took shape, he foresaw the success it would one day attain, and confidence was restored. He had rested in "Carmen" all his artistic faith, his whole soul; he had, so to say, breathed into it his whole life; he was certain that his work was good and must triumph; but gradually, as the date of the first representation drew near, he would again grow uneasy, and the acute anguish that overcomes the artist when the day set for these bloodless battles approaches finally broke down his robust health. The failure of "Carmen," his favorite work, dealt the last blow: Bizet passed away June 3, 1875, at Bougival, in the arms of his young wife,[1] and surrounded by the members of his family. The nature of the disease that bore him off so swiftly was never exactly understood: some say it was *angina pectoris*; others, an embolism. The saddest version of his case would appear the truest: an excess of toil, ever-renewed deceptions, and, most trying of all things, the deep wound dealt him on the gloomy night when he beheld his "Carmen," the work dear to him above all others and upon which he founded his most legitimate hopes, misunderstood, almost disdained.

After Bizet's death his apotheosis commenced. How saddening are these incomprehensible reversals of the judgment of the throng, how instructive should be the unjust charges of the critics! After Bizet was gone no one thought of discussing his tendencies, of classing him, of "labeling" him; men were willing to listen, to judge, to applaud. It was these endless comparisons that so distressed him in life,— comparisons that led one to believe that he had no character of his own, that he was but an imitator, a reflection of others. One oft-repeated epithet that infuriated him most was "fierce Wagnerian!" It is astounding that such a designation should have found an echo; one need but look into Bizet's work, from its first to its last measure, to be convinced that nothing warrants it. Bizet admired Wagner greatly, but his admiration never attained to idolatry. "Art is art," and Bizet's worship went to Mozart as to Beethoven; to Verdi as to Schumann; to Berlioz as to Gounod—"Mossieu Gounod," as our young and quite decadent musicians are wont to say.

A sworn foe to school prejudices, Bizet detested "processes." Like all great minds, like all enthusiastic and generous souls, he was an eclectic; the adjective is contemned by some authors who pretend that eclecticism implies lack of ideal. No, eclecticism in art is the love of the Beautiful, wherever it may exist. Art is of all times and all lands; happy are they whose souls are sufficiently exalted, whose minds are sufficiently open to understand and admire the eternal master-works.

But admiration is not imitation, and Bizet's eclecticism had no in-

[1] Bizet married, in 1869, Mlle. Geneviève Halévy, daughter of the illustrious composer of "La Juive."

fluence upon his sharply defined individuality.   Art, it has been declared, has no country; but the artist has, and the true artist sets the seal of his race on all sincere work.   If we claim Bizet with pride, it is because he is one of our purely national glories.

THE GRAVE OF BIZET.

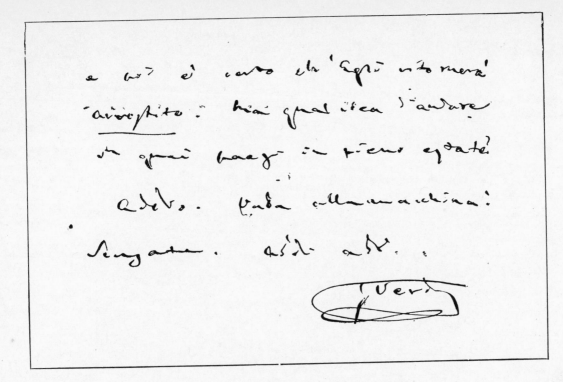

GIUSEPPE VERDI

BY

F. A. SCHWAB

THE long and active life of the musician that held, with Richard Wagner, the ear of the world during the second half of the nineteenth century, furnishes a simple record of labor, success, and, presumably, happiness. Giuseppe Verdi, though born of humble parentage, never knew the pangs of extreme poverty. His genius had early recognition. Popularity clung to him to the close of his career; and his days, made bearable by sturdy health, extended far beyond the period allotted to man by Biblical authority. There is an ancient proverb that says, "Call no man happy until he is dead." It had no application in the case of the great Italian composer; and, as he sank into his final sleep, his latest memories must have reassured him as to his place in the history of his art, and soothed him with thoughts of the Horatian "non omnis moriar."

The composer of the best-known operas of the age was born at Roncole, a small village in the district of Parma, three miles from Busseto. His father and mother, Carlo and Luigia Verdi, kept a wretched *osteria;* and as the patronage of the whole population of two hundred souls would have been insufficient to yield a living income, they carried on, besides, a petty trade in tobacco, coffee, sugar, and groceries. The exact date of their son's birth has never been ascertained, but the baptismal entry in the register of the church of San Michele being dated October 11, 1813, it is pretty certain that the infant must have been between twenty-four and forty-eight hours old when christened Fortuninus Josephus Franciscus, to quote the Latin names embodied in the formal certificate. His childhood went by quietly enough. We learn that his mother bestowed most attention upon his education; that the lad was passionately fond of her; that he was rather timid, reserved, and even serious for his age; and that the first indications of his liking for music were afforded by his partiality for hand-organs, which he invariably followed about until their owners were far beyond the last houses of the village. Circumstances proved favorable to the development of his musical talent. There was no school at Roncole; but the Church of San Michele was possessed of an organ, and the boy's parents, recognizing that their son would ere long have to earn his livelihood, thought that by confiding him to the care of the local organist he might, in due season, be appointed his successor. After a three years' course of study the wishes of Verdi's parents were gratified, and the lad became organist of the parish church. He was then in his eleventh year, and tolerably ignorant, no doubt, in matters familiar to school-boys generally; so his father at once decided that he should take up his abode at Busseto, where he could at least obtain elementary instruction, while discharging his duties as village organist on Sundays and holidays. Verdi sustained the double part of pupil and *maestro* for seven years. On week-days he studied at Busseto, and on Sundays, and whenever the numerous *feste* of the church were celebrated, he was beheld at the organ of San Michele. Small as were his emoluments, they were not to be despised, for his parents were well-nigh as poor as people in sunny Italy can be. The honoraria were insignificant enough, for all that; including fees for funeral services, christenings, and marriages, they did not exceed one hundred lire (twenty dollars) per annum,—this slender amount, however, being somewhat augmented by the collection which, in accordance with established usage, the organist always took up at harvest-time. Two years rolled by, and young Verdi learned to read, write, and cipher. As a reward for his industry, his father found him employment in a distillery managed by one Antonio Barezzi, an amateur of no mean ability.

Verdi's admission to Barezzi's household finally determined the bent of his career. Busseto is a small town with a population of two thousand souls. It was, too, in a diminutive way, a sort of musical center; and Verdi's surroundings were most helpful. He studied hard, won the good graces of Fernando Provesi, his teacher, and when the latter resigned the conductorship of the local Philharmonic Society he put his pupil in his place. But Busseto proved, ere long, a "pent-up Utica" for the growing talents of the young enthusiast, and, with the assistance of Barezzi and other friends, he was sent to Milan. The Milan Conservatory was then directed by Francesco Basily, whose name will go down to posterity, one may believe, not because of his ability as a musician, but because he refused to accept Verdi as a conservatory student, on the ground that "he showed no disposition for music"! The applicant was disappointed, but not discouraged, and looked elsewhere for introduction. This he secured from Vincenzo Lavigna, whose view of his pupil's future was as roseate as Basily's was gloomy. Verdi had opportunities to compose works for public performances and to direct a band, and none went by unheeded.

In 1833 Verdi returned to Busseto, where he conducted an orchestra and carried on a lively contest with a rival *maestro*. During his sojourn at Busseto, which ended in 1838, when he quitted the town and took up his abode in Milan, one important event in his private life demands mention. Barezzi, although the father of a numerous family, had always treated his protégé as a son. The terms of intimacy upon which Verdi lived with his benefactor's children ripened, in the case of Barezzi's eldest daughter, into a stronger feeling. His boyish attachment for Margherita Barezzi, who is described as having been comely and intelligent, developed into love. Margherita was impressed with the talent and industry of the youth, and she believed in his future. The young people sought Barezzi's consent to their marriage, and the father met the request with a reply that he would never refuse a child of his in marriage to a worthy young man whose capacity and steadiness he regarded as quite as valuable possessions as wealth. The wedding was celebrated in 1836, when Verdi was in his twenty-third year. Two years afterward, when Margherita had borne him two children, his engagement with the municipality having expired, and the annual honorarium of three hundred lire being quite insufficient for the support of the composer and his family, his lares and penates were made ready for removal, and once again the musician journeyed toward Milan.

From the day of his arrival in the chief city of Lombardy, Verdi became possessed

"OTELLO."

From "Album de l'Opéra."

of a single thought and object: success on the lyric stage. Fortune served him admirably from the first. He became acquainted with a young poet, Temistocle Solera by name, whose ambition ran in the same groove. Solera was but nineteen, and a good musician as well as a clever librettist. The two aspirants to fame, having determined to strike up an alliance, Solera wrote a libretto entitled, "Oberto, Conte di San Bonifacio," to which Verdi composed the music. The first performance of "Oberto" was given at La Scala on the evening of November 17, 1839, and the work was received with so much favor that Merelli, who was then the impresario of the house, bound Verdi by con-

tract to supply him with three additional operas. If Merelli had stipulated that the novelties were to be *opere serie*, the result would have been more felicitous for both manager and artist. Unluckily, he did not, and one of the few failures of Verdi's art life was the consequence. For some occult reason, he chose an old libretto by Felice Romani that one Gyrowetz had already set to music, and addressed himself to the task of furnishing it with a score. The current of the composer's talent never lay in the direction of *opera buffa* or *mezzo carattere* music, and circumstances made his attempt to produce comic music more hopeless still. While busy with his new work an event occurred that

531

almost broke his heart and unsettled his reason. His beloved wife was stricken down by brain fever, and after a few days' illness she died, leaving the composer in a condition more easily imagined than described. Though beside himself with grief, he had to finish the opera he had begun, and it will be generally conceded that, under the influence of such a misfortune, the production of music of a light order was out of the question. "Un Giorno di Regno," under which title the fresh setting of "Il finto Stanislao" was made known at La Scala on September 5, 1840, had a memorable downfall; it proved, to use an Italian term, *un fiasco d'una sera.*

The limits set the writer of this article make it impossible to more than enumerate the operas composed by Verdi during his protracted career. Room can be made only for their titles and for a mention of their fate. "Nabucco" followed "Un Giorno di Regno," and its success at once placed Verdi on a plane with Donizetti, Mercadante, Pacini, and Ricci. Next came "I Lombardi" and "Ernani," two triumphs; "I Due Foscari" and "Giovanna d'Arco," which were but mildly impressive; "Alzira," "Attila," and "Macbeth," which were but moderately successful; "I Masnadieri," which was coolly received; "Il Corsaro" and "La Battaglia di Legnano," which found little favor; "Luisa Miller," which won applause; and "Stiffelio," which was less fortunate. The more striking achievements are next in order: "Rigoletto," "Il Trovatore," "La Traviata," and "Un Ballo in Maschera." All these operas were characterized by a profusion of melodies that were sung and played the world over. It was at the stage of his career marked by the composition of "La Forza del Destino" that a change was observable in Verdi's style. "Don Carlos," written for the Paris Opera House, and "Aïda," composed by order of the Khedive, made still clearer the musician's purpose to meet the severe demands of the age; and to this part of his record, which binds him more closely to the readers of the present and the immediate future than do most of his earlier performances, somewhat less hurried consideration may be accorded. Between the production of "Aïda" and that of "Otello" sixteen years, unmarked save by the composition of the "Messa da Requiem," went by. Five years before the new setting of Shakspere's tragedy was revealed, Richard Wagner, the composer's only peer among the musicians of the age, had passed away, and of two masters but one remained. Of Verdi's plans during that long period of repose nothing was known even to his intimates. The Italian newspapers occasionally printed stories of forthcoming achievements, and some particularly well informed writers held out hopes of a "Nero" and a "Francesca da Rimini," but nothing came of items that the composer never took pains even to contradict. In 1883, however, trustworthy information got abroad simultaneously with the frequent appearance at Sant' Agata of Arrigo Boïto, himself a poet and composer of no mean ability. Verdi was quick to perceive, not merely Boïto's merits, but his modernity both literary and musical, and the book of "Otello" was the outcome of the discovery. On January 1, 1885, the composer sent to his publisher, Giulio Ricordi, a magnificent tart concealing in its depths a tiny Moor. On the following New Year a second tart was forwarded, and this time the baby Moor had attained fair proportions. On January 1, 1887, emerged from the third tart a virile *Otello*, armed cap-a-pie. Rehearsals were at once begun at La Scala, and on February 5, 1887, in presence of an audience of some four thousand spectators, assembled from all parts of Europe, the curtain rose upon the first representation of the opera.

Detailed review or criticism, even of the later works of the master, not being compressible within the boundaries of a mere outline of his art record, it must suffice to say in respect to "Otello" that, as "Don Carlos" and "Aïda" denoted an advance on earlier efforts, so did "Otello" in truthfulness of dramatic expression and elaborateness of instrumentation disclose still greater progress in the new direction given to music within the last half century. Even as Boïto's book comes closer to Shakspere than does the wretched Rossinian libretto still remembered by hoary-headed dilettanti, Verdi's score comes closer to a possible tone-painting, enriching, if not illuminating, the poet's work. Melodists generally and hundreds of musicians and music-lovers that descry the influence of Wagner wherever rich instrumentation abounds, were not slow to pro-

CLARA LOUISE KELLOGG IN "AÏDA."

claim that Verdi had gone over to the new faith, and that "Otello" was distinctly Wagnerian. In point of fact, there is no trace of Wagner in "Otello." Verdi's intimates, indeed, have united in declaring that the master was familiar with but three of the German composer's performances: "Rienzi," "Lohengrin," and "Der Fliegende Holländer." The score of "Otello" is not the efflorescence of a germ. The *leit-motif* system has no recognition; the human voice is supreme in its every scene; and the orchestration, however resounding, harmonious, and complex, simply sustains the song. Verdi's sole intent in "Otello" has been the expression of the sentiments of the personages, their characterization being effected simultaneously by the message delivered. The old-fashioned aria, with recitative, andante, and final cabaletta,

was long ago discarded. In "Otello" no concession whatever is made to virtuosity, and there is not a measure in the opera that can be held up as in disaccord with the dramatic situation. Whether the opera, with its admirable modern characteristics, will carry the name of its composer down to generations unborn as surely as will many of his less realistic, less finished, and more tuneful achievements, is a question that need not be mooted in this place. There is little melody, in the exact popular sense of the word, in "Otello." A fine Italian ensemble at the close of Act III, a simple and touching "Ave Maria" in Act IV, and passages of a love duet are the only parts of the score that have anything of the sensuous charm of Verdi's earlier music. But, as Hanslick puts it, "youth in music is melody,'

533

and Verdi was just seventy when he wrote "Otello."

The success of the opera was immediate and undisputed, and ere long it was performed in every large city of America and Europe. In most of the capitals its impres-

Only six years separated the first night of "Otello" from that of "Falstaff." Verdi, however, according to his own story, had long cherished the idea of setting to music "The Merry Wives of Windsor." Writing from Genoa, under date of December 3, 1890, to

SOPHIE CRUVELLI.

She created the rôle of *Hélène* in Verdi's "Sicilian Vespers"; she also sang the leading rôle in "Fidelio" when
it was produced in Paris in 1852, and won a great success in "Ernani."
From a French lithograph.

siveness was greatly heightened by its chief interpreters, Signor Tamagno and M. Maurel. The tenor, endowed with a voice of extraordinary compass and resonance, was excellently fitted to portray the violent and cruel Moor; and the ferocity of the murderer in the last scene has never had, at the hands of far more intelligent and experienced tragedians, even equally adequate representation. M. Maurel's *Iago* rose to the highest plane of lyric and dramatic art, and the happiest portrayals of this personage that his contemporaries have essayed have been more or less felicitous copies of his masterly effort.

the Marquis Gino Monaldi, the composer observes:

"What can I say to you? For forty years I have wished to write a comic opera, and I have been familiar with 'The Merry Wives of Windsor' these fifty years; but . . . the usual 'buts' that are everywhere have prevented me from gratifying my wish. Now Boïto has silenced them all, and has fashioned me a lyric comedy that resembles no other. I am amusing myself making music for it, without projects of any kind, and I do not know, even, whether I shall end it. . . . I repeat, I am amusing myself.

"*Falstaff* is a mischief-maker who does

all sorts of bad deeds, . . . but in a diverting form. He is a 'type.' And 'types' are so varied! . . . The opera is wholly comic."

Further proof of the composer's long-harbored scheme is given by M. Maurel, who visited him in 1890.

"One afternoon," relates M. Maurel, "Verdi spoke at length of his old-time intention to write a musical comedy. He said he had found no text that quite satisfied him, either in Molière or in the French playwrights of the actual period. I insisted upon Shakspere. He appeared impressed, but, with his wonted inclination to silence, made no further remarks, beyond mentioning that he would like more information on the subject.

"A few days afterward I addressed to Verdi the manuscript of 'The Taming of the Shrew' recently adapted by M. Paul Delair for Coquelin. Verdi's letter of acknowledgment ran textually thus: 'The comedy pleases me vastly, but, to deal with it, composers such as Cimarosa, Rossini, Donizetti, etc., are needed. The composers of the period are too much harmonists and too much "orchestrists" [sic]; they have not courage enough to stand aside, to renounce instrumentation *malgré tout*, to think only of the accuracy of the accent, the truthfulness of the personages, the strength of the situations. As for myself, I can only say to you: "It is too late."'"

M. Maurel was not a little puzzled by the closing words of the letter, but they were explained, two years afterward, when, after supper in the Palazzo Doria at Genoa, Verdi said to him, with a smile: "Do you know that you quite alarmed me two years ago? You spoke to me so enthusiastically concerning Shakspere that I fancied some one had been indiscreet. . . . Now I can tell you that Boïto and I had then laid the plan of a lyric comedy founded upon Shakspere. It is almost completed, and its title shall be 'Falstaff.'"

The rehearsals of "Falstaff" began in January, 1893. They were extremely fatiguing, but the energy of the composer stimulated the artists, and on February 9 the first representation took place. As in "Otello," M. Maurel, as *Falstaff*, offered a portrayal that must be described as absolutely unique in its combination of the singer's and the comedian's art; the artist has remained to this day, in fact, the single representative of the personage, performing in French at the Paris Opéra Comique and in Italian in the principal cities of the old and new worlds.

Without entering into details concerning the score of "Falstaff," it may be noted that there is more youthful exuberance in its measures than in any part of "Otello." The comic Shaksperian personages and incidents are quite as felicitously illustrated as are the scenes and characters of the tragedy; and, strange to say when one remembers the advanced age of the composer, an air of extraordinary juvenility pervades every scene. Some idea of Verdi's intentions in respect to the import of his music, as well as an indication of his rare power of intuition, may be gathered from two extracts from letters addressed to M. Maurel while the latter was studying his part. In the first Verdi says: "You have already the book of 'Falstaff.' As soon as the music is engraved you shall have the score. Study, examine as much as you wish the verses and words of the libretto, but do not busy yourself too much with the music. Do not find what I am telling you strange. If the music have the requisite character, if the character of the personage be rightly apprehended, if the accent of the word be true, the music goes of itself and is born, so to say, of itself. There may be for you some technical difficulties, but there must be no difficulties of expression. There may be, perhaps, too, some intentions, some shades, some colors to find; but all this is hard to understand in a piano score, and we shall seek it out together."

A week later, Verdi wrote another letter, in which his thoughts were still more clearly bodied forth:

"You have already received from Ricordi some numbers of 'Falstaff'; you will shortly receive the remainder. I admire study generally, and I admire the study you have bestowed and will bestow upon the personage of *Falstaff*. But take care: in art the predominance of the reflective tendency is a sign of decadence. This means that when art becomes a science the result is something odd (*baroque*) that is neither art nor science. Do well: yes! Do too much: no! You yourselves in France say, 'Seek not noon at fourteen o'clock.' This is right! So do not weary yourself in fitting your voice, but keep to the voice you have. With your great talent as a singing actor, with the accent and pronunciation you possess, the character of *Falstaff*, once learned, will come forth all-created. It is useless to rack your brain and carry on studies to vary the vocal effects, for those studies might be injurious to you."

It may be well to add that M. Maurel took little heed, in some ways, of the composer's advice, which lacked the basis of personal experience; and that the expressiveness of the performance was undeniably heightened by methods that only the comedian and singer's personal judgment could sanction and commend.

"Falstaff" was to be the "song of the swan" of the great operatic composer. He composed, however, in his eighty-sixth year, four pieces of sacred music: an "Ave Maria," a "Stabat Mater," "Laudi alla Vergine," and a "Te Deum,"—works of a sufficiently secular character to bear performance in the concert-room. But the end of a long and glorious career was close at hand. He was in fairly good health when, toward Christmas, 1900, he arrived in Milan. On New Year's day there were gathered about him his warmest friends: the aged prima donna, Teresa Stolz (who was the original heroine of "Don Carlos," "La Forza del Destino," and "Aïda," and who withdrew from public life in 1876), Arrigo Boïto, Giulio Ricordi, and the romantic poet Pascarella, a guest in the same hotel, whose witty conversation afforded the composer much entertainment. Nothing then foreshadowed the last summons. It came on the morning of January 21, when an apoplectic stroke stretched him speechless on his bed. He never rallied. At his bedside were Maria Carrara Verdi (daughter of a cousin, who had accompanied him to Milan), Arrigo Boïto, the two Ricordis, Mme. Stolz, Giuseppe Giacosa, and Carlo Mancini. In the corridors of the hotel scores of journalists stood, day and night, awaiting the hourly bulletins that were transmitted to every part of the world as quickly as received. In the streets crowds were gathered about the newspaper offices, and spoke with bated breath of the impending loss. Throughout Italy the feeling was such as might have preceded a national calamity. Toward midnight on January 26 a change came over the features of the dying man, and his breathing grew more labored;

at a quarter to three on the morning of January 27 he quietly passed away.

In accordance with Verdi's instructions, his obsequies were performed with absolute simplicity. But his dread of ostentation was powerless to prevent the extraordinary demonstration of sorrow and respect that attended the funeral in Milan, and prompted, later on, memorial services in most European capitals. In Paris notably impressive exercises took place at the Sorbonne, under the auspices of the leading Italian residents. Minister Leygues and Academician Larroumet spoke; the barytone Delmas sang the gloomy and powerful "Credo" from "Otello"; the band of the Opera House and that of the Garde Républicaine performed some numbers from Verdi's early operas and the march from "Aïda"; and Clovis Hugues, deputy from the Seine—a singularly unromantic and almost caricatural personage with a high, squeaky voice—read an original poem, whereof the soaring eloquence was in singular contrast with the droll delivery of the orator. Verdi's body was laid beside that of Giuseppa Strepponi, his second wife, in the Cimitero Monumentale in Milan. This, however, will be only its temporary resting-place, the composer having left instructions that, later on, both caskets be placed in the vault of the "House of Rest for Musicians," an asylum founded and richly endowed by him. Some months after Verdi's death, his formal wishes as to the disposal of two large chests, presumably filled with manuscripts, were faithfully carried out. The chests, unopened, were burned to ashes. There will be no posthumous works to reveal early feebleness or, still more saddening, later decay.

Verdi's life was one of extreme plainness and regularity. He married twice, his second wife being Signorina Strepponi, who was the heroine in his first successful opera, "Nabucco." He seldom quitted his native land, "the love of the steeple"—"*l'amore del campanile*," as the Italians put it—being strong to the end. He habitually passed the winter in Genoa and the summer at his splendid country-house not far from Busseto. The estate stands almost in solitude in the center of a vast plain, a church and two or three peasants' houses being the only buildings in proximity to the *maestro's* dwelling. The surroundings are not at all picturesque; the soil is under thorough cultivation, but the well-tilled fields have no charm for the eye, and the long rows of poplars and the shallow brook babbling beside them are totally devoid of pictorial suggestiveness. The visitor comes suddenly upon two weeping-willows, and, beyond, a row of close-planted trees half conceals a simple dwelling from the glance of the passer-by. Beyond the house a fine garden extends down to a small artificial lake. The *maestro* usually wrote in his bedroom, situated on the ground floor and looking out upon the garden. The apartment was furnished with artistic profusion: a magnificent piano, a library, a massive inkstand, numberless sketches, statuettes, vases, and knickknacks courted and repaid inspection. Above the piano was an oil-painting of the aged Barezzi, Verdi's earliest friend and Mæcenas, whose memory he revered.

The composer was an early riser. At Sant' Agata he was stirring at five in the morning. After the habitual cup of black coffee he took a stroll in the garden. Then he rambled through the fields and gave orders to his gardener, previous to visiting the stables and barn-yard. In a couple of hours one stroke upon a bell summoned him to a cup of café-au-lait, partaken of with his wife. At half-past ten the bell sounded again, and this time a more substantial meal, to be followed by a game of billiards or a long walk, was shared. The letter-carrier was due at two o'clock, and, with his appearance, the one hour of excitement of the day was welcomed. What with reading and writing, five o'clock was soon at hand and dinner was served. Then the composer indulged in a ride, and the evening was whiled away in conversation. At ten Verdi set an example of early retirement: he disappeared, and everybody did likewise.

Time and space are lacking for a hasty estimate, even of the active influence, if any, exercised by Verdi's work upon the music of the age. Whether, by dimming the mild light diffused by the gentle strains of Cimarosa and Paisiello, by counteracting what Scudo calls the "debilitating irony" of Ros-

sini's writings, and by swaying the masses through appeals to their senses rather than to their imagination and intellect, he contributed as largely to the development of his art and the bettering of taste as a more skilled and thoughtful musician, endowed

GABRIELLE KRAUSS.
As *Desdemona* at the Théâtre Italien, Paris. Born 1842.

with the same splendid creative power, might have done, is at least doubtful. It is gratifying to note, however, that, despite his easy victories over audiences in a land whose sons wax wildly enthusiastic over a single *cantabile*, and where one mellifluous or stirring theme will save a trivial achievement from oblivion, the story of the last twenty years shows that Verdi did not disregard the ever-widening influence of German thought. If he did not aim at conciliating the disciples of pure Wagnerism, he freed his latest performances from the absurdities that marred many of his earlier productions. From the period in which he wrote "La Forza del Destino," his operas bear no resemblance to the old-time processions of ballads and dance themes. As a creative composer he stands without a rival. No one since Rossini has possessed the gift of melody and natural, unforced tone-color in so eminent a degree; and the feeblest of his operas would enrich for life, as to material, any of the over-ambitious and hard-working (after the fashion of the mosaic-makers of Venice) modern composers of France, Italy, and Germany. As to the future, Verdi's admirers need entertain no apprehensions. Half a century hence the complex civilization of the age may render "Tristan und Isolde" musical food for infants, while the Verdian repertoire will appear as remote as do now the operas of Lulli and Monteverde; but some noble monuments of the Italian composer's matchless powers will surely remain. Even as the sextet from "Lucia" will never be suffered to pass away, the quartet from "Rigoletto" and the "Miserere" from "Il Trovatore" will endure for eons, and stir to the depths the emotions of sentient throngs.

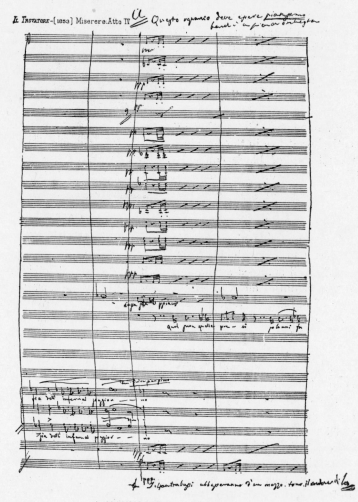

A MANUSCRIPT OF VERDI.

The "Miserere" from "Il Trovatore."

d'après mon portrait
peint par Leyraud, et placé
au plafond de la salle à manger
de l'académie de France à Rome
(X^{bre} 1865)   J. Massenet
Villa Médicis.

AUTOBIOGRAPHICAL NOTES
BY THE COMPOSER MASSENET

YOU are so kind as to write to know what was the beginning of my musical career, and you ask me, "How did I become a musician?" This seems a very natural question, but nevertheless I find it a very awkward one to answer. Should I tell you that, like many of my brothers in art, I had followed my vocation, I might seem slightly conceited; and should I confess that it caused me many a struggle to devote myself entirely to music,

then you might have the right to say, "Why, then, did you become a musician?"

My father was a superior officer under the First Empire. When the Bourbons were restored he sent in his resignation. As he had been a distinguished pupil of the Polytechnic School, he devoted himself to manufactures, and started important iron-works near St. Etienne (Loire). He thus became an iron-master, and was the inventor of those huge hammers which, crushing steel with extraordinary power by a single blow, change bars of metal into sickles and scythes. So it was that I was born to the sound of heavy hammers of brass, as the ancient poet says.

My first steps in my future career were no more melodious. One day, six years later, my family then living in Paris, I found myself

such good effect that within a year I became "lauréat" of the Conservatory. At this period my father's ill health forced us to leave Paris, and so put a stop to my music for several years. I took advantage of this period to finish my literary studies. But the pain of separation from the Conservatory gave me courage enough to beg my parents (whom my

MASSENET IN HIS STUDY.

in front of an old piano, and, either to amuse me or try my talent, my mother gave me my first music-lesson. It was the 24th of February, 1848, a strangely chosen moment, for our lesson was interrupted by the noise of street-firing that lasted for several hours. The revolution had burst forth, and people were killing one another in the streets.

Three years later I had become — or my parents affectionately thought I had become — a clever enough little pianist. I was admitted to the piano classes at the Imperial Conservatory of Music. To my mother I now was "an artist," and even though my education took up six hours of my day, she found time to make me work at my piano to

wish distressed) to permit me to return; and I did not again leave Paris until the day when I departed for Rome with a scholarship from the Académie de France, the "first grand prize" of musical composition (1863).

Did the progress made in these years of work really prove my vocation? I had won the "Prix de Rome," and taken prizes for piano, counterpoint, and fugue. No doubt I was what is called a good pupil, but I was not an artist in the true sense.

To be an artist is to be a poet; to be touched by all the revelations of art and nature; to love, to suffer, — in one word, to live! To produce a work of art does not make an artist. First of all, an artist must be touched by all the manifestations of beauty, must be interpenetrated by them, and know how to enjoy them. How many great painters, how many illustrious musicians, never were *artists* in the deepest meaning of the word!

Oh, those two lovely years in Rome at the dear Villa Medici, the official abiding-place of holders of Institute scholarships — unmatched years, the recollection of which still vibrates in my memory, and even now helps me to stem the flood of discouraging influences!

It was at Rome that I began to live; there it was that, during my happy walks with my comrades, painters or sculptors, and in our talks under the oaks of the Villa Borghese or under the pines of the Villa Pamphili, I felt my first stirrings of admiration for nature and for art. What charming hours we spent in wandering through the museums of Naples and Florence! What tender, thoughtful emotions we felt in the dusky churches of Siena and Assisi! How thoroughly forgotten was Paris, with her theaters and her rushing crowds! Now I had ceased to be merely "a musician"; now I was much more than a musician. This ardor, this healthful fever still sustains me; for we musicians, like poets, must be the interpreters of true emotion. To feel, to make others feel — therein lies the whole secret!

But a few days separated me from the hour in which I had to say good-by to the Villa Medici, to my happy life — a life full of work, full of sweet tranquillity of mind, a life such as I never have lived again.

It was on December 17, 1865, that I had to prepare for my departure; nevertheless, I could not persuade myself to bid adieu to Rome. It was Rome that bade me adieu, and this is how she did it. It was six o'clock in the afternoon. I was alone in my room, standing before the window, looking through the glass at the great city outlined in gray against the light still remaining from a lovely clear sunset. This view is forever imprinted on my memory, and at the time I could not detach myself from it. Alas! little by little a shadow crept over one corner of the sky, spreading and spreading until finally Rome had disappeared altogether. I have never forgotten those moments, and it is in remembering them that I evoke my youth.

I notice that I am saying but little of music, and that I seem to care more for what strikes the eye than for what charms the ear. Let us open together some of my orchestral scores. Thereon I am in the habit of writing the day and the hour, and sometimes an account of events of my life. Some of these have afforded me suggestions for my work. The first part of "Mary Magdalene" begins "At the gates of Magdala, evening." It was in truth of Magdala that I was then thinking; my imagination journeyed to far Judea, but what really moved me was the remembrance of the Roman Campagna, and this remembrance it was that I obeyed. I followed the landscape I had really known; therein was its accent, its exact impression. Afterward, in writing the "Erinnyes," the love that I felt for an exquisite Tanagra terra-cotta dictated to me the dances for the first act of Leconte de Lisle's admirable drama. Later, while I was arranging the score of the "Roi de Lahore," near me was a little Indian box whose dark-blue enamel spotted with bright gold continually drew my eyes to it. All my delight, all my ardor came from gazing at this casket, wherein I saw the whole of India!

Mournful recollections also take up a great part of the life of the musician whose modest beginnings were saluted by firing in the streets. In 1870 — a dismal date for my poor loved country — the Prussian cannons, answering those of Mont Valérien, often lugubriously punctuated the fragments that I tried to write during the short moments of rest that guard duty, marching around Paris, and military exercises on the ramparts left us. There the musician, in the physical weariness of this novel life, vainly trying to find a few moments of forgetfulness, did not altogether abdicate his rights. In the leaves of a finished score, but one which will never be brought before the public, "Méduse," I find annotated the patriotic cries of the people, and the echoes of the "Marseillaise," sung by the regiments as they passed my little house at Fontainebleau on their way to battle. And so in other fragments I can read the bitter thoughts that moved me when, having returned to Paris before it was invested, I was inspired by the woeful times that were upon us during the long winter of that terrible year.

"ROI DE LAHORE."

Drawn by R. D. MacKenzie, after a photograph by Johnston and Hoffmann.

Oh, the unforgettable pain and sorrow of those dismal days when our hearts plunged so quickly from comforting enthusiasm to the darkest despair! — when weeks of uncertainty and of waiting were scarcely brightened by rare letters, received one knew not how or whence, and bringing us news of ancient date concerning the far-off families and the dear friends we no longer hoped to see again! Then came the last effort, the last struggle at Buzenval; the death of my poor friend, the painter Henri Regnault; then the most terrible trial of all, whose shameful reality made us forget cold, hunger, all that we had endured — the armistice, which in our wearied but far from resigned

542

hearts rang the knell of our last and righteous anger! Yes, truly, during those dark days of the siege of Paris it was indeed the image of my dying country that lay bleeding in me, feeble instrument that I was, when, shivering with cold, my eyes blinded with tears, I composed the bars of the "Poëme du Souvenir" for the inspired stanzas written by my friend the great poet Armand Silvestre," "Arise, belovèd, now entombed!" Yes, both as son and musician I felt the image of my poor country imprint itself on my bruised heart in the sweet and touching shape of a wounded muse, and when with the poet I sang, "Tear off thy winding sheet of flowers," I well knew that, though buried, she would come forth from her shroud, with blanched cheeks, indeed, but lovelier and more adorable than ever!

I have already said how dear to me is, and how faithfully true remains, the recollection of my Roman years; and I should like to be able to convince others how useful it is for young musicians to leave Paris, and to live, were it but for a year, in the Villa Medici, among a set of intelligent comrades. Yes, I am thoroughly in favor of this exile,— as it is called by the discontented. I believe in residing there, for such a residence may give birth to poets and artists, and may awaken sentiments that otherwise might remain dormant.

But, you answer, genius cannot be given to any one, and if these young men be merely good students, already masters of their trade, it is not possible to give them the sacred fire they need.

Yes! I believe that being forced to live far away from their Parisian habits is a positive advantage. The long hours of solitude in the Roman Campagna, and those spent in the admirable museums of Florence and Venice, amply compensate for the absence of musical meetings, of orchestral concerts, of theatrical representations,— in short, of music. How few of these young men, before leaving France, ever knew the useful and penetrating charm of living alone in close communion with nature or art! And the day in which art and nature speak to you makes you an artist, an adept; and on that day, with what you have already learned, and with what you should already know, you can create in strong and healthy fashion. How many garnered impressions and emotions will live again in works as yet unwritten!

In order to give more weight to my personal opinions, let me have the pleasure of quoting a fragment of the speech made at one of the last prize-day distributions of the Académie des Beaux-Arts by my whilom comrade at Rome, now my colleague at the Institute of France, the celebrated engraver Chaplain:

During their stay at the Villa Medici, these young artists are far from spending all the treasure of thoughts and impressions which they there amass. What delight, and often what rare good luck, later to find a sketch made from some lovely scene, or an air noted down while traveling through the mountains! On the road from Tivoli to Subiaco, one summer day, a little band of students were on a walking excursion through the beautiful mountains which, like an amphitheater, surround and rise up around Rome. We had halted in order to contemplate at our leisure the wonderful panorama of the Roman Campagna unrolling itself before us. Suddenly, at the foot of the path we had just climbed, a shepherd began to play a sweet, slow air on his pipe, the notes of which faded away, one by one, in the silence of the evening. While listening, I glanced at a musician who made one of the party, curious to read his impressions in his face: he was putting down the shepherd's air in his notebook. Several years later a new work by a young composer was performed at Paris. The air of the shepherd of Subiaco had become the beautiful introduction to "Mary Magdalene."

I have quoted the whole, even the friendly praise given me by my dear comrade of Rome, in justification of my enthusiasm for those blessed years to which, it seems to me, I owe all the good qualities wherewith people are kind enough to credit me.

If I speak to you of Rome, it is because the Villa Medici is unique as a retreat,— is a dream realized. I have certainly been enthusiastic over other countries, and I think that scholars should travel. When I was a scholar, I left Rome during many months. Two or three friends would join forces and start off together. We would go to Venice or down the Adriatic; running over perhaps to Greece; and, on our return, stopping at

Tunis, Messina, and Naples. Finally, with swelling hearts, we would see the walls of Rome; for there, in the Academy of France, was our home. And then, how delightful to go to work in the healthful quiet, in which we could create without anything to preoccupy us — with no worries, no sorrows! What joy to return to "our villa," and to meditate under its evergreen oaks!

The ordinary traveler never can know this repose, because it is to us alone — we scholars of the Institute — that France gives such a shelter. The remembrances of my youth have almost always been my consolation for the years of struggle that have made up my life. But I wish to bring to your great country also my tribute of personal gratitude. It is to a woman of America, to Miss Sibyl Sanderson, the incomparable interpreter of "Esclarmonde," that I owe the impulse to write that lyric drama.

Yes; I acknowledge that until that moment I had been a musician through experience and through the vision. Now I have not only looked, I have listened!

J. Massenet.

DETAIL FROM THE HEMICYCLE OF THE SORBONNE.
Painted by Puvis de Chavannes.

MICHAEL WILLIAM BALFE

AS a composer of popular operas, Balfe is worthy of a place among those who have done work for the musical world, especially for those lovers of music who are most interested in its English development.

Michael William Balfe was born at Dublin, Ireland, May 15, 1808. When he was four years old his family resided at Wexford, and it was here, in the eager pleasure he took in listening to a military band, that Balfe gave the first sign of his musical aptitude. At five years of age he took his first lesson on the violin, and at seven was able to score a polacca composed by himself for a band. His father now sought better instruction for him, and placed him under O'Rourke (afterward known in London as Rooke), who brought him out as a violinist in May, 1816. At ten years old he composed a ballad, afterward sung by Madame Vestris in the comedy of "Paul Pry," under the title of "The Lover's Mistake," and which even now is remarkable for the freshness of its melody, the gift in which he afterward proved so eminent.

When he was sixteen his father died, and left him to his own resources; he accordingly went to London, and gained considerable credit by his performance of violin solos at the so-called oratorios. He was then engaged in the orchestra at Drury Lane, and when the director had to appear on the stage (which was sometimes the case in the important musical pieces), he led the band. At this period he took lessons in composition from C. F. Horn, organist of St. George's Chapel, Windsor, and father of the popular song-writer. In 1825 he met with a patron, the Count Mazzara, whom he accompanied to Italy. At Rome he was located in the house of his patron, and studied counterpoint under Frederici, afterward head of the Conservatorio at Milan. He next went to Milan, and studied singing under Filippo Galli. Here he made his first public essay as a dramatic composer by writing the music to a ballet entitled "La Pérouse," the melody and instrumentation in which created a favorable sensation.

Balfe was now in his twentieth year. Visiting Paris, he was introduced to Rossini, then director of the Italian opera. The maestro was not slow to perceive his talent, and offered him an engagement as principal barytone, on condition that he should take a course of preparatory lessons from Bordogni. He made his first appearance at the close of 1828 in "Figaro," with decided success. At the close of his Paris engagement he returned to Italy, and was welcomed by a new patron, the Count Sampieri of Bologna. In the carnival season of 1829-30 he was principal barytone at Palermo, and here produced his first complete opera, "I Rivali di se stessi," written in the short space of twenty days. This was followed in rapid succession by "Un Avvertimento ai gelosi," produced at Pavia, and "Enrico Quarto" at Milan, where he was engaged to sing with Malibran at La Scala. At Bergamo he met Mlle. Rosen, a German singer, whom he married. He continued to sing on the stage in Italy until the spring of 1835, when he returned to London, and appeared at several public and private concerts.

Balfe's career as a writer of English operas commenced from this year, when he produced his "Siege of Rochelle" at Drury Lane with distinguished success. It was played for more than three months without intermission, and completely established the composer's fame. "The Maid of Artois" came out in the following spring, its success heightened by the exquisite singing of Malibran. "The light of other days" in this opera, in the judgment of one of his biographers, was perhaps the most popular song in England that those days knew. In the autumn of this year Balfe appeared as a singer at Drury Lane. In 1837 he brought out his "Catherine Grey" and "Joan of Arc"—himself singing the part of Theodore; and in the following year "Falstaff" was produced at Her Majesty's Theater, the first Italian opera written for that establishment by an English composer since Arne's "Olympiade." Two months previously "Diadeste" was given at Drury Lane. In 1839 he was much on the boards, playing Farinelli in Barnett's opera of that name at Drury Lane, and in an English version of Ricci's "Scaramuccia" at the Lyceum. In 1840 he entered the field as manager of the Lyceum (the English opera house), and produced his "Keolanthe" for the opening night, with Madame Balfe in the principal character; but with all its merited success the opera did not save the enterprise from an untoward close.

Balfe now migrated to Paris, where his genius was recognized, and Scribe and St. George furnished him with the dramatic poems which inspired him with the charming music of "Le puits d'amour" (performed in London under the title of "Geraldine") and "Les quatre fils d'Aymon" (known as "The Castle of Aymon"), both given at the Opéra Comique. While thus maintaining his position before the most fastidious audience of Europe, Balfe returned to England and produced the most successful of all his works, "The Bohemian Girl" (November 27, 1843). This opera has been translated into almost every European language, and has been as great a favorite on our side of the Atlantic as on his. In 1844 he brought out "The Daughter of St. Mark," and in the following year "The Enchantress"—both at Drury Lane. In 1845 he wrote "L'Etoile de Séville" for the Académie Royale, in the course of the rehearsals of which he was called to London to arrange his engagement as conductor of Her Majesty's Theater, which office he filled to the closing of that establishment in 1852. "The Bondman" came out at Drury Lane in the winter of 1846, Balfe having arrived from Vienna specially for the rehearsals. In December, 1847, he brought out "The Maid of Honour"—the subject of which is the same as Flotow's "Martha"—at Drury Lane. In 1849 he went to Berlin to reproduce some of his operas, when the King offered him the decoration of the Prussian Eagle, which as a British subject he was unable to accept. Between this year and 1852 Balfe had undertaken to conduct a series of National Concerts at Her Majesty's Theater: the plan of these performances was devised with a view to the furtherance of the highest purposes of art, and several important works were produced in the course of the enterprise, which did not, however, meet with success.

At the close of 1852 Balfe visited St. Petersburg with letters of introduction from the Prince of Prussia, and was received with all kinds of distinction. Besides popular demonstrations and imperial favor he realized more money in less time than at any other period. The expedition to Trieste, where his next work, "Pittore e Duca," was given during the carnival, with such success as the failure of his prima donna could permit, brings us to 1856, when, after an absence of four years, he returned to England.

In the year after his return Balfe brought out his daughter Victoire (afterward married to Sir John Champton, and subsequently to the Duke de Frias) as a singer at the Italian opera at the Lyceum; and his next work, "The Rose of Castile," was produced by the English company also at this theater on October 29, 1857. This was succeeded, in 1858, by "La Zingara," the Italian version of "The Bohemian Girl," at Her Majesty's Theater, and by "Satanella" at the

Lyceum. "Satanella" had a long run, and one of the songs, "The power of love," became very popular. His next operas were "Bianca," 1860; "The Puritan's Daughter," 1861; "The Armourer of Nantes" and "Blanche de Nevers" in February and November, 1863.

In December, 1869, the French version of his "Bohemian Girl" was produced at the Théâtre Lyrique of Paris under the title of "La Bohémienne," for which the composer wrote several additional pieces, besides recasting and extending the work into five acts. The success attending this revival procured him the two-fold distinction of being made Chevalier of the Legion of Honor by the Emperor of the French, and Commander of the Order of Carlos III by the Regent of Spain.

In 1864 Balfe retired into the country, became the proprietor of a small landed property in Hertfordshire, called Rowney Abbey, and turned gentleman farmer. Here he amused himself with agriculture and music, making occasional visits to Paris. He had several severe attacks of bronchitis, and suffered much from the loss of a favorite daughter, which much weakened his constitution. In September, 1870, he caught a violent cold, which caused a return of his old complaint, and on October 20 he expired.

"Il Talismano," the Italian version of Balfe's last opera, "The Knight of the Leopard," was produced at Drury Lane on June 11, 1874; and on September 25 in the same year a statue to his memory, by a Belgian artist, M. Mallempre, was placed in the vestibule of Drury Lane, the scene of so many of his triumphs.

Balfe's miscellaneous pieces are numerous, including the operetta of "The Sleeping Queen," performed at the Gallery of Illustration; three cantatas—"Mazeppa," performed in London; and two others composed at Paris and Bologna. Some of his ballads are not likely to be soon forgotten. His characteristics as a composer are summed up by a brother artist, Sir George Alexander Macfarren, in the following words: "Balfe possesses in a high degree the qualifications that make a natural musician, of quickness of ear, readiness of memory, executive facility, almost unlimited and ceaseless fluency of invention, with a felicitous power of producing striking melodies. His great experience added to these has given him the complete command of orchestral resources, and a remarkable rapidity of production. Against these great advantages is balanced the want of conscientiousness, which makes him contented with the first idea that presents itself, regardless of dramatic truth, and considerate of momentary effect rather than artistic excellence; and this it is that, with all his well-merited success with the million, will forever prevent his works from ranking among the classics of the art. On the other hand it must be owned that the volatility and spontaneous character of his music would evaporate through elaboration, either ideal or technical; and that the element which makes it evanescent is that which also makes it popular."

"Balfe's claim to particular notice," says another English critic, "rests less on the intrinsic merits of his works than on their undoubted success; and, most of all, on the fact of his being one of the few composers of British birth whose names are known beyond the limits of their own country."

To these judgments we may add the following observations of a recent American writer: "Balfe lacks depth, serious musical discipline, and individuality; his style is a mixture of English-ballad sentimentality and the Italian manner of the Rossinian period. But his gift of simple melody, his strong comic vein, his facility of writing, his peculiarly English half-spoken, half-sung dialogue, and his feeling for effect have won for him a prominent place among English composers."

FÉLICIEN CÉSAR DAVID

ONE of the most prominent of French composers is David, who was born at Cadenet, Vaucluse, April 13, 1810. His father was an accomplished musical amateur, and it is said that Félicien at the mature age of two evinced his musical taste by shouts of applause at his father's performances on the fiddle. At the age of four the boy was able to catch a tune. Two years later Garnier, first oboe at the Paris Opera, happened to hear the child sing, and strongly advised his mother to cultivate Félicien's talent. Soon afterward the family removed to Aix, where David became a chorister at the cathedral. He is said to have composed hymns, motets, and other works at this early period, and a quartet for strings, written at the age of thirteen, is still preserved.

In 1825 he went to the Jesuit college at Aix to complete his studies. Here he continued his music, and acquired some skill on the violin. He also developed an astonishing memory for music, which enabled him to retain many pieces by Mozart, Haydn, Cherubini, and Lesueur, by heart. When he left the college, at the age of eighteen, want of means compelled him to enter the office of his sister's husband, a lawyer, but he soon afterward accepted the appointment of second conductor at the Aix theater, which he occupied till 1829, when the position of maître de chapelle at the cathedral was offered to him. During the one year he occupied this place he wrote several compositions for the choir of the church; one of these, a "Beatus Vir," afterward excited the admiration of Cherubini.

In 1830 David went to Paris to finish his musical education. He had a small allowance from his uncle, but his wants were moderate and his enthusiasm great. Cherubini received him kindly, and under his auspices David entered the Conservatoire, and studied harmony under Millot. He also took private lessons from Réber, and thus accomplished his course of harmony within six months. He then entered the class of Fétis for counterpoint and fugue. An "Ave verum" composed at this time proves his successful advance. On the withdrawal of his allowance David had to support himself by giving lessons. At the same period he narrowly escaped the conscription.

In 1831 we have to date an important event in the composer's life—his joining the Saint-Simonians. David lived for some time in the kind of convent presided over by the Père Enfantin, and to his music were sung the hymns which preceded and accompanied the religious and domestic occupations of the brethren. When, in 1833, the brotherhood was dissolved, David joined a small group of the dispersed members, who traveled south, and were received with enthusiasm by their coreligionists at Lyons and Marseilles. The music fell to the composer's share, and several of David's choruses were received with great applause.

At Marseilles David embarked for the East, where he remained for several years, at Constantinople, Smyrna, in Egypt, and in the Holy Land. The impressions he received were of lasting influence on his talent. He managed wherever he went to take with him a piano, the gift of an admiring manufacturer at Lyons. Soon after his return, in 1835, he published a collection of "Mélodies orientales" for piano. In spite of the melodious charm and exquisite workmanship of these pieces they met with total neglect, and the disappointed composer left Paris for several years, and lived in the neighborhood of Igny, rarely visiting the capital. Two symphonies, twenty-four quintets for strings, several nonets for wind, and numerous songs belong to this period. One of his symphonies, in F, was in 1838 performed at the Valentino concerts, but without success.

In 1841 David again settled in Paris, and his name began to become more familiar to the public, owing to the rendering of some of his songs by M. Walter, the tenor. But his chief fame is founded on a work of very different import and dimensions—his ode-symphonie "Le désert," in which he embodied the impressions of his life in the East. It was produced December 8, 1844. The form of this composition is difficult to define. Berlioz might have called it a "melologue." It consists of three parts subdivided into several vocal and orchestral movements, each introduced by some lines of descriptive recitation. The subject is the mighty desert itself, with all its gloom and grandeur. On this background is depicted a caravan in various situations, singing a hymn of fanatic devotion to Allah, battling with the simoom, and resting in the evening by the fountain of the oasis.

Whatever one's abstract opinion of programme music may be, one cannot help recognizing in "Le désert" a highly remarkable work of its kind. The vast monotony of the sandy plain, indicated by the reiterated C in the introduction, the opening prayer to

Allah, the "Danse des almées," the chant of the muezzin, founded on a genuine Arabic melody—are rendered with a vividness of descriptive power rarely equaled by much greater musicians. David, indeed, is almost the only composer of his country who can lay claim to genuine local color. His Arabs are Arabs, not Frenchmen in disguise.

"Le désert" was written in three months. It was the product of spontaneous inspiration, and to this its enormous success is mainly ascribable. None of David's subsequent works have approached it in popularity. "Le désert" was followed, in 1846, by "Moïse au Sinaï," an oratorio written in Germany, where David had gone on a concert tour, and where he met with much enthusiasm not unmixed with adverse criticism. "Moïse," originally destined for Vienna, was performed in Paris, its success compared with that of its predecessor being a decided anticlimax. The next work is a second descriptive symphony, "Christophe Colomb" (1847), and its success was anything but brilliant. "L'Eden," a mystery, was first performed at the Opéra in 1848, but failed to attract attention during that stormy political epoch.

His first genuine success since 1844 David achieved with an opéra comique, "La perle du Brésil" (1851). His remaining dramatic works, "La fin du monde," "Herculaneum," "Lalla Roukh," "Le saphir," and "La captive," had varying fortunes, "Lalla Roukh" faring best of all.

David's power as an operatic writer seems to lie more in happy delineation of character than in dramatic force. Hence his greater success with comedy than with tragedy. "Lalla Roukh" particularly is an excellent specimen of felicitous expression, and easy but never trivial melodiousness. Here again his power of rendering musically the national type and the local surroundings of his characters becomes noticeable. This power alone is sufficient to justify the distinguished position he holds. As to his final place in the history of his art it would be premature to give a definite opinion. David died near Paris, August 29, 1876. Since his death several of his works—"Le désert" and "Lalla Roukh" among the number—have been revived with much success. David has had many followers, some of whom have in turn been influential composers in their respective fields.

JACQUES OFFENBACH

THE composer and master of burlesque comic operettas, Jacques Offenbach, was born at Cologne, Germany, June 21, 1819, of a Jewish family, one of the members of which, a chorister in the synagogue of that city, published songs commemorative of the exodus from Egypt, with a German translation, and ancient traditional melodies, in 1838. Offenbach's musical talent displayed itself at a very early age; and his father, a distinguished kapellmeister, taught him until he was thirteen, when he sent him to the Conservatoire of Paris, then under the direction of Cherubini, where he remained until 1837, after which he played the violoncello in the orchestras of different theaters, and finally in that of the comic opera. In 1841 he brought out some of his own compositions, and became known as concert cellist.

At this time the young musician manifested his originality and taste for parody and eccentricities. Thinking, doubtless, that the sound of the violoncello was insufficient in itself, he imitated the violin and other instruments. He imitated the bagpipe so well that he misled his hearers, and excited the enthusiasm of the uneducated class, who formed the majority in the concerts of that time. In 1848 he went to Germany, but returned to Paris in 1850, when he was engaged as leader of the orchestra in the Théâtre Français.

The deplorable state into which the orchestra had fallen was proverbial. Offenbach wished to make this the starting-point of his fortune. He got up the characters, composed pretty little airs, preluded parodies of La Fontaine's "Fables," the publication of which

obtained for him considerable success. The manner in which he made his orchestra execute Gounod's beautiful music for the choruses of "Ulysses" did him great honor. Meanwhile his talent for jesting, drollery, and buffoonery was becoming more and more known in his circle of acquaintances. Artists and writers pressed him to take advantage of it in the music he wrote for theaters. But while he found no difficulty in getting texts, he for a while could find no theater willing to bring out such works as he was desired to write.

Finally, in June, 1855, Offenbach's wishes were fully realized: he had a theater for himself. He obtained a privilege for the Bouffes-Parisiens, which he installed in the Champs-Elysées. The new theater was inaugurated by the performance of "Les deux aveugles." His success was so great that hardly had a year expired when he was obliged to exchange his theater in the Champs-Elysées for the large Salle-Comte in the center of the city.

His "Orphée aux enfers," played for the first time in 1858, is a grotesque and clownish parody, which commences by transforming Orpheus into a master of the violin giving private lessons, and finishes by a vulgar dance. This work obtained immense success. It was given over four hundred times in Paris alone. "Orphée" was in every way advantageous to its authors: it not only drew full houses, but even the honorary favors that government voluntarily bestowed to success, if not always to the beautiful, the good, and the useful. This work served as a sort of signal for the fabrication of pieces of the same stamp; so

Giulia Grisi.

GIULIA GRISI AS DESDEMONA.

FROM A LITHOGRAPH PUBLISHED IN LONDON IN 1836.

DESDEMONA. "Nè più ripeta l'aura
Dé miei lamenti il suon."

that all the French theaters became inundated with them, to the great detriment of good taste, wit, and art. Before long it was perceived that they had entered upon a dangerous path; but the impulse had been too strongly given, and they could not bridle it. Such buffoonery replaces the pleasures of the mind, the ear, and the emotions of the heart, by unhealthy sensations. Many of the melodies, however, are charming: we would willingly acknowledge their artistic merit; but then we cannot forget that they are associated with the grossest scenes.

In "Daphnis et Chlóé" (1860) there are fine melodies; and the same may be said of the operetta "Fortunio." Offenbach, who had the singular idea of competing and offering prizes, made a musical tour through England with his troupe in 1857, and through Germany in 1858. In 1860 he tried a ballet with the opera, but did not succeed.

In 1861 the composer tried "Barkouf" upon the stage of the comic opera; which had the reception it merited in this theater, where it was out of place. The failure of this piece was partly owing to Scribe, the author of the libretto, who had chosen a dog for the hero of the piece. The frequenters of the comic opera, though not very particular in their selections, protested against this novelty.

Offenbach resumed the direction of the theater, which he had given up for a while, and brought out several pieces: one of the most amusing was "Lischen und Fritzchen." The latter, an Alsatian domestic, murders the French language so outrageously that his master turns him out of doors. Just at the moment he is venting his grief in comic complaints, he meets Lischen, also a young Alsatian; and the two speak so extravagant a language that they astonish each other. This little work is filled with pleasing melodies, and is very comical.

"La belle Hélène," a burlesque composition, put upon the stage in 1864, had unparalleled success in France, not particularly creditable to the French taste of the times. Except the introduction, in which is a fine hautboy solo, there is nothing but dance music and drolleries.

"La grande-duchesse de Gérolstein" also attracted a crowd, although the music is less interesting than that of the preceding works of the composer. Such was the infatuation which this piece caused, that at the time of the *Exposition universelle,* in 1867, many of the sovereigns of Europe, who were then in Paris, went to see it.

To do Offenbach justice, it must be said that his talent as cellist was genuine. He was a remarkable virtuoso before he became a composer; he had great facility for composition, as his numerous works prove. Besides, he possessed originality, drollery, and good humor. With such natural gifts, had he set a higher standard he might have produced works that would have placed him in the ranks of the greater masters.

In 1876 Offenbach made an unprofitable tour in America, of which he gave an account in his "Notes d'un musicien en voyage," published in 1877. He died in Paris, October 5, 1880.

A GREEK MURAL TABLET.

Showing the rhythmic and melodic origin of metric motion.

GREAT VOCALISTS

SOME GREAT VOCALISTS OF THE PAST
From Contemporary Prints

GREAT VOCALISTS

CHAPTER I

FROM THE BEGINNINGS OF OPERA TO CATALANI

Early Exponents of Vocal Art—Francesca Cuzzoni—Farinelli
—Catterina Gabrielli—Madeleine Sophie Arnould—Gas-
paro Pacchierotti—Gertrude Elisabeth Mara—Antoinette
Cécile Saint-Huberty—Elizabeth Billington—A List of
Other Noted Artists.

THAT there is ample evidence of the influence of
vocal music among ancient peoples—whether in
religious procession, bardic recital, or dramatic chorus
—is abundantly shown in the historical section of the
present series. There, also, it appears that during the
Middle Ages vocal music continued to play its part in
the life of European nations. It was kept alive largely
in one of two ways—by the services of the Church, or
by the minstrel who appeared under various names
and by whom several more or less distinct phases were
developed. Here and there a name emerges, such as
that of Taillefer, whose martial chant rang forth to
lead the invading host of Normans at the battle of
Senlac; or Wolfram, whose poetic gifts have been
celebrated by Wagner in "Tannhäuser." It is not,
however, until the establishment of opera that a record
of great singers begins sufficiently authentic and detailed to supply material for definite biography.

It was in 1600 at Florence that the first regular public performance of opera was given. The growth of
opera on the Continent and in Great Britain was rapid,
and this soon became the most elaborate and lavish of
all forms of public entertainment. The impetus that
it gave to the development of musical art was great,
and through it most of the historic singers have risen
to eminence. As Italy was the original home of opera
and center of instruction in the art of song, the important vocalists were at first largely of Italian origin.
In France, however, progress was rapid, and a French
school of opera, with its own methods and traditions,
shortly came into being. In Germany and Great
Britain, also, native singers gradually arose. In London the opera soon became extremely popular, and the
choicest talent was secured from abroad by means of
most liberal inducements.

It has seemed best to give, in this opening chapter, a
brief biographical survey of the leading early exponents of the vocal art. The selection of names has
been carefully made from an extensive list, and includes those who played the most distinguished parts
in that stage of musical evolution and to whom testimony and tradition have assigned a peculiar place. The
arrangement is chronological.

In addition to the names that we have here treated

at some length, we have also given a list of a few
others in regard to whom the reader may find full information in musical encyclopedias and other works
of reference. This preliminary chapter is followed by
several others of which each is concerned with one of
the great names identified with opera, from Catalani
to Jenny Lind; and the section is concluded by a chapter devoted to a few artists of more recent times whose
names have already become classic in the annals of
song.

Certain rather definite limits having been set to the
extent of this portion of the work, many well-known
singers have necessarily been omitted. Furthermore,
it has been deemed impossible to accord any space to
operatic favorites of the present, to whom no decisive position can as yet be assigned.

FRANCESCA CUZZONI.—This great contralto was born
at Parma (or, according to others, at Modena) about
1700, received her first instruction from Lanzi, a noted
master, and became one of the most famous singers of
the eighteenth century. She made her début at Venice
with Faustina Bordoni in 1719 in Gasparini's "Lama-
no," being described as "virtuosa di camera" of the
Grand Duchess of Tuscany; and she appeared again,
with Bordoni and Bernacchi, in the "Pentimento Gene-
roso," in the same year and at the same place. After
singing on most of the principal stages of Italy she
went to England. On her first arrival there she married Sandoni, a harpsichord-master and composer of
some eminence. Her first appearance in London was
on January 12, 1722, as Teofane in Handel's "Otho."
Her singing of her first air, a slow one, "Falsa im-
magine," fixed her reputation. A story is told about
this song which illustrates her character as well as
that of Handel. At rehearsal she took a dislike to the
air, and refused to sing it; whereupon Handel seized
her by the waist, and swore he would throw her out
of the window if she persisted. She gave way, and in
that very song achieved one of her greatest triumphs.
Success followed her in "Coriolano," in "Flavio," and
in "Farnace"; and she became a popular favorite.

In the following year she sang in "Vespasiano" and
"Giulio Cesare," and her triumphal career was continued in "Calfurnia," "Tamerlane," and "Artaserse";
and in "Rodelinda" (1725) she created one of her
most successful parts, gaining great reputation by her
tender singing of the song "Ho perduto il caro sposo."
French applause met her in "Dario," "Elpidia,"
"Elisa," "Scipio," and finally "Alessandro" (Handel),

when she first encountered, on the English stage, the redoubtable Bordoni. In this opera her style and that of her rival were skillfully contrasted by the composer; but the contest was the first of a series which did the Italian opera much harm.

In 1727 she created a great effect in the song "Sen vola" ("Admeto"), which displayed her warbling style. Her next part was in "Astyanax." The violence of party feeling had now become so great that, when the admirers of Cuzzoni applauded, those of Bordoni hissed; and vice versa. This culminated during the performance of "Astyanax," when shrill and discordant noises were added to the uproar, in spite of the presence of the Princess Caroline. Lady Pembroke headed the Cuzzonists, and was lampooned in the following epigram:

UPON LADY PEMBROKE'S PROMOTING THE CAT-CALLS OF
FAUSTINA.

Old poets sing that beasts did dance
    Whenever Orpheus play'd,
So to Faustina's charming voice
    Wise Pembroke's asses bray'd.

At the close of the season, the directors, troubled by the endless disputes of the rivals, decided to offer Faustina one guinea a year more than the salary of Cuzzoni. The latter had been persuaded to take a solemn oath that she would not accept less than her enemy, and so found herself unengaged. About this time she yielded to the invitation of Count Kinsky, and went to Vienna. She sang at court with great éclat; but her arrogant demands prevented her from getting an engagement at the theater.

At Venice she next sang at one theater, while Faustina performed at another. In London again, a few years later (1734), she appeared in Porpora's "Ariadne"; and, with Farinelli, Senesino, and Montagnana, in "Artaserse" as Mandane, and also in other operas. Hawkins says that she returned again in 1748, and sang in "Mitridate"; but this is not recorded by Burney, who puts her third visit in 1750, when she had a benefit concert (May 18). The concert was a failure, and she disappeared again. She then passed some time in Holland, where she soon fell into debt, and was thrown into prison. Gradually she paid her debts by occasional performances given by the permission of the governor of the prison, and returned to Bologna, where she was obliged to support herself by making buttons. She died there in poverty in 1770.

It was difficult to decide whether she excelled more in slow or in rapid airs. A "native warble" enabled her to execute divisions with such facility as to conceal their difficulty. So grateful and touching was her natural tone that she rendered pathetic whatever she sang, when she had the opportunity to unfold the whole volume of her voice. Her power of conducting, sustaining, increasing, and diminishing her notes by minute degrees acquired for her, among professors, the credit of being a complete mistress of her art. Her trill was perfect: she had a creative fancy, and a command of tempo rubato. Her high notes were unrivaled in clearness and sweetness, and her intonation was so absolutely true that she seemed incapable of singing out of tune. She had a compass of two octaves, C to C in alt. Her style was unaffected, simple,

and sympathetic. As an actress she was cold, dressed badly, and her figure was short and ungraceful. Yet the fine ladies imitated the costume (brown silk, embroidered with silver) which she wore in "Rodelinda," and it became the rage. There are no good portraits of her; but she figures in several of the caricatures of the time, and notably in Hogarth's "Masquerades and Operas," where she is the singer to whom the Earl of Peterborough is presenting £1000.

CARLO FARINELLI.—The real name of this singer was Broschi. He was born at Naples, January 24, 1705, according to his own statement made to Burney, who saw him at Bologna in 1770. He soon left the care of his father, who taught him the rudiments, to enter the school of Porpora, of whom he was the first and most distinguished pupil. In spite of his explicit statement to Burney, it is not possible that Farinelli could have made his début at Naples in 1720 at the age of fifteen in Metastasio's "Angelica e Medoro"; for the latter did not leave Rome till 1721, and "Angelica e Medoro" was not written before 1722. In that year Farinelli, already famous in Southern Italy under the name of *il ragazzo* (the boy), accompanied Porpora to Rome, and made his first appearance there in "Eomene," composed by his master for the Teatro Aliberti. There was a German trumpet-player at that time in the capital, who excited the admiration of the Romans by his marvelous powers. For this artist Porpora wrote an obbligato part to a song, in which his pupil vied with the instrument in holding and swelling a note of extraordinary length, purity, and volume. Although the virtuoso performed this in a wonderful manner, Farinelli excelled him in the duration, brilliance, and gradual crescendo and diminuendo of the note, while he carried the enthusiasm of the audience to the highest pitch by the novelty and spontaneity of the trills and difficult variations which he introduced into the air.

Having remained under the instruction of Porpora until 1724, Farinelli made his first journey to Vienna in that year. A year later he sang for the first time at Venice in Albinoni's "Didone abbandonata," libretto by Metastasio; and subsequently returned to Naples, where he achieved a triumph in a "dramatic serenade" by Hasse, in which he sang with the celebrated songstress Tesi. In 1726 he appeared in Ciampi's "Ciro" at Milan; and then made his second visit to Rome, where he was anxiously expected. In 1727 he went to Bologna, where he met, for the first time, the famous Bernacchi, the "King of Singers." In a grand duo with Bernacchi, Farinelli poured forth all the beauties of his voice and style without reserve, and executed a number of most difficult passages, which were rewarded with tumultuous applause. Nothing daunted, Bernacchi replied in the same air, repeating every trill, roulade, or cadenza that had been sung by Farinelli. The latter, owning his defeat, entreated his conqueror to give him some instruction, which Bernacchi, with equal generosity, willingly consented to bestow; and thus was perfected the talent of one who has through tradition been ranked as perhaps the most remarkable singer who ever lived.

After a second visit to Vienna, in 1728, Farinelli went several times to Venice, Rome, Naples, Piacenza, and Parma, meeting and vanquishing such formidable rivals as Gizzi, Nicolini, Faustina, and Cuzzoni, and everywhere loaded with riches and honors. In 1731 he visited Vienna for the third time. It was at this point that he modified his style, from one of mere brilliance and bravura, which, like a true pupil of Porpora, he had hitherto practised, to one of pathos and simplicity. This change is said to have been suggested by the Emperor Charles VI. "You have," he said, "hitherto excited only astonishment and admiration, but you have never touched the heart; it would be easy to you to create emotion, if you would but be more simple and more expressive!" Farinelli adopted this admirable counsel, and became the most pathetic, as he was still the most brilliant, of singers.

Returning once more to Italy, he revisited with ever-increasing renown Venice, Rome, Ferrara, Lucca, and Turin. In 1734 he made his first journey to England. He arrived at the moment when the opposition to Handel, supported by the nobles, had established a rival opera, with Porpora for composer, and Senesino, who had quarreled with the great German, for principal singer. The enterprise, however, did not succeed, but made debts to the amount of £19,000. At this juncture Porpora naturally thought of his illustrious pupil, who obeyed the summons, and saved the house. He made his first appearance at the Lincoln's Inn Opera, in "Artaserse," the music of which was chiefly by Riccardo Broschi, his own brother, and Hasse. The favorite airs were "Pallido il sole," set by Hasse and sung by Senesino; "Per questo dolce amplesso," by the same, and "Son qual nave," by Broschi, both the latter being sung by Farinelli. In the last, composed specially for him, the first note was taken with such delicacy, swelled by minute degrees to such an amazing volume, and afterward diminished in the same manner to a mere point, that it was applauded for full five minutes. After this, he set off with such brilliance and rapidity of execution that it was most difficult for the violins of those days to accompany him.

He sang also in "Onorio," "Polifemo," and other operas by Porpora; and excited an enthusiastic admiration among the dilettanti which finally culminated in the famous ejaculation of a lady in one of the boxes (perpetuated by Hogarth in the "Rake's Progress")— "One God and one Farinelli!" His salary was only £1500, yet during the three years (1734-36) which he spent in London, his income was not less than £5000 per annum. On his return to Italy, he built, out of a small part of the sums acquired there, "a very superb mansion, in which he dwelt, choosing to dignify it with the significant appellation of the *English Folly*."

Toward the end of 1736 Farinelli set out for Spain, staying a few months in France by the way; where, in spite of the ignorance and prejudice against foreign singers which then distinguished the French, he achieved a great success. Louis XV gave him his portrait set in diamonds, and 500 louis d'or. Though the singer, who had made engagements in London, intended only a flying visit to Spain, his fortune kept him there nearly twenty-five years. He arrived in Madrid, as he had done in London, at a critical moment. Philip V, a prey to melancholy depression, neglected the affairs of the state, and refused even to preside at the Council. The Queen, hearing of the arrival of Farinelli, determined to try the effect of his voice upon the King. She arranged a concert in the next room to that which the King occupied, and invited the singer to perform there a few tender and pathetic airs. The success of the plan was instantaneous and complete; Philip was first struck, then moved, and finally overcome with pleasure. He sent for the artist, thanked him with effusion, and bade him name his reward. Farinelli, duly prepared, answered that his best reward would be to see the monarch return to the society of his court and to the cares of the state. Philip consented, allowing himself to be shaved for the first time for many weeks, and owed his cure to the powers of the great singer. The Queen, alive to this, succeeded in persuading the latter to remain at a salary of 50,000 francs, and Farinelli thus separated himself from the world of art forever.

He related to Burney that during ten years, until the death of Philip V, he sang four songs to the King every night without change of any kind. Two of these were the "Pallido il sole" and "Per questo dolce amplesso" of Hasse; and the third, a minuet on which he improvised variations. He thus repeated about 3600 times the same things. It is not true that Farinelli was appointed prime minister by Philip; but under Ferdinand VI, the successor of Philip, he enjoyed the position of first favorite, superior to that of any minister. This king was subject to the same infirmity as his father, and was similarly cured by Farinelli, as Saul was by David. His reward this time was the cross of Calatrava (1750), one of the highest orders in Spain. From this moment his power was unbounded, and exceeded that ever obtained by any other singer. Seeing the effect produced on the King by music, he easily persuaded him to establish an Italian opera at Buen-retiro, to which he invited some of the first artists of Italy. He himself was appointed the chief manager. He was also employed frequently in political affairs, and was consulted constantly by the minister La Enseñada.

In all his prosperity, Farinelli ever showed the greatest prudence, modesty, and moderation. Having one day heard an officer in the antechamber complain of the King's neglect of his thirty years' service, while riches were heaped on "a miserable actor," Farinelli begged a commission for the grumbler, observing mildly that he was wrong to tax the King with ingratitude. According to another anecdote, he once requested an embassy for a courtier, when the King asked him if he was not aware that this grandee was a particular enemy of his. "True," replied Farinelli; "but this is how I desire to take my revenge upon him."

Shortly after the accession of Charles III to the throne (1759), Farinelli received orders to leave the kingdom, owing probably to Charles's intention to sign the family pact with France and Naples, to which the singer had ever been opposed. He preserved his salary, but on condition that he should live at Bologna and not at Naples. Once more in Italy, after twenty-five years of exile, Farinelli found none of his friends remaining. Some were dead; others had quitted the country. He passed the twenty remaining years of his life in a splendid palace, a mile from Bologna, contemplating for hours the portraits of Philip V, Elisabeth and Ferdinand. He received the visits of strangers courteously, and showed pleasure in conversing with them about the Spanish court.

When Burney saw him at Bologna in 1771, though he no longer sang, he played on the viol d'amour and harpsichord, and composed for those instruments. He had also a collection of keyed instruments in which he took great delight, especially a piano made at Florence in 1730; and a fine gallery of pictures by Murillo and Ximenes, among which were portraits of his royal patrons, and several of himself, one by his friend Amiconi, representing him with Faustina Bordoni and Metastasio.

Fétis falls into an error in contradicting the story of Farinelli's suggesting to the Padre Martini to write his "History of Music," on the ground that he only returned to Italy in 1761, four years after the appearance of the first volume, and had no previous relations with the learned author. He was in correspondence with him certainly as early as April, 1756, when he writes in answer to a letter of Martini, and, after adverting to the death of Bernacchi, orders twenty-four copies of the "History," bound in red morocco, for presents to the Queen and other notabilities of the court. It is, therefore, quite possible that their correspondence originated even long before this. They remained in the closest intimacy until separated by the decease of Farinelli, July 15, 1782.

Martinelli speaks in glowing terms of this great artist, saying that he had seven or eight notes more than ordinary singers, and these perfectly sonorous, equal, and clear; that he had also much knowledge of music, and was a worthy pupil of Porpora. Mancini, a great master of singing and a fellow-pupil of Bernacchi with Farinelli, speaks of him with yet more enthusiasm. "His voice," he says, "was thought a marvel, because it was so perfect, so powerful, so sonorous, and so rich in its extent, both in the high and the low parts of the register, that its equal has never been heard in our times. He was, moreover, endowed with a creative genius which inspired him with embellishments so new and so astonishing that no one was able to imitate them. The art of taking and keeping the breath, so softly and easily that no one could perceive it, began and died with him. The qualities in which he excelled were the evenness of his voice, the art of swelling its sound, the portamento, the union of the registers, a surprising agility, a graceful and pathetic style, and a shake as admirable as it was rare. There was no branch of the art which he did not carry to the highest pitch of perfection. . . . The successes which he obtained in his youth did not prevent him from continuing to study; and this great artist applied himself with so much perseverance that he contrived to change in some measure his style and to acquire another and superior method, when his name was already famous and his fortune brilliant."

CATTERINA GABRIELLI.—Daughter of Prince Gabrielli's cook, Catterina was born at Rome, November 12, 1730. She became one of the most beautiful, accomplished, and capricious singers that ever lived. When she was fourteen the Prince, walking in his garden, heard her singing a difficult song of Galuppi's, sent for her, and after listening to her performance promised her his protection and a musical education. She was placed first under Garcia, lo Spagnoletto, and

afterward under Porpora. A great success attended her début (1747) as prima donna, at Lucca, in Galuppi's "Sofonisba." Guadagni gave her some valuable instruction in the style in which he himself excelled—the pure and correct cantabile. This she was therefore now enabled to add to her own, which was the perfection of brilliant bravura, with a marvelous power of rapid execution and an exquisitely delicate quality of tone. At other theaters in Italy she met with equal success, singing in 1750, at Naples, in Jommelli's "Didone," after which she went to Vienna. Here she finished her declamatory style under the teaching of Metastasio, and fascinated Francis I, who went to the opera only on her nights. Metastasio is said to have been not indifferent to the charms of this extraordinary singer, still known as la Cochetta or Cochettina, in memory of her origin; but she did not respond. Her capricious treatment of her numerous adorers gave rise to hundreds of stories.

In 1765 she quitted Vienna, laden with wealth, and went to Sicily, where she excited the same furor, and exhibited the same caprices. She was imprisoned by the King because she would not sing her part in the opera above a whisper. During the twelve days of her imprisonment she gave sumptuous entertainments, paid the debts of poor prisoners, and distributed alms in profusion. Each evening she assembled the other inmates of the jail, to whom she sang her favorite songs. The King was obliged to set her free, and her reputation with the public stood higher than ever. In 1768 she went to Russia; where she astonished Catharine II by demanding 5000 ducats as salary, a sum, as the Empress objected, larger than the pay of a field-marshal; to which Gabrielli simply replied, "Then let your field-marshals sing for you"—as Caffarelli once replied in similar circumstances.

She appeared in London in the season of 1775-76. Burney says of her that "she had no indications of low birth in her countenance or deportment, which had all the grace and dignity of a Roman matron." The public was prejudiced against her by the stories current of her caprice; and she remained during only one season. Burney extols the precision and accuracy of her execution and intonation, and the thrilling quality of her voice. She appeared to him "the most intelligent and best-bred virtuosa with whom he had ever conversed, not only on the subject of music, but on every subject concerning which a well-educated female, who had seen the world, might be expected to have information." She sang with Pacchierotti at Venice in 1777, and at Milan in 1780 with Marchesi, with whom she divided the public into two parties. After this, Gabrielli retired to Rome with her sister Francesca, who had followed her everywhere as seconda donna. She died in April, 1796, of a neglected cold.

MADELEINE SOPHIE ARNOULD.—This famous actress and singer, and the original Iphigénie in Gluck's opera of "Iphigénie en Aulide," was born in Paris, February 14, 1744, in the same room in the Rue de Bethisy in which Admiral Coligny was murdered, August 24, 1572. The Princess of Modena, having heard the child sing in the church of Val de Grâce, was so charmed that she recommended her to the royal intendant of music. Against the will of her mother, Sophie became a member of the Chapelle Royale, and was taught comedy by Mlle. Hippolyte Clairon, and singing by Mlle. Tel. Madame de Pompadour on one occasion was so much struck by the young artist that she characteristically said, "With such talents you may become a princess." She made her début on December 15, 1757, and remained on the stage till 1778, the most admired artist of the Paris Opera. In that year she left the boards and retired to private life. Arnould was not less renowned for her wit and power of conversation than for her ability as a singer and actor. A volume of table-talk, called "Arnouldiana," contains a host of her caustic and witty speeches. At her house was long maintained a salon frequented by many persons of prominence. Her fame as an artist rests very largely on her connection with the operas of Gluck. She appeared with great success in the "Orphée" and "Alceste" as well as "Iphigénie." In Gluck's subsequent works her place was taken by a Mlle. Levasseur. Her acting was quite as much admired as her singing, and Gluck's new ideas found in her an able interpreter. She died in 1803.

GASPARO PACCHIEROTTI.—Perhaps this artist was the greatest singer of the second half of the eighteenth century. He was born in 1744 at Fabriano, near Ancona.

Having been prepared for the career of a sopranist, he studied long and carefully before he began, at the age of sixteen, to sing secondary parts at Venice, Vienna, and Milan. Endowed with a vivid imagination, uncommon intelligence, and profound sensibility, but having, on the other hand, a tall and lean figure, and a voice which, though strong in the lowest register and rising easily to the high C, was often uncertain and nasal, Pacchierotti required much determination and strength of character to overcome the defects, and take advantage of the qualities, with which he found himself provided by nature. This he accomplished only by painful and laborious study, retiring to a garret in Venice, where he practised the most difficult exercises which the masters of those days prescribed as necessary to the education of the voice. Success at last crowned his endeavors.

Milan was the last place in which he sang a secondary rôle. Having returned to Venice in 1769, he took the place of Guarducci, primo musico at the San Benedetto, then the chief theater in that city. Successful here, he was immediately invited by the impresario of the opera at Palermo for the season of 1771. On the way thither he visited Naples, where he was informed that the celebrated prima donna De Amicis had protested against the proposition that she should sing with him, "a player of second parts." The Venetian minister, to whom he was recommended, comforted him in this juncture, but only with the humiliating permission to show his powers by singing two pieces, with full orchestra, at the San Carlo, before Lacillo, Piccinni, and Caffarelli, as judges. Here he was brilliantly successful, and was immediately offered his choice between the theaters of Palermo and Naples. He proudly chose the former, where he met the great De Amicis, and had to submit to another ordeal in a duet with her at the first general rehearsal of "Didone." Even De Amicis herself, however, was surprised into sincere and kindly admiration.

This set the seal on Pacchierotti's reputation, and for twenty-five years he delighted the cognoscenti of Europe. He remained for a time in Italy, singing at Parma, Milan, Florence, Forli, and Venice. After this, he sang at Milan in the carnival of 1778, then at Genoa, Lucca, and Turin; but in the autumn of that year he went to London with Bertoni, and made his first appearance there with Bernasconi in the pasticcio "Demofoönte." Great expectations had been formed of him, not only from his continental reputation, but from the account given by Brydone in his "Tour through Sicily and Malta," and from some airs sung "in his manner" by Piozzi, "in a style that excited great ideas of his pathetic powers." These expectations were not disappointed; and Burney's warm but intelligent praise of his beautiful voice, his perfect command of it, the taste and boldness with which he invented new ornaments, the truth and originality of his expression, and his other musicianly qualities, must be read by those who would form an idea of the truly great singer that Pacchierotti was. Lord Mount Edgcumbe also speaks in the highest terms of the talent of Pacchierotti, whom he calls "decidedly the most perfect singer it ever fell to his lot to hear." Though intimately connected with his friend Bertoni, Pacchierotti sang with no less ardor and energy the music of Sacchini and other rival composers.

After a second visit to London Pacchierotti again returned to Italy. He sang at the Tuileries in Paris on his way back again to England from Venice, where Bertoni had written fresh operas for him. Galuppi had died there in 1785, and at his funeral Pacchierotti took part in a requiem. "I sang very devoutly indeed," he wrote to Burney, "to obtain a quiet to his soul." Pacchierotti arrived in London, on his third visit, in 1790, and sang at the Pantheon, and at the festival in Westminster Abbey in 1791. At the opening of the Fenice at Venice in 1792, he took his leave of the stage, after which he settled in Padua. In 1796, however, he was compelled to appear once more to sing before General Bonaparte, who was passing through the city. He sang, but most unwillingly.

At Padua he enjoyed the society and the esteem of all the literati of the city. In a letter to Catalani, which he had intrusted to Dragonetti, who was on the point of escaping from Italy, he lamented the French occupation. Both fugitive and letter were intercepted; and the unlucky Pacchierotti was thrown into prison, where he was detained for a month. Not long before his death he was visited by Rossini, to whom he deplored the depraved modern taste in singing, and the growth of a noisy and rococo style, for which, doubtless, the old singer thought Rossini in great degree to blame. "Give me another Pacchierotti," Rossini replied, "and I shall know how to write for him!"

During his remaining years, Pacchierotti did not cease his daily practice and enjoyment of singing, in private; but mainly devoted himself to Benedetto Marcello's setting of Giustiniani's paraphrase of fifty psalms, "from which," he said, "he had learned the little that he knew." From the midst of this quiet life he departed October 28, 1821. Only a few moments before his death he had repeated, as usual with him, some of Metastasio's sacred verses, in the most pathetic tones; and he died praying "to be admitted to one of the humblest choirs of heaven."

"An anecdote illustrating Pacchierotti's pathos," says Ferris, "is given by the best-informed musical authorities. When Metastasio's 'Artaserse' was given at Rome with the music of Bertoni, Pacchierotti performed the part of Arbaces. In one place a touching song is followed by a short instrumental symphony. When Pacchierotti had finished the air he turned to the orchestra, which remained silent, saying, 'What are you about?' The leader, awakened from a trance, answered with much simplicity in a sobbing voice, 'We are all crying.' Not one of the band had thought of the symphony, but sat with eyes full of tears, gazing at the great singer."

GERTRUDE ELISABETH MARA.—Among great singers Mara presents many interesting characteristics. She was born at Cassel, February 23, 1749. Her mother died soon after the birth of this child, and her father, a poor musician, named Schmeling, is said to have adopted the plan of securing his little daughter in an armchair while he attended to his affairs. From this cause, it appears, she fell into a rickety state, from which it was long ere she recovered, if indeed she ever recovered entirely. Schmeling contrived to increase his income by mending musical instruments, and the little Gertrude one day, when only four years old, got hold of a violin, and began to draw musical sounds from it. For this she was punished by her father; but the temptation was too strong to be resisted, and she seized every opportunity when Schmeling's back was turned of practising on such instruments as she could find. Before long, to his astonishment, he found her playing on a violin, of which she had mastered the scale. Struck with her genius, he gave her a few lessons, and found her so apt a pupil that, not long afterward, he was able to play duets with her before a few amateurs.

By favor of an amateur, Schmeling and his child were enabled to visit the fair at Frankfort, where the little girl's performance excited great wonder. A subscription was set on foot, a better education was given to her, and when she had reached the age of nine her health had improved, and she was able to proceed to Vienna with her father, and there give some concerts. The English ambassador advised Schmeling to take the child to England, advice on which the poor musician, furnished with letters of introduction by the ambassador, gladly acted. He soon obtained for his wonderful child the patronage of many noble and influential persons, including the Queen. The little girl, petted and admired by all the great ladies, was, however, persuaded by them to give up the violin, which they thought an unfeminine instrument, and was encouraged to sing. Her voice was already resonant and clear, but she had, of course, had no instruction. Schmeling, by the help of her protectresses, placed the young Gertrude under the tuition of Paradisi.

Having returned to Cassel, Schmeling found it impossible to get an engagement for his daughter at the court; for the King would not hear of any but Italian singers. Hiller now received her into his music-school at Leipzig, where she remained for five years. In 1771 she came from this academy with a voice remarkable for its extent and beauty, a great knowledge of music, and a brilliant style of singing. She was the first great singer that Germany had produced. Her education had been formed on the music of Hasse, Graun, Benda, Jommelli, Pergolese, Porpora, and Sacchini; but Hasse, with his vocal passages and facile style, was her favorite master. Her voice extended from the middle G to E in alt. She made her début in an opera of Hasse's at Dresden, and was successful. With difficulty, the King, Frederick II, was persuaded to hear her; and, though strongly prejudiced against her on account of her nationality, he was immediately converted by her singing at sight an air of Graun's, and finally engaged her for life to sing at court. Here she profited by the hints of Concialini and Porporino, and perfected her singing of slow and legato airs.

It was at this juncture that, in spite of all advice, and although the King twice refused his consent, she married the violoncellist Mara. She soon discovered her folly, and regretted it when too late. The King allowed her no liberty or indulgence. On one occasion she was actually brought from her bed, by his orders, transmitted through an officer and guard of soldiers, and, though complaining of indisposition, forced to sing at the Opera. She at length succeeded in escaping to Dresden, where she was detained by the Prussian ambassador. Frederick, however, who had lost some front teeth and could no longer play the flute, cared now but little for music, and gave her a tardy permission to cancel her engagement. Mara, free at last, arrived in 1780 at Vienna, where Storace was playing in opera buffa, for which the Emperor had a great liking. To this, however, Mara was not well suited, and she was coldly received. Provided with a letter from the Empress to Marie Antoinette, she passed through Germany, Holland, and Belgium, singing at various places on her way. At Munich Mozart heard her, but was not favorably impressed. He wrote, November 13, 1780, "Mara has not the good fortune to please me. She does too little to be compared to a Bastardella (yet this is her peculiar style), and too much to touch the heart like a Weber [Aloysia], or any judicious singer."

She was again at Vienna in March, 1781, and Mozart mentions her as giving a concert there. She reached Paris in 1782. Here she found the celebrated Todi, and a rivalry immediately sprang up between these two singers, which divided society into factions, as when Handel and Bononcini, or Gluck and Piccinni, were opposed to each other by amateurs incapable of admiring both.

Two years later, in the spring of 1784, Mara made her first appearance in London, where her greatest successes awaited her. She was engaged to sing six nights at the Pantheon. Owing to the general election, she sang to small audiences, and her merits were not recognized until she sang at Westminster Abbey, in the Handel commemoration, when she was heard with delight by nearly 3000 people. She sang in the repeated commemoration in 1785, and in 1786 made her first appearance on the London stage in a serious pasticcio, "Didone abbandonata," the success of which was due entirely to her singing. In March, 1787, Handel's opera of "Giulio Cesare" was revived for a benefit, and Mara played in it the part of Cleopatra, which Cuzzoni had sung in 1724. It was so successful that it was constantly repeated during the season. Mara again took a leading part in the festival in Westminster Abbey in 1787, and she remained connected with the opera in London till 1791, after which, though she sang occasionally on the stage, and even in English ballad operas, she was more frequently heard in concerts and oratorios. For these she was better suited, as she was not a good actress.

In 1788 she was singing in the carnival at Turin, and the following year at Venice. She returned to London in 1790, went to Venice in 1791, and again in the next season to London, where she remained for ten years. After this time, she found her voice losing strength, and she quitted England in 1802, having received a splendid benefit of over £1000 at her farewell concert. She sang without effect at Paris; and then, after passing through Germany, took up her residence at Moscow.

By teaching she acquired a small competence, which was lost to her (1812) in the fire of Moscow, which destroyed the merchant's house in which she had placed it. Forced to begin once more to seek a means of subsistence, when almost sixty-four years old, Mara traveled in Livonia, where she was kindly received, and settled in Revel. She now supported herself again for about four years by teaching, and then formed the strange desire to revisit London, the scene of her former glory. Here she arrived in 1819, according to Fétis, though Lord Mount Edgcumbe puts her visit before the burning of Moscow. In any case, announced in a mysterious manner by Messrs. Knyvett as "a most celebrated singer whom they were not at liberty to name," she appeared at the King's Theater, when it was discovered that not a shred of her voice remained—and it never appeared again. She returned to Livonia, and died at Revel, January 20, 1833, at the age of eighty-four, soon after receiving from Goethe a poem for her birthday, "Sangreich war dein Ehrenweg," dated at Weimar, 1831.

ANTOINETTE CÉCILE SAINT-HUBERTY.—In this group of artists belongs the eminent French operatic actress whose real surname was Clavel. She was born at Toul, about 1756. Her father, who had previously served in the army, became stage manager to a French opera company at Mannheim, and afterward at Warsaw, where she studied for four years with Lemoyne, conductor of the orchestra. Her first public appearance was in an opera of his, "Le Bouquet de Colette." She then went to Berlin, and subsequently for three years sang at Strasburg, as Mlle. Clavel. Thence she went to Paris, and made her début at the Académie in the first performance of Gluck's "Armide" (September 23, 1777).

For a considerable time she played only in subordinate parts. Her appearance was not striking; she was fair, thin, and below middle height, with a face expressive but not beautiful. Her voice was produced badly and with effort, her stage action was spasmodic and exaggerated, and she had a strong German accent. But Gluck found in this ill-trained actress qualities he may vainly have sought for in more finished singers. She appeared one morning at rehearsal in an old black gown in the last stage of patched decrepitude. "Here comes Madame la Ressource," remarked some gay rival (alluding to the character of that name in "Le Joueur"). "Well said," answered Gluck; "that woman will some day be the *resource* of the opera." She

labored to improve herself, and on the retirement of two leading singers succeeded to their parts.

Her first great success was as Angélique in Piccinni's "Roland," and was followed by others in Floquet's "Le seigneur bienfaisant," Gossec's "Thésée" (March 1, 1782), and Edelmann's "Ariane" (September 24, 1782), all tragic rôles. As Rosette in Grétry's "L'embarras des richesses" (November 26, 1782), she showed all the versatility and vivacity necessary for comedy. As Armide (in Sacchini's "Renaud"), in "Didon," "Chimène," "Les Danaïdes," "Alceste," and "Phèdre," she had a succession of triumphs. "Didon," Piccinni's masterpiece, made no impression till she undertook the title rôle, and the composer declared that without her his opera was "without Dido." On her first appearance in that part (January 16, 1784) she was crowned upon the stage.

She was never a perfect vocalist; "less violent and extravagant in her singing than the generality of French singers, but still with too much of the national style," says Lord Mount Edgcumbe, who admits, however, that she was an excellent musician. But her power lay in her extreme sensibility. In truth and force of expression she was unequaled; her declamation was impassioned, her byplay "terrible," her silence "eloquent." Having studied the Greek and Roman statues, she abandoned the hoops and powder previously used in the costume of ancient characters, and adopted appropriate robes.

In 1785 she made a journey to Marseilles, which resembled a royal progress. The excitement she created amounted to frenzy, and when she left Provence she carried away more than a hundred crowns, many of them of great value. But on her return to Paris she found new rivals to dispute her sway. She failed, too, as Clytemnestra, a part altogether unsuited to her. It ended four years later by her marrying the Count d'Entraigues, of strong royalist sympathies, in which she participated warmly. In 1790 he had emigrated to Lausanne, and there their marriage took place, at the end of that year. It was not acknowledged, however, till 1797, after the Count, imprisoned at Milan by Bonaparte, had been released by his wife, who found means of enabling him to escape, and of preserving his portfolio, which was filled with political papers.

The Count afterward entered the Russian diplomatic service, and was employed on secret missions. After the peace of Tilsit, he possessed himself in some manner of a copy of the secret articles of the treaty, and hastened with them to England to communicate them to the government. He established himself, with his wife, at Barnes, near Richmond, where, July 22, 1812, they were assassinated by their servant, who stabbed them as they were getting into their carriage, and blew out his own brains afterward. This man had been bribed by emissaries of Fouché's, sent to watch the proceedings of the Count d'Entraigues, had allowed them to take copies of correspondence with the Foreign Office, intrusted to his care by his master, and had reason to think that his treachery was being discovered.

ELIZABETH BILLINGTON.—This celebrated English singer was the daughter of Carl Weichsel, a native of Freiberg in Saxony, and principal clarinet at the

King's Theater. Her mother was for several years a favorite singer at Vauxhall Gardens, London, and elsewhere. Elizabeth was born in London, probably in 1768. She and her brother Carl were from the earliest possible moment trained to music, and on March 10, 1774, performed on the pianoforte and violin at their mother's benefit concert at the Haymarket Theater. At fourteen years old she appeared as a singer at Oxford, and at sixteen became the wife of James Billington, a double bass player. Immediately after their marriage they went to Dublin, where Mrs. Billington commenced her career as a stage singer in the opera of "Orfeo ed Euridice."

On her return to London she obtained a trial engagement of twelve nights at Covent Garden, where she appeared February 13, 1786, as Rosetta in "Love in a Village." Her success was such that the managers immediately engaged her for the remainder of the season at a large salary. She speedily attained a position at the Concert of Ancient Music, where she disputed with Mara for supremacy. Mrs. Billington remained in England until 1794, when she went with her husband and brother to Italy. At Naples Sir William Hamilton, the English ambassador, induced Mrs. Billington and her brother to perform in private before the King, who immediately prevailed on Mrs. Billington to sing in public at the San Carlo Theater. Accordingly in May, 1794, she made her appearance there in Francesco Bianchi's opera "Inez di Castro," written expressly for her. Her success was complete, but her triumph was suddenly interrupted by the death of her husband. On renewing her performances she met with the most favorable reception, and sang successively in operas composed for her by Paisiello, Paer, and Himmel.

In 1796 she went to Venice, where, being attacked by illness, she performed only once. She and her brother next visited Rome, and all the principal places in Italy. In 1798 she married a M. Felissent, from whom, however, she soon separated. In 1801 she re-

turned to England, and as the managers of Drury Lane and Covent Garden competed for her services it was arranged that she should perform at each house alternately. She accordingly appeared at Covent Garden Theater, October 3, 1801, as Mandane in Arne's "Artaxerxes," still retaining the name of Billington. From this time until 1809, when she retired from public life, her services were in constant request. Once afterward she quitted her retirement to perform at a concert given in Whitehall Chapel on June 28, 1814, in aid of the sufferers by the war in Germany. In 1817 she was reconciled to her husband, and quitted England with him for her estate, situated near Venice, and there she died, August 28, 1818. Mrs. Billington's compass was extensive (three octaves from A to A in altissimo), the upper notes being exquisitely beautiful. She excelled in passages of execution, but her powers of expression were limited. This limitation, however, was compensated by her natural and artistic gifts.

The reader may also be interested in seeking information regarding the following. All will be found treated in Grove's well-known "Dictionary of Music and Musicians."

Francesca Margherita de l'Epine.
Catherine Tofts.
Anastasia Robinson (?-1750).
Margherita Durastanti (c. 1695-?).
Faustina Bordoni Hasse (1700-83).
Lavinia Fenton (Beswick) (?-1760).
Regina Mingotti (1728-1807).
Nicolino Grimaldi, called Nicolini (c. 1673-?).
Giovanni Battista Rubinelli (1753-1829).
Luigi Marchesi (1755-1829).
Girolamo Crescentini (1766-1846).
Josephina Grassini (1773-1850).
Charles Benjamin Incledon (1763-1826).
John Braham (1774-1856).

CHAPTER II

ANGELICA CATALANI

ONE of the first among the queens of song, Catalani presents a figure of striking interest. In her case marvelous vocal powers were allied with personal beauty. She was borne along a tide of success that carried her to fortune and splendor, and yet left her a pure-minded and amiable woman, unspoiled by the world's flatteries, full of charities and good works.

Angelica Catalani was born in October, 1779, at Sinigaglia, near Rome, where her father was a tradesman, and from about her twelfth year was educated

at the convent of Santa Lucia, at Gubbio, to which she had gained admittance through the influence of Cardinal Onorati. At the convent the extreme beauty of her voice attracted great attention, and the abbess, a woman of ability and culture, did all in her power to develop the rare gift. Catalani sang solos in the choir, and the flexibility, compass, and beauty of her voice became famous in the district, attracting large congregations. On fête-days the chapel was thronged by a wondering and delighted crowd, and numbers were unable to obtain admission or to catch a glimpse of *la maravigliosa* Angelica. The pleasure of the congregations frequently expressed itself in applause, and the abbess was at last enjoined by the bishop to discontinue the solos. An ingenious compromise was thereupon effected. The pieces previously given as solos were sung in concert, and the brilliancy of Angelica's soul-moving notes was tempered by the voices of the novices, among a group of whom she was veiled from the eyes of mere secular curiosity. Angelica remained three years at the convent, receiving such musical tuition as it afforded—an imperfect tuition, under which she contracted meretricious tricks of execution, never afterward wholly overcome.

Catalani later received instruction from Marchesi, who was much struck by the phenomenal beauty of her voice, and taught her to control its luxuriance. While pursuing her studies at Florence under this master, she heard a distinguished prima donna at the theater. The skillful execution of the vocalist moved her to tears, and she exclaimed, "Alas! I shall never attain such perfection." Subsequently she was introduced to the artist, who, after hearing her sing, embraced her with great tenderness, saying, "Be assured, my child, in a few years you will surpass me, and it is I who shall weep at your success."

In 1795 Catalani obtained her first engagement. The proprietor of the theater of La Fenice at Venice was in a dilemma. A new opera had been prepared with great care, and arrangements were complete for its production on a magnificent scale, when the prima donna suddenly died. Zamboni, the prompter, suggested to the despairing manager that the young Catalani should have a trial. The suggestion was adopted, and the youthful singer, trembling with emotion, yet sustained by the ardor of genius just kindled to ambition, made her début in the title-rôle of Mayer's opera of "Lodoïska."

Her success was instantaneous; nothing was wanting to insure triumph. Her face and figure constituted a vision of loveliness, and the rare quality of her voice added to these an angelic charm. Such a combination had never before been witnessed, even in Venice. Histrionic power was deficient; but this defect was lost or ignored among so many perfections crowned by such a gift of song. The impression left upon the audience was expressed in loud cries of admiration culminating in the wildest enthusiasm. The critics vied with each other in praise. Catalani's voice, a soprano of the purest quality, embracing a compass of three octaves from G to F, and so powerful that no band could drown it, was described as "full, rich, and magnificent beyond any other voice ever heard," and could only be compared to the tones of musical glasses when magnified to equal volume. Without the experience and training of other artists, and, indeed, being only imperfectly studious of the rules of art, she could ascend at will from the least audible sound to the most magnificent crescendo. This power constituted an original charm which raised her above all minute criticisms, and astonished and delighted her audiences. "One of her favorite ornamental caprices was to imitate the swell and fall of the sound of a bell, making her tones sweep through the air with the most delicious undulations, and showering her graces in wasteful profusion."

In 1798 Catalani, having greatly extended her powers as a vocalist, sang at Leghorn with Crivelli, Marchesi, and Mrs. Billington, and subsequently appeared at La Pergola in Florence. In 1801 she was received with enthusiasm at Milan, where she appeared in Zingarelli's "Clitennestra" and Nasolini's "Baccanali"; thence she proceeded to Florence, Triest, Rome, and Naples, adding to her triumphs at each city. In 1804 she was engaged by the Prince Regent of Portugal for the Italian opera at Lisbon, with Gafforini and Crescentini, at a salary of 24,000 cruzados (about $15,000). It was while at Lisbon that Catalani was introduced to Captain Valabrègue, a handsome young officer of noble family, and attached to the French Embassy. A mutual attachment sprang up. and, in spite of the opposition of Signor Catalani, they were married at Lisbon. Catalani was devoted to her husband, who repaid her by his constancy, and by absorbing his identity in the public character and fame of his wife, whose enormous gains he drew upon without stint, and dissipated at the gambling-table. This failing, it appears, constituted no barrier to her affection and unselfish generosity. An anecdote—related, also, of Barbaja, impresario of La Scala—is told of Valabrègue to the effect that once, when at rehearsal his wife complained that the piano was "too high," he had a carpenter saw six inches off the legs of the instrument.

Having entered into an agreement to appear in London at the King's Theater, Haymarket, Catalani left Lisbon to appear at Madrid and Paris before crossing the Channel. Her concerts at Madrid, under the patronage of the Queen, created a great sensation, and the rush for seats was often the occasion of tumult. She obtained for the best seats as much as four ounces of gold, equal in value to twenty-one guineas, per seat; and for three concerts in Paris she realized 72,000 francs. She sang twice at St. Cloud; and Napoleon, who desired to retain her services for the French capital, summoned her to the Tuileries. The world-conqueror was unusually gracious to the conqueror of hearts; but his manner was still sufficiently awful. When informed that she was about to visit London, he said, "You must remain here. I will pay you well, and your talent will be better appreciated. You shall have 100,000 francs per annum, and two months for *congé*. Come! that is settled. Adieu, madame." The fair songstress, who had hitherto bowed before kings and queens with conscious indifference, trembled in the presence of the Emperor; but she left the palace without acquiescence. Determined to fulfill her London engagement, and being denied a passport, she disguised herself as a nun and took passage for England, where her contract with the proprietors of the King's Theater provided for a salary of £2000, £100 extra for traveling expenses, and a clear benefit.

The London début took place on December 15, 1806. She appeared in "Semiramide," expressly composed for her by Portogallo. She took London by storm; she was caressed, fêted, adored. Her subsequent concerts and operatic engagements throughout the United Kingdom were equally successful.

Exorbitant demands in Catalani's money contracts were all traceable to Valabrègue. On one occasion he named a sum so preposterous that the manager declared it would disable him in the engagement of additional talent for the opera. "Talent!" exclaimed Valabrègue, "have you not Madame Catalani? My wife, with four or five puppets, is quite sufficient." These tactics were tacitly admitted by Catalani, who grew at length to regard them as both wise and desirable. Her operas were one-part operas; the music was hacked and hewed to suit her exact vocal requirements, and subsidiary parts were dispensed with; a few puppets to fill in the tableaus seemed sufficient for her.

Catalani left the King's Theater at the close of the season of 1813—the last of her regular operatic engagement. Having returned to Paris, she obtained the management of the Italian opera there, with a subvention of 160,000 francs. After an unfortunate period, she left Paris at the return of Napoleon (1815) and went on tour, visiting Hamburg, Denmark, and Sweden, and exciting wild enthusiasm in the principal cities. After the Restoration she reappeared in Paris, and resumed the direction of the opera. The system which had temporarily ruined opera in London was established. All expenses were cut down; scenery, orchestra, and chorus were diminished; operas were rearranged and variations by Rode introduced, until little more than the names of the original works remained.

In May, 1816, Catalani went to give concerts in Munich, and thence proceeded to Italy, returning to Paris in August of the following year. In April, 1818, she abandoned opera management and entered upon a concert tour that lasted nearly ten years. In 1824 we find her in London, performing a certain number of nights, but with no regular engagement. We learn from Lord Mount Edgcumbe that "her powers were undiminished, her taste unimproved." An attempt to engage her for the opera stage in London in 1826 was frustrated by the exorbitant terms proposed by Valabrègue. She visited Germany, Italy, Paris once more —singing here without the usual success—Russia, Poland, and North Germany, reappearing in England for the York Festival in 1828. Lord Mount Edgcumbe, who heard her this year at Plymouth, describes her as having "lost, perhaps, a little in voice, but gained more in expression," as "electrifying an audience with her 'Rule Britannia,'" and as "still handsome, though somewhat stout." Eventually Catalani retired to her beautiful villa in the neighborhood of Florence, where she founded a school of singing for young girls. She was attacked by cholera while on a visit in Paris, and died there, June 12, 1849.

She had achieved the supremest heights of popularity, and the honors showered upon her were justly due. The King of Prussia sent her a complimentary autograph letter, and the medal of the Academy. From the Emperor of Austria she received a superb ornament as a token of admiration. By the Emperor and Empress of Austria she was laden with rich presents and high distinctions. The magistracy of Vienna struck a medal in her honor. In England she realized more than £50,000 in a few years.

And while kings, potentates, and peoples rained honors upon her, Catalani remained unspoiled by fortune, preserving to the stage an ideal of pure womanhood in art, and retaining a virginal charm of domestic truth and deep religious simplicity. Her charities were boundless. The amount earned by public concerts for various institutions is estimated at 2,000,000 francs, and her private purse supplied the most exquisite gratification of a noble heart which overbrimmed with benevolence.

Of the great prima donna's style of singing there is much conflict of opinion. Her voice, for clearness and purity, for richness, for height and depth of grandeur and vocal power, was allowed on all sides to be transcendent; but her style, it was said, was artificial, lacking both artistic method and intellectual breadth, and being especially deficient in artistic restraint. To arrive at some degree of sureness on this point, it would be necessary to examine the critical estimates of her contemporaries, the majority of whom agree, in the main, that though she lacked the essential qualifications of the highest artistic expression, the charm of her vocal power was unrivaled. Her singing instinct was true—even equal to her vocal range and power; but her taste was false; and her mind—still limited by imperfect culture—was not equal to her artistic sense and enjoyment.

In an interesting passage, quoted by H. Sutherland Edwards in his "History of the Opera," Jacques Godefroi Ferrari, a pupil of Paisiello, unconsciously suggests this distinction, possibly without being aware of its entire significance. "Her voice," says Ferrari, "was sonorous, powerful, and full of charm and suavity. This organ, of so rare a beauty, might be compared for splendor to the voice of Banti; for expression, to that of Grassini; for sweet energy, to that of Pasta; uniting the delicious flexibility of Sontag to the three registers of Malibran. Madame Catalani had formed her style on that of Pacchierotti, Marchesi, Crescentini; her groups, roulades, triplets, and mordenti were of admirable perfection; her well-articulated execution lost nothing of its purity in the most rapid and most difficult passages. She animated the singers, the chorus, the orchestra even, in the finales and concerted pieces. Her beautiful notes rose above and dominated the ensemble of the voices and instruments; nor could Beethoven, Rossini, or any other musical Lucifer, have covered this divine voice with the tumult of the orchestra. Our vocal virtuosa was not a profound musician; but, guided by what she did know, and by her practised ear, she could learn in a moment the most complicated pieces."

Here the critic hints at a limited musical knowledge on the part of Catalani. But it is clear that her chief defect was in taste and not in knowledge, and in understanding even more than in taste. Castil-Blaze, another authority quoted by Edwards, accentuates this view, with the same unconscious naïveté as Ferrari, and amidst a similar blaze of panegyric.

"Her firm, strong, brilliant, voluminous voice," he says, "was of a most agreeable timbre; it was an admirable soprano of prodigious compass, from *la* to the upper *sol*, marvelous in point of agility, and producing a sensation difficult to describe. *Madame Catalani's manner of singing left something to desire in the noble, broad, sustained style.* Mesdames Grassini and Barilli surpassed her on this point, but with regard to difficulties of execution and *brio*, Madame Catalani could sing out one of her favorite airs and exclaim *Son Regina!* She was there without a rival. I never heard anything like it. She excelled in chromatic passages, ascending and descending, of extreme rapidity. Her execution, marvelous in audacity, made talents of the first order pale before it, and instrumentalists no longer dared figure by her side." Tulou, the flautist, once performed after the great singer and achieved signal success, but the experiment was regarded as a very dangerous one to undertake. We have ventured to italicize the sentence in which the writer, to adopt a colloquialism, unconsciously "gives away" the artist.

Lord Mount Edgcumbe, the severest critic of Catalani's faults of style, also confirms the view here suggested, and his remarks are worth quoting on account of their testimony to the phenomenal powers of the vocalist. "Her voice," he says, "is of a most uncommon quality, and capable of exertions almost supernatural. Her throat seems endued (as has been remarked by medical men) with a power of expansion and muscular motion by no means usual, and when she throws out all her voice to the utmost, it has a volume and strength that are quite surprising, while its agility in divisions, running up and down the scale in semitones, and its compass in jumping over two octaves at once, are equally astonishing. It were to be wished she was less lavish in the display of these wonderful powers, and sought to please more than to surprise; but her taste is vicious, her excessive love of ornament spoiling every simple air, and her great delight (indeed her chief merit) being in songs of a bold and spirited character where much is left to her discretion (or indiscretion) confined by accompaniment, but in which she can indulge in ad libitum passages with a luxuriance and redundancy no other singer ever possessed, or if possessing, ever practised, and which she carries to a fantastical excess. She is fond of singing variations on some known simple air, and latterly has pushed this taste to the very height of absurdity, by singing, even without words, variations composed for the fiddle."

Catalani's knowledge and culture did not embrace the high things of the intellect, and her mental range was limited in the extreme. A lovely creature, endowed with many graces, and gifted beyond measure in one phase of her art, she was the idol of society; but her strange ignorance of general subjects was often the cause of unfriendly remark, and sometimes led her into ludicrous mistakes. Once at the court of Saxe-Weimar she noticed the majestic presence of the illustrious Goethe, and, observing the marked attention paid to him, she inquired who he was. "That, madame, is the celebrated Goethe," was the reply. "Goethe—Goethe?" she asked, with a puzzled air. "On what instrument does he play?" "He is the renowned author of 'The Sorrows of Werther,' madame." "Oh, yes, I remember," she said: then, addressing the great man with abrupt vivacity, added, "Ah, sir, what an admirer I am of 'Werther'!" Goethe, always amenable to feminine charm, bowed profoundly. "I never," she continued, "saw anything so laughable in my life. What a capital farce it is!" "'The Sorrows of Werther' a farce, madame?" the poet murmured icily. "Oh, yes," said Catalani, with a burst of laughter, "never was there anything so exquisitely ridiculous." The great prima donna was innocently referring to a stage burlesque travesty of the famous book. Goethe did not recover himself the whole evening.

CHAPTER III

LUIGI LABLACHE

A GREAT heart in a great body, a great soul in a great voice, such was Luigi Lablache. He was born at Naples, December 6, 1794. His mother was Irish, and his father, Nicolas Lablache, a merchant of Marseilles, had quitted that place in 1791 in consequence of the Revolution. But another revolution, in 1799, overwhelmed him with ruin in his new country, and he died of chagrin. His family was, however, protected by Joseph Bonaparte, and the young Luigi was placed in the Conservatorio della Pietà de' Turchini, afterward called San Sebastiano. Gentilli taught him the elements of music, and Valesi instructed him in singing; while, at the same time, he studied the violin and violoncello under other masters. His progress was not at first remarkable, for he was wanting in applica-tion and regularity; but his aptitude was soon discovered by a singular incident. One day a contrabassist was wanted for the orchestra of San Onofrio. Marcello-Perrino, who taught young Lablache the cello, said to him, "You play the cello very well: you can easily learn the double bass!" The boy had a dislike for that instrument; nevertheless, he got the gamut of the double bass written out for him on a Tuesday, and on the following Friday executed his part with perfect accuracy. There is no doubt, in fact, that had he not been so splendidly endowed as a singer he might have been equally brilliant as a virtuoso on any other instrument that he chose.

The beautiful soprano for which he was renowned was last heard on a memorable occasion. Haydn died in 1809, when Lablache was fifteen years of age. At the performance of Mozart's "Requiem" in honor of the dead master, the young singer sang the soli. So much was he in earnest, when really put to a congenial task, that he overstrained his voice and became perfectly speechless after the performance. Fears were entertained that the loss of voice might be permanent, and indeed the soprano was gone never to return; but in a few months the most magnificent bass took its place.

In speaking of Mozart's "Requiem" it is interesting to note that on a much later occasion Lablache was again a principal performer in it. It was when Beethoven was carried to his last rest. Lablache not only traveled to Vienna for the interment, but defrayed out of his own pocket the expenses of the opera singers, and took a leading part as one of the torch-bearers gathered around the grave of the great master. So freely was this acknowledged that Schubert composed and dedicated to him three songs set to Italian words.

The new vocal development only increased Lablache's desire to go on the stage. No doubt he felt in him the dramatic gifts of which he gave proof in later years. No less than five times did he run away from the Conservatorio, only to be recaptured after a short spell of liberty. He signed an engagement for Salerno, accepting very small compensation, the most tempting feature being the payment of one month's salary in advance. The possession of this turned his head completely; he did not leave Naples until he had gone through all the money, a feat which did not take him more than two days. When he appeared at Salerno with a well-filled portmanteau, the impresario received him kindly, but became very cool when a few days later a director of the Conservatorio turned up to reclaim the truant. Still there were the contents of the portmanteau to recoup the manager for the salary advanced; at least so he fondly imagined, until an inspection proved them to consist of sand. When the number of these withdrawals had reached five, the government thought it necessary to intervene. A law was passed that no theater in the kingdom should engage a pupil of the Conservatorio without special permission, and a penalty sufficiently formidable was imposed. This was effective in returning Lablache to his studies and preventing him from leaving the Conservatorio until his time had expired.

When, in 1812, eighteen years old, he had at last gained that freedom which he had so longed for, he lost no time in devoting himself to the career of his choice. His first engagement was as buffo at the San Carlino Theater at Naples, and his début was in "La Molinara." He further increased his connection with the stage by marrying Teresa Pinotti, the gifted daughter of a clever actor. Though a marriage in which the early age of eighteen represents all the wisdom and experience of the husband cannot be recommended without reserve, his was a happy one. Lablache, naturally indolent and devoid of the quality of application, needed a stimulating influence to force him into study; his wife had sufficient judgment and ambition to see that his talents were wasted as a suburban buffo. In fact, a man of inferior physical resource probably would have been ruined by the strain of two performances per day. Lablache, easy-going

and satisfied with his present position, was not easily prevailed upon to sever his connection with the Carlino; above all, he dreaded the necessary study of good Italian to replace the patois which was all he knew and all he had thus far required. But Teresa was determined, and womanlike, she carried her point by sheer perseverance.

Accordingly the couple left for Sicily, where the husband procured without great trouble the appointment as *primo basso cantante* of the opera at Palermo. He achieved wonders here in the part of Ser Marc-Antonio, and his reception by the public was so gratifying that he made Palermo his home for five years. Gradually his fame spread beyond the confines of the island. The directors of La Scala at Milan heard of his voice, and engaged him without hesitation. His first appearance there was in "La Cenerentola"; his acting and singing were excellent, and more than made up for the faulty pronunciation, which would have damned any inferior performance. But Lablache was not blind to his faults, and soon determined to rectify them. Not unlike Rossini, he acquired in later life that culture which want of opportunity and indolence had prevented him from acquiring during boyhood and youth. Already, in Naples, he had commenced to fill out the lacunæ in his education.

The Milan season established the fame of the singer throughout Europe. Mercadante, at that time at the height of his renown, wrote "Elisa e Claudio" expressly for him. Travel was now the only thing needed to make his reputation universal. Until 1824 his time was divided between Milan, Turin, and Venice; then he crossed the Alps and appeared in Vienna, where he soon became a prime favorite. A medal with a flattering inscription still bears testimony to the enthusiasm of the excitable Viennese. From Vienna he returned to Naples, the birthplace he had left twelve years before, and which he now reëntered as first singer to Ferdinand I, with an engagement at the San Carlo. For a number of years he devoted himself to that theater, alternating his engagement with frequent tours through Italy, but not going beyond the boundary of that country.

English and French impresarios tried in vain to secure him for their theaters. It was not until 1830 that he appeared in Paris and London, where he was received with the greatest admiration. His triumphs were not limited to his voice; wherever he appeared there were enthusiastic and sincere admirers of his talent for the stage, his striking appearance, and his social successes as a finished man of the world. There were, indeed, competent critics who doubted whether he was greater as a singer or as an actor. His head and features were imposing, his figure tall enough to set off his bulk. A critic writes: "One of his boots would have made a portmanteau, one could have clad a child in one of his gloves." His strength was truly Herculean; as Leporello he used to carry off under his arm Masetto, represented by a fairly powerful man. On one occasion he was seen lifting a heavy contrabass from the orchestra on to the stage by one hand, and replacing it without an effort. To all these accomplishments must be added a perfect balance of temper and a probity and broad-mindedness not generally met with. His repertoire was exceedingly large, ranging from low comedy to high drama and tragedy. It was considered an undecided point whether he was better as Géronimo in "Il Matrimonio segreto" and the Podesta in "La Gazza ladra," or in the serious parts he took in "Norma" and "Semiramide." Critics united in considering his conception of the rollicking part of Leporello unique and unrivaled, while, at the same time, he had great success in the title-rôle of "Don Giovanni."

In 1833 Lablache paid one last professional visit to Naples, and received the unbounded applause of his countrymen as Dulcamara in "L'Elisire d'amore," and in "Don Pasquale." From that year he divided his time between London and Paris, appearing also in some of the oratorio performances for which the English provincial towns are celebrated. His kindly disposition was ever exerted on behalf of his brethren in the theatrical profession. "Lablache acts toward me as a father," said Jenny Lind to Queen Victoria. At the English court he was *persona gratissima*. Both the Queen and the Prince Consort distinguished him, and toward the former and some of her children he acted for a time as teacher.

In 1852 he accepted an engagement for the season at St. Petersburg, and created the greatest possible sensation, but this was his last regular connection with the stage. Feeling, perhaps, that his health was giving way, he retired to his beautiful country-seat, Maisons-Laffitte, near Paris, and henceforth limited his musical activity to a few lessons and an occasional reappearance on the boards. He never composed.

At Maisons-Laffitte he passed some of the happiest moments of his life. Though his health was giving way, he felt no suspicion that his days were numbered, until 1856, when grave disorders in his system commenced to preoccupy his mind. At Kissingen, the watering-place recommended by his physicians, he met one of his old admirers, the Emperor Alexander II of Russia, who treated him in the most friendly manner. An appointment as court singer, and a Russian decoration, may have gladdened his heart for the moment, though he felt that he could not hold them for long. "It will be an ornament for my burial," was the remark he made to the Emperor in regard to the order.

He returned to his French country-seat only to find that his apprehensions were well founded. Even the mild air of August struck chilly on his constitution. A move to Posilipo, and afterward to Naples, afforded only temporary relief. He asked and obtained the solace of religion administered by an old comrade who had exchanged the stage for a convent of Dominicans. On January 23, 1858, the celebrated singer passed away. He lies buried at Maisons-Laffitte, whither his body was removed in accordance with the terms of his will.

Tradition teems with charming anecdotes of the wit, genius, and generosity of Lablache; and here let us relate a touching instance told by one who was a witness of the great singer's quixotic act of kindness. One night while taking his accustomed walk of exercise after the opera, enjoying his solitary cigar and cogitations, he came suddenly upon a ragged street singer, trolling out his miserable song and disturbing the harmony of the peaceful moonlight night. Lablache, impatient of so rude an interruption to his thoughts, and disgusted by the efforts of the desecrator of music, strode up to the beggar in order to bid him cease his mournful attempts at song. A glance revealed to him that the singer was old, decrepit, and trembling with exhaustion. In a moment the ill humor of Lablache changed to pity, and addressing the man, who was evidently frightened by the formidable size of his interlocutor, he very gently said: "Why do you make such a noise, my friend? what can I do to help you?"

"Nothing, monsieur," answered the man with a sad attempt at dignity. "I don't beg; I sing for the few sous thrown by those who care to listen."

"Oh! ho!" exclaimed Lablache with assumed irony, "then, since you succeed so badly, let me assist you!"

Whereupon the great singer lifted up his voice in a strain so grand and sweet that the poor old man would have fallen at his feet in the ecstasy of his surprise and joy had not Lablache supported him. But others heard him and came trooping from café and restaurant, lured by the rich and glorious tones. "Lablache, 'tis Lablache," whispered the crowd as they gathered round. One, two, and three chansons followed, and then the great singer, seizing the tattered hat of the old man, passed it round. Gold and silver glittered in the moonlight as they fell into that shabby hat, a fortune for the miserable votary of music, whom Lablache placed in a comfortable home with the proceeds of those few moments of perfect song. The next day all Paris knew of this latest act of benevolence of their idol, and very proud indeed were the witnesses to retail their participation in that midnight romance of the boulevards.

Rossini, who loved him with an affection as deep as it was sincere, was very fond of telling the following story of Lablache's humor. A provincial rang his bell one day by mistake. Lablache by some chance opened the door himself. "I wish to see Tom Thumb," said the visitor in some trepidation. "I am he!" exclaimed Lablache in deep overpowering tones. "You!" gasped the other; "but they told me he was a very little fellow." "Oh! that is when I perform in public," replied Lablache with an air of surprise and sincerity, "but when I get home to my own rooms I let myself out and enjoy myself." It seems that General Tom Thumb, who was then appearing in vaudeville, was really quartered under the same roof with Lablache, which gave point to the humor of the situation.

CHAPTER IV

GIOVANNI BATTISTA RUBINI

RUBINI divides the palm with Mario. In many respects it is difficult to decide how much of the palm should be given to either, or whether it should be equally divided. The weight of sympathy is doubtless on the side of Rubini, whose splendid powers were unrivaled in delicacy of expression, and whose florid execution—a phrase wofully abused by charlatans and pretenders—was a perfect wilderness of sweets. His name, too, is inalienably associated with the fame of Bellini and Donizetti, composers whose genius his voice touched into expression, and whose fame he extended among their contemporaries.

Giovanni Battista Rubini was born at Romano, near Bergamo, April 7, 1795. His father, from whom he learned the rudiments of his art, was a poor musical professor. The infancy of Rubini was chequered by poverty and family straits, but not uncheered by music; for the child had within him a gift of song that expressed itself with spontaneous enthusiasm after the manner of birds. When only eight years of age he sang in the church choir, and played a violin in the orchestra. Don Santo, priest and organist at Adro, to whom at this period the child was committed for instruction, declared that he had no talent for singing, and sent him home again. Poor Don Santo—sole depositary of the musical wisdom of that small world—much he knew about it!

At the age of twelve Rubini appeared in a woman's part at the theater of Romano with considerable success. At the conclusion of his part of the performance he sat at the front door of the theater with a plate before him to receive his reward from the public. So it appears that he was not in the regular salary list. Shortly afterward we find him at the Bergamo theater, playing the violin in the orchestra between the acts of comedies, and singing in the opera chorus. At a pinch he served the manager well by singing in a drama a cavatina by Lamberti; the vocalist was enthusiastically applauded by the audience, and received an extra five-franc piece from the management. Rubini always remembered this event with pleasure, and in his prosperous days often sang the old cavatina for his friends.

In his nineteenth year, after various vicissitudes in a troupe of wandering singers—he danced in a ballet at Piedmont, and so badly that he was hissed—he obtained an engagement as tenor at Pavia at a very small salary. But the young artist was cheerful and courageous, happy to have found employment, ready to profit by every opportunity, and eager to commend himself to the management, which, somehow, did not set a high value upon his services. Rubini himself could not have foreseen the triumphs that waited upon his future song, the crowds wild with adulation, the deference of potentates, the jeweled loveliness of the civilized world, careful of the smiles of the awkward,

commonplace, pockmarked tenor, with a voice of gold, a mouth cradle-kissed by all the bees of melody. When singing and acting on a pittance, tossed by wayward Fortune from pillar to post, how should he dare to dream of that future of fabulous sums, of a palatial residence in beloved Bergamo, of a princely revenue in England and France, of $100,000 a year in St. Petersburg!

Rubini sang at the carnival at Brescia; shortly afterward at the San Mosè Theater at Venice, then at Naples with Pellegrini and Nozzari, in two operas written by Fioravanti for Barbaja, the famous impresario. His success was undoubted. The public recognized his great merits as a singer, and the resonance and beauty of his voice were acclaimed on all sides. It was the beginning of fame. Still Barbaja consented to retain his services only on a reduced salary. Rubini accepted the situation with all its hardships, including the galling reduction of salary, for the sake of being near Nozzari, from whom he was taking lessons.

Even Barbaja, not slow to recognize artistic merit that paid well, was soon to acknowledge the value of the new tenor. Of Barbaja many humorous anecdotes are told. Once, after Rubini had attained to great fame, the impresario was complacently regarding the tenor from a box in the theater of La Scala, when some wags in the auditorium, bent upon astonishing the manager, set up a discordant hiss. It was one of Rubini's most successful parts, and the singer looked up in confused amazement. Barbaja leaned out of his box in a towering rage, and, shaking his fist at the hissers, caused general consternation by shouting: "Bravo, Rubini! never mind those pigs. It is I who pay you, and I am delighted with your singing."

In 1819 Rubini was married to Mlle. Chomel, known at Naples as La Comelli, a singer of reputation, and pupil of the Paris Conservatoire. The marriage appears to have been a very happy one. Rubini had a simple, kindly nature, pleased with success but not dazzled into moral blindness by it, and his head was never turned by flattery or good fortune.

Rubini, having made vast strides as a singer in all the Italian cities, now looked toward Paris. He made his début in the French capital, October 6, 1825, in "La Cenerentola," which was followed by "Otello" and "La Donna del Lago." His triumph was complete. Paris was taken by storm; Rubini was hailed as the "king of tenors." His glorious voice, his brilliant execution, his power in dramatic vocalization, his thrilling pathos, were declared to exceed all the best traditions of the lyric stage. He united the power of expressing deep tragic feeling to the most melting tenderness. *"Qu'il avait des larmes dans la voix!"* (What tears are in his voice!) said one of his critics. From this time forward his artistic career was one continuous triumph. Barbaja, having now no doubt of his value, insisted upon his return at the end of six months to fulfill his engagement at Naples, Milan, and Vienna.

Rossini's music, in which Rubini made his first appeal to fame, was soon to be displaced by the new school of opera which the singer himself helped to create. Bellini and Donizetti both wrote operas under the direct influence of Rubini, and the former composer got Rubini to sing over the airs of "Il Pirata" and "I Puritani" during the composition of these operas. Donizetti also wrote the tenor parts of his later operas with an eye to Rubini. "Every one," says H. Sutherland Edwards, "who is acquainted with 'Anna Bolena' will understand how much Rubini's mode of singing the airs, 'Ogni terra,' etc., and 'Vive tu,' must have contributed to the immense favor with which it was received." The succession of operas after "Anna Bolena"—"Lucia," "Lucrezia," "Marino Faliero," etc.—all evince the dependence upon each other of artist and composer.

The influence of Bellini upon the style of Rubini was salutary. It helped to moderate his love of ornamentation, and induced a juster conception of the value of simple and chaste expression in singing. It showed him that force and animation were weakened rather than enhanced by too much decoration; and that true art gained strength and massive grandeur from simplicity. Rubini's voice was a revelation to the composer, who lost no opportunity of convincing the artist that its singular purity, freedom, and majesty were best displayed in passages expressing simple dignity and pathos. Although he had carried the art of florid execution to the highest degree of perfection, his real forte lay in the expression of the gems of melody, abounding in the touches which reach the heart and overbrim the eyes. To this end Bellini wrote the tender, moving strains of the tenor parts originally intrusted to Rubini, and prevailed upon him to abandon the falsetto voice, which, although he employed it with the greatest tact and delicacy, would not be tolerated in our day even from a Rubini. Rubini's voice extended from E of the bass to B of the treble clef, and commanded a falsetto register as high as F and G above. Simple emotion, expressed with the vocal power of a great singer, afforded a golden key to the sympathies of the audience—this was the principle applied by Bellini and adopted by Rubini. As illustrating their spirit of coöperation, more than one pleasant record might be cited. Edwards tells us that when Bellini was putting the finishing touches to the part of Arturo in "I Puritani," Rubini (singing the music as it had just been written down by the composer) inadvertently displaced a D flat by an F natural, which both surprised and pleased Bellini, who accepted it as an emendation, saying, "If he can sing it, he may as well have it." In Rossini's music Rubini had climbed to a high position in the artistic world; but it was really as an exponent of the school of Bellini and Donizetti, and especially in the enunciation of the principles laid down by Bellini, that he won his great fame as a singer.

After the conclusion of his engagement with Barbaja, Rubini appeared in London in 1831. His contracts had allowed him only a moiety of his earnings, which he now received in full to his own account. He was in a position of positive affluence, with prospects that placed the scantily remunerated engagement at Pavia, seventeen years before, in the dimmest shade of the backward vista of a dream. Not long previously Rubini and his wife had been offered engagements at a joint salary of $30,000 a year; now these figures were more than doubled. Rubini, blest with simple tastes, and having no delight in mere extravagance, did not squander his money. He lived much in society, with hearty enjoyment of the good things of life; but he laid by a great fortune. A clinging to old ties and associations ever remained with him. He never forgot that he was once a poor chorister, and when a dismissed member of the chorus besought his intervention with an obdurate manager, he signed his plea for the defaulter, "Rubini, *ancien choriste.*" In a like spirit he purchased a property and residence at his birthplace, where he spent his last days. The years from 1831 to 1843 were divided between Paris and London. Rubini was the lion of the greatest two capitals in the world. He sang in operas, concerts, festivals, and created a furor wherever he appeared. A history of his triumphs would fill a volume.

It is remarkable that during the most eventful years of his life the great tenor sang with undiminished force and attained the zenith of his fame with a broken clavicle. The story of the accident was told by Castil-Blaze in the "Revue de Paris," and is thus condensed by Edwards: "Pacini's 'Talismano' had just been produced with great success at La Scala. Rubini made his entry in this opera with an accompanied recitative, which the public always applauded enthusiastically. One phrase in particular, which the singer commenced by attacking the high B flat without preparation, and holding it for a considerable period, excited their admiration to the highest point. Since Farinelli's celebrated trumpet song no one note had ever attained such a success as this wonderful B flat of Rubini's. The public of Milan went in crowds to hear it, and having heard it, never failed to encore it. *'Un' altra volta!'* resounded through the house almost before the magic note itself had ceased to ring." The theater was thronged for the eighth performance of "Il Talismano." "The orchestra," says Edwards, "executed the brief prelude which announced the entrance of the tenor. Rubini appeared, raised his eyes to heaven, extended his arms, planted himself firmly on his calves, inflated his breast, opened his mouth, and sought, by the usual means, to pronounce the wished-for B flat. But no B flat would come. *Os habet, et non clamabit.* Rubini was dumb; the public did their best to encourage the disconsolate singer, applauded him, cheered him, and gave him courage to attack the unhappy B flat a second time. On this occasion Rubini was victorious. Determined to catch the fugitive note, which for a moment had escaped him, the singer brought all the force of his immense lungs into play, struck the B flat, and threw it out among the audience with a vigor which surprised and delighted them. In the meanwhile, the tenor was by no means equally pleased with the triumph he had just gained. He felt that in exerting himself to the utmost he had injured himself in a manner which might prove very serious. Something in the mechanism of his voice had given way. He had felt the fracture at the time. He had,

indeed, conquered the B flat, but at what an expense!
—that of a broken clavicle."

However, Rubini continued his scene. He was
wounded but triumphant, and in his artistic elation he
forgot the positive physical injury he had sustained.
On leaving the stage, he sent for the surgeon of the
theater, who, by inspecting and feeling Rubini's clavicle, convinced himself that it was indeed fractured.
The bone had been unable to resist the tension of the
singer's lungs. Rubini may have been said to have
swelled his voice until it burst one of its natural
barriers.

"It seems to me," said the wounded tenor, "that a
man can go on singing with a broken clavicle." "Certainly," replied the doctor, "you have just proved it."
"How long will it take to mend it?" he inquired. "Two
months, if you remain perfectly quiet during the whole
time." "Two months! And I have only sung seven
times. I should have to give up my engagement. Can
a person live comfortably with a broken clavicle?"
"Very comfortably indeed. If you take care not to lift
any weight you will experience no disagreeable effects."
"Oh! there is my cue," exclaimed Rubini; "I shall go
on singing."

"Rubini went on singing," says Castil-Blaze, "and
I do not think any one who heard him in 1831 could
tell that he was listening to a wounded singer—wounded gloriously on the field of battle. As a musical doctor, I was allowed to touch the wound, and I remarked
on the left side of the clavicle a solution of continuity,
three or four lines (that is to say, a quarter or a third
part of an inch) in extent between the two parts of the
fractured bone. I related the adventure in the 'Revue
de Paris,' and three hundred persons went to Rubini's
house to touch the wound and verify my statement."

Rubini was idolized in Paris and London, and, indeed, in all the first capitals of Europe. He was the
darling of society, and his popularity never diminished
during his lifetime. The public adored the great singer,
and great nobles and mighty potentates paid him
marked attention. In 1842, at the conclusion of a concert at Wiesbaden, Prince Metternich invited him to
the château, where on the following day he met a distinguished company. After dinner Rubini sang two
of his favorite songs unsolicited. The delighted prince,
famous for his rare and costly wines, gave him a
basket of his Johannisberg—the choicest selection of
that vintage in the world—at the same time offering
him the freedom of the château, and instructing the
servant to receive Rubini at all times as if he were its
master. With princely courtesy and generosity the
stately mansion with all its magnificent appointments
was placed absolutely at the disposal of the great
tenor. It was the Prince of Courtesy's fitting *devoir*
to the King of Song. "And the cellar also?" asked
Rubini, with slyly amiable vivacity. "The cellar also,"
replied the Prince gaily: "the cellar at discretion."

In 1843, accompanied by Liszt, Rubini undertook a
tour through Holland and Germany. They separated
at Berlin, and Rubini proceeded alone to St. Petersburg, where he was received with great *éclat*, and his
singing created the wildest enthusiasm. His first concert realized 50,000 francs. The Czar Nicholas con-
ferred upon him the rank of colonel, and appointed him
director of singing in the Russian dominions. His

artistic career may be said to have terminated in Russia. After a return visit to Italy in the summer, with
a call, *en passant,* at Vienna, he reappeared at St.
Petersburg in 1844. The climate at length seriously
affected his health, and permanently injured his voice.
He retired to his estate at Romano, where he died.
March 3, 1854.

There can be no doubt of the high merit of Rubini.
He was a great singer of the highest order, and thoroughly deserved the fame he enjoyed during his lifetime. It was expected by the partisans of Mario that
the latter would eclipse Rubini at the very outset of
his career. But Mario, ever confident, and relying
wholly on the quality of his voice, had the mortification
of exciting an unflattering comparison in the minds
of his first audience. "Rubini!" they shouted with a
deafening clamor of disapproval—"*Pas d'amateurs—
Rubini—pas d'amateurs!*" Rubini was a master of
style, knew every vibration of his tones, and had
learned the utmost command of his fine organ by intense study. Though he never became a finished actor, the care he bestowed upon perfecting the quality
and adaptability of his voice was unrivaled; and in
this respect, if in no other, Mario was greatly his
inferior. "Mario," says Louis Engel, "cannot be said
to be the greatest tenor of the century, because his
wonderful gifts were not developed by persevering
study like the equally wonderful voice of Rubini, who
surpassed in this respect every singer before or after
him." And again: "The intense persevering studies
of Rubini and Lablache, the greatest singers of their
age, were never made by Mario, who at first was only
an amateur." Rubini paid no attention to declamation, and in concerted pieces nearly always remained
silent, reserving himself for supreme efforts, when
the effects produced on his audiences were almost
magical. Chorley, whose testimony is always valuable,
notes his defects as an artist. "He would walk through
the third of an opera languidly," he says, "giving the
notes correctly and little more—in a duet blending
his voice intimately with that of his partner (in this he
was unsurpassed); but when his own moment arrived
there was no longer coldness or hesitation, but a passion, a fervor, a putting forth to the utmost of every
resource of consummate vocal art and emotion, which
converted the most incredulous, and satisfied those till
then inclined to treat him as one whose reputation had
been overrated."

He is charged with too much indulgence in head
notes; "but," says Escudier, "so perfect is his art that
the transition from one register to the other is imper-
ceptible to the hearer. . . . Gifted with immense
lungs, he can so control his breath as never to expend
more of it than is absolutely necessary for producing
the exact degree of sound he wishes. So adroitly does
he conceal the artifice of respiration that it is impossible to discover *when* his breath renews itself, inspiration and expiration being apparently simultaneous, as
if one were to fill a cup with one hand while emptying
it with the other. In this manner he can deliver the
longest and most drawn out phrases without any solution of continuity."

Rubini's figure was short and awkward, and his
features were seamed and scarred by smallpox; but
these disadvantages were counterbalanced by his

agreeable smile, the intelligence and brightness of his expression, and the amiability of his manner. He never excelled as an actor; indeed rarely tried to act at all—a disposition hardly conceivable of one who had been associated in art with the incomparable Pasta and the brilliant Grisi, who belonged to the age of Malibran and Lind and Mario. Grisi is said to have made an actor of Mario; and it is difficult to imagine Rubini playing Ægeus to the Medea of Pasta without catching inspiration from that truly great actress, who woke admiration and envy in the breast of the aged Siddons. A French critic remarked: "He did not trouble himself much about anything but the particular scene which placed him in the foreground. When this was past, he retired, without caring much for the story of the drama, or the conduct of the other performers. In the air, the duet, or the finale, in which he had a preponderating part, Rubini would suddenly rouse himself and display all the energy and charm of his incomparable talent. It was in the tone and sonorousness of his organ, in the artistic management of his voice, that all Rubini's dramatic power consisted."

Such a talent is excellent in oratorio, or on the concert platform, where its limitation is in due order and propriety. On the lyric stage, however, it is a reproach to find it unaccompanied by the histrionic arts which add to the grace, strength, and triumph of the situation. Without these the singer—as in the case of the great Catalani—is liable to the charge of commanding attention merely in the capacity of a musical instrument with finer lights and shadows—of being *vox et præterea nihil*. And if Rubini escaped the imputation, it was because he sang like one inspired, adding to the splendor of his voice, with its Orphic sweetness and entrancing majesty, the feeling of a true artistic nature, a just conception of ideal and dramatic qualities, a charm of energy, of reposeful peace, and a massive intellectual power, such as he was denied the ability of imparting to stage action and gesture. Whatever his defects may have been, he is among the greatest true singers of the world.

CHAPTER V

GIUDITTA PASTA

GIUDITTA NEGRI, a Jewess, was born in 1798; according to some at Saronno, near Milan, to others at Como. Her first publicity as a vocalist of eminence was attained after her marriage to Signor Pasta, a tenor, which took place about the year 1816. She was first instructed at the cathedral of Como, and later at the Milan Conservatorio. In 1815, having left the Conservatorio, she appeared in the minor theaters of Leghorn, Parma, and Brescia; and in the following year at Paris in the train of Catalani. Without bursting into sudden splendor, she played subordinate parts, and matured her voice by incessant practice and care. It was said of her that she left nothing to chance, and proved the truth of the axiom that genius is the art of taking pains.

She made her first appearance at the King's Theater, London, January 11, 1817, in the part of Arsinoë in Cimarosa's "Penelope," the title-rôle being played by Madame Camporesi. This was followed by Cherubino in "Le Nozze di Figaro," and subordinate parts in several other operas. She failed to excite general notice. Her voice was lacking in clearness and purity, and she had not yet attained complete command of it. But her style was expressive, and her acting was characterized by ability such as indicated a reserve of histrionic power of the highest order.

Pasta returned to Italy, withdrew temporarily from the stage, and for over a year applied herself to a rigorous course of study. The reward of patience and assiduity was won on her reappearance in Venice, where she created a profound sensation in 1819, and at once asserted the claims of genius developed by conscientious study. A season in Rome during the same year was attended by the most gratifying success, which was followed by triumphs at Triest and Milan in the following year. In 1821, at Paris, she succeeded in making a complete conquest of the public, which, after a flattering reception at Verona, was ratified in March of the next year, when in the opera of "Romeo e Giulietta" she was received with enthusiastic homage.

By perseverance she had conquered defects of tone, and the surprising beauty of her voice was now the theme of universal admiration. Its range and power were remarkable. The critics found that she had extended it to two octaves and a half, from A above the bass clef to C flat, and even to D in alt. Its quality was marked by a rare sweetness which permeated its volume, and her exquisite taste was reinforced by deep feeling and accurate judgment. Her trill was exceptionally beautiful and artistic.

A writer who met her in retirement many years afterward gives an interesting account in her own words of her achievement of the trill. "I had no natural shake or trill," she says, "and as the music of forty years ago was very elaborate, this was a great drawback to me. For five years I struggled to obtain the power of trilling; one day it came to me as by inspiration, and I could shake perfectly. I kept the secret at rehearsal. I was then at Bergamo, acting in 'Niobe,' an opera containing an aria, 'Il soave e bel contento,' which suited my voice in every respect, but which I had hitherto been obliged to partly omit, as a long trill obbligato opens the quick movement. I simply told the conductor of the orchestra to suspend the instruments at this passage, as I wished to introduce a long cadenza. When I came to the passage in question I stood in the middle of the stage, and commenced a shake in a low key, gradually increasing in power, finally diminishing, and ending in a cadenza which perfectly linked it to the aria. For a minute or two there was a dead silence, then the musicians laid down their instruments, while both orchestra and public applauded me to the echo."

Pasta's fame speedily attained the zenith. Her rare powers, ripened by time and developed and refined by study, burst upon an astonished world with the splendor and brilliancy of a constellation. Whatever defects still lingered in her voice were concealed by her intellectual refinement, her marvelous pathos, her transforming energy in heroic situations, her profound but restrained tragic power. She was among the greatest actresses of her time—of all time. Her lower notes had tears in them, and thus her command of pathetic emotions was heightened and intensified; her movements and gestures were indescribably graceful, deepening into grandeur or tragic abruptness as the situation required. Passion and fire, held in artistic restraint, like hounds in the leash, gave to supreme moments inimitable and decisive touches. A perfect grace in pause or movement, added to facial charm, made every pose, accentuated by true art, but never artificial, a study for a painter or sculptor. Niobe, Tancredi, Romeo, Desdemona, Medea, Semiramide—each character was infused with life and individuality, and borrowed distinction and grandeur from real emotion. "Here is a woman," exclaimed Talma, "of whom I can still learn!"

Pasta reappeared in London, April 24, 1824, as the reigning queen of that stage which, only seven years before, she had left almost unnoted. She took the town by storm. In 1825-26 she appeared alternately in London and Paris. Owing to a disagreement with Rossini, at that time director of the Italian Opera, she quitted Paris and went to Naples. In 1827, however, she returned to London for a season of twenty-three nights, for which she received three thousand guineas, and a free benefit which realized fifteen hundred guineas. During this season she played Desdemona, and elicited a comparison with Malibran, who also essayed the part. Malibran's superiority in vocalization was admitted, but she failed to wrest the palm from Pasta, whose conception of the part and finished acting were beyond her rival's scope. Pasta's impersonation of Queen Mary in Coccia's "Maria Stuarda," first produced that season, still further increased her fame and popularity. The farewell in the last scene is said to have been a crowning triumph of queenly grandeur and pathos. She felt the situation deeply, and when she appeared before the curtain in response to a tumultuous call she was still suffering from ex-

treme agitation. After a triumphal season at Dublin she went to Triest.

The story is told that either at Dublin or Triest she one day met a child of three, who in artless tones solicited alms for her blind mother. Pasta, bursting into tears, gave the child all the money in her purse. To the friends who began praising her bounty she said: "I will not accept your compliments. This child demanded charity in a sublime manner. I have seen at one glance all the miseries of the mother, the wretchedness of their home, and all that they suffer. I should indeed be a great actress if at any time I could find a gesture expressing profound misery with such truth."

In 1828 Pasta was again in England, and during a most brilliant series of successes, including "Tancredi," Mayer's "La Rosa bianca e Rosa rossa," and "Zelmira," she achieved a great triumph in the part of Armando in "Il Crociato in Egitto," an opera originally composed for the celebrated male soprano Velluti. She had already taken the rôle in Paris. There a spirit of partisanship was maintained, rising at times to serious outbreaks during the performance. The palm, however, was awarded to Pasta. Her tempo was faultless, her conception of the part was strikingly original, and Velluti could not hope to compete with Pasta in histrionic power. On the night of the first performance in London a humorous incident occurred. At the conclusion of a scene, Pasta hastened to her dressing-room to change, but the audience clamored for an encore, and amid laughter, she hurried on to the stage again half Crusader and half Mameluke.

For her benefit she selected "Otello," appearing herself as the jealous Moor, Sontag being the Desdemona. The experiment was a daring one. The transposition of the music marred the effect of some of the concerted pieces. But the tragic intensity of the great actress conquered prejudice, and carried away the audience. In this year (1828) Pasta excelled herself as an actress; doubtless stimulated to the expression of her highest powers by the presence of her "two young and glorious rivals," Malibran and Sontag.

In 1829 the Emperor of Austria created her first court singer. During this year she purchased a charming villa on the Lake of Como, and at Bologna performed in twelve operas by Rossini, the master himself conducting. A medal was struck in her honor by the Societa del Casino. In the following year she was at Milan, singing with Rubini and Lablache. Donizetti in that year wrote and produced "Anna Bolena," with Pasta, Galli, and Rubini specially in mind. In 1831 Pasta and Rubini surpassed themselves as Amina and Elvino in Bellini's "La Sonnambula," written for Pasta.

Pasta, Lablache, and Rubini appeared together (1831) in London in "Medea." If possible, Pasta's tragic acting was grander than ever; she was said to have revived the memory of the great Siddons, and the tragedienne, who witnessed one of her performances, is stated to have exclaimed: "I am thankful that she lived not in my time." Her versatility was remarkable, and her genius for comedy was shown in "Prova d'un Opera Seria," a burlesque of the rehearsals of grand opera. She evoked roars of laughter by her droll singing, which was free from the slightest trace of vulgarity. The quarrel scene between the prima donna and the composer (Lablache) was rendered irresistibly amusing by the superb comic power displayed by Pasta. In that year she bade farewell to the Parisian stage.

In 1832 Bellini's "Norma" was produced at La Scala. Pasta, as the druid priestess, achieved the crowning triumph of her career; she was supported by Donzelli (Pollione) and Giulia Grisi (Adalgisa). When "Norma" was produced during the next season in London for Pasta's benefit, it did not create en-thusiasm, although it was conducted by the composer; indeed, the superb acting of Pasta and the singing of Grisi, then rising into fame, alone saved it from failure —its great beauties not being readily discriminated by the English public, with whom it shortly afterward be-came a prime favorite. After 1841 Pasta lived in retirement at her Lake Como villa and in Milan, de-voting herself to advanced vocal instruction, which she was eminently fitted to impart. She died at the villa, April 1, 1865.

CHAPTER VI

HENRIETTE SONTAG

FEW lives of celebrated singers have been more sensational than that of Henriette Sontag. Not one do we call to mind in which the fabric of reality has been interwoven with so much romance, the course of incident more thrilling, the sequence of circumstances bordering more closely on the province of the fairy tale.

Sontag was born in the beautiful Rhenish town of Coblentz, May 13, 1805. It was a modest household, that of the Sontags; father and mother were both actors. The child was barely six when she made her first appearance at Darmstadt in Kauer's "Donauweib-chen," and created some sensation by the sterling quality of her voice. Three years later the father died, and mother and children went to Prague, where Henriette continued to appear in children's parts, anxiously awaiting the time when she would be allowed to enter the Conservatory.

At last, in 1815, though under the age prescribed, she was admitted. When she was fifteen, a fortunate accident occurred that was to lift her at once into a prominent position. The regular prima donna sud-denly fell ill, and the director of the theater had to confide her part as Queen in "Jean de Paris" to Hen-riette. Always petite, at that time she looked a mere child. She used to dwell in after years on the many innocent stratagems adopted to add to her apparent age, one of the principal items being a pair of red shoes with soles four inches in thickness. Though she was naturally somewhat timid, the sweetness of her voice was such as more than to compensate for all de-ficiencies. The Prague audience was so generous in its applause that the reputation of the singer traveled fast beyond the limits of both town and kingdom. Vienna was still the Mecca of all aspirants to musical honors. Henriette was soon installed in the "Kaiserstadt," over which the shadows of Haydn and Mozart seemed yet to linger, where the mighty genius of Beethoven was still battling against poverty and physical adversity; where Weber, Moscheles, Hummel appealed for judg-ment, and Fodor-Mainvielle enchanted mighty audi-ences.

Four years Sontag remained in the gay capital, al-ternating her time between close study and occasional appearances on the stage. Ever afterward she ac-knowledged freely that she owed much, and perhaps everything, to Madame Mainvielle, who took a friendly interest in the young singer. But the Vienna public, slow to recognize new talent, was not very apprecia-tive until Weber set the seal on her name by confiding to her the title-rôle in his opera "Euryanthe," which she carried through triumphantly, October 25, 1823. Composer and singer were in every one's mouth; even Beethoven, whose interest was not easily aroused, and whose deafness had kept him at home on the night of the performance, asked how "little Sontag" had ac-quitted herself. From this date the German, and we may say the European, reputation of Sontag was es-tablished. She was soon to leave Vienna—not, however, before she had sung at the first performance of Bee-thoven's Ninth symphony and his mass in D, works which tax the powers of a singer.

After a short engagement in Leipzig, she signed a contract on excellent terms for Berlin. Here she was received with the greatest enthusiasm, and acquired a popularity never known before. The court, affable and art-loving, was additionally impressed by her Ger-man birth. The nation was delighted. Many are the tales related of the exaggerated form this worship took. On one occasion a set of boisterous students at Göttingen overturned her post-chaise into the river, that nobody might use the vehicle after her. Luckily the coach was empty at the time.

In 1826 Sontag first appeared in Paris as Rosina in "Il Barbiere," and was warmly applauded. The critics were unanimous in her praise. Catalani is reported to have said of her: *"Elle est la première dans son genre mais son genre n'est pas le premier"* (She is first in her class, but her class is not the first). And yet there may have been just a grain of truth concealed in this malice. In comic and light opera, such as "Il Barbiere" and the graceful, if somewhat shallow, productions of the French school, she was as near perfection as can be imagined; but when she turned to more serious parts, as in "Semiramide," it was stated—and perhaps not quite without reason—that she was somewhat lacking in highly dramatic quality. Where she was wanting Pasta excelled, and the earnestness with which Sontag watched that great actress and tried to frame herself on her model forms one of the many proofs of the modesty which was a prominent feature in her character.

In England she appeared first on April 19, 1828, at the King's Theater, London, as Rosina, and met with a most flattering reception, sharing with Malibran the honors of that and the succeeding season. The story of the coolness existing between the two, and of how, after singing together the duet from "Semiramide" at a concert, mutual admiration transformed their estrangement into warm friendship, is well known. Sontag appeared here in other rôles, and her artistic fame was enhanced by her popularity in society.

At Berlin Sontag had made the acquaintance of Count Rossi, of the Sardinian diplomatic service. In 1829 their private marriage took place.

After a time Count Rossi's efforts to procure court sanction to his union were successful—the King of Prussia bestowed a patent of nobility on the lady, who bade farewell to artistic life. As Countess Rossi she accompanied her husband to The Hague, where he was representative of the Sardinian court. Occasionally she would sing for public charities, in concerts or oratorio —a style in which she is said to have been unrivaled; still, for nearly half her lifetime she remained lost to the musical public and followed the career of her husband at the courts of Holland, Germany, and Russia. But the disorders of 1847-48 had impaired their fortunes, and she was tempted to return to the opera.

Lumley, of Her Majesty's Theater, London, was in the throes of one of those crises which more than once threatened that theater with imminent ruin. Jenny Lind, on whose reappearance he had counted, was not to be weaned from the repose she enjoyed in her Brompton villa. There was nobody to replace her, and the public protested emphatically against any singer not of the very first merit. Before any knowledge of the financial embarrassments of the Rossis could have reached him, the wary impresario had scented from afar the possibility of securing the great singer to repair his falling fortunes. A first attempt to approach the subject through the Earl of Westmorland, British ambassador at Berlin, was doomed to failure; but where the diplomatist had failed the virtuoso was successful. Thalberg, passing through Berlin, called on the Countess, and laying siege to the half-willing victim, succeeded in breaking down the last barriers of her resistance. The overjoyed impresario was enabled to announce in a flourish of language her immediate return to the stage.

It was, in truth, a great risk. She had been for operatic purposes dead for over twenty years, and this half-forgotten singer of a previous generation was now to be unearthed and placed in juxtaposition to the mature power of Jenny Lind. Lumley himself confessed that he thought it impossible that a voice could be

preserved intact for such a length of time. Had there been another singer at his command it is more than likely that the idea to reëngage Sontag would not have occurred to him. But all his doubts were dispelled. Her voice and charms were unimpaired, and the unanimous opinion seems to have been that, in the words of Adolph Adam, she now united to youth and freshness the qualities of a finished artist. Her former deficiencies were in some measure compensated by study and less girlish appearance. As Amina, though Jenny Lind was fresh in the public memory, she was rapturously received; as also in Desdemona, and Susanna in the "Nozze di Figaro," one of her favorite parts, and pronounced by a German critic the most perfect thing he had seen on any stage. Her extraordinary preservation of her powers was partly due, no doubt, to long exemption from the wear and tear of incessant public singing, but Sontag was always extremely careful of her voice, discarding any rôle that did not lie well within her register. Thus, in an early contract at Berlin, she expressly stipulates that she shall not be bound to sing in the operas of Spontini.

After a tour in the English provinces in the winter of 1849, she went to Paris, where a successful series of concerts, also under Lumley's management, preceded in the spring of 1850 her reappearance at Her Majesty's to win fresh laurels as Norina in "Don Pasquale," Elvira in "I Puritani," and Miranda in Halévy's new opera "La Tempesta." As Zerline and in "La Figlia del Reggimento," she appeared for the first time, and with preëminent success. In the autumn of 1850 she sang in Italian opera at Paris, Lumley again being director of the company. During this season Alary's "Tre Nozze" was produced, and the polka-duet between Sontag and Lablache never failed to send the public into ecstasies. It was brought out in London in 1851, with similar results. During this season, Sontag's last in London, she sang in a round of her favorite parts, and in the production of "L'Enfant prodigue." In Germany, wherever she went she carried all before her. At a concert at Munich she was expressly requested to stay to hear the last piece. It proved to be a "Huldigungs Chor"—verses composed expressly in her honor by the Crown Prince and set to music by Lachner.

In 1852 Sontag received offers from the United States, which tempted her thither with her husband in the autumn. The results were brilliant. Her voice was strengthened by the climate, and at this time she could sing in "Lucrezia Borgia" and "La Figlia del Reggimento" on a single evening without overfatigue. Her last appearance was made in "Lucrezia" at the City of Mexico in 1854. She was attacked by cholera, and on June 17 a brief illness cut short a life of uncheckered prosperity.

Berlioz, remarking on the fact that Sontag had less to suffer than other equally famous singers from hostile criticism and party spirit, ascribes it to her having united so many favorite qualities. Her figure was slender and *mignonne*, her hair between auburn and blonde, her eyes large, and her features delicate. Her voice, a soprano of clear and pleasing quality, was specially good in the upper register, reaching the E in alt with facility, and in perfection of execution she seems to have been unsurpassed by any singer of her time. But she was deficient in dramatic power, and only appeared to the highest advantage in works of a light and placid style. On her return to Paris, in January, 1828, she essayed parts of a different order, such as Donna Anna and Semiramide, with success, but in passion and emotion never rose to the distinction she attained as a songstress. She was a thorough and conscientious artist, and her style won her the special favor of eminent musicians. Mendelssohn entertained the highest admiration for her, and she obtained a like tribute of praise from connoisseurs in every country. It fell to her lot to achieve an international popularity and fame never before accorded to a German singer.

CHAPTER VII

MARIO

THÉOPHILE GAUTIER, on hearing for the first time the exquisite voice of Mario, listened in rapt attention. When the aria ceased, he seemed lost in wonder, and said, the soft tone of the last note still lingering in his ear, "It is a nightingale singing in a thicket"; then, after a pause, "Yes, he excels in the rendering of tender thoughts—love, melancholy, regret for an absent home, and all the soft sentiments of the soul."

Never was youth more richly gifted for the operatic stage than was Mario. Beauty of voice, face, and figure, with the most winning grace of Italian manner, were all his. For the stage he was born, and to the stage he remained faithful during his artistic life. To the brilliance of his success in opera he brought one great helping quality, the eye for color and all the important details of costume. His figure on the stage looked as if it had stepped out of the canvas of Titian, Veronese, or Tintoretto. Never was an actor more harmoniously and beautifully dressed for the characters he impersonated—no mean advantage, and no slight indication of the complete artistic temperament.

Mario, Marchese di Candia, was born in 1812 at Genoa, of an old and noble family. His father had been a general in the Piedmontese army; and he himself was an officer in the Piedmontese Guard, when he first came to Paris in 1836, and immediately became a great favorite in society. But he was then only an amateur, and as yet all unfitted for public singing. Tempted as he was by the offers made to him by Duponchel, the director of the Opera—which are said to have reached the sum of 1500 francs a month, a large sum for a beginning—and pressed by the embarrassments created by expensive tastes, he still hesitated to sign such a contract. Finally persuaded to do so, he compromised the matter by signing only the Christian name, under which he became afterward so famous—Mario.

After a course of training under Michelet, Ponchard, and Bordogni, he made his début, November 30, 1838, in the title-rôle in "Robert le Diable." His success was pronounced from a vocalistic point of view, but he had yet to learn to be dramatic as well as musical. In 1840 he passed from the Académie to the Italian opera, as best suited to his nationality. His first appearance in London was in "Lucrezia Borgia," June 6, 1839; but it was not until 1846 that he took the place of Rubini, and was acknowledged as the most perfect stage lover ever seen. The only failure, if it can be so called, was in his attempt to sing the title-rôle in "Don Giovanni," a part in which Nourrit and Garcia had failed to succeed. In Mario's case this failure is to be accounted for by the fact that the character of reckless profligate was not in keeping with his temperament; in fact, he was too amiable to secure the approval of his audience. Mario seldom sang in oratorio, although passionately fond of sacred music, which strongly appealed to his sensitive nature. At the Birmingham Festival in 1849 he sang "Then shall the righteous," in "Elijah"; and at Hereford in 1855, "If with all your hearts," in the same work.

Mario sang, after this, in each season at Paris and in London, improving steadily both in acting and singing, though it fell to his lot to create but few new characters—scarcely another besides that of the "walking lover" in "Don Pasquale," a part which consisted of little more than the singing of the serenade "Com è gentil." In other parts he only followed his predecessors, though with a grace and charm which were peculiar to him, and which may possibly remain forever unequaled. "It was not," says Chorley, "till the season of 1846 that he took the place of which no wear and tear of time had been able to deprive him." He had then played Almaviva, Gennaro, and Raoul, and had shown himself undoubtedly the most perfect stage lover ever seen, whatever may have been his other qualities or defects. His singing in the duet of the fourth act of "Les Huguenots" raised him again above this; and in "La Favorita" he achieved, perhaps, his highest point of attainment as a dramatic singer.

For five and twenty years Mario remained before the public of Paris, London, and St. Petersburg, constantly associated with Grisi. In the earlier years (1843-46) of that brilliant quarter of a century, he took the place of Rubini in the famous quartet, with Tamburini and Lablache; this, however, did not last long; and he soon remained alone with Grisi, the sole remaining star of the original constellation. To this gifted prima donna Mario was united, after the dissolution of her former marriage; and by her he had three daughters. He left the stage in 1867, retired to Paris, and then to Rome. There he was subsequently appointed curator of the Museum, and there he died, December 11, 1883. He made two tours of the United States, in 1854 (with Grisi) and in 1874.

Mario never got over his nervousness. *"Gli assi, gli assi mi fanno tremare"* (Your footlights make me tremble), he used to say. Once he was asked by a lady to sing at her evening reception; and would he think 1500 francs sufficient remuneration? Mario refused, telling the messenger he was sorry, but he was engaged. When remonstrated with he said, "Is it worth while putting on a dress coat for the sake of 1500 francs ($300)?"

Again, when the Czar Nicholas ordered Mario to shave off his beard, he refused. The Czarina, knowing that the Czar brooked no contradiction, asked him to comply for her sake; but Mario said he would rather leave St. Petersburg than run the risk of losing his voice, and he kept his beard. It is needless to say that whenever Mario walked in London he was recognized. One day, as he was walking in Piccadilly, a young lady saw him, and involuntarily exclaimed, "Mario!" *"A votre service, mademoiselle,"* said the handsome tenor, removing his hat, while the young lady blushed crimson.

Many other stories are told in connection with Mario. Well known is that of the lady who, though she had never been introduced to Mario, yet was present during her lifetime at every performance (all but three, say some) in which he sang, no matter in what part of the world it was, and who died without ever having spoken or written a word to the artist she so highly esteemed.

An interesting incident is related of his first visit to Queen Victoria, when commanded to sing before her Majesty at Balmoral. Upon this occasion a carriage had been ordered for the great tenor to enable him to enjoy the lovely scenery of Deeside without tiring himself; but Mario wearied of the carriage, stopped the coachman, and desired him to return home, continuing the excursion on foot. When, on his return, he entered the grounds of the castle, he lost his way and suddenly found himself close to a very plainly dressed woman, who, in a sunbonnet of capacious proportions, was engaged, watering-pot in hand, in refreshing a thirsty flower-bed. Mario advanced, hat in hand: "Your pardon, mademoiselle," he said, "but I am a stranger, a guest of her Majesty; she has asked me to sing. I have lost my way, and it is near the hour. Could you tell me the path to reach the Queen's apartment?" "You wish to see the Queen?" "Yes, mademoiselle." "Well, signor, you see her now—I am the Queen; follow me."

CHAPTER VIII

MARIA FELICITA MALIBRAN

THIS great singer was born at Paris, March 24, 1808, where her father, Manuel Garcia, had arrived only two months before. When three years old she was taken to Italy, and at the age of five played a child's part in Paër's "Agnese," at the Fiorentini, Naples. So precocious was she that, after a few nights of this opera, she actually began to sing the part of Agnese in the duet of the second act, a piece of audacity which was applauded by the public. Two years later, she studied solfeggi with Panseron, at Naples; and Hérold, happening to arrive about the same time, gave her her first instruction on the piano. In 1816 Garcia took her to Paris with the rest of his family, and in the autumn of 1817 to London. Already speaking fluently Spanish, Italian, and French, Maria picked up a tolerable knowledge of English in the two and a half years she spent in London. Not long after, she learned German with the same facility. Here, too, she had good teaching on the piano, and made such rapid progress that on her return to Paris in 1819 she was able to play Johann Sebastian Bach's clavier works, which were great favorites with her father. In this way she acquired sound taste in music.

At the age of fifteen she was made by her father to learn singing under his own direction; and, in spite of the fear which his violent temper inspired, she soon showed the individuality and originality of her genius. Two years had barely elapsed when (1824) Garcia allowed her to appear for the first time before a musical club he had just established. There she produced a great sensation, and her future success was confidently predicted. Two months later Garcia returned to London, where he was engaged as principal tenor; and here he set on foot a singing-class, in which the education of Maria was continued, if not completed. It is not quite certain whether an illness of Pasta, prima donna at the King's Theater, was the occasion of Maria's first public appearance, or whether it was due to Ronzi's not fulfilling an engagement; but there is no doubt she was the means of helping the management out of a very awkward situation, while making for herself a name. Her début was in "Il Barbiere di Seviglia," and her performance of Rosina made her at once a favorite with the London public. Lord Mount Edgcumbe says that "she was too highly extolled and injudiciously put forward as a prima donna, when she was only a promising débutante"; but this was not the opinion of the public, nor of the ruling powers, who forthwith engaged her for the remaining six weeks of the season for $2500, the playbills including a *première* of Meyerbeer's "Il Crociato in Egitto."

The stay in London was, however, predestined to be short. Garcia had engaged himself and family to perform in New York, and they consequently left England for that destination. Although the company, with the exception of the Garcias, was made up of the poorest material, the performances were fairly sustained, Maria, of course, taking the principal parts. This tour was of the greatest possible benefit to her in her later career, for she acquired that experience and confidence without which the best of artists fail to impress an audience. Her voice, also, which needed constant practice, improved as time went on. She appeared in a great number of operas, of which we may mention "Otello," "Don Giovanni," "Tancredi," "La Cenerentola," besides two operas specially composed for her by her father, "L'Amante astuto" and "La figlia dell' aria." The American public treated the company with cordiality; yet the venture was, from a pecuniary point of view, a failure.

We come now to a period in Madame Malibran's life which various biographers have treated in different ways—that of her marriage to François Malibran, a merchant. The fact is to be recorded that the marriage settlement contained a clause by which Garcia was to receive $25,000 as a *solatium* for the loss of his daughter's services; also the further fact that Malibran's financial position, already seriously compromised, drove him into the bankruptcy court before the first year of married life was over. There could be no question as to the future career of Madame Malibran; she had nothing but her voice, and to exercise it in New York was out of the question, as all the money she made would have been seized by her husband's creditors. The parting was as much *à l'amiable* as it could be under the circumstances. The terms have remained secret, but there is reason to believe that a portion of the wife's earnings in Europe were to be sent to her husband.

Madame Malibran arrived in Paris in December, 1827. Her first operatic appearance occurred in January, 1828, and the occasion was the performance of "Semiramide" at the Grand Opéra for the benefit of Galli. She was laboring under many disadvantages: for the first time in her life she felt nervous, nor was the part one she would have chosen; nevertheless she scored an immediate and striking success. Henceforth there was never any want of engagements; the difficulty was rather to choose among a surfeit. Her début at the Théâtre des Italiens was in "Otello," an opera to which she remained partial all her life. The novelty and originality that distinguished her style from that of all other prime donne earned her great applause.

So far her receipts had been moderate, averaging little more than sixty pounds per night, both in London and Paris, while twenty-five pounds was her fee for singing at concerts. When Sontag retired, it was felt that the remuneration was not adequate. The next offer, from Alfred Bunn of Drury Lane, was made at the respectable figure of £125 per night for nineteen nights. At this time Malibran made two notable additions to her repertoire, "La Gazza ladra" and "La Cenerentola," in both of which operas her success was prodigious; the combination of singing and acting was on all hands admitted to be unequaled. It was remarked that though not the first to act in "La Gazza ladra," she was yet the first to bring out hidden beauties of the prison scene which nobody had suggested before. Her representation of the neglected heroine in "La Cenerentola" was also true to life, and may have awakened reminiscences of her own by no means too happy childhood. In 1830 an attachment sprang up between her and Charles de Bériot, the celebrated violinist; and this ended only with her life. They built in 1831 a handsome villa in a suburb of Brussels, to which they returned after every operatic campaign. (In 1836 they were married at Paris.)

During the next few years her time was fully taken up between London and Paris. In 1832 Lablache, passing through Brussels on his way to Italy, suggested more in joke than in earnest that she should accompany him. The clock had barely struck five on the next morning when a traveling-carriage containing Malibran drew up at his door, ready to start for Italy. Lablache could scarcely credit his eyes; but those who knew this creature of impulse hardly wondered at her adopting a course which commended itself to her mind by its originality and caprice. During this tour, Milan, Rome, Naples, and Bologna were visited with equal success.

In the spring of 1833 she went to London, and sang at Drury Lane, in English opera, receiving 80,000 francs for forty representations, with two benefits which produced not less than 50,000 francs. The prices offered to her increased each year to an unprecedented extent. She received at the Opera in London, during May and June, 1835, £2775 for 24 appearances. Sums, the like of which had not been heard of before in such cases, were paid to her at the provincial festivals in England.

Having played in English versions of "Sonnambula" and "Fidelio," Malibran returned to Naples, where she remained until May, 1834, proceeding then to Bologna, and thence to Milan. She soon returned to London for a flying visit; and was singing at Sinigaglia in July. On August 11 she went to Lucca, where her horses were taken from her carriage, which was drawn to her hotel by enthusiastic admirers after her last appearance. She next went to Milan, and thence to Naples, where she sang during the carnival. Here she met with an accident, her carriage being upset at the corner of a street; and she suffered injuries which prevented her from appearing in public for a fortnight. Even then, she made her first appearance with her arm in a sling, which added to the interest of the occasion. From Naples she went, in the same triumphant manner, to Venice, her arrival being announced by fanfares of trumpets. There she was besieged with fresh enthusiasm, which followed her in her return to Paris and London.

Early in April, 1836, she arrived in London. Prospects looked bright for the young prima donna. Her reputation showed no signs of decrease; every performance added vigor and subtlety to her voice; there was hardly a rival to challenge her. It was during this visit that while riding an unmanageable horse she was thrown and dragged some distance before the stirrup gave way and left her on the road, unconscious and bedraggled with mud and blood. Even then matters might have mended had she listened to rational advice; but her only object was to keep the affair secret from her husband. She would see no physician, neither would she take that repose of which she stood in the greatest need. On the same evening she performed as usual, her hair being so arranged as to conceal the heavy injuries to her head; and it cannot be doubted that this accident, aggravated by her obstinacy, led to her premature death. About the end of July she left England for Brussels, where, unheeding severe pain, she gave a concert on August 12, following it by a performance of "La Sonnambula" at Aix-la-Chapelle.

In September she again came to England for the Manchester Festival, during which her short, brilliant life ended. She had arrived, with her husband, after a rapid journey from Paris, on Sunday, September 11, 1836. On the following evening she sang in no less than fourteen pieces. On the Tuesday, though weak and ill, she insisted on singing both morning and evening. On Wednesday, the 14th, her state was still more critical, but she contrived to sing with thrilling effect the last sacred music in which she ever took part, "Sing ye to the Lord." That same evening her last notes in public were heard with Mme. Caradori Allan, in the duet "Vanne se alberghi in petto," from "Tito Andronico." This was received with immense enthusiasm, the last movement was encored, and Malibran actually accomplished the task of repeating it. It was her last effort. While the concert-room still rang with applause, she was fainting in the arms of her friends; and, a few moments later, she was conveyed to her hotel. Here she died, after nine days of nervous fever, September 23, 1836. She was buried on October 1, in the south aisle of the collegiate church, Manchester. Her remains were soon afterward removed to Brussels and there reinterred in the cemetery of Lacken, where a mausoleum was erected by Bériot, containing a bust of the great singer by the celebrated sculptor Geefs.

It is difficult to appreciate the charm of a singer whom one has never heard. In the case of Maria Malibran it is exceptionally difficult, for the charm seems to have consisted chiefly in the peculiar timbre and unusual extent of her voice, in the excitable temperament which prompted her to improvise passages of strange audacity upon the stage, and on the strong musical feeling which kept those improvisations nearly, but not quite, always within the bounds of good taste. It was, after all, her mind that helped to enslave her audience; without that mental originality, her defective vocal organ would have failed to please where, in fact, it provoked raptures.

The life of Malibran is an attractive study from many points of view. While unstinted admiration is due to the actress and singer, we linger with pleasure over highly amiable traits of character, such as courage, sincerity, tact, generosity, and immutable attachment to friends. And if we regret her obstinacy, for which she had to suffer severely, we must not forget that it was the outcome of a daring and an energy rarely met with among the favorites of fortune. In artistic circles her death left a great void. It is true, great singers were among her survivors; but until Jenny Lind fascinated her audiences, none had arisen to approach Malibran in the combined arts of singing and acting. Malibran composed and published many nocturnes, songs, and chansonnettes. Some of the unpublished pieces were collected and published under the title of "Dernières Pensées musicales de Marie-Félicité Garcia de Bériot."

CHAPTER IX

GIULIA GRISI

OF Giulia Grisi a critic thus wrote in the London "Times": "There are certain striking features in every one of her impersonations, to forget which is utterly impossible for those who are able to feel and appreciate such traits in the exhibition of vocal and dramatic art. She was equally admirable in lyric tragedy, lyric comedy, and lyric melodrama; such traits were as plentiful as with less gifted artists they are rare." Grisi combined with this remarkable versatility a capacity for study and love of improvement in her art truly wonderful, an example by which many of the young singers of to-day might profit were they to lay it to heart; in fact, her whole artistic life was one of constant effort to attain perfection. No vocalization was too trivial for her careful study, no part beneath her creative instinct. She loved her public with a devotion amounting to reverence; with the veneration of a priestess she made her offering of song at the altar of art; her profession was to her a holy duty. Her noble appreciation of the public was strikingly shown in her unvarying promptitude to keep her part in the fulfilment of their pleasures. She rarely disappointed them; ill or well, she was ready to appear when announced. The public knew they were sure of her, and sought the opera in a comfortable state of confidence that no sudden announcement of change of bill would confront them, as in the case of more than one capricious prima donna of those days.

Giulia Grisi, the daughter of Gaetano Grisi, an officer of engineers under Napoleon, was born at Milan in 1812. The tastes of the family were decidedly musical and artistic, the father having dramatic ability, and the mother taking delight in vocal work. An elder sister, Giuditta, who was born in 1805 and died in 1840, was a singer of considerable ability and fame; but the name of Grisi, as known to the world, was made famous by the celebrated Giulia. Grisi was the niece of the famous Grassini, and a cousin, Carlotta Grisi, was distinguished as a dancer.

Giulia's vocal talent manifested itself at a very early period, and it was carefully fostered and cultivated by Giuditta. Her subsequent teachers were Filippo Celli, Madame Boccabadati, and Guglielmi. At the age of seventeen she made her début at Bologna, creating a very favorable impression, and raising glowing hopes about her future. Her voice and personal charms were both pronounced to be eminently distinctive, and the grace of her style, and the promising dramatic force of her acting, at once secured the sympathy of the audience. Like Pasta, she carried off a moderate stature by a noble bearing and handsome features, which expressed an intellectual variety and a charming individuality. To Pasta she was also akin in dramatic genius and fire.

Her progress was unusually rapid. Within a year after her début Rossini predicted a great future for her. At the conclusion of a short engagement at Florence, Grisi appeared at La Scala in Milan, where she met Pasta, then at the zenith of a splendid career, who aided her with counsel and instruction. She also attended a course of study under Mariani, and was further aided by Rossini and Bellini. Rossini was exceedingly gracious to the fair young aspirant, and Bellini recognized in the young artist all the qualifications for a perfect Adalgisa. Strangely enough, when the opera was first brought out, the first act proved almost a fiasco; and it was not until the duet for Norma and Adalgisa in the second act that the audience began to applaud. Dissatisfied with her engagement at Milan, and unable to get herself released from it by ordinary means, the impulsive Giulia took to flight, and escaping across the frontier reached Paris, where she found her aunt, Madame Grassini, her sister Giuditta, and Rossini, who was then director of the Théâtre des Italiens.

The patronage of Rossini soon procured her an engagement, and she made her first appearance in the title-rôle of his new opera, "Semiramide." She was supported by Eckerlin and Tamburini, and her success was immediate and triumphant. For sixteen consecutive years she was engaged at the Italiens.

On April 8, 1834, she made her first appearance in London in "La Gazza ladra"; but her principal triumph was achieved in "Anna Bolena," in which opera she had the coöperation of Lablache and Rubini. This was the period of phenomenal casts. The celebrated quartet of Grisi, Lablache, Tamburini, and Rubini was world-renowned. It lasted for some time. A substitute for Rubini was found in Mario; but when Lablache and Tamburini fell out there were no reserves to draw upon. The quartet dwindled to a duet; but the duet of Mario and Grisi became equally famous. These delightful artists are now invariably associated together. Heine ("Parisian Letters") coupled them in a poetic simile as "the rose, the nightingale among flowers, and the nightingale, the rose among birds."

Between 1834 and 1861 Grisi missed only one season in London—that of 1842. Her health was robust, and enabled her to undergo severe and repeated exertions. In 1854, with Mario, she made a tour of the United States. She was received very coldly at Madrid in 1859, and at once relinquished her engagement. Rest was prescribed. In 1861 Gye, director of the Royal Italian Opera of London, proposed a contract stipulating that Grisi should not appear in public for five years. As soon as the term had expired she surprised the public by appearing at Her Majesty's Theater in "Lucrezia Borgia." The performance was a comparative failure. Grisi withdrew from the opera, but continued to sing at occasional concerts with undiminished popularity.

She had for years made London her headquarters, and on leaving it in 1869 to pay a visit to Berlin had no intention of not returning to the capital where she had obtained her greatest and most prolonged successes. Inflammation of the lungs, however, seized her, and after a short attack she died at the Hôtel du Nord, Berlin, November 25, 1869.

Grisi was married in 1836 to the Count de Melcy, but the union proved a most unhappy one. A warm attachment sprang up between her and Mario, and received the sanction of the Church after she had succeeded in procuring a divorce from her first husband. By Mario she had three daughters. The Emperor Nicholas jestingly referred to them as "grisettes." "Pardon me, sire," was the reply, "they are marionettes."

Her splendid voice, in its prime, had no flaw, and her superb histrionic talent added luster to the brightest laurels of the lyric stage. Chorley tells us that her voice had a compass of from C below to C above the staff, and had not "a break or a note which had to be managed." He further speaks of the "clear, penetrating beauty of her reduced tones, differing in quality from the whispering ventriloquism which was one of a rival's most favorite effects." "I have never," he declares, "tired of Madame Grisi during twenty-five years, but I have never been, in her case, under one of those spells of intense enjoyment which make an epoch in life."

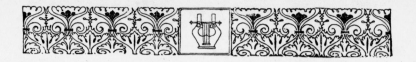

CHAPTER X

JENNY LIND

JENNY LIND was a native of Sweden. She was born at Stockholm, October 6, 1820. Her parents were respectable, laborious, and poor—her father a teacher of languages, her mother a schoolmistress. Jenny was the first child of their marriage, and there was afterward born to them a son named John. Jenny could sing the airs of her native land with correctness, and even with some expression, when she was but twenty months old. By the time she was three years of age singing was her delight; she was always singing; and she had the faculty of catching every song she heard, and repeating it with remarkable exactness. She was a lonely and timorous child. The absence of her father, who was abroad all day pursuing his vocation, and the constant occupation of her mother in her school, left her very much alone; and during her solitary hours her voice and her music were the unfailing solace of her existence. The first nine years of her life were marked by no particular event. The Swedes are a musical people, and many children in Stockholm, besides Jenny Lind, were fond of singing.

When she was about nine years of age the silvery tones of her voice chanced to catch the ear of an actress named Lundberg, who at once discerned its capabilities. Madame Lundberg went to the parents and told them how delighted she had been with the singing of their child, and advised them to have her educated for the opera. The child was more than willing, and very soon Madame Lundberg had the pleasure of conducting her to Crœlius, one of the most noted music-masters of Stockholm. Crœlius soon became an enthusiast respecting his new acquisition, and at length he resolved to present her to the manager of the royal theater.

When the enthusiastic Crœlius presented her to the manager, that potentate saw before him a pale, shrinking, slender, undersized child, between nine and ten years of age, attired with Sunday stiffness in a dress of black bombazine. "You ask a foolish thing," said he. "What shall we do with that ugly creature? See what feet she has! and then her face! She will never be presentable. No, we cannot take her. Certainly not!" The old music-teacher was too confident of the value of the talent which the child possessed to be abashed by this ungracious reception. "Well," said he, with some warmth, "if you will not take her, I, poor as I am, will take her myself, and have her educated for the stage." The old man's enthusiasm piqued the curiosity of the manager, and he consented at length to hear her sing. Undeveloped as her voice then was, it already had some of that rapture-giving power which it afterward possessed in such an eminent degree. The manager changed his mind, and Jenny was at once admitted to the training-school attached to the royal theater. There she had the benefit of highly competent instructors, as well as the inspiring companionship of children engaged in the same pursuits.

The pupils of the training-school were required, now and then during the season, to perform in little plays written and arranged expressly for them. It was in one of these, in the eleventh year of her age, that Jenny Lind made her first appearance in public. The part assigned her was that of a beggar-girl—a character which her pallid countenance and slight person fitted her to represent. She acted with so much simplicity and truth, and sang her songs with such intelligent expression, as to secure the favor of the audience in a high degree. She made what we now call a "hit." Other children's plays were written for her, in which for two winters she delighted the people of Stockholm, who regarded her as a prodigy.

At the height of her transient celebrity, her brilliant prospects clouded over. She observed with alarm that her upper notes grew weaker, and that her other tones were losing their pleasure-giving quality. By the time she was thirteen years of age her upper notes had almost ceased to exist, and no efforts of her teachers could restore them. The scheme of educating her for the opera was given up, though she continued for four years longer to be an assiduous member of the school, studying instrumental music, and the theory of composition. One of the severest of her trials was that of being forbidden to use her voice, except for a short time every day in very simple music.

Her seventeenth birthday came round. The master of the training-school was about to give at the theater a grand concert, in order to display the talents and improvement of his pupils. The chief part of this concert was to consist of the celebrated fourth act of "Robert le Diable," in which Alice has but one solo assigned to her, and that not a favorite with singers. When all the parts had been distributed except that of the undesirable Alice, the director thought of Jenny Lind, and offered it to her. She accepted it and began to study the music. A strange thing happened to her on the night of the concert. Her upper notes suddenly returned to her in all their former brilliancy, and every note in her voice seemed at the same moment to recover its long-lost sweetness and power.

No one had anticipated anything from the Alice of that evening, and thunders of applause greeted the unexpected triumph. Except herself, no one was so much surprised as the director of the school, whose pupil she had been for six years. Besides warmly congratulating her that evening, he told her on the following morning that she was cast for the important part of Agathe in "Der Freischütz." The evening came. We have an account of her début from the pen of her friend and kindred genius, Fredrika Bremer: "I saw her at the evening representation. . . . She seemed to move, speak, and sing without effort or art.

All was nature and harmony. Her singing was distinguished especially by its purity, and the power of soul which seemed to swell in her tones. Her 'mezzo voice' was delightful."

But her probation was not yet finished. After this dazzling success, she remained for a while the favorite of the Stockholm public, adding new characters to her list and striving in every way known to her to remedy certain serious defects in her voice and vocalization. In her efforts to improve her voice while performing at the opera she overstrained it, and the public of Stockholm, limited in number and fastidious in taste, left her to sing to empty boxes. She felt the necessity of better instruction than her native city afforded. Garcia was then living at Paris, at the height of his reputation as a trainer of vocalists. She desired to place herself under his instruction; but although she had been a leading performer at the Stockholm opera for a year and a half, she was still unable to afford the expense of a residence in Paris. To raise the money she gave concerts, accompanied by her father, in the principal towns of Sweden and Norway.

Her first interview with Garcia was disheartening in the extreme. "My good girl," said he, after hearing her sing, "you have no voice; or, I should rather say, that you *had* a voice, but are now on the point of losing it. Your organ is strained and worn out; and the only advice I can offer you is to recommend you not to sing a note for three months. At the end of that time, come to me again, and I will do my best for you." At the appointed time she stood again in the master's presence. He told her that her voice was improved by rest and capable of culture. She placed herself under his instruction, and profited by it; but, strange to say, Garcia never predicted for her a striking success, either because her voice had not yet regained its freshness, or the old master's ear had lost its acuteness. He used to say that if she had as much voice as she had intelligence, she would become the greatest singer in Europe, and that she would have to sing second to many who had not half her ability.

During her residence at Paris, she had the honor of singing before Meyerbeer, who instantly perceived the peerless quality of her voice. He arranged a grand rehearsal for her, with a full orchestra, when she sang the three most difficult scenes from three favorite operas. She delighted the company of musicians and the great master who heard her, and she narrowly escaped being engaged at once for the Grand Opera of Paris.

Her musical education was now complete. Returning home she gave a series of performances at Stockholm, which enraptured the public, carried her local reputation to the highest point, and secured for her a pressing invitation to sing at Copenhagen. It seems that she was still distrustful of her powers, and shrank from the ordeal of appearing in a country not her own. Her scruples at length gave way, and she appeared before the Danes in the part of Alice, in "Robert le Diable." We have an interesting account of her success at Copenhagen, in the autobiography of Hans Christian Andersen, who not only heard her sing, but became acquainted with her.

"It was," he says, "like a new revelation in the realms of art. The youthful, fresh voice forced itself into every heart; here reigned truth and nature, and everything was full of meaning and intelligence. At one concert she sang her Swedish songs. There was something so peculiar in this, so bewitching, people thought nothing about the concert-room." The students of the university gave her a serenade by torchlight, and she was the first to whom such a compliment was paid. Her success incited her to fresh exertions.

From this time forward, she knew little but triumph. When she left Stockholm again to enter upon an engagement at Berlin, the streets were crowded with people to bid her farewell. At Berlin, the Countess Rossi (Madame Sontag) pronounced her "the best singer in Europe." At Hamburg, a silver wreath was presented to her at the end of a most brilliant engagement. At Vienna, her success was beyond all precedent, and when she reappeared at Berlin the enthusiasm was such that it became a matter of great difficulty to procure admission to the theater.

After four years of such success as this, her popularity ever increasing, she accepted an engagement to sing in London. She arrived there in April, 1847, and soon began her rehearsals at the Queen's Theater. When her voice was first heard in that spacious edifice at a rehearsal, no one was so enchanted as Lablache, the celebrated basso. "Every note," he exclaimed, "is like a pearl!"

One morning at rehearsal she said to him: "Will you do me the favor, Signor Lablache, to lend me your hat?" Much surprised, he nevertheless handed her his hat, which she took with a deep courtesy, and, tripping away with it to the back part of the stage, began to sing an air into it. She then brought back the hat to Lablache, and, ordering that portly personage to kneel, returned it to him with the remark: "I have now made you a rich man, signor, for I have given you a hat full of pearls!"

When the eventful evening came the theater was crammed to its utmost capacity. She sang the part of Alice, in "Robert le Diable." By the time she had completed her first aria every one present felt that the greatest singer of the time, if not of any time, was this stranger from Stockholm. At Edinburgh a concert was given, for performing in which she received a thousand pounds sterling. Her charities constantly increased in number and amount. In almost every place she gave a part of her gains to charitable institutions. After two years of continual triumph, she resolved to take her leave of the stage, and to sing thenceforth only in the concert-room. Her last operatic performance was in May, 1849, in the part of Alice.

Her fame had long ago crossed the Atlantic. In October, 1849, P. T. Barnum, who had recently returned home after a three years' tour with the famous General Tom Thumb, conceived the happy idea of bestowing upon his countrymen the delight of hearing the voice of "the Swedish Nightingale." "I had never heard her sing," he said. "Her reputation was sufficient for me." He cast about him at once for a fit person to send to Europe to engage the songstress, and John Hall Wilton was instructed to engage Jenny Lind on shares, if he could; but he was authorized, if he could do no better, to offer her a thousand dollars a night for one hundred and fifty nights. Besides this, all her expenses were to be paid, including servants, carriages, and secretary, and she was to have the privilege of selecting three professional persons to accompany her. Barnum further agreed to place the whole amount of money for the one hundred and fifty nights in the hands of a London banker before she sailed. Negotiations were speedily concluded on a basis satisfactory to both parties.

Long before the great songstress landed all America was on the *qui vive*. On Sunday, September 1, 1850, at twelve o'clock, the steamer "Atlantic," with Jenny Lind on board, came to opposite the quarantine ground, New York. The wharves and ships were covered with thousands of people on that pleasant Sunday afternoon to see her step on shore. Nineteen days elapsed before her first appearance in public, during which she was the center of attraction, and the theme of every tongue. The acute and experienced Barnum, perceiving that his enterprise was an assured success, endeavored to guard against the only danger which could threaten it. Two days after the arrival of the "Nightingale" he told her that he wished to make a little alteration in their agreement.

"What is it?" she asked, much surprised.

"I am convinced," replied he, "that our enterprise will be much more successful than either of us anticipated. I wish, therefore, to stipulate that you shall always receive a thousand dollars for each concert, besides all the expenses, and that after taking fifty-five hundred dollars per night, for expenses and my services, the balance shall be equally divided between us." Jenny Lind was astonished; and supposing that the proposition was dictated by a sense of justice, she grasped the manager by the hand, and exclaimed: "Mr. Barnum, you are a gentleman of honor! You are generous. I will sing for you as long as you please. I will sing for you in America—in Europe—anywhere!" Barnum hastened to let people know that the change in the agreement was not the dictate of pure generosity. He feared that envious persons would create discontent in her mind, and he thought "it would be a stroke of policy to prevent the possibility of such an occurrence." The tickets for the first concert were sold at auction, and produced the astonishing sum of $17,864. Jenny Lind instantly resolved to give her portion of the proceeds to the charitable institutions of the city.

Five thousand persons assembled at Castle Garden, who had paid for the privilege sums which varied from two dollars to two hundred and twenty-five. It was the largest audience before which she had ever appeared, and she was considerably agitated. When the conductor of the concert led her forward, attired in white, with a rose in her hair, the audience stood up and gave her three thundering cheers, and continued for several seconds to clap their hands and wave their hats and handkerchiefs. She had a singularly pleasing way of acknowledging the applause of an audience. She had a timid, shrinking look, which appealed powerfully to popular sympathy, and inflamed the enthusiasm of the spectators to the highest degree. The orchestra began to play the prelude to "Casta Diva"— a piece which displayed all the power, all the thrilling sweetness, and some of the defects of her wonderful organ. Never had an assembly come together with such high-wrought expectations. Nevertheless, those

expectations seemed to be more than realized, and the last notes of the song were lost in the irrepressible acclamations of the people.

This success was the beginning of a splendid career in America. Under Barnum's management, she gave ninety-five concerts. The total receipts were $712,-161. The average receipts of each concert were $7,496. The sum received by Jenny Lind was $176,-675. Mr. Barnum's receipts, after paying her, were $535,486. After enchanting the United States it remained for Jenny Lind to conquer the fastidious and difficult public of Havana. A striking scene occurred on the occasion of her first appearance there. The people were much offended by the unusual prices charged for admission, and came to the concert determined not to be pleased—a circumstance of which Jenny Lind was ignorant. But a report of that time tells us that "not a vestige .of opposition remained. Again, again, and again did they call her forth, and at every appearance the thunders of applause rang louder and louder." In Havana, as in every other large city in America, she bestowed immense sums in charity, and gave charity concerts which produced still larger benefactions. During her residence in America, she gave away, in all, about $58,000.

The precaution which Barnum had taken against the intermeddling of envious persons proved to be insufficient, and after the ninety-fifth concert, Jenny Lind desired the contract to be annulled, and to give concerts on her own account. The manager gladly assented, and they separated excellent friends. Among the performers at her concerts was Otto Goldschmidt, a pianist and composer, whom she had formerly known in Germany, and with whom she had pursued her musical studies. Her friendship for this gentleman ripened into a warmer attachment, and ended in their marriage at Boston, in 1852. After residing some time at Northampton, Mass., they returned to Europe, where they afterward resided, finally settling in England. Occasionally, Madame Goldschmidt appeared in public concerts and oratorios. She died at her cottage, Wynd's Point, Malvern, England, November 2, 1887.

Her voice was a soprano of bright, thrilling, and remarkably sympathetic quality, from D to D, with another note or two occasionally available above the high D. The upper part of her register was rich and brilliant, and superior both in strength and purity to the lower. These two portions she managed, however, to unite in the most skillful way, moderating the power of her upper notes so as not to outshine the lower. She had also a wonderfully developed "length of breath," which enabled her to perform long and difficult passages with ease, and to fine down her tones to the softest pianissimo, while still maintaining the quality unvaried. Her trill was true and brilliant, her taste in ornament altogether original, and she usually invented her own cadenze. In a song from "Beatrice di Tenda," she had a chromatic cadence ascending to E in alt, and descending to the note whence it had risen, which could scarcely be equaled for difficulty and perfection of execution. The great secret of her success as a singer was well expressed by her friend Jules Benedict: "Jenny Lind makes a conscience of her art."

CHAPTER XI

SEVEN ARTISTS OF THE RECENT PAST

Adelina Patti—Christine Nilsson—Amalie Materna—Jean and Edouard de Reszke—Nellie Melba—Marcella Sembrich.

ADELINA PATTI.—No one has ever been more extravagantly eulogized than Madame Patti under the well-worn phrase of "the queen of song." If to be "queen of song" means to have reigned over countless admirers and to have fed all her life on the rose-leaves of acclamation, to have enforced the largest premium from managers ever given for such artistic service, to have preserved better than any of her contemporaries the traditions of the Italian bel canto in her vocal form, the diadem fits her charming head worthily. Nature endowed her with a voice of only moderate power, but of bell-like, voluptuous sweetness, which, if one may compare the things of sound and sight, suggests the round perfection of the pearl. Her notes were remarkably even and emitted with the bird-like facility which does not impress the listener more with its gush of melody than with the sense of artlessness, the extreme achievement of the art which conceals art. The compass when Madame Patti's organ was in its mellowest prime reached F in alt, and the power to take the perfect high notes at long intervals was always a noticeable feature of her skill, though singers shun this fatiguing leap of the voice as warily as misers guard their treasure-boxes. In purity of style and artistic finish of vocalization it is within bounds to say that no cantatrice of her immediate generation quite reached her level.

Adela Juana Maria Patti was born in Madrid, February 19, 1843. The father, Salvatore Patti, was a Sicilian tenor; the mother, known as Signora Barili, a beautiful Roman of the Trastavere. This musical couple came to the United States shortly afterward and made the country their home. Little Adelina's talent, shown almost in infancy, was carefully cultivated by her parents, and at the age of seven she made her début in New York, at Tripler Hall, in the difficult air of "Casta Diva" from Bellini's "Norma." Two years after this the little girl appeared as Rosina in "Il Barbiere," and sang all the fioriture with exquisite ease. Alboni, then singing in America, remembered having seen her "put on a table, or at least a high platform, where she walked up and down as if it were a stage and sang and acted like a grown-up person, with the sort of inspiration that moved an Italian improvisatore." After four years of this "infant prodigy" touring, it was deemed wise to give the voice a rest for two years, and then Adelina began to study seriously with Moritz Strakosch, who had in the meanwhile married Amalia Patti, her elder sister. She was not yet fifteen when she sang in a concert tour with Gottschalk throughout the United States, and a year later she made her serious bow to a New York audience in the rôle of Lucia, November 24, 1859. She appeared in opera and concert for nearly two years under the management of her brother-in-law Strakosch, and then went to London, where she made her début in Gye's Royal Italian Opera Company as Amina in "La Sonnambula," May 14, 1861. Unheralded by fame, she made an instant and magnificent conquest, ranking among the great first appearances in the musical history of that capital. The next year she sang at the Théâtre des Italiens in Paris and met a no less enthusiastic recognition. Thenceforward it was a primrose path, and Europe metaphorically was at her feet. The detailed record of her triumphs would be a monotonous rehearsal—the streams of gold and jewels showered on her, and the no less golden stream of homage and flattery, the world of fashion wooing a modern Danaë. For more than thirty years she was the cynosure of the musical public in so far as it bows before perfection of vocal art. Her sister Carlotta was also a brilliant vocalist of the florid school, though lameness debarred her from the opera stage.

Madame Patti had a repertoire of thirty-six operas, among which may be specially mentioned "Don Giovanni," "Le Nozze di Figaro," "Otello" (Rossini), "Il Barbiere," "La Gazza ladra," "I Puritani," "La Sonnambula," "Lucia di Lammermoor," "Linda di Chamounix," "Don Pasquale," "La Figlia del Reggimento," "Ernani," "Il Trovatore," "La Traviata," "Giovanna d'Arco," "Esmeralda," "Don Desiderio," "Villeda," "Aïda," "Crispino e la Comare," "Dinorah," "Les Huguenots," "L'Africaine," "L'Etoile du Nord," "Marta," "Faust," "Romeo e Giulietta," "Fra Diavolo," and "Semiramide." Her great fame was made in the lighter operas, which involve the singing of florid music and the acting of sparkling comedy, her dainty symmetry of person fitly symbolizing her art. She was, *par excellence,* the best-paid singer of the age, her terms for America having been, for many years, five thousand dollars a night, and for Europe twenty-five hundred dollars. It need scarcely be said that she accumulated a great fortune. Her country-seat, Craig-y-Nos, near Swansea, Wales, became one of the show-places of Great Britain. She was thrice married—in 1868 to the Marquis de Caux; in 1886 to Ernesto Nicolini, a well-known tenor; in 1899 to Baron Cederström.

CHRISTINE NILSSON.—Jenny Lind, whose star shone so fixedly beside the luster of such rivals as Garcia-Viardot, Persiani, Grisi, and Sontag, had a worthy successor in the singer who embodied, musically and dramatically, the most acceptable idea of Marguerite in Gounod's "Faust" known to the stage, and whose creation of Ophelia in Thomas's "Hamlet" still sets the tide-mark for succeeding aspirants.

Peasant in blood like Jenny Lind, Christine Nilsson was born August 20, 1843, in a forester's hut near the market town of Wexiö, Sweden, and when scarcely more than a baby sang and fiddled at the country fairs. The provincial judge, Tornerhjelm, a musical enthusiast, one day was attracted by a large crowd, and found the center of it a tiny, barefooted, golden-haired thing of three. He was enchanted with the quality of the voice, and did not rest till he had seen the parents and secured their unwilling assent to give this tot with a nightingale in her throat an adequate education. She was placed in the care of Baronne de Leuhusen (a gifted Swedish writer under the pen-name of Mademoiselle Valerius), who insured the child every advantage of musical and literary training. She had the best teachers which Sweden could furnish in French, German, and Italian, in singing and violin-playing and the higher branches of harmony, till she was sixteen, and then Judge Tornerhjelm told the enraptured girl that she must go to Paris for further instruction— Sweden was exhausted. Christine was even then undecided whether she would be singer or violinist, following the example of Fräulein Schmöling, the wonderful child-player, who ultimately became the great singer, Madame Mara. She gave a concert in Paris, where she fiddled and sang to the great delight of her audience, and then voice won the day.

The eccentric but great teacher Wartel took her in hand for three years, and kept her sol-faing till the last six months, when he gave her words to sing. Under this terrible gymnastic drill her organ acquired that firmness and solidity of tone which it retained unimpaired till her retirement from the stage. Meyerbeer was enraptured with the brilliant young voice, and offered her Ines in "L'Africaine" for her début, but Christine was obstinately set on Italian opera, and accepted a Brussels engagement, from which she was miraculously saved by the bankruptcy of the impresario. The great French singer Miolan Carvalho heard her and induced her husband, the manager of the Théâtre Lyrique, to give Christine an opening in "Traviata," including a three years' engagement. Her success was as instantaneous as it was brilliant, and she became the idol of the Paris public. There was at once recognized something setting her apart from all actors—that poignant, thrilling quality in the vocal timbre, not to be confounded with mere sweetness, or richness, or even nobility of tone. She sang in quick succession in "Marta," "Don Giovanni," "Sardanapale," "Les Bluets," and "Die Zauberflöte." In the latter opera, as Astrafiammante, she showed her great compass of register, reaching up to F in alt, and the astonishing speed and crispness of her staccati. Rossini, it is said, during this season warned her against employing her highest three notes as dangerous, and she gradually discontinued their use.

She appeared in London in 1866 with equal éclat, and sang a wide range of parts, among them Marguerite, in "Faust," then first heard in England. The original representative, Miolan Carvalho, crossed the Channel for the performance, and added her own praise to the public plaudits. The spirituality, tenderness, and pathos of the interpretation made it one of the great original conceptions of the stage. In 1868 Thomas selected the dreamy, poetic-looking Swede to

create his Ophelia in "Hamlet" at the Grand Opera, and her singing and acting confirmed the opinion that she was one of the greatest singers of the generation. After another London season, Mlle. Nilsson accepted an American engagement under Max Strakosch for concert and opera. This tour, it is said, brought her $200,000, and the American public was no less warm in recognition than transatlantic audiences. Here she sang for the first time one of her greatest parts, Elsa in "Lohengrin." Here, too, she made her first profound impression as an oratorio singer—a musical genre, in which her reputation became as great as in dramatic singing, owing to the peculiarly crystal-line ethereal quality of her voice. A noted English critic once said of her, with pardonable exaggeration, "When Patti sings, one fancies the notes of the lark rising to the gates of heaven, but Nilsson's voice is a strain from the other side of the gates."

Nilsson was married in 1872 to Auguste Rouzaud, a young French merchant, who had won her affections amid a throng of titled admirers. She returned to Drury Lane, London, in 1872, where she created the rôle of Edith in Balfe's "Il Talismano." The next year saw the diva back in America to repeat her triumphs, and she visited this country again in 1884. It is said that in 1880 Nilsson lost a large portion of her fortune by Rouzaud's business speculations. He died a paralytic in 1882. For two years the devoted wife had retired from her profession to minister to the sick husband. While the professional life of this artist was mostly spent in France and England, she made splendidly successful tours in Germany, Russia, Spain, and Italy, as well as in the United States. In 1887, having retired from the stage, she espoused a Spanish nobleman, Count de Miranda.

Nilsson's voice, though of moderate power, was noted for its crystalline brilliancy, resonance, and purity of tone. Perfectly even in its register, it extended from G natural to D in alt. The singer, after her first three years of stage singing, only used two and a half out of her three and a half original octaves. When one had exhausted ordinary musical terms to describe this voice, there was still something strange left which no one could quite define, and it was the secret of her unique power. Lacking the velvet voluptuous sweetness of Patti's organ; lacking, perhaps, the perfect mechanism of Patti's vocal art, this poignancy in her tones had its transcendent effect. Her fame shines most brilliantly about such pathetic characters as Marguerite, Mignon, Ophelia, Elsa, and Valentine ("Huguenots").

AMALIE MATERNA.—As a notable example of a singer equipped by nature and training to interpret the Wagner stage music, and in similar degree the heavy rôles of the great dramatic operas, none can be cited in comparison with Amalie Materna. Her name has become specially famous through the world in connection with Brünnhilde in the Nibelungen trilogy, and Kundry, the heroine of "Parsifal."

She was born at Saint Georgen, Styria, in 1847, her father being the village schoolmaster. She had that early domestic training in the art in which she was to became famous, almost inevitable in a land of musical people, and at the age of thirteen her voice in the church service gave her a local name. She does not appear to have made any extraordinary juvenile success in operatic singing. Her first stage appearance was at the Thalia Theater in Gratz, where she sang very acceptably in operetta and gave speedy indications of her latent dramatic resources. Here she married Karl Friedrich, and was soon engaged with him to sing at the suburban Karls Theater of Vienna. Her remarkable gifts could not long be hidden under a bushel, for her singing and acting became the common gossip of the greenroom and clubs of one of the most musical of cities. In 1869 she was engaged as dramatic prima donna at the Imperial Opera House, and made her début as Selica in "L'Africaine." The impression she produced was powerful and lasting. She immediately took her place among the first German singers, and became a famous exponent of the heavy rôles of one of the leading opera houses of Europe. She perpetuated the grand traditions of Schröder-Devrient in the massive style of her singing and acting, in such operas as "Fidelio," "Les Huguenots," "La Juive," "Le Prophète," "Il Trovatore," "La Favorita," "Iphigénie," "Faust," etc., which tax the extreme capacities of musical passion; though she seems never to have attained that marvelous flexibility which, with noble quality of voice and histrionic power, made another celebrated German singer, Titiens, equally with Pasta, an exponent of all schools wherein dramatic fitness is not entirely lost in bravura singing.

Eminent as Materna had become in Germany, it was not till 1876 that her fame was trumpeted to the ends of the musical world. She was selected by Wagner to interpret the rôle of Brünnhilde at the Bayreuth Festival of 1876. For such a creation as that of the Valkyr heroine she was fitted by nature, appearance, and endowment, and Wagner could have hunted the world in vain for her match. A stately figure, instinct with superb health and vitality, a face molded to convey the loftier emotions, a genius for dramatic impersonation, which would have made her famous without her voice, an organ of great compass and volume in which sweetness is married to strength, and of almost tireless power—these gifts made her the picked of "ten thousand." Bayreuth rendered Materna almost as famous as Wagner himself, so intimately was her performance associated with the success of his unique enterprise. The composer, too, has put on record his enthusiastic recognition of this singing tragedienne as the perfect incarnation of his art-ideal.

Materna's brilliant London success in 1877 in the Wagner concerts was followed by further triumphs in her own country, and in 1882 she visited America for the musical festivals of New York, Boston, and Cincinnati, held under the direction of Theodore Thomas. She also appeared in concert in Boston and Philadelphia. She did not then have the advantage of the illusions of the stage, but her great audiences could readily grasp, in the nobility of her voice and the fervor of her dramatic method, the secrets of the glamour by which she had taken the whole art and musical world captive at Bayreuth. She was recalled from America to create the part of Kundry in "Parsifal," at the Wagner Festival of 1882, and on the night of July 28 she again displayed that imaginative power and equipment of executive gifts which distinguished her Brünnhilde in the "Nibelungen Ring."

When Leopold Damrosch directed the season of German opera in New York in 1884-85, the Nibelungen trilogy constituted the chief feature of his season, and Materna was here to repeat her magnificent impersonations of the heroine, though, of course, the realistic background of the Bayreuth performances was absent. She also sang in other operas of her repertoire, such as "Tannhäuser," "Lohengrin," "Les Huguenots," and "Le Prophète," with scarcely less pleasure to the public. She repeated her tour in America in 1885-86, and in 1893-94 she again sang in concert and opera in New York, Boston, Philadelphia, and other Eastern cities, her more notable appearances being in Brünnhilde, Elisabeth ("Tannhäuser"), and Valentine ("Les Huguenots").

Materna's voice was remarkable for volume and compass, spanning three octaves, and great evenness of register. Its full sonorous quality and tireless vigor chiseled each note out of the loudest tumult of the orchestra. Her dramatic fervor separated her from all other great singers of her period. She could not, indeed, sing the sparkling fioritura which makes one think of diamond-dust, wherewith Patti delighted the public, any more than Patti could sing the musical heartbeats of Brünnhilde, throbbing with heroic energy. The genre is antipodal. Materna, though she made her highest fame as a "Wagner" singer, it must be remembered also plucked splendid laurels in other fields, and therefore escapes any narrow criticism which denies to the music of Wagner value as the vehicle of the finer qualities of the vocal art. She who could sing the music of Fides, Marguerite, Valentine, Fidelio, and Alice, as Materna has so often done, with enthralling effect and beauty of style, is entitled to be ranked with the greatest, aside from her distinction in a special school.

JEAN and EDOUARD DE RESZKE.—Of stage tenors since Mario, the most popular with Americans, and the most versatile if not the greatest in all respects, was Jean de Reszke. The De Reszke brothers, Jean and Edouard, belonged to the most celebrated family of singers of modern times. Their mother was a distinguished amateur; a sister, Josephine, achieved great success as a soprano in nearly all the capitals of Europe. The eldest of the family, Jean, was born in Warsaw, January 14, 1852. When only twelve years old he sang in the cathedral, and the rare quality of his voice aroused the interest of all Warsaw. He passed his examination and obtained his degree as advocate; but his underlying artistic sentiment was too strong to be subdued. He took lessons from Ciaffei, then in Italy studied under the famous barytone Cotogni, and with him visited London and St. Petersburg, where he heard such singers as Mario, Tamberlik, Faure, Graziani, and Patti. In 1874 he made his first appearance in Venice in "La Favorita," under the name of De Reschi, and a few months later was introduced to the London stage in the same rôle. Although the critics called attention to the fact that his voice lacked the deeper quality and resonance of a barytone, being more like a low tenor, he persevered in his career, and attained considerable celebrity. But his physical strength began to suffer from the strain of singing parts that were written much too low for him; so, acting upon the advice of Sbriglia, he decided to retire temporarily from the stage and prepare himself for the tenor repertoire.

After two years of study, aided by the wise counsels of Sbriglia, he made his début as a tenor at Madrid in "Robert le Diable." His success was great and immediate, and his career one long, uninterrupted, and ever-increasing triumph. Yet in no country did he create such a furor or arouse such enthusiasm as in America, where he was the idol of the public and accounted "the very Prince Charming of opera." His repertoire embraced "Faust," "L'Africaine," "Aïda," "Le Cid" (written for him by Massenet, and in which he made his Parisian début, November, 1885), Raoul in "Les Huguenots," Launcelot in "Elaine," and Roméo in "Roméo et Juliette," which was revived for him and placed in the ranks of grand opera, as originally intended by Gounod. In Wagner's operas he was admirable as Siegfried, Lohengrin, Walther, and especially as Tristan. But whether he represented one of Wagner's legendary knights or the impassioned lover and hero of Meyerbeer or Gounod, he was equally charming. His matchless voice and the exquisite art with which he sang were rivaled only by the picturesque grace and manly beauty that characterized each and all of his impersonations.

"I am a singer, not a writer," he once said, when asked to give his opinion regarding certain musical compositions and their authors. "I prefer to speak only of what lies directly in my province—i.e., the interpretation, not the creation, of those works. To the composer belongs the analysis, to the interpreter the inspiration. I rarely, if ever, sing or act the same rôle twice alike. Of course, on general grounds, the basis of my work is the same; my conception of a rôle, once thought out and executed, does not change; but variations and new ideas are constantly suggesting themselves, and, though always on the same canvas, one embroiders a different pattern; a touch here and there, a dash of color against a deeper background, a paler tint or a tenderer tone—who can foresee or measure and calculate what the actual moment may inspire?"

Jean de Reszke retired from opera in 1904, and opened a singing-school in Paris. His brother Edouard (born in Warsaw, December 23, 1855), who was associated with the great tenor in so many of his engagements in America and abroad, continued to appear in basso rôles a few years longer, but finally bade farewell to the lyric stage, devoting the greater part of his time to pupils in London.

NELLIE MELBA.—Though she is known to the world as Madame Melba (from her birthplace), this singer's family name is Mitchell. She was born in Melbourne, Australia, May 19, 1865, and at the town hall there she made her first public appearance at the age of six. Her father, David Mitchell, was strongly opposed to her choice of a musical career, and had he been permitted to decide the matter she would never have become a professional singer. As a young girl, however, she was allowed to receive instruction in piano, harmony, and composition, and when she was offered a place as organist in a church, the stern old Scotchman made no objection. The inevitable happened. The young girl found that she possessed a voice, and it became the one ambition of her life to employ it to the best advantage. In 1882 she married Captain Charles Armstrong, and, removed from parental authority, was encouraged to follow her natural bent. In due course of time the young singer sailed away from the colonial capital from which she took her stage name, and eventually placed herself under the tutelage of Madame Marchesi. Her voice, a pure and flexible soprano, admirably suited to the coloratura music of the Italian composers, developed an even compass of from B flat to F'''. On October 27, 1887, she made her début in opera, appearing at the Théâtre de la Monnaie, Brussels, as Gilda in Verdi's "Rigoletto." Her success was immediate. Engagements followed for Covent Garden, London, and a few years later she was one of the leading sopranos at the Metropolitan Opera House, New York. With the predominance of German opera in New York, however, Melba found it desirable to devote herself to Covent Garden and the Paris Opera, and with the exception of occasional concert tours she was heard no more in America until 1906, when she was engaged as leading soprano at the Manhattan Opera House. Among the best of her many rôles may be noted Juliette in Gounod's "Roméo et Juliette," Violetta in "La Traviata," Rosina in "The Barber of Seville," the Queen in "Les Huguenots," Nedda in "I Pagliacci," Marguerite in "Faust," the name part in Saint-Saëns's "Hélène," Ophelia in "Hamlet," Micaëla in "Carmen," and Elsa in "Lohengrin." She made several triumphal tours of Australia, and in England was in great demand for concert and oratorio.

MARCELLA SEMBRICH.—Like many another great singer, Sembrich was wise in the "choice of her parents"—both were musicians. She was born February 15, 1858, at Wisniowczyk, Galicia. Her father was Kasimir Kochanska; her mother, born Sembrich, was a singer. She was christened Praxede Marcelline, but it is doubtful if these names and the cognomen were ever used on a musical programme after her first public appearance at the age of twelve. At her operatic début she assumed her mother's name for stage purposes, and as Marcella Sembrich she was known and admired by all lovers of music.

While other little girls devoted most of their time to dolls, Marcelline was playing piano and violin, and when she was first brought into notice it was as a violinist and pianist. Those who heard the great prima donna in "The Barber of Seville" are aware that she had not forgotten her skill at the piano; for Rosina is compelled to interpolate a number of songs at the "music-lesson," for which Rossini's music is missing, and it was Sembrich's custom as Rosina to play her own accompaniment at the piano. Nor did she abandon the violin. It is of record, indeed, that she played it at a great concert in New York in the early eighties; but as she was endowed by nature with a finer instrument than any made in Cremona, her skill in this respect has been forgotten. One may suspect that the little Marcelline acquired a knowledge of other instruments than these, but one thing is certain—she played with vigor and precision on the side drum. As the heroine of "La fille du régiment" it was her custom to march in to a roulade of her own drumming which aroused the admiration, not only of the gods, but of the percussion section of the orchestra.

To return to the child débutante: she had evinced enough talent to justify her parents in placing her with Wilhelm Stengel, of the Lemberg Conservatory, where she studied piano. Her progress was rapid, and she passed from the supervision of Stengel to that of Brustermann, and then for a time had lessons from Liszt, in Vienna. Her first vocal master was Rokitansky. Next she studied for a while with Richard Lewy, completing her education under the direction of the two Lampertis.

On June 3, 1877, Marcella Sembrich made her operatic début in Athens as Elvira in "I Puritani." Her exquisite voice, perfect musicianship, and charming stage presence won instant recognition. The following year she appeared with equal success at the Royal Dresden Opera. Thereafter she was in demand at the chief European opera houses, and from 1878 until 1908, when she retired from the operatic stage, one of the most popular members of the Metropolitan Opera House Company, New York.

To mention the rôles in which she distinguished herself during this notable career is to catalogue the fine coloratura parts now in repertoire. Let these suffice: Amina, Lucia, Marguerite de Valois, Dinorah, Violetta, Constance, Susanna and Astrafiammante.

By many competent authorities, both in America and abroad, Sembrich was regarded as the chief exponent in her generation of the Italian style of singing when Italy was at its best. She was always a conscientious artist in her relation to the public, and a favorite in the recital and concert-room as well as on the operatic stage.

CHAPTER XII

STARS OF MODERN OPERA

LILLIAN NORDICA.—Outstanding as an American singer Nordica also ranks as one of the great singers of the world, a solid proof of the fact that a great artist can come out of American environment and receive an adequate training in the United States. Nordica is a stage name taken by the singer in deference to the notion prevailing in her time that a plain American surname was a handicap to an opera singer. He real name was Norton and she was born at Farmington, Me., May 12, 1859. Both parents were of the old Puritan stock.

When Lillian was five years old the family removed to Boston. In her girlhood she worked in a book shop. Her talent for singing showed itself and she became a student at the New England Conservatory, in Boston, where she was a pupil of John O'Neill. Her concert début in 1876 was only the beginning of a life of hard study. Combined with her fine talent was a strong character and definite personality. She won her first important engagement as soloist with Gilmore's Band by reason of her confidence in her ability and steady persistence in seeking an opportunity to show her art. A tour in the United States was followed by one in Europe in 1878, and encouragement to enter the operatic field. Under the instruction of San Giovanni, in Milan, she prepared a number of rôles and made her début in TRAVIATA at Brescia, April 30, 1879. Her first appearance at Paris was in FAUST in 1882; her American début was in New York, also as *Marguerite*, in 1883; her first engagement at Covent Garden, London, was in 1887.

The passing years established her reputation as a singer of the first rank. Her first engagement at the Metropolitan Opera House, New York, was in 1893, in which she competed for honors with Melba, Calve and Eames. During this period she worked hard—she learned a rôle slowly but held it tenaciously—and was gradually moving on to the highest position, that of a singer of Wagnerian rôles, a dramatic part essentially different from the coloratura singing she had previously done with so great success. In 1894 she sang the part of *Elsa* at Bayreuth, and then set to work to learn other rôles. From then she rarely sang in other than Wagnerian dramas. Her finest work was done as *Isolde*. Of this role William Armstrong, a well-known critic, wrote: "Her splendid trumpet tones, her tones of subdued, passionate tenderness, were of supreme beauty." Mme. Schumann-Heink, commenting on Nordica's earlier rôles, said: "Her velvety tones were better than those of any singer among them all. Her high C in Verdi's REQUIEM spun out like a thread of golden light."

The late years of her life Nordica gave up mainly to concert tours throughout the world. It was on one of these that she died at Batavia, in the East Indies, May 10, 1914. Her career shows the power of genius and diligence to raise one from poverty to high artistic eminence.

ENRICO CARUSO.—Ask any music lover in almost any part of the world his verdict as to who was the greatest tenor in recent times and the reply will be, "Caruso." Of course, only a small number of persons, comparatively, heard him personally. But wherever the phonograph has been carried Caruso's golden voice has been heard through the medium of records, in operatic arias, concert songs, folk songs and other gems of vocal music. While he lived he was a vital character in the world of art. His untimely death was a tragedy to music.

Enrico Caruso was born of humble parents, a member of a large family, in Naples, February 25, 1873. As a youth of ten he sang in church choirs. He set himself to study under various teachers without, apparently, any conception on their part or his own of the splendid natural endowment that he possessed. Military service intervened but fortunately did not injure his voice. His training was again taken up by Lamperti, Vergine and Lombardi who set him with serious purpose and steadfast mind on the way of art. He made his début at Caserta, near Naples, in April, 1895, taking the part of *Faust*. A year later he won real success at Naples in the tenor rôles of LA TRAVIATA, LA FAVORITA and GIOCONDA. An engagement in Milan made his position as an artist secure. Appearances in other Italian cities followed, in Petrograd and in Buneos Aires. A first appearance in London was made in 1902 in RIGOLETTO, winning the favor of the public before that of the press.

On November 23, 1903, Caruso first came before an American audience at the Metropolitan Opera House in New York in the rôle of the *Duke* in RIGOLETTO. From that time on he was the great favorite of the American musical public and ranked as one of the outstanding artists of his time. He was probably the highest paid singer, not only for opera performances but for concert appearances. It has been stated that he was paid, at the zenith of his fame, as high as $10,000 a performance. Aside from this his royalties for the numerous records he made for the phonograph were figured at upwards of $100,000 annually.

In the latter years of his life he developed trouble in the larynx due, in all probability, to the prodigality with which he lavished the treasure of his voice as a tribute to the enthusiasm of the public. Operations seemed to relieve the trouble but other complications set in and death resulted at Naples, August 2, 1921.

His tone was unrivalled in sweetness and power backed by the ringing resonance of the true dramatic tenor. He was an indefatigable student of his art and obtained a control of breath worthy of the stories told of some of the singers of the golden age of Italian song. He was at home in the stormy, passionate music of modern opera, the tranquil beauty of lyric song and the simple style of the folksong.

GERALDINE FARRAR.—Prominent among the singing artists of her time and lauded for the vigor and dramatic quality of her impersonating of opera rôles, Geraldine Farrar became a favorite with the American public. Like Lillian Nordica she offers an example of the fact that the Anglo-Saxon race can produce successful artists in a line which had been supposedly reserved for the foreigner. It is true that Farrar studied in Europe, but the groundwork of her musical education was laid in Boston.

Geraldine Farrar was born at Melrose, Mass., a suburb of Boston, on February 28, 1882. Her parents were amateur musicians and sang in church choirs. The father was a storekeeper and played baseball in his leisure. In 1884 he was engaged professionally in the sport as a first baseman, which he followed for the summer, in winter occupied in business. As a child Geraldine showed talent for music, especially singing, but disliked the necessity for practice in piano playing. In 1894 she sang in public with so much success that she was brought to the attention of a fine teacher of singing in Boston, Mrs. J. H. Long, who consented to take the girl as a pupil. Mrs. Long's first victory was in overcoming Geraldine's distaste for the practice of scales and other technical exercises. Concert appearances in Melrose were mingled with persistent study. In May, 1896 she sang for the first time in Boston at Mrs. Long's annual pupils' recital. Attendance at opera performances roused an ambition for a career on the stage. Advice from Jean de Reszke to study in New York was followed and some time was spent with Mme. Cappiani and Emma Thursby. The encouragement of well-known singers and critics seemed to justify the young singer in her ambition.

She was now seventeen. Handicapped by the inability of her father to undertake the expenses of finishing training in Europe it was impossible to pursue her studies further. At this juncture a wealthy woman music-lover agreed to provide for the expense of the training in Europe by a loan of a large amount. In Paris she studied with Travadello. On the advice of Nordica and her husband the next study was made in Berlin under Graziani, supplemented later by Lilli Lehmann. Her début was made as *Marguerite* in FAUST at the Berlin Royal Opera House in 1901, followed by engagements in other European cities, including Paris and Monte Carlo. The American début was at the Metropolitan Opera House, in November, 1906, as *Juliet* in ROMEO AND JULIET. Her repertoire included the standard works from the French, Italian and German literature including several of the Wagnerian operas and Humperdinck's KÖNIGSKINDER. Her success with American audiences duplicated her reception in Europe.

Her voice was of the lyric order yet so definite was her control and so vivid her power to take up a character and identify herself with it, that her presentation of a part was spontaneous, her voice responding to the need for expression and subtlety in delivery. Further proof of her histrionic gift and power was given by her extraordinary work in her film representation of *Carmen*, produced in 1915. Miss Farrar was married to the actor, Lou Tellegen, in 1916.

MARY GARDEN.—Rated as an American singer Mary Garden is of Scotch ancestry. Perhaps those qualities of personality have had much to do with the way she worked up to the heights of success. She believed that she could bend fate to her will. She is of that type that rules, and works for what she wants. She has the Scotch feeling for melody and music and the practical qualities which make the race remarkable in achievement. "Battles never frighten me," she said.

Mary Garden was born in Aberdeen, Scotland, February 20, 1877. Her family came to the United States in 1883 and first settled in Chicopee, Mass., then in Hartford, Conn., going to Chicago in 1888. Mary's talent for music showed when she was a child. The first studies were made on the violin, followed by instruction in piano playing. Her training in singing began in 1893 under the direction of Mrs. S. R. Duff. Teacher and pupil went to Paris in 1895. With her characteristic efficiency she shut herself out from all things not French until she felt herself at home in the vernacular. Seven teachers were tried before she felt that she had met the right ones for her: Trabadello and Fugère of the Opera Comique. Her first appearance was to have been in the part of *Micaela* in CARMEN. Meanwhile she had studied the part of *Louise* in Charpentier's opera of that name. Attending a performance of LOUISE as a listener she took the place of the prima donna who was suddenly taken ill and sang the part from the third act to the close with success. This was followed by an immediate engagement.

English-speaking artists have won success in Italian and Wagnerian operas, but French modern works demand something different. This something Mary Garden showed great ability to grasp and assimilate. Her success as a histrionic artist was as great as her success as a singer. A proof of this power of dramatic impersonation is that she was chosen by Debussy to create the rôle of *Melisande* in 1902. The same vivid qualities were recognized by the French public in other productions.

Oscar Hammerstein, of the Manhattan Opera Company, New York, with his keen sense of artistic stature, engaged Mary Garden for his organization. Her New York début was in the rôle of *Thaïs,* November 25, 1907, and was an extraordinary success. In 1910 she joined the forces of the Chicago Opera Company and remained with them. Her greatest rôles were *Salomé* (Strauss), *Sapho, Griselidis, Marguerite, Carmen,* and *Jean* in LE JONGLEUR DE NOTRE DAME. She was artistic director of the Chicago Opera Company during the season of 1921-1922. Her voice may not have been a great one and her vocalism less perfected than that of some other singers, but her marvelous acting and her power of assimilating a character and of representing it with vivid expression made her work phenomenally successful.

MENDELSSOHN'S MUSE.

FROM A PAINTING BY BOUTET DE MONVEL.
A portrait study of his sister, Fanny Mendelssohn.

WOMAN IN MUSIC

BY

LOUIS C. ELSON

I

ANCIENT INFLUENCES

ALTHOUGH millions of young ladies have studied music more or less thoroughly during the past two or three centuries, there is as yet no female figure as prominent in musical creation as Rosa Bonheur in painting, or George Eliot in literature. I have often questioned eminent teachers and composers as to their views of this matter and their opinions as to the cause of the apparent male supremacy.

Svendsen, the famous Norwegian, stated that he found the girl student much more teachable than the boy, up to a certain point. The girl, he said, had a quicker perception of the meaning of the composition and always caught the points of its interpretation more readily. When it came to individualizing, and more especially to creating new musical thoughts, he found a distinct slowing-up, and that here the male student of talent would forge ahead perceptibly.

Reinecke, for a long time the head of the Leipsic Conservatory and the leader of the Gewandhaus Orchestra, should certainly be entitled to an opinion, not only because he trained thousands, but because he had ten daughters of his own, and his opinion almost exactly coincided with that of Svendsen. I shall show in later chapters why I venture to differ from these authorities, and why I believe that a great woman composer may soon arise.

Let us first examine what influence has been exerted by women upon the recognized masters of composition. It will form a fitting preamble to the study of woman's actual musical achievement that is to follow.

* * *

IN THE DAYS of the troubadours and minnesingers, from about 1200 to 1450, a great change took place in the appreciation of womanhood in France and Germany. Woman had been degraded to an unjustly low position, but was now elevated to an exaggeratedly high one. She became the queen to whom all homage was due, the arbiter of fate, the ruler of kings. She inspired music and poetry to an unlimited degree.

Walther von der Vogelweide sang of the women of his native land all through his wanderings in foreign climes. Once he burst forth with the sentiment—

> Many lands have I seen
> And many ladies fine,
> Yet none are like the German dames
> With form so divine.

Which did honor to his loyalty, even if we may doubt the question of "form." Henry of Meissen never wrote a poem or sang a song that had not for its topic the idealization of German womanhood. They changed his very name to *Frauenlob*, "Homage to Women." When he died, the noble dames of Germany came to his funeral at Mainz in such numbers that when they threw in their rosebuds and poured their libation of wine into the open grave it overflowed with the numerous tributes.

In France, too, women inspired the troubadours to numerous songs. There was this distinction between the minnesinger and the troubadour; the former often sang of the entire sex, praising their gentleness, their fidelity, while the troubadour usually was more specific, choosing some one special object of his devotion and giving all his musical homage to her; praising her beauties with commendable detail, but usually giving her some pastoral pseudonym, as "Amaryllis," "Daphne" or "Chloe." Sometimes there were rather imaginative songs also. I cannot think of anything more fanciful than the affection of Geoffrey Rudel for the Countess of Tripoli. He had never seen her, but the descriptions of knights coming from the East so worked upon his imagination that he indited song after song to his lady. Finally, he plucked up courage and went to Tripoli.

This was dangerous for such an excitable nature as his seems to have been, for when he stepped on shore, the thought that he was now to meet his idol so moved him that he fell down in a swoon. They carried him to a hostelry near by, and the Countess, moved by such intense affection, came to the room where he lay ill. That was the most dangerous of all, for he now became so overjoyed that he died at once, and the lady erected a monument to his memory.

Sometimes the troubadour sang a song of etiquette to his lady love, and these songs are among the most curious effusions inspired by the women of the Middle Ages— although not by the middle-aged women. In one of these songs of etiquette the singer leaves very little to the imagination; he sings of cleaning the teeth, eating daintily with the fingers (forks had not yet come in)

and washing the hands thereafter. In another of these songs the lady has asked her adoring adviser what she shall do, if at a banquet a knight who has taken too much wine should pay her too marked attention. The troubadour advises her, in poetry and tone, to introduce some topic for discussion, to ask the knight if he thinks the Gascon ladies are more beautiful than English ones.

> And if he says "The Gascon"
> You by the English bide,
> But if he says "The English"
> Then take the Gascon side.

And he suggests immediately calling some other women in the room to give their judgment in the matter—

> And when they enter in the fight
> You're not alone with this bold knight.

Which is good enough advice even in the twentieth century.

In one of these German songs similar to these *Essenhamens*—as they were called—a lady is advised to study "cooking, sewing, surgery and chess," which will seem a strange combination to many a female reader even if she assents to the first two. The study of surgery was essential in those days. If the lady of the castle was handsome and gracious many a knight would carry a lance in her honor in the tournaments that were so common, and one of these knights might be brought to the castle with a broken arm or a cracked pate. Then the fair chatelaine must be ready to give first aid to the injured. The knowledge of chess was also of use, for many a knight would stay as a guest in the castle for weeks, and if the time hung heavy on his hands the lady would invite him to play chess with her, usually for a stake.

*   *   *

IT IS A tempting subject and very much more could be said about it, but I have shown that woman influenced music of various kinds in the medieval times. Of the women who actually made music I shall tell in connection with the story of female composers. One belated troubadour may be mentioned here, and the lady who inspired his music. The latter was Madame D'Hauteville, and the singer was Louis XIII. of France.

The reader will at once think of the composition called "Amaryllis" by Louis XIII., arranged by Ghys. This is one of the false compositions in music. Many such exist. "Stradella's Prayer" was not composed by Stradella, but probably by Gluck; Beethoven's "Farewell to the Pianoforte" was not his farewell, nor was it his last composition, but a trivial work in a lady's album, it is thought, and certainly composed long before his death; "Weber's Last Waltz" was not his last waltz, nor his waltz at all, since it was composed by Reissiger; and Mozart's celebrated "Twelfth Mass" has probably not a note of Mozart from beginning to end.

In similar manner, "Amaryllis, by Louis XIII.," as it is played on the piano by many young musicians, was not composed by the French king, but by an Italian named Baltazarini before Louis XIII. was born, and it is not "Amaryllis," but was named by its composer "La Clochette," from the fact that a little bell sounded all through the chief theme. Yet, curiously enough, Louis XIII. did write an "Amaryllis," and it was a four-part song in praise of Mme. D'Hauteville, whom he named as above in accordance with the troubadour custom.

AMARYLLIS

English version by Louis C. Elson

LOUIS XIII (1620)

II

THE WIVES OF COMPOSERS—BEETHOVEN AND FEMALE INSPIRATION

AS we approach later days we find composers much influenced by their wives or women who won their affection. This was naturally not so much the case in the early days when music was contrapuntal and leaned heavily to the intellectual side. We hear but little of the wives of Palestrina or of Orlando di Lasso, the two earliest really great composers. Nor did the first or second marriage of Bach influence his music greatly save in the fact that as he had twenty-one children and trained most of them in music he must have had a fair-sized orchestra in his own family circle. Handel never married, although it is said two Englishwomen were deeply in love with him. He certainly paid more attention to affairs of the stomach than to affairs of the heart if the caricature published during his lifetime which portrays him with a pig's head, seated at an organ which is garnished with hams and sausages, be a correct representation.

We may doubt if Mozart or Haydn were influenced by woman in the composition of their music. There is an odd similarity in their wooing and wedding. Haydn fell in love with the younger daughter of the wig-maker Keller, but this young lady was deeply religious and soon became a nun. Keller, *père*, did not wish to lose so promising a son-in-law—for Haydn was then a permanent orchestral director in the household of Prince Nicolas Esterhazy—and therefore he urged him to take the elder sister instead, which he did. She led him a furious dance the rest of his life. When he was beginning to win a larger income in London, she wrote to him urging the purchase of a certain dwelling in Vienna, "which will just suit me when I am a widow!" The house was not bought, but a separation was finally achieved.

Mozart's courtship began in much the same way. He fell in love with a daughter of a musician named Weber, in Mannheim. But Aloysia Weber was piqued when, at the command of his father, the young Mozart left for Paris. She presented him with a prophetic gift, at parting—a pair of mittens—and soon after she married an actor named Lange, whereupon Mozart transferred his affections to her sister Constance, whom he married. It was not an unhappy match, yet Constance Mozart was a wretched helpmate for a struggling composer. The pair spent money when they had it, and tried to borrow when they had none. The name of Constance Mozart can only be directly associated with one composition of the master, the overture to "Don Giovanni."

The opera had been announced, rehearsed, and was to be given the next day, but Mozart had delayed writing the overture until the very last minute. At last, within twenty-four hours of the performance, he began work upon it. To refresh him during moments of rest, Constance sat by him and told him all the gossip of the neighborhood. The boy from the opera house came for each page of the score as it was completed, and rushed with it to the copyist, that the different instruments might have their parts in time. Sometimes an hour of sleep was sandwiched in, and Constance sat by to wake the composer when it was necessary to resume the task. Sometimes, too, it is said, she brewed him a stimulant of which he was fond.

The haste with which the work was written may be shown by the fact that there was no time for a rehearsal, and Mozart, who conducted the first performance, was obliged to say to the musicians—"Gentlemen of the brasses, I fear that I have written either six measures too many or too few in your part, but watch me carefully and it will come out all right."

The overture was played, and proved to be a masterpiece, and a few over-sapient critics claim to be able to detect the very places where the composer went to sleep and was waked up again! So much to Constance's credit.

It stands against Constance Mozart that, being somewhat ill on the day of his funeral, she did not go to Mozart's grave, which was one of the common receiving tombs and shared with others. Nor did she visit it when she got well. She subsequently married Baron von Nissen, and it was about ten years later that von Nissen suggested to her that it might be well for them to try to find the grave of Mozart. It was then too late. The old sexton had died, and there was no record of where the body had been laid. It has never been discovered. Constance outlived her second husband and died, quite well-to-do, at eighty years of age.

Nor was Mozart himself so very poverty-stricken as some of the musical histories would have us believe. He was improvident, and continually borrowing money which he seldom repaid, but here is a letter to his wife, written October 7th, 1791, very near the end of his life (Krehbiel's translation), when she had gone to Baden for her ill health.

"As soon as you were gone I played two games of billiards with Herr von Mozart [himself], who wrote the opera for Schicka-neder's Theatre; then I sold my nag for fourteen ducats; then I had Joseph call my *primus* [a janitor valet] and bring a cup of black coffee, to which I smoked a glorious pipe of tobacco. . . . What do I see! What do I smell! It is the *primus* with a cutlet. Gusto! I eat to your health!"

Billiards, coffee, a "nag," tobacco, a semi-valet, a meat supper. These are not signs of pressing poverty!

It is only when we come to Beethoven that we begin to find the female influence exerted directly upon the works of a great tone-master. Beethoven was continually falling in love. As each fall was entirely platonic, and led to noble music, the world may be glad he was so susceptible. Beethoven had the loftiest ideal of pure womanhood. He longed for some great-minded companion to stimulate the best that was in him. There was a long procession of those who awakened his muse. In his youngest days it was Eleonora von Breuning, whose brother and mother were close friends, and who taught him the beauties of German literature. The guidance of this noble and well-educated woman undoubtedly influenced his later compositions in a large degree. It is, however, a pity she did not include Shakespeare in her curriculum, since no one could have set that poet to music as well as Beethoven.

He was in love with the Countess Erdoedy, if his letter beginning "Liebe, liebe, liebe, liebe, Gräfin," counts for anything, and he dedicated Op. 70, two trios, and Op. 102, two sonatas, to her. The Countess Babette von Keglevics ruled his heart for some time, as the piano sonata, Op. 7, may show. Bettina Brentano, and the Baroness von Ertmann also had their influence and were duly translated into tones.

The seventh and eighth symphonies, the brightest of his entire series, were an outcome of his courtship of Amalia Seebald, a charming singer, who seems to have been very fond of him. Why no marriage ensued is something of a mystery, yet the episode crystallized in two of the most charming tone-poems in the world: the eighth symphony being the most exquisite embodiment of humor, while the seventh is, at least to me, the most perfect of Beethoven's symphonies.

But there was one affection which seems to have been deeper and stronger than all the others put together. This was revealed by two letters, found after his death, in a secret drawer in Beethoven's desk. These breathe a fervor that is almost volcanic. We do not know to whom they were addressed. Many believe that it was Giuletta Guicciardi, but Beethoven seemed to allude to her with marked indifference at a later epoch of his life. The fact remains that the great sonata, Op. 27, No. 2, which is called "The Moonlight Sonata," is dedicated to Giuletta Guicciardi. The name "Moonlight" was never given by Beethoven to the work, and the silly story about his wandering in the forest and improvising for a blind girl, is one of the gushy, sentimental fictions of music, but the fact remains that one may readily imagine this work a direct inspiration of passion.

Beethoven's later notes seem to show that a painting of a woman at prayer had inspired the work. It is possible that various influences were at work here, and it is also possible that Beethoven, who was very shy and sensitive, did not care to wear his heart on his sleeve and to reveal all about this romantic work. The influence of woman upon the later composers was not less marked than in the case of Beethoven, and the details can be yet more definitely traced.

III

FEMALE INSPIRATION—SCHUBERT, SPOHR AND WEBER

IT is a question how much Schubert was influenced by female surroundings. His music was something that bubbled up spontaneously and needed no external stimulus. We come nearest to the divine fount of inspiration in the works of Schubert. People who are not trained in music have an utterly false idea of how a composer achieves his work. In the first place, a real master of tones does not use any instrument while he is thinking out a composition. Mozart said he always composed best while playing billiards. Stephen C. Foster, the famous writer of American folk songs, used to seek inspiration by riding up and down Broadway in a five-cent 'bus. Beethoven did his greatest musical work during long walks, jotting down his ideas in a memorandum book.

If we compare the Beethoven ideas as found in some of these memorandum books which have been preserved, with the works as finally printed, we find most striking changes, most marked improvements, showing that the original inspiration was not accepted by him.

In Schubert we find one great instance of spontaneous composition. He wrote the splendid setting of "Hark, Hark, the Lark," from Shakespeare's "Cymbeline," on the back of a bill-of-fare, in an open-air restaurant just outside of Vienna while waiting for his breakfast one Sunday morning. He jumped out of bed one night and wrote out "The Trout," and spilled a lot of ink on the manuscript afterward while he was half asleep. He composed best when he was unhappy, and once said the public seemed to like best those songs which were wrung from his adversity. Unfortunately too often

> The anguish of the singer
> Makes the beauty of the strain.

One looks in vain for female influence here, either to crush his heart or to uplift it. We have been thus minute in describing Schubert and his work because of an apocryphal story told in many musical histories. When he was teacher in the family of Prince Esterhazy, at Zelesz in Hungary, he fell in love, the story runs, with Countess Caroline Esterhazy, one of the Prince's daughters whom he taught. One day she asked him why, among his numerous dedications, he had never dedicated a single composition to her. "Because," was the reply, "all that I achieve is dedicated to you!"

We are sorry to throw doubt on so pretty a tale, but if Schubert had dared say that to a countess in the early nineteenth century, he would certainly have been thrown out of the castle. Countess Caroline never mentioned this incident. She married Count Von Crenneville, "and lived happily ever afterward." The chief point to be made against the story is the fact that Schubert did dedicate a piece to the Countess, the Fantasie in F minor for piano duet (Op. 103) which was published after his death. This work is so inferior to most of his compositions that we cannot by any stretch of fancy imagine it to be the tribute of a secret and lifelong devotion. Unfortunately, musical history is full of such false anecdotes.

A much more direct and traceable female influence is found in the case of Louis Spohr, a composer who is unjustly neglected in recent days. Spohr began violin study at five years of age, and at six was able to take part in chamber concerts. He began to compose when he was six. In 1805 he became conductor at the court of Gotha. While there he met and married a charming young harp player named Dorette Scheidler. A better match could not have been imagined. Spohr was the leading violinist of Germany, and Dorette Scheidler probably the best harpist. A great change had just taken place in the harp. This instrument, which had been used for thousands of years, had always been a diatonic one, requiring retuning at certain changes of key. In 1810 Erard invented a system, in use to-day, of double-action pedals, by which each string could be tuned instantly as flat, natural or sharp, and this gave the harp entrance into all keys.

With the new instrument, and with his new wife, Spohr began a series of concerts in which there was both conjugal and musical partnership. Harp and violin duets, and works in which these instruments were employed with orchestra, were produced by him copiously, and concert tours were made through many countries. It may be of interest to state here that Spohr was probably the first conductor to lead regularly with a baton. The use of a short stick in directing is scarcely one hundred years old.

It is in the life of Carl Maria von Weber that we find a more elevating example of female influence than a musical partnership. To understand what a noble, womanly nature accomplished in this instance we must know something of the career and nature of Weber before he met Caroline Brandt. His father was a scion of a noble family, and financial counselor to the Archbishop of Cologne. But he was a selfish and dissipated character and although "financial counselor," he took mighty little heed to his own finances, being a sad spendthrift. The son was a delicate child, afflicted with hip disease from birth, unable to walk at four years of age. At that age he was able to sing and to play the piano with amazing ability. In my companion work, "The Childhood of Composers," one will find how Beethoven's father tried to make a money-making prodigy of his son, inspired thereto by the example of Mozart. Weber's father attempted something of the same sort. In spite of the irregularity of life entailed by this injudicious proceeding, the lad received some fairly good musical training. Beethoven, who had emphatic quarrels with Weber, has misled many musical historians by saying of him—"He studied music so late that he never attained more than the art of pleas-

FUGHETTA BY WEBER

Composed at the Age of Eleven

ing." We disprove this statement by printing herewith a fughetta in excellent counterpoint which was one of six which the boy composed when he was eleven years old.

But it was a vagrant life at the best that the boy lived. His constant theatrical associations often produced footlight flavor in his music which can be discerned even in his sonatas. His youth was full of escapades. He became an official—not musical—at the court of Stuttgart and the dissipated life here almost wrecked his career before it had fairly begun. The King of Württemberg often quarreled with the young secretary of his brother's household. Once, after a stormy interview with the king, young Weber met a peasant woman in the ante-chamber who inquired of him as to where she could find the royal washerwoman. "In there," responded Weber, pointing to the king's chamber, and in she went. Weber went into imprisonment to pay for his audacity. Finally the Weber family, including the father, was banished forever from Württemberg.

Then came theatrical life, and in the course of this the meeting with the singer, Caroline Brandt, whom Weber brought from Vienna to Prague to sing in the opera com-

pany which he directed there. There was much affection on both sides, even from the beginning. Fraulein Brandt was at first unwilling to sacrifice her promising career to become the wife of such a wandering troubadour as Weber. Once, indeed, she attempted to disentangle the bonds which bound them, and wrote to Weber that they had better part. Weber's response was bitter enough, for he accused her of only estimating art as a means of getting soup, meat and shirts.

This lover's quarrel soon blew over and when Weber returned to Prague his faithful Caroline announced herself willing to wait until he should have attained a fixed position that would enable him to support a household. This position soon came.

Weber was appointed operatic conductor in Prague for life. Not long afterward marriage followed, and then a very successful concert tour as a honeymoon.

Weber's married life was one of absolute and entire happiness. It enabled him to bear the many trials which always beset an operatic manager in a small European city. Caroline Brandt, too, became greater because of this marriage. She had been a favorite of the public and a spoiled child of the theatrical world. She now became an earnest domestic helper and merged herself entirely into her husband's career; and that career grew astonishingly greater. Prague was soon left behind and Germany witnessed the great triumphs that were to come in Weber's short life. All the great operas that Weber wrote came during his married life and, it is no exaggeration to say, because of it. His whole existence seems to have been bound up in the happiness of his wife and children.

They shared the tremendous triumph of "Der Freischütz." The dissipated, spendthrift wastrel had vanished, and in his place there was a true man, loving art and idolizing his family. The final act of Weber's life shows this devotion most pathetically.

London had come under the spell of his operas and wished to see the great master. An offer of a thousand pounds came from the Covent Garden Opera House for an opera composed to an English text, to be performed in London and conducted by the composer. Weber was now far gone in consumption and knew well the danger of the task, but he wanted above all things to provide for his wife and family. Dr. Hedenus was consulted about the trip to England. "If you give up composing and conducting, and take a vacation in Italy, you may live five or six years yet. If you go to London you may not live as many weeks," was the emphatic reply. "As God wills," said Weber, and then began studying English that he might make the opera of "Oberon" more thorough.

The London performance was a great success. Weber's contract was that he should conduct the first twelve representations and this he carried out loyally. But his strength was ebbing fast and suddenly a dire premonition that the end was near came upon him. Quick preparations were made for the return journey, for Weber had a great longing to see his family once more. It was too late. On the morning of the fifth of June, 1826, they found him dead in his bed, in the house of his host, Sir George Smart (in Great Portland Street, London). Among his papers they found a manuscript which they supposed was his final work, and it was at once published under the title of "Weber's Last Waltz." Many of our readers know it under this title, or as "Weber's Last Thought," but it is not Weber's at all. It was given to him as a souvenir, when he started on his fatal journey, by the composer of it—Reissiger.

A great funeral in London followed Weber's death. All England paid tribute to the great composer. They would have paid still greater tribute, had they known the story we have detailed, to the man who cheerfully laid down his life for those he loved.

IV

THE AFFECTIONS OF CHOPIN AND BERLIOZ

IF the influence of a good woman was clearly marked in the life and musical career of Weber, it was still more so in the compositions of Robert Schumann, but, as Clara Schumann was herself a composer, it will be more fitting to examine her life and influence in the series of women workers in music, which is to follow. The same is true of Fanny Mendelssohn, whose influence was also exerted in this dual manner.

Chopin was strongly under female influence at times, and this was, in his case, not an unmixed blessing. His affection for the young soprano, Constantia Gladkowska, was the immediate cause of some of his music. The natural outpouring of the affection of a musician would seem to be in song, but only Schumann has lived up to this statement, while Chopin was almost entirely devoted to one kind of composition—pianoforte—and is the only one of the great masters who has thus limited himself. He left a few songs, but these were published only after his death, and they are to a great degree piano works in disguise.

Constantia Gladkowska, when Chopin first met her, was just graduating from the Warsaw Conservatory of Music. Chopin gave concerts with her, wrote reviews in praise of her vocalism, and even before this had embodied his devotion in a musical composition. He writes about her, in a letter dated October 8, 1829, as follows:

"I have, perhaps to my misfortune, already found my ideal, whom I worship faithfully and sincerely. Six months have passed and I have not yet exchanged a syllable with her, although I dream of her every night. My thoughts were with her when I composed the *adagio* of my concerto."

This leads to some confusion. There is no *adagio* in either of his piano concertos. But he used this term indiscriminately for any slow movement, as the French often use the word *andante*. Investigation and comparison of dates leads to the conclusion that the *larghetto* of the *F* minor piano concerto was the movement indicated.

Another woman exerted some influence upon Chopin, without, however, exciting the tender passion. This was the Countess Delphine Potocka, to whom he dedicated several of his works. The Countess was a very talented amateur. Kviatkowski says that she took as much trouble with, and pride in, her musical *soirées* as other people took in giving successful dinners. She had a beautiful soprano voice. When Chopin was on his deathbed, she sang to him, having hurried from Nice to Paris on hearing the sad news. A famous picture commemorates this deathbed concert. There was another woman who exerted an intense and perhaps evil power over Chopin's life. Of her we shall speak next.

Although Chopin was at one time engaged to Marie Wodzinski this seems not to have had any marked influence upon his career; the engagement was soon broken and Marie married Count Skarbek. But the influence of the great French novelist George Sand (Madame Dudevant), upon his life was of the most marked character. It would not be the place, in these pages, to re-try the celebrated case of musical history. William H. Hadow, George Eliot, Elizabeth Browning, Matthew Arnold, and other eminent commentators, have held the connection of these two natures to have been nobly platonic and that Madame Dudevant martyred herself in elevating the character and ideals of Chopin. Huneker takes an opposite view. Here is Grenier's description of this remarkable woman:

"She was short and stout and her eyes attracted attention immediately. They were wonderful eyes, set rather too close together, large, black, very black, but by no means lustrous. They reminded one of velvet and gave a strange, dull, cold look to the face. Those large, fine and tranquil eyes with strong eyebrows over them gave a strength and dignity to her countenance which the lower part of the face seemed to contradict. The nose was rather thick, the mouth coarse, chin small."

It was with this great woman that Chopin went to Majorca, when her son, Maurice, was ill. Chopin was ill himself, and what with bad weather, chilliness, and dreary surroundings, the invalid must have been rather a burden to Madame Dudevant. One can read the details of all this in her "History of My Life," for, if she inspired some music in Chopin, he furnished her with considerable copy for her writings and novels. She once said, "Chopin is a detestable invalid," and the remark was undoubtedly true. In her novel of "Lucrezia Floriani," George Sand has drawn a picture—rather a caricature—of Chopin as Prince Karol.

But there is one piece of Chopin's music which George Sand was unintentionally instrumental in producing. It came after the pair had quarreled at Nohant. Chopin returned to his room in Paris, and, seating himself at the piano, began to improvise. He generally composed at the keyboard, which other great masters very seldom did. As he improvised he says that he seemed to see the folding doors swing apart and the nobility of Poland march by his piano. The richly dressed aristocratic dames, the lordly cavaliers, the troops going out to war, all seemed passing by. He grew terrified at his own vision and finally rushed from the room into the street. But he afterward wrote out this composition which was evolved under such nervous strain. It was probably the polonaise in A, known as the "Military Polonaise," although some authorities identify the work as the "A flat Polonaise," and consider the repeating bass figure of four descending notes, in the middle part of this composition, as being the portrayal of the tramp of the cavalry marching to battle.

* * *

BERLIOZ, the great French composer, who was, with Liszt, the pioneer of the modern school of program music, was tremendously influenced by a woman, in two of his greatest works. It is a strange love story, the one which culminated in the "Symphonie Fantastique" and the "Romeo and Juliet" symphony. Berlioz was very poor and very ambitious. In his youth he had already suffered much, for he was entering a musical career with only the reluctant acquiescence of his father, and with the ardent opposition of Cherubini, who was at the head of the Paris Conservatoire, where he was studying, and who could not understand the romantic modern school of composition in the least degree.

On the evening of September 11, 1827, the young composer went to a performance of Shakespeare, at the Odéon, in Paris. The chief actress was an Irish woman named Harriet Constance Smithson (Henrietta Smithson), and the play was "Hamlet." The young man was at once enamored of the *Ophelia*. Four days later he saw the actress again, this time as *Juliet*. Then a great, an overwhelming passion entered his breast. It is said that he then and there declared that the *Juliet* should become his wife, and that upon the play he would write his greatest musical work. He has denied this story, but the fact remains that his movement picturing the balcony scene is his most tender composition, and the one which he valued highest among all his works.

However, the "Symphonie Fantastique" is the more important work. It is not only the most graphic tone picture in the whole repertory, but it is the most definite love letter that was ever written in tones. The five movements portray the story of a young artist who has fallen hopelessly in love and who in his despair attempts suicide by taking opium. (The father of Berlioz was an opium eater.) It does not kill him, but causes this dream:

FIRST MOVEMENT. The Obsession by the Passion of Love. Here a love theme is introduced that runs all through the work.

SECOND MOVEMENT. A Ball. In the midst of the revelry the lover still dreams of his beloved.

THIRD MOVEMENT. In the Fields. The young lover hears a shepherd and shepherdess breathing their soft avowals. A thunderstorm ensues and the shepherdess is killed by a bolt.

FOURTH MOVEMENT. March to Punishment. The lover in a fit of jealous rage has killed his sweetheart and is being led to the guillotine. The menacing crowd around the tumbril, the pause at the scaffold, the last thought of the condemned man, of his beloved whom he has slain, the fall of the ax, the quivering corpse, are all relentlessly given. But even this is not the end.

FIFTH MOVEMENT. A weird last movement pictures the soul of the murderer arriving in the infernal regions. Here everything that was good and noble in his love is derided and parodied.

There was a strange alteration in this love letter, for Berlioz heard many slanders about Miss Smithson while she was in London, and he parodied her and turned her character to baseness in this strange finale. The slanders were disproved, and before Miss Smithson heard the work the heroine in the symphony was restored to nobility.

The seemingly impossible actually happened. Miss Smithson had an accident which retired her from the stage. The young composer became more famous, and finally they were affianced and at last were married. It is a pity that we cannot add that "they lived happily ever after." Madame Berlioz became insanely jealous as Berlioz's passion became gradually calmer. It was so notoriously wretched a partnership that the poet Heine, always satirical and often malicious, suggested that Berlioz probably wrote the "March to Punishment" for his own wedding. The passions are all stilled now, the actors are dust, but the musical love-letter remains imperishable in the concert repertoire.

* * *

IN THE CASE of Wagner we can also find female influence exerting strong power in some of his compositions. It is only recently that Wagner is coming to be judged dispassionately by musical historians and even yet there are virulent partisans who are cloaking and concealing many of his undeniable faults. We must bear in mind that the artistic temperament does not always imply morality or unselfishness. No amount of whitewashing will take away the stain of his separation from Minna Planer, Wagner's first wife, who sacrificed her entire career to his comfort.

The uncomplaining devotion of this first wife can scarcely be exaggerated. During the Paris days of poverty she trudged about seeking and obtaining loans for her husband (a Wagnerian loan was practically a gift), she took in lodgers in their humble apartments, she blacked the boots of husband and lodger, and she sewed and washed and drudged, only to be set aside when the days of prosperity came, and when she objected to her husband seeking inspiration from the wives of other men. Such inspiration he found in Mathilde Wesendonck, who was the chief factor in bringing forth "Tristan and Isolde."

But the reader should imagine two distinct Wagners, almost a real Dr. Jekyll and Mr. Hyde: "Wagner the Little" and "Wagner the Great." The latter it was who never forsook his highest ideal in art; who worked a quarter of a century upon a great music drama ("The Ring of the Nibelungs") without the hope of ever seeing it given, and wrote to a friend, "If I live to complete it I shall have lived gloriously, and if I die before it is finished I shall have died for something beautiful." It must be acknowledged that poor Minna Planer could not grasp such an ideal. If the reader seeks to discover more about "Wagner the Little," Ernest Newman's recent "Wagner as Man and Artist," Kapp's "Richard Wagner und die Frauen," and Praeger's "Wagner as I Knew Him," will present the seamy side. It is possible that Bernard Shaw, in "The Doctor's Dilemma," pictured this Wagnerian double nature in his character of the unscrupulous artist. It is much pleasanter to dwell upon the loftier side of Wagner's nature.

The second wife of Wagner was Cosima, the daughter of Liszt. She had been the wife of Wagner's friend and supporter, Hans von Bülow, but Wagner won her away from her husband. If any happiness can be justified that is founded upon the unhappiness of others, one may dismiss the lonely and deserted Minna Planer and the tortured Von Bülow from the mind, and confess that the happiness of the Wagner pair was ideal. Cosima Wagner was a helpmate indeed for her imperative and very erratic husband. She was his secretary; she stood as the buffer between him and troublesome visitors; she was the diplomat who smoothed out many a trouble that was caused by Wagner's impolitic, arrogant and irritating ways; and next to himself, Wagner loved her as well as anything on earth.

Which brings us to another love-letter in instrumental music. The Wagners were living in Triebschen, near Lucerne, in 1870. There had been born to them a son, Siegfried Wagner. Cosima's birthday was approaching. She was born on Christmas Day, 1837. Wagner determined to give her a birthday and Christmas gift to commemorate their happiness. He began composing an idyl made up of themes from his opera of "Siegfried," but worked out instrumentally and in an entirely different manner from their use in the opera.

December fourth he gave the score to his friend, Hans Richter, who at once wrote out the parts and set about engaging an orchestra to rehearse the new work. The musicians came to Lucerne secretly on December twenty-fourth and Wagner rehearsed them himself in the Hôtel du Lac. Christmas Day, in 1870, fell on a Sunday, and on that Sabbath morning, quite early, they all came very quietly to the Villa Triebschen. The music desks were noiselessly placed upon the stairs leading up to Madame Wagner's chamber— the family called the "Siegfried Idyl" "stair-music" after that — and then the musicians slipped into the kitchen to tune up. They took their places, one contrabass and one violoncello at the foot of the stairs, then two horns, one bassoon, two clarinets, an oboe and a flute, two violas, two second violins and two first violins, and at the very top of the stairs, Wagner with the conductor's baton, ready to lead the work. All this was early in the morning, before there was any chance of the family being up. At 7:30 Wagner stepped into the chamber and handed his wife the following poem, which I have translated rather freely, keeping its loving sentiment intact as far as possible.

Thy sacrifices have my victory gained me,
　And to my work have given lofty aim.
In many hours of trial they sustained me,
　Till strength and daring to my labor came.
Oft in the land of legend we were dreaming,
　Those stories which contain the Teuton's
　　fame,
And when a son upon our lives was beaming,
　Siegfried, we felt, must be the hero's name.
For him and thee in tones I now am praising;
　What thanks for deeds of Love could better
　　be?
Within my soul the grateful song upraising
　Which in this music I have now set free.
And in the cadence I have held united
　Siegfried, our dearly cherished son, and thee.
And all the harmonies that I am bringing
But voice the thought that in my heart is ringing.

After handing this poem to his wife Wagner came to his post at the head of the stairs again, and the music began. The musicians were invited to spend the Sunday at the villa and the "Siegfried Idyl" was repeated several times during the day.

The themes of the composition are especially appropriate to their subject, with a tranquil cradle song, and much use of a guiding figure, "Siegfried, the Treasure of the World." Hans Richter, the great conductor, had helped amazingly in bringing this surprise to success. He played the viola in the orchestra, he arranged the orchestra and copied the parts; he rehearsed the men, and, as there were a few measures of trumpet in the work, he borrowed a trumpet from a band man and went to the military barracks every day to practice on the instrument, which was new to him, as he was chiefly a horn player. The daily excursions for this purpose, and to Zurich for some of the band, led Madame Wagner, always keen for her husband's interests, to think that he was growing dilatory in his duties as musical secretary, but it was all cleared up after that Christmas morning.

Cosima Wagner idolized her husband as well. When he died, suddenly, in Venice, in 1883, she was almost bereft of reason. Wagner had always praised her beautiful long hair, and this she cut off and placed in his coffin. Six months after the death of the master I was in Bayreuth at the Wagner home. But still his widow would see no one. Even her father, Franz Liszt, was not allowed in her presence. Only the son Siegfried became her solace in those dark days. Every day, in sunshine or storm, she would sit some hours by the tomb, which is in the garden, just back of Villa Wahnfried, their home. The devotion at times seemed to surpass love and become idolatry.

*   *   *

Two women, besides these mentioned, have exerted a great influence upon the composition of music — Fanny Mendelssohn and Clara Schumann—but as they were musicians in their own right, and as I am to write of great women musicians later on, I reserve these for a subsequent chapter. I may passingly mention that many great female singers have exerted a direct influence on certain composers. Mendelssohn wrote his "Hear Ye, Israel" in the key of B, because it brought in F sharp very often, and this was a glorious note in Jenny Lind's register, of which the composer was thinking when he wrote the aria. Massenet changed a large

part of his "Jongleur de Notre Dame" for the sake of Mary Garden. But Massenet wrote an entire opera because of his admiration of the high notes of the delightful American soprano, Sybil Sanderson. Few Americans have any conception of the beauty of Sybil Sanderson's voice when it was at its best, during her sojourn in Paris. She could then take G in altissimo with purity and ease. Massenet wrote the opera of "Esclarmonde" especially for her, and brought in that G (the Parisians called it the "Tour d'Eiffel note") twice for her especial benefit. How much Massenet prized the work of our American singer may be judged by the accompanying letter. (See opposite page.)

V

EMINENT WOMEN ACTIVE IN MUSIC: MUSICAL QUEENS!

IN preceding chapters I have spoken of the influence which woman has exerted upon certain of the great masters of music, and the compositions—often masterpieces—resulting from this inspiration. It is now in order to study what woman herself has accomplished in the field of musical creation. It is true that we may not find as important works as George Eliot or George Sand have produced in literature, or Rosa Bonheur in painting, but we shall nevertheless find much of value evolved by women composers, and we may also find indications which point to a possible female Chopin or Mozart in the future.

In the earliest days of history we find women active in music and even occupying certain fields of art to the exclusion of men. The mourning women, so often alluded to in the Scriptures (Jeremiah 9:17-21, for example) must have been musical and poetic improvisers something like the "keeners" still to be heard at wakes in some of the remote parts of Ireland. Miriam's song (Exodus 15:20) was improvisational music, and so was that of Deborah (Judges 5).

We must bear in mind, in reading the musical allusions in the Bible, that very much of the ancient music was never written down, but was composed, together with the words, upon the spot. One must also picture the musician of the Bible as giving many expressive gestures along with the singing, for "dancing," in the Scriptural sense, was generally what we would call "dramatic action" to-day. Always imagine a liberal amount of pantomime in picturing Miriam or Deborah giving their music. There is one pictorial proof of this existing upon the wall of a tomb in Thebes (given by Lepsius in his great folio), in which is pictured a musical conservatory of about 4,000 years ago, most of the students females, dancing or pantomimic action indicated with each of the vocal lessons. And there is not a scrap of written music in the picture, every detail being taught orally.

Ancient Greece gives us the first woman composer—poet and musician were one in those days—in the person of Sappho. She is, however, a vague figure, dating from the beginning of the sixth century B. C.; and even the story of her suicide on account of disappointed love does not bear the test of analysis. But that she wrote beautiful poetry which was chanted to impressive music, and that she taught others, may not be doubted. Corinna, a century later, was also a famous poet-composer and a teacher as well, while Lamia, during the age of Pericles, was the most important female instrumentalist—she was a flute player—of the ancient epoch.

The first musical saint that we find in history is a woman—St. Cecilia—but here, too, everything is vague and doubtful. We are told that she was a noble Roman who, about A. D. 230, was forced to marry a pagan named Valerian; that she succeeded in converting him and his brother to Christianity, and that they all were martyred together in one of the persecutions. As one version gives

FACSIMILE OF A LETTER OF JULES MASSENET.
(See p. 600.)

her demise in the year 176, another in 180, and a third about 250 A. D., we are forced to conclude that she died a very lingering death; but, as she is said to have united instrumental with vocal music in praising the Lord, Raphael has painted, Dryden rhymed, Maderno sculptured her, and she is regarded as the beginning of female skill in music.

But all the music of the ancient world must have been in a large degree an inspirational affair. It was rather an art than a science, and it is doubtful whether anything more than melody—without harmony or counterpoint—was attempted. The troubadours and minnesingers, about whom so much has been written, never went beyond mere tune-writing in their compositions. There was, however, a romantic female adjunct to this school of composers, especially in England, in what were called the "glee-maidens." These were minstrels who wandered about the country, composing songs and singing them, sometimes to the people, sometimes to the lords and ladies in a castle, and sometimes even in the courtyards of a monastery to the monks. A goat or dog was often their only guardian or escort. They usually sang their songs and played the melody on the violin or harp simultaneously.

That they had some standing is shown by the fact that William the Conqueror gave an estate to one of them named Adeline. But the chief figure among these "gleemaidens" comes in the reign of Henry III. This was Marie de France. She was probably born in Brittany, but spent most of her life in England, which was then a decidedly French nation in its aristocracy and court life. Twelve of her songs, in manuscript, are treasured in the British Museum at present. One of them is a setting of the story of "King Arthur and the Round Table," a topic much prized in England. She also set many of Æsop's fables to verse and music. She was familiar with French, English, and Latin, and translated some of her songs from the last-named tongue. But few of the "gleemaidens" had such attainments, and their art gradually tended toward vagabondage.

It was very different with the troubadours, who were the aristocratic secular composers—always with melody only—of the Middle Ages. There were also female troubadours, although they were by no means so numerous as the male. Probably the most remarkable female composer—in this primitive school—that ever existed, was Eleanor of Aquitaine, who was successively wife of Louis VII of France and Henry II of England. She obtained the permission of Louis VII to accompany him in his crusade, and she headed a company of charmingly armored amazons, chose the route of the expedition, dallied a while in Turkey to try to convert a handsome young emir in the court of Sultan Noureddin, and wrecked the expedition generally. When these amazons left France, they sent their spinning wheels, as a spicy sarcasm, to the knights that stayed at home.

In England Eleanor instituted "courts of love" in which the ladies tried many cases relating to the tender passion, and occasionally formulated such rules as these:

A true lover eats but little.

A true lover grows pale when he sees his sweetheart.

No one can truly love two persons at the same time.

A true lover is always anxious and ill at ease.

Once her court of love debated the question as to whether one could continue to love after marriage, and it is to be regretted that it was decided in the negative. This energetic and highly sentimental queen composed several love songs and had the troubadour's gift of improvisation.

But this simple art of melody-writing soon merged into something greater—the science of composition. The practice of combining melodies, or melody and accompaniment, gradually evolved itself during the twelfth and thirteenth centuries, and we shall now find real composers among our musical women. Since we have begun, however, with a royal composer, let us cite a few more gifted queen musicians.

The next royal figure after Queen Eleanor who displayed musical tendencies was a rather pathetic one. It was poor Anne Boleyn, who may have charmed Henry VIII with her music—her letters show that she threw herself at that monarch's head—but the only composition that is now ascribed to her is one which she wrote when she had lost the king's favor and was approaching her doom. It begins:

Oh, Death, rock me asleep.
  Bring me to quiet rest;
Let pass my weary, guiltless life
  Out of my careful breast.
Toll on the passing bell,
Ring out my doleful knell.
Death doth draw near me.
There is no remedy.

The king's daughters were both musical. Queen Mary played the virginals, which was the primitive predecessor of the piano, a a thin-toned, tinkling instrument of about four octaves compass. Queen Elizabeth counted herself a well-equipped musical critic, although there is considerable doubt regarding how far her technical abilities extended.

There is a quaint account of her musical conceit left to us by Sir James Melville, who was at one time an ambassador at her court from Queen Mary of Scotland. He says that as he was about to leave the palace and London an English courtier came to him and asked him if he cared to hear Queen Elizabeth play the virginals. Naturally Sir James responded in the affirmative, whereupon the Englishman led him through a secret passage which ended at a silken curtain. Standing there quietly, after a little while he heard the instrument sounding. Growing bolder he softly entered the room, but the queen heard him and frowned and struck at him. He threw himself upon his knees and begged her pardon for his intrusion, but said that he had ardently desired to hear the queen's great skill at the instrument. Elizabeth was quickly mollified, but asked him which was the better musician, she or his own queen. A diplomat can easily sit on both sides of the fence, and Sir James replied that Mary Stuart played very well for a queen, but that Elizabeth's skill was something amazing. Naturally with this compliment the queen was more than satisfied.

What did she play to him? Unfortunately on this point Sir James is silent, but there is extant a certain dance which the queen loved greatly, so much so that her music teacher, Dr. Byrd, made an arrangement of it expressly for her. She often played it; she may have played it to Sir James Melville.

In playing this dance — Sellinger's Round—one must give a constant staccato, as the virginals could neither shade nor sustain a note. The queen seems never to have attempted composition.

* * *

ONE OTHER QUEEN may appear in our list of composers, however, and a sovereign yet more unfortunate than Anne Boleyn—the unhappy Marie Antoinette. As a child at the Austrian court she had shown musical capacity. She was attracted toward the young boy, Mozart, who played the spinet in Vienna, and romped with her in the palace. She took lessons in music of no less a master than Christoph Willibald Gluck.

Long after, when, in 1775, Gluck was in Paris, there took place one of the greatest

SELLINGER'S ROUND

musical battles in history. Gluck was trying to establish dramatic music in opera. He maintained that the music in opera should absolutely portray the meaning of the poetry. In this he was the forerunner of Wagner and his music-drama. But the Italians and French were by no means ready to accept this theory, and demanded sweet melody first, foremost, and all the time, irrespective of the text. They set up as their champion a very fluent composer, Nicolo Piccini.

In 1779 the rival parties hit upon the idea of having the two composers set the same text to music, and "Iphigenie en Aulide" was the result. Gluck's victory was complete and decisive. The verdict undoubtedly came from the public, but it is also true that had not his old pupil, Queen Marie Antoinette, fought for him during the preceding years he would not have made any headway against his enemies in Paris. Therefore dramatic music owes a debt to this queen that is not generally recognized.

In the queen's own composition—" 'Tis My Friend" *—one finds little of this dramatic power, but rather a gentle, pastoral sweetness which is not without its charm.

* This song by Marie Antoinette is found on p. 1544, Vol. VI of the Vocal Edition of MODERN MUSIC AND MUSICIANS.

'TIS MY FRIEND

FLORIAN
English version by
Louis C. Elson

QUEEN MARIE ANTOINETTE

Andantino con moto

1. In   your   vil - lage   should you dis-
2. If   he   sings with   ca - dence so
3. If   he   charms you   e'en_ with-out

cov - er   Wand' - ring   lone, a   shep-herd young and   fair,__
sweet - ly,   If   his   voice each   bos - om can   thrill,__
speak - ing, Mere - ly   by   his   glance so__   bright,_

With this we finish the royal line of musical women. We may now permit the rank and file of female composers to pass in review.

VI

FEMALE COMPOSERS—FANNY MENDELSSOHN AND CLARA SCHUMANN

LET us now examine the list of women who have been actual music composers in the full sense of the word. If I enumerate only those who have been really great in the creation of music, as yet, the list will be very small, while if I give the names of all those who have composed agreeable, pleasing, and correct music, it will be a catalogue as long as a city directory, and about as interesting. I shall therefore confine myself to describing only those who have become, in some degree, epoch-making, and who can serve as models for those women who are at present at-

tempting the thorny path of musical composition.

We must turn to Italy for the earliest name of the list. In Brescia, before 1540, there was born a woman who might have been very great had she lived in the twentieth century, when the opposition to female composers has almost entirely vanished. Maddalena Casulana published two entire volumes of madrigals, in 1568 and 1583, and Vittoria Aleotti, Orsina Vizzani, and Francesca Baglioncella soon followed in the same school.

One must remember that the madrigal was the most severe exhibition of skillful counterpoint. The word has often been misused in later days and its very origin is obscure. Some derive it from madre, mother, and think that it was originally a song in praise of the Virgin; others derive it from mandra, a sheepfold, and think that it was pastoral music, and still others imagine that it was a morning-song of bright character. The true madrigal, however, was always unaccompanied, and the melody was dispersed among the different parts, never being carried on in one voice. At this epoch the composers did not write songs for a single voice—that was left to the people to evolve for themselves (the folk song)—but always composed their vocal music for several voices intertwining. Early in the seventeenth century two ladies composed solo songs, which were then called "monody"; these were Francesca Caccini and Barbara Strozzi, both of good family and of fine education. Several Italian women also composed sacred music during the seventeenth century, and this was again severely contrapuntal. By this I mean that several melodies intertwined simultaneously.

Germany gives us one great female name in the sixteenth century, a trifle later than

Maddalena Casulana — Madelka Bariona. France had a female composer who may have been contemporaneous with the fair Maddalena, Clementine de Bourges, who composed most excellent and skillful music. Her career was cut short, however, by a great misfortune. She was engaged to a young officer in the royal army, and when this man was slain in an encounter with the Huguenots, in 1560, she at once died of grief.

But it was in the nineteenth century that the real and continuous race of female composers began, and even then the opposition to woman entering this profession was very great. As recent a musician as Anton Rubinstein found great fault with the attempt of women to become composers. And we shall find a startling instance of this opposition depriving the world of possibly its greatest female composer, in studying the career of Fanny Mendelssohn.

She was the elder sister of the famous Mendelssohn and the two, as children, were the closest chums. They studied their music together and the mother—herself a most cultivated woman—used to say of them, at their piano lessons, "they both have Bach-fugue fingers." At that time there was no thought of either one of them becoming a composer; they were studying music as part of a liberal education. But when Felix Mendelssohn began composition Fanny was as well equipped as he and used to help him by giving him themes and melodies. At a later period she composed many works of her own, chiefly songs and other short musical forms. But her entire family, including her brother, were inflexibly opposed to having a woman composer in the family, and she gently gave way to their dictum, giving her compositions to her

brother, who published some of them as his own.

There is not much doubt but that some of the "Songs without Words" were composed by Fanny Mendelssohn. Some of the vocal songs certainly were, as the following anecdote may prove: Mendelssohn had become famous and was, in his adult years, idolized in England. Queen Victoria herself joined in this worship, as did her consort, Prince Albert, himself a composer. They had invited the composer to Windsor Castle where he paid a most informal visit. He had visited the nursery with the royal pair, and then they had gone to the music-room together. Here Queen Victoria offered to sing one of Mendelssohn's songs, and told him that her favorite was "Italy." Mendelssohn blushed and acknowledged that that particular song was composed by his sister Fanny. We give the song herewith:

ITALY
ITALIEN

English version by
Louis C. Elson

FANNY MENDELSSOHN

Queen Victoria was twenty-two years old at this time. Mendelssohn asked her to sing the song for him, and he says in one of his letters—"She sang charmingly, in good time and tune, and with excellent execution. Only, where it goes down to D [B in our transposed version given] and comes up again chromatically, she sung D-sharp each time. With the exception of this trifling error it was really beautiful and the long high note near the end I have never heard taken clearer or purer by any amateur. After I had confessed that Fanny had written the song (which I found very hard, but pride goes before a fall) I begged her to sing one of my own works."

The chumship of brother and sister lasted all through their brief lives. How musical was their communion may be shown by a letter written to Fanny when Felix was on the west coast of Scotland. He had just visited Fingal's cave and wrote to his sister: "This is how the island impresses me," and then followed twenty measures of music which afterward became the chief theme, the first measures of the "Hebrides Overture," where my readers may play them to-day. It was a charming instance of a musician writing to a fellow-musician in that language which goes beyond words.

And thus close in life, in death they were scarcely divided. When the news of Fanny's death was brought to Mendelssohn, he gave a scream and fell down in a swoon. He had burst a blood vessel in his brain. He temporarily recovered and sought recuperation in Italy, but on his return he went to his sister's room, in their dwelling in Berlin, where everything had been carefully kept as when Fanny was alive, and this undid all the benefit of the tour, Mendelssohn dying soon thereafter. Yet with all this affection the brother kept his sister from the career in which she might have shone resplendently. She married a painter named Hensel and lived a domestic life, instead of composing.

* * *

BUT WE CAN now turn to a greater pair than the Mendelssohns, and find a great composer fostering his wife's talent and taking pride in it. Robert Schumann first met Clara Wieck when she was a mere child, yet a piano prodigy. Among the great affections of the world one constantly reads of Héloïse and Abelard, of Petrarch and Laura, but beside these the musician may justly place the affection of Robert Schumann and Clara Wieck. Just as Romeo has a fancied love for Rosalind before he meets Juliet, so Schumann had an affection for Ernestine von Fricken before he saw Clara budding into womanhood. As he turned every event of his life into music one can find his love-letter to Ernestine in his Carnival scenes for piano, in which he constantly spells out the name of her birthplace in notes. She was born in the city of Asch, and in the German nomenclature E-flat is called "ES" and B-natural is named "H" —whence "A, ES, C, H." Also A-flat is called "AS," whence we can obtain the variant of "AS, C, H." The reader will be astonished, if he examines Schumann's "Carnival," to find how much of this great piano suite is founded on these notes, a notable instance of music inspired by female influence. But the greater passion was to produce infinitely greater music. There was trouble and stress enough. Frederic Wieck, the father of Clara, who had assured Schumann's mother that her son would make a worthy career in music, found him altogether too doubtful for a son-in-law and opposed the union.

Here we may contradict one of the many false stories regarding musical compositions. The sentimentalists tell a tale regarding Schumann's "Warum" which is altogether false. They say that Schumann, separated from his Clara by a stern parent, wrote the questioning composition upon a leaf of music paper and sent it to his beloved. She read it and understood its questions—"Why are we separated? Why must we suffer?" and wept over it. She took it to her father and he also wept over it (it must have been rather damp by that time), and he at once sent for Schumann, said "Bless you, my children," and they lived happily ever afterward.

There is not a particle of truth in all this rigmarole. "Warum" is one of the "Phantasiestücke," a set of eight pieces, that were dedicated to Anna Robena Laidlaw, a Scottish woman who was one of Schumann's most gifted pupils. To settle this silly anecdote once for all let me quote a letter of Schumann to Miss Laidlaw regarding these same pieces. He writes:

The time of your stay here will always be a most beautiful memory to me, and that this is true you will soon see in eight "Phantasiestücke" for pianoforte that will shortly appear bearing your name upon their forehead. It is true that I have not asked for permission to make this dedication, but they belong to you, and the whole "Rosenthal" with its surroundings of romance is in the music.

The winning of Clara Schumann was a more laborious task than the writing of a composition. Schumann had won the heart of the young lady who was now a pianist of world-wide celebrity; but the father was inflexibly opposed to the match. Schumann therefore tried in every way to achieve fame quickly, that he might thereby win his bride. He went to Vienna, hoping to better his position there. While he was in that city he discovered Schubert's C major symphony, which came very near to being lost to the world. He also visited the grave of Beethoven, and found a pen upon the tomb. It was an odd discovery, and Schumann, being very impressible, saved that mysterious pen and wrote his first symphony with it. He gave a set of musical lectures in a German university, that he might receive from it the title of "Doctor," and his letter notifying Clara of his being "Doctor Schumann" is full of glee.

But the final victory was won by means very different from the composition of "Warum." In some parts of Germany it was legal, if a couple were desirous of matri-

LOV'ST THOU FOR BEAUTY
LIEBST DU UM SCHÖNHEIT

FR. RÜCKERT
English words by
Louis C. Elson

CLARA SCHUMANN
Op. 37, No 4

FIRST PAGE OF A SONG BY CLARA SCHUMANN

It will be apparent to the reader, by this song, how much Clara Schumann was influenced by the vein of her husband's composition. Were this song published without the composer's name, many a critic would ascribe it to Robert Schumann.

mony, were both of legal age, and were opposed by the parents, for the young man to bring suit requiring the opposing parents to show cause why the marriage should not take place; and if it was proved that there was no real impediment, and that the would-be bridegroom was able to support a family, the court "advised" the parents to give their consent. This "advice" was equivalent to a command, and this is the way in which Schumann won his bride.

After the marriage—in 1840—Schumann burst forth into song. He wrote a cycle of songs entitled "Poet's Love" and followed it up with his most joyous and triumphant symphony, the one in B-flat. But the cycle which was most directly inspired by Clara Schumann was that entitled "Woman's

Life and Love." This cycle of songs was almost a prophecy. It pictures the awakening of love, the struggle for union, the marriage, and then the death of the husband, and at the end the composer brings back the first themes—the awakening of love as if the widow only lived in the memory of her dead husband. It all came true in later years, and Clara Schumann lived on, after her husband had died in an insane asylum, only with the purpose of making his greatness known to the world, a task in which she succeeded gloriously.

But Schumann did not, as Mendelssohn, try to oppose the female composer. In fact he effaced himself sometimes so thoroughly that once, in Russia, when Clara Schumann had made a brilliant success in a concert, both as pianist and composer, an effusive nobleman, after showering his compliments upon Mme. Schumann, turned to the husband, who stood by, and asked: "Are you, also, musical?"

Schumann published some of his wife's songs with his own, but always under her own name. Clara Schumann composed in almost every branch of musical form. It is not too much to say that probably she is the greatest female composer who has as yet arisen. Concerts have been given, made up entirely of her compositions. She composed chamber-music, piano works, many songs, a piano concerto, etc. Her trio in G-minor for piano, violin and violoncello holds its own against any masculine compositions.

She devoted much of her life, however, to making her husband's work known, and his piano concerto, the piano quintette, Op. 44, and the piano quartet, owe their acceptance chiefly to her.

In her tastes Mme. Schumann was decidedly conservative. Her grandson, Ferdinande Schumann, has recently published extracts from her diary, which show this very clearly. She was a decided Brahmsite, and Brahms was always an intimate friend of the Schumann family. Mme. Schumann and he were "Clara" and "Johannes" to each other, and it was natural that she should have imbibed some of the master's Toryism in Music. How far that conservatism extended with Brahms may be judged by the following incident. He had been a warm friend of Herman Levi, who was a man of the broadest musical culture, conducting Wagner's operas and revising those of Mozart with equal fidelity. One day, in conversation with Brahms, Levi spoke of Gluck and of Wagner, whereupon Brahms angrily exclaimed: "These two names are not to be spoken in the same breath!" and brusquely left the room, becoming antagonistic to Levi from that time.

Mme. Schumann, in her old age, had somewhat similar ideas. She told Stockhausen that although Wagner was a genius, his music would one day totally disappear. It was, she thought, too unhealthy,—the coloring good, but the drawing bad. But one might make an endless list of the mistakes of composers in criticism, for Tschaikowsky despised Beethoven's latest quartets. Brahms scorned Bruckner, Handel had a contempt for Gluck and Purcell, Mozart derided Abt Vogler, Beethoven sneered at Weber, Weber thought Beethoven quite fit for an asylum, and one might extend the list much further. But Mme. Schumann was probably the best female pianist that has lived, and her personal character was most lovable. Therefore, of all the female composers I am inclined to give the first place to Clara Josephine Schumann.

VII

OTHER EUROPEAN FEMALE COMPOSERS

GERMANY has not been so definitely preëminent in music and its women composers as with its male geniuses. It is probable that Clara Schumann will head the list for some time to come. The nation's appreciation of her was evidenced at her jubilee, which marked the completion of fifty years of labor in the field of music. Enthusiastic crowds attended the concert she gave on that occasion. She played her husband's piano concerto, and at the end was presented with a gold crown, on each laurel leaf of which was inscribed the name of some famous composer. This gifted woman always preferred to be known as Schumann's widow, rather than as a composer in her own right, and to the last she played his compositions in preference to her own.

In Germany royalty has always busied itself somewhat with music, and almost every queen or princess has composed to some extent. It is unnecessary to give the list here. It begins with the sister of Frederic the Great, the Princess Anna Amalia, and extends to the Princess Beatrice of Battenberg. But in Austria in the eighteenth century, we find a woman composer who may well be balanced against even some of the great masters. Maria Theresa von Paradies was born in Vienna in 1759. She met with an accident at the age of three, which caused her to be blind for life. The Empress Maria Theresa heard her, when she was eleven years old, singing a soprano air from Pergolesi's "Stabat Mater," and playing her own accompaniment upon the organ, and was so impressed by the excellence of her work that she took the girl under her protection and procured the best teachers for her. Maria Theresa von Paradies became very prominent as a performer, but soon retired from the public stage to devote herself to composition. She composed several sonatas, operas, etc., of considerable merit. Mozart admired her compositions, and showed his esteem by dedicating one of his concertos to her.

Another Viennese lady, Marianne Martinez, left a large list of compositions, including an oratorio. The compositions of these ladies, when preserved, are regarded rather as curiosities than as living numbers of the repertory. In the nineteenth century Germany gives us Emilie Mayer, Agnes Bernouilly, and a long list of lesser celebrities. Perhaps the most noted woman composer at the end of the nineteenth century was Louisa Adolpha Lebeau. She was born at Rastadt in 1850, and has recently lived in Baden-Baden. Her compositions have won prizes, and have become in some degree standard in Germany. She has composed in all the large forms of music, but her best work has been in chamber music, her string quartets being of excellent quality.

Americans might recall to mind, when they are singing the ever-popular "Soldier's Farewell," that this chorus, and a cantata, too, are the work of a woman— Johanna Kinkel. Another excellent composer is Ingeborg Stark. She was born in St. Petersburg, or Petrograd, of Swedish parents, but belongs to Germany because her life-work has been chiefly done there. Ingeborg Stark went to Liszt at Weimar, a beautiful northern girl who seemed much more adapted to society than to the stern work of composition. Liszt looked at the compositions she had brought, and perhaps doubting them somewhat, gave her a fugal subject to write up as a test. She at once worked on the theme in good counterpoint and handed it to the master. He played it, acknowledged that it was good, but added: "You don't look at all like that"; whereupon the young lady replied, "I should hope that I didn't look like a fugue!" This retort won Liszt's admiration and he was always interested in her work thereafter. A scion of noble family fell in love with Miss Stark, and she soon became Ingeborg von Bronsart, the name by which she is known throughout Germany.

There are literally dozens of German ladies who are composing good songs and piano pieces to-day, but to give the list would serve no purpose whatever. England also has an extremely long list of good women composers. Let me speak only of the greatest of these. The two chief ones bear the name of Smith, and when we remember that the composer of the tune of "The Star-Spangled Banner" was an Englishman named John Stafford Smith, it will be seen that the Smith family are to be honored in English music, and that Oliver Wendell Holmes's line, "Fate tried to conceal him by naming him Smith," has lost its point. Alice Mary Smith (1839-84) composed symphonies, concertos and fine chamber music which is deservedly popular. Ethel M. Smyth (a slight deviation from "Smith") has won about as high a reputation as any other woman composer. She has composed operas which have become standard. Her one-act opera, "Der Wald," has been given in Germany, England, and America; and her three-act work, "The Wreckers," began

a triumphant career in Germany just before the war.

The daughter of an English general, Miss Smyth was born in London, April 23, 1858. Her music is modern in the sense that it follows Wagnerian continuity, but it is free from the ugliness which permeates so much latter-day music. She has composed very much besides the two operas mentioned, especially a beautiful Mass, an opera entitled "Fantasio," and many other works. Perhaps the future will rank Miss Smyth as the greatest woman composer of the present.

Agnes Zimmermann, born in Cologne, but closely identified with England in her musical career, has composed violin sonatas, instrumental trios, etc. The names of Liza Lehmann, Frances Allitsen, Guy d'Hardelot (Mrs. Rhodes), and Maude Valerie White may be mentioned as prominent in the smaller forms of composition.

France gives a long list of women composers also, but among these two stand pre-eminent. Augusta Mary Ann Holmès was born at Paris in 1847, and died there in 1903. She was of Irish parentage, but afterward became naturalized as a Frenchwoman. She has been larger in her musical conceptions than any other woman composer of the present. Opera, symphony, overture, triumphal odes, have all been composed by this great Irishwoman. She has been more virile in thought and broader in

execution than many male composers. Her name, originally "Holmes," has been Gallicized into "Hol-mès," with two syllables and a French pronunciation.

The other most prominent French woman composer is Cécile Louise Stéphanie Chaminade, whose name is known all over the civilized world. She was born in Paris in 1861. When Ambroise Thomas heard some of her earliest compositions he remarked: "This is not a woman who composes, but a composer who happens to be a woman." Bizet also was full of encomium for her early work. Perhaps the best point in Mlle. Chaminade's work is its grace and fluency. She has not yielded to the temptation to do something overwhelming, but has generally kept to the smaller forms, of which she is a complete master. Yet she has done one or two large works with success, notably a grand ballet and symphonic scene, entitled "Callirrhoë," and a piano concerto. But it is her short piano pieces, and also her poetic songs, which have won her a fame that is now world-wide.

VIII

WOMEN COMPOSERS OF AMERICA

IT may be well again to repeat that no attempt is made in these articles to give a list of women who have become prominent in music, but only to point out some shining examples which may serve as guides to those who are following in the tonal path. It is pleasant to note that America has given brilliant examples. In America there has never been the prejudice which has opposed the entrance of women into the field of musical creation, the prejudice which caused Rubinstein to say to the brother-in-law of Chaminade, "I hear you have a sister-in-law who is composing music. *She ought not to do that!*"

About one hundred and fifty names might be cited of American women who have done creditable work in composition, but only the leaders can be mentioned. Margaret Ruthven Lang, the daughter of that eminent musician, B. J. Lang, was born November 27, 1867. Brought up as she was in a musical family, she began composing at the age of twelve. She studied with John K. Paine, J. C. D. Parker, and George W. Chadwick. Her orchestral works, chiefly overtures, have been performed by the Boston Symphony Orchestra and by Theodore Thomas's orchestra. She has composed in many of the larger musical forms. Her most recent compositions have been chiefly songs.

Miss Lang has done some piquant and excellent work in the domain of children's songs, which, although intended for juveniles, will certainly interest children of a larger growth. Her settings of Lear's Limericks, and of "Grandma's Song Book," are only comparable with Liza Lehmann's daintily humorous works in England.

An American woman-composer who is of great promise is Miss Mabel Daniels. She is unaffected in her work, melodic yet sufficiently developed to interest the musician. She is also an authoress and has written a very interesting volume of musical life in Germany. Her father, although a prominent merchant, was much interested in music and was for some time president of the Handel and Haydn Society of Boston.

Miss Grace Marshall was born near Nineveh, Indiana, in 1885. After music-study in Boston she became the wife of Mr. Clough-Leiter, who is himself a prominent American composer. She has hidden her identity under the cacophonic name of G. Marscal-Loepke, and has written many charming juvenile pieces and also much more ambitious work.

Mary Turner Salter, born in Peoria, Ill., in 1856, has done good work in several original songs which have made their way into concerts of the highest rank. She is also the wife of a prominent musician—Mr. Sumner Salter. She is, thank Heaven, not given to dissonant progressions or mystic musical riddles in the modern vein.

Helen Hopekirk (Mrs. William Wilson), although Scottish by birth has resided so long in America that she may be spoken of under the classification of American composers. She was born in Edinburgh, May 20th, 1856, and won much success as a pianist in Europe before coming to America. For more than twenty years she has been resident in Boston where she is a prominent teacher. She has composed an excellent piano concerto, a Concertstuck for piano and orchestra, many piano works, a large number of songs, has arranged many of the Scottish folk songs, and has received success in all these varied fields. There is a strength and virility in her works that places all of them in a very high rank.

MRS. H. H. A. BEACH

Gena Branscombe deserves mention as being beautifully melodic in her work and having a degree of expressiveness that puts her in the class of Cécile Chaminade. And this is, fortunately, the good influence which many American female-composers are exert-

ing upon our Art at present: while some of
the native males are trying to out-Herod
Herod by terrific progressions and impossible chord resolutions, while the motto of most
of them is "Leave Richter behind, all Ye
who enter Here," while the only deceptive
cadence left in their music is to resolve the
dominant chord into the tonic,—the Ameri-

FAY FOSTER

can woman-composers have upheld the banner of "Beauty in Music," and may yet succeed in guiding their masculine brethren
from the thorny paths which they have
chosen.

It is almost an injustice to give especial
names where so many have succeeded in this
pleasant field. Generally the composers
have chosen the smaller forms, songs or
piano works of drawing-room calibre. Lola
Carrier Worrell, Eleanor Freer, Mary
Knight Wood, Helen Hood, Fay Foster,
Cara Roma, Mana Zucca, Amy Woodford-
Finden, Mrs. Carrie Jacobs-Bond, Jessie
L. Gaynor, Mary Helen Brown, Edith
Noyes-Green, and a host of others have done
good work. Perhaps they will yet teach the
more radical composers the truth of Beethoven's sentence: "Music, even when picturing something that is ugly, must itself
remain beautiful."

* * *

THE MOST prominent figure in this field of

music is Mrs. H. H. A. Beach. Here we find
a woman who requires not the slightest
concession on account of her sex. She has
written many works which are standard and
which have won recognition in their own
right. Her maiden name was Amy Marcy
Cheney, and she was born in Henniker, New
Hampshire, September 5, 1867. She is a
descendant from the early colonial settlers,
and belongs to one of the oldest American
families. She had the sense of absolute
pitch (the ability to name a note the instant
it is sounded) from the very beginning, and
is said to have astonished her family with
this gift when she was still a baby. At a
very early period she was able to sing some
forty different songs, although her favorite
was the old anthem, "The Moon Shines Full
at His Command." She would sternly correct any deviations in the singing of any of
these songs with the command, "Sing it
clean."

At two years of age she was taken to be
photographed. While sitting and waiting
for the focusing of the camera she suddenly
burst out singing, "See the Conquering
Hero Comes," to the utter amazement of
the photographer.

From the age of four the precocious Miss
Cheney was allowed access to the piano,
and she played with full harmony the hymn
tunes she had heard in church. She also
made up a few pieces of her own, which she
named "Mamma's Waltz," "Snowflake
Waltz," etc. She could transpose easily at
this time. I recall meeting her when she had
begun systematic work under a teacher, and
well remember her transposing a Bach
fugue to any key that I called for. She
studied with Ernst Perabo, Junius W. Hill
and Carl Baermann. Her teachers justly
considered her the greatest musical prodigy of America. It is a point worth noting
that this great woman-composer was entirely
trained in America. There was an intention of sending her abroad when she grew
up, but a wealthy physician, Dr. H. H. A.
Beach, frustrated this plan by marrying
her. The struggle of the rising composer was
thus entirely eliminated from her life. She
was a fine pianist, she had appeared in public at sixteen years of age—she was then

still Miss Cheney—and she even appeared on the programs of the Boston Symphony concerts. After her marriage she appeared only for charitable purposes, but fortunately with some frequency.

Mrs. Beach has composed in all the musical forms, large and small. Her song, "The Year's at the Spring," is known everywhere, and her other songs and piano works are very numerous. She has, like Augusta Holmès, won laurels in much vaster compositions. Her first work of great dimensions was a Grand Mass in E-flat major, performed by the Handel and Haydn Society in Boston, in 1892.

Another of her great works is the "Gaelic Symphony," which has been performed by the chief American orchestras. It was completed in 1896 and is made up of several genuine Gaelic themes. A sonata in A minor for violin and piano also deserves mention. Numerous works have been written by Mrs. Beach for public occasions and festivals. I consider Mrs. Beach's piano concerto in C-sharp minor to be a remarkable composition. Its Scherzo is altogether charming, and the Finale is most powerful. She has written some excellent cantatas for women's voices. "The Sea Fairies" and "The Chambered Nautilus" among them, and a piano quintet. Some quaint Eskimo pieces for piano are made on actual Eskimo themes. Other important works of Mrs. Beach are "Variations on a Balkan Theme" and the "Festival Jubilate," the latter written for the dedicatory exercises of the World's Columbian Exposition at Chicago in 1893. One of the most interesting things about Mrs. Beach's creative activity is the astonishing rapidity with which she is able to compose.

I may well close my discursive writings about woman in music with the important figure of Mrs. Beach. This composer is not only an American, but also an entirely American art product. It is reasonable to believe that with the freedom that is accorded the woman-composer among us, with the numerous great conservatories here opening wide their doors to women and offering them the most thorough instruction, America may yet bring forth a woman-composer of the magnitude of Mozart, Chopin, or Haydn.

A BACCHANTE FROM POMPEII

CHILDREN IN MUSIC

BY

LOUIS C. ELSON

I

THE BEGINNINGS OF MUSICAL TRAINING

IT is only in modern times that the training of the child in music has attracted the attention of eminent authorities, the best modes of instruction have been sought out, and the needs of the juvenile student carefully analyzed. The records of children in music, in ancient times, are remarkably brief. Children were allowed to sing in Old Rome, on special holidays, and even took part in some of the historical triumphs of long ago. Their training, as all the school training in ancient Rome, was probably very severe, with frequent recourse to the rod.

In the Middle Ages children often sang and acted in the religious festivals and mysteries. We have the story of the death of "one of the angels" who appeared in Rome in a religious pageant. This particular angel, a child, had been gilded from head to foot, and died because of the stoppage of all the pores of the skin. It is to the training of choir-boys in the monastery of Arezzo that we owe our vocal scale of to-day. Guido, their teacher, about A.D. 1000, found that he could fix the musical intervals of the scale in their minds by the hymn which they sang to St. John. It ran:

> *Ut*-quænt laxis,
> *Re*-sonare fibris,
> *Mi*-ra gestorum,
> *Fa*-muli tuorum,
> *Sol*-ve polluti,
> *La*-bii reatum,
> *Sa*-ncte Johannes.

And each line began one degree higher than the one before it. Notice how the first syllables give the names of the first six notes of the vocal scale and the origin of *Do, Re, Mi,* etc., will at once be seen. The unvocal Ut—still used in France—was soon changed to *Do.* It is very appropriate that the vocal syllables should have their origin in a hymn to St. John, since in the Catholic Church that saint is the especial patron of singers.

About A.D. 940, we find the first musical child prodigy, appearing at the French court. The youngster of nine years played upon the ponderous pipe organ of that time, an instrument which had keys as large as bricks, which dipped about eight inches before a tone was sounded, and which were pressed, not by the fingers, but by the fist. Our little prodigy fisted so well that he is recorded in history.

The children of the olden days have, however, made their mark in history rather by their songs than by their fists. The juvenile songs of a thousand years ago have percolated down through the centuries in a wonderful manner; but of that we will write in a later chapter. Let us now rather study what has been developed in the musical training of children of the present.

When may the training of a child in music begin? It really commences with the infant in its mother's arms. Robert Franz, the great German song composer, remembered a great choral which he heard when less than three years old, he had been carried to a festival by his nurse. The present writer recalls a nursery song which his grandmother used to sing to him, and judging by the date of her death he must have heard this melody in his cradle. Therefore, even the infant receives musical impressions which may prove to be a foundation for subsequent musical taste.

The mother, however, can begin to guide the child in a more systematic manner at a very early age. How often one hears a very young child go to the piano and bang the notes, amused at the sound it creates. A sensible mother will guide this exuberance into a very much better channel, by causing the child to strike single notes at first, and then training it to strike two notes together, thirds or sixths, causing an agreeable concord instead of a noise. The chances are that the child will enjoy the results better than the untrained one does its own banging.

While not out of sympathy with musical games for certain stages of musical kindergarten work, we do not believe in giving them much prominence; the child does not crave them so much as is imagined; it usually tolerates them—at least we have found this to be the case with really musical children. Rhythmic games, with singing, or a musical accompaniment are quite another matter.

But many parents will ask, "How can I tell if my child is really musical?" The fact that a young child can hum a tune proves little; it merely shows that it is not unmusical. Other tests may be applied with more certainty of result. Try to discover what tunes are the favorites with the child. See if it likes them best quite alone or with harmony. Most children love third and sixth progressions. If you find one who cares for a work which has some dissonance in it you have probably discovered a musical nature. Not one child in a thousand will care for anything contrapuntal, but the thousandth one is an artist in embryo.

Lest any reader imagine that I am overestimating the appreciative powers of very young children let me give two examples from my own researches in this matter. Years ago I was told of the infant daughter of an eminent New York musical critic— that she was remarkably susceptible to music. In testing this I held her in my arms and sang a rollicking melody. The little one laughed and crowed in delight. Then I changed the tune to a sorrowful Russian folk-song, and the little face became overcast and soon the tears were coursing down the cheeks. Another very similar case was that of a very young lad, of four years, who sat by the piano while I gave one of Schubert's most plaintive melodies. Here there was no thought of experiment, but I suddenly found our young auditor in tears. I stopped at once, but he called out, "I like it!"

It may be accepted as an ascertained fact that feeling precedes intellect in most children. Surely the above instances may prove it. But such exhibitions of feeling as those described above are almost to be regarded as danger signals. Such children are not to be pressed on in music, but rather restrained. The mother may realize the precious possession, but she must also become aware of its fragility. In such cases John Stuart Mill's pregnant sentence, "First a healthy animal," must be taken to heart, and out-door exercise and hearty play must counteract the evidently morbid tendency.

There are different opinions as to musical audition during the years of childhood. Some have demanded that the child should often hear music beyond its capacity for appreciation, in order that it may grow up to the more advanced or complicated music. I am of a contrary opinion. The concert should be almost entirely an enjoyment to the young auditor and when the program is too heavy he should not be taken to hear it. Concerts and boredom should not become synonyms in this case. I tender my respectful sympathy to the musical children that I have sometimes seen sitting through a Brahms symphony or a Strauss symphonic poem at the Boston Symphony Concerts. Just as carefully as the mother looks over the reading matter of her child, so should she examine the lists of music which that child is to be obliged to hear. At the same time one need not fear a composition which is partly in advance of the child's status. Many children would enjoy the larger part of a Mendelssohn symphony, for example.

Such abnormal developments have recently taken place in some musical children that one is almost afraid to set down a hard-and-fast rule in these matters. What with an Erich Korngold writing involved modern compositions at nine years of age, and a Willy Ferrero leading an orchestra in Wagnerian selections at seven years, we may expect to find the baby's rattle discarded for the conductor's baton, or the infant writing double fugues for its own cradle-songs very soon, yet the above rules of early concert audition may hold for the average young musical talent for a time.

* * *

AND now we approach the time for the first music lessons. How early may they begin? Again we answer that the musical mother may begin with some points during the earliest years. Fix the names and sounds of a few notes in the mind as early as it is receptive of these impressions. Test also if the child can identify the notes by name on hearing their sounds. Such absolute pitch is not so rare as many imagine. Do not be unduly elated if your child has it, and do not think it unmusical if it has not this style of musical memory. I have known some very famous musicians who were quite innocent of absolute pitch, and I also have known some musical mediocrities who had this peculiar faculty even from early years. Almost all of my

blind pupils have had absolute pitch, no matter what their grade of musical ability was. Gounod, when quite a child, was exhibited by his parents to many admiring friends, to show his ability to name any note when sounded on the piano; but many a child has done this who has not grown up into a composer.

Naturally, the reading of notes now follows. I do not wish to discourage those teachers who pin their faith upon an artificial system of memorizing these. If the spelling of "Face" will help the child to remember what notes come upon the spaces in the G clef, well and good, and the first letters of "Every Good Boy Deserves Fudge" may similarly inculcate the E, G, B, D and F, which come upon the lines. I have not, in my experience, found any necessity for such artificial aids, nor do I especially incline toward too many music-study games to help along the child in the early stages of work. These may do well enough with those who need to be coaxed to a disagreeable task, but the child who loves music will find enough attraction in it without any such sugar-coating of the pill.

But there is one general defect in training the child in the early stages of music that may well be spoken of here. It is the tendency to keep the exercises in the key of C for far too long a period. There is a certain German piano method which begins with a course of about three months, never once departing from the key of C. By that time the child has gained the impression that all normal music ought to be in that key and regards all other keys as something artificial, and this impression will continue for a much longer time than the teacher imagines.

Our advice is to begin transposition almost at once. After some simple exercise is mastered in the key of C, let the pupil try to put it in B, or D, by ear. Later, when the scales are taken up, do the same kind of transposition. As a matter of fact, the scale of B is easier to play—as regards position of the hand and passing the fingers over and the thumb under—than the key of C, although it is harder to read.

If there should be any young mother among my readers who is giving the first lessons, let me counsel strongly against using any old instruction book that happens to be in the house. There were some very faulty instruction books in vogue in America one or two generations ago. There was a piano method which sold more than a million copies in its time, yet it is one that the careful teacher of to-day would consider very poorly graded for elementary instruction.

Do not use the old-fashioned "American Fingering." The pupil will have to unlearn it when he gets deeper into music. As many do not understand how two methods of fingering came about, let me here digress a moment to explain a bit of musical history.

Fingering began upon the violin, and the first finger-markings of music are found in early violin studies and pieces. As the thumb is never used in violin music only the four fingers received marks: 1, 2, 3 and 4. Later, when fingering was applied to piano, or spinet, or clavichord music, these same markings were followed; especially as in this early playing—in the seventeenth and eighteenth centuries—the thumb was seldom used in piano work, but was suffered to hang down along the edge of the keyboard. When the thumb was employed it was marked, at first with an "0," so that the fingering ran, 0, 1, 2, 3, and 4. But as this "0" was sometimes apt to be mistaken for a whole note, it was soon changed into a mark somewhat like an "X." We append an illustration which shows the shape of this old thumb-mark and also illustrates how careless was the old system of fingering.

No one would dream of fingering any passage in this manner to-day, but it served well enough for the old spinet, on which every note was short and sudden (*staccato*), so that it really made very little difference which finger was employed.

Thus arose the so-called "American Fingering," which is not in the least American; it had its beginning in England. It was copied by the Colonies from the mother-country, whence the name, and England is the only country where it is tolerated to-day, while even there it is beginning to die out. Therefore we beg the teacher of children not to use it, but to hasten its early demise.

Let the earliest pieces have some pictorial idea to them. It awakens the imagination of the young player to carry out a tonal sketch—"A Woodland Ramble," "A Swing-song," "Catching a Fish," or something of that kind. There is now a large repertoire of really good music of this kind to choose from. Good old Kapellmeister Carl Reinecke had a very large family of children and he wrote many pieces on the plan we have indicated. Oesten, Jungmann, and many other Germans have written the same kind of juvenile music, and in America we have E. R. Kroeger, Mortimer Wilson, Newton Swift, Ænris Ravina and many other good composers who have also used their skill to give simple pictures to the child-musician.

Using some concerted music in the early stages will cause the young musician to think of blending his performance with that of somebody else, and will bear good fruit in the later stages of study. The accompaniment of a song, of a violin melody, and the playing of four-hand music with either a comrade or with the teacher is to be encouraged. There are some extremely simple works written to supply this want. The duets by Diabelli give the pupil only five notes to play, while the teacher's part is

Aurettis Minuet

much more developed and causes the music to be of real interest to the beginner.

Although I have spoken of the musical mother being of great help in the advancement of the musical child, yet I must maintain that the earlier a systematic teacher is engaged, the better. What that teacher should be like, and the further points of progress will be indicated in a future chapter.

II

THE CHILD'S HAND

The use of Bach. Exercises and studies

SINCE the child's piano practice has fairly begun, attention must be paid to various details of the work. The piano seat should be broad enough for comfort, not a narrow or rickety stool upon which the child must balance itself. The feet must not dangle in the air, but a comfortable footstool must be provided. When, a little later on, the pedals begin to be used, the child must not stretch downward for them, at the risk of slipping from his perch, but an extension of wood must be set over the pedals, so that they reach to the level of the feet.

Study the shape of the hand of the young player. It should have an influence upon the studies and exercises that are to be given. If he grows up with a very small hand it must make up by dexterity what it lacks in reach. A small hand is not a disadvantage. One of the very greatest of American pianists, Mr. Wm. H. Sherwood, had a phenomenally small hand, yet could sweep the widest chords so swiftly that the notes seemed to be played simultaneously. The ideal piano hand is a long-fingered, slender, sinewy one. Yet the great artist, Moritz Rosenthal, once told me that he dreaded to see the long-fingered, slender-handed young lady come to him as a pupil, since the long finger almost always was a wabbly one.

A few years ago there was a peculiar theory afloat that the stretch of the hand could be improved by cutting the ligaments between the fingers. All these improvements upon nature must be laughed to scorn. The improvement of the hand by surgery, the benefiting of the voice by tonsillotomy, may be looked at very much askance. One may recall the fact that Clara Butt, the great contralto, was actually in the surgeon's chair when she suddenly decided to allow her throat to remain as God had made it, and it has charmed tens of thousands since then.

The young surgeon is far too ready to experiment upon the musician, even from the time when Sir Robert Hunter said that he would gladly give a thousand pounds to dissect a pianist's hand; meaning, probably, that he suspected changes in muscles and tissues because of the constant practice. But if there are no pianist's hands to be bought in this manner, at least the investigators have taken care to obtain casts and photographs of the hands of the most celebrated keyboard artists, and they form an interesting study in comparisons. We are somewhat surprised to find that they are not so long-fingered as we had supposed; some of them are even short-fingered. Liszt's hand was slender, somewhat bony, but evidently very muscular. Rubinstein's was rather short-fingered, but very broad, and he could take long stretches easily. There was a cavity in his right hand, which came about in a rather odd manner. If he grew out of patience at a lesson he would crash down upon the piano lid (or upon the keyboard) with his open hand, scaring the pupil greatly. The habit led to the formation of a callous which he was constantly trimming, until the cavity was the result.

But if the child's hand bids fair to be unusually small, special attention should be paid quite early to velocity studies and rapid finger work. There is no harm in sugar-coating the pill of such practice a little. Many a piano piece which is given some attractive title is a good velocity study in disguise.

There should not be too much practicing at first. Remember that enthusiasm is worth more than routine. Let the emotional side of music precede the intellectual, but later on both must develop together. The periods of practice might well be alternated with occasional listening to good music. If the mother is the teacher she can do very much to interest the young student by playing certain pieces to him, explaining some points and questioning about others. Short pieces by Schubert, Mendelssohn's "Songs Without Words," Schumann's "Scenes from Childhood," and even short movements from the sonatas of the masters could be employed.

A little explanation of the simpler architecture of music might be interwoven with this audition. I have done this with both children and adults and found that interest in music was intensified by it. People are too much afraid of so-called "classical" music. Yet even contrapuntal music if it be carefully chosen can be made very interesting both to non-musicians and to musical children. The servant in the family of a Boston musician recently heard the master playing a Bach fugue, and exclaimed to her mistress, "Isn't he ever going to let one hand catch up with the other?" She had caught the scheme of the fugue intuitively and certainly more correctly than Browning did in his "Master Hugues of Saxe-Gotha."

Occasionally one finds an old-fashioned teacher of piano who holds that all technical preparation is found in the scales, and allows scale-practice to preponderate over everything else in his lessons. A very little reflection will show how mistaken this view is. In playing the scales, through several octaves, the first, second, and third fingers get equal work, and the most of it. The fourth finger gets just half as much exercise as these. The little finger gets practically no employment at all, only striking a single note—at the beginning, in the left hand, and at the top, in the right hand. Such practice might easily form an unequal set of fingers.

It is well, in order to offset this, when playing the scales through several octaves, to give a slow trill at the top with the fourth and fifth fingers of the right hand, and with the same fingers of the left hand when reaching the lowest notes. Always supplement the scales with sufficient finger exercises. One of the most effective finger exercises for equalizing the fingers is to play triplets as follows:

Right hand: 1-2-1; 2-1-2; 1-2-1; 2-3-2; 3-2-3; 2-3-2; 3-4-3; 4-3-4; 3-4-3; 4-5-4; 5-4-5; 4-5-4; 5-4-5; 4-5-4; 5-4-5; 4-3-4; 3-4-3; 4-3-4; 3-2-3; 2-3-2; 3-2-3; 2-1-2; 1-2-1; 2-1-2; *1.*

Left hand: 5-4-5; 4-5-4; 5-4-5; 4-3-4; 3-4-3; 4-3-4; 3-2-3; 2-3-2; 3-2-3; 2-1-2; 1-2-1; 2-1-2; 1-2-1; 2-1-2; 1-2-1; 2-3-2; 3-2-3; 2-3-2; 3-4-3; 4-3-4; 3-4-3; 4-5-4; 5-4-5; 4-5-4; *5.*

Practice this simple exercise first with each hand alone, then with two hands together, DAILY, increasing the speed gradually as the fingers become supple, until finally the exercise becomes a triplet trill. No finger exercise that I know of will do so much to equalize the hand. Give a slight accent on the first of each group.

How much ought Bach to be used in juvenile instruction? Unfortunately there are some old-fashioned pedants who force Bach down the pupil's throat just as anxious parents used to crowd down sulphur and molasses. With some pupils Bach and contrapuntal intellectuality need not come upon the scene at all. But with the best student the case will be different. Be careful not to tire out the young mind with too complex a study of musical ideas. Let him make friends with Bach by means of some of the sarabands from the English or French suites, since the sarabands contain the least contrapuntal and the most melodic ideas of Bach's instrumental works.

Perhaps it may be well to explain here the difference between harmonic and contrapuntal music. In harmonic music (homophony) there is a single, clear, melodic voice which is supported by chords; in counterpoint (polyphony) melody is supported by melody; that is, two or more melodies are intertwined. When we remember that Jean Jacques Rousseau once wrote that he doubted whether the human mind could fully grasp more than two melodies at a time, we can understand why a child, unless phenomenal, might readily be repelled by intricate contrapuntal music.

Nevertheless, we can make a start with an

especially gifted pupil and use some of
Bach's two-part inventions. But we must
beware of allowing the young musician to
think that they are merely scales and exercises. The figures and their combinations
must be explained, and here at least the
child must understand something of musical
architecture before trying to play the lesson.

Let us take invention No. 2, for example.
The first eight measures in the right hand
are a theme, or melody. Two measures
later, starting with measure No. 3, the left
hand plays the SAME MELODY below it, as an
accompaniment to the right hand melody.
This is called a canon. Directly after the
left hand has finished its melody—ending
two measures after the right hand had completed its part—that is in measure No. 11—
the left hand starts the same theme, and
two measures later the right hand commences the same melody, but this time
ABOVE IT, and imitates it clear through.
That is called double counterpoint. It is
decidedly in contradiction of the Scriptural
injunction, "Let not thy right hand know
what thy left hand doeth."

We do not intend to make these suggestions too technical, but it is self-evident that
the hundreds of young pupils who are forced
to play such an invention without knowing
anything about these imitations and inver-
sions cannot play intelligently and will
probably dislike the entire piece.

Some of the movements of the suites may
be used in the place of exercises. The
courantes and gigues make good velocity
exercises. The gigues—or jigs—have the
rollicking spirit of the Irish dance in them.
The gigues and courantes, however, are too
difficult to be taken in the early lessons.
Nevertheless, if Bach forms a good part of
the early training of the talented pupil, it
will be a seed from which a noble harvest
will grow later on.

III

RHYTHM SCALES. PUBLIC SCHOOL WORK

RHYTHM is implanted in all animate
nature. Spiders, mice, horses, and ele-
phants, all fall under the spell of rhythm.
It is small wonder then that a child is
rhythmic by nature. It would be a foolish
teacher who would discard attractive
rhythms in music because deeper things
exist. Rhythmic games are most attractive
and helpful with young children and play
their part in developing the musical instinct. Jaques Dalcroze, the eminent Swiss
composer, is now beginning to apply this
love of rhythm to the musical education of
adults as well, in the new art of Eurhyth-
mics, which is being taught both in Europe
and America. Possibly in the near future
we shall have this art either replaced by,
or more probably combined with, children's
musical games.

In the public schools we shall find our
young pupil gaining something in music,
and yet not nearly enough. He will be
made to sing, and sing, and sing. He begins singing in chorus when he enters the
primary school, and he will continue chorus
work, until he gets through high school. It
is strange that no classes exist to teach correct appreciation of music, its forms, history, schools, etc.; instead of forcing the
musical and unmusical to form one grand
continuous chorus.

In high school and college the history of
art and of literature are taught, without
forcing the students either to paint or to
write novels and poems, but nothing of
the kind has yet been introduced into the
musical scheme of our public schools. The
young man, or woman, who has been duti-
fully singing all the way from primary
school to college usually leaves the eight or
ten years' public educational course without any practical knowledge of music. He
does not know what a fugue is telling him;
he does not comprehend the meaning of a
sonata or symphony; he does not understand the simplest architecture of music;
he cannot classify the different schools of
composition, nor tell of their chief repre-
sentatives, or their influence. And yet these
and a hundred other points could readily
be taught to non-musicians.

We therefore must supply these important adjuncts to our young musician in the
home since we cannot rely upon public
school music to give him this essential education. We must begin to give the growing

child a broader outlook into the musical field. Just as we taught him (Chapter I) that all keys were made to be played in, so now we may show him that there are other scales in existence besides our diatonic major and minor. Here are a few other tonalities which can be used in music:

A scale of five tones. This is our regular scale, but with the fourth and seventh notes left out. This pentatonic scale is used very much in China, but it is more to our purpose—since we are not studying Chinese music—that it is used in many popular Scottish songs, such as "Auld Lang Syne," "Ye Banks and Braes o' Bonnie Doon," etc.

A scale of white keys only, from D to D, a Gregorian mode used very much in the Middle Ages and found in several of Bach's chorals and fugues.

Other scales, such as from C to C with E flat, F sharp and A flat (Hungarian), or C to C with D flat and A flat (Byzantine), will sometimes be found, and a little taste of the flavor of these will show our young musician how broad the field of musical construction really is.

An acquaintance with the orchestra will be a great factor in the development of the child's appreciation of music. Here perhaps the public school course may, in exceptional cases, be of help. It may possibly be that a small band or orchestra has been formed among the scholars. If such a band exists we would advise the teacher to allow the player of each instrument to explain colloquially, the working of his instrument, to the rest of the class. It will be an object lesson that they will appreciate.

The young student will soon comprehend that just as an oil painting is of a higher school than an etching, so an orchestral piece tells us much more than a piano composition.

There may be some readers who imagine that such a varied line of musical work is far beyond the average pupil, but this is really not the case. The varied work will make the whole study of music more interesting. It is usually the young pupil who is confined entirely to a few humdrum pieces and exercises upon the piano, who is never allowed a glimpse of the broader field

of music, who gets tired of the whole business and cannot be brought to any sustained interest.

I have given some 240 concerts to adult audiences in the public schools of Boston. In some districts the audiences were wage-earners, laborers, and many who had not had any opportunities for the study of music. After popular demonstration and explanation, these audiences grew heartily enthusiastic over Mozart's "Magic Flute" overture, Bach fugues, symphonic movements, and other intricate music. If this can be done with an average public of the working classes, how much more may be taught an intelligent child who is interested in its studies and who is endowed with a love of music to start with!

But how much depends upon the teacher! How few study the personality of the child that they are to train. If ever the wind is to be tempered to the shorn lamb it must be in the early stages of music teaching. We cannot work entirely by the standards of "best music." What is digestible for one may be totally indigestible for another.

We pity that martinet teacher who believes himself strictly honest because he treats all his pupils alike, giving them all one system and one degree of attention. Not only will he wear himself out, but he will wear out some of his pupils as well. Such a teacher cannot see that there are cases where the rules must be relaxed. There are some examples of these martinets in musical history. Wagner's first regular teacher, Mueller, could not see that he was dealing with a genius, and wanted to treat a mountain torrent as if it were a canal. The result was mutual dissatisfaction and a final explosion. Beethoven's counterpoint teacher, Albrechtsberger, only saw that his pupil broke rules which the teacher supposed were immutable, and he warned his other pupils not to associate with this black sheep.

The teacher who treats his pupils alike is comparable to a man who is filling several bottles of various sizes. He is determined to put a quart in each. What the result will be with the pint and the gallon bottles can readily be imagined. In fact the overuse of "method" is baneful. We in America bow down too much to this fetich. Even the great Leschetizky once wrote to a friend in America: "I have no method." In fact, in this matter one can transmute Shakespeare and change his "Methinks there is some method in this madness," into "Methinks there is some madness in this method."

IV

DIFFERENT TYPES OF PUPILS

THERE are often two opposite kinds of juvenile pupils for the teacher to deal with. One is overbold and the other too timid. By their results they might be called the Scrambler and the Stammerer.

Every music teacher, and every mother who has superintended the musical education of several children knows these two types. There is a kind of pupil who will undauntedly plow through everything no matter what havoc is made. False notes, errors in counting the time, omissions, none of these things stop her, and she finally gets through somehow and ends with emphasis.

The other type, the opposite of this, is mortally afraid of a single mistake. With her, one error always breeds many. A single false note and she will probably stop at once, and the mortal dread of making errors is very likely to cause them.

Of course these two pupils require opposite treatment. It is well to stop the "scrambler" at the slightest mistake. As this sort of pupil is apt to overuse the damper pedal to blur over her errors, it is best to forbid the use of this pedal altogether until the piece or study is almost perfect. (I shall soon give remarks upon the use and abuse of the damper pedal.) With this pupil it is well to use the metronome very much. She is a devout disciple of Young's poetic line:

We take no note of time,

and there is no fear of the counting machine ever making her too mechanical.

With such a pupil much four-hand playing is a benefit, since it enforces some regard for strict time-keeping.

The "stammerer" must have quite different treatment. The teacher must often choose some new pieces which are somewhat below her technical ability. These pieces must be played through, from beginning to end, without stopping. No error should be corrected at the time that it takes place, although the teacher should take note of such faults, and correct them after the piece is ended.

Such a pupil should take part in four-hand playing also, because she feels that her errors are less noticeable and the fact of the other player's going on prevents her from stopping.

How much more confidence a nervous soloist may display in a duet may be illustrated by a case which took place in Leipsic years ago. If the reader looks at Reinecke's "Spring Song" he will find a beautiful vocal solo with piano accompaniment, and a violin obbligato, or added part. Dr. Reinecke once told me the story of how it came to have that shape. It was originally a soprano solo, and it was to be sung by one of the advanced pupils at a Conservatory concert. The night before the concert the young lady who was to sing came to Reinecke's house. (The great director of the Leipsic Conservatory lived very modestly in the Querstrasse, up four flights.) She was suffering from an attack of anticipatory nervousness and stage fright.

Dr. Reinecke asked her if she would be as scared if the song were a duet. Amid tears and sobs she replied in the negative. Thereupon the composer sat down and wrote the violin support, and his son at once rehearsed it standing beside the singer. The next day it achieved an entire success and the singer did excellently. So also our "stammerer" may do well if the playing is shared with another performer.

Just as a child learns language in the first stages without a grammar it should, at first, learn music naturally and without too much rule. There are certain elements of music which are natural. Rhythm appeals to all animate creation, and much may be made of it from the earliest stages of musical work. The identification of different rhythms on hearing them played will be an easy task and a useful one. The characteristics of rhythms might also be explained so as to interest a musical child.

The most cradling, soothing rhythm is six-eight in medium or slow tempo, and therefore almost all of the cradle songs, slumber songs, boat songs (barcarolles), and swing songs are in this rhythm. But the same rhythm taken rapidly becomes the snappiest and brightest in music, and quick-steps and other spirited music will be found in quick six-eight or in two-four rhythm. The three-four rhythm is often very expressive and emotional, and most of the slow movements of sonatas will be found in it. The most rickety rhythm imaginable is five-four, and even though the child will not be called upon to play such a rhythm for a long time it may sense its effect even in the early stages of musical study.

We have already spoken of the necessity of accustoming the young pupil to different keys in the early stages of practice; let us now add to that the necessity of an early use of two clefs. There is a defect in many instruction books for the young in that the *G clef* is often used alone, for so long a time, that when the child is brought face to face with the *bass clef* the foundations of the universe seem disturbed. The earlier the *bass clef* is brought into play the better. As regards the sense of absolute pitch we have said that is a good indication of the musical sense, but not an unfailing proof of a musical genius. It is a species of musical memory which recalls the sound of every tone and enables its possessor to name any tone on hearing it. The blind almost invariably have this faculty. Nevertheless we have known some prominent musicians who do not possess it and some mediocre musicians who do.

The faculty can be cultivated, but it is unnecessary to harass the youngster with an effort to acquire it. The sounding of a tuning fork, or a pitch pipe, many times a day, always humming its tone in imitation, often results in fixing one tone in the mind, with which all others can be compared mentally. The writer recalls an ocean voyage in which he struck two consecutive days of fog. The whistle of the ship happened to sound "A." He heard that note every minute for about forty-eight hours. He heard it mentally for a good many days after!

Relative pitch is another matter altogether, and ought to be cultivated as early as possible. This means the identifying of any tone after some other tone has been sounded and named, as a clue. It is the science of intervals. It is taught in many public schools and is the best part of their musical curriculum. The study of such interval work is called *solfeggio*. We have already spoken against the great preponderance of vocal instruction in our public-school musical system, but the *solfeggio* part of it is valuable to every musical student.

A real musician must be able to read a page of music exactly as people read a printed page, without actually hearing the sounds. *Solfeggio* is the first step toward this desideratum. Even singing itself is of some help to the pianist, since he gets a better sense of phrasing by means of it. There was once a famous piano teacher in the Paris Conservatoire who always made his pupils take a term or two of singing lessons as a direct aid to piano phrasing and sense of expression.

To come back to our young pupil; among the musical tests which can be made into a game is that in which the parent or teacher plays a short passage of music, putting a false note in one of the chords. See if the pupil can detect the error and pick out the note which is wrong. Occasionally play a musical period, but omit the final cadence, letting the young bystander add the omitted chord. Rhythmic tests can be varied greatly and many kindergarten games are merely such tests in pleasant disguise. The young musician might be taught very early to count music by beats of the hand. In such counting one need not hamper him with many rules at first, merely insisting upon a down beat at the beginning of each measure.

V

METHODS: MUSICAL PRODIGIES

WE have been asked frequently as to what particular method is to be used in the earliest stages of piano study. There are many good methods. Any that takes up the two clefs in the primitive stages of work, and does not cling to the key of *C*, like a shipwrecked sailor to a floating mast, will do. But it is well to remember that the method is not so important as the teacher, as we have intimated. The great Leschetizky once wrote two letters to Carl Stasny, the eminent pianist, in which he said:

I could never come to a decision to publish a Piano School, since such a work would demand a definite line of study which would need to be logically followed. "All roads lead to Rome," they say, and there is something true in the saying. But the by-paths are, in my opinion, a matter of considerable importance. Therefore I hold, above all things, to a correct beginning, which is very seldom made, since few beginners seek a teacher who understands the course of preparation for future virtuosity. Even in the beginning the most various attempts must be made to bring to this or that pupil the technical art-touch, without overstraining the differently organized hands.

The writer personally examined the two letters, from one of which he has made the above literal translation. In the other the famous teacher adds:

My motto is that without a good, yes, a *very* good, teacher, no printed method will be effective. And only he who can demonstrate practically every possibility to his pupils is a good teacher.

In another sentence he disclaims having any special method, but advises special work for every type of pianist's hand. There is one point we wish to emphasize here. The "very good teacher" that Leschetizky speaks of need not necessarily be a foreigner. Too many Americans imagine that a well-trained foreign teacher must be the best attainable, while they have a certain condescension toward the American musician. This is a mistake. Often the native-born teacher is more sympathetic

with the pupil and understands his nature better than the professor from overseas. The sympathetic bond between teacher and pupil must never be lost sight of in the matter of musical education; it is a most important factor.

Another earnest word may be spoken here about the pupil of especial talent. Let there be no "prodigy" work; no giving of juvenile concerts or recitals, except in the intimacy of the teacher's studio or at home. They always dwarf the growth of the musician. One could make a very long list of prodigies that were great only while they were little; musicians who diminished, artistically, as they grew up. Beethoven, Wagner, Brahms, were not child-prodigies; while Mozart and Liszt, both of whom fulfilled the great promise of their precocious musical childhood, are exceptions.

The most wonderful child-prodigy in music that we ever heard was Josef Hofmann. At nine years of age he was pianist, composer, conductor, and an improviser be-

JOSEF HOFMANN AT THE AGE OF TWELVE

yond compare. We recall giving him a theme for improvisation, before an audience of over 3,000 people, and from the way he worked it out spontaneously, with rhythmic changes, contrapuntal devices, etc.—one certainly felt that here was a new Mozart, a boy who would easily become the greatest composer of the world. He has become a very superior pianist, a thorough musician, a good composer, but Richard Strauss is still one of the foremost of living composers, and yet is not nearly as great as we expected this prodigy to become.

This is an example of fairly successful growth, but sometimes the prodigy fails altogether to keep the promise of a phenomenal childhood. Maurice Dengremont was a wonderful violinist when very young. When he grew up he was more remarkable as a billiard-player than as a musician. We know of another young violinist who, when he was seven years old, played before the King of Holland, but when he was thirty-seven he was a successful merchant.

Rubinstein's mother acted most wisely when she declined to allow the boy to give concerts, even though the family needed the money which his juvenile piano recitals would have won. Brahms, after a successful musical début at fourteen years of age, disappeared from public view for five years' further study. The excessive applause which a juvenile musical prodigy receives is almost always fatal to further rigorous and conscientious study.

But we are dealing, in these articles, not with the musical phenomenon, but with the average young American pupil who desires to develop normally the musical good that is in him. We need scarcely say that a one-sided education is to be avoided. The musician who is interested in history, poetry, painting, belles-lettres, is more proficient in his music because of the knowledge of the sister arts. The day is past when the musician is not expected to know anything besides his notes and their execution; the musician of the future is to be a man of general culture, and it is noticeable how our large American conservatories of music take heed of this and add general studies to their curriculum.

VI

THE VOCAL STUDIES. COMPASS OF THE CHILD'S VOICE—GENERAL MUSICAL COMPASS

WE have not spoken much as yet of the vocal side of the child's education. Almost everybody has a musical voice to start with, although this is usually supposed to be the privilege of a favored few. The voice can be trained from earliest childhood, and its training is usually a pleasure rather than a task to the musically inclined boy or girl. How little the child's voice has been understood may be gathered from the fact that until recently the compass of the juvenile voice was not comprehended. Look over most of the children's songs of even a few years ago and it will be found that the compass was made quite narrow—about from middle *C*, to *D*, a ninth above. Careful investigation has shown that the average juvenile voice runs about a fourth higher, and in works such as Pierne's ''Children's Crusade,'' we find a compass from *C* to *G*, naturally avoiding the extremes.

A few words regarding musical compass in general may here be pertinent.

When we look at the keyboard of the modern piano, with its seven and a third octaves, we are apt to imagine that music demands a very wide compass for its best expression. Such is by no means the case. One of the noblest collections of contrapuntal music in existence—Bach's ''Well-tempered Clavichord,''—consisting of ninety-six intricate and most ingenious compositions—could be played upon a piano which has but four octaves instead of more than seven. Almost all orchestral works, especially the classical symphonies, could readily be transcribed for a piano of six octaves. The highest instrument of the orchestra, the piccolo, does not go as high as the piano, while the deepest regular instrument, the contrabass, goes only to the deepest *E* of the keyboard.

Proceeding from the works of widest musical compass to those of the narrowest, we find that sometimes an effective melody can be composed within much more restricted limits than is generally supposed. Get out the hymn book and look at the good old tune "Hamburg." It is made up of only five notes, and has a compass of only a diminished fifth. And the lowest of these notes (*E*) is used but once and could readily be altered to *G*, leaving the melody but four notes—*F, G, A, B*-flat. The reason of the narrow compass of this famous tune is that Dr. Lowell Mason arranged it from an old Gregorian chant, and the Gregorian melodies were much more restricted than the modern.

There is, however, a more modern tune of narrow compass, and operatic, too, which may be found in Meyerbeer's "Robert le Diable." It is a melody of four notes— *G, C, D, E*—ascending, and it was written to be played entirely by *kettledrums!* It is a fairly long march tune, and, when repeated by the full orchestra, is quite effective. Kettledrums formerly were treated as transposing instruments, the key to which the drums were to be tuned indicated in the score; now composers write notes for them, but without accidentals.

The German composer, Cornelius, once composed a song in which the voice has one note only, but here the melody is largely committed to the piano. It is entitled "Ein Ton." Mendelssohn did something akin to this in the part of the *Mayor* in the operetta, "Son and Stranger." The *Mayor* repeats one single note throughout his entire part. Mendelssohn did this in order that his unmusical brother-in-law, the painter Hensel, might take part in the performance, which was arranged as a surprise to the composer's parents at their silver wedding. It is said that Hensel had even then great difficulty in singing his "melody," so that the *Mayor* was greeted with laughter by the assembled family.

Regarding vocal study during the change of voice, opinions differ. Our own view is that it is safer to let vocal study drop for a time at this period, resuming it very gradually after the voice has become fixed in its new register. Yet some hold that very light practice may be continued through all the period of change.

There is one more point that may be touched upon in ending this subject; it is the question of how far heredity enters into the matter of musical ability. Studying the

lives of great composers we find that Beethoven's father and grandfather were musicians of ability; Mozart's father was a prominent musician; the Bach family were musicians for generation after generation, beginning with Veit Bach in the sixteenth century; Puccini, the modern operatic composer, can trace prominent musicianship in his father, grandfather, great-grandfather, and great-great-grandfather, all of whom achieved high reputation in the art. On the contrary, Haydn's father was a peasant; Schubert's a schoolmaster; Wagner's a chief-of-police; Handel's a barber-surgeon; and such instances might be multiplied either in support or in contradiction of musical heredity.

It is more than possible that segregation and environment may have had much to do with the cases classed as hereditary. We must remember that it was the line of least resistance for the old composers to train their children in their own profession and that this in itself might account for the succession of composers in a single family. We might also remember that while some of the sons of Johann Sebastian Bach were great musical figures, one son, David, on the other hand, was an idiot. The sole surviving son of Palestrina was not musical. The brother of Beethoven was but a mediocre musician.

Perhaps the writer may be excused for citing a case in his own family. Of four brothers he himself and one other were fond of music, while the other two were decidedly unmusical, scarcely able to distinguish one tune from another, and unable to sing or to whistle a tune correctly. Altogether then, heredity might indicate a possibility of musical talent, or even a probability, but it would not be a sure indication, and the lack of musical ability in a family would not prove that a child was certain to be unmusical.

VII

THE PIANO PEDALS

THE first pianos had no pedals and the tones were not checked by the dampers when the finger left the key. In the 18th century there were, however, attempts to work the dampers by means of knobs, drawn like organ stops. Finally, in 1783, Broadwood invented the device of working the dampers by the feet, but he applied it only to the largest instruments. The general use of the pedals belongs to the 19th century, beginning in its earliest days.

There may be two or three pedals on the pianoforte of the pupil, the central one of the best instruments sustaining any single note or chord if the pedal is put down while the keys are held. This is called the Sostenuto Pedal. In much music it is marked as if it were the ordinary damper pedal, but sometimes it is more carefully designated as "Sos. Ped.", SP or TSPd—the latter indicating "tone sustaining pedal."

In less developed pianos the central pedal may be a Bass Damper Pedal, and is intended to sustain the bass notes only. Both pedals were invented to meet the need of the player to sustain the lower notes without blurring the upper ones, since more than half the time the bass notes are the ones which we desire to sustain. In some instruments the only use of the middle pedal is for a "muffler", a strip of felt which falls between the hammers and the strings, supposedly minimizing the tortures of piano practice to those unsympathetic auditors who must remain within hearing distance during the practice hour of the young aspirant.

In any case the child-pupil need not be troubled with this central pedal until quite advanced. But the use of the damper pedal demands most careful teaching to the young, for they are very apt to overuse it. It is often called the "loud pedal." The teacher must not make the mistake of telling the child that it does not make the music louder, for the pupil will readily recognize the fact that it *does* somewhat increase the sound. It will be much better to say that the mis-called "loud pedal" is not used to make the music louder but to sustain the tones, even though it does incidentally increase the tone in heavy passages. The surest way to impress this upon the child is to choose for the first study of the damper pedal some composition that is to be played *pianissimo*. The effort to play very softly, while con-

stantly using the "loud pedal" will do more to give an understanding of this matter than any long explanation on the teacher's part.

Carefully impress upon the young student that every note is somewhat impure when the damper pedal is used, and this can be easily demonstrated. Impress the fact that the lifting of the pedal must wipe out one harmony before the next is played or there will be the utmost blurring. Perhaps, later on, some work can be played where the pedal is purposely used to blur the tones, as in the clangor of bells, the roar of thunder, etc.

It is a pity that the marking of the pedal is not more definite and uniform. The usual mark is "Ped." for its use and a star as the sign of its discontinuance. In some Pedal Studies it is written on a single-lined staff with notes which must be counted, to indicate the exact length of its continuance. These may be used with an advanced pupil. Several very simple yet intelligible modes of marking have been invented in America which give the exact length of continuance. A comparing of these markings may be seen in the accompanying illustration, as also an example showing appropriate use for the "Sostenuto Pedal."

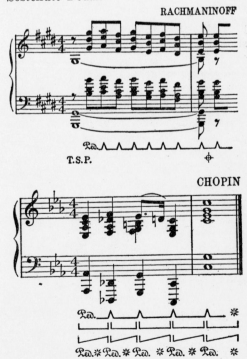

Beethoven added to the vagueness of pedal marking by sometimes using the term *senza sordine* (without dampers) for the use of the loud pedal, and *con sordine* (with dampers) for its discontinuance, which is very apt to mislead even the teacher, who mistakes *con sordine* for an indication of the use of the "soft" pedal. He uses this in the first movement of his "Moonlight Sonata," and no less an editor than Eugen d'Albert fell into the error. In this sense the word "dampers" refers to the individual dampers which accompany each hammer, thus stopping the tone immediately on the release of the key—unless the action of these dampers is suspended by the use of the "loud" or damper pedal.

The soft pedal need not be used in the early stages of study, since the pupil should be able to achieve *pianissimo* by touch alone. But when it is used the pupil can be easily made to perceive that while it is a great fault to hold down the "loud" pedal for any length of time, the "soft" pedal can often be used continuously, and also both pedals can be used simultaneously, the "soft" one continuously—if need be—and the other intermittently.

It might be well to show the pupil that the soft pedal alters the touch of most upright pianos, and that it causes an unpleasant sound on the square piano. If the student has a grand piano it would be well to explain by demonstration the true meaning and action of *una corda* and *tre corde*.

I always hold it good, when possible, to give some instruction about the mechanism of the pianoforte even to the young pupil. A visit to a pianoforte manufactory, a view of the sounding-board, the stringing, the pedal mechanism, and above all the action, will only result in a child taking more interest than ever in her own pianoforte.

VIII

SCIENCE OF SOUND

IT is a disputed point as to whether a child should be instructed at all in the physical laws underlying Music. While I should not counsel adding acoustical studies to the work of a very young student, I should certainly tell him some stories about the wonders of sound, and let him make a few primitive experiments. Such a proceeding would only add to his interest in Music. Here are a few points not beyond the comprehension of many children.

Every musical instrument has a sounding-board. The bell of a cornet or of a trombone is its sounding-board. The voice has the hard palate and the whole top of the head as a resonator—especially the back of the nose. The sounding-board should magnify the tone, much as a Fresnel lens in a light-house intensifies the light of a paraffin lamp.

Stringed instruments should have especially effective sounding-boards. All musical sounds are regular vibrations of the air; irregular vibrations produce only noise. A string swinging to and fro in space moves very little air, and the sound of the string itself is not audible a few feet away. But when the vibrations set up by the string go through the bridge of the violin, or other stringed instrument, and thus strike the sounding-board, which begins to vibrate in sympathy with them, they become very powerful. The Stradivarius has a rich tone because the sounding-board is perfectly elastic and vibrates freely. A sound-box is the best sounding-board, and the box of a violin is made to vibrate both front and back, by a post which carries the vibrations to the back-board. If we put a clamp on the bridge of the violin it restricts the vibrations on their journey to the sounding-board and at once the tone is "muted." But the power of sound vibrations is so tremendous that no muting could absolutely stop them.

Wonderful things have been discovered in the application of vast sounding-boards. In some modern halls, as in Symphony Hall, Boston, there are large sounding-boards set in the ceiling to increase the tone of the orchestra which plays underneath them.

If you will look at the back of your upright pianos you will see the sounding-board, quite free and open. It is made of many spruce or fir planks of finest quality, well-seasoned and glued together. If you will now examine the wires at the other side of the sounding-board, you will find that they all run over a bridge made of strips of maple, which carries their vibrations to the sounding-board. Without this sounding-board and bridge, the tone of the strings of the piano would be almost inaudible.

We have just explained that all musical sounds are regular vibrations of the air; if the air vibrates slowly we get a deep tone; if it vibrates rapidly the result is a high tone. Pitch, therefore, depends upon the rate of vibration. Strike the deepest note on your piano keyboard. If it is A it has a trifle more than twenty-seven vibrations a second; if it is C it has a fraction more than thirty-two. If you listen carefully to these deep tones you will hear a rumbling mingled with them, so that you can actually perceive that they are made of regular vibrations even if you cannot count them.

If you played the pedals of a large church organ you could go deeper and deeper until you came to C, an octave below the deepest C of the piano, when the separate vibrations would be clearly perceptible. If you could sound a tone still lower—which could be done by a longer pipe—it would no longer be audible as a tone, for sixteen vibrations a second is as low as the human brain can perceive tone; it would fall apart into separate puffs, or vibrations, no longer connecting together.

Now as regards the upper end, probably the highest C of the piano is the highest tone you have ever heard. It has about 4,150 vibrations a second. But we can actually hear more than three octaves above that—up to nearly 38,000 vibrations a second, though the faculty to distinguish these vibrations differs greatly with different brains. Women can hear higher tones than men; but as cats can hear higher than women, there is no reason for women to get conceited about this.

The use of the "tempered scale" may be a little beyond the childish comprehension, yet one can explain that each scale in each different key ought to be tuned in a certain proportion from its own key-note. If we were to give all these differences accurately we should need to have a separate keyboard for each scale—twelve keyboards for the major and twelve more for the minor scales.

To avoid this and yet remain in tune in different keys, the piano tuner tries to divide the octave in twelve equal semitones, each a trifle out of tune—but none very much so—and equally out of tune in each scale. In this "tempered scale" the octaves are absolutely true in pitch. The fourths and fifths are so slightly out of tune that none but the finest ear could detect it; but thirds and sixths are noticeably off pitch.

A very simple experiment will show this. Nature always produces a little roughness, or throbbing, when an interval is not in perfect tune. This throbbing is called "the beats." Strike an octave upon your piano or organ and if it is in tune you will hear a smooth sound, the two tones coalescing perfectly. Now strike a third or a sixth, in the middle or lower register, and you will hear the roughness that was absent from the octave—which shows that the interval is not in perfect tune. This is more perceptible on the organ than on the piano.

Two centuries ago, when this system of equal temperament had not been introduced, they never used keys which were distant from the key of C. Such keys as D-flat (five flats) or B (five sharps) were never used and were deemed entirely theoretical. It was Bach, who in 1722 tuned his clavichord—the predecessor of the piano—in the tempered scale, and composed twenty-four fugues and preludes in each of the several major and minor keys. In 1742 he composed a second volume of this "Well-tempered Clavichord," in which he repeated the experiment. He probably adopted the idea from the writings of Andreas Werckmeister, a German, who was born in 1645, and died 1706.

We never hear any musical tone quite alone. With every tone that is heard there mingle faint, high tones called overtones, which blend with the tone that is heard and make its quality good or bad. If these overtones are present in good proportion, the lower ones rather full and the upper ones faint but clear, we get a beautiful quality of tone. The lower overtones make the richness of the tone, the upper ones its delicacy.

Everyone knows that music sounds better

on a cold, dry day than on a muggy, warm, and damp day. The reason is that the heavy air smothers some of the high overtones and renders the tone less delicate. If you hear a violin played in Denver or Leadville it will sound better than in Chicago, simply because the elasticity of the air at the high altitude makes it possible for the high overtones to vibrate very freely.

When the overtones are faint, we get a dull and lifeless tone, like that of a tuning-fork when its sound has almost ceased or the tone of the stopped diapason on an organ. When they are too strongly present we get a very incisive tone, such as that of the oboe, or of some mandolins, or of a very old "tin-panny" piano. If one were to hear a tone quite by itself, without any of the mingled overtones, it would be very muddy, dull, and unpleasant.

If the child wants to hear some of these overtones separately, let him try the following experiment. Strike a moderately deep note, *Great C* for example. While this is sounding—or before it is struck—press down the key an octave higher without sounding it. Now take the finger away from the deeper note, and the higher note—which was not sounded—will be heard. Do the same with the note a fifth above the octave, and you will get the same result—a tone. Do it with any of the keys between and there will be no result—no sound. This certainly shows that the higher notes were sounding together with the deeper one. Such simple experiments and stories about the science of sound will certainly be better for the child than some of the false and ultra-sentimental stories attached to certain famous compositions.

One of the chief mistakes in the study of music in America is the tendency to rhapsodize or "gush" over romantic compositions. Some pupils are fed on this kind of false enthusiasm until they demand a story for each piece they play. Some women's clubs carry this story-telling fad into even the more advanced branches of music. As a consequence, a great deal of false history has been made up to meet the demand thus created. Here are a couple of the false stories:

It is said that Stradella, the Italian composer (1645-1681), won the affection of a patrician lady in Venice and that her brother hired assassins to murder him. The assassins went to a church where Stradella was giving a new composition, hoping to kill him as he came out. As he sang his beautiful song, the murderers were moved to tears. When he came out they revealed the plot to him and even gave him money that he might escape from the city. This story is connected with the composition called "Stradella's Prayer." The story is entirely untrue; the song was not even composed by Stradella. It is ascribed, by investigators, to Gluck.

The story that Beethoven's "Moonlight Sonata" was improvised by the composer on his discovering a blind girl in a cottage in a wood near Vienna; that he sat down at the piano while the moonlight streamed in, and enraptured the blind girl with his harmonies, is entirely untrue. A sonata is never improvised; it is planned as carefully as a house. Beethoven did not even name this work "Moonlight Sonata"; that was done by an enterprising publisher.

All such sentimental stuff should be avoided with the young music student.

IX

THE CHILDHOOD OF THE GREAT COMPOSERS

IN the preceding chapters we have studied the development of the child in music. It may be pertinent to such a subject to examine the childhood of some of the great composers and note the character of their genius in its incipient stages. Yet so many divergent phases will be found in the boyhood of the chief musicians that it is doubtful if a definite lesson can be drawn from the subject, which is, however, interesting in itself. Pertinacity and perseverance will be found in almost every instance.

The great Bach was left an orphan at ten years of age. One of his elder brothers, John Christoph Bach, took the boy to live with him in Ohrdruff, in Thuringia, and became his teacher. It was a quiet and sober home, and the brother taught him music, chiefly of the sacred school. Few details are left of his juvenile study, yet one anecdote may serve to show the ardor of young Bach's work. His brother had a collection of organ and other compositions locked up in a bookcase with a lattice front. Bach, after vainly trying to induce his brother to let him study it, managed to extract it through the lattice work. He took it out nearly every night after the family had gone to bed, and sat up for hours copying the work by moonlight.

When he had the copying nearly completed his brother discovered the copy and took it from him. It is quite possible that the strain upon his eyesight, caused by this kind of night work, laid the foundation for the blindness which came upon Bach in his later years. The brother has been held up in some musical histories as a severe tyrant, because of his action in this case, but nothing of the kind is proved, since the works may have been beyond the lad's capability, and John Christoph may have been only a conscientious teacher. Bach studied diligently in the Lyceum of Ohrdruff, where he certainly learned a good amount of Latin, some chorus singing, and received a fair general education.

Handel's childhood was more erratic. There was a combat between his father and the boy on the matter of music. The father was body surgeon to the Duke Augustus of Saxony, and although he had begun life as a barber was at this time a man of considerable importance. He was quite an old man when Handel was born. An English musical history puts it rather quaintly when it says, "Handel's father was 63 years old *when he was born*," which makes the father the oldest baby on record.

Handel's father intended him for a legal career, and was dismayed at the love for music which the young boy displayed. He caused all his musical toys to be burned at once, and packed the child off to school when he was only five years of age. It may have been his mother, or possibly his Aunt Anna, who helped him to smuggle a clavichord into the garret at this time. As a small clavichord was not much bigger than a large book, and as its tone could not be heard even a few yards away, the boy's

musical practice went on unmolested for a while.

One day the father made up his mind to make a journey to Weissenfels and pay his respects to the Duke. The boy begged urgently to be allowed to go along. The father refused his request. But when he had gone about ten miles on his journey, he found that his obstinate youngster had "caught on behind," and was riding with him on the coach. It was too late to send him back, so he was perforce allowed to make the journey.

The fates seem to have ordained that journey, for when the boy arrived at the court at Weissenfels the musicians all made a pet of him. One day he was playing to some of them on the organ in the chapel when the Duke himself came in. He was astounded at the natural musicianship of the boy and after a long argument with the father succeeded in extracting from him a promise that he would give the lad a good chance at a musical education—all of which came from the obstinacy of the seven-year-old in forcing his trip to Weissenfels.

At ten years of age Handel composed remarkable trios and other concerted music, and he himself said, during his later years in England, that Zachow, his teacher, "made him work like the devil." We shall find that almost all the great masters had plenty of hard work during their earliest years.

Mozart's childhood was a most interesting one. The boy was a strange, old-fashioned kind of child, and his parents had grave doubts as to whether he would grow up. He had a mortal terror of the sound of a trumpet, and would run away terribly frightened if he heard one played. But he loved the spinet, on which his elder sister, Maria Anna, took her lessons from their father, Leopold Mozart, who was an estimable man and an excellent violinist.

After the lesson the three-year-old boy would climb to the keyboard and try to imitate some of the chords and progressions which he had heard. At four years he played a little piece which he had composed —a Minuet—and his father wrote it down and perpetuated it. But soon after this the boy was trained to write his own notation, as may be seen from the manuscripts at the Salzburg Mozarteum, which he composed and wrote down when only seven years of age.

Naturally the father began the training of such a precocious nature very early. Since both brother and sister were prodigies they were placed before the public very early. In Vienna the boy received a dress suit and sword from the Empress Maria Theresa, and he romped about the palace with the little Princess Marie Antoinette, who was to end her days upon the guillotine, in Paris. In London there were many especial attractions advertised at the concerts of the pair. The young Mozart was to play a piece of music with a cloth spread above his hands, so that he could not see the keyboard. He was also to improvise upon a theme given by anyone in the audience. He was to read a concerted piece at sight, and to do many other tricks. This was not real musicianship. Fortunately, however, it did not result in vitiating his taste or in lowering his abilities. His subsequent growth was much more normal.

Haydn was born in a one-story hut, occupied by peasants, in the village of Rohrau. Naturally there could be no musical training in the tiny farm where his childhood was spent, but a cousin, named Frankh, discovered that the boy had a good voice and a musical ear, and offered to train him in the art. We can imagine the kind of training that the young peasant received from one who was scarcely of a higher station. Blows, buffetings and beatings were of daily occurrence in the curriculum. For all that, Frankh meant to deal honestly with the lad and a little later got him an appointment as a

pupil in the choir of St. Stephen's cathedral, in Vienna, Georg Reuter, the director, promising him a good musical education. This promise he utterly failed to keep, therefore Haydn was almost entirely self-taught. His subsequent study of the works of Philipp Emanuel Bach helped him greatly, and he picked up crumbs of musical knowledge while acting as accompanist and semi-servant for Porpora, the great singing teacher. They called him "Porpora's boot-black," and his menial position all through his younger years left a trace of servility which he could not shake off in later and more prosperous times.

The childhood of Beethoven was unpleasantly influenced by that of Mozart. Beethoven's father was an improvident drunkard and he read with envy about the money which Leopold Mozart had gained through his two prodigies. Suddenly he began to think that his own son might be made into

MENUET AND TRIO

(Composed at 5 years of age)

W. A. MOZART

something of the same sort by a forcing process. But Beethoven was not of the prodigy type; he had great musical ability as a child, but he was destined to ripen more slowly and healthily. Nor was his father a character of the Leopold Mozart style; he was irregular in his instruction and joined with him was a boon companion named Pfeiffer, who assisted at the so-called lessons. It is a wonder that the severity, irregularity and lack of system did not cause Beethoven to hate music. Friends of the family have left it on record that they had seen the young Beethoven sitting in tears at the piano many times. Finally, however, the father and the unenlisted volunteer decided that they could not waste their time in the hopeless task of making a prodigy, and a real teacher, Neefe, was called in. Then only did Beethoven's musical instruction begin. He ad-

vanced rapidly enough to be able to compose a two-voiced fugue at about ten years of age, and the accompanying sonata even earlier.

Franz Schubert was, like Haydn, chiefly self-taught. When we state that he was the son of a poor schoolmaster, in a suburb of Vienna, and that his father had eighteen other children, one can imagine that the childhood of this composer was not very roseate.

But if they were very poor, at least they were a loving family, and there was music in the crowded home. His father and an elder brother taught the young Franz the musical elements. He was rather an ugly duckling in these early years, unattractive personally, near-sighted and shabbily clothed. But he had a love for music and a sweet voice, and these two good gifts led him to be placed in the parish choir, where the director Holzer, began to give him systematic training in music. But he seems to have comprehended the science of this art almost intuitively. Holzer once exclaimed: "Whatever I try to teach him he seems to know already."

His excellent voice and his musical abilities soon procured him a place in the choir of the Imperial Chapel in Vienna. This position was by no means as glittering as it sounds, for the lads were half-starved by the authorities, and received only desultory musical training. But this little was enough for the young Schubert and he began composing with a fervor that was phenomenal. There are stories of how he scribbled melodies on the backs of menus and odd scraps of paper. This had to do, perhaps, with a very acute limitation to his fever of creation —he did not have the money

SONATA

(Composed at the age of 9 years)

L. VAN BEETHOVEN

to buy music paper. A few lessons in thorough-bass seem to have comprised the extent of Schubert's musical training. Just before his death he made arrangements to take some lessons in counterpoint, but these were prevented by his untimely decease. One rather odd error in connection with Schubert's boyhood may be corrected here. The school attached to the Imperial Chapel is called the "Konvictschule." A few careless translators have stated that Schubert studied in a school for convicts.

Frederic Chopin as a baby was averse to music. The playing of a piano would cause him to cry violently. Whether this expressed disapproval cannot be ascertained at this late day. We have seen that sometimes excess of emotion may cause the infant's tears to flow. But biographers seem to have decided that Chopin disliked the piano in his youngest years. At any rate he soon got over this aversion — if such it was—and was a prodigy at the age of nine, when he appeared in a charity concert in Warsaw. He had one piano teacher, Zywny, and one theory teacher, Elsner, both of whom laid a good foundation, but the boy's own individuality did more than their instruction. After the charity concert, in which the lad was prouder of his new lace collar than of his playing, the "Chopinek" was invited to the homes of the highest aristocracy of Poland.

A little later Catalani heard him play, and this great singer gave the boy a gold watch as a token of her appreciation. He began to compose before he had taken any lessons of Elsner, when he was only ten years of age. One of his marches so pleased the Grand Duke Constantine that he had it arranged for a military band and played on parade. The Czar of Russia also gave him a diamond ring at the time. Chopin was an unspoiled lad, full of vivacity and youthful pranks.

Such a childhood as the one described above was in vivid contrast with the privations of a Bach, a Haydn, or a Schubert. It is pleasant to find, once in a while, a composer who has not had his gold melted in the crucible of adversity. Certainly the childhood of Mendelssohn is a picture of everything that is genial and happy. Well did they change his given name of Jacob to "Felix" (the happy one) for no other musician had as prosperous and sunny a childhood. His father was rich and respected.

At first, and in fact all through his childhood, Mendelssohn studied music merely as

POLONAISE
A-FLAT MAJOR
(Composed at the age of 9 years)

FREDERIC CHOPIN

an adjunct of a liberal education, just as he studied Latin, drawing, belles-lettres. Yet he must have become a very good executant, since he appeared in public as early as his ninth year. The mother would sit by as Felix and Fanny took their lessons or did their piano practice. "They have Bach-fugue fingers," was her graphic comment on one occasion.

In his tenth year Felix began the study of composition, still merely as an accomplishment. But the standing and wealth of the family made possible certain things which have been denied to all other child composers. When the young Mendelssohn had completed an orchestral work the father would engage musicians, the boy composer would direct them, and the new work would be given at the Sunday afternoon musicale in a large hall in the garden before a host of admiring friends.

There was a little of self-conceit mingled with the great talent that was developing. But if the giant power of the works of Beethoven were absent from his compositions the geniality which was in his childhood was reflected sunnily through all Mendelssohn's musical life.

At the end of his childhood Mendelssohn was already fully equipped in everything pertaining to skill. No boy of eighteen ever wrote a masterpiece such as the "Midsummer Night's Dream" Overture. Yet the conceit which we have alluded to bubbled up occasionally. Especially was this the case when he attempted his first and only opera, "Camacho's Wedding." The critics all found fault with it, and justly, too. But young Felix vented his anger in a satirical poem on music critics generally.

If the composition's long,
  Then their yawns they're stifling;
If you try to make it short,
  Then they call it "trifling."

If the work is plain and clear
  Then it's childish stuff;
If it should be more complex
  Then they call it tough.

Let a man write as he will,
  Critics snarl and bite;
Therefore let him please himself
  Then he'll be all right.

Schumann and Wagner were alike in their childhood in the fact that they both showed greater predilection for poetry and drama than for music. Schumann had some piano instruction in his boyhood, but Wagner had none. When Wagner's stepfather, Geyer, was upon his deathbed, he heard the boy trying to pick out some of Weber's melodies and said "What if the lad should possess musical talent?" But at school Wagner only showed inclination toward poetry. During his boyhood he wrote a drama in which he made such sanguinary work that he found all of his characters dead at the end of the second act. Not wishing to end the play at so early a stage he peopled the next act with their ghosts.

There was not an inkling of Wagner's musical abilities in his childhood. Even in his youth, when the hearing of a Beethoven symphony inflamed him with a passion for music, he was largely self-taught, studying the scores of Beethoven. His first teacher tried to turn the mountain torrent into a canal, and of course there was an explosion before many lessons. Subsequent work with Theodore Weinlig helped Wagner more. Wagner could not play decently upon any instrument. There is no especial moral to be drawn from this except the fact that genius is amenable to no known laws.

There have been girl prodigies in Music as well as boys. In my article on "Women in Music" I have given an account of the childhood of Mrs. H. H. A. Beach, which tells of remarkable traits of precocity. Not all of these prodigies bear out their promise so well as this eminent woman composer has done. There was born in Paris, Oct. 4, 1885, a girl named Jeanne Blancard, whose musical precocity was of a remarkable sort. She was the daughter of a government official and her grandmother was a teacher of Music. Jeanne knew the names of the notes in her second year, and was soon able to name any note that was sounded for her.

At two years of age she played on the piano with one hand—either right or left, it seemed to be the same to her—the popular melodies which she heard sung in the streets. At seven years of age she composed an Impromptu, which one may compare with the Minuet of the six-year old Mozart. In her little composition the young Jeanne seems to waver doubtfully between 6/8 and 2/4 rhythm. With such precocity we may soon expect babies to compose their own nursery songs and possibly score them for orchestra. But Jeanne Blancard has not fulfilled her early promise and Chaminade is still the chief woman composer of France.

Germany has given us Erich Korngold, who composed large works in the modern vein when he was ten years of age, and Italy has given us Willy Ferrero, a child who conducted Wagnerian works with a full orchestra at the ripe age of seven! Such phenomena are not healthy, and I can only repeat what I have said in a preceding chapter, that prodigies are to be discouraged in the interests of real art. Both Liszt and Rubinstein were denied admission to the Paris Conservatoire when they came as prodigies, and the young Verdi was similarly rejected from the Milan Conservatory, chiefly because the directors did not care for juvenile phenomena. In this they were not altogether unwise, even though these instances became brilliant exceptions to the "prodigy" rule.

X

HISTORY IN CHILDREN'S MUSIC

VERY few musicians, and still fewer of the general public, know how much of history is embedded in many of the songs which every child and adult sings. Possibly the song that is most widely spread about the earth is the one which would be the least suspected of antiquity or of historical importance. It is the bacchanalian ditty known in America as "We Won't Go Home till Morning." In England this is known as "For He's a Jolly Good Fellow." In France it is known as "Malbrooke s'en

va-t'en Guerre." In Arabia it is known as one of the chief songs of the fellaheen peasantry. But among the crusaders of the twelfth century it was known as the Song of Mambron.

Mambron was a crusader-knight who fell fighting bravely under the walls of Jerusalem. His comrades sang the well-known melody in his praise. When the crusaders went back to France the melody took root in Brittany, where old legends are preserved almost as flies in amber, and was sung along the countryside. By and by a Bretonne nurse went up to Paris and took service in the royal family. The queen heard her singing the old song, but could make nothing of the words, "Mambron s'en va-t'en Guerre," and changed them into "Malbrooke s'en va-t'en Guerre"—"Marlbrough has gone to the War"—and thus it entered into French history. Beethoven uses it in this sense in his "Battle" Sym-

IMPROMPTU
(Written at the age of 7 years)

JEANNE BLANCARD Op. 3

phony ("The Battle of Vittoria"). Most curious of all, this tune was once played in Cairo, where a wealthy Frenchman was giving a band concert to the people. They seemed rather bored by the music, and the leader, somewhat piqued, finally cried out, "Give them 'Marlbrough,' they can't understand anything better"; and, sure enough, when the melody was played, the Arabian and Egyptian auditors suddenly woke up to fervor. He had unconsciously given them a tune with which all of them were familiar, a tune which had been planted in the East by the crusaders.

But if the songs of adults go back to a remote past, in certain instances, those of the children certainly rival and sometimes surpass them in antiquity and historical importance. From the earliest days of the Christian Church, the voices of children were heard in public. One of the best compliments paid to the power of children's singing was given by the Roman Emperor, Julian the Apostate, who tried to imitate the early Christian idea, and have children sing in the worship of the pagan deities. In a letter written to one of his officers, in Egypt, A.D. 361, he says:

I consider no study more worthy of attention than that of music. I wish you to choose from the population of Alexandria some well-born lads who shall be supplied with clothes, corn, wine, oil, and money, by the comptroller of my treasury. These boys are to be selected for a definite time, according to the quality of their voices. Should any of them show signs of giving great ability in the Art of Music let them know that we will give to such very great rewards. The souls of these boys will, independent of any rewards that we may offer, be cleansed and benefited by the power which good music exerts. So much for the new candidates. As for those who are now being instructed by the music teacher Dioscurus, tell them to practice all the more diligently, and we will see to

it that they are assisted in any way that they may desire.

Thus we see that children's voices were well appreciated more than fifteen hundred years ago. We shall see, a little later on, that the religious songs of children have sometimes a peculiar significance. Before pursuing this topic, however, let us examine the song which takes us back much further than that of Mambron, spoken of above, and much beyond the epoch of Julian and ancient Rome. As dancing and music were united in the most ancient music, so in this song we find the two arts joined. It is not the melody which we are able to trace here, but the combination of singing and circular dancing. It is the music game of "Little Sallie Waters." We suppose that our adult readers have often seen the children dancing in a circle around one or two who are placed in the center, while the moving circle-dancers chant,

Little Sallie Waters,
Sitting in the sun.

A similar song and dance is executed in Russia, Norway, England—even the Maypole dance comes in this classification—France, in short in almost every country of the earth. At once the ethnologist surmises that this universal custom is the survival of something very ancient, and his researches prove his supposition to be quite correct. All through the Middle Ages we can trace the "Reigen" or circular dances. Rome and Greece furnish specimens of such dances carried on by adults. The dance of the Israelites around the golden calf was one of this class of dances—a circle around a central object. This Scriptural dance was however only copied from the circular dance of the Egyptians around the bull-god Apis, and these only copied a still earlier dance of the primitive sun-worshipers around a more dreadful central object, a human sacrifice.

The religious side of children's music is wonderfully widespread. In France the children sang "Noëls" before the time of Charlemagne. The word itself is derived from "Nouvelles" or "News," and meant about the same as "Glad Tidings"—the story of Redemption. Often in ancient France the processions were headed by children singing these "Noëls," which was a much prettier escort than the modern brass band.

But this religious music found its most congenial soil in Old England, where the music of the waits has existed for many centuries. At present one can find the waits in England, about Christmas time, in the shape of rather woebegone wanderers, who sing more or less dismal carols in the hope of extracting a small Christmas gift from the passers-by. Down to the year 1820 this right of pecuniary serenading was vested by law in certain persons. From the rather vagabond character of this singing some philologists imagined that the word "wait" was derived from a Scotch word meaning to "wander." But it is probably derived from the German word "wacht" (to watch); for the early English waits were by no means wanderers, but well-nourished pages in the royal court, where they probably sang couplets at each hour as the watchmen did in Old Germany. Here is a rule regarding the waits which we have culled from the roll book of the time of Edward IV.:

The Wait eateth in ye halle with mynstrieles and taketh at Nyghte a Loffe, a Galone of Ale, and for Somere two candeles pich, a bushele of Coles; and for Winter nyghtes a half-loffe of Bread, a Galone of Ale, four Candeles pich, a Bushele of Coles. Iffe he be syke, he taketh two loves, two messes of great meat, one Galone of Ale.

And what with so much ale we should scarcely think that the youngster had much chance of recovery. One example of what these old waits sang may be appended here, with the music. The tune will be recognized as a typical example of the sturdy old English carol. It ran thus:

The words were as follows:

Joseph was an old man,
An old man was he,
He married sweet Mary
And a virgin was she.

As they went a-walking
In the garden so gay,
Maid Mary spied cherries
Hanging down from yon tree.

Mary said to Joseph
With her sweet lips so mild,
"Pluck those cherries, Joseph,
For to give to my child."

"Oh, then," replied Joseph,
With words so unkind,
"I will pluck no cherries,
For to give to thy child."

Mary said to cherry tree,
"Bow down to my knee,
That I may pluck cherries
By one, two, and three."

The uppermost sprig then
Bowed down to her knee.
"By this you may see, Joseph,
These cherries are for me."

Oh, eat your cherries, Mary,
Oh, eat your cherries now,
Oh, eat your cherries, Mary,
That grow upon the bough.

Then follows a religious homily upon the worship of the Heavenly Infant, and Joseph is convinced that he did not act rightly in declining to gather cherries.

In some of these old carols there are "refrains" or "burdens"—a line, or a phrase recurring without making sense in each case. Sometimes, however, these "burdens" have a meaning which is veiled in antiquity. Thus "Hey tol-de-rol," which is found in many an old drinking-song as well as in love-songs, originally was "Hey troly-loly," which was equivalent to "alack and alas." The refrain of "Willow," which will recur to many who have read their Shakespeare, alluded to a disappointed love, as the "Broom" indicated a violent death. But the oldest of these refrains is "Derry, Derry Down," which some philologists trace to ancient druidic times, believing it to be a pagan incantation. Very strange are the metamorphoses of words, and there is often more of history in a word than in a monument. How many, for example, are aware of the fact that the innocent exclamation "By Jiminy," comes from the most sacred old Roman oath by the "Gemini" (the twins), or the Dioscuri, Castor and Pollux? Our everyday exclamation of "Dear me!" is but a phonetic imitation of the Italian "Dio Mio," which brings it into the field of profanity. Learned commentators have tried to prove that our "Hurrah" is but the ancient Egyptian morning cry to the god of the rising sun, Amon Ra.

But we are wandering from our songs of childhood. Not all of the ancient ones can be traced to their sources, yet it is odd to see how some of them have changed their meaning during the centuries. The comical ballad of "There Were Three Crows Sat on a Tree," was once an earnest praise of loyalty. The crows speak of the knight who had died in the Holy Land, and describe the faithful hound who guards his master's body, and the hawks who fly about him and chase off the ravens. One old version of this song tells of a woman leaning over the parapet of her castle, forever gazing in the distance in the hope of seeing her knight return; the second verse (related by the second crow) tells of three children wandering through many lands, seeking their father and never finding him, while the third verse, and crow, relate his death in a far-off land.

Probably every child knows the song "London Bridge Is Falling Down," but not one of the juvenile singers is aware of the fact that this song was sung in 1205, when good old Peter of Colechurch was building old London Bridge of stone, and the people laughed at the idea, and predicted, in this song, that the top-heavy structure would fall in before it was completed.

Sometimes there is a quaint vein of humor in antique songs of childhood. Often this takes the shape of paradoxical or contradictory lines. The Irish (adult) song of the "Groves of Blarney" is a specimen of this contradictory style, but the juvenile song of "Three Children on the Ice," is fully as good an example as any. It runs:

Three children sliding on the ice,
　All on a summer's day,
It so fell out, they all fell in,
　The rest they ran away.

Now had these children been at home,
　Or sliding on dry ground,
Ten thousand pounds to one penny
　They had not all been drowned.

You parents all, who children have,
　And you, too, that have none,
If you would keep them safe abroad,
　Pray keep them safe at home.

There are a few variants of this song, but it has been traced back to the year 1659. "Sing a Song o' Sixpence" is older, for it was sung in the sixteenth century with the words and tune of the present.

When we come to the subject of rounds we find that many of those which children now delight in had their origin in the Elizabethan era. This is but natural, since one of the great delights of that epoch was the singing of rounds and catches. There was an enormous amount of social singing about the year 1600, in London. One very pretty custom was the singing of duets, not as the singers do to-day, standing side by side, but with the two vocalists seated at a table, OPPOSITE each other. The music was between them, printed so as to be easily read from two sides at once, as the selection here reprinted from an old English volume of such music will show.

The round of "Three Blind Mice" was sung as early as 1609, and was very popular because of its simplicity. There is, however, one famous round which is much older than those cited. It is the one which is now sung to the words:

Turn again, Whittington,
Thou worthy citizen,
Lord Mayor of London.

This had its origin, with the same music as is sung to-day, in the year 1453. In that year Sir John Norman was elected lord mayor of London. Up to that time the lord mayors had always made their progress in procession through the streets of the old city, and there was great festivity on Lord Mayor's Day. Sir John Norman kept up this wild festivity, but determined to introduce a novelty by making his parade upon the Thames in barges. The watermen were so delighted with this innovation that they made an especial round for that day and sang it in honor of the new Lord Mayor. The boatmen sang:

> Row the boat, Norman, row,
> Heave-ho and rum-be-low
> Row to thy Leman.

The second line is an example of the old "burden," this time a sailor's call, while "leman" meant "mistress," or "sweetheart."

This topic has already caused us to wander through many countries and centuries. There have been scientific investigators at work upon the old favorite, "Ride a cock-horse to Banbury cross," but we somewhat doubt their conclusions. Of course the "cross" was always the market place, or the open square in the center of the medieval town. But they ride the cock-horse a good deal further back than Banbury. They drive it away back into Grecian mythology, when it becomes the hippogriff, half-horse, half-dragon. With this long horseback ride we may well end a subject which has in itself far more of history, mythology, and religion, than juvenile singers dream.

XI

CONCLUSION

THE present is the age of scientific pedagogy. There was never a time when such care was taken in teaching the young. The word "education" is derived from the Latin *educo,* meaning "to bring out," and nowadays every teacher tries to bring OUT what is in the child, instead of merely laboring to pump things IN. It was by no means always thus in music. When we look at the method of musical training of a hundred years ago we are appalled at its severity and its tactlessness. Haydn suffered many a flogging; Beethoven was wofully abused by his first teacher, his father. Paganini was kept at practice hour,

after hour, through almost the entire day, and, on making the slightest error in his violin-playing, was forced to practice into the night as well.

To-day we find the greatest masters glad to write works to interest children in music. Bizet, Rheinberger, Reinecke, Schumann, and many others have created musical works which are simple enough for the youngest students to play and to comprehend. The first efforts of the composers in this field, toward the end of the eighteenth century, were most elephantine in their clumsy attempts to sugar-coat the pill of juvenile instruction. Here is a translation of the preface to J. F. Reichardt's collection of songs for children, which appeared in 1781.

My desire, in publishing these songs for you, dear children, is to cheer you so that you shall try to sing correctly and clearly. When one gives one's self labor or trouble in any matter, one asks beforehand of what special use it is to be. Isn't it so, my little dears? Then look and I will explain it to you at once, of how much use it will be that you should sing sweetly and pleasantly. How often when you are in church you are disturbed and annoyed by the evil-sounding screaming of some children, yes, and sometimes of grown people too! You look around to see who it is and sometimes you burst out laughing. Are you not distressed by this, and is not your own singing disturbed by it, my loves?

We can imagine how a twentieth century child would scorn such a sirupy attempt to cajole it into study. And when we find Johann A. Hiller, at about the same time, presenting to children such topics as "On Death," "On Resignation" etc., we are not much impressed by the common sense of the pioneers of children's song-books.

All of this has been changed. There is at present a truer comprehension of the needs of the child, a closer sympathy with the juvenile mind and aspirations. We have endeavored to sum up some of these advances and to make clear those points which are not universally understood. The subject is of the first importance in this branch of education, for in music "Just as the twig is bent, the tree's inclined."